For Reference

Not to be taken from this room

NOVELS

for Students

Advisors

Jayne M. Burton is a teacher of English, a member of the Delta Kappa Gamma International Society for Key Women Educators, and currently a master's degree candidate in the Interdisciplinary Study of Curriculum and Instruction and English at Angelo State University.

Mary Beth Maggio teaches seventh grade language arts in Schaumburg, Illinois.

Tom Shilts is the youth librarian at the Okemos branch of Capital Area District Library in Okemos, Michigan. He holds an MSLS degree from Clarion University of Pennsylvania and an MA in U.S. History from the University of North Dakota.

Amy Spade Silverman has taught at independent schools in California, Texas, Michigan, and New York. She holds a bachelor of arts degree from the University of Michigan and a master of fine arts degree from the University of Houston. She is a member of the National Council of Teachers of English and Teachers and Writers. She is an exam reader for Advanced Placement Literature and Composition.She is also a poet, published in *North American Review*, *Nimrod*, and *Michigan Quarterly Review*, among others.

Mary Turner holds a BS in Secondary Education from East Texas State University and a Master of Education from Western Kentucky University. She teaches English 7 and AP English 12 literature and composition at SBEC in Southaven, Mississippi.

Brian Woerner teaches English at Troy High School in Troy, Ohio. He is also a Program Associate of the Ohio Writing Project at Miami University.

NOVELS
for Students

**Presenting Analysis, Context, and Criticism
on Commonly Studied Novels**

VOLUME 38

Sara Constantakis, Project Editor

Foreword by Anne Devereaux Jordan

GALE
CENGAGE Learning®

Detroit • New York • San Francisco • New Haven, Conn • Waterville, Maine • London

Novels for Students, Volume 38

Project Editor: Sara Constantakis

Rights Acquisition and Management: Margaret Chamberlain-Gaston, Tracie Richardson

Composition: Evi Abou-El-Seoud

Manufacturing: Rhonda Dover

Imaging: John Watkins

Product Design: Pamela A. E. Galbreath, Jennifer Wahi

Content Conversion: Katrina Coach

Product Manager: Meggin Condino

For product information and technology assistance, contact us at **Gale Customer Support, 1-800-877-4253.** For permission to use material from this text or product, submit all requests online at **www.cengage.com/permissions.** Further permissions questions can be emailed to **permissionrequest@cengage.com**

Gale
27500 Drake Rd.
Farmington Hills, MI, 48331-3535

ISBN-13: 978-1-4144-6701-6
ISBN-10: 1-4144-6701-X

ISSN 1094-3552

This title is also available as an e-book.
ISBN-13: 978-1-4144-7367-3
ISBN-10: 1-4144-7367-2
Contact your Gale, a part of Cengage Learning sales representative for ordering information.

Printed in Mexico
1 2 3 4 5 6 7 16 15 14 13 12

Table of Contents

The Informed Dialogue:
Interacting with Literature

When we pick up a book, we usually do so with the anticipation of pleasure. We hope that by entering the time and place of the novel and sharing the thoughts and actions of the characters, we will find enjoyment. Unfortunately, this is often not the case; we are disappointed. But we should ask, has the author failed us, or have we failed the author?

We establish a dialogue with the author, the book, and with ourselves when we read. Consciously and unconsciously, we ask questions: "Why did the author write this book?" "Why did the author choose that time, place, or character?" "How did the author achieve that effect?" "Why did the character act that way?" "Would I act in the same way?" The answers we receive depend upon how much information about literature in general and about that book specifically we ourselves bring to our reading.

Young children have limited life and literary experiences. Being young, children frequently do not know how to go about exploring a book, nor sometimes, even know the questions to ask of a book. The books they read help them answer questions, the author often coming right out and *telling* young readers the things they are learning or are expected to learn. The perennial classic, *The Little Engine That Could, tells* its readers that, among other things, it is good to help others and brings happiness:

"Hurray, hurray," cried the funny little clown and all the dolls and toys. "The good little boys and girls in the city will be happy because you helped us, kind, Little Blue Engine."

In picture books, messages are often blatant and simple, the dialogue between the author and reader one-sided. Young children are concerned with the end result of a book—the enjoyment gained, the lesson learned—rather than with how that result was obtained. As we grow older and read further, however, we question more. We come to expect that the world within the book will closely mirror the concerns of our world, and that the author will *show* these through the events, descriptions, and conversations within the story, rather than *telling* of them. We are now expected to do the interpreting, carry on our share of the dialogue with the book and author, and glean not only the author's message, but comprehend how that message and the overall affect of the book were achieved. Sometimes, however, we need help to do these things. *Novels for Students* provides that help.

A novel is made up of many parts interacting to create a coherent whole. In reading a novel, the more obvious features can be easily spotted—theme, characters, plot—but we may overlook the more subtle elements that greatly influence how the novel is perceived by the reader: viewpoint, mood and tone, symbolism, or the use of humor. By focusing on both the obvious and more subtle literary elements within a novel,

Novels for Students aids readers in both analyzing for message and in determining how and why that message is communicated. In the discussion on Harper Lee's *To Kill a Mockingbird* (Vol. 2), for example, the mockingbird as a symbol of innocence is dealt with, among other things, as is the importance of Lee's use of humor which "enlivens a serious plot, adds depth to the characterization, and creates a sense of familiarity and universality." The reader comes to understand the internal elements of each novel discussed—as well as the external influences that help shape it.

"The desire to write greatly," Harold Bloom of Yale University says, "is the desire to be elsewhere, in a time and place of one's own, in an originality that must compound with inheritance, with an anxiety of influence." A writer seeks to create a unique world within a story, but although it is unique, it is not disconnected from our own world. It speaks to us *because* of what the writer brings to the writing from our world: how he or she was raised and educated; his or her likes and dislikes; the events occurring in the real world at the time of the writing, and while the author was growing up. When we know what an author has brought to his or her work, we gain a greater insight into both the "originality" (the world of the book), and the things that "compound" it. This insight enables us to question that created world and find answers more readily. By informing ourselves, we are able to establish a more effective dialogue with both book and author.

Novels for Students, in addition to providing a plot summary and descriptive list of characters—to remind readers of what they have read—also explores the external influences that shaped each book. Each entry includes a discussion of the author's background, and the historical context in which the novel was written. It is vital to know, for instance, that when Ray Bradbury was writing *Fahrenheit 451* (Vol. 1), the threat of Nazi domination had recently ended in Europe, and the McCarthy hearings were taking place in Washington, D.C. This information goes far in answering the question, "Why did he write a story of oppressive government control and book burning?" Similarly, it is important to know that Harper Lee, author of *To Kill a Mockingbird,* was born and raised in Monroeville, Alabama, and that her father was a lawyer. Readers can now see why she chose the south as a setting for her novel—it is the place with which she was most familiar—and start to comprehend her characters and their actions.

Novels for Students helps readers find the answers they seek when they establish a dialogue with a particular novel. It also aids in the posing of questions by providing the opinions and interpretations of various critics and reviewers, broadening that dialogue. Some reviewers of *To Kill A Mockingbird,* for example, "faulted the novel's climax as melodramatic." This statement leads readers to ask, "Is it, indeed, melodramatic?" "If not, why did some reviewers see it as such?" "If it is, why did Lee choose to make it melodramatic?" "Is melodrama ever justified?" By being spurred to ask these questions, readers not only learn more about the book and its writer, but about the nature of writing itself.

The literature included for discussion in *Novels for Students* has been chosen because it has something vital to say to us. *Of Mice and Men, Catch-22, The Joy Luck Club, My Antonia, A Separate Peace* and the other novels here speak of life and modern sensibility. In addition to their individual, specific messages of prejudice, power, love or hate, living and dying, however, they and all great literature also share a common intent. They force us to *think*—about life, literature, and about others, not just about ourselves. They pry us from the narrow confines of our minds and thrust us outward to confront the world of books and the larger, real world we all share. *Novels for Students* helps us in this confrontation by providing the means of enriching our conversation with literature and the world, by creating an *informed* dialogue, one that brings true pleasure to the personal act of reading.

Sources

Harold Bloom, *The Western Canon, The Books and School of the Ages,* Riverhead Books, 1994.

Watty Piper, *The Little Engine That Could,* Platt & Munk, 1930.

Anne Devereaux Jordan
Senior Editor, TALL (Teaching and Learning Literature)

Introduction

Purpose of the Book

The purpose of *Novels for Students* (*NfS*) is to provide readers with a guide to understanding, enjoying, and studying novels by giving them easy access to information about the work. Part of Gale's "For Students" Literature line, *NfS* is specifically designed to meet the curricular needs of high school and undergraduate college students and their teachers, as well as the interests of general readers and researchers considering specific novels. While each volume contains entries on "classic" novels frequently studied in classrooms, there are also entries containing hard-to-find information on contemporary novels, including works by multicultural, international, and women novelists. Entries profiling film versions of novels not only diversify the study of novels but support alternate learning styles, media literacy, and film studies curricula as well.

The information covered in each entry includes an introduction to the novel and the novel's author; a plot summary, to help readers unravel and understand the events in a novel; descriptions of important characters, including explanation of a given character's role in the novel as well as discussion about that character's relationship to other characters in the novel; analysis of important themes in the novel; and an explanation of important literary techniques and movements as they are demonstrated in the novel.

In addition to this material, which helps the readers analyze the novel itself, students are also provided with important information on the literary and historical background informing each work. This includes a historical context essay, a box comparing the time or place the novel was written to modern Western culture, a critical essay, and excerpts from critical essays on the novel. A unique feature of *NfS* is a specially commissioned critical essay on each novel, targeted toward the student reader.

The "literature to film" entries on novels vary slightly in form, providing background on film technique and comparison to the original, literary version of the work. These entries open with an introduction to the film, which leads directly into the plot summary. The summary highlights plot changes from the novel, key cinematic moments, and/or examples of key film techniques. As in standard entries, there are character profiles (noting omissions or additions, and identifying the actors), analysis of themes and how they are illustrated in the film, and an explanation of the cinematic style and structure of the film. A cultural context section notes any time period or setting differences from that of the original work, as well as cultural differences between the time in which the original work was written and the time in which the film adaptation was made. A film entry concludes with a critical overview and critical essays on the film.

To further help today's student in studying and enjoying each novel or film, information on media adaptations is provided (if available), as well as suggestions for works of fiction, nonfiction, or film on similar themes and topics. Classroom aids include ideas for research papers and lists of critical and reference sources that provide additional material on the novel. Film entries also highlight signature film techniques demonstrated, and suggest media literacy activities and prompts to use during or after viewing a film.

Selection Criteria

The titles for each volume of *NfS* are selected by surveying numerous sources on notable literary works and analyzing course curricula for various schools, school districts, and states. Some of the sources surveyed include: high school and undergraduate literature anthologies and textbooks; lists of award-winners, and recommended titles, including the Young Adult Library Services Association (YALSA) list of best books for young adults. Films are selected both for the literary importance of the original work and the merits of the adaptation (including official awards and widespread public recognition).

Input solicited from our expert advisory board—consisting of educators and librarians—guides us to maintain a mix of "classic" and contemporary literary works, a mix of challenging and engaging works (including genre titles that are commonly studied) appropriate for different age levels, and a mix of international, multicultural and women authors. These advisors also consult on each volume's entry list, advising on which titles are most studied, most appropriate, and meet the broadest interests across secondary (grades 7–12) curricula and undergraduate literature studies.

How Each Entry Is Organized

Each entry, or chapter, in *NfS* focuses on one novel. Each entry heading lists the full name of the novel, the author's name, and the date of the novel's publication. The following elements are contained in each entry:

Introduction: a brief overview of the novel which provides information about its first appearance, its literary standing, any controversies surrounding the work, and major conflicts or themes within the work. Film entries identify the original novel and provide understanding

of the film's reception and reputation, along with that of the director.

Author Biography: in novel entries, this section includes basic facts about the author's life, and focuses on events and times in the author's life that inspired the novel in question.

Plot Summary: a factual description of the major events in the novel. Lengthy summaries are broken down with subheads. Plot summaries of films are used to uncover plot differences from the original novel, and to note the use of certain film angles or other techniques.

Characters: an alphabetical listing of major characters in the novel. Each character name is followed by a brief to an extensive description of the character's role in the novel, as well as discussion of the character's actions, relationships, and possible motivation. In film entries, omissions or changes to the cast of characters of the film adaptation are mentioned here, and the actors' names—and any awards they may have received—are also included.

Characters are listed alphabetically by last name. If a character is unnamed—for instance, the narrator in *Invisible Man*—the character is listed as "The Narrator" and alphabetized as "Narrator." If a character's first name is the only one given, the name will appear alphabetically by that name.

Variant names are also included for each character. Thus, the full name "Jean Louise Finch" would head the listing for the narrator of *To Kill a Mockingbird*, but listed in a separate cross-reference would be the nickname "Scout Finch."

Themes: a thorough overview of how the major topics, themes, and issues are addressed within the novel. Each theme discussed appears in a separate subhead. While the key themes often remain the same or similar when a novel is adapted into a film, film entries demonstrate how the themes are conveyed cinematically, along with any changes in the portrayal of themes.

Style: this section addresses important style elements of the novel, such as setting, point of view, and narration; important literary devices used, such as imagery, foreshadowing, symbolism; and, if applicable, genres to which the work might have belonged, such as Gothicism or Romanticism. Literary terms are explained within the entry but can also be found in the Glossary. Film entries cover how the director conveyed the meaning, message, and mood of the work using film in comparison to the author's use of language, literary device, etc., in the original work.

Historical Context: in novel entries, this section outlines the social, political, and cultural climate in which the author lived and the novel was created. This section may include descriptions of related historical events, pertinent aspects of daily life in the culture, and the artistic and literary sensibilities of the time in which the work was written. If the novel is a historical work, information regarding the time in which the novel is set is also included. Each section is broken down with helpful subheads. Film entries contain a similar Cultural Context section because the film adaptation might explore an entirely different time period or culture than the original work, and may also be influenced by the traditions and views of a time period much different than that of the original author.

Critical Overview: this section provides background on the critical reputation of the novel or film, including bannings or any other public controversies surrounding the work. For older works, this section includes a history of how the novel or film was first received and how perceptions of it may have changed over the years; for more recent novels, direct quotes from early reviews may also be included.

Criticism: an essay commissioned by *NfS* which specifically deals with the novel or film and is written specifically for the student audience, as well as excerpts from previously published criticism on the work (if available).

Sources: an alphabetical list of critical material used in compiling the entry, with full bibliographical information.

Further Reading: an alphabetical list of other critical sources which may prove useful for the student. It includes full bibliographical information and a brief annotation.

Suggested Search Terms: a list of search terms and phrases to jumpstart students' further information seeking. Terms include not just titles and author names but also terms and topics related to the historical and literary context of the works.

In addition, each novel entry contains the following highlighted sections, set apart from the main text as sidebars:

Media Adaptations: if available, a list of audiobooks and important film and television adaptations of the novel, including source information. The list also includes stage adaptations, musical adaptations, etc.

Topics for Further Study: a list of potential study questions or research topics dealing with the novel. This section includes questions related to other disciplines the student may be studying, such as American history, world history, science, math, government, business, geography, economics, psychology, etc.

Compare and Contrast: an "at-a-glance" comparison of the cultural and historical differences between the author's time and culture and late twentieth century or early twenty-first century Western culture. This box includes pertinent parallels between the major scientific, political, and cultural movements of the time or place the novel was written, the time or place the novel was set (if a historical work), and modern Western culture. Works written after the mid-1970s may not have this box.

What Do I Read Next?: a list of works that might give a reader points of entry into a classic work (e.g., YA or multicultural titles) and/or complement the featured novel or serve as a contrast to it. This includes works by the same author and others, works from various genres, YA works, and works from various cultures and eras.

The film entries provide sidebars more targeted to the study of film, including:

Film Technique: a listing and explanation of four to six key techniques used in the film, including shot styles, use of transitions, lighting, sound or music, etc.

Read, Watch, Write: media literacy prompts and/or suggestions for viewing log prompts.

What Do I See Next?: a list of films based on the same or similar works or of films similar in directing style, technique, etc.

Other Features

NfS includes "The Informed Dialogue: Interacting with Literature," a foreword by Anne Devereaux Jordan, Senior Editor for *Teaching and Learning Literature* (*TALL*), and a founder of the Children's Literature Association. This essay provides an enlightening look at how readers interact with literature and how *Novels for Students* can help teachers show students how to enrich their own reading experiences.

A Cumulative Author/Title Index lists the authors and titles covered in each volume of the *NfS* series.

A Cumulative Nationality/Ethnicity Index breaks down the authors and titles covered in each volume of the *NfS* series by nationality and ethnicity.

A Subject/Theme Index, specific to each volume, provides easy reference for users who may be studying a particular subject or theme rather than a single work. Significant subjects, from events to broad themes, are included.

Each entry may include illustrations, including photo of the author, stills from film adaptations, maps, and/or photos of key historical events, if available.

Citing Novels for Students

When writing papers, students who quote directly from any volume of *NfS* may use the following general forms. These examples are based on MLA style; teachers may request that students adhere to a different style, so the following examples may be adapted as needed.

When citing text from *NfS* that is not attributed to a particular author (i.e., the Themes, Style, Historical Context sections, etc.), the following format should be used in the bibliography section:

> "*Night.*" *Novels for Students.* Ed. Marie Rose Napierkowski. Vol. 4. Detroit: Gale, 1998. 234–35.

When quoting the specially commissioned essay from *NfS* (usually the first piece under the "Criticism" subhead), the following format should be used:

> Miller, Tyrus. Critical Essay on "*Winesburg, Ohio.*" *Novels for Students.* Ed. Marie Rose Napierkowski. Vol. 4. Detroit: Gale, 1998. 335–39.

When quoting a journal or newspaper essay that is reprinted in a volume of *NfS*, the following form may be used:

> Malak, Amin. "Margaret Atwood's *The Handmaid's Tale* and the Dystopian Tradition." *Canadian Literature* 112 (Spring 1987): 9–16. Excerpted and reprinted in *Novels for Students.* Vol. 4. Ed. Marie Rose Napierkowski. Detroit: Gale, 1998. 133–36.

When quoting material reprinted from a book that appears in a volume of *NfS*, the following form may be used:

> Adams, Timothy Dow. "Richard Wright: 'Wearing the Mask.'" In *Telling Lies in Modern American Autobiography.* University of North Carolina Press, 1990. 69–83. Excerpted and reprinted in *Novels for Students.* Vol. 1. Ed. Diane Telgen. Detroit: Gale, 1997. 59–61.

We Welcome Your Suggestions

The editorial staff of *Novels for Students* welcomes your comments and ideas. Readers who wish to suggest novels to appear in future volumes, or who have other suggestions, are cordially invited to contact the editor. You may contact the editor via e-mail at: **ForStudentsEditors@cengage.com.** Or write to the editor at:

Editor, *Novels for Students*

Gale

27500 Drake Road

Farmington Hills, MI 48331-3535

Literary Chronology

1789: James Fenimore Cooper is born on September 15 in Burlington, New Jersey.

1840: James Fenimore Cooper's *The Pathfinder; or, The Inland Sea* is published.

1851: James Fenimore Cooper dies of chronic liver disease on September 14 in Cooperstown, New York.

1890: Nevil Shute is born on January 17 in London, England.

1897: William Faulkner is born on September 25 in New Albany Mississippi.

1900: Margaret Mitchell is born on November 8 in Atlanta, Georgia.

1919: Doris Lessing is born on October 22 in Persia (now Iran).

1928: James Lincoln Collier is born on June 27 in New York City.

1929: Chaim Potok is born on February 17 in the Bronx, New York.

1930: Christopher Collier is born on January 29 in New York City.

1935: E. Annie Proulx is born on August 22 in Norwich, Connecticut.

1935: Thomas Keneally is born on October 7 in Sidney, Australia.

1936: Margaret Mitchell's *Gone With the Wind* is published.

1938: William Faulkner's *The Unvanquished* is published.

1939: The film *Gone With the Wind* is awarded eight Academy Awards for Best Actress in a Leading Role, Best Actress in a Supporting Role, Best Art Direction, Best Cinematography, Best Director, Best Film Editing, Best Picture, and Best Screenplay; in addition to an honorary award for outstanding achievement in the use of color for the enhancement of dramatic mood, awarded to William Cameron Menzies.

1939: The film *Gone With the Wind* is released.

1941: Anne Tyler is born on October 25 in Minneapolis, Minnesota.

1948: William Gibson is born on March 17 in Conway, South Carolina

1949: Margaret Mitchell dies after being struck by a car on August 16 in Atlanta, Georgia.

1950: Nevil Shute's *A Town Like Alice* is published.

1955: William Faulkner is awarded the Pulitzer Prize for Fiction for *A Fable*.

1956: Chitra Banerjee Divakaruni is born on July 29 in Calcutta, India.

1958: Cristina García is born on July 4 in Havana, Cuba.

1960: Nevil Shute dies of a stroke on January 12 in Melbourne, Australia.

1962: William Faulkner dies of a heart attack on July 6 in Byhalia, Mississippi.

1963: William Faulkner is awarded the Pulitzer Prize for Fiction for *The Reivers*.

1966: Sherman Alexie is born on October 7 in Spokane, Washington.

1972: Chaim Potok's *My Name Is Asher Lev* is published.

1974: James Lincoln Collier and Christopher Collier's *My Brother Sam Is Dead* is published.

1982: Thomas Keneally is awarded the Man Booker Prize for *Schindler's Ark*.

1982: Thomas Keneally's *Schindler's Ark* is published in Australia. It is published in the United States as *Schindler's List* in 1983.

1983: The film *Schindler's List* is released.

1984: William Gibson's *Neuromancer* is published.

1988: Anne Tyler is awarded the Pulitzer Prize for Fiction for *Breathing Lessons*.

1988: Doris Lessing's *The Fifth Child* is published.

1992: Cristina García's *Dreaming in Cuban* is published.

1993: E. Annie Proulx's *The Shipping News* is published.

1993: The film *Schindler's List* is awarded the seven Academy Awards, for Best Picture, Best Director, Best Adapted Screenplay, Best Cinematography, Best Art Direction, Best Film Editing, and Best Original Score.

1994: E. Annie Proulx wins the Pulitzer Prize for Fiction for *The Shipping News*.

1999: Chitra Banerjee Divakaruni's *Sister of My Heart* is published.

2002: Chaim Potok dies on July 23 in Merion, Pennsylvania.

2006: Anne Tyler's *Digging to America* is published.

2007: Doris Lessing is awarded the Nobel Prize for Literature.

2007: Sherman Alexie's *The Absolutely True Diary of a Part-Time Indian* is published.

Acknowledgements

The editors wish to thank the copyright holders of the excerpted criticism included in this volume and the permissions managers of many book and magazine publishing companies for assisting us in securing reproduction rights. We are also grateful to the staffs of the Detroit Public Library, the Library of Congress, the University of Detroit Mercy Library, Wayne State University Purdy/ Kresge Library Complex, and the University of Michigan Libraries for making their resources available to us. Following is a list of the copyright holders who have granted us permission to reproduce material in this volume of *NfS*. Every effort has been made to trace copyright, but if omissions have been made, please let us know.

COPYRIGHTED EXCERPTS IN *NfS*, VOLUME 38, WERE REPRODUCED FROM THE FOLLOWING PERIODICALS:

Booklist, no. 12, February 15, 2006. Copyright © 2006 by the American Library Association. Reproduced by permission of the publisher.—*Film Criticism*, no. 2, 1997. Copyright © 1997 by *Film Criticism*. Reproduced by permission of the publisher.—*Knickerbocker*, January, 1841.—*Los Angeles Times Book Review*, July 18, 1993. Copyright © 1993 by *Los Angeles Times Book Review*. Reproduced by permission of the publisher.—*MBR Bookwatch*, February, 2008. Copyright © 2008 by *Midwest Book Review*. Reproduced by permission of the publisher.—*MELUS*, no. 2, Summer, 2004. Copyright © 2004 by *MELUS*: *The Society for the Study of Multi-Ethnic Literature of the United States*. Reproduced by permission of the publisher.—*National Review*, no. 11, June 10, 1988. Copyright © 1988 by National Review, Inc., 215 Lexington Avenue, New York, NY 10016.—*New Literary History: A Journal of Theory and Interpretation*, no. 2, Spring 1992. Copyright © 1992 by The Johns Hopkins University Press. Reproduced by permission of The Johns Hopkins University Press.—*Notes on Contemporary Literature*, no. 2, March, 2009. Copyright © 2009 by William S. Doxey. Reproduced by permission of the publisher.—*Publishers Weekly*, no. 32, August 9, 2004. Copyright © 2004 by Reed Publishing USA. Reproduced from *Publishers Weekly*, published by the Bowker Magazine Group of Cahners Publishing Co., a division of Reed Publishing USA, by permission.—*School Library Journal*, no. 8, August, 2007. Copyright © 2007 by Library Journals LLC, a wholly owned subsidiary of Media Source, Inc. No redistribution permitted. Reproduced by permission of the publisher.—*Science-Fiction Studies*, no. 1, March, 1990. Copyright © 1990 by SFS Publications. Reproduced by permission of the publisher. —*Studies in American Jewish Literature*, no. 2, 1982. Copyright © 1982 by The Kent State University Press. Reproduced by permission of the publisher.—*Studies in American Jewish Literature*, v. 29, 2010. Copyright © 2010 by Purdue University Press. Reproduced by permission of the publisher.—*West Virginia University Philological Papers*, Fall

2004, for "Scarlett O'Hara as Confederate Woman" by Katharine Lane Antolini. Copyright © 2004 West Virginia University. Reproduced by permission of the author and publisher.—*Western American Literature*, no. 3, November, 1986. Copyright © 1986 by The Western Literature Association. Reproduced by permission of the publisher.—*World Literature Today*, no. 2, Spring, 1995; no. 4, Autumn, 1999; no. 1, Winter, 2000. Copyright © 1995, 1999, 2000 by *World Literature Today*. All Reproduced by permission of the publisher.

COPYRIGHTED EXCERPTS IN *NfS*, **VOLUME 38, WERE REPRODUCED FROM THE FOLLOWING BOOKS:**

Bourke, Roger. From "'A Town Like Alice' and the Prisoner of War as Christ-figure," in *Prisoners of the Japanese: Literary Imagination and the Prisoner-of-war Experience*. University of Queensland Press, 2006. Copyright © 2006, University of Queensland Press. Reproduced by permission of the publisher.—Clarke, Deborah. From "Gender, War, and Cross-Dressing in 'The Unvanquished,'" in *Faulkner and Gender: Faulkner and Yoknapatawpha*. Edited by Donald M. Kartiganer and Ann J. Abadie. University Press of Mississippi, 1996. Copyright © 1996, University Press of Mississippi. All rights reserved. Reproduced by permission of the publisher.—Curran, Trisha. From "'Gone with the Wind': An American Tragedy," in *The South and Film*. Edited by Warren French. Southern Quarterly, 1981. Copyright © 1981 by the University of Southern Mississippi. Reproduced by permission of the publisher.—Scapple, Sharon. From "Divided Loyalties: Why Is My Brother Sam Dead?," in *Phoenix Award of the Children's Literature Association 1990-1994*. Edited by Alethea Helbig and Agnes Perkins. Scarecrow Press, 1996. Copyright © 1996 by University Press of America, Inc. All rights reserved. Reproduced by permission of the publisher.—Sceats, Sarah. From "Flesh and Bones: Eating, Not Eating, and the Social Vision of Doris Lessing," in *Theme Parks, Rainforests and Sprouting Wastelands: European Essays on Theory and Performance in Contemporary British Fiction*. Edited by Richard Todd. Amsterdam: Rodopi, 2000. Copyright © 2000 by Editions Rodopi B. V. Reproduced by permission of the publisher.—Short, Kathy G. From "'My Brother Sam Is Dead': Embracing the Contradictions and Uncertainties of Live and War," in *Censored Books II: Critical Viewpoints, 1985-2000*. Edited by Nicholas J. Karolides. Scarecrow Press, 2002. Copyright © 2002 by University Press of America, Inc. All rights reserved. Reproduced by permission of the publisher.—Zelizer, Barbie. From "Every Once in a While: 'Schindler's List' and the Shaping of History," in *Spielberg's Holocaust*. Edited by Yosefa Loshitzky. Indiana University Press, 1997. Copyright © 1997 Indiana University Press. Reproduced by permission of Indiana University Press.

Contributors

Bryan Aubrey: Aubrey holds a Ph.D. in English. Entry on *The Fifth Child*. Original essay on *The Fifth Child*.

Cynthia A. Bily: Bily teaches English at Macomb Community College in Michigan. Entry on *The Absolutely True Diary of a Part-Time Indian*. Original essay on *The Absolutely True Diary of a Part-Time Indian*.

Catherine Dominic: Dominic is a novelist and a freelance writer and editor. Entries on *The Shipping News* and *A Town Like Alice*. Original essays on *The Shipping News* and *A Town Like Alice*.

Charlotte M. Freeman: Freeman is a writer, editor, and former academic living in small-town Montana. Entry on *A Bend in the River*. Original essay on *A Bend in the River*.

Diane Andrews Henningfeld: Henningfeld is an emerita professor of English who writes widely on literature and current events for educational publications. Entry on *Neuromancer*. Original essay on *Neuromancer*.

Michael Allen Holmes: Holmes is a writer and editor. Entries on *Dreaming in Cuban* and *Sister of My Heart*. Original essays on *Dreaming in Cuban* and *Sister of My Heart*.

David Kelly: Kelly is a professor of creative writing and literature. Entries on *Gone with the Wind* and *Schindler's List*. Original essays on *Gone with the Wind* and *Schindler's List*.

Michael J. O'Neal: O'Neal holds a Ph.D. in English. Entries on *My Brother Sam is Dead* and *The Pathfinder; or the Inland Sea*. Original essays on *My Brother Sam is Dead* and *The Pathfinder; or the Inland Sea*.

Kathy Wilson Peacock: Wilson Peacock is a writer and editor specializing in literature and science. Entry on *My Name Is Asher Lev*. Original essay on *My Name Is Asher Lev*.

Bradley A. Skeen: Skeen is a classicist. Entry on *The Unvanquished*. Original essay on *The Unvanquished*.

The Absolutely True Diary of a Part-Time Indian

The Absolutely True Diary of a Part-Time Indian (2007) is the seventh book of fiction by Sherman Alexie, probably the most well-known Native American writer of the twenty-first century. It is his first book written specifically for young-adult readers. Based on Alexie's own life, it tells the story of one year in the life of Arnold "Junior" Spirit, a fourteen-year-old boy from the Spokane Indian Reservation in Washington who transfers to the wealthy all-white Reardan High School at the beginning of his freshman year. By choosing Reardan, Junior finds that he is considered both a traitor on the reservation and an outsider at school. His names reflect his internal split: he is called Junior at home and Arnold at school. He is, in his words, only a "part-time Indian," and his challenge is to find his way and his identity through this complex life. The novel is narrated by Junior himself and includes the vulgar language, sexual references, and gritty situations common to adolescent boys. One important feature of the novel is the illustration by Ellen Forney. Junior is a cartoonist, and the novel is sprinkled with his funny and touching drawings of people and events.

The Absolutely True Diary is typical of Alexie's work in its setting—the Spokane Indian Reservation where the author himself grew up—and in its realistic portrayal of the harshness of many Native American lives. The novel won several important awards, including the National Book Award for Young People's Literature and the

SHERMAN ALEXIE

2007

Sherman Alexie (Getty Images)

Boston Globe-Horn Book Award for Excellence in Children's Literature in Fiction. It has been published in twelve countries other than the United States. It has also become one of the most frequently challenged books in schools and libraries, as many adults have found the book too crude or too negative for young readers.

AUTHOR BIOGRAPHY

Alexie was born on October 7, 1966, in Well-pinit, Washington, a small town on the Spokane Indian Reservation. His father was a member of the Coeur d'Alene tribe, and his mother was Spokane. While Alexie's father, a logger and trucker, was often away from the family, either working or drinking, his mother supported her six children with an office job and part-time sewing.

Alexie was born with hydrocephalus, also known as "water on the brain." After many childhood struggles, including a life-threatening

surgery and years of seizures, he largely overcame the condition. Like many children who grow up to be writers, he was an avid reader and serious about his education. Alexie attended schools on the reservation through eighth grade and then asked to be sent to Reardan High School, an all-white school in the small but wealthy town of Reardan, Washington, about twenty miles from Wellpinit. There, he was teased and bullied because of his enlarged head and because he was the only Native American at the school, but he gained some respect by excelling on the basketball court and in the classroom. During Alexie's teen years, one of his older sisters was killed in a fire in her mobile home.

After high school, Alexie attended Gonzaga University for a couple of years, but he began drinking heavily and dropped out. Months later, he decided to start over and enrolled at Washington State University, where he found his way to a poetry workshop and discovered his talent for writing. He graduated in 1991 with a degree in American Studies and published his first book, a collection of poems, *The Business of Fancy Dancing*, the next year. The book received good reviews and more national attention than a first book of poetry typically draws; soon he published two more books of poetry, followed by the story collection *The Lone Ranger and Tonto Fistfight in Heaven* (1993) and the novel *Reservation Blues* (1995). In less than five years, he became the most well-known Native American writer of his generation. He wrote poetry, short stories, novels, essays, and reviews, and his first film, the award-winning *Smoke Signals* (1998), was the first nationally distributed feature film written, directed by, and starring Native Americans.

Alexie has worked throughout his career to find new outlets and new role models for Native American teens. In 2005, he became one of the founders of Longhouse Media, an organization that trains young people to make films. His first book for young readers is *The Absolutely True Diary of a Part-Time Indian* (2007). The book's central character, Arnold "Junior" Spirit, shares many qualities and experiences with the author. The novel won several awards, including the 2007 National Book Award for Young People's Literature.

As of 2011, Alexie has published several books of poetry and fiction and has written and produced three films. He is outspoken against the practice of converting books to electronic formats and does not allow his own books to be made available for electronic readers. He is a popular speaker and reader and also occasionally does stand-up comedy. He lives in Seattle with his wife Diane Tomhave and their two sons.

PLOT SUMMARY

The Black-Eye-of-the-Month Club— Revenge Is My Middle Name

In the first sentence of *The Absolutely True Diary of a Part-Time Indian*, the first-person narrator names the physical disability that identifies him: "I was born with water on the brain." Later in the first chapter, the narrator, Arnold "Junior" Spirit, describes his many physical abnormalities: he has an enlarged head, he stutters and has a lisp, and he has large hands and feet. He is frequently teased and roughed up, which is why he claims membership in the "Black-Eye-of-the-Month Club." In his free time he is mostly alone, reading or drawing cartoons.

Junior next describes his family. They are desperately poor—so poor that, when Junior's dog Oscar becomes ill, his Dad shoots the dog to end his suffering because they have no money to pay a veterinarian. Junior would like to hate his alcoholic parents for their weakness and their poverty, but actually he loves them and depends on them. He knows that his mother would have liked to go to college and his father would have liked to be a musician, but life on the reservation offers few opportunities for dreamers. He climbs out of his depression over the dog with the help of his best friend Rowdy, the meanest kid on the reservation. Rowdy encourages Junior to go with him to the Spokane Powwow, an annual celebration, but Junior's fears are realized when he is bullied there by three brothers in their thirties. To revenge his friend, Rowdy waits until the brothers are passed out drunk, then sneaks into their camp and cuts off their braids.

Because Geometry Is Not a Country Somewhere Near France—Rowdy Sings the Blues

Junior's first day of high school arrives, and he is excited about school, especially his geometry class. However, when he opens his textbook he sees "Agnes Adams," his mother's name, written inside and realizes that the reservation school has not had new textbooks in more than thirty years.

MEDIA ADAPTATIONS

- *The Absolutely True Diary of a Part-Time Indian* was recorded as an unabridged audio book, read by Sherman Alexie, by Recorded Books in 2008. The recording, which won the 2009 Odyssey Award for recorded fiction, is available on CD or as a download.

In frustration, he throws the book and hits his teacher, Mr. P, in the face; he is suspended from school.

A week later, Mr. P comes to Junior's house. He tells Junior that he is ashamed of the way he and other teachers tried, in the earlier days, to "kill the Indian to save the child." He reveals that Mary, Junior's sister who lives in the basement and never goes out, was the smartest student he ever taught and that she had secret dreams of being a romance writer, and he encourages Junior to leave the reservation before he is trapped forever.

Junior asks his parents to let him transfer to Reardan High School, an all-white school in the wealthy town twenty-two miles away. Without hesitating, they agree, although his dad points out that transportation will be a problem. Rowdy does not take the news so well. He screams at Junior, punches him in the face, and storms off. Junior realizes that "my best friend had become my worst enemy."

How to Fight Monsters—Tears of a Clown

On Junior's first day at Reardan, which has an Indian for its mascot, he confirms what he has suspected: he is not like the other kids. They are so white as to seem translucent, and he knows that most of them will be going to college. When he gets to his first class—late—everyone stares at him. He tells Penelope, the most beautiful girl he has ever seen, that his name is Junior, but when the teacher calls him "Arnold" she makes fun of him for not knowing his own name.

The boys at Reardan tease him mercilessly, calling him every anti-Indian name they can think of. Finally, one of the biggest boys, Roger, tells a joke that is racist and vulgar. Junior feels he has no choice but to punch Roger in the face. The boys are shocked; apparently, white boys at Reardan do not settle their differences with hitting.

Junior turns to his grandmother for advice, and she suggests that Roger did not hit Junior back because he respects Junior. Eugene, Junior's dad's best friend, gives him a ride to school one day on his motorcycle and tells Junior that he admires his courage in braving the white school, but Junior's growing confidence does not last. The next time he sees Penelope, she snubs him again.

Halloween—Thanksgiving

On Halloween, both Junior and Penelope dress as homeless people, and she begins to chat with him in a friendly way, but as fall moves on Junior is lonelier and lonelier. He does not have any friends at school, and back home Rowdy has turned his back on him. One bright moment happens in science class, when the teacher makes fun of Junior's explanation of how petrified wood is formed and Gordy, the class genius, supports Junior's explanation.

However, a low moment follows soon after, when the family discovers that Mary, Junior's sister, has married a man from Montana and left home without warning. Junior's parents are upset, but Junior is secretly glad that Mary has gotten away and gone in search of something better. Slowly, he and Gordy become friends, or at least study partners. Gordy encourages Junior to find joy in books and in cartooning, and Junior comes to understand what he means.

Thanksgiving is another mixed day for Junior. The family meal is delicious and full of laughter, but Rowdy, still angry, does not come over afterward for the traditional pie-eating contest. Junior draws a cartoon of the two of them and takes it over to Rowdy's house, but Rowdy refuses to see him.

Hunger Pains—My Sister Sends Me a Letter

When Junior excuses himself from class one day to use the bathroom, he hears Penelope next door vomiting and learns that she is anorexic. She denies that she has a problem, just as Junior's dad denies his alcoholism, and Junior

promises to keep her secret. He also falls in love with her, and the two become a couple, in part so Penelope can annoy her racist and domineering father. Penelope dreams of getting out of Reardan and traveling around the world, but she fears that she will be stuck in her small town forever. One day, Junior sends Rowdy an email from the school computer lab, confessing that he loves a white girl and asking for advice. Rowdy replies, but only with insults.

In December, Junior takes Penelope to the Winter Formal. He cannot afford formal clothes, so he borrows an old polyester suit from his father. He does not have gas money, so he arranges to meet Penelope at the dance. All is going well until the dance ends and Roger suggests they all go out for pancakes. Junior know he cannot pay for his and Penelope's food, but he cannot think of a way to get out of going. He goes along, dreading the moment when he will have to reveal that he is poor, but Roger has guessed, and he slips Junior some money in the restroom. Penelope finds out, and Junior discovers that neither Roger nor Penelope will shun him for his poverty; instead, they are happy to drive him home. Junior realizes, "If you let people into your life a little bit, they can be pretty damn amazing."

While he is building friendships at school, Junior is reminded of his old life. He emails Rowdy again and gets more insults in return, and Mary sends Junior a letter raving about her beautiful home and her struggle to find work.

Reindeer Games

Junior's dad encourages him to try out for basketball, and to Junior's surprise, he makes the varsity team. The coach remembers him as good shooter for the Wellpinit team, and Junior shows his determination when he goes one-on-one against the much bigger Roger and refuses to give up. Reardan's first game of the season is against Wellpinit, and when Junior enters his old gym, everyone in the crowd and on the Wellpinit team goes silent and turns their back to Junior. The only exception is Rowdy, who faces Junior with hatred in his eyes.

During the first period, someone in the crowd throws a quarter at Junior's head, opening up a deep cut. Eugene, who is now an EMT, cleans and stitches the cut so Junior can get back into the game; he tells Junior again how cool he is. Junior goes back on the court, where Rowdy throws an elbow and knocks him unconscious.

Wellpinit wins the game by thirty points, but Junior is not there to see it; he has been taken by ambulance to the hospital. Later, the coach stops by the hospital to check on Junior, to apologize for putting him into the game at all, and to say that he respects Junior's commitment. Junior is not supposed to sleep because of his head injury, so he and the coach sit up all night telling stories.

And a Partridge in a Pear Tree—Wake

As he has done on many Christmases before, Junior's dad takes the family's meager savings and disappears for several days, drunk. When he returns, Junior is hurt, but he loves his dad and tells him it is all right. Mary sends Junior several postcards of Montana, revealing that she still cannot find a job but that she has begun writing a book. Junior thinks about his family and how they show their love and realizes that many of his white friends have more money and security but also have parents who ignore them.

Junior's grandmother, he says, is the best thing about Wellpinit. She is smart and loves to travel, and Junior finds that she is more tolerant of different kinds of people than other Indians he knows. She has no patience with homophobia, for example, and she makes friends with homeless people whenever she goes to Seattle. She loves to attend powwows, where she could meet new people from far away. Suddenly, however, she is dead, killed by a drunk driver while walking home. Her last wish is that the family should forgive the driver.

At her funeral, thousands of people come, and none of them treat Junior unkindly. Mary is not able to be there, but the rest of the extended family gathers and mourns. Into the gathering comes a white man, Billionaire Ted; he is "yet another white guy who showed up on the rez because he loved Indian people SOOOOOOOO much." Ted explains that he collects Indian artifacts and that for several years he has owned a beaded powwow dance outfit. At great expense, he has hired an expert to research the outfit, and the expert has traced the dress to the Spokane people and to Grandmother Spirit herself. Billionaire Ted has come to give the dress back, but none of the crowd recognizes the style of beadwork, and Grandmother Spirit was never a powwow dancer, so Junior's mother hands the dress back. Ted leaves, followed by the laughter of the crowd.

Valentine Heart—My Final Freshman Year Report Card

More sadness comes. Eugene is shot in the face and killed by a friend when the two men, both drunk, quarrel over the last drink from a bottle of wine. Junior blames himself for the deaths, becomes more and more depressed, and starts missing school. When he returns, one of his teachers makes a sarcastic comment about his attendance. Gordy stands up, slams his book down on the desk, and walks out, followed by all of the other students in the class. Junior has friends.

Junior becomes the best shooter on the basketball team but never becomes comfortable playing. In fact, he throws up before every game. When Reardan faces Wellpinit again, Junior is determined to win. Rowdy is assigned to guard Junior, and for the first time, Junior leaps higher than Rowdy and steals the ball out of his hands. He outscores Rowdy throughout the game, and the Reardan team wins easily. However, as Junior watches his old Wellpinit classmates after the game, he realizes that, for many of them, basketball is all they have. None of them will go to college, many of them had no breakfast that morning, and most of them have alcoholic parents. Winning the game seems less glorious now, but when Junior and Rowdy exchange their next emails, Rowdy's insults seem less angry, and Junior is hopeful.

The hopefulness does not last. Junior is called out of class one day, and the school counselor awkwardly tells him that Mary has died. Apparently, she and her new husband had a party in their trailer. A fire started, and Mary was drunk and passed out; she never realized the trailer was on fire. Junior thinks that if he had never left for Reardan, Mary would never have left for Montana; he feels responsible for her death. After Mary's funeral, Junior runs into Rowdy, who has been watching from a distance. Rowdy also blames Junior for Mary's death, and he tells Junior, "I hate you!" before running away. At school, the white kids hug Junior and slip him notes of sympathy.

Remembering—Talking about Turtles

Junior and his parents take a picnic lunch and Dad's saxophone and go to the cemetery to clean the family graves. They hug and express their love, and Junior finds himself crying for all the missed opportunities and all of the lonely people in the world. He realizes that he is going to be all right and thinks of those—including Rowdy—who will never reach their dreams. He remembers a day when he and Rowdy were ten and they climbed the biggest tree on the reservation. They were able to see their whole world from the top, and it was beautiful.

School ends, and Junior sits at home alone. Then Rowdy shows up. They trade insults, shoot some hoops, and talk about the future.

CHARACTERS

Billionaire Ted
Billionaire Ted is a wealthy white man from Montana who appears at Grandmother Spirit's funeral. He is typical of a kind of white person who is fascinated by Indians and full of misinformation about them; these fanatics become a target for mockery by Indians who see, as the white people themselves do not, that this fascination is superficial and condescending. Billionaire Ted has come to return a beaded dress that he believes once belonged to Grandmother Spirit, but the research that he has paid for turns out to be worthless. Junior's Mom examines the dress and rejects it, and Billionaire Ted drives away while two thousand Indians laugh.

Coach
"Coach" is the only name Junior ever gives for the man who coaches the Reardan High School basketball team. Coach seems to have no racist leanings; he wants the best players on his team and treats Junior the same way he treats the others. Coach understands young men: he knows what Junior is up against as the only Indian student at Reardan and what it means to Junior to be at odds with Rowdy. When Junior is hospitalized after Rowdy knocks him unconscious during the first Reardan-Wellpinit basketball game, Coach comes to see him in the hospital to apologize for putting Junior in the game and for putting him in an untenable situation. He stays the whole night talking with Junior, but Junior does not narrate any details about their conversation because "that night belongs to just me and my coach."

Dad
Junior's dad, Arnold Spirit, Sr., is an alcoholic, discouraged that he was not able to have the musical career he dreamed of. He spends most of his time drinking or watching television alone.

Sometimes Junior joins him, but the two sit and watch without speaking. Although Dad is frequently angry and depressed, he does not beat his children, as Rowdy's father does, and he never misses one of Junior's basketball games. Still, he cannot support his family, and in the beginning of the book, Dad shoots Junior's sick dog because the family cannot afford to take him to the veterinarian. When Junior transfers to Reardan, Dad drives him to and from school—when he remembers and when he has enough money for gas. At the end of the novel, after Mary has died, Dad tells Junior that he loves him. Junior is pleased to hear it, although he has never doubted that it was true.

Eugene
Junior's dad's best friend, Eugene, rides around the reservation on a 1946 Indian Chief Roadmaster motorcycle. Like many of the adults on the reservation, Eugene is an alcoholic, but he is kind to Junior. He gives Junior a ride to school on his motorcycle and, after he has had some EMT training, stitches up Junior's cut face during a basketball game. Eugene dies when he is shot in the face by a good friend; both drunk, they are fighting over the last swig of alcohol in a bottle.

Gordy
Gordy is a student at Reardan High School. Like Junior, he is a bookish nerd who does not fit in. Gordy supports Junior when the science teacher at Reardan is mocking him for his explanation of how petrified wood is formed, but he explains later that he has not spoken up to help Junior. "I did it for science," he says. Gordy and Junior form a distant friendship, spending time together studying in the library. Gordy speaks with a vocabulary and a wisdom beyond his years, and he helps Junior see better ways to learn. After Grandmother Spirit is killed and Junior misses several days of school, Gordy leads his classmates in walking out of social studies to protest the teacher's unkind remarks to Junior, and Junior realizes that his white classmates have become friends.

Junior
Fourteen-year-old Junior, whose given name is Arnold Spirit, is the novel's main character. He is an Indian living with his alcoholic parents and his depressed sister on the Spokane Indian Reservation. Because he is small and nerdy, because he stutters and has a lisp, and because hydrocephalus

has given him an enlarged head, he is a constant target of bullying and teasing. His only friend is Rowdy, an angry bully himself who has always stuck up for Junior.

Junior, who is most expressive when he is drawing cartoons, feels that his life is depressing and hopeless, but the feelings are crystallized when he discovers, on his first day of geometry class, that his reservation school has been using the same textbooks since his mother was a student there. His resulting outburst leads his teacher to urge Junior to leave the reservation and try to get a better education somewhere else before it is too late.

Junior transfers to Reardan High School in a small, all-white, wealthy town nearby, and soon discovers that he is smarter than he thought he was and a better basketball player. At first an outcast, he gradually wins the respect and friendship of his classmates, who can see that he does not give up easily when things go against him. Junior knows that doing well at Reardan is his only chance to escape the reservation, his only chance to realize his dreams though his parents never realized theirs. He does his best to keep his new friends from discovering how poor his family is, and he works hard at school and at basketball. But he sees that he is at best only a "part-time Indian"; at school, where everyone calls him "Arnold," he will always be thought of as Indian, and therefore as different, while on the reservation, where he is known as "Junior," his decision to attend Reardan is seen as a betrayal, as an attempt to be white.

As he moves through his freshman year of high school and faces the rejection of his best friend and three devastating deaths, Junior learns how to accept himself as an individual with strengths and weaknesses rather than as a representative of a group or tribe. He begins to see the limitations that held back his parents and his sister and that will hold back Rowdy, and even as Junior and Rowdy resume their old friendship at the end of the novel, the reader knows that one day Junior will leave Rowdy behind.

Mom

Junior's mom's real name is Agnes Adams Spirit, but Junior, the narrator, always refers to her as "Mom." She is a recovering alcoholic and poor, but she is very smart, an avid reader with a good memory. Junior thinks she might have become a community college teacher "if somebody had paid attention to [her] dreams" and she

had been able to go to college. Indirectly, she is the reason Junior transfers to Reardan High School. On the first day of geometry class, Junior finds her name, "Agnes Adams," written in his textbook and realizes that the school in Wellpinit is so ill-equipped that even the textbooks are at least thirty years old. Mom does not hesitate when Junior says he wants to transfer to the all-white school; she knows that getting off the reservation will be his only chance of realizing his dreams.

Mr. P

Mr. P is the white geometry teacher at Wellpinit High School on the reservation; he is eccentric and forgetful and has been teaching on the reservation for decades. Junior neither respects nor trusts him, seeing him as merely a white do-gooder who has been foisted on the school because no one really cares about the quality of Indian kids' education. After Junior throws a book at Mr. P one day in class and is suspended, Mr. P drives out to Junior's house to advise him to leave the reservation and look for a better education in Reardan. He confesses that, in his early days of teaching on the reservation, he harmed children by trying to force them to give up their culture. He reveals that he knew Junior's sister Mary, the smartest student he ever taught, and that she had secret dreams of being a writer. The reservation makes people give up, Mr. P says, and if Junior does not leave he will eventually give up, too.

Penelope

Penelope is a pretty, smart, and popular white girl with beautiful blue eyes. Junior meets her on his first day at Reardan High School, when she chats with him and then turns against him, making fun of him because he gives his name as "Junior" while the teachers call him "Arnold." For weeks she is cold and mean to him, but she warms up to him when Junior discovers but keeps the secret that she is anorexic. Junior and Penelope become something of a couple. Penelope never really loves Junior, but she likes him, and she knows that it irritates her father to see her dating an Indian. Penelope is deeply unhappy, believing that she will never escape her small town and see the world. When Junior and Penelope go to the Winter Formal together, Penelope discovers the depth of Junior's poverty and accepts it as he accepts her anorexia.

Roger

Roger, sometimes called Roger the Giant, is a big young man, a member of the Reardan varsity basketball team. In the beginning, he teases Junior with racial slurs, until the day he tells a joke that is so racist and infuriating that Junior punches him in the face. From then on, Roger leaves him alone. During basketball tryouts, Junior is paired with the much bigger Roger in a one-on-one game; Junior's determination to keep playing after he is knocked down wins the respect of Roger and the coach. Soon, Roger becomes something of a big brother to Junior, as he is to Penelope, and he slips Junior some money after the dance when he realizes Junior does not have any.

Rowdy

Rowdy is Junior's best friend, born only two hours after Junior on November 5, 1992. He was born screaming and seems to have been angry ever since. Rowdy's family is as poor as Junior's, but Rowdy's father is also physically abusive, and Rowdy frequently comes to school with bruises. He is a bully and frequently gets into fights with the other boys, but he is always ready to defend Junior against other bullies. The two boys have a strong bond, which they typically demonstrate by insulting each other, wrestling, and acting indifferent.

When Junior decides to leave the reservation for school, Rowdy takes the decision as personal rejection and turns his anger and jealousy toward Junior. He refuses to have any contact with Junior and does not even come by for his traditional pumpkin pie at Thanksgiving. During the first basketball game between Wellpinit and Reardan, held on the reservation, Rowdy knocks Junior unconscious and puts him in the hospital on the way to soundly defeating the Reardan team. His anger is amplified when Junior helps defeat Wellpinit in a second basketball game, and Junior realizes that for Rowdy and the other boys stuck on the reservation, winning at basketball is one of few ways to gain attention and pride.

At the end of the novel, Rowdy shows up at Junior's house. Neither boy says anything warm or sentimental (Rowdy says that he has come by only because he is bored), but it appears that they will spend at least summer vacation as friends again.

Agnes Adams Spirit

See Mom

Arnold Spirit, Jr.

See Junior

Arnold Spirit, Sr.

See Dad

Grandmother Spirit

Junior's maternal grandmother is a tough and sensible woman who gives Junior advice about how to deal with other men. A widow, she wears bandannas, goes to garage sales, and makes delicious salmon mush. She is open-hearted, arguing that homophobia is wrong and making friends with homeless people when she visits the big city. When she is fatally hit by a drunk driver, her last request is that the family forgive the driver, rather than seek revenge.

Mary Spirit

Mary is Junior's older sister. She is smart and funny and tough, and she never lets her family know that she used to read romance novels all day long and dreamed of writing them herself. After graduating high school, she seems to collapse, perhaps realizing that her future offers few options. She lives in her parents' basement for seven years, never goes out, and rarely speaks, and the family nicknames her "Mary Runs Away."

One day, she actually runs away without warning; she marries a young man she met in the casino and moves with him to the Flathead Reservation in Montana. Occasionally she sends postcards to Junior, describing her beautiful life. In fact, she is living in a trailer and struggling, unable to find a job but using the time to try to write an autobiography. During Junior's first year at Reardan, she is killed when her trailer catches fire. Passed out drunk, she never wakes up.

THEMES

Identity

The central question facing Junior, the protagonist in *The Absolutely True Diary of a Part-Time Indian*, is over his identity: Who is he? Does he have to turn his back on being an Indian in order to have the kind of life he dreams of? From the beginning, Junior is not the kind of kid who fits in. He has an enlarged head, large hands and feet, a stammer and a lisp, and even on the reservation

TOPICS FOR FURTHER STUDY

- Watch the movie *Smoke Signals* (1998), for which Sherman Alexie wrote the screenplay, and read the short story "This Is What It Means to Say Phoenix, Arizona," from Alexie's collection *The Lone Ranger and Tonto Fistfight in Heaven* (1993). Is it possible to imagine Thomas Builds-the-Fire and Victor Joseph as the adult versions of Junior and Rowdy? What do the younger and older characters have in common, and how are they different? Write a paper in which you predict what happens to Junior and Rowdy several years after *The Absolutely True Diary* ends, drawing on Thomas Builds-the-Fire and Victor Joseph as appropriate. If you wish, write an illustrated "Epilogue" to the novel instead, setting it ten or more years in the future and echoing the narrator's voice.

- Research the history and development of the Spokane Indian Reservation, and prepare a digital presentation for your class including maps, important dates, and statistics. Be sure to point out the locations of Wellpinit and Reardan, a description of the Spokane Powwow, and any other information that helps readers understand the references in the novel.

- Research the controversy over Indian mascots for school athletic teams, and decide for yourself whether you think they are respectful or disrespectful. If possible, contact the administrations of several of these schools (for example, the University of Louisiana at Monroe) and ask about the financial implications of these changes. Prepare a Power-Point presentation of typical mascots and fans, possibly incorporating videos if appropriate, to persuade your classmates to accept your position.

- *The Lone Ranger*, a popular television show from 1949 to 1957, featured the Lone Ranger himself (a masked hero who rode into town to do good deeds) and his Indian companion, Tonto. Out of more than two hundred episodes made, seventy-eight are available on DVD and about a dozen can be watched for free at hulu.com. Watch an episode of the show, perhaps with your class. Write a character analysis of Tonto, making note of any stereotypes you find.

- Read Sandra Cisneros's short novel, *The House on Mango Street* (1984), about a Latina girl who dreams of escaping her impoverished Chicago neighborhood. Write a paper in which you compare Junior's dreams and struggles with those of Esperanza Cordero, and bring in other characters—or real people—you may know who dream of leaving home (you might include Jay Gatsby, Jane Eyre, or even Luke Skywalker). Is the experience different for boys and for girls? For Indians and for Latinas? For modern people and those living in the past? What can you generalize about the need to leave home and make one's own way?

- Choose one of the chapters in *The Absolutely True Diary of a Part-Time Indian* that is not illustrated, and create a cartoon for it in the style of those in the book.

- Prepare a short video or podcast of tips for students who will soon spend their first day at your school. Use humor to give advice and to point out common mistakes that new students sometimes make. Ask permission from your principal to post it on YouTube or show it on your school news station.

---

he is constantly teased and beaten up. Although he has never been accepted on the reservation, he is rejected in a more profound way once he transfers to Reardan, the white high school.

When he tells Rowdy, his only friend, that he is transferring, Rowdy punches him in the face and shouts, "You always thought you were better than me." In the drawing Junior makes after the argument, Rowdy is calling Junior a "white lover." When Reardan plays basketball at Wellpinit, the reservation crowd taunts Junior by shouting the name he is called at Reardan, "Arnold," and turns away from him. In their minds, he is no longer an Indian.

However, Junior knows that he does not belong at Reardan, either. "I woke up on the reservation as an Indian," he says, "and somewhere on the road to Reardan I became something less than Indian." For the first several weeks, no one at school will even speak to him. Once he has made a few friends and begun to fit in with the white students, his identity becomes even more confusing. He notes, "Traveling between Reardan and Wellpinit...I always felt like a stranger. I was half Indian in one place and half white in the other."

Junior's learning to shape his two lives into a coherent whole is the major theme of the novel. He has to learn to cherish the traditions and strengths of his native culture while rejecting the weaknesses, including hopelessness and alcoholism, and he must incorporate values that are seen as "white," including a new way of thinking about education. In the end, Junior realizes that he belongs to many groups: "I was a Spokane Indian. I belonged to that tribe. But I also belonged to the tribe of American immigrants. And to the tribe of basketball players. And to the tribe of bookworms." Junior claims membership in fourteen tribes, and concludes, "That's when I knew that I was going to be okay."

Friendship

One of the most appealing threads running through *The Absolutely True Diary of a Part-Time Indian* is the friendship between Junior and Rowdy. They boys were born only hours apart, and they have been best friends ever since. Junior is awkward and weak and nerdy, and Rowdy is an angry bully; for each of them, their friendship is essential, because each has only one friend. However, these are adolescent boys, and they do not permit themselves to express their affection for each other directly. Instead, they insult each other, punch and wrestle each other, and exchange trash talk on the basketball court.

When Rowdy learns that Junior is transferring to Reardan, he cannot say that he will miss Junior or that he would be afraid to go. He cries,

is ashamed of crying, and ends up punching Junior in the face. When Junior misses Rowdy at Thanksgiving, he shows his longing by drawing a cartoon of the two boys together and bringing it to Rowdy's house. Rowdy will not come to the door, will not admit that he likes the cartoon, and makes an obscene gesture at Junior, but Junior guesses from the fact that Rowdy does not tear up the cartoon that there is some lingering respect.

At the end of the novel, when Rowdy breaks down and comes over to see Junior, he cannot admit that he misses his friend or that he admires his bravery. He says that he still hates Junior but has come over because "he's bored." When Rowdy yells "I hate you" and when Junior realizes that "my best friend had become my worst enemy," the reader knows that the friendship will endure, even if the boys do not dare believe it or show it. As the two friends play basketball in the final chapter, they come the closest they have ever come to having a heartfelt conversation, but Rowdy laces his sentimental talk with vulgarities and insults.

Family

Junior's relationship with his parents is a complicated one. On one level, it is straightforward and positive: he loves his parents, and they love him and each other. His parents do not hesitate in allowing him to transfer to Reardan High School, although it is twenty-two miles away and coming up with gas money is a struggle. They do their best to get him new clothes for school, to give him rides when they can, and to lend him a suit for the formal. Before Junior leaves for Reardan, Rowdy spends a lot of time at Junior's house because his own father is frequently drunk and violent, but Rowdy knows he is safe with Junior's parents. In addition to his parents, Junior has an older sister and a grandmother who are also positive influences, sharing advice and affection.

However, *The Absolutely True Diary of a Part-Time Indian* is not a 1950s family television show, and Junior's family is not a model family. They are poor, and Junior reveals early on, "My mother and father are drunks." His mother does not drink much, but Junior's father is frequently drunk, and Junior knows that, although his dad means well, he cannot be relied on. Often his dad drives Junior to school, but sometimes he simply

Arnold lives on the Spokane Indian reservation. *(Fusion Photography | Shutterstock.com)*

forgets or has spent all of the family's money on drinking. At Christmastime, Junior's dad "did what he always does when we don't have enough money. He took what little money we did have and ran away to get drunk." Mary, Junior's sister, is a smart woman who dreams of being a writer, but her own alcoholism and severe depression lead her to run away to get married, live in a trailer, stay unemployed, and die young. Eugene, "a good guy and like an uncle" to Junior, dies in a drunken fight with a friend, and Junior's beloved grandmother is killed by a drunk driver.

Junior begins his journey surrounded with his family's love, but he loses three members to death, and he knows that he will have to leave the others behind in order to "have a better life out in the white world." In the novel's second-to-last chapter, Junior and his parents go to the cemetery to clean the family graves. "I'm crazy about you," his father says, and his mother tells Junior, "I'm so proud of you." Alexie deliberately makes this the last look the reader has of Junior's family—a scene of love and pride and support.

STYLE

Bildungsroman

The Absolutely True Diary of a Part-Time Indian is an example of a type of novel called a *bildungsroman,* or the "coming of age" novel. Typically, this kind of novel tells the story of a young person who moves from innocence to insight or from youth to maturity and who faces challenges and learns lessons along the way. Also, the character is typically pushed away from home out into the wider world early in the novel. Here the protagonist, Junior, leaves his home—or his feeling that he is home on the Spokane Indian Reservation—and heads out into a wealthy all-white town to find knowledge and experiences that would not otherwise be available to him. At first he is rejected by his new society, but he gradually acquires the skills he needs to be accepted and to succeed.

Junior's development begins with formal education. He realizes, with the help of Mr. P and his mother's old textbook, that he will never be able to get a decent high school education in his local school; in fact, he rejects two better schools on the reservation to select Reardan High School, the best school in the area. However, his education goes beyond school. He also learns that white people can be friends, that he is smart and capable, and that the only way he will ever realize his dreams—as his parents were never able to realize theirs—is to eventually leave the reservation forever behind him. This last lesson is a bittersweet one. As he watches his Reardan basketball team celebrating its win over the Wellpinit team, he realizes with sadness and shame that Rowdy and the others will never go to college, never succeed financially, and never escape the burden of alcoholism. Like many protagonists in the coming-of-age novel, Junior learns that, once he sets out on his journey, he can never go back.

Illustrations

Perhaps the most unusual element of *The Absolutely True Diary of a Part-Time Indian* is the inclusion of the illustrations by Ellen Forney. The protagonist, Junior, is constantly drawing cartoons that introduce the important people in his life or express his deepest, most complex feelings. As he puts it, "I draw because I want to talk to the world. And I want the world to pay attention to me. I feel important with a pen in my hand." As an adolescent with multiple disabilities, including a lisp and a stammer, Junior has found that he can express himself better with his pen than through speaking. When his best friend Rowdy refuses to speak to him, Junior makes his first approach by drawing a cartoon of the two boys together and delivering it to Rowdy.

There are sixty drawings in the novel, all of them ostensibly drawn by Junior; several of them are made to look as though they have been drawn on notebook paper, crumpled up in a backpack, smoothed out, and taped into the book. Junior includes drawings of his parents, his sister, his grandmother, his friend Rowdy, Eugene, Penelope, and others, labeled with their favorite clothing and most revealing possessions. Many of the drawings show Junior feeling lonely or nervous or embarrassed.

In an important cartoon in the chapter "How to Fight Monsters," drawn on Junior's first day at Reardan, he illustrates the feelings that give the novel its title: he shows a high school kid with a line drawn top to bottom down his middle. On one side, the kid is white, full of hope, with nice

clothes and "a bright future"; on the other side he is Indian, with "bone-crushing reality" instead of hope, inexpensive clothes, and "a vanishing past." As time passes, Junior becomes more like the white kids and becomes like both sides of the drawing at once. He *becomes* a part-time Indian. Junior as narrator is not reticent about sharing his feelings in words with his readers, but Junior the character keeps most of his feelings to himself, expressing them mainly through his private drawings.

HISTORICAL CONTEXT

Native American Literature

Although Native American oral traditions reach back hundreds of years, it was not until the second half of the twentieth century that Native American authors began writing and publishing books that reached a large, mainstream readership. Many critics use the year 1968, the year that N. Scott Momaday's novel *House Made of Dawn* won the Pulitzer Prize, as the beginning of what they call the Native American Renaissance. Several events contributed to this Renaissance: the honorable service of many Native Americans in the Vietnam War, the success of the civil rights movement and the feminist movement, and an increased awareness among whites of Native American culture and social issues. James Ruppert, in "Fiction: 1968 to the Present," notes that this period was important for Native American writers, for "suddenly it seemed possible that they could be successful with their writing and still remain true to their unique experience."

Ruppert walks his readers through the decades after 1968. He notes that the 1970s produced writing that often reflected a romantic view of the past, celebrating the old ways and saving the old stories from being forgotten, and the 1980s brought a flourishing of Native American writers, including Leslie Marmon Silko and Louise Erdrich, who reached large audiences and won major awards. He credits Erdrich, whose *Love Medicine* (1984) won the National Book Critics Circle Award for Fiction, with introducing humor.

By the time Alexie began publishing poetry and then fiction in the 1990s, there was already a place for Native American literature in the bookstores and the schools. One strand of this writing is exemplified by Joseph Bruchac, who has published several popular retellings of traditional tales, including the collection *Between Earth and Sky: Legends of Native American Sacred Places* (1996). Alexie and his contemporaries have attempted to write in a new voice and to explore what it means to be a Native American today. This new fiction is not set in a romantic past or out in the desert or the forest, but on the poverty-stricken, alcohol- and despair-filled reservation. As Ruppert writes, Alexie's "reservation dwellers do not contemplate myth or pronounce wisdom about nature."

Alexie is typical of Native American writers in the twenty-first century in his need to address two distinct audiences. In a 2007 interview with James Mellis, Alexie discussed his hope that *The Absolutely True Diary* would reach "a lot of native kids certainly, but also poor kids of any variety who feel trapped by circumstance, by culture, by low expectations." However, as he explains, a writer cannot make a living—or even find a publisher—by appealing only to poor children. Instead, he acknowledges that "college-educated white women" make up the largest share of book buyers, teachers, and librarians: "They seem to be the people who are most willing to ignore barriers and boundaries and to reach across, so that's who my audience is in reality." This need to be true to authentic experience while still appealing to a white readership has been a continual challenge and opportunity for Native American writers since the 1960s.

Through this period, even the terminology used by and for these writers has changed. "Native Americans" was used, beginning in the 1960s, as a polite and respectful term, and it was the term used by the federal government to take in all of the "native" groups, including Hawaiians. Later, many writers and activists, including Sherman Alexie, came to reject this bureaucratic term in favor of "Indian" or "American Indian." In the twenty-first century, many say that either term is acceptable, and "Native American" is the term used most in the classroom and in scholarship. Many individuals prefer to be labeled with the name of their tribe, rather than lumped together with other indigenous groups. Alexie is typically referred to by critics as a Coeur d'Alene/Spokane Indian, designating the tribes of which his father and mother were members, and Junior calls himself either a Spokane or an Indian.

A Native American teen is torn between cultures.
(Mona Makela / Shutterstock.com)

CRITICAL OVERVIEW

The Absolutely True Diary of a Part-Time Indian, Alexie's first book written for young-adult readers, was widely praised from its publication in 2007 and has become a popular book in schools and school libraries. It won dozens of awards, including the 2007 National Book Award for Young People's Literature, the 2008 American Indian Library Association American Indian Youth Literature Award, the 2008 *Boston Globe-Horn Book* Award for Excellence in Children's Literature in Fiction, and the 2008 Pacific Northwest Book Award. It was named to several "best books" lists in 2007, including those of the *New York Times*, *Los Angeles Times*, *School Library Journal*, *Horn Book*, and *Kirkus Reviews*.

Reviewers almost universally praised the book. Bruce Barcott, reviewing *The Absolutely True Diary* for the *New York Times*, notes that, although this was Alexie's first young-adult novel, "it took him only one book to master the form.... [T]his is a gem of a book." In the Minneapolis-St. Paul *Star Tribune*, Jim Lenfestey compares Alexie to J. D. Salinger and calls the novel "an absolutely honest, scary, and very funny bright light among the lost." *Los Angeles Times* contributor Susan Carpenter describes Alexie as a "masterful" writer who has been able "to transform sociological issues into a page turner that resonates with adolescent readers."

Many reviewers believe that the book could be helpful to young readers. Ian Chipman's review in *Booklist* comments that "younger teens looking for the strength to lift themselves out of rough situations would do well to start here." Writing for *Teenreads.com*, Jana Siciliano finds that "Junior's remarkable ability to weather even the worst possible storms...makes this an uplifting yet very emotional reading experience."

The book has also been well-received outside the United States. Reviewing the novel for the London *Guardian*, Diane Samuels writes,

> Maybe it's the combination of drawings, pithy turns of phrase, candour, tragedy, despair and hope that makes this more than an entertaining read, more than an engaging story about a North American Indian kid who makes it out of a poor, dead-end background without losing his connection with who he is and where he's from.

She concludes that the novel is "humane, authentic and, most of all, it speaks." Beyond Great Britain, the novel has been published in twelve foreign editions.

Scholars have begun to examine the novel, as well, tying it to Alexie's earlier novels and short stories for adult readers and encouraging its use in classrooms. Jan Johnson, in an essay published in 2010, sees in *The Absolutely True Diary* and in the novel *Flight* (2007) that "empathy, compassion and forgiveness mark a possible way out of suffering and grief" and concludes that they "convey hopefulness not apparent earlier in Alexie's career." In a 2009 essay, Bryan Ripley Crandall recommends the novel for teachers of adolescents interested in issues of inclusion, arguing that "the story has the potential to promote discussions among a wide variety of students: those with disabilities, those who are seen as able, those from majority-dominant backgrounds, and those from minority cultures."

However, *The Absolutely True Diary* has not been universally admired. After a parent complaint about sexual references, the novel was removed from ninth grade English classes at Crook County High School in Prineville, Oregon, in 2008, and parents in Antioch, Illinois, tried to have the book removed from their local school's ninth grade summer reading list in 2009. In 2010, the book was officially banned from school classrooms in Stockton, Missouri. One of the school board members who voted in favor of the ban and who found the book offensive told Mike Penprase in the Springfield, Missouri *News-Leader*, "We can take the book and wrap it in those 20 awards everyone else said it won and it still is wrong." The novel was the second most frequently challenged book in schools and libraries in 2010, as listed by the American Library Association. The newsletter *Education Services News* listed the reasons for the challenges: "offensive language, racism, sex education, sexually explicit, unsuited to age group, violence."

CRITICISM

Cynthia A. Bily

Bily teaches English at Macomb Community College in Michigan. In the following essay, she discusses the themes of death and rescue in The Absolutely True Diary of a Part-Time Indian.

One of the most admired qualities of Sherman Alexie's *The Absolutely True Diary of a Part-Time Indian* is its humor. Using a fourteen-year-old boy, Arnold "Junior" Spirit, as a narrator, Alexie infuses the novel with funny reflections on good chicken, squabbling between siblings and friends, nerdiness, and self-consciousness—not to mention the cartoons that Junior draws to express and to deflect painful thoughts. However, the humor is bittersweet; it is so genuine and warm that it is easy to overlook how dark the novel actually is. Just as Junior uses humor to help him get through bad times, Alexie uses humor to help readers maintain hopefulness as they experience his novel's strong undercurrent of death.

When Mr. P comes to talk to Junior near the beginning of novel, shortly after Junior has hit him in the face with a thrown book, he tells Junior, "If you stay on this rez...they're going to kill you. I'm going to kill you. We're all going to kill you. You can't fight us forever." Junior is not sure what to make of this remark. He has failed to understand Mr. P's confession that, in his early days of teaching, he was taught to "kill the Indian to save the child," that is, to force the

WHAT DO I READ NEXT?

- Alexie's first book of fiction was *The Lone Ranger and Tonto Fistfight in Heaven* (1993), a collection of short stories set on the Spokane Indian Reservation. Written for adults, the stories contain the humor and grittiness that mark his later works, as they depict the grinding poverty and struggles over identity faced by Alexie's characters.

- *Reservation Blues* (1995), Alexie's first novel, tells the story of Thomas Builds-the-Fire and his magical blues guitar. Thomas and some of his friends from Wellpinit form a blues band, Coyote Springs, and set out on the road, where they must find ways to balance this exciting new art form with elements of their Native culture.

- In his memoir *At the End of Ridge Road* (2005), Abenaki Indian writer Joseph Bruchac describes how he was raised in upstate New York by his grandparents and taught to love nature and to respect his ancestors. As a young boy, he was drawn to reading and writing but found acceptance from the other boys through sports.

- Tom, the Mohawk protagonist of Erik E. Esckilsen's novel *Offsides* (2004), is good enough to be a star player on the soccer team at his new high school, but he refuses to play for a school whose mascot is a stereotypical Indian warrior.

- In Charlotte Brontë's classic novel *Jane Eyre* (1847), Jane must overcome the expectations and limitations of a young woman without money in England and find a way to use her intelligence in a society that has little use for bright, capable women.

- *The Spokane Indians: Children of the Sun* (2006), by Robert H. Ruby and John A. Brown, is a history of the Spokane people from their early salmon-based life in the central plains of Washington, through their confinement on reservations, to twentieth century struggles to balance heritage and modern life.

- *American Born Chinese* is a young-adult graphic novel written by Gene Yang in 2006. It is similar in theme and style to *The Absolutely True Diary of a Part-Time Indian* in that is a bildungsroman novel, uses illustration to help tell the story, and addresses the difficulties and stereotypes of minority students in an American school.

---

children to give up anything that tied them to their Indian culture and kept them from being more "civilized," more white. Now, when Mr. P speaks of the rez killing Junior, the boy—and the reader—thinks Mr. P is again speaking metaphorically. One of the lessons that Junior learns as the novel moves forward is Mr. P's warning is not a metaphor—getting away from the reservation could literally save Junior's life.

Alexie eases into the theme of death with the sad story of Junior's dog, Oscar. Like many adolescent boys, Junior feels his closest relationship is with his dog: "He was the only living thing that I could depend on. He was more dependable than my parents, grandmother, aunts, uncles,

cousins, and big sister." When Oscar becomes sick, the family has no money to pay for a vet, and finally there is nothing left to do but shoot the dog to end its suffering. The death of Oscar is thus tied up with the family's poverty, which comes from being Indians on a reservation with few opportunities. Junior does not blame his family for their poverty or for Oscar's death, but Oscar's death makes him pause to contemplate what kind of life his family might have had if his parents had been able to realize their dreams.

Junior, the reader learns in the novel's first chapter, has been fighting off death since he was born. He was born with hydrocephalus and underwent a life-threatening surgery when he

THE HARDER LESSON TO ACCEPT, BUT THE REAL ONE, IS THAT IF JUNIOR IS TO SAVE HIS OWN LIFE HE WILL HAVE TO REJECT SOME OF HIS INDIAN WAYS AND JOIN THE WHITE WORLD—HE WILL HAVE TO BECOME A PART-TIME INDIAN."

was only six months old. Since then, he has had a cloud of death hanging over him, worrying that a high fever or a head injury could kill him.

Another life-threatening danger—alcoholism—faces many of the people in Junior's world. Both of his parents are alcoholics, and although there are no scenes in the novel of Junior's mother drinking or being drunk, his father is frequently shown to be drunk, depressed, and undependable. Rowdy's father is often drunk and beats Rowdy and his mother. The Andruss brothers pass out drunk at the powwow after assaulting Junior.

Eugene, Junior's father's best friend, is one of the men Junior can count on when his father forgets his promises or when others in the town turn against him. As Junior describes him, "Eugene was a good guy, and like an uncle to me, but he was drunk all the time. Not stinky drunk, just drunk enough to be drunk." Eugene dies drunk, "shot and killed by one of his good friends, Bobby, who was too drunk to even remember pulling the trigger." Soon afterward, Bobby hangs himself. Even Junior's grandmother, friend to the poor and the gays and the homeless, a woman who "had never drunk alcohol in her life," is killed by a drunk driver as she walks home from a powwow.

Junior is surrounded by death, and his first response is anger: "I could easily have killed myself. Killed my mother and father, killed the birds, killed the trees, and killed the oxygen in the air. More than anything, I wanted to kill God." Junior knows that he has seen too much death in his young life. "I'm fourteen years old," he says, "and I've been to forty-two funerals. . . . And you know what the worst part is? The unhappy part? About 90 percent of the deaths have been because of alcohol."

Junior sinks into a depression, and tries to pull himself out of it by writing and drawing. He is gradually rescued by his white friends, who dramatically stand by him and embrace him at school, but as the novel makes brutally clear, just getting away from the Spokane Indian Reservation will not be enough to save Junior. After all, his sister Mary escapes, marrying a man she meets in the casino and moving with him to the Flathead Reservation in Montana. For a while, it seems that Mary is heading toward a better life. She loves her husband, she loves Montana, and she has begun writing a book in fulfillment of a lifelong dream. However, Mary does not get away from alcohol, the scourge of Indian life, and she dies in a trailer fire, too drunk to wake up and save herself. For a while, Junior blames himself, as Rowdy blames him, believing, "She had burned to death because I had decided that I wanted to spend my life with white people." This is not where the novel leaves Junior; it is not his fault, and he should not give up his plan to leave. The harder lesson to accept, but the real one, is that if Junior is to save his own life he will have to reject some of his Indian ways and join the white world—he will have to become a part-time Indian.

Junior understands this by the time he and his parents go out to the cemetery to clean the family graves. Instead of blaming himself for making Mary decide to leave home, he honors her for pursuing her dreams, even though she did not catch them, and he resolves to keep trying himself. He explains his grief:

> I was crying because I knew five or ten or fifteen more Spokanes would die during the next year, and that most of them would die because of booze. I cried because many of my fellow tribal members were slowly killing themselves and I wanted them to live. I wanted them to get strong and get sober and get the hell off the rez.

In the last chapter, Junior is reunited with Rowdy, and he remembers a summer day when the boys were ten years old and decided to climb the tallest pine tree on the reservation. Alexie brings the novel back to a metaphoric, childlike view of death, to subtly highlight the seriousness of Junior's new understanding. As a child, Rowdy and Junior climbed a tall tree. They told each other, "We're going to die," and Junior kept thinking a branch would break "and send me plummeting to my death." That was a child's understanding of death; there is no real terror in the comments, and the boys were rewarded for their bravery with a few hours of peace and beauty.

Coming out of his memory, Junior reflects that he "can't believe I survived my first year at Reardan." Again, with the word "survived," Alexie reminds the reader that there are different kinds of survival, and different kinds of death. He has no objection to this casual talk, but he underscores the fact that his lesson for Junior is serious: to live, Junior must leave. Junior himself understands this. As he and Rowdy play basketball in the final scene, he has already begun to think of his friend as a part of his past. He thinks, "I would always love Rowdy. And I would always miss him, too. Just as I would always love and miss my grandmother, my big sister, and Eugene."

Critic Jan Johnson, in an essay titled "Healing the Soul Wound," emphasizes the "compassion and empathy" of *The Absolutely True Diary*, explaining that Junior's

> father is an alcoholic, but he deeply loves his son. [Junior] expresses love for his father, his family, his tribe and his reservation but believes he must leave to escape the hopelessness and despair that can overwhelm even wonderful, loving people.

Alexie himself has often acknowledged that he also had to leave to become the man he is. In a 2007 interview with Tanita Davis and Sarah Stevenson, he comments

> Politically, I want all those folks, Indian or not, who celebrate me to realize that they are also celebrating the fact that I left the rez. All of my books and movies exist because I left.

The Absolutely True Diary of a Part-Time Indian is the story of one Indian young man, Junior, and the novel emphasizes the particular dangers that face young men like Junior. However, Alexie does not limit his warning only to Indians, and he does not believe physical death is the only kind there is. In his interview with Davis and Stevenson, he demonstrated the universality of the novel's message:

> I think Arnold, by leaving the rez, is escaping a slow-motion death trap. But I would also love my readers to recognize that a small white 'mainstream' town can be a kind of death trap, too.... Metaphorically speaking, we all grow up on reservations, don't we?

He addressed this idea again in a 2008 essay "Every Teen's Struggle," writing, "Teenagers of every class, color and creed, feel trapped by family, community and tribal expectations. And teenagers have to make the outrageous and heroic decision to recreate themselves."

Native American boy in ceremonial head dress
(Lori Martin / Shutterstock.com)

Source: Cynthia A. Bily, Critical Essay on *The Absolutely True Diary of a Part-Time Indian*, in *Novels for Students*, Gale, Cengage Learning, 2012.

Emily Judah

In the following review, Judah, age thirteen, explains why she recommends the novel.

The Absolutely True Diary of a Part-Time Indian was a very interesting book. When I read the first chapter it was totally different than what I expected as I picked it out without knowing anything about the book.

Arnold, who prefers the nickname Junior, is a 14-year-old Spokane Indian who lives on a reservation in Des Moines, Iowa. He was born with too much cerebral spinal fluid in his skull. When he was a baby he had to have surgery to remove some of the excess fluid from around his brain. The surgery resulted in some physical problems—like Junior having forty-two teeth, being nearsighted in one eye, farsighted in the other, his feet being size eleven in third-grade, and having a stutter and a lisp. Because of his appearance and lisp, Junior is picked on by everyone except his best friend, Rowdy, who is one of the meanest Indian kids that ever lived. On top of all of that, Junior's family is poor just like all of the other Indians on the reservation.

All the Spokane kids go to the same school that their mothers and fathers, grandmothers and grandfathers went to. All of the kids seem to fall into the same cycle as other generations. They graduate, get a small, low-paying job, drink too much alcohol, and live the rest of their life without hope. Junior knows that he will end up just like the others if he doesn't work for his dreams and leave the depressing ways of reservation life. One day Junior's white math teacher, Mr. P, stops by to talk to him. As they talk Mr. P explains that going to the school on the reservation will likely crush all of his chances of making something of himself and suggests Junior transfer to Reardan, a more promising school 22 miles away from the reservation. After long and careful thinking Junior makes the difficult decision to leave the reservation school and go to Reardan. Junior knows he is the first student ever to leave the reservation school and understands how hard the transition will be. The remainder of the book is about Junior's struggles in a new environment, constant battles with old friends and finally the struggle to do the best you can and never give up.

I thought that *The Absolutely True Diary of a Part-Time Indian* had a very good storyline. I learned what minorities go through in their everyday life, and how they feel. In the book there were some places with very mature subject matter, but the author did a good job of putting them in places that helps the reader peek into the struggles of youth. I felt like I knew exactly how Junior felt. Overall, I really liked this book. I would recommend *The Absolutely True Diary of a Part-Time Indian* to ages 14 and up.

Source: Emily Judah, Review of *The Absolutely True Diary of a Part-Time Indian*, in *MBR Bookwatch*, February 2008.

Rick Margolis
In the following review, Margolis interviews Alexie about the origin and evolution of this novel.

You were born with hydrocephalus (water on the brain), and you grew up poor on the Spokane Indian Reservation with alcoholic parents. How did you learn to read by the time you were three?

Partly it was because my dad was a major genre reader. He read a lot of, like, *The Executioner*

and *The Punisher* and a lot of Zane Grey and Louis L'Amour. He was way into the John F. Kennedy assassination; so there were dozens of those books around the house. Even though my dad was a randomly employed, blue-collar alcoholic, he was also very much into reading. And then the other thing was, ironically, because I was so sick and because Indian health service has such great contracts with major health-care providers, I ended up in a lot of therapy—physical therapy, occupational therapy, speech therapy. Because they thought I was going to be mentally disabled, they had me in a lot of educational therapies. So my brain disease and my brain surgery got me the kind of early childhood education that I never would have gotten otherwise.

When you were five, you read The Grapes of Wrath, *which remains one of your favorites. Back then, what appealed to you about the story?*

Fleeing poverty. Getting in the car and going and trying to find a way, and being stopped at nearly every turn—the struggle against poverty.

You understood that concept at such a young age?

One of the things that I've always said is that you measure the quality of a person's life by the age at which they had their first political thought. I was about four, standing in line to get government food on the reservation. And it struck me that all over the news I was watching Russians standing in line to get government food—and they were the enemy.

The Absolutely True Diary of a Part-time Indian *is the tale of a 14-year-old Native American who transfers to an all-white school in hopes of finding a better life. Essentially, it's your real-life story. Why not just write a memoir?*

The material in *True Diary* was actually first part of a memoir. I've been working on a family memoir about my family's history with war. So I wrote this entire huge section about the first year I spent at the white high school, and it didn't fit whatsoever, thematically. So I put it aside, I had 450 manuscript pages that didn't seem to be going anywhere. Then a YA editor called me, as she had been calling me over the years, about every six months: "So where's that YA novel?" She called me on this day that I had printed out those pages, and as I was talking to her, I was looking at my desktop and there was the manuscript, sitting there, and I thought, "Wow! I think that's a novel." So it was really sort of a coincidence. And then partly I made it a novel simply because—this is weird to say—nobody would actually believe it as a memoir.

Boys are going to love the book, because it's funny and entertaining and has great illustrations. Also, one of its characters equates the joy of reading to getting a "metaphorical boner." Did you coin that phrase or did you hear it in high school?

All my metaphorical and metaphysical boners are recent.

How did you come up with it?

It was literally while lying in bed, talking to my wife about loving books and loving her—and loving her and books together.

You're a successful poet, novelist, screenplay writer, and filmmaker. Did you ever imagine your life would turn out so well?

You know, I worked hard, and I got lucky. I always think of that movie *Broadcast News*, when William Hurt says to Albert Brooks, "What do you do when your reality exceeds your dreams?" And Albert Brooks says, "You keep quiet about it."

Source: Rick Margolis, "Song of Myself: Sherman Alexie's First YA Novel, *The Absolutely True Diary of a Part-Time Indian*," in *School Library Journal*, Vol. 53, No. 8, August 2007, p. 29.

SOURCES

Alexie, Sherman, *The Absolutely True Diary of a Part-Time Indian*, Little, Brown, 2007.

———, "Every Teen's Struggle: Speaking to a Universal Need," in *Publisher's Weekly*, Vol. 255, No. 7, February 18, 2008, p. 160.

Barcott, Bruce, "Off the Rez," in *New York Times*, November 11, 2007, http://www.nytimes.com/2007/11/11/books/review/Barcott3-t.html (accessed March 30, 2011).

Carpenter, Susan, "Misfit," in *Los Angeles Times*, September 16, 2007, http://articles.latimes.com/2007/sep/16/books/bk-carpenter16 (accessed March 30, 2011).

Chipman, Ian, Review of *The Absolutely True Diary of a Part-Time Indian*, in *Booklist*, August 1, 2007.

Crandall, Bryan Ripley, "Adding a Disability Perspective When Reading Adolescent Literature: Sherman Alexie's *The Absolutely True Diary of a Part-Time Indian*," in *ALAN Review*, Vol. 36, No. 2, Winter 2009, pp. 71–78.

Davis, Tanita, and Sarah Stevenson, "Sherman Alexie," in *Conversations with Sherman Alexie*, edited by Nancy J. Peterson, University of Mississippi Press, 2009, pp. 187–91.

Grassian, Daniel, "Understanding Sherman Alexie," in *Understanding Sherman Alexie*, University of South Carolina Press, 2005, pp. 1–14.

Guth, Amy, "Proposed Sherman Alexie Book-Ban in Suburban Chicago High School," in *Chicago Now*, June 22, 2009, http://www.chicagonow.com/blogs/chicago-subtext/2009/06/sherman-alexie-book-ban-antioch-chicago-suburban-high-school.html (accessed May 26, 2011).

Johnson, Jan, "Healing the Soul Wound in *Flight* and *The Absolutely True Diary of a Part-Time Indian*," in *Sherman Alexie: A Collection of Critical Essays*, University of Utah Press, 2010, pp. 224–40.

Lenfestey, Jim, "Straight Shooter," in *Star Tribune* (Minneapolis-St. Paul, MN), September 13, 2007, http://www.startribune.com/entertainment/books/11381521.html (accessed March 30, 2011).

Mellis, James, "Interview with Sherman Alexie," in *Conversations with Sherman Alexie*, edited by Nancy J. Peterson, University of Mississippi Press, 2009, pp. 180–86.

Penprase, Mike, "Stockton Book Ban Upheld 7–0 in Packed Public Forum," in *News-Leader.com* (Springfield, MO), September 9, 2010, http://www.news-leader.com/article/20100909/NEWS04/9090375/Stockton-book-ban-upheld-7-0-in-packed-public-forum (accessed May 26, 2011).

"Prineville Board Bans Book after Parent Complains," in *KATU.com*, December 12, 2008, http://www.katu.com/news/36051944.html (accessed May 26, 2011).

Ruppert, James, "Fiction: 1968 to the Present," in *The Cambridge Companion to Native American Literature*, Cambridge University Press, 2005, pp. 173–88.

Samuels, Diane, "A Brave Life," in *Guardian* (London, England), October 4, 2008, http://www.guardian.co.uk/books/2008/oct/04/teenage.sherman.alexie (accessed May 3, 2011).

Siciliano, Jana, Review of *The Absolutely True Diary of a Part-Time Indian*, in *Teenreads.com*, http://www.teenreads.com/reviews/9780316013697.asp (accessed March 30, 2011).

"2010 ALA 'Banned Books List,'" in *Education Services News*, April 14, 2011, http://educationservicesnews.blogspot.com/2011/04/2010-ala-banned-books-list.html (accessed May 26, 2011).

FURTHER READING

Banner, Stuart, *How the Indians Lost Their Land: Law and Power on the Frontier*, Belknap Press, 2005.
    This thorough and serious analysis by a law professor explains how the Europeans moved across North America, acquiring land and pushing the Native Americans ever westward. Although the book is detailed and tells a complex story, it is written in clear language for general readers.

Berglund, Jeff, and Jan Roush, eds., *Sherman Alexie: A Collection of Critical Essays*, University of Utah Press, 2010.

This volume gathers fourteen critical essays about Alexie's fiction, poetry, and films. While a few of the pieces are rather technical, Berglund's introduction, Jan Johnson's essay on *Flight* and *The Absolutely True Diary*, and Angelica Lawson's analysis of gender roles in *Smoke Signals* offer interesting insights for general readers. The book also includes an extensive bibliography of primary and secondary sources.

Bruce, Heather E., Anna E. Baldwin, and Christabel Umphrey, *Sherman Alexie in the Classroom*, National Council of Teachers of English, 2008.

Part of the National Council of Teachers of English High School Literature Series, this volume provides ideas for teaching Alexie's films, short stories, poems, and novels. The chapter on *The Absolutely True Diary* and the novel *Flight* emphasizes Alexie's determination not to shield young people from the real world and the need to teach students about "understanding, reconciliation, responsibility" in a post-9/11 world.

Mihesuah, Devon A., *American Indians: Stereotypes and Realities*, Clarity Press, 2009.

In an easy-to-follow two-part format, this book presents twenty-five common stereotypes about Indians, each followed by images, texts, and explanations that show why the stereotype is false. Also included is a list of "do's and don'ts for those who teach American Indian history and culture."

Moore, David L., "Sherman Alexie: Irony, Intimacy, and Agency," in *The Cambridge Companion to Native American Literature*, edited by Joy Porter and Kenneth M. Roemer, Cambridge University Press, 2005, pp. 297–310.

Published before *The Absolutely True Diary of a Part-Time Indian*, Moore's essay is a critical overview of Alexie's poetry, fiction, nonfiction, and film, placing his work in the larger context of Native American writing since 1968. Moore identifies several topics and themes—including identity racial tension, absent fathers, and basketball—that also inform *The Absolutely True Diary*.

Truer, David, *Native American Fiction: A User's Manual*, Graywolf Press, 2006.

In this collection of essays, novelist Truer suggests ways to read Native American fiction purely for its literary qualities rather than as historical or cultural artifacts. He analyzes works by several authors, including Leslie Marmon Silko and Louise Erdrich, and includes Alexie's *Indian Killer* and *Reservation Blues*.

SUGGESTED SEARCH TERMS

Sherman Alexie

The Absolutely True Diary of a Part-Time Indian

Native American literature

Sherman Alexie AND diary

Sherman Alexie AND award

Sherman Alexie AND challenged books

Sherman Alexie AND coming-of-age

Sherman Alexie AND bildungsroman

Sherman Alexie AND Native American literature

Spokane Indians

Spokane Indians AND Sherman Alexie

banned books AND The Absolutely True Diary of a Part-Time Indian

The Absolutely True Diary of a Part-Time Indian AND controversy

Digging to America

ANNE TYLER
2004

Digging to America, Anne Tyler's seventeenth novel, published in 2004, centers on two families who meet in 1997 in the Baltimore-Washington airport while awaiting the delivery of their adopted Korean daughters. The Donaldson-Dickinson clan arrives with great fanfare; grandparents and cousins and aunts and uncles, bearing balloons and video cameras and sporting large buttons proclaiming "I'm a Grandma!" and "I'm a Mom!" The Yazdans are a smaller group—Sami, his wife Ziba, and his mother Maryam—and they go almost unnoticed until their baby arrives and the Donaldson-Dickinsons realize there are two babies on the plane. Bitsy Donaldson tracks down Ziba Yazdan and a friendship ensues, cemented over the years by the ritual Bitsy invents, an Arrival Party, held each year on the anniversary of the day the girls arrived.

The point of view of the novel alternates between the Yazdan and Donaldson-Dickinson clans, a device that demonstrates the different ways the two families handle their adoptions and the different customs they keep. The Yazdans are Iranian. Maryam immigrated in her early twenties, while Ziba's family, the Hakimis, came in the 1980s. Although the Yazdans are eager to downplay the double difference their daughter carries as a Korean-born child in an Iranian family in American society, the Donaldsons are just as eager to maintain their daughter's cultural markers. Over the course of the

novel, we see how the girls' personalities develop as they grow and follow the course of friendship between the two families. It is a friendship that will be tested when the grandparents, Dave Dickinson and widowed Maryam Yazdan, begin dating after Dave's wife, Connie, dies, and it is in this way that the novel takes on not just issues of adoption but also those of immigration and assimilation and how these issues affect the personal identities of all parties concerned.

AUTHOR BIOGRAPHY

Tyler was born on October 25, 1941, in Minneapolis, Minnesota, the eldest child of Lloyd and Phyllis Tyler. Her parents were Quakers, and the family, which came to include three younger brothers, moved several times in search of an intentional community (a planned, communal arrangement where several like-minded families live together cooperatively) before settling, in 1948, in the Celo Community in rural North Carolina. Tyler was home schooled until she was eleven, when the family moved to Raleigh, where she was enrolled in public school. In her essay "Still Just Writing," Tyler notes of that transition, "I had never used a telephone and could strike a match on the soles of my bare feet." The experience of finding the outside world peculiar, and being considered peculiar in turn, instilled in Tyler that sense of being an outsider that seems common to many writers. In the same essay, she notes, "I have given up hope, by now, of ever losing my sense of distance; in fact, I have come to cherish it." Tyler completed high school at sixteen and got a scholarship to Duke University. There, she majored in Russian and studied creative writing with the novelist Reynolds Price.

After college, Tyler moved to New York to complete a master's degree in Russian at Columbia University, and in 1963, she married Taghi Mohammed Modarressi, an Iranian medical student. They moved to Montreal so he could finish his residency and then to Baltimore in 1967, where Tyler has lived ever since. They had two daughters, Tezh, born in 1965, and Mitra, born in 1967. Her husband died in 1997, and while Tyler is adamant that she never uses real people in her books, she has said in an interview with Jennifer Morgan Grey, published in the reader's guide included in the Ballantine paperback edition

of the novel, that her decision to include Iranian characters in *Digging to America* allowed her to draw on "many fond memories of my late husband's gigantic family."

Digging to America is Tyler's seventeenth novel. Six of her novels have been made into movies. She won the National Book Critics Circle award in 1985 for *The Accidental Tourist* and the Pulitzer Prize in 1989 for *Breathing Lessons*. Tyler is a fiercely private writer who has for decades refused most requests for interviews and who does not go on book tours or teach in a university. In "Still Just Writing," she wonders, "Why do people imagine that writers, having chosen the most private of professions, should be any good at performing in public, or should have the slightest desire to tell their secrets to interviewers from ladies' magazines?" And so, while we know the biographical outlines of Tyler's life, the reader will have to be content with the product of her vigorous imagination, the more than seventeen novels she has produced over a long career.

PLOT SUMMARY

Chapter 1
In the first chapter of *Digging to America*, two families converge in the Baltimore-Washington airport to wait for a flight to arrive bearing their newly adopted Korean daughters. The Davidson-Donaldson family comprises many members bearing gifts and balloons and video recorders. The Davidson-Donaldsons are unaware that there are two babies arriving that night, especially as the Yazdan family is a much smaller group comprised simply of the parents and a single grandmother. The first baby to emerge from the plane is Jin-Ho, sturdy, round, with a fringe of black hair cut straight across her forehead. She is delivered to the Donaldsons. The second baby is named Sooki, and she is a tiny baby with a wisp of black hair. Upon seeing a second baby arrive, the Donaldsons introduce themselves and invite the Yazdans back to their house to celebrate the girls' arrival. The Yazdans pass on the offer.

Chapter 2
Maryam Yazdan takes care of her granddaughter two days a week while Ziba, her daughter-in-law, works. Sooki has been renamed Susan, a name that is close to her Korean name, but is American

MEDIA ADAPTATIONS

- An unabridged audiobook version of *Digging to America* is available at Audible.com. It is narrated by Blair Brown. It was released in 2006 by Random House Audio and runs for eight hours and thirty-three minutes.

- Lorelei King narrates an abridged version of *Digging to America*. It runs for five hours and forty-four minutes and was released in 2006 by Random House Audiobooks. It is available at Audible.com.

and easy for her extended Iranian family to pronounce. Maryam calls her Susie-june, "june" being an Iranian diminutive that connotes a familial and affectionate relationship. The Donaldsons have reached out to Sami and Ziba Yazdan, Susie's parents, and the two mothers have been comparing the progress of their babies. Jin-Ho's seemingly easy adjustment causes Ziba to doubt herself, but within weeks, Susan settles in. Maryam loves taking care of Susan and worries that she will overstep with Ziba; several times she checks her own opinions and refrains from contributing how she might do things differently.

Meanwhile, the Donaldsons invite the Yazdans to a leaf-raking party. Bitsy, Jin-Ho's mother, wants the girls to get to know one another since she believes their common Korean origins give them a shared cultural heritage. Ziba is nervous because Brad and Bitsy are half a generation older than she and Sami, and she is a little bit intimidated by Bitsy's enthusiastic and specific opinions.

The families begin to meet regularly, and the Donaldsons are invited to Susan's first birthday and then to Maryam's Iranian New Year's party. Maryam quarrels with Sami when he takes her shopping and then realizes with regret that she has become increasingly critical with age.

On the day of the party, everyone is on edge. Ziba is nervous about the Donaldsons coming and snaps at her mother-in-law for speaking Farsi. Bitsy asks about Maryam's journey to America,

investing it with false exoticism. Sami offends his mother by telling the story of her arranged marriage and proxy wedding to his father as an example of old-world backwardness when Maryam knows that she married Kiyan for love. Maryam retreats to the kitchen where Bitsy's parents follow, helping to clean up and commiserating about the ways that family gatherings are stressful for everyone. Bitsy's mother, in particular, strikes Maryam as a person of great warmth.

Chapter 3

In Chapter 3, Bitsy Dickinson plans the first Arrival Day party, which becomes an annual event. Brad's confidence in Bitsy causes her to remember her short first marriage to the son of her parents' best friends. Bitsy and Stephen met when they attended the same college their parents had, and they married shorty after graduating. Bitsy realized when she met Brad that she had made a terrible mistake in marrying Stephen. Bitsy has always been shocked at the "shameless, ruthless, single-minded" way that she left Stephen for Brad, especially when it turned out that she could not have a biological child, even after years of trying.

Bitsy feels that her inability to conceive was all part of some cosmic plan to bring Jin-Ho to her, and for her, the Arrival Day signals a moment of enormous importance. Bitsy decides that they need a ceremony to commemorate the event, and so when all the family are gathered, she asks Linwood, the oldest cousin, to light the candles on the enormous American Flag cake she has ordered, while Brad waits outside the door to escort the girls in while the family sings "She'll be Comin' Round the Mountain." Bitsy thinks the song lacks dignity, but the kids all love it.

The Donaldsons then show the videotape of Jin-Ho's arrival in Baltimore. Bitsy apologizes that Susan is not featured, but Ziba reassures her that it is fine, because she has a clear memory of the day. Bitsy is amazed by this, she was so overwhelmed by emotion that she does not remember it herself. Watching the video, Bitsy is overcome. That little person in the arms of the Korean adoption official hardly seems like the daughter she has come to know and love. Ziba and Bitsy bond afterward about the experience of waiting for their daughters to arrive, and Bitsy gives in to speculation about how the girls will grow closer as they grow older, almost like sisters in their shared bond of being adopted.

Feeling off kilter from her intense emotions, Bitsy finds her mother, Connie, in the other room and is surprised when Connie hands her a piece of paper with the name of a nurse Maryam suggested. Connie is ill and fears that her husband, Dave, is overwhelmed with the work of caring for her. Connie asks Bitsy to help her convince Dave to hire this nurse. Bitsy finds herself inexplicably resentful that it was Maryam who came up with the solution to Bitsy's family problem.

Chapter 4

Chapter 4 opens with an amusing dissection of American customs that Sami does for Ziba's relatives. Maryam disapproves of this performance, in part because she thinks Sami, who refused from childhood to speak Farsi, is making fun of the country that afforded them safety and prosperity. Maryam also teases him that she never expected him to marry an Iranian girl, as he had always only dated blonde "American" girls before Ziba. Sami reflects that the familiarity he found in Ziba was a surprise to him, even as he knew his mother would disapprove of her family, who are more recently arrived, who support the Shah, and who evince a fondness for flashy clothing and designer labels. After Ziba and Sami married, Ziba's father offered Sami a job in his real-estate business, and to his surprise, Sami does not regret having given up his graduate work. Sami resents Bitsy Donaldson for what he views as her affected opinions on politics and childrearing, as well as her insistence on exoticizing both the girls' Korean heritage and his family's Iranian heritage.

It is the Yazdans' year to host the Arrival Party, and Ziba's female relatives spend a week preparing while the male relatives gather in the adjoining room, eavesdropping on the women's gossip and telling stories of their own. On the day of the Arrival Day party, the Donaldsons arrive with Bitsy's father, who is still deeply grieving the recent death of his wife, Connie.

Over dinner, Bitsy is appalled that Ziba is enrolling Susan at the preschool where Maryam works. Bitsy lectures about how the children are too young and questions Ziba for working at all. Ziba's brother tries to deflect the conversation, but Sami can see that Ziba's feelings are hurt and that she is no longer enjoying her own party. Sami loses his temper with Bitsy and tells her she owes Ziba an apology, but Bitsy is completely confused. Brad comes outside to the barbecue to

discuss it with Sami, who tells Brad that Bitsy is pushy and self-righteous. The two men get into a shoving match, after which they begin to laugh and wind up hugging one another.

Chapter 5

Chapter 5 opens with Dave Dickinson's astonishment that Bitsy and Brad are thinking of adopting a second child. He remembers how jealous he was of how his own children took all of Connie's attention, how chaotic and noisy things were when his kids were very young. Jin-Ho has been such a wonderful addition to the family, he thinks it is tempting fate to try it again. Mostly though, Dave is grieving. The paradox of his situation is that, as much as he hates being alone, he cannot imagine being with anyone other than Connie.

It is the Donaldsons' year to host the Arrival Party, and when Dave arrives he finds the girls outside on the sidewalk riding their bikes while inside Bitsy is fussing over a house full of Iranian guests. When they play the video, Dave only has eyes for Connie and is surprised to see how healthy she looked. Maryam tells him of her own experience when Kiyam died and how difficult it had been to see him change and fade and become fractious as his illness progressed. Dave admits the same and finds himself cheered up by their discussion.

When Dave returns home after the party, he tackles cleaning out the house, discovering old sewing patterns, photo albums, and tax records. It takes him several days, and at the end he is so exhausted from missing Connie and trying to bring some order to his grief, that he falls into a deep sleep, during which he dreams that Maryam comes to him. In the dream, he takes her hand.

Chapter 6

Chapter 6 is written from Maryam's point of view and opens with her surprise when she learns that Sami and Ziba have bought a new house in the Donaldsons' neighborhood without consulting her. On moving day, Maryam brings Susan home from school with her, and Dave calls and offers to bring Jin-Ho over to play. Clearly lonely, Dave angles to stay for the afternoon, but Maryam shoos him off so she can cook dinner for Sami and Ziba in peace. She likes Dave, but his neediness wears on her.

In July, Maryam goes to Vermont to visit her cousin Farah, who is married to an "American" named William. Farah is Maryam's only extended family member in America, and while Maryam loves her dearly, she also thinks that Farah has exaggerated her Iranian heritage in order to fulfill her husband's desire for an exotic wife. When both Bitsy and Ziba also pressure her to go out with Dave, Maryam thinks how much the younger generation does not know about her and reminisces about her girlhood in Tehran.

It was Maryam's arrest by the secret police for demonstrating at university that started her family's search for an overseas husband, and it was just their luck that Kiyan happened to be visiting relatives at the time. Although at first they only went out in order to make their families happy, they realized after a few weeks how much they liked one another and agreed to be married. Because Kiyan had to return to Baltimore before the wedding could be arranged, they married by proxy, and Maryam boarded a plane with only a single piece of luggage. They came to love one another deeply.

Chapter 7

When Bitsy and Brad fly to China for three weeks to adopt Xiu-Mei, Dave agrees to stay at their house with Jin-Ho. Although he is nervous about three weeks alone with a young child, they get along quite well. Maryam invites them to her house along with Sami, Ziba, and Susan, and Dave is discomfited by the family's discussion of feeling alien in both their home and adopted cultures. When the day arrives to greet Xiu-Mei, Dave is surprised to see Maryam arrive at the airport. The occasion lacks the drama of Jin-Ho's arrival, because Bitsy and Brad are exhausted from the long trip, and the family is no longer allowed to meet them at the gate. Xiu-Mei is tiny and sucking vigorously on a pacifier.

Maryam offers Dave a ride back to the house, and on the way they discuss their families. Maryam admits that she finds being foreign exhausting at times. No matter how hard she tries, she feels she can never get being American right. When she explains that Susan complained about Christmas, Dave laughs and notes that all children complain that other families' Christmases are better. When they arrive at the Donaldsons', Dave takes her hand and gently tells her to come inside to the party.

Chapter 8

Ziba is deeply confused about Maryam's growing relationship with Dave. No one can quite figure out if they are a couple or simply enjoying one another's company, and because Maryam has always been so self-possessed, no one is brave enough to ask. Among Ziba's family, Maryam is known by the nickname Khanom, which means "Madame" but connotes a person who thinks she is better than others. Despite the curiosity of the family, it seems that Maryam and Dave are spending a lot of time together, and when Ziba consults Bitsy, Bitsy seems to think they are dating. Although Ziba's affection for Bitsy has not waned, she no longer feels intimidated by her, especially not now that Bitsy is exhausted by the new baby. Xiu-Mei is having difficulty adjusting. She is reluctant to eat and has been hospitalized several times with infections and intestinal blockages.

When Maryam goes to Vermont to visit Farah, Dave surprises Ziba while she is watering the plants at Maryam's house. He confesses to Ziba that he loves Maryam but that he has no idea how she feels about him. The next Arrival Day party is at the Yazdans', and when Dave arrives, he makes a point of asking Maryam which dishes are hers. Everyone remarks on the manner in which both Maryam and Dave light up in one another's presence. Ziba finds herself becoming impatient as Maryam holds Dave at arm's length.

At the Donaldsons' leaf-raking party, Dave surprises everyone, especially Maryam, by proposing to her. Stunned, she accepts, and they all celebrate. In the morning, Maryam arrives at Sami and Ziba's house to tell them she has changed her mind. It was a surprise. She only accepted to be polite. She should have refused. It was too much. Ziba tries to dissuade her, but Maryam's mind is made up, and she leaves to go tell Dave. Ziba finds herself furious at her stiff mother-in-law, who she thinks has been unnecessarily cruel.

Chapter 9

In Chapter 9, Jin-Ho narrates the saga of Xiu-Mei and her pacifier. Xiu-Mei refuses to be separated from her pacifier even for a moment and screams inconsolably when her parents try to break her of the habit. Bitsy has had it with the pacifiers, so she invents a ritual. Bitsy tells the girls that there is a Binky Fairy, and when little girls get big enough, the Binky Fairy comes down and takes away all the binkies, leaving a present behind. Jin-Ho has questions, but her mother tells her not to worry, that it is all going to work out.

Because of the broken engagement between Dave and Maryam, Bitsy wonders whether or not to invite the Yazdans, and when she tries to impress upon Jin-Ho the importance of being friends with Susan and how they might someday go back to Korea together to find their biological mothers, Jin-Ho is appalled. "Why would we want to do that?" she asks. Xiu-Mei fights the plan to give up her pacifiers, refusing to participate in the Binky Fairy story, and Dave, who has taken to stopping by daily since Maryam broke things off, suggests that perhaps Bitsy is making too much of the binky issue.

On the eve of the Binky Fairy party, a huge storm blows into Baltimore, cutting the electricity and knocking over two big trees. The girls are frightened by the storm, but despite the upheaval, Bitsy is determined to have the Binky Fairy party. When the guests arrive, they are handed helium balloons with binkies tied to them, and they go outside to set the binkies free. The Donaldsons' neighbor points out that there are now binkies draped over the fallen trees and Bitsy promises to clean them up. The Binky Fairy brings Xiu-Mei a toy stroller.

Jin-Ho overhears her mother and her grandfather talking about Maryam again, and Bitsy admits that it was clear they both loved one another. At the end of the party, Xiu-Mei has swiped her friend Lucy's pacifier and is sucking on it vigorously.

Chapter 10

While picking Susan up from ballet class, Maryam runs into Dave, who is there picking up Jin-Ho. Maryam is relieved that Dave seems relaxed around her, and they chat for a moment before he blurts out that Bitsy is sick with the same cancer that killed Connie. Maryam instinctively responds with concern and then retreats to her normal reserve when Dave asks if she will be at the Arrival Day party this year. Maryam writes Bitsy a note, expressing her concern and offering whatever help she can give. She also begins to examine her life. While she loves the peace and order of her days and her house, she realizes that she is lonely and that, as she gets older, it becomes more and more tiring to go out in public. She feels her English slipping.

As Bitsy's chemotherapy progresses, Maryam hosts Jin-Ho and Xiu-Mei on her afternoons with Susan. Bitsy begins to recover and calls Maryam to thank her for her note and her help and to urge her to come to the Arrival Party. Maryam is touched and thinks back to that terrible morning when she told Dave she had changed her mind about accepting his proposal. Ziba shocks Maryam by suggesting sushi for the Arrival Day party instead of Iranian food, but determined to learn not to care so much about what people think, Maryam buys a bottle of sake for the occasion.

Maryam does not sleep well the night before the Arrival Day party and feels out of sorts all morning. She tries to rest and is shocked to be awakened by the telephone—she meant to lie down only for a moment. Sami is calling, angry at her for not showing up at the party. He tells her the Donaldsons have all left, and Ziba is upset. Maryam apologizes and says she will be right there, and then she sees Brad Donaldson on her front walk and Dave's car pulls up. The Donaldsons have come to get her, and Maryam finds herself frozen in place. She hears Jin-Ho's disappointed voice saying she must not be home, and as the Donaldsons return to their cars, Maryam springs to life, rushing down the stairs and out the front door, calling after them: "Don't go!" and "Wait for me!"

CHARACTERS

Mrs. Barber
Mrs. Barber is the director of the Julia Jessup preschool where Maryam works. She spends her summers in Maine.

Stephen Bartholomew
Stephen Bartholomew was Bitsy's first husband. He and Bitsy went to Swarthmore College together, just as their parents had. The parents had been best friends, and Bitsy and Stephen found one another and dated all through college. They married right after college, and Bitsy realized that they were not a good match because Stephen was very critical. The marriage lasted less than a year before she left him for Brad.

Abe Dickinson
Abe is Bitsy's younger brother. He is married to Jeannine, and his daughters are Polly, Deirdre, and Bridget.

Bridget Dickinson
Bridget is the daughter of Abe and Jeannine and older cousin to Jin-Ho and Xiu-Mei.

Connie Dickinson
Connie Dickinson is Bitsy's mother and Dave's wife. She is a warm presence who reaches out to Maryam when Sami embarrasses her by telling her marriage story. She dies of cancer shortly after Jin-Ho and Susan arrive from Korea. Dave and Bitsy grieve bitterly for her after she dies.

Dave Dickinson
Dave is Bitsy's father and Connie's husband. He is a high school physics teacher who retires after Connie dies. He hates being single, and his courtship of Maryam forms one of the central plots of the novel. He is a big rumpled man who loves his family and finds himself wondering, after the death of his wife, how he can possibly live alone. He falls hard for Maryam and is brokenhearted when she refuses his marriage proposal.

Dierdre Dickinson
Dierdre is the daughter of Abe and Jeannine and older cousin to Jin-Ho and Xiu-Mei.

Jeannine Dickinson
Jeannine is the wife of Abe and mother to Bridget, Dierdre, and Polly. She oversteps with Bitsy early in the novel when she suggests that Bitsy arrange home care for her mother despite her father's objection. She is a school principal.

Jin-Ho Dickinson-Donaldson
Jin-Ho is one of the two Korean children who arrive in Baltimore on the same day to be adopted by American families. She is a big sturdy child who settles in easily. Although her parents keep her Korean name and worry about maintaining a connection to her ethnic heritage, she only wants to be American as she grows up. In the chapter written from her point of view, she admits that she has not once watched the video of her arrival from Korea, and when she begins school, she changes her name to Jo, although her family forgets and continues to call her Jin-Ho.

Laura Dickinson
Laura is the Bitsy's sister-in-law, Mac's wife, and mother of Stephanie and Linwood.

Mac Dickinson
Mac is Laura's husband and father of Stephanie and Linwood. He is Bitsy's younger brother.

Polly Dickinson
Polly is the daughter of Abe and Jeannine and older cousin to Jin-Ho and Xiu-Mei.

Bitsy Dickinson-Donaldson
Bitsy is the mother of Jin-Ho and Xiu-Mei, the wife of Brad, and the daughter of Dave and Connie. She seeks out the Yazdans after the two babies arrive and takes Ziba under her wing. Ziba is at first enthralled with the older Bitsy, who has such specific opinions about parenting and politics. Bitsy is often described, especially by Dave, as gawky and awkward and is a person who filled up the long fifteen years in which she tried to have a child with a number of hobbies, including weaving. She comes off as overbearing at times, but she has a big heart and truly wants to nurture an extended family that includes the Yazdans. She becomes ill with breast cancer, but by the novel's end, she seems to have recovered.

Xiu-Mei Dickinson-Donaldson
Xiu-Mei is the Donaldsons' second adopted daughter. She is Chinese and nearly five years younger than Jin-Ho. She is a more difficult child than Jin-Ho was, refusing to eat and becoming entirely dependent on her pacifier.

Brad Donaldson
Brad Donaldson is Bitsy's second husband and father to Jin-Ho and Xiu-Mei. He is a high school teacher and adores Bitsy. She married him in large part because he was so supportive and kind to her. He agrees with all of her political and parenting decisions and is her biggest supporter.

Lou Donaldson
Lou is Brad Donaldson's father and the husband of Pat. He is a retired lawyer who is more conservative politically than Bitsy or her parents, and she worries that he disapproves of her. He disappoints Bitsy regularly by choosing to go on vacation or on cruises rather than come to her parties marking the girls' milestones.

Pat Donaldson
Pat is Brad Donaldson's mother and Lou's wife. She's a very conventional person who enjoys cruises with her husband.

Gita Hakimi

Gita Hakimi is Ziba's mother and the wife of Mustafa. Maryam finds it difficult to warm up to her and continues to address her as Mrs. Hakimi long after she should have switched to the more intimate Gita, or Gita-june. Gita is not comfortable in English and often reverts to Farsi, to the embarrassment of her daughter Ziba.

Mustafa Hakimi

Mustafa Hakimi is Ziba's father. He is a big hearty man, who builds suburban subdivisions and who hired Sami after he married Ziba. He is a supporter of the Shah, and Maryam disapproves of his politics and thinks he is too flashy. He is the patriarch of a large extended family that often gets together for big parties.

Farah Karimzadeh Jeffreys

Farah is Maryam's double first cousin, that is, she is the daughter of an uncle on her father's side and an aunt on her mother's side. She is younger than Maryam and lives in Vermont with an American she met as a student in Paris. Maryam thinks Farah exaggerates her Iranian background, dressing in extravagantly Iranian clothing. She is the only person Maryam has in her life who knew her as a child and with whom she shares a family history.

William Jeffreys

William is Farah's husband. She met him in Paris, and Maryam considers him something of a hippie. They live in Vermont, and Maryam disapproves of William's love of all things Iranian. Maryam thinks that William is too invested in Farah's otherness and fears that Dave feels the same about her. William provides an example of everything Maryam fears about dating an American.

Kari

Maryam's friend, Kari, is a widow of Turkish origin. When Maryam asks Kari about dating, Kari tells her that she makes up a story about it being forbidden in her culture for widows to go out with strange men.

Moosh

Moosh is Maryam's cat. He was a stray, and she named him for the Farsi word for "mouse" due to his grey coat.

Mrs. Simms

Mrs. Simms is the assistant director of the Julia Jessup preschool where Maryam works.

Kiyan Yazdan

Kiyan was Maryam's husband, Sami's father, who died when Sami was fourteen. Nine years older than Maryam, he was a doctor who had already emigrated from Iran to the United States when they married. Although they had an arranged marriage, they were deeply in love. He died after a long illness from cancer after nearly twenty years of marriage.

Maryam Karimzadeh Yazdan

Maryam is Sami's mother, widow of Kiyan, and grandmother to Susan. Maryam participated in protests against the Shah in Iran as a girl and was arrested once, so her family sought to find her a husband who could get her out of the country. Although her marriage to Kiyan was arranged, they loved one another deeply. She feels estranged from both Iran and America and struggles with her own feelings of superiority, judgment, and foreignness.

Maryam wants very much not to be a bother to her son and to Ziba, which causes her too often to err on the side of reserve. Her appearance is important to her, and she finds both the casual clothing of most Americans and the bright designer attire of Iranians like the Hakimis equally repugnant. The Hakimis, who hail from a lower Iranian social class than Maryam, call her "Khanom" behind her back, a nickname that means "Madame" but implies that Maryam thinks that she is an aristocrat and hence, above them.

After the death of his wife, Dave Dickinson falls in love with Maryam, and at the annual leaf-raking party, he surprises her with a proposal. She accepts but then backs out the next day, saying she felt pressured in public like that and that Dave is too American. Later she regrets turning him down and is relieved when the Donaldsons come to fetch her for the Arrival Day party at the end of the novel. It is left open whether she and Dave reconcile or not.

Sami Yazdan

Sami is the son of Maryam, husband of Ziba, and father of Susan. Sami lost his father to cancer when he was in his early teens and treats his mother with a mixture of deference and good-natured teasing. He was surprised to find himself attracted to Ziba in college because of their shared Iranian heritage after he had spent his entire childhood trying to be as American as possible. He and Ziba have a good marriage, and she appreciates that he is American enough to help out around the house and with Susan in ways a more traditional Iranian man would not. Sami retains some of the reserve of his mother, but loves Ziba's big Iranian family and, after a while, even finds himself speaking to Susan in Farsi, a language he refused to learn as a child.

Susan Yazdan

Susan is the daughter of Sami and Ziba, granddaughter of Maryam, Gita, and Mustafa. Her original Korean name was Sooki, but the Yazdans renamed her Susan when she arrived in Baltimore because it was a name that was equally easy for Americans and Iranians to pronounce. She is often called Susie-june, "june" being an Iranian diminutive that indicates an affectionate or familial relationship. She is markedly smaller than Jin-Ho but has a determined personality. Although Ziba's parents had some initial objections to international adoption, Susan quickly becomes a favorite among their grandchildren, and Mustafa is always pointing out "Hakimi" traits she embodies. As she grows, she is described as bossy by the Donaldsons and as determined and particular by her own parents.

Ziba Hakimi Yazdan

Ziba is the wife of Sami, the mother of Susan, and Maryam's daughter-in-law. She emigrated from Iran to Baltimore with her family when she was in high school. Ziba is an outgoing person, who initially impresses Sami by her direct manner and her combination of American and Iranian good looks. When the children first arrive, Ziba is somewhat enthralled with the older Bitsy, impressed by her definitive opinions on parenting and politics, even as she is sometimes surprised by the things to which Bitsy objects. Unlike Bitsy, Ziba continues to work after Susan arrives, relying on Maryam and the Julia Jessup Preschool as a matter of course. Like Bitsy, Ziba has a warm heart, and the two women form an enduring bond over their shared struggles to have a biological child and their parallel adoption stories.

THEMES

American Identity

What does it mean to be an American? In *Digging to America*, this question is posed in any number of ways, by almost all of the characters. The characters in this book comprise a number of ethnicities, from the Iranian American Yazdans and Hakimis, to the Korean-born babies, Jin-Ho and Susan, to the native-born Donaldsons and Dickinsons. All of these characters must define for themselves what it means to be an American.

Tyler introduces this theme from the very beginning when she shows the different ways the two families approach naming their babies. The "American" family, the Dickinson-Donaldsons, is concerned with maintaining their daughter's ethnic identity and so retain her Korean name, Jin-Ho (they later do the same for their Chinese daughter, Xiu-Mei). The Yazdans, who have made the journey of immigration themselves, are more concerned with finding a name that will seem native to both their Iranian heritage and their adopted American citizenship, so they change their child's name from Sooki to Susan. The naming issue is further complicated when Jin-Ho asks to be renamed "Jo." While standing out and being unique is seen as a positive value by Bitsy, to Jin-Ho, it is a sign of difference that she rejects.

The character who muses most on questions of identity is Maryam Yazdan. Maryam immigrated in her early adulthood and struggles even decades later with the sense that she belongs neither in America nor in Iran. She often finds fault with the Americans she meets, including the Donaldsons. She recoils from what she views as an easy familiarity and resents inquiries into the customs of her native country. When Sami and Ziba invite the Donaldsons for the Iranian New Year, Maryam thinks impatiently, "Why should they have to put on these ethnic demonstrations? Let the Donaldsons go to the Smithsonian for that!" Despite her U.S. passport, Maryam does not think of herself as American. "It was important to keep up appearances," she thinks. "Let the Americans lounge about in their sweatsuits! She was not American.... She was a guest, was what she meant. Still and forever a guest, on her very best behavior."

Despite being white and born in the United States, the Donaldsons are also forced to confront

TOPICS FOR FURTHER STUDY

- Read Sherman Alexie's young-adult novel *The Absolutely True Diary of a Part-time Indian*. While Alexie's book is set in a different place and time than *Digging to America*, both works take as a central concern the experience of feeling alienated in one's community. Make a list comparing the ways that Arnold Spirit's challenges compare with those faced by Maryam, Jin-Ho, Sami, or Bitsy. Using your list, write a short story or poem in which the protagonists of the two works encounter one another at school. Feel free to add graphics like Alexie does in his novel.

- The major characters in *Digging to America* have very different views on the importance of ethnic heritage to one's contemporary life. While Bitsy Donaldson, who is the most "American" of the characters, is concerned about maintaining her daughter's ties to the culture in which she was born, the Yazdans and Hakimis want to assimilate. Interview your parents and grandparents about your own ethnic background. Where did your family originate? How long ago did they immigrate to America? Is ethnic background important to your family and how? What role do stories, poetry, or music play in the cultures from which your family originates? Build a Web page with elements that include video interviews with your family, visual representations of their immigration story, recordings of traditional performers, and links to research about ethnic organizations working to keep those traditions alive.

- Food is a major theme in *Digging to America*, especially festive food served at celebrations. The Donaldsons are fascinated by the Iranian dishes served by the Yazdan and Hakimi families for the arrival parties and New Year celebrations. Interview some relatives and ask them about a traditional family dish. Compile a written recipe for this dish. Pretend you are producing a cooking show, and create a video presentation that explains the origins of your family dish and that can be used to teach someone else how to make it.

- Maryam Yazdan had to leave Iran in part because she got into trouble for protesting the repression in that country after the revolution. Research the Iranian revolution. What was its cause? Who was ousted from power and what group came to power? Why did the new regime seek to crack down on dissent? What was the experience of living in this new regime like for most Iranians? What was the experience of Iranian women under the new regime? With several classmates, create a dramatic production or documentary that illustrates the challenges and hopes of the Iranian revolution, and perform it for your classmates or post it on YouTube or your Web page.

- Every family is a small culture that has catch-phrases and nicknames for one another (Ziba's family refers to Maryam as *Kha-nom*). Collect catchphrases, nicknames, and foreign phrases that your family uses as a sort of family shorthand, and make a list of them. If there are members of your family who speak other languages, be sure to collect their sayings as well. Once you have ten to fifteen phrases, write each on a slip of paper and use them as the starting point for a story. Rearrange the order of the slips of paper until a story suggests itself to you. What do these phrases mean to the person who uses them? Do they have one meaning to that person and another meaning to others in the family or those outside the family? What do they mean to you? How do they illustrate something about your family or culture? Write a short story that express these feelings.

The Dickinson-Donaldsons and the Yazdans both adopt Korean babies. (Mastering_Microstock / Shutterstock.com)

what it means to them to be American. After Maryam breaks off her engagement to Dave, Dave and Bitsy feel that their very American identities have been rejected. "The way she observed the Iranian New Year but never ours," Dave says, trying to parse why Maryam rejected him. He continues, "Well, sometimes it seems to me that most of the adapting in this country is done by Americans."

Although the Donaldsons never examine the paternalism inherent in their feeling that they have rescued Jin-Ho and Xiu-Mei by bringing them to America, they find the confrontation with Maryam's refusal to assimilate threatening. By maintaining her difference, she belies their belief that all other cultures are really like the American one. This renders the final scene in the novel so touching; the Dickinson-Donaldsons reach out to Maryam despite the gulf she feels she needs to maintain between herself and others, and in turn, Maryam reaches out across her own instinct to retreat. Both parties have moved toward a new understanding of one another.

Family

In many ways, the manner in which characters feel they belong, or do not belong, to their families is a microcosm of those characters' feelings about belonging in their country. Maryam's feelings of alienation in American culture are mirrored in her relationships with her family. She works very hard to be a "good" mother-in-law, refraining from meddling in Sami and Ziba's life, maintaining her independence, and keeping up appearances. She also distinguishes herself from Ziba's family, noting, "To be honest, the Hakimis were only one generation removed from the bazaar. Maryam's family would never even have met them if they were back home."

Sami, on the other hand, was always the boy who refused to speak Persian, who assimilated entirely, and who dated blonde American girls in high school, yet when he met Ziba, who was both Iranian and also American like he was, "he noticed how much they understood about each other without discussion. A cloak of shared background surrounded them invisibly." It is the combination of familiarity and strangeness that draws Sami to Ziba, and later into her family, and finally back into the Persian language itself. Ziba, her family, and the family they make together forms the bridge for Sami between his Iranian and his American personalities and allows him to merge them at last.

Bitsy's relationship between family and identity is a little more complicated. Bitsy feels that she has never really accomplished anything:

> She had never completed her education courses, never held a full-time job. She had busied herself with dribs and drabs like teaching yoga and attending pottery seminars. . . . little made up activities without steady pay or health-care benefits.

Therefore, the adoption of Jin-Ho and later Xiu-Mei strikes her as being "*better* than childbirth? More dramatic, more meaningful." Bitsy projects her own desires for uniqueness and specialness onto her daughters by maintaining their birth names and dressing them in ethnic costumes for special occasions, insisting to herself that their very difference is what gives them meaning. For the girls, who grow up wanting to fit in, as is seen in Jin-Ho's wanting to be called Jo and admitting to never *ever* watching the video of her arrival, Bitsy's urgent need to stand out becomes the family drama against which they rebel. Where Bitsy seeks drama and meaning, Jin-Ho seeks belonging and fitting in.

Family dramas are the core theme of all of Tyler's novels. She seems fascinated with the ways that people fit into or rebel against their family roles and identities, and in this, *Digging to America* is typical of her work. That she adds the element of ethnic and national identity only gives her more to work with, because these characters must negotiate not only their familial roles but also their ethnic identities.

STYLE

Point of View

A work of fiction uses the third-person point of view when the narrator is separate from the protagonist(s) and narrates the events of the story from outside the protagonist's point of view. One can often identify a third-person story by its use of the pronouns "he," "she," and "they." The narrative point of view in *Digging to America* is considered limited because the narrator filters all knowledge through the sensibility of the point-of-view character. For instance, in the chapters from Maryam's point of view, the reader only has access

to the information Maryam knows, so for example, the reader, like Maryam, is surprised to discover that Sami and Ziba have bought a new house in Bitsy and Brad's neighborhood. By using a third-person limited point of view, Tyler allows the reader to share in Maryam's shock and her feeling of having been excluded from an important decision.

Point of view is further complicated in this novel by the manner in which Tyler changes the point-of-view character. The novel alternates between the point of view of a member of the Yazdan family and that of one of the Dickinson-Donaldson family. Although the first chapter is narrated from an omniscient point of view, that is, the point of view of someone who can see the entire story, the subsequent chapters are narrated, in order, by Maryam, Bitsy, Sami, Dave, Maryam, Dave, Ziba, Jin-Ho, and then Maryam again. By alternating the points of view, Tyler allows the reader access to the minds of all of these characters, and by extension, we learn how they feel about one another. For example, it is not until Jin-Ho's chapter that we learn that she has absolutely no curiosity about Korea and, in fact, never watches the video during the annual Arrival Day party. During Dave's chapters, we learn that, although he loves his daughter Bitsy, he also has a clear understanding of her character flaws.

A hallmark of Tyler's work is the clarity with which she draws her characters and the manner in which she is clear about their faults while showing a sort of radical acceptance of the ways in which people are different from one another. By limiting the point of view to the knowledge that individual characters have and then rotating among the characters, she allows the reader to see how this group of people struggles to know, accept, and finally love one another.

Comedy

Although the categories of comedy and tragedy are traditionally applied to dramatic works, as fiction has merged with the movies in the twentieth century, these categories have come to be seen as applying to works of fiction as well. Although comedies are often funny, it is not humor that distinguishes a comedy from a tragedy so much as structural elements, including a focus on ordinary people rather than heroic or mythical characters, concentration on the exposure of these characters' shortcomings, and ending on a happy note, often, in the case of Shakespeare, a marriage. Despite a lack of slapstick humor, *Digging to America* is a comedy because it fits these criteria.

The novel concerns itself with two rather ordinary families, the Yazdans and the Dickinson-Donaldsons. Although both families contain interesting characters, none of them is an aristocrat, hero, or figure out of myth; they are teachers and widows and real-estate developers, perfectly ordinary modern American identities. While Maryam's imperious attitude earns her the nickname *Khanom*, or Madame, she is not an actual member of an aristocratic class, and this sort of exposure of a character's foibles forms the second major characteristic of a comedic work.

Although Tyler is never cruel to her characters, she does not shy away from exposing their shortcomings. Bitsy has a warm and enthusiastic heart, yet she is also bossy and overbearing and far too convinced of the value of her own opinions. Ziba is glamorous and young but perhaps overly swayed by Bitsy's definitive take on life, whereas Sami's agreeable nature belies an aggressive streak when he thinks his family has been disrespected. Dave is good-natured and kind but also stubborn and, like many Americans, blind to the experience of foreigners. Maryam is kind and loving but also stiff and overly reserved, with a stubborn streak of her own. That Tyler chooses to play these characters' foibles off one another, rather than inflict some kind of negative consequence, is another sign that this is a comedic novel rather than a tragic one. In a tragedy, the hero must be punished for his mistakes of judgment, whereas in a comedy, the characters' mistakes will be exposed, then discharged with laughter, and forgiven by the happy ending.

Thus, one can read the ending of this novel as a classic comedic one. Maryam has isolated herself through a combination of character flaw and accident and has put herself in a dangerous position where she could suffer punitive consequences from her actions. A classic comedy of errors ensues. Sami and Ziba realize their guests have all left the Arrival Day party and surmise that they are angry, that the friendship is broken. Sami calls Maryam, who begins to rush to correct her error only to find that they were all mistaken. The Dickinson-Donaldsons have not left in a huff, they have left in order to descend on Maryam's house, to bring her back into the family fold, and end the novel happily. That

Maryam hesitates before joining them demonstrates how close the line can be between comedy and tragedy. Had she refused, she would have been a tragic figure, brought down by her own flawed character. Instead, she joined the celebration, thus fulfilling the essential task of the comedic work, to incorporate a community into a celebration and to end on a happy note.

HISTORICAL CONTEXT

Although *Digging to America* is a novel in which many of the characters seek to minimize the historical events that instigated their migrations to America, nonetheless, historical events did precipitate the migration stories of the Iranian and Korean characters. The novel also spans the time period in which the attacks of September 11, 2001, occurred, and while this does not form the central event of the novel, its effects are felt both in the airport scenes and in the manner in which the Iranian characters feel they are treated in the aftermath of the attacks.

Iranian Diaspora

The dispersion of a people from its homeland is known as a diaspora, and there have been two major waves of Iranian migration in this century. The first occurred between the mid-1950s and the Iranian revolution in 1979 and consisted mainly of students who came to the United States to be trained in professions. As Iran industrialized with the advent of an oil-based economy, it sent many of its young people abroad to learn the skills the nation needed. The second wave occurred after the Iranian revolution and peaked in 1990, when the U.S. Census Bureau reported an estimated 24,977 Iranian immigrants.

Over half of all Iranian immigrants live in California, followed by the New York and Washington-Baltimore metropolitan areas. Over 50 percent of Iranian immigrants have bachelors' degrees or higher, and the majority are employed in professional, managerial, and sales jobs. The self-employment rate for Iranian immigrants is nearly twice that of other foreign-born populations. The Yazdan and Hakimi families are very representative of both the early and later waves of Iranian immigration, and their blending of Iranian and American traditions is also typical of this immigrant population.

Korean Adoption

After the Korean War (1950–1953), in which the United States, with United Nations backing, staged a military operation to enforce the division of the Korean peninsula along the thirty-eighth parallel, relations between soldiers and Korean women resulted in the out-of-wedlock births of several thousand mixed-race children. South Korea was a very traditional and patriarchal culture and was unable to incorporate these children, who were abandoned and sometimes abused. Henry and Bertha Holt founded Holt International, an adoption agency that specialized in international adoption. Adoption of any children is rare in Korea, a society in which family name and blood ties are deeply tied to traditions of honor and respect for one's elders. There are several factors of the Korean adoption system that appeal to foreign parents seeking to adopt, including the availability of infants and toddlers, that the children are fostered in families and do not spend their early years in orphanages, and that the agencies will escort children on the flight to America, as happened in *Digging to America* with Susan and Jin-Ho.

Attacks of September 11, 2011

On September 11, 2001, the United States was attacked by nineteen Al Qaeda terrorists who took control of four commercial airliners. Two of the planes were flown into the World Trade Center towers in New York City; one flew into the Pentagon in Washington, D.C.; and the fourth was crashed into a field in Pennsylvania. Subsequently, President George W. Bush declared a "War on Terror," aspects of which included the invasion of Afghanistan, whose Taliban government had given safe haven to Al Qaeda, and the passage of the Patriot Act, which granted the government increased powers of surveillance and search (several of which were later struck down by the courts).

Although the attacks of September 11, 2001, were not the first attack by a foreign power on American soil, the spectacular and unexpected nature of the event and the deaths of so many civilians shocked the nation. While historians and pundits continue to wrestle over the ultimate meaning of the events, it is safe to say that they brought a new sense of physical vulnerability to much of the population. The effects of these attacks are seen in *Digging to America* in two ways, that the families cannot meet Xiu-Mei at the airport gate as they did Jin-Ho and Susan

Maryam, a traditional Muslim, begins a relationship with Dave, a widower, that further binds the two families. (Zunjeta / Shutterstock.com)

and that the Iranian American characters report being treated with increased suspicion due to their skin color, religious affiliation, and accents.

CRITICAL OVERVIEW

Digging to America, published in 2004, is Tyler's seventeenth novel. Tyler has enjoyed a particularly successful career; several of her novels have been made into movies or television movies, and she has an enormous and dedicated fan base. She won the Pulitzer Prize in 1988 for *Breathing Lessons* and the National Book Critics Circle Award in 1985 for *The Accidental Tourist*; both *Ladder of Years* and *Digging to America* were short listed for the Orange Prize for Fiction, and *Noah's Compass* was short listed in 2010 for the Mann Booker Prize. Tyler's quiet talent has long appealed to other novelists.

Writing in the *New Yorker* in 1977, the novelist John Updike notes Tyler's "unmistakable strengths—her serene, firm tone; her smoothly spun plots; her apparently inexhaustible access to the personalities of her imagining; her lack of any trace of intellectual or political condescension," but also points out "her one possible weakness: a tendency to leave the reader just where she found him." Updike explains that, in Tyler's work, "the impending moral encloses the excitements of her story in a circle of safety that gives them the coziness of entertainment." It is that quality of coziness that was for many years interpreted as a lack of seriousness, an impression that is finally, as Tyler enters the later years of her career, being reconsidered as her work is nominated for prizes like the Mann Booker, which generally rewards not just a single work but the trajectory of a career.

A number of critics noted that with *Digging to America*, Tyler seemed to have broken new ground in her fiction. Tyler's fictional territory has always been Baltimore, but with *Digging to America*, her Baltimore suddenly became a much more multicultural place. Although she is adamant that her personal life does not appear in her novels, Tyler was married to an Iranian American doctor and was widowed after nearly thirty years of marriage. In an interview with USINFO, the U.S. Department of State's Bureau of International Information Programs, found on the America.gov Archive Web site, Tyler noted:

> I knew from my own real-life experience that Iranians are wonderful storytellers, that they love to discuss interpersonal intrigues and family complications; but the actual stories that those women tell in the kitchen are entirely imaginary. I made them all up from scratch.

Michiko Kakutani, writing in the *New York Times*, was one of the first critics to notice this new expansiveness in *Digging to America*. She calls the novel

> arguably her most ambitious novel yet: a novel that not only provides an intimate portrait of a Baltimore family (or, in this case, two Baltimore families), as almost all of her books do, but also unfolds gently to look at what it means to be an American.

Kakutani notes further, "With Maryam Yazdan, the novel gives us an affecting portrait of a woman caught between two cultures and two countries," explaining that Tyler portrays Maryam as "a woman pulled between the expectations of her clamorous family and her own

temperamental inclinations toward solitary independence."

Ron Charles, writing in the *Washington Post*, agrees. "With her 17th novel, Tyler has delivered something startlingly fresh while retaining everything we love about her work," he writes in a review published when the novel was released. "*Digging to America* delivers...a daring expansion of Tyler's range, the people who are really at the heart of this novel come from Korea, China and Iran." Charles also notes,

> Her success at portraying culture clash and the complex longings and resentments of those new to America confirms what we knew, or should have known, all along: There's nothing small about Tyler's world, nothing precious about her attention to the hopes and fears of ordinary people.

Liesl Schillinger, writing in the *New York Times*, notes a structural change in this novel as well, pointing out that "usually, she begins with a close focus on one or two characters and then widens it to reveal their ensnarement in family and local ties." Schillinger comments that "Tyler's characters face the future, not the past, so she doesn't let the freight of personal history freeze their forward motion, although it sometimes slows them down." Finally, Schillinger points out that *Digging to America* "starts in the present and mostly stays there, traveling backward just enough to give us clues about her characters' impulses."

CRITICISM

Charlotte M. Freeman

Freeman is a writer, editor, and former academic living in small-town Montana. In the following essay, she examines how Anne Tyler uses third-person limited point of view as a structural device to achieve her comedic goal of separating each character from his or her family group in order to reunite them in a classical comic celebration at the end of Digging to America.

Anne Tyler's novels are known for their graceful writing, their quirky characters, and their happy endings. Thus, although she is not a writer known primarily for her humor or for telling jokes, she is, in the classical sense, a comic writer. Her interest lies in examining the lives of ordinary people as they go about their daily lives. Her plots usually revolve around the ways in which those characters have become estranged

WHAT DO I READ NEXT?

- Jane Jeong Trenka was six months old and her sister Carol was four and a half when they left Korea and were adopted by the Trenkas, a childless white couple from rural Minnesota. In her memoir, *The Language of Blood* (2005), Trenka recounts the experience of growing up with loving parents in a family where no one ever mentioned the girls' Asian ethnicity. Beautifully written, this book has become a touchstone for American families who have adopted Asian children.

- Like Maryam Yazdan, Marjane Satrapi had a period of teenage rebellion in post-revolutionary Iran that put herself and her family in danger. *Persepolis* (2004) is her memoir in graphic novel form and tells the story of her family's struggle to find a life in a repressive society. The story begins when Satrapi is a child, during the Iran-Iraq war, and follows her through her teenage years in an Austrian boarding school and then back to Iran where she attends college, marries, and divorces. By the book's end, Satrapi has fled Iran for Paris, where she begins work on the manuscript that becomes *Persepolis*. Satrapi's art is minimalist and shot through with humor. The book was also made into an animated film in 2007.

- Gene Luen Yang's prizewinning graphic novel for young adults, *American Born Chinese* (2008), is the story of Jin Wang, a lonely Taiwanese American boy navigating the challenges of middle school in San Francisco. The novel filters Jin Wang's feelings of being born in the wrong body through the story of the Chinese folk hero the Monkey King and through the figure of Chin-kee, an amalgamation of ugly Chinese American stereotypes. This lively and emotionally affecting book was the first graphic novel nominated for the American Book Award.

- *The Accidental Tourist* (1985) is one of Tyler's most beloved novels. The story of Macon Leary, a travel writer who hates to travel, the novel begins shortly after the senseless murder of Macon's son in a burger-joint holdup. Macon and his wife drift apart and separate, and after an accident, Macon returns to his childhood home, where his eccentric siblings still live. Slowly he comes back to life, in part through his budding relationship with Muriel Pritchett, a dog trainer he hires for his unruly dog. Much like the main character in many of Tyler's novels, Macon is eventually forced to choose between his new and his old lives.

- In *Reading Lolita in Tehran: A Memoir in Books* (2003), Azar Nafisi recounts the story of the illegal reading group she started after being forced to resign her professorship at the University of Tehran. She chooses her seven best students, and they read through Jane Austen, William Faulkner, and the great, if controversial, Vladimir Nabokov novel *Lolita*. The books are banned in Iran, so the women often share photocopies, and as their group coheres, the shy become less so, and they find small ways to rebel against the oppressive government.

- Rose Kent's novel *Kimchee and Calamari* (2007) follows fourteen-year-old Joseph Calderaro as he struggles with a school assignment about ancestry. Adopted as a child, Joseph is ethnically Korean, yet his father insists that he "became Italian" on the day he was adopted. In a panic, Joseph appropriates a famous Korean marathoner and writes an award-winning essay about how the man is his biological grandfather, a move that eventually backfires on him. While rewriting the essay, Joseph finds more details about his birth family and strengthens his relationships with his adoptive parents and siblings.

> *DIGGING TO AMERICA* IS A COLLECTIVE NOVEL,
> A NOVEL IN WHICH THE GATHERED VOICES AND
> EXPERIENCES OF THE ENTIRE GROUP OF PEOPLE
> ARE GIVEN MORE VALUE THAN THE SINGLE
> EXPERIENCE OF ANY ONE OF THEM."

from their families or communities and are resolved when the characters are reintegrated into those social groups.

Writing in the *New Yorker* in 1977, the novelist John Updike praises Tyler's "unmistakable strengths—her serene, firm tone; her smoothly spun plots; her apparently inexhaustible access to the personalities of her imagining; her lack of any trace of intellectual or political condescension," while noting that "her one possible weakness: a tendency to leave the reader just where she found him." One could argue with Updike that this tendency is not a flaw but rather the fulfillment of the promise a comic work holds out, for unlike tragedy, which is designed to challenge the reader or viewer to address the tragic flaws that cause the powerful to fall, a comic work offers a glimpse of a familiar world turned askew, then righted once more. The pleasure is in the righting of the fictional ship, in returning the reader to his or her starting place. This fulfillment of reader expectation is one reason Tyler has not always been taken seriously by the critics who have tended to agree with Updike, who noted in that same *New Yorker* article that "the impending moral encloses the excitements of her story in a circle of safety that gives them the coziness of entertainment."

However, as the critic Joseph C. Voelker points out in his critical examination of Tyler's first ten novels, *Art and Accidental in Anne Tyler*, her method owes much to her Quaker upbringing. She is, therefore, working in a spiritual and ethical framework that goes unrecognized by those of her peers, like Updike, who are more indebted to the authoritarian Puritan framework that informs their own works. Voelker notes that Tyler's work is characterized by "the distrust of glamour, the quiet resistance toward moral authority, the conviction of human goodness, and the calm insouciance toward sexuality

that Baltzell identifies as essentially Quaker," whereas an Updike novel "naturally gravitates toward hellfire sermon."

The sensibility that informs the novels of an author like Updike cannot help but inform his critical writing as well. His stature as both a critic and novelist ensures that his judgments will thus become the conventional wisdom on the subject. Updike's admiration for Tyler is genuine, but it is also clear that the differences in their sensibilities are such that he cannot see the quiet completion in her works for the comic accomplishment it is. Voelker points out another Quaker trait in Tyler's work that seems particularly applicable to *Digging to America*:

> Invariably, Tyler hands over spontaneous inspiration to one of her characters, none of whom is denied at least the potential to see and speak the gently surprising truth, each of whom is permitted captainship of his or her destiny within the confines of a random and ungovernable external world.

The clearest example of Tyler allowing her characters "captainship" of their lives can be seen in the way she rotates the points of view in *Digging to America*. While the book opens with one short chapter in the third-person omniscient point of view, it then proceeds to rotate among the characters, alternating between the Yazdan family and the Dickinson-Donaldson family. Each chapter is told from the point of view of a different character, including their interior monologues. This allows the reader access to that character's thoughts about the others, as well as to their feelings of belonging or being estranged from their family and community.

Maryam Yazdan is the first character to whom Tyler gives a chapter, and there are three others (chapters 2, 6 and 10) also written from her point of view. It is the arc of Maryam's relationship with Dave Dickinson that forms the spine of the plot. In Maryam's first chapter, we learn that she thinks of herself as an optimist, "or on second thought, not an optimist: a pessimist. But her life had been rocky enough that she faced possible disasters more philosophically than most." She describes her life, her son, her daughter-in-law, her worries for them, and the joy she takes in Susan, yet Maryam's anxiety about how other people see her runs through it all like a thread.

At the end of a day of babysitting Susan, she declines Ziba's invitation to stay to tea, letting "herself out the front door. She was trying to be the perfect mother-in-law. She didn't want Ziba to consider her a nuisance." We also learn that Maryam can be acerbic, even if only in her own head, a trait that is usually brought out by people she thinks of as "Americans." When invited to the Donaldsons' for a leaf raking party, she thinks to herself about Bitsy:

> There was something aggressive about her plainness . . . her blatant lack of makeup, her chopped hair and angular, rawboned body. She might almost be making a statement. Next to her, Ziba looked very glamorous, but also a little bit flashy.

By showing us Maryam from both the inside, in her own chapters, and from the outside in the chapters narrated by the other characters, Tyler grants Maryam captainship of her own destiny.

Maryam is not the only character into whose mind the reader is allowed by Tyler. The other chapters are narrated by Bitsy, Sami, Dave, Ziba, and Jin-Ho. It is perhaps in Jin-Ho's chapter that the sensibility Voelker describes as Quaker comes most into view. Jin-Ho's age is not entirely clear, but she is in her first few years of elementary school; she is old enough to understand most of what is going on around her, but not old enough to care deeply about adult subjects like her grandfather's feelings for Maryam. Tyler is careful, however, not to make her merely cute. Like the adult characters, Jin-Ho is allowed to captain her own ship.

The clearest example of this is when Bitsy, in encouraging Jin-Ho to be patient with Susan, who Jin-Ho finds bossy, tells her that the friendship will grow in importance as the girls grow up. "Someday you might even travel to Korea together and look up your biological mothers," Bitsy suggests. Jin-Ho is horrified by this thought. "Why would we want to do that?" she replies. Bitsy replies with her usual effusiveness, assuring Jin-Ho, "We wouldn't mind! We would support you and encourage you!" Jin-Ho is unmoved, and in her interior monologue, we learn that she rejects everything Korean, the food and the costumes. Most crucially, we learn that "she never, ever, even once in her life had watched that stupid videotape." Where Bitsy sees foreignness as exotic and special, Jin-Ho rejects it entirely. By giving Jin-Ho an interior life that is private only to her and allowing the reader inside Jin-Ho's experience of being in this family, Tyler demonstrates an anti-authoritarian approach to the novel.

Digging to America is a collective novel, a novel in which the gathered voices and experiences of the entire group of people are given more value than the single experience of any one of them. In rotating among these points of view, Tyler makes the point that truth is both individual and collective, that while each of us has a private story that we tell ourselves about our lives, there is also this separate collective story of our family and our community in which we are embedded. In giving equal weight to both the individual and the collective narratives, she undermines the idea that any one of us can know the entire truth.

Tyler carries this anti-authoritarian approach to plot into the comedy plot as well. While the primary plot of the novel is the broken romance between Maryam Yazdan and Dave Dickinson, each of the other characters experiences smaller versions of the comedy drama as well. Each point-of-view character, at some point in the novel, feels himself or herself exiled from the larger community, and each is eventually brought back into the fold. Although Sami's primary sense of alienation has to do with being an outsider in the Iranian community, an experience that is rectified as he finds himself speaking Persian to Susie, he also nearly exiles himself from the Dickinson-Donaldson friendship when he lets his irritation at Bitsy erupt into a shoving match with Brad. The comedy plot is fulfilled when the fight, instead of escalating, reveals itself as ridiculous to the two men, and they wind up hugging and laughing at their own behavior. A potential rupture in the community fabric is thus mended.

Ziba too finds herself feeling alienated early in the novel by her own sense of awe and timidity in the face of Bitsy's certitude. Bitsy is older than Ziba, and her child seems to fit in more quickly and grows faster than Ziba's. Bitsy has specific opinions on so many subjects. However, when Bitsy finds herself exhausted by Xiu-Mei's frailty and her iron-clad determination not to give up her pacifier, Ziba finds that "lately, she had become Bitsy's moral support—almost her elder—as various difficulties arose with little Xiu-Mei." The tables turn, and in being needed, Ziba feels herself to be brought into the communal fold and finds her niche.

As for Bitsy herself, the event that threatens to exile her from the community is not so much a character flaw as an external event: she gets cancer. Becoming ill, Bitsy, whose personality is forceful, even bossy, finds herself being folded

The relationships continue with the annual Arrival party celebrations. *(Thomas M. Perkins / Shutterstock.com)*

into the community as her family and friends step up to help her, at exactly the same time when she is in danger of being exiled from the community by death itself. However, the nature of a comedy is to supply a happy ending, and although Bitsy's illness and recovery hang over the plot like a shadow, she is officially recovered as the book ends.

All of these subplots serve primarily to reinforce the main plot, the romance plot between Dave Dickinson and Maryam Yazdan. It is more common for the romance plot in a comedy to concern a young couple, but in this case, it is the widowed elders who become involved, and the inability of the other characters to determine the nature of their romance provides a humorous subplot of its own for much of the novel. For Maryam, the first obstacle is becoming a part of the community at all. Maryam is a reserved person, the kind of person who finds herself gravitating to the corner at the Hakimis' big parties and who has always felt herself a stranger, and she resists becoming part of the Donaldsons' orbit, an orbit she sees as belonging to her son and daughter-in-law. However, slowly, she does.

Maryam becomes fond of them all, but when Dave shows signs of becoming attached to her after his wife dies, she resists. She has been widowed a long time. She tells herself she likes her quiet life. She tells herself he is too American. She complains to Ziba that "he takes up so much space. He seems to be unable to let a room stay as it is, always he has to alter it." Ziba replies, "But, Mari-june, That's not American; it's just . . . male." Maryam's broken engagement is the danger point for her. She exiles herself from the community afterward, not wanting things to be awkward, and it is not until the entire Dickinson-Donaldson clan comes to physically get her for the Arrival Day party that Maryam is reconciled to the group once again. In a classic comedic plot, the novel would end with a wedding, and while it is not explicit that Maryam and Dave will rekindle their romance, Maryam's second thoughts and the actions of the family indicate that it may very well be so.

Although Tyler's work is sometimes considered mere entertainment, her deft use of the tools of classic comic structure reveal an author working at the top of her game. That her novels fulfill the expectations of their readers simply marks them as comedies, even if they are comedies of gentle rather than broad humor. Whether it is her Quaker background or simply her personal sensibility, Tyler also seems deeply invested in exploring the human foibles of all of her characters, and this is arguably the key to her long-term success.

Source: Charlotte M. Freeman, Critical Essay on *Digging to America*, in *Novels for Students*, Gale, Cengage Learning, 2012.

Swati Guleria

In the following essay, Guleria and Neelakantan focus on the transnational themes represented by the Iranian American couple and the adopted Korean children in the novel.

Anne Tyler's *Digging to America* (London: Vintage, 2007) offers an insightful critique into the phenomenon of transnationalism. The present paper focuses on the liberating and constricting aspects of the transnational experience on two generations of Iranian-Americans and also on the first generation of Korean children being raised in the USA.

Significantly, the experience of Maryam who had immigrated to America in Tyler's novel is a happy one in that it helped her to leave behind a rigid theocratic society and relocate to a predominantly secular culture that values individual freedom. Young and well-educated and rendered a misfit in Iran precisely for the same reason, she seeks an escape in her marriage to Kiyan, a fellow Iranian, employed in America. The first kind of freedom that immigration brings Maryam involves shedding the purdah. Soon after reaching America, Maryam adopts the western attire and even acquires a driving licence which acts as her passport to mobility and independence.

Likewise, for the first generation Kiyan, immigration holds out the promise of the American Dream. Ambitious, he succeeds as "a pathologist with a good-paying nine-to-five job." However, obsession with work incapacitates him for social life in America. Significantly, the range of vocabulary available to immigrant men like Kiyan often becomes restricted to technical terms. Thus his social ineptitude is discovered for the reader by the narrator's comment that he [Kiyan] "didn't always get [the] jokes [of his colleagues] and his knowledge of colloquial English [was] surprisingly scanty."

The novel also shows how the notion of space in America that is often geared to human comfort proves liberating for Maryam. Memories of her family sleeping together in Iran on the terrace in full view of other families often arouse feelings of shame in her. The celebration of privacy as a value in America appeals to Maryam since an "unprivate way of life had [always] gone against her grain."

Maryam comes into such private as well as personal space only after Kiyan's death. Typically "very moody" and "demanding," Kiyan in seeking her "constant attendance" reduces her to a glorified slave. Interestingly, Mahler in an intelligent essay highlights a style of behaviour that perfectly answers to the description of Kiyan and Maryam in *Digging to America*: "Men wish to return home where they recoup higher status, while women try to settle the family in the 'host' country" (Mahler, J. Sarah. "Theoretical and Empirical Contributions towards a Research Agenda for Transnationalism." *Transnationalism from Below*. Ed. Michael P. Smith and Luis Eduardo Guarnizo. 6 vol. New Brunswick: Transaction Publishers, 1998, p. 83). However, Maryam gets a chance to be herself and live a life of her own only when her fortunes change following the death of Kiyan as well as the subsequent marriage of her son, Sami. Soon she understands that such freedom comes with a price. Realizing the futility of living bereft of companionship, she finds herself drawn towards Dave, an American widower.

Fortunately, social mores in America that encourage free mixing of men and women create no barriers for Maryam to fall in love with Dave. While no one disapproves of their relationship, it is also ironically true that it is fraught with complications. In the bargain, she remains an eternal outsider. Maryam's migration to America betrays her preference for being an outsider rather than live a life of unfreedom in Iran: "[the issue concerns] whether one sacrificed freedom and independence to take on inherited responsibility [of one's own patriarchal culture in Iran] or risked rootlessness and alienation by leaving home and hearth" (Michiko Kakutani, "Belonging to a Family, Belonging in America." Rev. of *Digging to America*, by Anne Tyler. *The New York Times Book Review* 19 May 2006. 24 May 2008. http://www.nytimes.com/2006/05/19/books/19book.html).

For second generation Ziba, unlike Maryam, life as a young woman in America is far less regimented. As an adolescent, however, Ziba had to endure parental surveillance. And such a cultural practice contrasts sharply with the American parents' perception of their teenagers as individuals who could very well take care of themselves. Assimilated into American ways, Ziba escapes the smothering effect of parental concern by living an independent life on campus. She eventually marries Sami Yazdan, her college mate, who is no less Americanized than her. Their union exemplifies a departure from the world of their first generation parents in many ways.

Unlike Kiyan and Maryam, Sami and Ziba share a happy married life free from gender stereotyping. Considering that both of them are employed, Sami is wise enough to reject role stereotyping altogether and happily assists Ziba with household responsibilities including child care, a circumstance which makes women in Ziba's family envy her. Appropriately enough, she feels "a flood of appreciation for all the ways that he [Sami] was different from his father."

More importantly, the transnationalism of *Digging to America* is exemplified in the adoption of Korean children by second generation American and American-Iranian families, which curiously turns out to be a mixed experience. Undoubtedly, adoption provides the Korean children a genial family environment in America. Adopted by couples without children, the fate of the children transforms dramatically from being homeless to becoming scion of their foster parents and grandparents. In America, the girls not only have access to basic education but are also provided "all the possibilities" such as ballet dancing and art camp.

Significantly, the upbringing of both the adopted female children conforms to practices in a typical American family. If anything, the second generation Yazdans' adopting a Korean rather than an Iranian child betrays their cultural anxieties about their American credentials.

Despite all the advantages adoption confers on the Korean children, they run the risk of being stereotyped like the second-generation Ziba. For instance, Bitsy Donaldson's stereotypical thinking gives rise to the hypothetical assumptions such as the likelihood of the girls becoming bosom friends or the future possibility of their visiting Korea to trace their biological mothers and the happenstance of the mothers turning out best friends too. Not so surprisingly,

it is Bitsy's "blithe assumption that their [American] way was the only way!" which, in refusing to concede any merit to Ziba's style of bringing up her child, undermines Sami's and Ziba's belief in their assimilation.

In skillfully portraying the concerns which are in the foreground of transnationalism, Anne Tyler clearly shows the resiliency of hyphenated identities. *Digging to America* refuses to view America as a melting pot and instead privileges the more inclusive notion of salad bowl that resonates with the social realities of a transnational globalized America. Fittingly, both Yazdans and Donaldsons eventually overcome their bitterness arising out of their cultural differences and learn to accept each other. Thus Tyler's vision of America posits its faith in human togetherness that celebrates diversity and difference over divisions and conformity.

Source: Swati Guleria and G. Neelakantan, "Transnationalism in Anne Tyler's *Digging to America*," in *Notes on Contemporary Literature*, Vol. 39, No. 2, March 2009.

Donna Seaman

In the following review, Seaman deems Digging to America *one of Tyler's best works, lauding the novel for its insightful rendering of twenty-first century American society.*

The finest novelists of psychologically acute domesticity purposefully linger over the preparation of meals and the furnishing of rooms, and often turn special occasions into crucibles for conflicts and epiphanies. A master at these time-honored techniques, Tyler extends her reach in her seventeenth novel [*Digging to America*] and creates two very different households that serve as microcosms for twenty-first-century American society. The two families converge at the Baltimore airport, each nervously anticipating the arrival of an adopted Korean baby girl. Bitsy and Brad Donaldson appear to be stereotypical white middle-class Americans. The Yazdans—Ziba, Sami, and Sami's glamorous, long-widowed mother, Maryam—are Iranian Americans. Hoping that the families will stay in touch so that their daughters can grow up together, Bitsy invents Arrival Day, an annual celebration that grows increasingly elaborate each year. Ultimately, these amusingly awkward and contentious events become the gauge of their lives. Each of Tyler's endearing characters is authentically rendered, but Jin-Ho and Susan, the two diametrically opposed young girls, are standouts, as is Maryam. As the novel's reigning consciousness, she reveals what it feels like to be viewed as "exotic" or "foreign" in America before and after 9/11, and how one can become detrimentally attached to the role of outsider. Handling time with a light touch, Tyler creates many blissful moments of high emotion and keen humor while broaching hard truths about cultural differences, communication breakdowns, and family configurations. This deeply human tale of valiantly improvised lives is one of Tyler's best.

Source: Donna Seaman, Review of *Digging to America,* in *Booklist,* Vol. 102, No. 12, February 15, 2006, p. 7.

SOURCES

"Adopting from Korea and Afterwards," in *Korean Adoption Option,* http://www.adoptkorea.com/Choosing_Korea/Choosing_Korea.htm (accessed May 3, 2011).

Charles, Ron, "The Roads to Home," in *Washington Post,* April 6, 2006.

Cuddon, J. A., "Comedy," in *Penguin Dictionary of Literary Terms and Literary Theory,* Penguin, 1997, pp. 148–49.

Evans, Elizabeth, *Anne Tyler,* Twayne Publishers, 1993, pp. xxii, 4–5.

"Interview with Novelist Anne Tyler," in *America.gov Archive,* http://www.america.gov/st/washfile-english/2007/August/20070807183753attocnich0.945492.html (accessed May 3, 2011).

Kakutani, Michiko, "Belonging to a Family, Belonging in America," in *New York Times,* http://www.nytimes.com/2006/05/19/books/19book.html?ex=1190260800&en=ccdc1b5fd4314d66&ei=5070 (accessed May 3, 2011).

Schillinger, Liesl, "The Accidental Friendship," in *New York Times,* http://www.nytimes.com/2006/05/21/books/review/21schillinger.html (accessed May 3, 2011).

"Spotlight on Iranian Foreign Born," in *Migration Information Source,* http://www.migrationinformation.org/USFocus/display.cfm?ID=404 (accessed May 3, 2011).

Tyler, Anne, *Digging to America,* Knopf, 2006.

———, "Still Just Writing," in *The Writer on Her Work,* edited by Janet Sternburg, Norton, 2000, pp. 13–15.

Updike, John, "Loosened Roots," in *New Yorker,* June 6, 1977, http://archives.newyorker.com/?i=1977-06-06#folio=130 (accessed May 3, 2011).

Voelker, Joseph C., *Art and the Accidental in Anne Tyler,* University of Missouri, 1989, p. 3.

Wheelwright, Julie, Review of *Digging to America,* in *Independent* (London, England), May 12, 2006, http://www.independent.co.uk/arts-entertainment/books/reviews/digging-to-america-by-anne-tyler-477765.html (accessed May 3, 2011).

FURTHER READING

Salwak, Dale, ed., *Anne Tyler as Novelist,* University of Iowa Press, 1994.

> This collection of seventeen essays examines those characteristics that make Tyler's fiction so powerful and so popular: her concern for the American family, her gift for illuminating the eccentricities and blind spots of those closest to us, her comic touch, and her interest in the life-changing potential of the chance encounter. Although the majority of contributors are academics, this collection also contains two fine essays on Tyler's work by the novelist John Updike.

Sternberg, Janet, *The Writer on Her Work,* W. W. Norton, 1980.

> This collection of essays by women writers is the source of one of Anne Tyler's few essays about her life and work. In "Still Just Writing," she discusses her childhood in the Celo Community in North Carolina as well as her journey to becoming a fiction writer. She also discusses the manner in which she juggles being a wife and mother with her work.

Tyler, Anne, *Breathing Lessons,* Knopf, 1988.

> Like Bitsy Donaldson, Maggie Moran, the protagonist of *Breathing Lessons,* is a meddler. Over the course of this very quiet novel, for which Tyler won the Pulitzer Prize, Maggie and her husband Ira make a ninety-mile round trip by car to attend the funeral of a friend. Over the course of the day, Ira contemplates his life, which he thinks he has wasted, as Maggie plots to reunite her son Jesse with his wife and baby. At times very funny, this novel examines the ways that life disappoints us and the means by which people carry on nonetheless.

Tyler, Anne and Shannon Ravenel, eds., *Best of the South: From the Second Decade of New Stories from the South,* Algonquin, 2005.

> This is the second of two short-story collections that Tyler edited with Ravenel for this series. For this volume, Tyler re-examined the 186 short stories that appeared in ten years' worth of the *Best of the South* annual anthologies and picked the twenty stories she liked best. The anthology contains an introduction by Tyler and stories by writers such as Chris Offut, Jill McCorkle, and Lee Smith. The book is a terrific anthology and an interesting glimpse of the sort of story that Tyler herself loves.

SUGGESTED SEARCH TERMS

Anne Tyler

Digging to America AND novel

Digging to America AND Anne Tyler

Korean AND adoption

Iran AND diaspora

international AND adoption

Anne Tyler AND Quaker

Anne Tyler AND Southern writers

Anne Tyler AND women writers

Anne Tyler AND John Updike

Anne Tyler AND novel

Dreaming in Cuban

CRISTINA GARCÍA

1992

In her debut novel, *Dreaming in Cuban* (1992), the Cuban American author Cristina García presents the oft-turbulent, occasionally magical lives of women in three generations of a Cuban family gradually divided by time, fate, and revolution. Critically admired and nominated for the National Book Award, the novel is widely deemed a stand-out text in the emerging canon of contemporary Latino literature. García originally launched a career as a journalist with national publications, but inspired by a visit back to her nation of birth and her reconnection with family and the culture there, she turned to fiction to fulfill her burgeoning creative impulse.

With her imagination fueled by poetry by the likes of the American modernist Wallace Stevens, she created a textually rich, imagistically powerful narrative that swirls around the young Cuban American Pilar—García's fictional counterpart—and her grandmother Celia. In fragmented postmodern fashion, the novel mixes third-person omniscient narration with first-person narration provided mostly by Pilar's generation as well as by Celia in epistolary form—old unsent letters that she ultimately bequeaths to her granddaughter. As reflected in her original title "Tropics of Resemblances" (taken from the Stevens poem that serves as the novel's epigraph), García sought to portray how the mothers, daughters, fathers, and sons in her story, in light of their differing experiences, form various and often conflicting conceptions of Cuban life and society.

Cristina Garcia (*AP Images*)

Dreaming in Cuban is aimed at a mature readership. The novel contains occasional scenes marked by sexual interaction or violent assault.

AUTHOR BIOGRAPHY

García was born on July 4, 1958, in Havana, Cuba, to a successful cattle rancher and his wife. In the Cuban revolution, along with many in the middle and upper classes, they suffered confiscation of their property and denunciation by the government, and in 1960, they left for New York City. Growing up in Brooklyn, García attended the Dominican Academy and worked for her parents' restaurant and retail business. She graduated from Barnard College of Columbia University in 1979 with a degree in political science, having taken only a single English class—one on the novella that instilled in her a lasting affection for literature.

Over the next decade, she would be inspired by the American authors Toni Morrison, Louise Erdrich, and Maxine Hong Kingston—of African, Native American, and Chinese descent, respectively—whose perspectives from outside of the dominant white American culture seemed to help make them exceptional observers. García next earned a master's degree in international studies from Johns Hopkins University and embarked on a career in journalism. Becoming a correspondent for various prominent publications through the 1980s, including the *Boston Globe*, the *New York Times*, and *Time* magazine, she relished the opportunities to delve into radically different worlds with each new assignment.

In 1984, she finally returned to Cuba, a visit that gave her the perspective of her grandmother and other Cuban kin, one vastly different from the anti-Castro stance maintained by her mother. In 1987, she was a *Time* bureau chief in Miami, where the vibrant Cuban community inspired her to further reconnect with her own past. She realized that the medium of fiction would offer more expansive opportunities for exploring and building on the memories and stories of her childhood and family.

In 1989, García began writing in extensive verse what would eventually become her first prose novel. Lauded by critics and nominated for the National Book Award, *Dreaming in Cuban* (1992) thrust García into the growing limelight accorded modern Latin American and Latino/a fiction. Garnering a Guggenheim fellowship and a National Educational Association grant, among other recognition, she has since published steadily and diversely, producing novels such as *The Agüero Sisters* (1997), further exploring life in Cuba and among Cuban exiles; anthologized short stories such as "Inés in the Kitchen" (1996), capturing her own feelings on the verge of motherhood (she has a daughter, Pilar García Brown, with husband Scott Brown); and edited collections such as *¡Cubanísimo!: The Vintage Book of Contemporary Cuban Literature* (2003). She has meanwhile served in various professorships, such as at Texas Tech University and, as of 2011, at the University of Miami. Her 2010 publication, *The Lady Matador's Hotel*, offers an atmospheric composite portrait of modern Latin Americans whose paths cross at a luxury hotel.

PLOT SUMMARY

Ordinary Seductions

OCEAN BLUE

Dreaming in Cuban opens in 1972 on the coast of Santa Teresa del Mar, Cuba, where Celia del Pino, a devout supporter of Fidel Castro's revolution, scours the northern coast from her porch after dusk for signs of foreign invasion. A vision of her husband, Jorge, draws her to the shore, but he disappears. He is ill and has recently departed for America for treatment. Reminiscing, Celia wades in, still in her house dress.

Their daughter, Felicia, unreconciled with her father, is consoled by her friend Herminia, who advises a spiritual cleansing at La Madrina's house. Felicia arrives for the session that night, where a Santeria priest and others enact the ritual sacrifice of a goat to Elleguá, god of the crossroads.

GOING SOUTH

Another del Pino daughter, Lourdes, rises early to walk to work at her bakery in Brooklyn. Sister Federica calls from the Catholic hospital there that has been treating Jorge to describe her vision of Jorge, aglow in divine light, announcing his departure from this life and passing out the window and along the river southward. After work, Lourdes visits the hospital and recalls her father's final years there. Her daughter, Pilar, seems to be missing.

That day, Pilar saw her father about town with another woman and decided to finally go back to Cuba, which her family left when she was two. On a bus to Miami, she meets Minnie, a seventeen-year-old girl seeking an abortion. Pilar thinks back on the phases of her family's life together.

THE HOUSE ON PALMAS STREET

Celia is waiting for her granddaughters, Luz and Milagro, to return from a camping trip. She recalls the Spaniard she loved in her youth, Gustavo. Despondent after he left for Spain, Celia was courted by Jorge but started writing letters to Gustavo that she never sent. She and Jorge married and moved in with his mother, Berta, and sister, Ofelia, on Palmas Street in Havana—where Celia now takes her granddaughters back to their mother, Felicia, and spends the night. Berta and Ofelia had treated Celia horribly.

In the morning, Celia goes to hear a speech by Castro, "El Líder," and decides to devote herself to national causes; she leaves for two weeks to harvest sugarcane. Upon returning, she finds Felicia unstable, feeding her three children nothing but coconut ice cream. Felicia guards her son, Ivanito, but Celia takes the twin girls back with her to Santa Teresa del Mar.

CELIA'S LETTERS: 1935–1940

Celia writes to Gustavo of her honeymoon, her first pregnancy (with Lourdes), her time in an insane asylum, her second daughter (Felicia), and Jorge's tragic milk-truck accident.

A GROVE OF LEMONS

In Miami in the evening, Pilar hopes to find her cousin Blanquito, who might help her flee to Cuba. She finds the house of his family, the Puentes, in Coral Gables and through a window sees her uncles watching television. After some rain, she falls asleep on a deck chair; in the morning, she is awakened by an aunt. Her mother will fly down to get her.

Forty days after Jorge's burial, Lourdes is visited by his ghost. The next day, she catches her new employee, Maribel, stealing fifty cents and fires her. She recalls her family's fleeing Cuba a decade ago, when she insisted they drive north from Miami until it felt cold enough. In Cuba before they left, she had a miscarriage after a fall from a horse, the revolutionary government appropriated the Puentes's estate, and a soldier raped her.

THE FIRE BETWEEN THEM

Deteriorating mentally, Felicia ponders her delusional states. During this "summer of coconuts," she dances with Ivanito, recalling her husband, Hugo, who swept her off her feet during a restaurant shift and impregnated her before leaving for sea work. Seven months later, they married, and he revealed his viciousness. When she was pregnant again—and infected with syphilis from him—she set fire to an oily rag and tossed it on his face.

Ivanito humors his mother as she neurotically collects coconuts for making ice cream, talks in colors with him, and banishes sunlight from the house. At the end of the summer, Felicia prepares a feast ending with pink medicine tablets crushed on ice cream, and she and Ivanito lie together to sleep.

Celia had visited that day; upon leaving, she sees two half-brothers in town and recalls her earliest years, before she was deposited with her great aunt, Alicia, in Havana. That night, she sleeps poorly and awakens to demand that the twins find Herminia to drive them to Havana to save Felicia.

CELIA'S LETTERS: 1942–1949

In her letters, Celia writes to Gustavo of war around the world, a lethal tidal wave, the plight of the Cuban poor, and giving birth to Javier.

Imagining Winter
THE MEANING OF SHELLS

Two years after the summer of coconuts, having nearly killed herself and her son, Felicia is hiking with a brigade of third-rate revolutionaries in training. Indifferent, she smokes while keeping distance from the others. Ivanito is at boarding school.

Celia has become the judge of a people's court that convenes in an old movie theater in Santa Teresa del Mar. At present, two women are contesting whether one's husband seduced the other. When the husband arrives, Celia sentences him to volunteer hours at a nursery. Back at home, she remembers Javier, who moved to Czechoslovakia at age twenty.

Luz tells of her and Milagro's increased distance from their neurotic mother since the summer of coconuts. Nine years after he was set aflame and fled, their father returns, and they meet him at a rented room in Havana; he is hideously disfigured. They start to care for him. They bring Ivanito once, interrupting their father in a private encounter with a masked woman.

ENOUGH ATTITUDE

Lourdes has become an auxiliary policewoman who patrols a Brooklyn neighborhood two nights weekly. She and her husband, Rufino, have grown distant; the cold disagrees with him. On her beat, she sees a figure leap into the river, and she dives in after him. It is the son of Mirabel, the Puerto Rican woman she fired, and he does not survive.

Pilar has a half-Mexican boyfriend from San Antonio, Max, who has a blues band. She listens to punk music while painting. Lourdes asks her to do a wall painting for the grand opening of her second Yankee Doodle Bakery, so Pilar paints a surreal Statue of Liberty with a safety pin in her nose, barbed-wire like figures floating around her, and "I'M A MESS" scrawled at the bottom. The customers are repulsed, but Lourdes defends her daughter.

BASKETS OF WATER

Ivanito tells of Mr. Mikoyan, a kindly Russian teacher. Mr. Mikoyan behaves inappropriately with students at Ivanito's school and gets fired.

Felicia, seeking a husband, consults a *santero*, who tells her, "What you wish for, daughter, you cannot keep." That day, she happens upon Ernesto, who has crashed his bicycle, and lures him into her backseat. They immediately marry, but days later, dutifully inspecting a restaurant, he is killed in a grease fire. Later, she finds herself married to an amusement-park

employee named Otto. They hop on a roller coaster for a thrill ride, but he somehow plummets from a great height.

Javier returns from overseas heartbroken, as his wife has had an affair with a visiting professor and taken their daughter. Celia nurses him, but he rises from bed only to start drinking. Cancer stricken, Celia has a breast removed.

CELIA'S LETTERS: 1950-1955

Celia writes Gustavo of her mother-in-law's death, Jorge's strictness with Javier, and her involvement in prerevolutionary activities.

A MATRIX LIGHT

Lourdes is exercising. She loses the 118 pounds she gained when her father moved to New York, surprising Pilar when she returns from art school for Thanksgiving. Still mourning the baby she miscarried long ago, imagined to have been a son, Lourdes resumes eating heartily.

Despite the years apart, Pilar still feels more connected to her grandmother in Cuba than to her mother. After a term in Italy, Pilar has left art school to study at Barnard College, in New York City. She drops by to see her boyfriend, Rubén, to find him cheating on her with an exchange student. She buys an acoustic bass.

GOD'S WILL

Herminia, who agreed to "save" Felicia at age six, tells how Felicia gained renewed interest in Santeria, despite Celia's misgivings, after Otto's death. She loyally attends ceremonies and reaches a final initiation, involving purification, possession, and sacrifice. She returns to an empty house, saddened but devoted to her new vocation. As time passes, her health weakens, until she dies in Celia's arms.

Ivanito gets a package at Celia's house. It is a radio, perhaps from his father.

DAUGHTERS OF CHANGÓ

In a final visit to Lourdes in Brooklyn, the ghost of Jorge tells about how he wronged Celia by leaving her with his rapacious mother and sister. He tells Lourdes to revisit Cuba.

Pilar, struggling to concentrate on midterms, visits a *botánica* (an expert in natural remedies) and is instructed to take herbal baths for nine days. In the park, some eleven-year-old boys fondle her at knifepoint and smoke some of her herbs. After her nine baths, she resolves to go with her mother to Cuba.

CELIA'S LETTERS: 1956–1958

In her letters, Celia writes of Lourdes's s marriage to Rufino, whose wealthy family is connected to President Fulgencio Batista. Rufino's parents ensure that their wedding is an extravagant affair.

The Languages Lost

SIX DAYS IN APRIL

After Felicia's funeral, Celia puts on her daughter's old bathing suit. Pilar and Lourdes arrive in Cuba, to find the house on Palmas Street deserted and drive to Santa Teresa del Mar. They find Celia on the porch, hair matted from a night swim. In town, Lourdes mocks the Cuban social realities. Felicia's children arrive, and after dinner at a tourist hotel, Lourdes feels the spirit of the music dancing with Ivanito.

Lourdes drives around, visiting the hotel of her honeymoon and the ranch where she and Rufino lived with his family before fleeing the country. Ivanito connects with Pilar, who predicts her family members' futures using the Chinese classic *I Ching*. Lourdes dotes on Ivanito. Herminia takes Pilar and Ivanito to her house, where they hear about Felicia's life and religion. Pilar paints pictures of Celia, who gives Pilar the box of letters to Gustavo.

Hearing that people are seeking asylum at the Peruvian embassy in Havana, Lourdes rushes there, to call Castro a killer. He leaves her be and tells the defectors they are free to go. Back at Celia's house, in the morning, Lourdes packs Ivanito a suitcase, gives him money and her New York address and phone number, and drops him at the Peruvian embassy. Pilar and Celia rush after them. Pilar squeezes past the gate and finds Ivanito, but then she leaves and tells Celia he must have flown away already. Back at home, Celia drifts into the sea.

CELIA'S LETTER: 1959

It is just after the revolution, and Celia tells Gustavo of Pilar's birth. She will no longer write him.

CHARACTERS

Alicia

At the age of four, Celia is dispatched by her divorced, indifferent parents to live with her great-aunt Alicia in Havana. Alicia provides Celia with a cultured upbringing, exposing her to piano playing, museums, symphonies, and films.

Gustavo Sierra de Armas

A married Spanish lawyer who buys a camera from Celia at El Encanto to document murders in the years leading up to the Spanish Civil War, Gustavo becomes young Celia's lover. She is despondent when he abruptly leaves. The pearl earrings he gives her do not leave her ears for good until the novel's end. By resembling Gustavo, Fidel Castro captures Celia's devotion.

Ernesto Brito

After crashing his bicycle, Ernesto is set upon by the yearning Felicia, who promptly marries him. Only four days later, Ernesto, a vigorous restaurant inspector, is killed on the job in a suspicious grease fire.

Otto Cruz

Otto is an amusement-park employee whom Felicia seduces behind a spare-parts warehouse. His visions of escape to Minnesota go up in smoke when he plummets from a roller-coaster joyride with his wife and is incinerated on high-voltage wires.

Herminia Delgado

Herminia is Felicia's best friend from childhood. She constitutes Felicia's connection to Santería, because her father is a *babalawo*, a high Santería priest. She collects herbal remedies and conducts spiritual rites on Felicia's behalf.

Sister Federica

Federica, a Catholic nun from the Sisters of Charity Hospital in New York, experiences a divine vision of Jorge leaving his earthly life and calls Lourdes to tell her about it.

Rubén Florín

A Peruvian who dates Pilar at Barnard, Rubén is caught cheating with a Dutch exchange student.

Minnie French

Minnie is a seventeen-year-old girl seeking an abortion who is Pilar's companion on the bus south to Miami.

Ilda Limón

Ilda is a neighbor in Santa Teresa del Mar who sometimes has news to share.

La Madrina

The house of La Madrina serves as a site of Santería ritual and sacrifice, and La Madrina guides Felicia through her initiation as a *santera*.

Max

Max, full name Octavio Schneider, is a boy from San Antonio who dates the teenage Pilar. His mother is Mexican, and he speaks Spanish. He likens Lourdes to a hostile goddess.

Sergey Mikoyan

Mr. Mikoyan, Ivanito's Russian teacher at boarding school, praises him highly, leading Ivanito to aspire to work in foreign diplomacy. Mr. Mikoyan embraces Ivanito inappropriately and is later fired.

Graciela Moreira

A frequent beauty-salon customer, Graciela is suspected of spying by Felicia after Ernesto's death and is given a caustic hair treatment.

Maribel Navarro

Maribel is a Puerto Rican woman whom Lourdes fires for stealing fifty cents. Maribel's wayward son kills himself by jumping into a river, despite Lourdes's attempt, acting as auxiliary police officer, to rescue him.

Berta Arango del Pino

Jorge's mother, who is overly attached to her son, proves a horrific mother-in-law to Celia. She treats Jorge's new wife with cruel derision and responds to her kindly overtures by dumping her casserole into a gutter. On her deathbed, Berta mistakes Jorge for her lover.

Celia del Pino

The del Pino matriarch, Celia spends much time looking out over the sea for invasion from the north and figuratively oversees all the actions of her descendants. She never quite overcomes her initial maternal coldness toward Lourdes. Her love of lyricism is inherited by Felicia, whose addled mind prioritizes aesthetic over meaning. During Celia's lukewarm marriage, her youthful affection for a socially minded Spaniard is eventually transferred to the charismatic Castro, and with an empty nest, she devotes herself to the revolution, serving as sugarcane harvester, judge, and coastal lookout. Although ambiguous, the novel's end suggests that, having unburdened herself of her letters to Gustavo, and in the wake of

Ivanito's departure, she releases her pearl earrings as well as herself to drown in the sea.

Felicia del Pino

Felicia's name connotes happiness, but her life takes one tragic turn after another. Jealous of her sister's bond with their father, she drifts out of the house into sketchy employment and a hasty union with a temperamental merchant marine who gives her three children as well as syphilis, which at least partly accounts for both her mental and physical deterioration later. After her father's death, she comes unhinged and ends up in reformatory boot camp, alienated from her children. Her second husband dies in a fire; her third she evidently pushes from a roller coaster to his death. Herminia believes that Felicia at last finds spiritual peace after her Santería initiation, but she nonetheless continues to deteriorate and dies.

Javier del Pino

Lourdes and Felicia's brother is present in very few scenes in the story. During childhood, he bristled at his father's capitalistic expectations, and as a young man, he left for Czechoslovakia, where he married Irina Novotny and had a daughter, Irinita. After his wife abandons him, he returns to Cuba, where, under his mother's care, he becomes a drunkard. Lourdes dreams that he drowns in a pool of rainwater, but his true fate is uncertain.

Jorge del Pino

Celia's husband, a traveling salesman fourteen years her elder, is jealous of her lingering affection for her departed Spanish lover. He sabotages his relationship with her when he leaves her with his mother and sister during her pregnancy; they sap her will to sustain a family, and when she renounces Lourdes upon birth, Jorge institutionalizes her. Several years later, he suffers a collision with a milk truck that leaves shattered glass in his spine; Celia knows then that she loves him, too. After spending years in New York being treated for cancer, he dies but lingers to revisit Lourdes as a ghost, expressing regret for his treatment of Celia. He asks her to apologize for him, but she never does.

Ofelia del Pino

Jorge's sister and the daughter of Berta Arango del Pino, Ofelia lives a sheltered life as her mother's closest companion. The two attend church, get their hair done, and whiten their mulatto skin together. Ofelia dies of tuberculosis.

Pilar Puente del Pino

Pilar, with a biography that aligns with García's own, proves to be the novel's pivotal character, serving as the most significant first-person narrator and reconnecting the remaining members of her family in her visit to Cuba with her mother. (The novel itself might be conceived as Pilar's presentation of her own diary, the stories she has recorded, and the letters her grandmother gave her.)

Pilar claims to remember everything she has experienced since birth, and she shares a special connection with her grandmother, whom she last saw when she was two years old, communicating telepathically in the evenings. Her rebellious attitude toward her by-the-book mother draws her toward abstract painting, punk music, and, ultimately, a visit back to Cuba. However, her tourist stint there leaves her to conclude that Cuba can no longer be her home and should not be Ivanito's, and she supports his escape despite the predictably tragic effect on Celia.

Blanquito Puente

Blanquito is Pilar's cousin who lives in Florida. She hopes that he will help her get to Cuba.

Guillermo Puente

Guillermo, the father of Rufino, is a wealthy Cuban (originally from Spain) affiliated with the Mafia and the dictator Fulgencio Batista. Because of these connections, the Puente family's estate is confiscated during the Cuban revolution. The family flees to Florida.

Lourdes Puente

An ethnically proud woman who marries her first love, Lourdes is heartbroken when she miscarries after a fall from a horse. She is traumatized when vengeful revolutionary soldiers, after seizing the Puentes' estate, rape and abuse her. After moving to Brooklyn with her husband and daughter, she becomes as American as apple pie, a hard-working entrepreneur who enrolls as an auxiliary policewoman in her neighborhood and defends freedom of speech by supporting Pilar's subversive Statue of Liberty painting. Rejected at birth by her mother, Lourdes remains close to her father even after his death. By visiting Cuba with Pilar, Lourdes condemns the backwardness of the place and manages to ensure Ivanito's escape.

Rosario Puente

An aunt of the Puente family living in Coral Gables, Florida, Rosario finds Pilar asleep in a lounge chair by the pool. Pilar had hoped that Rosario's son, Blanquito, would help her flee to Cuba.

Rufino Puente

Lourdes's s former classmate, Rufino is an earthy, inventive man who works his family's ranch and disappoints his wealthy mother by marrying Lourdes. Once the Puente family flees for America, Rufino's loyalty to Lourdes proves his undoing: by acceding to her demand to drive ever farther north, he ends up in a cold climate that compromises his well-being. In Brooklyn, the two are at first passionate but grow distant, and Rufino bonds instead with his daughter; he also gallivants about town.

Zaida Puente

The domineering mother of Lourdes's husband stage-manages the couple's wedding and scorns Lourdes's s redecoration of their villa. Zaida has eight sons, all immigrants to the United States.

Xiomara Rojas

Lieutenant Rojas strives to instill military discipline in her lackluster brigade of social deviants. Felicia is under her command at reformatory boot camp after the summer of coconuts.

Hugo Villaverde

Hugo Villaverde, descended from slaves on his father's side, ingratiates himself with Felicia with a touch of the hand, which prompts her to abandon her job for a fling with him. He proves a despicable husband, abusive and infected with a sexually transmitted disease. He later becomes a respected absentee father, whose daughters adore their gifts of Chinese scarves. After he is disfigured by their mother, the girls ally with him as opposed to her.

Ivanito Villaverde

When Felicia slips into a delusional state after her father's death, she keeps Ivanito close at hand. He dances with her, learns to talk in colors with her, and is fed a great deal of coconut ice cream—with the final spiked dose nearly killing them. Nonetheless, he remains devoted to her while at boarding school. After Felicia's death, this relationship transfers to his aunt Lourdes, who likewise dances with him and dotes on him.

His eyes are opened to the greater world by his radio, presumably a gift from his father, which lets him pick up U.S. stations. Ivanito's escape from Cuba, which is engineered by Lourdes and supported by Pilar (García's alter ego in the novel), suggests that the author imagines a better future for this uniquely bright boy outside of Cuba.

Luz Villaverde

The slightly older of the mixed-race twin daughters of Felicia, Luz (meaning "light"), who often speaks on behalf of her sister and narrates a portion of the story, develops a sense of identity distinct from her mother, whom she regards as insane. During the summer of coconuts, the twins gladly leave to stay with Celia. Luz sympathizes with and cares for her disfigured father and enjoys boarding school. Signifying the height of Cuban insularity vis-à-vis Americans, Luz and Milagro are deemed to inhabit a "tight sealed box" because they talk so little with Pilar.

Milagro Villaverde

Felicia's other twin daughter, Milagro (meaning "miracle"), is understood to generally follow her sister's lead. It is Milagro, however, who finds the way to their father's rented room.

THEMES

Separation

Among the array of interrelated themes present in the book, that of separation, especially between family members, stands out. Whether caused by differences in personality, defining episodes of conflict, or the rift of the Cuban Revolution, a sense of separation dominates the relationships between Celia and Jorge, Celia and Lourdes, Lourdes and Rufino, Lourdes and Pilar, Felicia and Hugo, and Felicia and her twin girls, and Celia and Lourdes.

While García illustrates much in the lives of all the characters, the bond between Celia and Jorge is never really portrayed. Their courtship is defined not by any romantic act of Jorge's but by Celia's lingering affection for the absent Gustavo and the letters she begins to write him. Those letters reveal how, even in coming to love Jorge, she remains emotionally attached to Gustavo and distant from Jorge. From this divide between parents stems another, as Celia

renounces Lourdes at birth, and the two never quite connect.

When the Puente family is exiled to America, Lourdes is so appalled by what has taken place that she insists on distancing herself from Cuba as thoroughly as possible. However, separating Rufino from his beloved homeland drives him to retreat inward, and he and Lourdes, in turn, eventually grow distant. Meanwhile, Pilar seems able to see through Lourdes's overenthusiastic patriotic and capitalist fervor, ideologically separating mother and daughter. This relationship is one of the few marked by the closing of the relational gap over the course of the novel, as they seem to bond in visiting Cuba—at least in their desire to deliver Ivanito from the island.

Felicia, in contrast, ends up separated from everyone she loves, burned husbands and questionably raised children alike, leaving her only the solace of religion and the ultimate resolution of death. Javier, likewise, is separated from his wife and daughter and ostracizes himself back in Cuba through excessive drinking. At the novel's close, the separation of Ivanito from Celia seems a final, definitive severed bond that brings about the del Pino matriarch's death by drowning.

As highlighted by the circumstances of Lourdes's family's migration to Brooklyn, the Cuban Revolution is held responsible not only for inflicting divides on families such as the Puentes but also for sustaining those divides through its political isolation. Pilar yearns to reestablish a physical connection with her grandmother in Cuba, but when she gets there, the place feels lost in time, and Pilar senses the island's magic but concludes that New York is where she truly belongs now.

Lourdes's derision of Cuban society turns into a comedy routine, but Pilar implicitly shows that she agrees with her mother by acting as an accomplice in staging Ivanito's escape. The reader may conclude that, as Ivanito would spiritually suffocate on the island, Pilar sympathizes with his desire to "talk to a million people at once"—that is, to be part of modern connected global society. Evidently the separation of Ivanito from his grandmother—which predictably breaks Celia's heart—is not a primary concern of Pilar's.

From the Puente women's perspective, Cuba is simply too separated and backward. This contention about Cuba's tragic self-containment is suggested early in the novel by an image conceived by Celia, who considers the westward drift of the American continents and "wonders

TOPICS FOR FURTHER STUDY

- Research the history of Cuba from 1959 until 1980, the concluding year of *Dreaming in Cuban*. In a research paper, summarize that history, marking significant events like the Cuban missile crisis. Discuss how the relationship between Cuba and the United States evolved, especially as a result of actions taken by Fidel Castro and various U.S. presidents, and analyze whether the positives of Castro's rule outweighed the negatives for the majority of the Cuban people.

- Write a short story about a visit to a strange place, employing at least one instance of magical realism with some symbolic significance.

- If García's novel were set in the twenty-first century, Pilar and Celia's telepathic connection might have been preempted by an electronic one. Choose three persons with whom you have stayed in touch from a distance by computer-mediated means, such as a sibling gone to college, a friend from a town you previously lived in, a friend who moved away, or cousins. For each person, send a questionnaire or conduct an interview asking about the quantity and quality of his or

her computer-mediated interactions with people near and far alike. (Questions may include: How much time do you spend daily interacting via computer? How much time interacting face to face? What is your relation to your closest electronic correspondent? How often do you see that person face to face? How are your relationships enhanced or detracted from by your electronic correspondence?) Write a blog post or essay discussing what you learned about the benefits and drawbacks of computer-mediated correspondence from your small ethnographic study, quoting your sources anonymously.

- Read *Finding Miracles* (2004), a book by Julia Alvarez for young adults, about a girl named Milagros from a Latin American orphanage who is adopted by an American family and comes to be called Milly. When a refugee named Pedro joins her class at school, she discovers a means to reconnect with her birth country. Write an essay comparing and contrasting the characters of Milly and Pilar from *Dreaming in Cuban*.

---

whether Cuba will be left behind, alone in the Caribbean sea with its faulted and folded mountains, its conquests, its memories."

Memory and Imagination

Imagination and memory are explored in García's narrative through many of the central characters. Celia's affection for poetry and habit of living in her memories of Gustavo—she tells him that "Memory is a skilled seducer"—perhaps instilled in her daughters the ability to inflict their own poetics on the past.

Regarding Lourdes, Pilar points out how her mother, with uncanny ability, "systematically rewrites history to suit her views of the world." Lourdes does this in an unconscious way, simply

remembering alternate versions of how things happened; that is, her imagination rewrites her memory. As Pilar remarks, "Telling her own truth is *the* truth to her, even if it's at the expense of chipping away our past." Felicia, at the end of the unbalanced summer of coconuts, presents a nearly identical notion to Ivanito: "Imagination, like memory, can transform lies to truths." She seems to mean that whatever your mind labels as a lie can be rewritten to be called—and thus believed to be—truth.

Pilar seems to differ from her mother and aunt with respect to memory, in the sense that instead of habitually rewriting it, she remembers everything accurately. Pilar comes across as loyal to objective truth, even if, like her depiction

At the heart of the story is the generational closeness of the family. (*Monkey Business Images | Shutterstock.com*)

of the Statue of Liberty, it is unpopular or provocative. She cherishes her memories of her grandmother but laments that they fade as the years pass, and she regrets that politicians were responsible for dividing her family, such that "there's only my imagination where our history should be."

The novel draws toward its conclusion when Pilar acts on her need to rejuvenate her Cuban memories by returning to the island. Ultimately, while Pilar consecrates her grandmother's letters, which reveal how Celia's memories of Gustavo sustained her, Pilar concludes that one cannot be sustained by memories alone. Her present life has taken shape in New York, and to remain in Cuba now would only actualize another separation, disconnecting her from her own memories of almost all her life.

Verse

It is notable and palpable that García began this novel as a poem. She later decided to transform the work to prose after it reached around one hundred pages. As she remarked in her interview with Scott Brown, inspired by poetry, she focused on "the musicality of each sentence" and tried to convey "the rhythm and syncopation of the Spanish language." The lyrical qualities in the characters originate with Celia, who recites verse by the Spanish poet Federico García Lorca and imparts her refined aesthetic sense on her language. Felicia inherits this affection for words, although her twin daughters find her locutions flowery but meaningless.

Color

The imagistic nature of the narrated text itself is perhaps most evident in the deployment of colors. Blue is associated with much that has to do with Cuba, such as Jorge's eyes, the glow of his ascension (whereby he returns to Cuba), and the ocean view by Celia's house. Blue is also linked with the medical treatments for both Jorge's and Celia's cancer, while green is the color of growth, leading Pilar—whose heightened sensitivity to colors is reflected in her abstract art—to wonder "why didn't the doctors change the color of those damn beams to green? We eat green, it's healthy." Later, Pilar shows particular interest in painting her grandmother, who "had lived all these years by the sea until she knew its every definition of blue," in all kinds of shades of blues—but when Celia sees these pictures, she asks, as if reading the blueness in her face, "But do I really look so unhappy?" In sum, the colorful poetic images do not just enliven the narrative but also connote, among other possible readings, the tranquil but arguably unhealthy isolation of this particular island surrounded by so much blue.

STYLE

Latino/a Literature

The twenty-first century has witnessed an outpouring of literature by authors of Latin American origin living in the United States, often referred to as Latinos/Latinas. A majority of these writers are of Mexican (Sandra Cisneros), Cuban (Oscar Hijuelos), or Dominican (Julia Alvarez) descent. While these authors have not intentionally formed any cohesive movement and employ various narrative styles, certain factors are common to many of their works.

Reflecting autobiographical circumstances, Latino texts often highlight what might be considered the central existential dilemma of the first- or second-generation immigrant to the United States—the feeling of fully belonging neither in the departed homeland nor in the family's adopted one. García presents this dilemma through Pilar, whose experience moving from Cuba to Brooklyn at age two matches García's own.

A corresponding shared feature in Latino literature is the return trip to the Latin American nation of origin, which may prove revelatory for various reasons, such as revived connections with long-lost relatives, enhanced understanding of the culture that shaped one's parents, or a visceral sense of how well one fits into that culture oneself. Pilar, for example, bonds with her grandmother as well as her cousin Ivanito, witnesses her mother's declamations against Cuban society, and feels for herself the ambience of Cuba. Ultimately, Pilar realizes that New York is where she now belongs. Similar characters in other Latino works have markedly different experiences and reach widely varying conclusions about themselves and their families.

In exploring Cuban culture, García devotes particular attention to Santería, the Cuban religion developed by African slaves who concealed their continued devotion to Yoruban deities by identifying them with Catholic saints. For example, Changó, the Yoruban god of thunder and lightning, is identified with Santa Bárbara—an ebony statue of whom, dubbed "the Black Queen," is prominent in La Madrina's house. Felicia, the descendant of Celia who becomes most involved with Santería, is linked with Changó through the fire and electricity that destroy her three husbands.

García has noted that she herself had no firsthand knowledge of Santería but recognized its significant role in Cuban society, and so in writing her novel, she conducted extensive research in order to portray aspects of the religion as accurately and respectfully as possible. The reader may draw his/her own conclusions about the fact that all of the predictions made by the Santería priests in *Dreaming in Cuban* prove true.

Magical Realism

One of the most common and appreciated features of modern Latin American and Latino/a fiction is the stylistic approach known as magic realism. The Cuban writer Alejo Carpentier first coined the term *loreal maravilloso*, or "the marvelous real," to describe the different reality experienced by the Latin American colonized—American Indians along with blacks—versus the white colonizers. That is, a mythic version of an event—such as, for example, a Haitian sorcerer turning into a bird to escape captors rather than being executed unseen in a melee—can be registered in the believer's mind as the true reality. What has become known as magical realism depicts such fantastic reality as truth.

The Colombian author Gabriel García Márquez, author of novels such as *One Hundred Years of Solitude* (1967), earned a Nobel Prize in 1982 largely in recognition of the nuanced mastery of magical-realist techniques demonstrated in his novels and stories. García has acknowledged that while writing her first novel, she was immersed in the works of García Márquez, whom she found to liberate her imagination, in a sense allowing the story in her mind to more purely tell itself with disregard for rational boundaries. In *Dreaming in Cuban*, events such as the ascension of Jorge, his ghostly conversations with Lourdes, the vanishing of the *santera*, and the electric annihilation of Otto Cruz all stretch the reader's conception of reality to incorporate what is likely considered impossible.

In such a literary ambience, the reader may in turn allow the aesthetic/karmic beauty to overshadow or obscure the extreme improbability of mirrored fates, such as Felicia fulfilling the curse of being named after a crazed husband-burner by becoming a crazed husband-burner, and biographical coincidences, such as Pilar being born exactly fifty years after Celia, as well as Felicia and Ernesto being born only minutes apart. Also, in this context, Pilar and Celia's separate claims of communicating with one another telepathically, claims that might ordinarily be considered illusory products of each's solitude, can be portrayed as a literal and true thought-to-thought connection. If the reader approaches a text such as *Dreaming in Cuban* with an open mind, he may find that there is as much, if not more, truth as well as beauty to be found in mythical, magical versions of the world than in literal, limited reality.

HISTORICAL CONTEXT

While *Dreaming in Cuban* takes place primarily in the 1970s, with flashbacks and remembrances reaching as far back as the 1910s, the relevant Cuban history and politics reach back at least as far as the Cuban War of Independence, fought against Spain from 1895 to 1898. Situated so close to its shores, the United States had vested economic and strategic interests in the island, leading President William McKinley to express and stir sympathy for the Cuban cause. When the U.S.S. *Maine* was mysteriously blown up in Havana Bay, U.S. public opinion tilted heavily toward entering the war, leading the conflict to blossom into the Spanish-American War of 1898.

The United States emerged victorious from this months-long conflict and signed a peace treaty with Spain, without involving any Cuban representatives. Thus, because no Cuban Republic had been established yet, the nation's political status was in doubt. To assist in governance, a U.S. military governor was installed in 1899, marking the onset of U.S. intervention on the island. Although the Cuban Constitutional Assembly sought to draw up a document signaling its full independence in 1901, the United States instead insisted that a special relationship between them be defined, threatening otherwise to prevent the formation of any republic at all.

The United States demanded that this relationship be as defined in the Platt Amendment, part of that year's U.S. Army appropriations bill, the conditions of which were narrowly approved by the Cuban assembly. This amendment allowed the United States to intervene in internal Cuban affairs whenever deemed necessary and to maintain naval bases and coaling stations. Before finally withdrawing from the island, the U.S. military governance invoked two military orders facilitating penetration of the island by U.S. railroad companies and investors seeking land. García's novel alludes to these colonial circumstances when Celia, writing to Gustavo, cites the Platt Amendment and "the way the Americans have interfered in our affairs from the very beginning."

While the novel otherwise refers little to these early circumstances vis-à-vis the United States, Cuba's history for the next century would be distinctly molded by their implications and Cuban reactions. Amassing control of the lion's share of capital in Cuba, U.S. interests were able to leverage political support for whoever they preferred to lead the nation, which would be whoever's policies most favored U.S. interests. One such president was Gerardo Machado y Morales—dubbed a "tyrant" by Celia—who took office in 1925. In that same year, a substantial workers' union and the Communist Party of Cuba were both formed, marking progress of the marginalized classes toward coalescing a nationalist movement.

The United States later assisted in bringing to power Fulgencio Batista, who headed Cuba's military in 1934 and had an intimate relationship with the U.S. embassy, lending him influence in the selection of heads of state. Batista was himself elected president in 1940. World War II saw concentrated Cuban production of sugar to supply the United States during its war effort as well as increasing Americanization of Cuban society, such as with the openings of U.S.-style department stores. Batista left office in 1944, but when succeeding presidents proved unable to improve Cuba's faltering economic situation or achieve political dominance, he aimed for reelection in 1952. Realizing, however, that his civilian political support was limited while regard for a Washington-favored strong man would be adequate among influential figures, he instead staged a military coup before the 1952 election. Certain parties and groups objected, but Batista retained the power he seized and became dictator. As Celia writes to Gustavo in March 1952, "The U.S. wants him in the palace. How else could he have pulled this off?"

COMPARE
&
CONTRAST

- **1970s:** In 1976, while retaining his position as first secretary of the Communist Party of Cuba, Fidel Castro, at the age of fifty, shifts from being the nation's prime minister to being its president.

  1990s: With Cuba remaining a one-party socialist state, Castro, entering his seventies, retains the same offices that he has held since 1976.

  Today: First appointed president by his elder brother (who was afflicted with intestinal illness) in 2006, Raúl Castro is elected to the post by the National Assembly in 2008, and in 2011, he is elected first secretary of the Communist Party.

- **1970s:** As the decade opens, Cuba's economy is stagnant, with blame placed upon low productivity among sugarcane harvest laborers. In attempts to reinvigorate revolutionary ideals, society is increasingly militarized, with officers appointed to civilian posts and military involvement in various national and local organizations.

  1990s: Having grown dependent on trade with the Soviet Union, Cuba suffers more economic troubles upon the collapse of the Soviet Union in the early 1990s, which leads to shortages of many kinds of raw and processed materials. Small-scale farmers' markets are allowed, and Cuba increases its openness to foreign investment.

Today: With the Cuban economy still faltering under the salaries of the expansive state workforce, Raúl Castro announces that small-business opportunities will be greatly expanded, and Cubans will be allowed to buy and sell homes, not a legal option since 1959.

- **1970s:** In 1979, Cuba provides substantial support to the revolutionary Sandinistas in Nicaragua, who manage to oust the despotic Anastasio Somoza Debayle—who had lent support to the failed U.S. Bay of Pigs invasion of Cuba—and establish a revolutionary junta government with social aims similar to Cuba's. Cuba is emboldened to aid insurgents in Guatemala, El Salvador, and Colombia.

  1990s: Needing support after the demise of the Soviet Union, Cuba tries to establish better relations with other Latin American nations, such as Venezuela under Hugo Chavez. Castro proves unwilling to compromise revolutionary values by engaging in relations with the United States.

  Today: Cuba has engaged in full diplomatic relations with the European Union since 2008, and in 2009, President Barack Obama announces that the United States seeks to form a new relationship with Cuba. However, as of 2011, the U.S. trade embargo, in place since 1962, remains mostly intact, and travel between the two nations is still heavily restricted.

It was at this time that Fidel Castro began making a name for himself as a revolutionary, history that García provides in snippets in Celia's letters. Then a lawyer in his mid-twenties, Castro organized a cohort of young, mostly impoverished nationalists who trained secretly to stage attacks on army garrisons in 1953. The attack on the Moncada garrison failed, leading to the capture and murder of many of the rebels;

Castro was sentenced to fifteen years in prison. The rebels had public opinion in their favor, and after winning a sham election in 1954, Batista was obliged to grant amnesty to Castro and his comrades.

Seeking asylum in Mexico, they issued the radical Manifesto to the People of Cuba in August 1955, calling for revolution to bring about a broad platform of social reforms, including labor laws in the interest of workers, the nationalization of U.S. utility monopolies, housing-development programs, and the elimination of corruption. A total of eighty-two revolutionaries returned to Cuban soil on the *Granma* in 1956, to be ambushed by government forces but regroup in the Sierra Maestra. In time, their forces grew, they won significant battles against government forces, and other nationalist groups on the island, including the student-led Revolutionary Directorate, joined the rebels' effort. The rebels' deciding offensive was staged in 1958, when Fidel and Raúl Castro and the Argentine guerrilla Ernesto Che Guevara led separate divisions that besieged the major cities of Santiago de Cuba, Guantánamo, and Santa Clara. Batista fled on January 1, 1959, and the Cuban Revolution had triumphed.

The ensuing years indeed saw positive changes for the majority of the Cuban people. As the holdings of Batista and his allies were nationalized, military funding was funneled instead to public health and education, and high sugarcane production bolstered the economy. Individual farm holdings were limited in size, shifting land from investors into the hands of laborers, and large cattle ranches were nationalized. With so many U.S. interests having lost masses of capital through these developments, the Central Intelligence Agency began developing and supporting plans to subvert the new Cuban government. As acts of sabotage and subversion increased, Cuba nationalized the major media outlets and more large landholdings, such as those of the U.S.-based United Fruit Company, and relations with the Soviet Union were initiated.

By October 1960, all U.S. concerns, from banks to factories to railroads, had been nationalized, and the United States banned trade with Cuba. The post-revolution turmoil came to a head in April 1961, when a force of C.I.A.-trained invaders landed in Cochinos Bay—the Bay of Pigs—but were quashed within days by militias and the rebel army. Thus ended the spate of U.S.-supported counterrevolutionary efforts, and the opposition between the United States and Cuba was firmly established: just off the shores of capitalist America, Cuba was now officially communist.

The Second Declaration of Havana of 1962 summarizes the opinion of many Cubans regarding U.S. involvement in Cuban affairs in the twentieth century: "Our wealth passed into their hands; they falsified our history, our administration and

Celia's letters tell much of the story in this novel.
(ARENA Creative / Shutterstock.com)

molded our politics to the interests of the intruders. The nation was subjected to 60 years of political, economic, and cultural asphyxiation." García's *Dreaming in Cuban*, through its kaleidoscope of interrelated characters, elucidates various perspectives on what the Cuban Revolution and the rule of Fidel Castro—mythologized as El Líder—have meant for the Cuban people, whether at home on the island or exiled.

CRITICAL OVERVIEW

Upon its publication in 1992, *Dreaming in Cuban* elicited consistently upbeat, admiring reviews in national newspapers. In *Latino Fiction and the Modernist Imagination: Literature of the Borderlands* (1998), John S. Christie notes García's nuanced use of multidimensional characters in exploring politics and Lorca's poetry to communicate her characters' sentiments. Christie asserts that "García's narrative subtleties and complexities...stretch her novel beyond editorial comment into imaginative, polyphonic literary art."

Similarly, Phillipa Kafka, in *"Saddling La Gringa": Gatekeeping in Literature by Contemporary Latin Writers* (2000), notes the impressive scope of García's objective presentation of so many variations on life in Cuban society. Kafka writes, "Amazingly, she never invalidates or disputes the diverse and conflicting perspectives of these different dreamers. She succeeds by giving readers a complexity of experience beyond binaries," where different viewpoints "circle around one another endlessly." In his essay "Matriarchy and Mayhem: Awakenings in Cristina García's *Dreaming in Cuban*," Joseph M. Viera calls the novel "a dynamic entry" in the growing canon of modern Latino/a literature. He approvingly deems the work a "representative microcosm of the Cuban condition" that is especially significant "since it focuses on the lives of female characters" and "is revelatory to the role of women in Cuban culture."

Lyn Di Iorio Sandín reads a little deeper into the fabric of García's novel in *Killing Spanish: Literary Essays on Ambivalent U.S. Latino/a Identity* (2004). Sandín finds it interesting that Pilar so easily concludes that she belongs in New York after only a three-week stay in her ancestral homeland, despite her connection with Celia and the claimed effects of the island's magic on her. Sandín thus concludes that the novel "never moves toward a definition of identity that gets beyond the internalization of exocitized images of Cuba, of a Cuba seen through Pilar's Americanized eyes." That is, "Like Pilar, the narrative is nervous about staying too long with the origin, as if too much focus on Cuba will indeed provoke an unpredictable 'chemical' change," as Pilar claimed was happening before she confirmed her attachment to New York. García delves deeper into questions of Cuban and Latina identity in her ensuing novels.

CRITICISM

Michael Allen Holmes

Holmes is a writer and editor. In the following essay, he explores possible symbolic significance in the character of Lourdes in Dreaming in Cuban.

Several of the Spanish names in García's *Dreaming in Cuban* have evident symbolic relevance. Regarding the central autobiographical

> WHETHER OR NOT GARCÍA INTENDS EXTENSIVE COMMENTARY ON THE CHRISTIAN GOD, LOURDES PERHAPS MORE SIGNIFICANTLY EMBODIES THE SENSE THAT IN THE MODERN ERA, CAPITALISM— EFFECTIVELY, THE WORSHIP OF MONEY—HAS BECOME THE TRUEST AMERICAN RELIGION."

character, *pilar* means "pillar," while *puente* means "bridge." These terms signify the character's architectural roles of bridging the gap between her American family and her Cuban relatives and, in keeping her own diary and guarding Celia's letters, of supporting the edifice of her family's history. Felicia's name, connoting *felicidad*, or "happiness," is sadly ironic, considering the successive tragedies that consume her life. Although Felicia meant the best in naming her daughters after "light," *luz*, and "miracle," *milagro*, her daughters consider the words she speaks "meaningless" and feel like "prisoners in her alphabet world." It may be fitting, then, that Luz and Milagro, their names connoting the height of spiritual grace, are like "a double helix, tight and impervious," that Felicia "can't penetrate"; spiritual grace eludes Felicia until her decline toward death.

The name Lourdes, taken by Jorge from "the miracle-working shrine of France," translates from the French as "heavy," "clumsy," or "dull," and these senses might be applied to Lourdes's character. However, as the final *s* in that name goes unpronounced in French, the phonetic similarity to the word "Lord" may bear greater significance. Several passages suggest that García plays upon this reference, and because Lourdes embodies American ideals as opposed to Cuban ones, the sense is allegorically fitting. Lourdes's introduction is presented behind curiously grand language, as if the stage is being set for the entrance of a god:

> The continents strain to unloose themselves, to drift reckless and heavy in the seas. Explosions tear and scar the land, spitting out black oaks and coal mines, street lamps and scorpions. Men lose the power of speech. The clocks stop. Lourdes Puente awakens.

WHAT DO I READ NEXT?

- In her second novel, *The Aguero Sisters* (1997), García further explores the divide between Cuba and America by presenting two sisters, one on the island and one on the continent, who are haunted by the mystery of their mother's death and who eventually reunite.

- García's *Dreaming in Cuban* might be considered a sister work to *Fallen Angels Sing* (1991) by Cuban American author Omar Torres. This novel is a fictional autobiography by a young Cuban poet who relocates to New York as a boy and, in seeking to figure out his relation to his past, eventually returns to Cuba.

- With experiences similar to those of Omar Torres, Pablo Medina wrote a memoir, *Exiled Memories* (1990), when he relocated to America. He relates the contented first dozen years of his life, spent in Cuba on his grandparents' farm and in Havana up until the revolution.

- A devoted reader of Latino literature, García is particularly fond of the Mexican American author Sandra Cisneros, whose best-known work is *The House on Mango Street* (1984), featuring first-person vignettes narrated by a young Latina growing up in a Chicago ghetto.

- Julia Alvarez, raised in the Dominican Republic before relocating to the United States, is one of the most acclaimed and prolific modern Latina writers. Her breakthrough novel, *How the Garcia Girls Lost Their Accents* (1991), focuses on the lives of four sisters who must adapt to life in New York City after their family is forced to flee the Dominican Republic.

- Dreaming plays a pivotal role in the plot of the young-adult novel *Donald Duk* (1991), by the American author Frank Chin, about a twelve-year-old boy who dreams that he is his great-great-grandfather in 1869, working on the Central Pacific Railroad with other Chinese laborers.

- The character Felicia in *Dreaming in Cuban* bears echoes from a book García has cited as an early inspiration, Gustave Flaubert's *Madame Bovary* (1856), about a woman with a fleeting mind who skips from one disastrous romance to another on her way to an untimely end.

- García has spoken of returning again and again to the stories of the Russian author Anton Chekhov, whose original use of stream-of-consciousness narration deftly illuminates the human condition. The volume *Stories: Anton Chekhov* (1968), translated by Larissa Volokhonsky and Richard Pevear, includes thirty of his most admired works.

Like a god or goddess, Lourdes proves domineering, self-assured, insistent, and righteous. She wields her authority with aplomb at her Yankee Doodle bakery—which she has christened with an almost comically patriotic name—and seeks additional authority as an auxiliary police officer. Pilar's boyfriend Max aptly identifies her "imperious disposition." When Pilar asks if he would call her a "frustrated tyrant," he posits "bitch goddess" as more fitting, and her quasi-divine status is confirmed.

Given her role in the novel, Lourdes would seem to be representing not just any god or goddess but in particular the Christian God. The narration reveals that Celia is perceived as having "an instinctive distrust of the ecclesiastical," while Felicia "suspected her mother of being an atheist and only hoped she wouldn't burn in hell for eternity as Lourdes and the nuns said." This passage—which surely plays upon the near homonym of "Lord"—suggests that Lourdes is devoutly Catholic, which is further affirmed when she invokes God's name and crosses herself upon being told of her father's death. Celia, then, a suspected atheist and diehard supporter of the socialist aims of the Cuban Revolution—which left Cuba allied with the godless Communism of the Soviet Union—is set in stark opposition to the Catholic and ultimately pro-American Lourdes. Celia can be seen to foreordain this religious/political rift with her daughter in pronouncing upon Lourdes's birth, "I will not remember her name," a line repeated an exceptional three times in the course of the novel.

If Lourdes is viewed as a stand-in for the Christian God, some of the descriptions of her are rendered subversively powerful. Where the muscles in her right eye are so weak that "every so often the eye drifts to one side, giving her a vaguely cyclopean air," the reader may glean the sense of a Lord whose depth perception is lacking—one who perhaps never foresaw that his name would be invoked by believers in such murderous campaigns as the Crusades and the Spanish Inquisition. As befits a God who sends believers to heaven and nonbelievers to hell and whose followers live by the clear-cut rules of the Ten Commandments, Lourdes "has no patience . . . for people who live between black and white." For an omnipotent God who supposedly dictates all people's fates, but without evident equality, Lourdes "is arbitrary and inconsistent and always believes she's right."

Whether or not García intends extensive commentary on the Christian God, Lourdes perhaps more significantly embodies the sense that in the modern era, capitalism—effectively, the worship of money—has become the truest American religion. Lourdes embraces capitalism with a rabid entrepreneurial fervor, perhaps as influenced by her ambitious salesman father, who readily adopted the American business ethos of his superior. One can hardly argue that Jorge was attending to a lamentable absence in Cuban people's lives with his electric brooms, a farcical product that the reader may suitably imagine as a ridiculous, useless contraption.

In a broader sense, however laudable it may be that capitalism allows any and all individuals to reap the financial harvest of their own hard work, the inescapable downside is that, if certain individuals are entitled to amass wealth, other individuals must be left relatively poor. Lourdes literally embodies the excessive accumulation of wealth in gaining 118 pounds through the manic consumption of her doughy confections. She manages to lose this weight, as market fluctuations might allow, but when the time-honored American ritual of Thanksgiving comes around, her weight is poised to balloon once more.

At length, embracing what Pilar recognizes as a pathetic version of the American dream, replete with endless barbecues and mindless parade gawking, Lourdes comes to fantasize about "a chain of Yankee Doodle bakeries stretching across America . . . her apple pies and cupcakes on main streets and in suburban shopping malls everywhere." By the time Lourdes returns to Cuba with her daughter, she has become monomaniacal in her belief in the pursuit of material wealth, to the extent that she cannot understand how Cubans can be content with what they have:

> You could have Cadillacs with leather interiors! Air conditioning! Automatic windows! You wouldn't have to move your arms in the heat! . . . Look how they laugh, Pilar, like idiots! . . . They're brainwashed, that's what they are!

Contrary to Lourdes's assessment, however, the reader may conclude that these Cubans, living in a society by and large purged of capitalist competition, do not particularly care about constantly improving and upgrading their possessions and their lives. They are capable of simply being content with what they have. Lourdes, rather, is the one who has been brainwashed, by American commercialism. One need look no further than the dollar bill to find the ultimate conflation of capitalism and the Christian Lord: in humble green letters, "In God We Trust."

Source: Michael Allen Holmes, Critical Essay on *Dreaming in Cuban*, in *Novels for Students*, Gale, Cengage Learning, 2012.

Suzanne Leonard

In the following excerpt, Leonard examines the use of a polyvocal narrative structure in Dreaming in Cuban *to express the responsibility and remembrance value of dreaming to the characters.*

RESPONSIBILITY AND REMEMBRANCE IN *DREAMING IN CUBAN*

. . . A somewhat more self-conscious rendering of the complexities that accompany the project of trying to "dream" a cultural history can be found in Cristina Garcia's *Dreaming in Cuban*, a text which also grapples with the relationship between imagination, inhabitation, and historical

The Cuban revolution is a defining event in the lives of the family in Dreaming in Cuban. *(Anthony Correia / Shutterstock.com)*

reconstruction. In *Dreaming in Cuban*, Garcia uses a polyvocal narrative structure to represent the lives of three generations of a Cuban family, a number of whose members have immigrated to the United States. The narrative, which focuses mostly on the female family members, switches between narrators and narrative forms. Pilar Puente is one of the few characters in the novel afforded a first person voice, although Pilar's grandmother Celia also imparts part of her story in epistolary form; the fact that both grandmother and granddaughter personalize their narratives enhances the thematic and narrative connection between them. Because Pilar's relationship with Celia, as does Donald's [in *Donald Duk*] with his great-great-grandfather, relies concurrently on acts of inhabitation and imagination, I have chosen to focus on this relationship for my analysis.

While Pilar lives in America, Celia remains in Cuba, devoted still to the political promises of Cuban leader Fidel Castro. Yet, despite the geographical distances, political affiliations, and national alliances that separate grandmother and granddaughter, both retain a spiritual and affective connection to their homeland. Although Pilar and her immediate family fled from Cuba

when Pilar was two, Pilar claims to remember everything that has happened to her since the time she was a baby. Pilar's longing for her birthplace originates in part from the knowledges of Cuba that her grandmother imparts via dreams since the two maintain a close psychic connection despite their physical separation. Pilar says, "Abuela Celia and I write to each other sometimes, but mostly I hear her speaking to me at night just before I fall asleep. She tells me stories about her life and what the sea looked like that day." Abuela Celia presents herself in the form of a narrative, represented as she is in the stories she tells about her life. In bringing descriptions of the sea to her granddaughter, Celia also suggests that the project of cultural and historical reconstruction relies in part on the existence of visual representations, as was also the case in *Donald Duk*. If Pilar can imagine the sea as her grandmother sees it, she can also bear witness to the Cuba that her grandmother knows.

Celia envisions her relationship with her granddaughter in similarly imagistic terms, which literalizes the cultural and psychic connection accomplished by dream work. Celia "closes her eyes and speaks to her granddaughter, imagines her words as slivers of light piercing the

> JUST AS HER GRANDMOTHER SPOKE TO
> PILAR FROM HER DREAMS, THANKS TO THE PROCESS
> OF 'DREAMING IN SPANISH,' CUBA AND HER
> GRANDMOTHER CONTINUE TO SPEAK THROUGH
> PILAR, HENCE THE NOVEL'S TITLE *DREAMING IN
> CUBAN.*

murky night," a statement which suggests that acts of imagination might indeed defy geographical boundaries and physical separations. This sequence also suggests the feasibility of achieving spiritual communion if one overcomes the limitations imposed by individual subject positions. Much like Donald's feeling that he is both himself and "the first Lee of the family in America" in his dream, Pilar and Celia use their dreams in order to achieve a spiritual communion that verges on inhabitation. Pilar writes, "I know what my grandmother dreams," and describes dreams that depict massacres in distant countries and pregnant women dismembered in the squares. These images witness horrible violations that Celia repeatedly calls on Pilar to remember, which suggests that the women are bound to one another in part by a mutual commitment to record and rectify cultural injustices.

Also like *Donald Duk*, *Dreaming in Cuban*'s narrative often privileges visual cues in order to remind its characters of their intergenerational affiliations. Pilar describes one dream, for example, in which she is put on a chair and brought to the sea, which recollects both her own departure from Cuba and also the many hours Celia spends staring across this vast expanse. Pilar continues, "They're chanting a language I don't understand. I don't feel scared, though. I can see the stars and the sky and the moon and the black sky revolving overhead. I can see my grandmother's face." The fact that Celia's image appears in Pilar's dream suggests that the women more often communicate through a semiotics of images (or what Luce Irigaray has called a "pictographic order") rather than a verbal or linguistic system of signification. Although Pilar cannot decode the chanted language she hears, Pilar does recognize her grandmother's

face. As Irene Brameshuber-Ziegler writes, the images "witness the insufficiency of regular language" (54), which suggests again that in the dream space the potential for pictographic communication is privileged over oral or spoken forms.

Repeatedly, in fact, images exist as the most resonant components of the dream-work one finds in *Dreaming in Cuban*. As Pilar reveals, "I have this image of Abuela Celia underwater, standing on a reef with tiny chrome fish darting by her face like flashes of light. Her hair is waving in the tide and her eyes are wide open. She calls to me but I can't hear her. Is she talking to me from her dreams?" Dreams seem to function here non-linguistically since Celia's "talking" to Pilar occurs through a moment of shared imagery, rather than as an act of explicit telling. Although Celia's words are obscured, the picture of her face is vivid. Moreover, Celia is calling from her dreams, which suggests that her communication is generated by, or from, the realm of the unconscious.

Such moments of shared imagery might even be said to encourage the erasure of difference between Celia and Pilar. This inhabitation differs from the type described by Chin because although Donald inhabits the body of his great-great-grandfather and participates in his experiences, Chin gives no indication that the men share thoughts or intimacies. Instead, Pilar comments of her grandmother, "She seems to know everything that's happened to me and tells me not to mind my mother too much. Abuela Celia says she wants to see me again. She tells me she loves me." Similarly, Celia remembers that even as an infant, her granddaughter "seemed to understand her very thoughts." The jouissance experienced by the women in fact seems commensurate with Luce Irigaray's notion of feminine syntax, a concept that is informed by female sexuality and is used by Irigaray to describe the privileging of feminine multiplicity and plurality over phallocentric oneness. Describing the syntax in *The Sex Which is Not One*, Irigaray writes, "there would no longer be either subject or object, 'oneness' would no longer be privileged.... Instead that 'syntax' would involve nearness, proximity, but in such an extreme form that it would preclude any distinction of identities, any establishment of ownership, thus any form of appropriation" (134). Fundamental to Irigaray's conception is the idea that in this feminine system, there are no clear boundaries between self and other or sub-ject and object, so that female experience is by nature dialectical. Calling for a subject not as an "I," but as an "I-she," Irigaray perceives that subject and object are intertwined and interre-lated positions. Such an interrelation might serve to clarify Pilar's position with respect to her cultural inheritances, in that Pilar is called to be both the "I" of her story and also the "she" of her grandmother's, and yet must hold the two positions in simultaneous constellation.

Indeed, it is the negotiation between the "I" and the "she" that makes Pilar's position with respect to her cultural identity so fraught, for Pilar realizes that she is called by her grand-mother to remember her grandmother's history rather than her own. When grandmother and granddaughter reunite at the end of the novel, Pilar writes: "As I listen, I feel my grandmother's life passing to me through her hands. It's a steady electricity, humming and true." The book's last page attests to a similar inheritance since Celia, on the day of her granddaughter's birth, ends a longtime letter-writing project that was meant to record Celia's life. Celia writes: "My granddaugh-ter, Pilar Puente del Pino was born today [. . .] I will no longer write to you, mi amor. She will remember everything."

The difficulty of being the "she" of her grand-mother's story, however, is that Pilar might need to be suspicious of the opinions she is being asked to perpetuate, given that Celia has spent the last thirty years of her life devoted to Fidel Castro. As the various characters profiled in *Dreaming in Cuban* articulate, many overlapping and contra-dictory strains of feeling toward Castro exist in Cuba. As a mediator who has spent her life living between the Cuban system and the American one, Pilar is cognizant of both the drawbacks and the potentialities of a mode of governance based, at least in theory, on the equal distribution of wealth. In America, for example, Pilar scorns her mother Lourdes' unabashed celebration of capitalist practices (Lourdes runs and owns the "Yankee Doodle Bakery" in Brooklyn) and Pilar attempts to mock Western democratic ideals by creating an irreverent painting of the Statue of Liberty. Yet Pilar also seems mindful of the enormous undertaking of negotiating between her story and her grandmother's, for to become the "she" of someone else's past, she understands, could necessitate an acceptance of political positions with which she simply cannot agree. In fact, despite Pilar's earlier longing for

Cuba, the end of the novel witnesses Pilar lying to Celia so that Ivanito, another of Celia's grand-children, might escape to the United States. In witnessing the violence of Cuba firsthand, Pilar realizes that there will be times when she must reject her grandmother's wishes and her commit-ments. Thus, Pilar resists what might have turned into an uncritical form of long-distance national-ism and affirms her responsibility to her extended family members. Her decision is complicated and perhaps even dangerous, however, for the cost of honoring her own impulses is that Pilar must defy her grandmother and also break the law. More-over, she is offered no guarantees of Ivanito's safety.

Although Pilar ultimately chooses to help Ivanito flee, she realizes that she is forever at a disadvantage in the sense that, as someone who has grown up in America, she will never fully understand Cuba's vexed political situation, nor will she be able to account for her position with respect to it. In part, she attributes her longing for Cuba to the fact that she has been denied the chance to develop a nuanced understanding of Cuba's history and implies that such losses con-stitute a structured absence in her life. While still in America, Pilar writes:

> Most days Cuba is kind of dead to me. But every once in a while a wave of longing will hit me and it's all I can do not to hijack a plane to Havana or something, I resent the hell out of the politicians and generals who force events on us that structure our lives, and dictate the memories we'll have when we're old. Every day Cuba fades a little more inside me, my grand-mother fades a little more inside me. And there's only my imagination where our history should be.

As this passage indicates, generals and poli-ticians are responsible for creating situations that change people's lives, and thus the cultural mem-ory of Cubans and Cuban Americans is struc-tured by events over which the people themselves have little control. Further, because accounts of war and battle take precedence, everyday stories, and especially tales of the marginalized or disen-franchised, barely register in the collective histor-ical consciousness. Pilar writes, "If it were up to me, I would record other things. Like the time there was a freak hailstorm in the Congo and women took it as a sign that they should rule. Or the life story of the prostitutes in Bombay. Why don't I know anything about them? Who choo-ses what we should know or what's important?"

Pilar's resentment of these hegemonic structures of remembrance and recognition resonates with Donald's frustration towards "official" accounts of Chinese American history since both characters realize that official versions of historical events supplant those that might be provided by the people themselves. Yet only Donald has the luxury of "fixing" these official truths, at least in the context of his classroom, because official representations are in such flagrant violation of what nineteenth-century Chinese American laborers actually accomplished. Pilar, however, is afforded no such opportunity for such corrective intervention, nor is she provided verification that there is one version of Cuban history to which she should or could remain faithful.

While Donald is granted external verifications that the version of history he has come to know in his dreams is indeed credible, Pilar gleans no such assurances of the legitimacy of her visions, or anyone else's for that matter. In fact, she realizes that the structures of remembrance to which she has access tend not to produce triumphant revisions, but rather lead to disappointing cultural erosions. As she laments the historical obfuscations that have and will take place, Pilar regrets that "every day Cuba fades a little more inside me," and, as a result, "there's only my imagination where our history should be." Pilar thus seems sadly conscious of the limitations of calling upon one's own consciousness, even one as fertile as hers and so intimately connected to her grandmother's subjectivity, in order to attempt the project of cultural reconstruction. Kathleen Brogan reads this passage similarly, suggesting that its ghostly imagery "points to the replacement of a vital cultural embeddedness with a merely invented ethnicity, an identity based less on collective memory than on an individual's fabrications" (95). Pilar's Aunt Felicia also voices dismay at the prospect of using a fallible imagination to record history when she says: "Imagination, like memory, can transform lies to truths." Unwilling to celebrate the purely "creative" aspects of the act of historical reconstruction, both Pilar and Felicia recognize that when removed from the cultural embeddedness that Brogan describes, imagination ceases to be a viable means through which to access cultural histories.

Despite Pilar's recognition of the pitfalls which attend the project of historical reconstruction, she remains unwilling to leave the imagining/imaging up to someone else. At the end of the novel, while in Cuba, she reveals, "I have begun dreaming in Spanish, which has never happened before. I wake up feeling different, like something inside me is changing, something chemical and irreversible. There's a magic here working its way through my veins." Spanish is a more intimate language for Pilar than is English, for she and her boyfriend used to speak Spanish when they made love. Her healthy skepticism about the project of learning through imagination notwithstanding, then, her rediscovery of the Spanish language enables her to create a vital link with her past. Just as her grandmother spoke to Pilar from her dreams, thanks to the process of "dreaming in Spanish," Cuba and her grandmother continue to speak through Pilar, hence the novel's title *Dreaming in Cuban*.

Pilar ultimately refuses to reauthorize her grandmother's sentiments toward Cuba or re-author herself in her grandmother's image; she decides to leave Cuba because, as she says, "sooner or later I have to return to New York. I know now it's where I belong—not instead of here, but more than here." In Cuba, Pilar learns perhaps not how to be her grandmother, but rather how to dream her, which is to say that Pilar learns to use dreams to negotiate successfully between the "I" and the "she" of her family history. In dreaming her grandmother, and also being dreamed by her, Pilar acknowledges that her grandmother and her grandmother's history will continue to constitute a persuasive, but also limited, presence in her life....

Source: Suzanne Leonard, "Dreaming as Cultural Work in *Donald Duk* and *Dreaming in Cuban*," in *MELUS*, Vol. 29, No. 2, Summer 2004, pp. 181–204.

Rocio G. Davis

In the following excerpt, Davis reflects on the use of the mother-daughter relationship theme in Dreaming in Cuban, *evaluating its use as a common theme in ethnic literature.*

The complex discourse of the mother-daughter relationship, as well as the imaginative inscription of the lost homeland, occupies a prominent place in the thematics of immigrant literature in the United States. Ethnic writing in general often reflects gender conflicts transmitted through culturally constructed but frequently misinterpreted roles, specifically those of mothers. Emblematic novels such as Maxine Hong Kingston's *Woman*

> THE POSITIVE EMPHASIS ON THE FATHER-
> DAUGHTER AND MOTHER-SON RELATIONSHIP,
> AS OPPOSED TO THE PROBLEMATIC MOTHER-
> DAUGHTER ONE, MAY ALSO HAVE ITS ROOTS IN
> SPANISH/CUBAN CULTURE."

Warrior and Toni Morrison's *Beloved* revolve around ambivalent relationships with the mother or mother figure, as well as other female members of the family. These texts are frequently narrated by protagonists who must necessarily deal with the implications of specific maternal discourse (or the lack thereof) in the process of self-identification and affirmation. The place of the mother—personally, socially, culturally—directs, modifies, and influences the daughters' responses to both individual and cultural demands. Ethnic texts such as these highlight questions of identification with and differentiation from the mother, emphasizing a need for understanding and bonding between mothers and daughters as a fundamental step toward self-awareness and mastery of the culture. Often the texts imply the need for the daughter to take on and continue maternal stories, transforming them literally and metaphorically with their own lives and experiences.

Cultural inscriptions by ethnic women offer an interesting analysis of the hermeneutics of female representation and access to the world, yet cannot be divorced from forms of orientation toward the mother or foremother. The pattern of the maternal figure as origin and daughter as perpetuation, extension, or completion repeatedly appears as a necessary starting point to the drama of the tenuous negotiation of identity and difference within the ambivalent universe of filiality. As Nancy Chodorow has pointed out, "In any given society, feminine personality comes to define itself in relation and connection to other people more than masculine personality does" (44). Emphasis on relationships leads to a reevaluation of personal and communal tragedies that oblige the daughters to look back to the mothers, whose image and personality are often inseparable from community history and values. These texts often involve a return to the maternal,

which leads to the appreciation of community history and forging of communal bonds with, first, the immediate family and then the larger gender and cultural group.

The novel here analyzed, Cristina Garcia's *Dreaming in Cuban*, centers on the complicated negotiations of mother-daughter bonds. Garcia tells the stories of three generations of Cuban women and their experiences with revolution and immigration through a blending of first- and third- person narrations, with epistolary sections that convey the rich texture of intersecting positionalities and overlapping worlds. At the center of the novel is Pilar Puente, born in Cuba and raised in Brooklyn, who must deal with her antipathetic relationship with her mother, Lourdes, and her longing for her grandmother, Celia. Similarly, Lourdes and Felicia, Celia's two daughters, struggle to unravel their complex ties with their mother as well as those with their own daughters. The novel thus presents a composite portrait of diverse mother-daughter relationships, offering a multiperspective vision of the possibilities for division and unity, adaptation and adjustment, separation and bonding.

The mother-daughter dance of approach and withdrawal is mirrored in the separate and interrelated sections on each of the characters, the shifts in temporality, geography, and narrative voice illustrating the tangled web of affinity between and among the characters and their homelands.

In the tradition of breaking silence that has become one of the shaping myths in ethnic writing by women, maternal storytelling becomes a medium of self-inscription and subjectivity, as well as an instrument of intersubjectivity and dialogue. The separate accounts of all the characters, mothers and daughters, are converted into chronicles of individual empowerment and self-affirmation. Garcia opts for a narrative stance that includes multiple voices, offering individual versions of events and engaging in complex dialogues. There is, further, a sense of collectivity in the text, according to which the diverse voices that speak discern self-referential hints at definition through the juxtaposition of the other voices in the narrative. The concept of the isolated self is continually questioned, as the individual accounts are repeatedly mirrored, contrasting or complementing preceding or succeeding stories. Thus, the individual voices that meditate on the mothers' and daughters' multilayered selves are inseparable from the other voices in the text, coalescing to represent the family to which these women belong. The process of unearth-ing maternal and communal stories becomes an essential part of the process of self-identification, linked to the discovery of the mother and the mother's history, cultural possibilities, and choices. Cultural identification, and the recovery of a bond with the heritage culture, arises from the irrevocable connection between self and community, as issues of origins and beginnings occupy center stage in the drama of self-affirmation. According to Lorna Irvine, the process of discovery—the "psychological journey"—of the daughter's own identity demands a revision of the relationship with the mother, and this often involves three stages: negation, recognition, and reconciliation (248). The need to go "back to the future" implies the urgency of appropriating the intricate truths about one's self and history as part of the process of self-affirmation. The immigrant characters in Garcia's novel—Lourdes and Pilar—need to return to Cuba in order to come to terms with the tangled meanings of mothering, language, and home, and renew their lives in the United States.

Ethnic and cultural factors, such as the serious difficulty of mutual decoding of social signs, are central to the linguistic misunderstanding between mothers and daughters. Language plays a central role in this process, as the exercise of female self-definition develops within the nuances of meaning, of understandings and misunderstandings, of significance misconstrued or unaccepted. In the isolation enforced by these misunderstandings, the characters explore a widening sphere of forms of communication: from telepathy to painting. The process of self-identification, therefore, involves issues of pain and resistance: remembering, understanding, and articulating significance within the female matrix. The most important lesson the daughters in the novel learn, as articulated by Chodorow, is that "differentiation is not distinctness and separateness, but a particular way of being connected to others" (11). They learn the distinction between division and differentiation, understanding that while division prevails, there can never be completion. As Chodorow explains, "In the process of differentiation, leading to a genuine autonomy, people maintain contact with those with whom they had their earliest relationships: indeed this contact is part of who we are" (10–11). Separation and death may be overcome by reconstructing both the cultural past and the image of the mother, achieving a reconciliation

with the maternal through and within language and by re-creating the idea of home. The final section suggests the protagonist's appropriation of the foremothers' voices and stories, to bring the cycle of generation and regeneration to completion.

Dreaming in Cuban explores the various dimensions of the drama of a family divided by Castro's takeover of Cuba in 1959. As William Luis points out, Garcia's novel weaves intricate layers of Cuban history, politics, literature, and culture, both on the island and in the United States, echoing the work of such Cuban literary masters as Cirilo Villaverde and Reinaldo Arenas, who also abandoned the island and lived in exile (203). Political events and loyalties lead Rufino, Lourdes, and Pilar Puente to immigrate to the United States in 1961, leaving behind Lourdes's parents, Celia and Jorge del Pino, as well as her sister Felicia and the latter's family. Jorge will eventually leave Cuba for medical treatment in the United States, and will die there. Events in recent Cuban history become the central subtext for the novel: Pilar was born ten days after the victory that forced Batista to flee the island and three days after Castro's triumphant march into Havana; the novel ends with Felicia's son Ivanito's escape to freedom.

The present time of the narrative develops between 1972 and 1980 and refers to specific events in the Revolution. Luis has analyzed extensively the specific events of recent Cuban history that Garcia incorporates into the subtext of her narrative: the failed ten-million-ton sugar harvest of 1970, the detention of the poet Heberto Padilla, and the seizing of the Peruvian embassy in April 1980, which was followed by the Mariel boatlift that enabled more than 125,000 Cubans to escape to Miami (206–8).

The blending of historical detail is central to Pilar's search for self, as she comes to terms with her position regarding the Cuban Revolution, the central point of contention with her mother. At the beginning of the novel, she rejects her mother's patriotic American values—"She bought a second bakery and plans to sell tricolor cupcakes and Uncle Sam marzipan. Apple pies, too. She's convinced she can fight Communism from behind her bakery counter"—sympathizing with the Cuban cause embodied in the figure of her grandmother. At the end, after witnessing life in Cuba for herself, and incorporating her grandmother's, aunt's, cousins', and mother's stories, she appears to become independent of her previous ideas. She lies to her grandmother about Ivanito's departure, implicitly assenting to his defection.

Pilar's process is highlighted by Garcia's complex ordering of the narrative. The author frequently juxtaposes present and past tense, blurring and confounding the two time frames: rather than presenting a chronological account, she invites the reader to reconstruct the sequence of events—from the first story, set in 1972, to the last piece, a letter written in 1959. Furthermore, as Jorge Duany explains, the geographic transition from Cuba to the United States is often imperceptible, because that is the way the characters experience the transition: "There is no radical discontinuity in time and space between the two sides of the del Pino family, one in Cuba, the other in the United States. The family is spiritually united by common memories and fantasies, by their image of Cuba" (177).

Section and story titles like "Imagining Winter" and "Going South" are paradigmatic of the journeys many of the characters have to take, away from and back to their original home, emphasizing the search for connection which will be completed in the final section, "The Languages Lost." The last line of the novel, from Celia's final letter to her Spanish lover, presents the charge given to Pilar, which she metafictionally completes through the novel. On 11 January 1959 she writes: "Dear Gustavo, The revolution is eleven days old. My granddaughter, Pilar Puente del Pino, was born today. It is also my birthday. I am fifty years old. I will no longer write to you, mi amor. She will remember everything." Pilar's trip to Cuba, when she inherits the letters her grandmother never sent to Gustavo, makes her understand that she belongs to a family as well as to Cuban history and culture. This discovery enables her to decipher the master codes of her increasingly complex subjectivity, allowing her to signify on her own, yet within the network of women of which she forms an inextricable part. Even Pilar's surname, "Puente," highlights her role as a bridge between the place and the people of the past and the future.

Thus, the recounting in Pilar's voice acquires a forceful emotional tone that rings clearly through the entire novel, transforming the story into a female bildungsroman. Furthermore, when questioned in an interview about the nature of the novel, Garcia admits that "emotionally, it's very autobiographical. The details are not. . . . Pilar is a kind of alter ego for me" (Lopez, 610). Cristina Garcia and Pilar Puente share biographical similarities, and the text may be read as both a valedictory and a catharsis for a young woman dealing with the events and characters in her past.

Crucial to the evolving relationship with the past is the figure of the mother, an image expanded in the novel to include both mother language and motherland. In the same movement, Lourdes abandons her mother and motherland, physically and emotionally, rejecting the communism that both espouse. Celia's relationship with her elder daughter is sour from the start, as she suffers from the loss of her Spanish lover and the abuse by Jorge's mother and sister. The awareness of her mother's rejection of her clouds Lourdes's infancy.

> She imagined herself alone and shriveled in her mother's womb, envisioned the first days in her mother's unyielding arms. Her mother's fingers were stiff and splayed as spoons, her milk a tasteless gray. Her mother stared at her with eyes collapsed of expectation. If it's true that babies learn love from their mothers' voices, then this is what Lourdes heard: 'I will not remember her name.'

Celia's other daughter, Felicia, also abandons her through her consistent indifference to the revolutionary cause, and her eventual sinking into madness: "After all, as her mother points out, the only thing Felicia ever did for the revolution was pull a few dandelions during the weed-eradication campaign in 1962, and then only reluctantly. Her lack of commitment is a source of great rancour between them."

The generational divisions extend to Lourdes and her daughter Pilar, who nonetheless has a powerful sense of connection with Abuela Celia, and also to Felicia and her revolutionary twin daughters, Luz and Milagro. Interestingly, familial and generational patterns develop to which all the characters adhere. The generational opposition between Celia and her two daughters, Lourdes and Felicia, is repeated in the next generation between Lourdes and Felicia and their own daughters, Pilar, Luz, and Milagro (Luis, 211). Still, similarities and connections are perceived between mothers and daughters, even those separated by an ocean. For instance, both Celia and Lourdes serve law and order, the mother as a civilian judge of her neighborhood defense committee and the daughter as an "auxiliary policewoman, the first in her precinct." Pilar also acknowledges seeing her mother in herself: "If I don't like someone, I show it. It's the one thing I have in common with my mother."

The difficulties between Lourdes and Pilar are a metaphor for all the other mother-daughter dyads. Both perceive clearly the gap between them. Pilar notes that "Mom's views are strictly black-and-white. That's how she survives," and Lourdes admits that she "has no patience for dreamers, for people who live between black and white," such as her own mother and daughter. Celia muses: "If I was born to live on an island, then I'm grateful for one thing: that the tides rearrange the borders. At least I have the illusion of change, of possibility," an attitude she shares with her granddaughter. On the one hand, Lourdes is consistently maddened by Pilar's immunity to threats, her "indifference," while the daughter suffers from her mother's unpredictability. When Lourdes asks Pilar to paint a mural for her new bakery, and agrees not to see it before the official unveiling, the daughter cannot fathom her mother's intentions. Lourdes looks at Pilar with an expression "as if to say, 'See, you always underestimate me.' But that's not true. If anything, I overestimate her. It comes from experience. Mom is arbitrary and inconsistent and always believes she's right. It's a pretty irritating combination."

Interestingly, both turn to the past—the dead father and the far-off grandmother—for advice. Jorge del Pino reassures Lourdes: "Pilar doesn't hate you, hija. She just hasn't learned to love you yet." Similarly, Pilar takes reassurance from Celia: "I might be afraid of her if it weren't for those talks I have with Abuela Celia late at night. She tells me that my mother is sad inside and that her anger is more frustration at what she can't change. I guess I'm one of those things she can't change." Yet when Pilar's blasphemous punk version of the Statue of Liberty is finally unveiled, the patriotic Lourdes rushes to her daughter's defense and protects the mural from a man who threatens to rip it with a knife: "Then, as if in slow motion, she tumbles forward, a thrashing avalanche of patriotism and motherhood, crushing three spectators and a table of apple tartlets. And I, I love my mother very much at that moment."

As opposed to other mother-daughter narratives, this text highlights the daughters' connections with their fathers, and that of the mothers with their sons. Lourdes and Jorge del Pino, Pilar and Rufino Puente, even Luz, Milagro, and Hugo Villaverde share a relationship that all the mothers envy. Celia perceives the affection between her husband and daughter, a world closed to her: "That girl is a stranger to me. When I approach her, she turns numb, as if she wanted to be dead in my presence. I see how different Lourdes is with her father, so alive and gay, and it hurts me, but I don't know what to do. She still punishes me for the early years." Moreover, "Lourdes is herself only with her father. Even after his death, they understand each other perfectly, as they always have." The disconnection between mothers and daughters finds a foil in the bond between mothers and sons. Javier del Pino returns to Cuba and his mother when his wife abandons him, taking their daughter. Felicia and Ivanito live happily for a while in a dreamworld of poetry and coconut ice cream. Lourdes fantasizes about the son she miscarried: "He wouldn't have talked back to her or taken drugs or drunk beer from paper bags like other teenagers. Her son would have helped her in the bakery without complaint. He would have come to her for guidance, pressed her hand to his cheek, told her he loved her. Lourdes would have talked to her son the way Rufino talks to Pilar, for companionship." She thus, at the end of the novel, adopts the motherless Ivanito and helps him escape from Cuba.

The positive emphasis on the father-daughter and mother-son relationship, as opposed to the problematic mother-daughter one, may also have its roots in Spanish/Cuban culture. Sons tend to be revered over daughters in these families, and Garcia blends this customary dynamic into her text, to complicate the central issue further. Sons traditionally enjoy preferential treatment in these families, though fathers are also inclined to pamper their daughters. The latter are, nevertheless, viewed by the mothers as extensions of themselves and are therefore treated more harshly, for they had to learn to be prepared for life. On the contrary, mothers openly indulge their sons, the future of the family and the country. This reality offers another layer of meaning to the text as a sociocultural construct: Garcia appears to suggest that the dynamic of conventional family relationships becomes another obstacle to the desired mother-daughter attachment.

Knowledge of a shared communication between Pilar and her grandmother serves to help reconstruct the matrilineal bond, forging the link with the mother country and its language as well. Between these two exists the attachment that both lack with Lourdes: "I wonder how Mom could be Abuela Celia's daughter. And what I'm doing as my mother's daughter. Something got horribly scrambled along the way." Celia provides Pilar with the connection to the maternal line, mother tongue, and homeland her mother had severed, as well as a sense of security and self-worth.

> I feel much more connected to Abuela Celia than to Mom, even though I haven't seen my grandmother in seventeen years. We don't speak at night anymore, but she's left me her legacy nonetheless—a love for the sea and the smoothness of pearls, an appreciation of music and words, sympathy for the underdog, and a disregard for boundaries. Even in silence, she gives me the confidence to do what I believe is right, to trust my own perceptions.

This link has loaded implications for the nature of narrating memory and the constructing of a multivoiced text. Because of their affiliation, Pilar can construct the text, the metafictional implication being the continuation of the cycle of women's stories within a culture-specific ambience: "Women who outlive their daughters are orphans, Abuela tells me. Only their granddaughters can save them, guard their knowledge like the first fire." The diary Pilar keeps becomes a repository of stories which will help her piece together her life, becoming the text the reader receives, as Isabel Alvarez-Borland suggests (46). She will thus appropriate the voices of the women who are part of the del Pino family saga— her grandmother, mother, aunt, cousins, and even her aunt's friend, Herminia Delgado—arriving at a deeper understanding of each one's motivations and actions. The metafictional detail suggests the continuance of the female line, and the narrative becomes the vehicle through which the wounds are healed and the pain of exile overcome....

Source: Rocio G. Davis, "Back to the Future: Mothers, Language, and Homes in Cristina Garcia's *Dreaming in Cuban*," in *World Literature Today*, Vol. 74, No. 1, Winter 2000, p. 60.

SOURCES

Alvarez-Borland, Isabel, "Displacements and Autobiography in Cuban-American Fiction," in *World Literature Today*, Vol. 68, No. 1, Winter 1994, pp. 43–48.

Archibold, Randal C., "In a Changing Cuba, Many Remain Skeptical," in *New York Times*, April 18, 2011, http://www.nytimes.com/2011/04/19/world/americas/19 cuba.html (accessed April 21, 2011).

Brown, Scott Shibuya, "A Conversation with Cristina García," in *Dreaming in Cuban*, Ballantine Books, 1993, pp. 249–56.

Christie, John S., *Latino Fiction and the Modernist Imagination: Literature of the Borderlands*, Garland, 1998, pp. 13–16, 44–54, 95–97.

Dalleo, Raphael, and Elena Machado Sáez, *The Latino/a Canon and the Emergence of Post-Sixties Literature*, Palgrave Macmillan, 2007, pp. 107–32.

Davis, Rocio G., "Back to the Future: Mothers, Languages, and Homes in Cristina García's *Dreaming in Cuban*," in *World Literature Today*, Vol. 74, No. 1, Winter 2000, pp. 60–68.

García, Cristina, *Dreaming in Cuban*, Ballantine Books, 2003.

Guerra Vilaboy, Sergio, and Oscar Loyola Vega, *Cuba: A History*, Ocean Press, 2010, pp. 30–78.

Kafka, Phillipa, *"Saddling La Gringa": Gatekeeping in Literature by Contemporary Latina Writers*, Greenwood Press, 2000, pp. 57–93.

Karim, Persis M., "Cristina García," in *Dictionary of Literary Biography*, Vol. 292, *Twenty-First-Century American Novelists*, edited by Lisa Abney, Thomson Gale, 2004, pp. 114–18.

Kellerhals, Merle David, Jr., "Obama Says U.S., Cuba Taking Critical Steps Toward a New Day," in *America.gov Archive*, April 21, 2009, http://www.america.gov/st/peacesec-english/2009/April/20090421102201dmslahrellek0.4116632.html?CP.rss = true (accessed April 21, 2011).

Kevane, Bridge, and Juanita Heredia, "At Home on the Page: An Interview with Cristina García," in *Latina Self-Portraits: Interviews with Contemporary Women Writers*, University of New Mexico Press, 2000, pp. 69–82.

Leonard, Suzanne, "Dreaming as Cultural Work in *Donald Duk* and *Dreaming in Cuban*," in *MELUS*, Vol. 29, No. 2, Summer 2004, pp. 181–204.

McCracken, Ellen, *New Latina Narrative: The Feminine Space of Postmodern Ethnicity*, University of Arizona Press, 1999, pp. 22–26, 109–17.

Payant, Katherine B., "From Alienation to Reconciliation in the Novels of Cristina García," in *MELUS*, Vol. 26, No. 3, Fall 2001, pp. 163–83.

Pérez Firmat, Gustavo, *Tongue Ties: Logo-Eroticism in Anglo-Hispanic Literature*, Palgrave Macmillan, 2003, pp. 139–41.

Sandín, Lyn Di Iorio, *Killing Spanish: Literary Essays on Ambivalent U.S. Latino/a Identity*, Palgrave Macmillan, 2004, pp. 5–19.

Suchlicki, Jaime, *Cuba: From Columbus to Castro and Beyond*, 5th ed., Brassey's, 2002, pp. 152–213.

Vasquez, Mary S., "Cuba as Text and Context in Cristina García's *Dreaming in Cuban*," in *Bilingual Review*, Vol. 20, No. 1, January/April 1995, pp. 22–27.

Viera, Joseph M., "Matriarchy and Mayhem: Awakenings in Cristina García's *Dreaming in Cuban*," in *Americas Review*, Vol. 24, Nos. 3–4, Fall/Winter 1996, pp. 231–42.

FURTHER READING

Carpentier, Alejo, *The Kingdom of This World*, translated by Harriet de Onís, Farrar, Straus and Giroux, 1949.

> Carpentier considered his use of *lo real maravilloso*—the marvelous real, precursor to magical realism—to be aesthetically superior to surrealism owing to its ability, like that of the Haitian Voudoun practitioners who inspired him, to release the reader's unconscious. This novel is his landmark tale of the Haitian Revolution.

García Lorca, Federico, *Gypsy Ballads*, translated by Robert Havard, Aris & Phillips, 1990.

> García Lorca, the Spanish poet in whom Celia finds so much inspiration, spent time with the Romany, or Gypsy, community of Spain and was inspired to write these poetic ballads that elevate the sense of their lives to mythic status. The collection was originally published in 1928 and is considered one of his most impressive volumes.

Guevara, Ernesto Che, *Che Guevara Reader: Writings on Politics and Revolution*, edited by David Deutschmann, Ocean Press, 2003.

> After meeting the Castro brothers in Mexico, the Argentine radical wanderer Che Guevara plunged himself into and made pivotal contributions to the Cuban Revolution. This volume offers a comprehensive selection of his letters, essays, and other writings on Marxist ideology and the need for revolution.

Núñez, Luis Manuel, *Santeria: A Practical Guide to Afro-Caribbean Magic*, Spring Publications, 1992.

> Although he was raised in Cuba until age ten, Núñez became Americanized and distanced from his parents' beliefs. Later, marriage to a Cuban woman brought him to embrace Santeria, which he recognizes as contrary to Western conceptions of religion and the workings of the mind. This book offers an intimate introduction to the religion.

SUGGESTED SEARCH TERMS

Cristina García AND Dreaming in Cuban

Cristina García AND Latina literature

Cuban Revolution AND literature

Cuban Revolution AND Fidel Castro

Cuba AND exiles AND Miami

Cuba AND Communism AND Soviet Union

Cuba AND United States AND embargo

Cristina García AND Miami AND journalist OR journalism

Cristina García AND interview

The Fifth Child

DORIS LESSING

1988

The Fifth Child, published in 1988, is a short novel by Doris Lessing, one of the most noted twentieth-century British authors. Set in England from the 1960s to the 1980s, *The Fifth Child* tells the story of a middle-class couple, David and Harriet Lovatt, who create an idyllic family life with their four children in a large Victorian house not far from London. Relatives come and stay during vacations, and there are long family parties. But the pleasant times fade with the arrival of Ben, the couple's fifth child. Ben is a strange, aggressive child who seems to the Lovatt family to be more alien than human. As they try to deal with him, their previously happy family life unravels. Harriet feels that the family blames her for what has happened, and Ben seems to have no future. As he reaches adolescence, he has learned nothing at school and fits in only with a crowd of soon-to-be dropouts who engage in petty crime.

Some critics saw the novel as a comment on British society in the 1980s, although Lessing said this was not her intention. Rather, she wanted to explore what might happen if some prehistoric, prehuman race was still somewhere present in the human gene pool and became incarnated in human form in a modern society. As she explored this idea, she produced a thought-provoking novel that deals with issues relating to the nature of the family and the role of women in family life, especially the notion of how to balance personal responsibility with the freedom to pursue personal and familial happiness.

Doris Lessing (AP Images)

AUTHOR BIOGRAPHY

Lessing was born Doris May Tayler in Persia (present-day Iran) on October 22, 1919. Both her parents were British. In 1925, the family moved to Southern Rhodesia, now Zimbabwe, which was then a British colony. Her father became a maize (corn) farmer. Doris was sent to a convent school and later a high school in Salisbury, the capital city. However, she dropped out of that school when she was thirteen and received no more formal education. She was, however, a voracious reader, especially of the great English and Russian novelists, such as Charles Dickens and Leo Tolstoy.

Lessing left home when she was fifteen and worked as a nursemaid. She also began writing short stories, two of which were published in a magazine in South Africa. She moved to Salisbury, England, and married Frank Watson at nineteen. They had two children, but Lessing left the family after a few years, while still living in Salisbury. She moved in left-wing political circles, where she met and married Gottfried Lessing. They had one son.

In 1949, Lessing moved to London with her son and published her first novel, *The Grass Is Singing*. Much of her writing was set in Africa in the 1960s and 1970s and exposed the inequities of colonial rule. During this time, she was banned from entering Southern Rhodesia or South Africa.

In 1962, she wrote *The Golden Notebook*, one of the novels for which she is best known. Notable novels of the 1970s included *Briefing for a Descent into Hell* (1971) and *Memoirs of a Survivor* (1974). Lessing also wrote many short story collections during this period, including *To Room Nineteen: Collected Stories, Vol. 1* (1978) and *The Temptation of Jack Orkney: Collected Stories, Vol. 2* (1978). She published a set of five related novels, collectively known as *Canopus in Argos*, from 1979 to 1983.

In 1985, she published the novel *The Good Terrorist*, and three years later *The Fifth Child*, which received the Grinzane Cavour Prize in Italy and was nominated for the 1988 Los Angeles Times Book Award. Another novel, *Love Again*, appeared in 1996, and in 2000, Lessing published a sequel to *The Fifth Child* titled *Ben, in the World*.

Lessing has also published plays, an autobiography, and two opera libretti (in collaboration with composer Philip Glass). She has won many literary awards, and in 2007, she was awarded the Nobel Prize in Literature.

PLOT SUMMARY

A Happy Family

Harriet and David meet at an office party in London in the 1960s. They fall in love almost immediately and decide to marry in the spring. They buy a large Victorian house within commuting distance of London and decide to have at least six children, even though they are not wealthy and do not know how they will afford such a large family. Molly, David's divorced mother, like the rest of his family, disapproves of their plans and tells David he will have to ask his wealthy father for money. When David's father, James Lovatt, visits, he says he will pay the mortgage for them. Harriet and David soon have their first child, Luke.

A pattern sets in at the Lovatt home. The whole family comes to visit at Easter and Christmas, and everyone enjoys feasting around the family table. Harriet soon becomes pregnant again, and her mother, Dorothy, lives with them most of the time to help out. Harriet gives birth to Helen, their second child, and then two years later to Jane, their third. Their family is a happy one.

Three years later, in 1973, Paul, the fourth child, is born. Harriet becomes very tired and irritable having to look after such a large family. However, she and David still want to have four more children. Although they plan to wait a few years, Harriet becomes pregnant again later that year. Dorothy is unhappy at all the work she has to do at their house, and Harriet and David agree to get someone else to help, although that is easier said than done. Harriet remains tired and unhappy.

Harriet's fifth pregnancy is not comfortable for her. She feels the fetus energetically moving around inside her, demanding attention. The family gathering at Christmas is not as happy as it usually is. Alice, a cousin of Frederick Burke, comes to help Dorothy. At five months, the fetus is large, but her doctor, Dr. Brett, says there is nothing abnormal about it. However, Harriet is in pain, which she must take drugs to control. The situation gets worse as the pregnancy advances. Harriet believes she is in a struggle with the fetus to survive, and she thinks of it as a monster.

Birth of Ben

The new baby is christened Ben. He is unusually large, weighing eleven pounds at birth, and his appearance is odd—unattractive although not actually deformed. Harriet does not bond with him and thinks of him as an alien or troll. As a baby, Ben is always struggling, fighting, crying out, perpetually restless and aggressive. Although he is healthy and has a huge appetite, he is not a normal baby. Harriet gets bruised breast-feeding him, he is so fierce and strong, so she decides to bottle-feed him instead.

That summer, the extended family comes to visit again. Ben is not social, and no one enjoys holding him. Harriet finds it impossible to love him. The other family members are anxious about Ben and even fearful of him. One day, Ben deliberately injures his brother Paul, spraining his arm. Ben is then mostly confined to his room, and anxiety spreads through the family.

In the summer of 1975, fewer people come to stay. Ben is now over a year old and comes out of his room more, but everyone is wary of him. Ben kills a small dog and a cat. At Christmas, only a few people come to the house.

When Ben is eighteen months old, Harriet takes him to Dr. Brett, but the doctor says Ben is normal, just hyperactive. He is against prescribing drugs to treat the condition. Now Ben is locked into his room at night and watched every moment during the day. Harriet is exhausted.

She, David, and the other four children take a vacation in France, leaving Dorothy in charge of Ben. When they return, Dorothy recommends that they institutionalize Ben. Harriet feels that Ben is destroying their family life and taking up all her time.

Ben Is Institutionalized

At Christmas when Ben is three, visitors come, including a dog. The dog loves Amy, the little girl with Down's syndrome, but is wary of Ben— rightly so, it turns out, as on one occasion he must be stopped when he seems about to strangle the dog. All the family members urge Harriet to institutionalize Ben; even David agrees. Harriet is reluctant but has to agree to it. Ben is sent away.

The entire family is relieved, and life appears to return to normal. However, Harriet is troubled by guilt and feels she must visit Ben. She drives several hours north to a grim institution, where reluctant officials allow her to see Ben only because she refuses to go away. Ben is naked except for a straitjacket and is unconscious from being drugged. Horrified, Harriet insists on taking Ben home with her. The two attendants are shocked but allow her to do so.

During the drive home, Ben wakes up, and Harriet is forced to inject him with a drug the institution gave her for him. When she gets home, the family is upset that she has brought Ben back. Ben screams and struggles in the straitjacket. Harriet feeds him and finds he is starving. Over the next few days, Harriet tries to get Ben to overcome his terror and behave better. Ben is able to join the family at meal times, but he does not trust his father and hisses at him.

Eventually Harriet finds a young man named John who works in the garden and seems to get along with Ben. She pays him to look after Ben, and John takes Ben away on his motorcycle during the days. They hang around with a group of unemployed youths, and Ben seems to fit in with them. They treat him a bit roughly, but he does not mind, and they accept him. At home at night, the other children lock their bedroom doors because they are afraid of Ben.

Ben Goes to School

When Ben is five, Luke and Helen announce that they want to go away to boarding school because they do not like Ben. Ben goes to school, even though Harriet believes he is not capable of learning. Ben does not want to go either, but John and his gang convince him he must. After school, he is picked up by the gang and remains with them until bedtime.

At school, Ben does better than expected at first, and his teachers say he tries hard. However, in the second term, he attacks a girl and breaks her arm. He does not seem to know that what he did was wrong. Harriet threatens to send him back to the institution, and John tries to explain to Ben that, if he hurts people they may hurt him back.

Harriet takes Ben to see Dr. Gilly, a specialist. Dr. Gilly tells her that the problem lies in her dislike of Ben. Harriet is upset because she thinks her family has blamed her all along for giving birth to this strange child. The doctor prescribes a sedative for Ben.

That Christmas, Luke and Helen prefer to go with other relatives. Ben spends most of his time with John, while Harriet tries to deal with Paul, who has become difficult and restless. Paul is sent to see a psychiatrist. He hates Ben, who threatened to strangle him on one occasion.

John and three of his friends depart to attend a job-training school in Manchester. Ben is upset and has a difficult time accepting that they have left. He spends long hours in front of the television, but he does not seem to understand what he sees. Harriet continues to believe that Ben is a throwback in the evolutionary chain, a Neanderthal creature. She is haunted by the fact that her rescue of Ben from the institution has destroyed her family, and the family blames her.

Ben turns eleven and goes to another school. He can barely read or write. He spends time with a group of loutish older boys, including Derek, Billy, Elvis, Vic, and others who come to the house, raid the refrigerator, and watch television. Harriet suspects they indulge in petty crime in the neighborhood. She and David realize it is time to sell the house.

Ben and his gang rob and beat a shopkeeper. Harriet thinks that, when they sell the house, Ben will drift off to London with his gang and live in some derelict building somewhere, stealing to survive. She wonders whether anyone will ever understand who he is, and she foresees a grim future for him.

CHARACTERS

Alice
Alice is a cousin of Frederick Burke who comes to help Dorothy and Harriet while Harriet is pregnant with Ben. She is capable and tough.

Amy
Amy is the youngest daughter of Sarah and William. She has Down's syndrome.

Angela
Angela is one of Harriet's two sisters. She is married with three children and copes efficiently with her life, although she resents the fact that her two sisters take up much of their mother's time.

Billy
Billy is one of the gang of youths who spend time at the Lovatt house with Ben. Harriet thinks he is stupid and violent.

Dr. Brett
Dr. Brett is Harriet's physician. Whenever he examines Ben, he finds him to be normal, although hyperactive.

Bridget
Bridget is a cousin of David's. She is fifteen years old and enjoys spending her holidays at the Lovatts' house, as she does not have much of a family life of her own. However, while Harriet is pregnant with Ben and in distress, Bridget becomes disillusioned with life there and returns to live with her mother.

Frederick Burke
Frederick Burke is the second husband of David's mother. He is a historian and lives in Oxford, England, where there is a famous university. As an academic, he is not wealthy, and he is rather distant in his manner. However, he is also kind, and David gets along well with him.

Molly Burke
Molly Burke is David's mother. She is divorced from David's father and remarried to Frederick Burke. They are both academics and live in Oxford. Molly does not approve of Harriet and David's desire to have many children and does not especially value family life.

Derek

Derek is an adolescent boy who is part of the gang that hangs out with Ben at the Lovatt house. He is unkempt and easy-going, ready to drop out of school.

Elvis

Elvis is one of the adolescent boys who come to the Lovatt house to hang out with Ben. He is polite, but Harriet also thinks he is nasty.

Dr. Gilly

Dr. Gilly is a pediatric specialist in London. Harriet takes Ben to see her. Dr. Gilly tells Harriet that the problem is with her, not Ben, because she does not like her own child.

John

John is a mostly unemployed young man who does some work for the Lovatts in the garden. He gets along well with Ben, and Harriet pays him to take charge of the boy during daytime hours. Later, he leaves for job-training school in Manchester.

Ben Lovatt

Ben Lovatt is the youngest son of Harriet and David. He is the "fifth child." His appearance is unusual and unattractive, and he is aggressive and very strong, even as a baby. Harriet is unable to bond with him and thinks of him as an alien creature, not human at all. Ben consumes twice as much food as a normal baby would. When he is less than a year old, he deliberately hurts his brother Paul, and before he is two, he kills a dog and cat. He is then sent to an institution where he is drugged and ill-treated, only to be rescued and taken home by Harriet. He remains a very difficult child, although he does get along with a youth named John, and John and his motorcycle gang adopts Ben as a kind of mascot. Ben attends school but does not learn much. He is also unable to grasp how people learn to get along with each other. He attacks a girl, and on another occasion, he is about to strangle Paul before Harriet stops him. However, whenever Harriet consults doctors about Ben, she is told he is a normal, if hyperactive, child. At eleven, Ben begins attending another school, and a gang of disaffected older boys forms around him. He appears to take part in robberies. When Harriet and David agree to sell their house, it appears that Ben's future is grim, and Harriet expects him

to drift to a large city and survive on the margins of society by criminal activities.

David Lovatt

David Lovatt is the husband of Harriet and the father of Ben. He is an architect by profession and is thirty years old when he meets and marries Harriet. His parents were divorced when he was a child. He was raised mostly by his mother and her second husband, occasionally visiting his wealthy father abroad. David is determined that life for his own children will be different; like Harriet, he gives priority to raising a large, happy family. He cannot really afford to support such a family on his salary, but he accepts help from his father. When their family life is disrupted by Ben, David's marriage comes under strain. He and Harriet no longer make love because they are worried they might conceive another child like Ben. He agrees much more readily than Harriet that Ben should be institutionalized, telling her there is no alternative. Later, he tries to persuade Harriet not to retrieve Ben from the institution. After Ben returns, there is a distance between Harriet and David; David feels hurt by what she has done, and he blames her for it. He spends more time at his office and comes home later. By the time Ben is about six, David has taken a part-time job at a college and is hardly ever at home. When he is at home, he is exhausted. Harriet realizes that he has become a different man. Spending almost all his time at work, he has become successful, but he no longer has time for his family. This is the opposite of what he had wanted and envisioned in the early days of their marriage.

Deborah Lovatt

Deborah Lovatt is David's sister. She is an attractive, unmarried young woman who is used to living the life of the rich. Later, she marries but soon gets divorced.

Harriet Lovatt

Harriet, the mother of Ben, is the oldest of three sisters and had a happy childhood, leaving home when she was eighteen. She trained as a graphic designer and is working in the sales department of a company when, at the age of twenty-four, she meets David. It is a fortunate meeting because Harriet has no interest in pursuing a career. She has always known that her happiness lies in getting married and having many children. She and David soon marry and create an idyllic family life with four children. But when Harriet conceives Ben, her life becomes difficult. The pregnancy is hard, and she fails to bond with the newborn boy. Ben is hard to control, and Harriet gets tired and finds that he takes up all her time, to the detriment of the other children. She tries to understand and love Ben but fails because he is so difficult. She reluctantly agrees to institutionalize him but is so racked with guilt at abandoning her child that she reclaims him, even though the family disapproves. She thinks of Ben as an alien creature but does her best to raise him, suffering because she knows that the family blames her for the situation. Her marriage suffers and she fears for Ben's future.

Helen Lovatt

Helen Lovatt is the eldest daughter of Harriet and David. Like Luke, she goes to boarding school because she does not like Ben. During vacations she prefers to stay with Molly, her grandmother, rather than with her parents. At sixteen, she is attractive and capable.

James Lovatt

James Lovatt is David's wealthy father. He is a boat builder and lives mostly abroad with his second wife, Jessica. He is a good-natured man who takes on David and Harriet's mortgage without complaint.

Jane Lovatt

Jane Lovatt is the third child of Harriet and David. She is a quiet girl, taking after her grandmother, Dorothy. Eventually, she prefers to live with Dorothy and her aunt Sarah rather than with her parents. At fourteen, Jane is not very good in school, but otherwise she seems fine.

Jessica Lovatt

Jessica Lovatt is James Lovatt's wealthy second wife. She is the same age as Molly but looks much younger. She does not like England because of its climate and prefers to be abroad.

Luke Lovatt

Luke Lovatt is the eldest son of Harriet and David. When he is eleven, he goes to boarding school. This is his choice because he does not like being around Ben. He also prefers to spend vacations with his grandfather rather than live at home. At eighteen, he is good-looking and reliable. His ambition is to be a boat builder, like his grandfather.

Paul Lovatt

Paul Lovatt is the fourth child of David and Harriet. Of all their children, he is the one most negatively affected by Ben's presence, and he hates Ben. By the time Paul is six, he turns from being a delightful child to one who is difficult and demanding and finds it hard to concentrate. He likes watching television, which calms him. At eleven, he is still very difficult. He hates his school and wants to go to boarding school, like his older brother and sister.

Sarah

Sarah, one of Harriet's two sisters, is unhappily married to William. She has four children, the youngest of whom, Amy, has Down's syndrome. She is annoyed with her mother Dorothy because she thinks Dorothy gives too much time to Harriet and not enough to her.

Dorothy Walker

Dorothy is Harriet's mother. She is a widow who stays for long periods at David and Harriet's house to help with the children. She is very capable but she gets exhausted with all the work.

William

William is married to Sarah. It is not a happy marriage, and he has left her twice, only to return. He has a poor-paying job in the building trade.

THEMES

Mother-Child Relationships

Central to the story is the relationship between Harriet and Ben. Harriet is a good mother whose relationships with her other children are normal, but Ben is the exception. Ben seems to be fighting her from the beginning, even while still in the womb. When he is born, Harriet dislikes him immediately, saying, "He's like a troll, or a goblin or something." Mother and child never succeed in bonding in a normal way. Nevertheless, she does her best to raise him in a responsible way. The effort involved in this leaves her exhausted and damages the life of the family. Still, Harriet only reluctantly agrees to send Ben away to an institution, and after that she is the only one in the family to be concerned about his fate. It is her sense of responsibility as a mother that compels her to reclaim Ben from the institution. However, the novel raises the

TOPICS FOR FURTHER STUDY

- When the Lovatt family disintegrates, who, if anyone, is to blame? Harriet thinks everyone blames her, but does David share any of the blame? What about Ben? Is it his fault? Do the parents fulfill their responsibilities to Ben or do they fail him? Give a short class presentation in which you discuss some of these issues and then lead a class discussion about them.

- Is Ben like a figure out of a science fiction or horror story, like the Frankenstein monster, or is he just a child with disabilities? What sort of disabilities might he have? Use online and traditional research resources to compile a list and description of common childhood disabilities that might match his behavior. Write an essay in which you discuss the different views taken of Ben by the family and the professional people Harriet consults. Why does Lessing make the story so ambiguous in that respect? Then try to diagnose what you think was "really" Ben's disability based on your research (keeping in mind that this is a work of fiction and may not exactly match any real medical issue). Address in your essay whether a precise diagnosis would have made a difference to Ben's family and to readers of *The Fifth Child*.

- Consult the young-adult nonfiction book, *Teen Minorities in Rural North America: Growing Up Different*, by Elizabeth Bauchnern (2007). In what sense might some of these stories about what it is like to be a minority and to feel different be Ben's story also? Lessing once commented that many students had told her they could relate to the book because they identified with Ben. Make an entry in your blog about a time when you felt "different" and share it with your classmates. Does recalling such a moment help you to understand Ben?

- With a group of students, imagine you are making a movie of *The Fifth Child*. Create a three- to four-minute movie trailer that brings out the most important theme of the novel, and upload it to YouTube. Invite your classmates to watch and review the trailer.

- Create an interactive time line that chronicles the changes in the education of children with disabilities in the past fifty years. Be sure to add all major legislation and groups that have to do with special education. Share your time line on a Web page.

question of whether Harriet is in some way to blame for the way Ben turns out because she does not love him. After all, the doctor and specialist to whom Harriet takes Ben both insist that, although Ben might be hyperactive, he is otherwise a normal child. Dr. Gilly puts it to Harriet quite bluntly: "The problem is not with Ben, but with you. You don't like him very much." Harriet also feels that her family blames her for the way Ben has turned out. This may suggest that the mother is used as a scapegoat by others who either do not see or do not wish to deal with the problem child. The blame then falls not on Harriet, but on an intolerant and prejudiced view of women. As Harriet says to David when she gets exasperated at being blamed,

"I suppose in the old times, in primitive societies, this was how they treated a woman who'd given birth to a freak. As if it was her fault. But we are supposed to be civilised!"

Responsibility

Harriet shows responsibility in the sense that she continues to try to look after Ben when everyone else has given up, but there is a wider question of responsibility that the novel raises. It suggests that the Lovatts are irresponsible in insisting on having a large family when they cannot afford it. David's father has to take on the mortgage, and then the Lovatts have to rely on Harriet's mother, Dorothy, to do the lion's share of the housework, which wears her out. The Lovatts'

The birth of Ben, the couple's fifth child, changes the family forever. (*Dmitriy Shironosov | Shutterstock.com*)

dream of a large house and lots of children seems increasingly selfish as the novel progresses. The extended family gathers there at Easter and Christmas and in the summer just because they want a good time, but the idyllic life cannot endure forever. It is as if the Lovatts are being punished not for their desire to be happy or their belief that they will be happy, but for developing a lifestyle that is more lavish than what they could reasonably expect, given their resources.

Society

The novel suggests that the happy family life with a large number of children that the Lovatts envision for themselves is impossible in the modern world. Sooner or later, the violence that is getting worse in society is going to intrude on their isolated world. This is hinted at early in the novel, when the narrator reports what the Lovatts hear on the radio: "Bad news from everywhere: nothing to what the News would soon become, but threatening enough." When the Lovatts are still a happy family, before the birth of Ben, the small town in which they live is deteriorating: "Brutal incidents and crimes, once shocking everyone,

were now commonplace." In particular, gangs of youths hang around and cause trouble. When Ben is born, it is as if the violence in the outer world has finally found its way into the Lovatt family. He is a symbol of a rogue element in society that people are unwilling to confront and have no idea of how to deal with.

STYLE

Horror Fiction

The novel does not fit easily into one genre. It is short enough to be a novella rather than a novel. (Exact definitions vary in terms of length, but a novella is a work that is longer than a short story but shorter than a full novel.) But what kind of novella is it? In many ways it is horror fiction. Horror fiction creates an atmosphere of fear and terror and may include elements of the supernatural. In *The Fifth Child,* Ben is often referred to as a creature from another world, an alien, and he has a will to harm others. Horror fiction goes back to the gothic novels of the eighteenth and nineteenth centuries. The genre originated with

Horace Walpole's *Castle of Otranto* (1764). Mary Wollstonecraft Shelley's *Frankenstein* (1818), which is sometimes mentioned in connection with *The Fifth Child*, is another example of the gothic novel.

Folklore, Fairy Tale, and Parable

The Fifth Child also has fairy tale and folklore elements. Ben is referred to as a changeling. A changeling, in mythology, is a child of a troll or some such creature who is substituted for a human baby. The baby is taken away to be raised by the elves, fairies, or trolls, while the offspring of the troll grows up in the human family. Shakespeare uses the myth of the changeling in his play *A Midsummer Night's Dream*.

A parable is a story that is designed to teach a moral or lesson. In *The Fifth Child*, the narrator tells the story in a rather distant manner, as if detached and uninvolved in the action. She seems to be telling an archetypal story—that is, an essential, timeless story that may lie at the heart of many other tales—from which the reader should learn a certain lesson. What that lesson might be, however, is open to interpretation. One possible meaning is the bleak advice: "Do not expect to be happy."

HISTORICAL CONTEXT

England from the 1960s to the 1980s

The Fifth Child begins in London in the mid-1960s. In England, as well as elsewhere in the West, the sixties was a decade of social change in which a vibrant, youth-based popular culture flourished. The more traditional, restrained culture of the 1950s gave way to something completely different as young people found new ways of expressing themselves in music, fashion, and politics. London was a center for this new wave of creative expression and earned the label "swinging London." England led the way in the popular music of the period, with bands such as the Beatles, the Rolling Stones, and the Who, among others. Styles of dress became more informal and flamboyant. Young men wore their hair long and young women wore miniskirts. Carnaby Street in London and the King's Road, Chelsea, were centers of fashion. An article in *Time*, "Great Britain: You Can Walk Across It on Grass," noted in April 1966:

London is switched on. Ancient elegance and new opulence are all tangled up in a dazzling blur of op and pop. The city is alive with birds (girls) and beatles, buzzing with minicars and telly stars, pulsing with half a dozen separate veins of excitement.

This is the culture that is hinted at in the opening pages of *The Fifth Child*, in the office party: "The women were dressed up, dramatic bizarre, full of colour: *Look at me! Look at me!* Some of the men demanded as much attention." Harriet and David do not fit in because they are throwbacks to the more conservative 1950s.

Another characteristic of the 1960s was the so-called sexual revolution. The near universal availability of a contraceptive birth control pill for women (often referred to, as it is in *The Fifth Child*, simply as "the Pill") meant that young unmarried couples, freed of the fear of pregnancy, could indulge in sex more casually and often with more than one partner. Standards of sexual morality therefore changed markedly from the 1950s.

The youth culture of the sixties was also referred to as the counterculture. It found political expression in a distrust of governments and large corporations, and a rejection of the materialism of Western culture generally. It was Left-oriented, anti-war, and pro-environment. This aspect of the sixties is epitomized by the popular slogan of the time, "Make Love Not War."

The sixties also gave rise to the women's movement, often known at the time as women's liberation. Women began to organize themselves and demand equal pay at work and more career opportunities. (In *The Fifth Child*, Harriet has no interest in becoming a career woman, instead choosing the traditional female role of mother and homemaker.)

By the early years of the 1970s, however, the counterculture was on the wane. By the end of the decade, Britain was facing an economic recession, and the mood of the nation was bleaker than it had been in the flamboyant sixties. In the early 1980s, the new Conservative government under Prime Minister Margaret Thatcher had to deal with a falling gross domestic product and steadily rising unemployment. From 1979 to 1983, unemployment more than doubled, from 1.2 million to 3 million. Many people were unemployed for long periods, including young people of low educational achievement, who faced a future that seemed to offer them nothing. It is these undereducated,

COMPARE
&
CONTRAST

- **1960s:** Because of the easy availability of the contraceptive birth control pill, people adopt more sexually active lifestyles.

  1980s: The new and deadly disease, AIDS, leads more people to adopt a cautious attitude to sexual activity.

  Today: In 2008, teenage pregnancies in Britain drop to their lowest levels in more than twenty years.

- **1960s:** More young people rebel against traditional authority, and a vibrant counterculture flourishes in Britain.

  1980s: Because of harder economic times in Britain, young people tend to be more conservative in their values. Unemployment is high, and many find it hard to get work.

  Today: A recession causes economic difficulties around the world. Although the British economy is slowly recovering, the youth unemployment rate is 20.3 percent in 2010, the highest since recordkeeping began in 1992.

- **1960s:** The average number of children in the British family at the end of the decade is two.

  1980s: A trend develops of couples having children later in life than people in previous generations. One reason for this is that more women are pursuing careers. This indicates that families will get smaller in the future.

  Today: The size of the average family in Britain is getting smaller: the average family has 1.8 children.

---

disaffected youths who inhabit the pages of *The Fifth Child* as the narrative moves into the 1980s.

CRITICAL OVERVIEW

The Fifth Child received many reviews, most of them positive. For Michiko Kakutani, in the *New York Times*, *The Fifth Child* was an examination of "the relationship between freedom and responsibility, between private suffering and societal disorder." Kakutani notes that these are issues with which Lessing was concerned throughout her career. Kakutani concludes that, although Lessing does not attain in this short novel the same "psychological density of her earlier novels or the mythic resonance of her outer-space fiction . . . she does manage to raise these provocative issues without ever wrenching her quicksilver narrative out of shape." Also in the *New York Times*, Carolyn Kizer refers to the novel as a "moral fable" that is "destined to become a minor classic." Kizer compares the novel to Mary Shelley's *Frankenstein* and George Orwell's *Nineteen Eighty-Four*, and sees it not only as a horror story but as a

"nightmare of social collapse," Lessing's pessimistic vision of the direction in which society is moving.

In *National Review*, Jeffrey Giles took a more critical view of the novel, commenting that Harriet Lovatt is similar to other Lessing heroines and "is the kind of heroine Miss Lessing uses to make a point. She is moody, stressed out, misunderstood by everyone, and inexplicably dull." Giles points out that Lessing has many times attacked stereotyped gender roles but comments that in *The Fifth Child* she "reinforces the very sexual stereotypes she appears to be battling. Harriet goes to reclaim her son, and the message seems to be that she alone is responsible for Ben's abnormality, and that women really are—above all else—mothers and wives."

The Fifth Child has also attracted the attention of scholars. For example, Roberta Rubenstein, in the essay "Doris Lessing's Fantastic Children," published in the collection *Doris Lessing: Border Crossings*, discusses the "disturbing moral concerns" raised by the novel. One of these is the question, "Is there any compromise possible between the needs of a family to maintain

Life inside the Lovatt home is not what it appears. *(Avella | Shutterstock.com)*

emotional cohesion and the needs of a profoundly anti-social, aberrant child?" Rubenstein points out that Lessing offers no simple answers to this or any other question that the novel raises.

CRITICISM

Bryan Aubrey

Aubrey holds a Ph.D. in English. In the following essay, he explores the issue that most interested Doris Lessing in The Fifth Child, *the effect Ben has on the Lovatt family.*

The saying "Sometimes a cigar is just a cigar" is a saying attributed to that pioneer of psychoanalysis, Sigmund Freud, who usually delighted in digging down below the surface of things to bring out their ultimate meaning. And by the same token, sometimes, too, a story is just a story—at least according to claims made by Doris Lessing in connection with her novel, *The Fifth Child*. When the novel was published in 1988, commentators

> ARE THE LOVATTS TEMPTING THE GODS BY REVELING IN THEIR HAPPINESS, SHOWING HUBRIS IN EXPECTING THEIR PERFECT LIFE TO CONTINUE UNINTERRUPTED?"

were reluctant to take it at face value, seeing it as an allegory about the deterioration of life in England in the 1980s. They did not for the most part want to take seriously Harriet Lovatt's belief that her problematic child Ben was quite literally a throwback in the genetic chain, a prehuman creature emerging in the late twentieth century, long after his own kind had become extinct. But this was indeed the way Lessing saw her story, and in writing it she wanted to explore the kind of issues that would be raised if such a being were ever to emerge. In an interview published in the *New York Times*, she told Rebecca Pepper Sinkler:

> I have always been fascinated by the legends of the little people, gnomes and goblins. And then I read an essay by [the anthropologist and poet] Loren Eiseley where he talked of walking up from the seashore somewhere in Maine at dusk. He had been thinking about the Ice Age, and he looked up and saw a girl. He said to himself, 'There is an Ice Age girl.' He speculated that the gene could have come down through the centuries.

This gave Lessing the seed of an idea for *The Fifth Child*, which grew further when she read a letter in a magazine from a mother who had given birth to three normal children, but the fourth was mean-spirited and was destroying the family. The mother considered her evil.

Lessing told Sinkler that when her publisher had offered the thought that the novel in fact depicted her "vision of England," she scoffed, saying that such a thought had not occurred to her.

The novel emerged, then, in response to the storyteller's imagination working on the question "What if . . . ?" What if those ancient genes were indeed mixed with human genes and were still circulating in the gene pool? What would happen if by some extremely remote chance those genes found their way into a human womb? How would people react? And how would such a creature cope, thrust into an alien setting?

WHAT DO I READ NEXT?

- Lessing's novel *Ben, in the World: The Sequel to the Fifth Child* (2000) takes up the story of Ben's life after he runs away from home. The story begins when he is eighteen. Ben does not have the skills necessary to succeed in society, and his awareness of this causes a build-up of anger. As he stumbles along his path, he is often betrayed and only occasionally befriended. The story has a wide range of settings, as Ben's wanderings take him to France and Brazil.

- *A Child Called It: One Child's Courage to Survive* (1995) by Dave Pelzer, is the best-selling account of the abuse Pelzer suffered at the hands of his alcoholic mother when he was a child. At the age of twelve, Pelzer was removed from his family home by the California authorities. This true story is a fascinating, if horrific account of the breakdown in the mother-son relationship. To Pelzer's mother, Dave must have appeared rather as Ben does to Harriet in *The Fifth Child*. To the reader, though, it is the mother who is the monster, not the child.

- *The Changeling*, by Zilpha Keatley Snyder, is a classic novel for young-adult readers. It was first published in 1970 and won several awards. Ivy Carson is a member of the disreputable Carson family in a suburban house in Rosewood, California. There is something magical about Ivy that makes her unlike the other Carsons, and it turns out she is a changeling with supernatural parents. The book is available in a 2004 edition.

- *The Dark-Thirty: Southern Tales of the Supernatural* (1992) by African American author Patricia McKissack won a Newbery Honor Award in 1993. It contains ten stories, all set in the South, and is appropriate for young-adult readers. Ghosts and magic abound, but McKissack also uses the opportunity to deal with historical themes such as slavery and freedom, covering a period from the nineteenth century to the civil rights movement of the 1960s.

- In *We Need to Talk about Kevin: A Novel* (2005), by Lionel Shriver, Kevin is a character not unlike Ben in *The Fifth Child*. He is hostile to his mother, and she lacks maternal feelings for him. As Kevin grows up, he has some of Ben's aggressive qualities, and he commits horrible acts of violence when he is seventeen. The novel has won praise from reviewers and readers.

- *Mothers and Sons: Stories* (2008), by Colm Tobin, contains nine stories, most of them set in Ireland, that explore relationships between mothers and their adult sons. The stories examine themes such as how such relationships may develop, get broken and healed, or, in some cases, remain unhealed.

These are the issues that Lessing wishes to explore; she is interested not only in Ben but in the effect Ben has on the Lovatt family, when the strangeness of the unknown erupts into the tried and trusted routines of the known. Ben himself should be thought of not as a monster or as an evil being. His tragedy is simply that he does not fit in; he has been born in the wrong place at the wrong time. As some kind of prehuman, Neanderthal creature, he simply does not have the mental or emotional equipment to understand human society. He is unable to learn anything at school. At home with the Lovatts, he has to observe others and pick up what he can by imitation, but he never really grasps or understands things naturally and intuitively, the way a human child would. He cannot get the hang of simple games such as snakes and ladders or repeat a story that has just been read to him, and Harriet is unable to guess what actually goes on in his mind, how his mental processes work, whereas she understands her other children easily. She does come to understand, however, that in his own terms, Ben is a complete being, just not a human being. When she observes him in his early teens, "She felt she was looking, through him, at a race that reached its apex thousands and thousands of years before humanity, whatever that meant, took this stage."

But what of Harriet and the family? Right from the beginning of the narrative, it seems that the author is setting this family up for a fall. Harriet and David seem too perfect in their big old house with their delightful young children. Nothing seems to mar their serene family life, but on at least one occasion the simplicity of the language the narrator uses to describe them seems almost ominous: "Happiness. A happy family. The Lovatts were a happy family. It was what they had chosen and what they deserved." Can one choose happiness? the reader might wonder. Does the triple repetition of the word here serve as something of a warning? In some kinds of literature, *hubris* is a pride or arrogance that seems to challenge the gods themselves, and events bring about the downfall and humbling of the person who shows it. Are the Lovatts tempting the gods by reveling in their happiness, showing hubris in expecting their perfect life to continue uninterrupted?

The Lovatts certainly do have a good number of happy years, and it seems for a while that they are immune to the bad luck that plagues other individuals and the society as a whole, as unemployment rises and people endure hardship. Their happiness seems almost to go against the grain. Indeed, Harriet made the kind of choice in her life that was at the time being brought into question— a woman's role as wife and mother. As women were discovering and fighting for new opportunities in work and careers during the 1960s, Harriet, although she did work as a graphic artist before her marriage, had no intention of becoming a "career woman," believing that happiness was best found in a family, not in one's work. When the break in the Lovatt's good fortune finally comes, the novel will show that in these changing times, Harriet's choice, although a traditional one, was not in fact the easy one. She too, like Ben, has come along at the wrong time. She would have been more at home in England in the 1940s and 1950s than in the 1960s and beyond.

It is also Harriet who suffers the most when their happiness begins to unravel with the arrival of Ben. She becomes extremely harassed as she tries to meet the incessant demands placed upon her. Her other children get neglected as Ben takes up all her time. This is where the story takes an especially interesting turn, as others in the family, including Dorothy, Alice, and David, appear to blame Harriet for the situation. She experiences "condemnation, and criticism, and dislike" from them. This seems largely because they are unwilling to deal with something that has so disrupted their expectations of what their family life should be like. Harriet is the only one who faces up to the situation. When she brings up the subject of who or what Ben is, the others say nothing, and their silence tells Harriet that "they would rather not face the implications of it." As for David, her husband, he disowns Ben completely. When Harriet says he is "*our child*," David replies emphatically, "No, he's not. . . . Well, he certainly isn't mine." So Harriet cannot put up much resistance when this previously perfect family, faced with something they do not understand, choose the most convenient course. They callously pack Ben off to the sort of institution that well-off families make use of when they want to get rid of a child they do not want. It is only Harriet who retains a sense of responsibility to her monster-child, which prompts her to bring him back from the institution, against the wishes of her family. Lessing here paints a rather chilling portrait of how the burden falls upon the mother to care for a child that has been rejected by the rest of the family—and Harriet also has to endure the attempts of the family to blame her for the entire situation. This is not a comfortable portrait of the burdens of motherhood.

However, Lessing does not make it that simple for the reader to assign sympathy and blame in the right proportions to the right people. She opens up a rich vein of ambiguity by having all the experts that Harriet consults declare that Ben is in fact a normal child. Dr. Brett, Harriet's physician, thinks so, but he is not surprised at her dislike of the baby. He says he sees such things frequently in his patients. This suggests that Harriet may indeed be the one with the problem. Mrs. Graves, the headmistress at the school Ben attends, sees nothing especially unusual in Ben.

Nor does the pediatrician, Dr. Gilly, who tells Harriet bluntly, "The problem is not with Ben, but with you. You don't like him very much." It is only the Lovatt family that regards Ben as an alien and a horror, which may perhaps say something about the narrow horizons that this particular family

The family is torn apart by the problem of Ben, the fifth child. *(ejwhite | Shutterstock.com)*

exhibit when faced with a child who does not fit their idea of what a child should be. Instead of expanding their boundaries to accommodate the newcomer, this nice upper-middle-class family chooses instead to close ranks and reject the infant outsider—with unwelcome consequences both for themselves and for Ben.

Source: Bryan Aubrey, Critical Essay on *The Fifth Child*, in *Novels for Students*, Gale, Cengage Learning, 2012.

Sarah Sceats

In the following excerpt, Sceats examines the representation of eating and food in Lessing's writing, particularly in terms of their roles in interpersonal or social relationships.

> [. . .] there is a terrible gap between the public and the private conscience [. . .]

'Dis-moi ce que tu manges,' wrote Antoine Brillat-Savarin in 1825, '[et] je te dirai ce que tu es. . . .' The potent suggestiveness of food is one of a writer's richest resources, and has been drawn upon and exploited ever since Homer. Literary food and eating, often enticingly (or revoltingly) evocative, are of great mimetic power and significance. It is fascinating and intriguing to read about what people eat, who they cook for, how

dinner—if it is—is served. Of still greater interest and significance, I think, are the aspects of food and eating which might be considered figurative: what is suggestive, speculative, intangible. Eating practices are in effect a currency, something 'understood,' broadly accepted, interpretable indeed, as Brillat-Savarin suggests. Encoded in appetite, taste, rituals and eating behaviours are all manner of apparent givens by which people are categorized and judged, and which disclose much about—to take a fairly random selection—class, generosity, rigidity, deprivation, power.

The revelatory use of eating in fiction is not simply a question of the elegance of metaphor, for eating and nourishment are at our core, essential in terms of survival, psychic development and primary social activities. (Hence the comparative rarity of novels without any mention of food or eating.) Their essential quality imbues food and eating with value, and this is one reason, in view of what I take to be her profound seriousness, for my focusing the discussion in this essay on the novels of Doris Lessing. Food and eating in Lessing's writing lie at the heart of a purposeful realism in which questions of psychological and political consequence

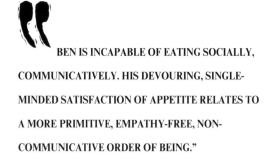

BEN IS INCAPABLE OF EATING SOCIALLY, COMMUNICATIVELY. HIS DEVOURING, SINGLE-MINDED SATISFACTION OF APPETITE RELATES TO A MORE PRIMITIVE, EMPATHY-FREE, NON-COMMUNICATIVE ORDER OF BEING."

are central. Here representation is rooted in the material and yet invades and embraces the metaphysical, the psychic, the mythical and the fantastic. And in all these spheres people hunger, provide, consume.

I want to look, briefly, at three aspects of food and eating in Lessing's writing, particularly as they relate to interpersonal or social connection. I will consider her representation of eating as a means of celebration and communication; focus on ways in which social eating might be problematic; and finally examine a pervasive trope in her work, that of not eating, of physical and mental breakdown and of some kind of ensuing enlightenment.

CELEBRATION AND COMMUNICATION

At its most basic level, eating is, of course, a necessity, a simple manifestation of the survival instinct, an expression of our essential physicality. This fundamental stoking is abundantly evident in Lessing's writing, from the hedonistic dinners and sundowner parties of the young whites in the African stories to the 'I want cake,' 'I want milk' of Ben, the uncompromising *Fifth Child*. Lessing's apprehension of the significance of feeding and nurturing to psychic development is (equally) widely evident, for example in the restless 'unappeasable mouth' of maternally-deprived Paul, again in *The Fifth Child*, or the compensatory cooking and caring behaviour of Alice Mellings in *The Good Terrorist*. In *The Marriages of Zones Three, Four and Five* much is made of the infant's need for 'feeding' in all senses by both physical and spiritual parents. The fact that Lessing repeatedly portrays maternal deprivation and abuse detracts not a bit from the perceived need; it is precisely because Martha Quest, for example, is half starved by her mother (albeit accidentally) that she in turn deprives her own child.

Lessing is, without doubt, a deeply committed writer, with a strong sense of political, ethical and aesthetic responsibility. She writes:

> The act of getting a story or a novel published is an act of communication, an attempt to impose one's personality and beliefs on other people. If a writer accepts this responsibility, he must see himself, to use the socialist phrase, as an architect of the soul, and it is a phrase which none of the old nineteenth-century novelists would have shied away from.(*A Small Personal Voice*)

The responsibility Lessing assumes is weighty. But she neither sees this as a restriction nor allows it to cramp her style. Like her esteemed nineteenth-century novelists (think, for example, of the jam-making scene in *Anna Karenina*), Lessing includes food and eating as part of her social and meta-physical vision. She has a relish, even a reverence, for the pleasures and sensuous materiality of food. Here is a sumptuous scene from *The Golden Notebook*:

> 'With strawberries, wine, obviously,' said Anna greedily; and moved the spoon about among the fruit, feeling its soft sliding resistance, and the slipperiness of the cream under a gritty crust of sugar. Molly swiftly filled glasses with wine and set them on the white sill. The sunlight crystallized beside each glass on the white paint in quivering lozenges of crimson and yellow light, and the two women sat in the sunlight, sighing with pleasure and stretching their legs in the thin warmth, looking at the colours of the fruit in the bright bowls and at the red wine.

There is a lively appreciation of mutuality in the shared enjoyment of eating here and elsewhere in the novel, in instances such as when, in the Blue Notebook, Anna shares her fellow Communist worker Jack's sandwich lunch or when, in the almost palpably evocative anticipation of shape, colour, touch and smell, she shops and cooks for a lover:

> It is a great pleasure, buying food I will cook for Michael; a sensuous pleasure, like the act of cooking itself. I imagine the meat in its coat of crumbs and egg; the mushrooms, simmering in sour cream and onions, the clear strong, amber-coloured soup [...] I unroll the veal that I remembered to batter out flat this morning; and I roll the pieces in the yellow egg, and the crumbs. I baked crumbs yesterday, and they still smell fresh and dry, in spite of the dampness in the air [...] All the kitchen is full of good cooking smells; and all at once I am happy, so happy I can feel the warmth of it through my whole body. (*The Golden Notebook*)

There is even an elegiac reprise, later on, when Anna shops for Saul Green. The potentially communicative importance of food is reinforced by inversion in the Yellow Notebook (Anna's draft fiction) by the healthy but limiting simplicity of her heroine Ella's dining and sexual relations with the boyish American she meets on the aeroplane. He eagerly orders 'the biggest steak they ha[ve] in the place,' swiftly drinks only Coca Cola or fruit juice, and happily completes sexual intercourse within seconds of getting into bed (*The Golden Notebook*).

The sharing of eating, food provision or cooking, like sex to a small extent and talk to a greater, is itself a connection, and may indeed be regarded as more intimate than either. The extraordinary intimacy of eating together is nowhere more clearly illustrated than in *The Marriages of Zones Three, Four and Five*, when the so-to-speak queen of Zone Three is brought to marry the ruler of Zone Four. Much suspicious and hostile circling, verbal sparring, discussion, rape, sleep, mountain-gazing and wary comradeship precede the betrothed couple's sitting to eat their—as yet—separate foods. It is only much later, when they have already reached a degree of intimacy figured in almost perpetual mutual nakedness, that they find they can no longer conjure separate foods, and are supplied with stewed beans and bread from the officers' mess, which they eat together with hungry relish.

PROBLEMATIC EATING

Communicative or social eating can, however, be problematic in a number of ways. Power relations of all kinds operate in and around the kitchen, and, as Foucault might suggest, acts (or discourses) of apparent communion mask the exercise of power. Dominance and subservience—whatever the ostensible positions of authority—are tenuous and slippery and interactions are subtle and frequently complex. That this is so much in evidence in Lessing's fiction is a measure of what Kate Fullbrook identifies as her being 'attuned to the position of the individual' as well as 'convinced of the power of collective decisions and potentialities. . . .' To take a couple of obvious examples: racist oppression and persecution are manifest in the world of the African novels and stories, yet the persecutors—Mary Turner in Lessing's first novel, *The Grass Is Singing*, Mrs. Quest and the colonial matrons of Zambesia in the Martha Quest novels, Mrs. Boothby in the Mashopi story of *The Golden Notebook*

may be mentioned as examples—perpetually feel themselves to be not *quite* in total control of the kitchen. In *The Good Terrorist* Alice Mellings strives to convert the group's anarchy to familial collectivity, battling to supplant their extravagant (though egalitarian) 'take-aways' with economical nourishing soups and stews. Functioning, according to Elizabeth Maslen, as 'both threat and victim,' Alice surrenders her will to her psychotic companion and devotes her considerable skills and energies to the physical good of the squat. Yet she attains a status and authority by means of this very submission, generating her acclaimed soups with maternal—and thus ambiguously powerful—bounty.

As these examples suggest, power relations in Lessing's writing always nudge from the simply private towards the public and the representative, and wider historical, political and social implications are invariably part of the picture, especially since her characters are frequently framed as 'representative.' But social eating can be problematic, too, in other ways. What happens, for example, when a group is invaded by the unsocialized? The arrival of Ben, in *The Fifth Child*, shatters Harriet and David's romantic idyll of family, setting child against adult, father against mother. Variously described as 'neanderthal,' a 'throwback,' an 'alien,' the infant Ben empties his mother's breast in seconds, always roars for more, and bites (literally) the hand that feeds him. As he grows he learns by imitation not to talk with his mouth full or eat with his mouth open, but this is mere semblance—'the energetic animal movements of his jaws confined behind closed lips' (*The Fifth Child*)—and his eating is never less than a subdued version of what is revealed when his mother finds him squatting on the kitchen table, grunting over an uncooked chicken he has torn apart. His response to her scolding on this occasion, in an echo from *King Lear*, is merely 'Poor Ben hungry.' (*The Fifth Child*)

Ben is incapable of eating socially, communicatively. His devouring, single-minded satisfaction of appetite relates to a more primitive, empathy-free, non-communicative order of being. While his siblings patiently instruct him in what is expected, in reality they progressively withdraw, at first in looks and conversation and finally by physical removal, until the family unit simply disintegrates. The great smooth table, with its palpable history of feasts and family, is scarred and darkened by the atavistic shadow of the unassimilable predatory individual. Not surprisingly, perhaps, Ben is especially associated with the 'barbarous eighties.'

I want now to recall my point about eating as positive intimate communication, and to suggest that the uniting effects of sharing food might themselves be expressly experienced as problematic, especially by men. On the two occasions quoted above, when Anna Wulf cooks so expectantly for her lover, he is about to leave her. What the men in both instances find threatening is precisely the intensity of mutuality, the shared body experience that dissolves some of the rigid boundaries of the individual. For Lessing's 'free women' food is part of the idyll, a means of conversation; by the men it is perceived as a trap.

On one level—that of the straightforward realist text—we could take such incidents as illustrating a male reluctance to take a subservient or passive role in female territory. Power relations and questions of dominance or subservience are crucial even to situations of 'shared' food, for the provider is almost inevitably in a dominant position, whether this is a man taking a woman to a restaurant or a woman cooking for her lover. In other words, Lessing's men's withdrawal from eating intimacy says as much about (gendered) power relations as about individual psyches.

This said, however, if men manifest fear of entrapment or commitment then the psyche clearly is relevant. On a less than conscious level a man may withdraw from a sensation of infantilization, of being mothered, as though convinced he must struggle to make the separation all over again. Maggie Kilgour suggests that the question of boundaries is inextricable from psychic gendering:

> While male sexual identity is achieved through the discovery of sexual difference and the need to turn from the mother to the absent father who represents separation, female development and discovery of sexual identity involves a continuing identification with the first love object because both are female. As a result of this, women tend to develop a less rigid sense of ego boundaries than men, and a more fluid sense of the relation between the self and the world outside.

This more fluid self, accessible to the contingent, has a natural inclination towards communication which endorses women's food sharing and offers an explanation, at least in part, for the almost exclusively female gender of the fasting communicants I am about to examine. Here, beyond the individual connection which may occur through

shared eating or sexual congress, a wider communication, a more significant breaching of the immured body of individualism, is what Lessing suggests is possible and indeed desirable. For this to happen, however, all kinds of fear and resistance have to be breached. . . .

Source: Sarah Sceats, "Flesh and Bones: Eating, Not Eating, and the Social Vision of Doris Lessing," in *Theme Parks, Rainforests and Sprouting Wastelands: European Essays on Theory and Performance in Contemporary British Fiction*, edited by Richard Todd, Rodopi, 2000, pp. 139–49.

Jeffrey Giles
In the following review, Giles is disappointed that the usually surprising Doris Lessing is so unsurprising in this short novel.

Harriet and David Lovatt won't stop having children. Throughout the "greedy and selfish Sixties," Harriet had been an anomaly: a Fifties throwback, an uptight wallflower, and, frankly, a husband-hound. David was an architect, a "judicious" drinker, and a "non-dancer." At the opening of Doris Lessing's latest novel, *The Fifth Child*, Harriet and David meet at a party and it's family-planning at first sight. They get married and set out to do the only thing either one seems capable of: tirelessly and ruthlessly churn out babies.

It has always been difficult to know what Doris Lessing will do next. She is an impatient, itinerant writer whose quest for perspective has taken her all over the map, both stylistically and politically. Perhaps the most surprising thing about *The Fifth Child*, then, is that it is quite unsurprising. Harriet is a familiar heroine for Miss Lessing. Like Alice Mellings from her earlier novel, *The Good Terrorist*, Harriet is the kind of heroine Miss Lessing uses to make a point. She is moody, stressed out, misunderstood by everyone, and inexplicably dull. David, unfortunately, doesn't fare as well. He is petty and selfish, and it's a safe bet that if Miss Lessing had given him a soul to sell, it would have gone to the devil long ago. For at least half of this slim, 133-page novel, the Lovatts seem little more than the butt of a joke about the nasty things that happen to people "brainwashed into believing family life is best."

Harriet and David have four children in the first six years of their marriage-each with "wispy fair hair and blue eyes and pink cheeks." While their in-laws are footing the bills and doing most of the housework, they spend their time collecting firewood and making jam. In these opening sections, Miss Lessing treats her characters with such disrespect that the reader can't help but cringe at the wicked fate she is surely arranging for them.

The Lovatts' fate is not long in coming. Harriet and David accidentally conceive a fifth child and Harriet's pregnancy is so extraordinarily painful that even Miss Lessing begins to feel sorry for her. The book finally divests itself of its smugness and the prose takes on a new energy: "People in passing cars would turn, amazed, to see this hurrying driven woman, white-faced, hair flying, open-mouthed, panting, arms clenched across her front.... Sometimes [Harriet] believed hooves were cutting her tender inside flesh, sometimes claws."

But just as Miss Lessing hits her stride, Ben is born and the novel goes utterly awry. Ben is such a preternaturally ugly and violent baby that Harriet is moved to remark, "He's like a troll, or a goblin, or something." Soon he's drinking ten bottles of milk a day and pulling toys apart with his bare hands. Try as they might, the doctors can't find anything wrong with him. And, for a while at least, the Lovatts put up with "Neanderthal baby," even as he emits "thick, raucous cries" and gives everybody "the creeps."

Predictably, the Lovatts turn out to be no match for Ben. How could they be? At one, Ben strangles both the cat and the dog. At six, he is hanging out on the street and "rush[ing] about on motorbikes or in borrowed cars." For someone with the right sense of humor, reading *The Fifth Child* can be an unbearably funny enterprise. Black comedy, of course, is not what Miss Lessing has in mind. She means to demonstrate the frailty—indeed the irrelevance—of traditional family roles in a world of "killing and hijackings; murders and thefts and kidnappings." Ben is the Lovatts' punishment "for thinking we could be happy. Happy because we decided we would be."

As the novel progresses, Harriet is overwhelmed with guilt at having given birth to such a shocking child. The "normal" society she lives in is more than willing to let her accept the responsibility. David is the worst of all. When Harriet refers to Ben as "our child," he responds, "Well, he certainly isn't mine." Eventually, David convinces Harriet to have Ben sent away to an institution where an indifferent staff will attempt to drug him into submission, then death.

Lessing has always written about women with candor and fierce loyalty. Her novel *The Golden Notebook*, for example, is a stunning, encyclopedic re-evaluation of gender roles. In *The Fifth Child*, Lessing again writes with considerable force as Harriet rejects the role she has been given as a woman and a mother. In the end, however, Lessing reinforces the very sexual stereotypes she appears to be battling. Harriet goes to reclaim her son, and the message seems to be that she alone is responsible for Ben's abnormality, and that women really are—above all else—mothers and wives. The novel complains about sexual stereotypes and conventional household politics, but it never manages to elude them.

Miss Lessing attempted to sketch out an alternative vision of the family in *The Good Terrorist* and was blunt about the difficulties such a project entails. In that book, Alice Mellings establishes a commune, hoping to come home at night "lit with the exaltation that comes from a day's satisfactory picketing and demonstrating and marching." With her young friends, she embraces every social issue she can think of: the plight of Ireland, the dumping of radioactive waste, "the ill-treatment of calves and chickens." Ultimately, however, concepts like family and property are just too strongly engrained: Alice's politics become fuzzy, and her commune becomes more and more like the Lovatts' house.

But while *The Good Terrorist* and *The Golden Notebook* are candid about personal and political conflicts, *The Fifth Child* is never anything more than vindictive. At times, the tone is arrogant and superior. At others, the prose is so lukewarm that one wants to blame the translator, only there isn't one: "It was a windy cold night, just after Christmas. The room was warm and wonderful. David wept. Dorothy wept. Harriet laughed and wept."

Miss Lessing has written more imaginatively and far more perceptively in the past. *The Fifth Child* is as angry a book as she has written, but in the end, the anger serves no purpose. There are no answers here—even the questions are hard to identify. Like Ella in *The Golden Notebook*, Doris Lessing seems to have found herself at an impasse: "All the time I'm thinking, we are all obsolete. What sort of doctor is it who sees his patients as symptoms of a world sickness?"

Source: Jeffrey Giles, Review of *The Fifth Child*, in *National Review*, Vol. 40, No. 11, June 10, 1988, pp. 51–52.

SOURCES

"Biography," in *DorisLessing.org*, http://www.dorislessing.org/biography.html (accessed April 3, 2011).

Giles, Jeffrey, Review of *The Fifth Child*, in *National Review*, Vol. 40, No. 11, June 10, 1988, p. 51.

"Great Britain: You Can Walk Across It on Grass," in *Time*, April 15, 1966, http://www.time.com/time/magazine/article/0,9171,835349,00.html (accessed April 8, 2011).

Hughes, Dominic, "The Size of the Average Family Is Getting Smaller," in *BBC News*, December 9, 2010, http://www.bbc.co.uk/news/health-11960183 (accessed April 4, 2011).

Kakutani, Michiko, "Family Relations, Society, and a Monstrous Baby," in *New York Times*, March 30, 1988.

Kizer, Carolyn, "Bad News for the Nice and Well-Meaning," in *New York Times*, April 3, 1988, http://www.nytimes.com/books/99/01/10/specials/lessing-fifth.html (accessed March 31, 2011).

Lessing, Doris, *The Fifth Child*, Knopf, 1988.

Ratcliffe, Anita, and Sarah Smith, "Fertility and Women's Education in the UK: A Cohort Analysis," in *Centre for Market and Public Organisation*, December 2006, http://www.bristol.ac.uk/cmpo/publications/papers/2007/wp165.pdf (accessed April 4, 2011).

Rothstein, Mervyn, "The Painful Nurturing of Doris Lessing's *Fifth Child*," in *New York Times*, June 14, 1988, http://www.nytimes.com/books/99/01/10/specials/lessing-child.html (accessed March 31, 2011).

Rubenstein, Roberta, "Doris Lessing's Fantastic Children," in *Doris Lessing: Border Crossings*, edited by Alice Rideout and Susan Watkins, Continuum, 2009, p. 69.

Sinkler, Rebecca Pepper, "Goblins and Bad Girls," in *New York Times*, April 3, 1988, http://www.nytimes.com/books/99/01/10/specials/lessing-fifth.html (accessed March 31, 2011).

"Teen Pregnancy Rates Lowest for over 20 Years," in *Direct.gov.uk*, February 8, 2008, http://www.direct.gov.uk/en/Nl1/Newsroom/DG_072829 (accessed April 4, 2011).

"The UK Family: In Statistics," in *BBC News*, November 6, 2007, http://news.bbc.co.uk/2/hi/uk_news/7071611.stm (accessed April 4, 2011).

Weardon, Graeme, "Youth Unemployment Hits Record High," in *Guardian* (London, England), January 19, 2011, http://www.guardian.co.uk/business/2011/jan/19/youth-unemployment-heads-towards-1-million (accessed April 4, 2011).

Young, Hugo, *The Iron Lady: A Biography of Margaret Thatcher*, Farrar Straus Giroux, 1989, pp. 316–18.

FURTHER READING

Ingersoll, Earl G., ed., *Doris Lessing: Conversations*, Ontario Review Press, 2000.
This book includes twenty-four interviews with Lessing, spanning a period of several decades.

Pickering, Jean, *Understanding Doris Lessing*, University of South Carolina Press, 1990.
This is a concise guide to Lessing's work up to and including *The Fifth Child*. It includes an annotated bibliography, or list of her works accompanied by brief descriptive notes.

Pifer, Ellen, *Demon or Doll: Images of the Child in Contemporary Writing and Culture*, University Press of Virginia, 2000.
Pifer discusses the ambivalent view of the child presented in a range of contemporary fiction, including *The Fifth Child*.

Robbins, Ruth, "(Not Such) Great Expectations: Unmaking Maternal Ideals in *The Fifth Child* and *We Need to Talk about Kevin*," in *Doris Lessing: Border Crossings*, edited by Alice Rideout and Susan Watkins, Continuum, 2009, pp. 99–106.
Robbins discusses the theme of maternity in *The Fifth Child*, pointing out that it breaks with the culturally accepted view.

SUGGESTED SEARCH TERMS

Doris Lessing

The Fifth Child AND Doris Lessing

horror fiction

changeling

troll

Swinging London

Thatcherism

England AND 1980s

Frankenstein

Neanderthal

horror fiction AND Doris Lessing

Gone with the Wind

1939 Margaret Mitchell's first and only novel, *Gone with the Wind*, was a best seller even before its first publication on June 30, 1936. Even with a higher-than-usual sales price, the initial printing of ten thousand copies quickly ran out, and by the time of the official release, a hundred thousand more copies were printed. The book has sold more than thirty million copies, often outselling the current best seller in any given year.

This phenomenal success carried over to the 1939 film version of the book, which producer David O. Selznick won the rights to make with a record-breaking bid a month after the book's release. Over the course of three years, the public watched as Selznick Studios underwent a very public process of auditioning famous and not-so-famous actors for the key roles that had so quickly become ingrained in the popular imagination, spending a fortune to design sets and costumes and to recreate the burning of Atlanta, one of the centerpieces of the novel. The resulting film was well worth the effort, earning thirteen Academy Award nominations (a record that would stand for the next twenty years) and yielding what many consider to be one of the finest examples of moviemaking ever to come from the Hollywood studio system. Adjusted for inflation, it is still the highest-grossing film of all time, beating out such blockbusters as *Star Wars*, *Avatar*, and *E.T.: The Extraterrestrial*.

Gone with the Wind, film and book, follows the story of Scarlett O'Hara, a spoiled rich girl

raised on a Southern plantation, and her struggles as the Civil War destroys the world she knew. Lying to get her way, marrying for money when she has to, and even killing when her own life is on the line, Scarlett is driven by both love and necessity to be a strong woman when she was raised to be genteel and decorative.

PLOT SUMMARY

Gone with the Wind opens with an overture, with selections from the soundtrack playing over a richly layered picture of the Georgia sky. The overture is a tradition in theater, to give audiences time to settle in their seats before the show. It is not necessary in a film because late audience members entering the theater cannot interrupt the performers who were filmed months or years earlier. The later intermission, which also plays music over a still screen shot, may not seem relevant to viewers who can pause or skip over parts of the film, but for audiences viewing this nearly four-hour film in theaters, the intermission afforded a necessary break.

The action begins with sixteen-year-old Scarlett O'Hara sitting on the steps of her family home, called Tara, talking with the Tarleton twins from a nearby plantation. The boys are excited about the coming war, but Scarlett finds this subject boring. The subject changes to the upcoming barbecue at the Wilkes plantation. When they tell her that Ashley Wilkes is to announce his engagement to Melanie Hamilton at that barbecue, Scarlett is stricken, unable to admit her secret love for Ashley. She later talks to her father, Gerald O'Hara, who worries that her interest in Ashley might be imprudent, reminding Scarlett her that most of the young men in the county want to marry her. Gerald gives a brief speech about the importance of owning land; this did not occur in the novel but was added for the film.

During the family's prayers, Scarlett decides that Ashley is marrying Melanie because he does not know how she feels about him, and she vows to tell him.

At the Wilkes's barbecue, Scarlett makes a point of flirting with all of the boys, to make Ashley jealous. Charles Hamilton, Melanie's brother, is dumbfounded by her attention, but the other women notice that she is being shameless.

While all of the ladies are supposed to be napping upstairs, Scarlett sneaks downstairs to tell Ashley about her love. She overhears Rhett Butler, a visitor from Charleston, South Carolina, anger the other men when he raises doubts about the South's prospects for the war. Ashley talks to Scarlett in the library of the house, and although Scarlett gets an admission of love from him, he repeats his intention to marry Melanie. When he leaves, Scarlett finds out that Rhett has heard her confession of love.

The firing on Fort Sumter, which began the Civil War, is announced, to general jubilation. Angry and jealous, Scarlett watches Ashley kiss Melanie as he prepares to go and enlist. Scarlett accepts a proposal of marriage from foolish Charles Hamilton out of spite.

A double wedding is held, and within a week comes news that Charles has died of measles and pneumonia before even reaching the battlefield.

Social standards require Scarlett to dress and behave as a widow, even though she does not miss Charles. Her mother offers to let her move to Charles's home town, Atlanta, to live with Melanie and Aunt Pittypat, who raised Charles. Scarlett accepts, hoping to see Ashley when he comes home to Melanie on furloughs.

Scarlett attends a ball to raise money to help the Confederate army, even though it is considered inappropriate for a widow to do so. Rhett Butler is introduced as a brave hero, a blockade runner who is getting goods through Union ships that are blockading Southern ports. When Dr. Meade announces an auction for dancing with the eligible women, Rhett offers an enormous sum for a dance with Scarlett. Her acceptance, done in the name of supporting the troops, scandalizes Aunt Pittypat and Mrs. Meade. Their displeasure pleases Scarlett.

Word comes of the massive casualties at the battle of Gettysburg. Scarlett and Melanie are relieved to hear that Ashley has survived, even though many others, including Dr. Meade's son and both Tarleton twins, have died. Ashley comes home for Christmas, and Melanie gives him a coat that she has made for him. Scarlett reasserts her love for him and gives him a sash made from one of her dresses. Ashley makes her promise to look after Melanie.

Scarlett and Melanie work with Dr. Meade in the hospital during the siege of Atlanta. Scarlett runs into Frank Kennedy, the beau of her

FILM TECHNIQUE

- *Gone with the Wind* is considered one of the most impressive early uses of the Technicolor film process, the most advanced system for filming movies in color known at the time. The Technicolor technique involves cameras that shoot footage with three strips of film at once, in red, blue, and green. These are later combined to reproduce the entire world of colors. Compared with modern methods, such as digital film, Technicolor films may seem pale, but at a time when most films were presented in black and white, the realism of Technicolor startled audiences.

- This film is presented using a full color palette, but the production designers have given particular emphasis to red. Red is the color of the Georgia clay and the dust that rises in the streets from it, as well as the skies when the sun is setting. When Scarlett and Rhett escape Atlanta, the background is filled with red from the fires behind them. It is the color of the staircase at the Butlers' Georgia house and, as the traditional signifier of harlotry, red is the color of the dress that Rhett forces Scarlett to wear to Ashley's birthday party. Red is the color of passion and intensity, contrasting war and its aftermath with genteel plantation life.

- Matte painting is a technique that is used to fill in landscapes and backgrounds without having to build intricate sets. Areas in the background of the set are painted black, and the scene is later filled in with paintings, which are added to the film during processing to imply the depth of the scene. Selznick used this technique to show the long drive to Twelve Oaks, for instance, and the fields surrounding Tara.

- A panning shot follows a character's motion, laterally (to the side), but panning out pulls the camera back to show a particular character in context, taking in more and more of the surroundings as the camera moves. One of the most famous panning out shots in film history is the scene of the wounded soldiers at the Atlanta train station. The scene begins with a close-up on Scarlett's face, but the camera moves back to reveal more and more injured men until it reaches a point where the scope of devastation, spreading into the distance in all directions, is almost unimaginable.

- An establishing shot shows the setting of a scene, often from a distance. In *Gone with the Wind*, establishing shots are used to give audiences a sense of the film's epic grandeur, reminding them of the story's big picture. There are establishing shots showing the great size of the plantations; the bustle in the streets of Atlanta under siege and, later, being rebuilt; the can-can show in New Orleans; and the shattering stained glass window that shows the struggle for normalcy during the shelling of Atlanta. Other films with tighter budgets would suggest these locales with smaller establishing shots, but here they serve to capture the sweep of history as a backdrop to the human story of Scarlett O'Hara.

- *Gone with the Wind* uses well-established conventions from live theater. The film begins with a long musical overture, pauses in the middle with an intermission that turns into an "Entr'acte," and ends with a title card that simply says "Exit Music." These segments were familiar to theater goers, but films usually use the beginning and the end for running credits. This film draws a comparison between itself and theater, which was, at the time, generally considered a more refined and important art form than motion pictures.

sister Suellen, on a stretcher. Disgusted with death and sorrow, she leaves and steps outside, only to find the streets of Atlanta in chaos, with enemy shells exploding not far away. She sees Big Sam, the foreman at Tara before the war, and learns that her mother is ill with typhoid fever. She wants to go home to Tara, but Melanie is having a difficult pregnancy and cannot be moved until her baby is born. Scarlett's maid, Prissy, says that she knows how to handle the baby's birth.

A title card tells viewers that the siege of Atlanta lasted thirty-five days. The streets are deserted, and a passing soldier tells Scarlett that the Union army is coming. He suggests that she leave town immediately, but she finds Melanie in labor upstairs. Scarlett goes to the hospital for the doctor and finds the streets jammed with thousands of injured soldiers. She returns to the Hamilton home and finds that Prissy lied about knowing how to deliver a baby.

After Scarlett delivers the baby, Prissy is sent downtown to find Rhett at a party in Belle Watling's place. He steals a horse and carriage and arrives at the house soon to pick them up. Scarlett breaks down and cries in Rhett's arms, so he offers to take her through the Union army lines to Tara. Their escape from Atlanta takes them past the ammunition depot, which the fleeing Confederate army has set on fire, providing one of the most famous scenes in film history.

On the road outside of town, Rhett leaves Scarlett to join the Confederate army, even though their defeat at Atlanta ensures the futility of their cause. Before leaving, he expresses his love for Scarlett and kisses her, but she stubbornly pushes him away. Scarlett, Prissy, Melanie, and Melanie's child Beau arrive to find Tara the only plantation in the area still standing. Scarlett's mother is dead of typhoid fever, and her father has been driven half insane. Scarlett takes charge, and the remaining servants (Pork, Mammy, and Prissy) pester her for instructions. Crazed with hunger, she digs a turnip out of the ground and eats it, though it makes her ill. Looking to the sky, Scarlett declares, "As God is my witness, I'll never be hungry again."

Music plays over a title card announcing "Intermission," which then changes to "Entr'acte" (a term from musical theater, indicating a musical interlude between the acts of a performance).

The second half of the film begins with Scarlett and her two sisters and the remaining servants working the fields of Tara themselves.

A lone Union soldier, a deserter (though in the novel he is one of Sherman's soldiers), comes into the house. With a pistol in one hand and her mother's jewel box in the other, he accosts

Scarlett, and she shoots him in the face. She and Melanie empty his pockets and hide the body before her sisters or other soldiers can find out about it.

The war is officially over, the South is defeated, and local governments are overtaken with politicians, usually from the North, called carpetbaggers. Tara falls under the power of Jonas Wilkerson, the Northern-born former overseer of Tara. Old neighbors move into Tara, including Suellen's boyfriend Frank Kennedy, who asks Scarlett, as head of the family, for Suellen's hand in marriage.

Ashley, presumed dead, returns after being released from a Union prison. Melanie runs to him; Mammy keeps Scarlett from running to him.

Scarlett finds out that the taxes have been raised to an amount too high for her to pay. When she finds that Ashley cannot help her raise the money needed, she breaks down crying, and they end up kissing. He admits his love for her but declares that he will not leave Melanie and their baby. Ashley tells Scarlett that she loves the land even more than she loves him.

Wilkerson comes to offer to buy Tara before it is taken away by the sheriff for unpaid taxes. Scarlett drives him away. Her father chases Wilkerson and, falling from his horse, is killed.

Scarlett decides to ask Rhett for the tax money. Thinking she needs to look like a woman of means, she makes a new dress from the curtains and visits him in the Atlanta jail where he is held. He can tell from her hands, however, that she is lying about being financially comfortable and has been performing hard labor. Scarlett offers herself to him, even though she knows he will not marry her, but he says he cannot access his money.

Leaving, she passes through Atlanta, which is being reconstructed, and sees the new store Frank Kennedy has opened. He mentions making thousands of dollars and wanting to live with Suellen in Atlanta, but Scarlett lies and tells him that Suellen is marrying someone else. She flirts with him, and in the next scene, she is married to him, writing a check to pay Tara's taxes.

Scarlett asks Ashley to start a lumber business to branch off from Frank Kennedy's store, but Ashley says that he is going to go to New York to work in a bank. Scarlett pretends to cry, which brings Melanie, who insists that Ashley stay in Atlanta and work for Scarlett.

At the Wilkes and Kennedy sawmill, Scarlett is a ruthless boss and a ruthless businesswoman, paying low wages to convicts to work in subhuman conditions and dealing with the carpetbaggers from the North. When Rhett meets her in the street, he is bemused that she is married to yet another man she does not love and is still pining for Ashley.

Going to her sawmill, Scarlett drives her carriage through Shantytown, where unemployed men live. She is attacked by two, but Big Sam steps forward to save her. Scarlett's husband, Frank, hearing about the attack, goes out to what he calls "a political meeting." As the women sit nervously sewing at the Wilkes' house that night, Rhett comes and tells Melanie that her husband and his friends are going to attack the vagrants of Shantytown, but the Northerners have set a trap for them. Northern troops come and surround the house, but Rhett and Dr. Meade bring Ashley home pretending to be drunk and to have spent the night at Belle Watling's house of prostitution. Actually, Ashley has been shot in the fight at Shantytown. Frank Kennedy has been killed.

Widowed again, Scarlett falls into a depression. She is afraid that she will go to hell for the way she treated Frank, and she drinks heavily. Rhett visits her and, with a sarcastic tone, proposes marriage. Scarlett accepts, but she admits that she has done so only for his money. They agree that this, at least, is honest.

On their honeymoon, Scarlett has nightmares about her past behavior. To comfort her, Rhett takes her home to Tara. They plan on rebuilding the plantation to the state it was in before the war.

When their baby, Bonnie Blue, is born, life seems perfect for Rhett and Scarlett. Rhett is delighted with his daughter, looking forward to a future in which she will be accepted into the highest realms of society. Scarlett, however, still dreaming of Ashley, withdraws her affection from Rhett, declaring that she will have no more babies with him. They continue to behave as a happy couple in public, though, courting the local matrons so that Bonnie will rise in society.

At the lumber mill, Scarlett becomes morose during a discussion about the old days before the war, and Ashley takes her in his arms to comfort her just as his sister, India, walks in. That night, Scarlett plans to stay home from Ashley's birthday party, knowing that everyone is gossiping about her, but Rhett insists she go and that she

wear a bright red dress, the color a prostitute would wear. Melanie welcomes her to the party, despite what she knows about the embrace between Ashley and Scarlett. Later, at home, Rhett is drunk when Scarlett comes downstairs. He threatens her and expresses remorse about her love for Ashley, and then he sweeps her off her feet and carries her upstairs, two steps at a time. For the first time in a long time, they spend the night together.

The next morning Scarlett feels good until Rhett enters the room and, unexpectedly, suggests that they should divorce. He leaves with Bonnie for a trip to Europe. Bonnie misses her mother, though, and so Rhett is forced to bring her home to Atlanta. He intends to drop Bonnie off and leave, but Scarlett announces that she is pregnant. When Rhett sarcastically suggests that an accident might spare her from having his baby, she swings at him and falls down the stairs, causing a miscarriage. In his grief and guilt, Rhett does not want to see her, but Melanie convinces him that Scarlett still loves him. She also explains that she is pregnant, even though the trauma of having her son Beau during the siege of Atlanta has weakened her.

While Rhett tries to convince Scarlett to try their marriage again, Bonnie rides by on her horse, announcing her intention to jump a hurdle. Scarlett remembers that her father died trying the same thing and shouts out, but it is too late: Bonnie falls from the horse and dies.

Rhett and Scarlett blame each other for their child's death. Melanie visits Rhett as he sits by Bonnie's body. When she leaves, she collapses before talking to Scarlett.

Two days later, Melanie is bedridden in her home, dying, and asks to see Scarlett. Dr. Meade warns her to not disturb Melanie by unloading her guilty conscience on her. Before Melanie dies, she makes Scarlett promise to look after Beau and Ashley. Her final words to Scarlett are that Rhett really does love her.

Leaving her room, Scarlett falls into Ashley's arms. Rhett leaves before he can hear Ashley tell her that he has always loved Melanie, not her.

Scarlett races home, realizing that she loves Rhett, only to find him packing his bag. She begs him to take her with him to Charleston, but he refuses. When Scarlett asks where she should go and what she should do, Rhett delivers one of the most famous lines in film history: "Frankly, my dear, I don't give a damn." In the novel, the line differs slightly; Selznick added the word "frankly," making it one of the most memorable lines in film history.

Scarlett, crying, recalls the voice of her father, telling her that land is the only thing that matters. She determines that she will go home to Tara and think of some way to win Rhett back.

CHARACTERS

Bonnie Blue Butler

Rhett and Scarlett's daughter is named Eugenia Victoria in the novel, after two European queens. In the film, that name is suggested, but she is immediately given the nickname "Bonnie Blue," which stays with her.

Bonnie represents Rhett Butler's hopes for the future. Although his life has been too scandalous for him to ever be accepted at the highest echelons of Georgia society, he thinks that Bonnie can be socially accepted when she grows up.

Rhett, angry at finding Scarlett in Ashley's arms, takes Bonnie away to Europe, hoping to keep her away from scandal. Bonnie is constantly terrorized in the night, calling out for her mother. Rhett returns to Atlanta to drop her off with Scarlett, and he stays as well.

Bonnie loves her horse. She dies in a horseback riding accident at a young age.

Rhett Butler

Rhett is played by Clark Gable. Throughout the film he is referred to as "Captain" Butler, one of the few indicators of his true profession: in the novel he is identified as the captain of a ship, his means of running through the Union's naval blockades. Although he is considered a hero of the war for defying the enemy so bravely, Rhett is very quick to note that he only does so for money. He is a rogue and a scoundrel, with a bad reputation for having been thrown out of West Point and for having ruined the reputation of a girl in Charleston, which caused his family to disown him.

Rhett has a cynical worldview. At the barbecue at Twelve Oaks, he alienates himself from the men who are enthusiastic about the coming war by pointing out the likelihood that the South will be defeated. During his relationship with Scarlett, he frequently makes frequent sarcastic remarks about her professed love for Ashley Wilkes. Still, he sees in Scarlett a person with the same ironic detachment that he has toward the world, and he is devoted to her throughout the war years. After she says she is glad that he did not try to be noble by joining the army, Rhett has an introspective moment, and he goes to join the army when it is on the verge of defeat. That, along with his respect for Melanie, shows that he is a decent man.

When he sees that his love for Scarlett will never amount to anything, he transfers his hopes to his daughter, Bonnie Blue, throwing himself into doing whatever is necessary to assure her place in the world. After Bonnie's death is followed by Melanie's death, he feels that there will be no way to win Scarlett's love. Even though she comes and declares her love for him, Rhett is cold to her and walks away from their torturous romance.

Scarlett Butler

See Katie Scarlett O'Hara

Dilcey

Dilcey is a character in the novel, but not in the film. She is a slave owned by John Wilkes. When she marries Pork, the valet of Gerald O'Hara, O'Hara goes to Wilkes and buys Dilcey and her daughter, Prissy, for three thousand dollars, so that their family can be together at Tara.

Johnny Gallagher

Gallagher is the man Scarlett hires to force convicts to work for low wages at her sawmill.

Charles Hamilton

Charles, played by Rand Brooks, is the brother of Melanie Hamilton. He is a visitor at Twelve Oaks during the barbecue that starts the film. Like most of the young men present, Charles is smitten with Scarlett, but he is awkward with her. The novel explains that his upbringing in the home of Aunt Pittypat Hamilton left him socially inept, nervous, and effeminate. When Ashley publicly announces his engagement to Melanie, Scarlett spontaneously announces that she and Charles are engaged too.

Charles is married to Scarlett for a week before shipping out to the army. He dies of pneumonia before ever engaging in battle. In the novel, his son Wade is born months after his death. Being his widow gives Scarlett an excuse to move into the Hamilton house with Melanie, to be close to news from Ashley.

Aunt "Pittypat" Hamilton

Aunt Pittypat raised Charles and Melanie in Atlanta after their parents died. The novel explains that she has a brother, Henry, who lives in town and manages her financial affairs. Pittypat is played in the film by Laura Hope Crews as a nervous woman who needs her smelling salts constantly at her side, to revive her when she faints, as she does frequently. As an upstanding member of Atlanta society, she is scandalized by the slightest things, such as seeing the recently widowed Scarlett dance with Rhett at the charity ball. Before the war comes to Atlanta and upsets the social order, Pittypat represents the delicate sensibilities of the Southern aristocracy, but she eventually has to leave town without facing the horrors that Scarlett and Melanie face while living in the war zone.

Scarlett Hamilton

See Katie Scarlett O'Hara

Wade Hamilton

Wade is Scarlett's child with her first husband, Charles Hamilton. This character does not appear in the film version of the story.

Ella Lorna Kennedy

Ella Lorna is the daughter that Scarlett has with her second husband, Frank Kennedy. She is a character in the novel, but she does not appear in the film.

Frank Kennedy

Frank Kennedy, played by Carroll Nye, is established early on as the romantic interest of Scarlett's sister Suellen. He is a quiet, shy man, much older than she is. When the war is over, he appears at Tara among the locals, those from the nearby plantations whose homes have been destroyed. When he asks Scarlett, who has become the head of the O'Hara family, if he can marry Suellen, her only reaction is to be amused that their marriage has not been arranged sooner.

When the taxes on Tara are due, though, and Scarlett is in Atlanta to see Rhett, she finds that Frank's store is prospering. She lies, telling him that Suellen, living miles away at Tara, is engaged to another man, and she seduces him. As Mrs. Kennedy, Scarlett takes over the business, running it in a more ruthless, unscrupulous way than Frank would have.

Frank Kennedy dies when he and several other men raid the camp of homeless men where Scarlett was attacked, mirroring the historical rise of the Ku Klux Klan.

Scarlett Kennedy

See Katie Scarlett O'Hara

Mammy

Mammy was the maid of Scarlett's mother when she was young. She is Scarlett's maid and later is a maid to Scarlett's daughter. She is played by Hattie McDaniel, who beat out Olivia de Havilland (Melanie) for the Academy Award for Best Supporting Actress that year.

Because she is such a long-time fixture in the O'Hara household, Mammy feels a responsibility for the family's social standing. She issues orders to young Scarlett that she is to behave like a young lady. Still, she is a servant and does not have the authority to enforce her orders.

When she moves to the Butler house with Scarlett, Mammy is suspicious of Rhett, who has a bad social reputation. He makes a point of winning her over with gifts and with honest talk, drinking whiskey with her to celebrate on the night that Bonnie Blue is born.

Dr. Meade

Dr. Meade is an older member of Atlanta society. During the war, he has the great responsibility of running the hospital, a nearly impossible task. He is one of the men who participates in the raid on the homeless camp, Shantytown, where Frank Kennedy dies and Ashley is wounded.

Mrs. Meade

Dr. Meade's wife, a respectable society matron in Atlanta, is scandalized by Scarlett's decision to dance with Rhett at a benefit ball. She is played by Leona Roberts.

Carreen O'Hara

Scarlett's youngest sister Carreen, played by film and, later, television star Ann Rutherford, is the first victim of Scarlett's acquisitive nature. When she was thirteen, before the novel or the film begins, Carreen (short for "Caroline Irene") was in love with Brent Tarleton, but her romantic hopes were dashed when Scarlett enchanted him. Carreen never gets over Brent, and the novel explains that she joins a convent when she grows up.

Ellen Robillard O'Hara

Ellen, played by Barbara O'Neil, is Scarlett's mother. The novel relates how her history mirrors that of her daughter: as a teenager, Ellen was in love with Philippe Robillard, her cousin, and agreed to marry Gerald O'Hara, who was nearly thirty years older than her, only when she found out about Philippe's death. She made this sudden reversal without revealing her secret sorrow, just as Scarlett accepts Charles Hamilton as her husband when she finds Ashley will not have her.

Ellen is a trained medical attendant. She delivers Emmy Slattery's illegitimate baby and promptly demands that her husband fire his overseer, Jonas Wilkerson, who fathered the child but will not marry Emmy. Later, while Scarlett is in Georgia, Ellen contracts typhoid fever when called to care for the Slattery household, and she dies the day before Scarlett returns home to Tara.

Gerald O'Hara

Gerald is Scarlett's father; he is played in the film by Thomas Mitchell, with a broad Irish brogue. Mitchell's novel recounts at length how he came to America with little money and proceeded to build his fortune as a cotton farmer, designing and building his dream house, Tara, in the North Georgia hills.

Gerald is an enthusiastic horseman. In the film, he walks with a limp, a reference to a fall he took while jumping his horse. Because he was once injured, he rides in secret, keeping his more dangerous moves out of sight of his wife. Scarlett sees him jumping his horse and uses the information to blackmail him into keeping quiet about her interest in Ashley.

After the Union army invades his house and burns his cotton stores and his wife dies of typhoid, Gerald is driven mad. He is left a puzzled, uncertain man who talks about his wife as if she were still alive.

Angered when his former farm overseer, Wilkerson, threatens to buy Tara, Gerald rides off after him like the champion horseman he once was. He falls from the horse, breaks his neck, and dies.

Katie Scarlett O'Hara

Scarlett O'Hara is the protagonist of both the novel and the film. She is played by Vivian Leigh, in a performance that won her the Academy Award for Best Actress. Scarlett is a vain, hardheaded, calculating, spoiled girl who finds herself frustrated by love and by war.

Scarlett is sixteen years old at the start of the film, and already her one weakness is present; though she takes a cynical view of everything else she encounters, she is at the mercy of her love for Ashley Wilkes. She believes he must love her too, and her scheme to make him acknowledge it leads her to expose her feelings to Rhett Butler, then a stranger. In the coming years, Rhett confesses that he loved her from the moment he met her.

Scarlett's first marriage, to Charles Hamilton, is meant to make Ashley jealous. Her second marriage, to Frank Kennedy, is to gain the money needed to pay the taxes, so that Tara will not be sold at auction. In each case, Scarlett steals her husband from a woman who has been in a long-term relationship with him. When each husband dies, she is annoyed that society forces her to pretend to grieve.

The one man on whom Scarlett's charm has no effect is Rhett Butler. When in need, she calls on him and acts coquettishly. Rather than bending to her will, as all other men do, Rhett is annoyed by her attempts to use him. Ironically, though, he is in love with her, and so will always do whatever he can to help her anyway. Still, Rhett is not afraid to incur her anger, which is usually a result of her frustration at being unable to control him.

Although Scarlett is willing to manipulate people shamelessly, she does have a sense of honor. She moves to Atlanta during the war to be near the home that Ashley will return to, but having promised him that she would look after Melanie, she sticks by Melanie's side through the siege of Atlanta. The coping skills she learns in the war zone are the skills that she applies to restoring Tara. She cares about her family estate more than she cares about most of the people in her life.

It is only after Melanie's death at the end of the film that Scarlett accepts the fact that Ashley does not love her, that he has truly loved Melanie all along. Free to follow her heart for the first time since her sheltered childhood, she realizes that she does love Rhett, but when she tells him so, he leaves her anyway.

Suellen O'Hara

Scarlett's sister, Suellen (short for "Susan Ellen"), has a relationship with Frank Kennedy at the beginning of the film. She waits for him through-out the war and is prepared to marry him, even though he is financially ruined. When he begins to prosper, however, her sister Scarlett tells Frank that Suellen has met another man and steals him away.

Uncle Peter

Uncle Peter is the ancient coachman in Aunt Pittypat's household. The novel explains his considerable role in the upbringing of Charles and Melanie in a house that lacked any other senior male presence. He is played by Eddie "Rochester" Anderson, a famous comic actor of the time who was much younger than his character.

Pork

The novel explains that Pork was Gerald O'Hara's valet when he was single. In the film, he is one of just a few servants who stay at Tara after the Union army has freed the slaves.

Prissy

When Gerald O'Hara buys Dilcey from John Wilkes, he also buys Dilcey's daughter, Prissy, whom he gives to Scarlett as a maid. Prissy accompanies Scarlett to Atlanta to live in the Hamilton house and to tend to Melanie's child, Wade. Prissy is lazy, deceitful, and proud, nearly causing catastrophe when she claims that she can handle the birth of Melanie's child but then, when Melanie is in labor, confessing that she actually knows nothing about childbirth. Actress Butterfly McQueen's exaggerated performance makes Prissy one of the most memorable characters in the film.

Big Sam

Big Sam, played by Everett Brown, is the field foreman at Tara until the war breaks out. Scarlett sees him briefly in Atlanta when he is passing through with other slaves who have been conscripted to dig ditches for the Confederate war effort. After the war, he is living in Shantytown when he hears her being attacked by road bandits, and he races to her rescue.

Emmy Slattery

Emmy is a member of the "white trash" family that lives near Tara. Ellen O'Hara is often called on to provide them with medical care. At the beginning of the film, Ellen comes home from delivering Emmy's stillborn baby, whose father is Jonas Wilkerson, the overseer at Tara. The

O'Haras dismiss Wilkerson because of this misconduct. After the war, though, Wilkerson, rich and powerful, has married Emmy, and he offers to buy Tara from the O'Haras, because Emmy has always wanted to live there.

Brent Tarleton

Brent and his twin brother Stuart are mischievous young men. They play cards, drink, flirt with Scarlett, and have been expelled from one college after another. The only person they claim to fear is their harsh mother. When war is announced, both Tarleton boys enlist immediately, and they are both killed at the Battle of Gettysburg.

Stuart Tarleton

Stuart Tarleton is played by George Reeves, who went on to fame in the title role of *The Adventures of Superman* on television. Stuart and his twin brother Brent compete for Scarlett's attention. They have both been expelled from a series of colleges and are eager to enlist in the army when the war breaks out. Both Tarleton brothers die at the Battle of Gettysburg.

Belle Watling

Belle, played by famed character actress Ona Munson, runs a saloon and house of prostitution, although the film only makes oblique references to her actual profession. She is a very good friend and confidante of Rhett Butler.

Although her job makes her wealthy, Belle is very self-conscious about her low social standing. When she wants to make a donation to help the Confederate cause, she is turned away, and has to seek out Melanie Wilkes to take her money. Still, she warns Melanie to be careful about being seen talking to her, a warning Belle repeats later after Melanie seeks her out to thank her for saving Ashley's life after the raid on Shantytown.

Ashley Wilkes

Ashley, played by Leslie Howard, is Scarlett's idea of a true Southern gentleman. He is educated, courtly, polite, and patriotic. Her love for him blinds her to who he really is, though. Again and again, Ashley expresses his doubts about the nobility of war, but Scarlett refuses to hear it. She also refuses to listen to him when he tries to turn away her romantic overtures. When he plans to move away from her after the war, to go to New York and work in a bank, Scarlett traps him by crying until Melanie insists that he must stay in Atlanta to help Scarlett work her lumber mill. He objects to the way she treats the employees of their business, but Ashley's personality is not nearly as strong as Scarlett's.

Ashley tries to resist Scarlett, but he falls for her charms; he comes close to kissing her when he is home on furlough and ends up kissing her passionately in the barn after the war is over. Scarlett assumes that his response to her advances is because he loves her as much as she loves him, and it seems for a time that Ashley believes that, too. After Melanie's death, however, it becomes clear that she, not Scarlett, was the one true love of Ashley's life.

Beau Wilkes

Beau is the infant son of Ashley and Melanie Wilkes, born during the siege of Atlanta.

India Wilkes

Ashley Wilkes's sister is promised to marry Melanie's brother, Charles, at the beginning of the film, since it is a tradition that the Wilkes always marry their cousins. Scarlett charms Charles and convinces him to marry her, though. India's revenge comes years later, when she sees Scarlett and Ashley embracing and she spreads word of it to Ashley's wife.

Melanie Hamilton Wilkes

Melanie is played by Olivia de Havilland as a paragon of virtue. Her instinctual response to everyone is kindness, as shown in her two scenes with Belle Watling: while others of Melanie's social standing, including Scarlett, shun Belle because it would hurt their reputations to be seen with her, Melanie welcomes her company. Her good-heartedness even extends to slights done to her, as when she hears that Scarlett and Ashley have been caught in an embrace but still welcomes Scarlett to her party and invites her to join her and Ashley.

The only time Melanie is anything but charitable comes after Scarlett has killed an invading Union army deserter who has been looting the house. Melanie says that she is glad Scarlett killed him, and comes up with a quick lie to help Scarlett hide the body.

When Melanie finds that she is pregnant after the war, she knows that having another baby will be dangerous for her, because her first labor, during the burning of Atlanta, took a heavy toll on her body. Still, she is delighted at the prospect of being a mother again. She is too fragile, however, and she dies of complications before the child is born.

Jonas Wilkerson

Victor Jory plays Wilkerson, the overseer of Tara at the beginning of the film. The O'Hara family does not think well of Wilkerson because he is a Northerner. After attending to the birth and immediate death of Emmy Slattery's baby, Ellen O'Hara insists that her husband fire Wilkerson for impregnating Emmy and abandoning her. After the war, Wilkerson finds himself socially respectable. He is married to Emmy and is politically powerful. He wants to buy Tara for Emmy when the O'Haras cannot pay the taxes, but Scarlett throws mud at him and chases him away.

THEMES

Honor

In the rolling text that follows the credits, *Gone with the Wind* compares the old South to a land of "Knights and Ladies Fair," but the actual story that follows raises questions about the system of honor that marked that place and time. In an early scene at the Wilkes plantation, for instance, most of the men are naïve in their excitement about the prospect of war. Even though Rhett and Ashley explain rationally why the South is destined to lose, their reason is viewed as a sign that they lack honor because they do not believe that the South must win. Throughout most of the film, in fact, Rhett is disdainful of the idea of the "Southern gentleman," yet he appears to the audience as more intelligent and practical than those who follow a pointless code of chivalry.

The rules pertaining to women's honor are even more directly skewed in the book and in the movie. Before the war, women are considered dishonorable for such obscure reasons as being out with men unchaperoned (which is why Rhett is considered to have "ruined" a girl in Charleston), for discussing financial matters, or for being seen in public during the year-long mourning period. These and hundreds of other unstated rules were taught to girls throughout their lives.

Though the novel and the book show some nostalgia for this system of honor, they also show

READ, WATCH, WRITE

- There is an ongoing controversy about Butterfly McQueen's portrayal of Prissy in this film. Some viewers feel that she is an ugly stereotype of an unintelligent and untrustworthy slave, but others see in the actress's performance an admirable slyness that indicates will and intelligence. Watch McQueen's scenes in *Gone with the Wind*, possibly in groups, and create an online blog to debate whether her character is admirable or offensive. Post your opinion, backed by facts from the film, and comment on at least three other posts on the same subject.

- Films are often identified by their directors, but *Gone with the Wind* is almost always discussed as the brainchild of its producer, David O. Selznick. Today, film reviewers recognize the touches of certain producers, such as Judd Apatow, Tyler Perry, Stephen Spielberg, or Avi Arid, regardless of who stars in or produces their films. Present scenes from your favorite film to your class using PowerPoint or Slideshare to explain what a producer does and how her or his vision ends up in the final film product. Be sure that the film is appropriate for classroom viewing.

- Read Harriet Beecher Stowe's novel about the lives of slaves, *Uncle Tom's Cabin*, published in 1852. This book, though sympathetic to its black characters, reinforced stereotypes that became ingrained in the minds of white Americans and that show themselves in *Gone with the Wind*. Use passages from Stowe's novel along with clips from *Gone with the Wind* that show characterizations that you believe have their basis in *Uncle Tom's Cabin*. Create a cause-and-effect chart or spreadsheet that shows the stereotypes in both the novel by Stowe and the film.

- Read *Olivia's Journey*, a young-adult novel by B. G. Lashbrooks, about an abused girl from Indiana who goes on the run with a fleeing Confederate deserter through Union territory at the end of the Civil War. Comparing this book with *Gone with the Wind*, make a list of stereotypes Southerners had about Northerners and vice versa. Do research to show what social factors these stereotypes were based on, and in an essay, explore their relationships with the truth.

- Watch *A Streetcar Named Desire*, the 1951 film that won Vivian Leigh her other Best Actress Academy Award. Her character in that film, Blanche Dubois, has much in common with Scarlett, if Scarlett were transplanted to a twentieth-century urban sitting. Show your class scenes from both films to identify acting techniques that Leigh used in fleshing out both Scarlett and Blanche, and use this explanation of acting technique to analyze the similarities between the two characters.

---

how foolish these rules can be. The most pointed example of this is the sense of shame carried by Belle Watling. Even though she is a generous supporter of the Southern cause and saves Ashley's life by providing him an alibi, Belle knows that, because she is a social outcast and a woman without "honor," it would poison Melanie's reputation to be seen with her. The film's position is more like Melanie's, viewing Belle for who she really is and not for her social position.

Antiheroes

The two most important men in Scarlett's life, Ashley and Rhett, represent two different aspects of the heroic ideal. Ashley is the traditional hero. He is handsome, intelligent, well-bred, and from a good family. He is a respected member of his community. He is strong, accepting his long internment in a prisoner of war camp without complaint. He is committed to the social order so completely that, as Scarlett views it, he marries a woman he does not love just to follow tradition, because Wilkeses always marry their cousins.

Rhett, on the other hand, is the antihero, the lone operator who follows his own individual moral code. He is a social outcast, having been driven away by his family in Charleston. He admits that he runs the Union army's blockades only because he can profit from doing so. When Scarlett comes to him desperate for money, he tricks her into agreeing to be his mistress, making it clear that he has no intention of marrying her, and then laughs at her when he reveals that he has no money to offer her.

Even though he does not match the image of heroism Scarlett was raised to admire, audiences can see the nobility in Rhett. He is modest, walking away from a challenge by Charles Hamilton even though, as Ashley explains, Rhett would almost certainly kill Charles in a duel. He is brave, driving a horse carriage through a burning city to save Scarlett and Melanie. He is loyal to Scarlett, courting her throughout her stay in Atlanta during the war even though she is interested in no one but Ashley. He is generous, redeeming Melanie's wedding ring for ten times its value so that she can feel that her obligation to the war effort is fulfilled. The fact that Rhett does all of these things with a bemused smile may make Scarlett think that he is not serious, but his ability to laugh in the face of adversity is a sign that he is a master of his fate.

Love

For all of the twelve years covered in this film, Scarlett believes that she is in love with Ashley and that he is in love with her. Ashley's interest in her is never entirely clear; before his marriage and when he is home on furlough from the army, he awkwardly avoids her advances, even though he is moved by her tears. After the war, when he is broken and filled with shame about his fear of the future and admires Scarlett's strength, he falls into a passionate kiss with her and admits that he does love her. When Melanie dies and there is nothing standing in their way, however, Scarlett realizes the truth, that Ashley really loved Melanie all along. At the same time, she realizes a greater truth: she loves Rhett, whom she has constantly pushed away throughout their relationship.

In Mitchell's novel, Rhett is less overt about his love for Scarlett, insisting that he admires her but has no illusions about romance. Film audiences, though, have a stronger, more immediate response to grand declarations of romance. Leaving her on the road between Atlanta and Tara, Rhett jokes about being a hero who deserves a hero's send-off, but then he also honestly and passionately declares that he loves her. Scarlett pushes him away, in that scene and through the coming years, because she is still holding out for Ashley. When she does return to Rhett, recognizing her love for him, he is in the process of leaving her, but she vows to herself that some day she will win him back.

Slavery

Like the novel, the film version of *Gone with the Wind* offers audiences a slave owner's perspective of slavery. For one thing, the black characters in the film seem content with the status quo. Unhappy or mistreated slaves are not shown, only slaves who feel at home in the slave system. Although the novel says that nearly a hundred slaves left Tara after the Union army invaded, the film shows only the few who stayed on the plantation, loyal to the O'Hara family. Their loyalty is understandable in the setting of the story, since they are accustomed to slave life. For instance, Mammy notes with pride that she has been a maid to three generations of O'Hara girls. Others feel a bond of loyalty with the people who owned them, as when, after the war, Big Sam, living in a camp of homeless men, runs to Scarlett's aid and becomes nearly homicidal with rage against her attackers.

As the film presents slavery, it is necessary for the former slaves to align themselves with their owners because most of the black characters lack sufficient intelligence or morals to live on their own. The most obvious example of this is Prissy, who is vain and deceitful but also cowardly and superstitious. Other black characters are treated only slightly better: Aunt Pittypat's footman Uncle Peter, for instance, is described in the novel as running the household while Pittypat dithers about decision making, but the film uses him as comic relief as he stalks a chicken in the rain. Prissy's mother, Dilcey, who Mitchell describes as bearing herself with grace and dignity, does not even appear in the film. In pre-Civil Rights era America, particularly in the segregated South, depictions of intelligent or independent black characters would have been opposed.

© *AF archive | Alamy*

STYLE

Epic

The word "epic" derives from the poetic tradition, where it was used to describe long poems that describe great sweeps of history, as in the *Iliad* and *Odyssey* of Homer, or the Mesopotamian *Epic of Gilgamesh*. Over time, the word has been applied to other literary forms, such as novels. Though it may be considered debatable whether a romantic film like *Gone with the Wind*, which uses the Civil War as its backdrop but never actually shows its battles, can be considered an epic in the truest sense, it is clear that Selznick intended the movie to capture the tone of an epic story. It takes place during a war, and it concerns the emotional extremes of love, death, betrayal, and desperation. It has a nationalistic theme, concerning itself with the Confederacy as a short-lived nation unto itself. Its central character, Scarlett O'Hara, overcomes the obstacles that hold her back. What is not epic in the story's scope is that its ending, in which Scarlett finally lets go of her obsession with Ashley, is more a personal decision than a heroic triumph.

One reason the film feels like an epic is the sheer grandeur of it. Its shooting budget was greater than had ever spent on any film production ($4,085,790), and audiences can see the effects of that budget on the screen, from huge, opulent sets to exact period costumes. The burning of Atlanta, for instance, presented a scene that was unimaginable for audiences accustomed to seeing films in black, white, and gray, showing Selznick's dedication to giving audiences a larger-than-life experience. Though not a traditional epic, this film fits the idea of the epic as a story that encompasses the sweep of history on a large scale.

Orchestration

Most people who have seen *Gone with the Wind* can hum at least the first phrase to its title tune, but though much has been written about the film's production, there has been little commentary on the work that Max Steiner did in composing its soundtrack. Steiner, previously known for composing the music for the 1933 blockbuster *King Kong*, went on to compose for Hollywood films for decades. In *Gone with the Wind*, audiences can hear traits that would continue throughout his works, such as separate motifs for the leading and supporting characters, the use of historically accurate music from the time the film took place, resilient melody and symphonic techniques mixed with nonsymphonic instruments, such as banjo, dobro, and harmonica. Though modern film composers have more leeway with their approaches to writing for film, Steiner imbued this film's soundtrack with more flair and creativity than audiences of the 1930s expected.

© *AF archive | Alamy*

CULTURAL CONTEXT

Historical Accuracy

Mitchell worked hard to establish the historical accuracy of the events surrounding the life of Scarlett O'Hara, checking the records for dates and locations of battles and troop movements mentioned in the story. From the general knowledge of the pending battle at Fort Sumter that starts the book to the resignation of Governor Bullock near the end in 1871, Mitchell, who was raised in Atlanta and was obsessed with Georgia history, specified the historic details of her novel.

In filming the story, David O. Selznick was scrupulous about getting the details right, faithful not only to the novel but also to historical accuracy. He had set designers pore through photographs of the Civil War era, for instance, to find details in drawing rooms and streets which they were to copy to make the movie's props. He ordered studio hands to find or, in some cases, create (from ground-up drainage tiles) soil that would resemble the red clay of Clayton County in northern Georgia. Actors were trained by vocal coaches suggested by Mitchell in the proper Georgia dialect that the author had in mind.

Where it served his purposes, Selznick diverged from Mitchell's vision. Tara, for instance, is described in the novel as a sprawling and unsightly place, but the film version of the mansion is stately and beautiful. It is hardly the sort of house that could be built by an uneducated immigrant with no

background in architecture, but it created the sort of visual effect that Selznick wanted, representing the genteel time that was in due course to be crushed by history.

Hayes Commission

Selznick's film was also hampered by the censors of the Hayes Commission, which enforced the production code of ethics that the Motion Pictures Producers and Distributors Association followed from 1930 until 1968. The Hayes Commission, named after Will D. Hayes, had the ultimate authority for what could and could not be depicted in movies, placing on them greater restraints than were placed on novels. Mitchell could, for instance, have Scarlett conclude that Wilkerson had fathered Emmy Slattery's baby, but the film could only allude obliquely to an out-of-wedlock pregnancy. Mitchell's novel also implied a sexual relationship between Belle Watling and Rhett and the clear acknowledgment that the establishment she ran was a house of prostitution, but the censors objected to both implications, and the screenplay was changed to accommodate them. Furthermore, the film standards board required Selznick to tone down some of the novel's sexual passion for the screen version. When Rhett takes Scarlett forcibly, Mitchell was able to render the scene with rough kissing, struggling, and bruising (though no explicitly sexual words), while Selznick had to suggest the violent passion of the scene with a sweeping camera shot of Clark Gable ascending a grand staircase with Vivian Leigh in his arms.

A clear distinction between the novel and the film is in the language: while the novel's Rhett used minor profanity casually, such words were forbidden by the code. His final line, telling Scarlett "I don't give a damn" had a resounding impact with audiences in 1939 because Selznick fought for use of the word "damn," which had not been heard in a film since the Hayes Commission was established.

CRITICAL OVERVIEW

When *Gone with the Wind* finally premiered in Atlanta, Georgia, in December 1939, the production had been in the public's attention since the novel's publication three years earlier. A cover story in *Time* magazine told the story of Selznick's long, public process of casting the key roles, especially the heavily covered search for the right actress to play Scarlett; the sequence of three directors (Michael Curtiz, Sam Wood, and finally Victor Fleming, whose name appears on the film); the ten or so writers who worked on the script; and the millions of dollars put into filming it. Ironically, the black actors who were so instrumental in the film's success were not allowed to attend the Atlanta premier because Georgia had Jim Crow (segregation) laws in place that prohibited integration in theaters.

The film was a success beyond anything Selznick could have hoped for. Reviews upon its release were almost universally glowing. However, as reported by Leonard J. Leff in *Atlantic Monthly*, the *Daily Worker*, published by the Communist Party of America, disapproved of the film's portrayal of race in the class system in the Confederacy.

More representative of the critical response was the review in the *Hollywood Spectator*, titled "David Selznick's Film Is the World's Greatest" (quoted in *Gone with the Wind as Book and Film*, a compilation edited by Richard Harwell). The author of that review notes that, among other things, "the picture is breath-taking in its visual beauty, for once Technicolor having justified its use in a dramatic multiple-reel production," and "the picture as a whole is truly the book in pictures and dialogue; it glorifies the book, makes it

live before our eyes." The reviewer also notes that "*Gone with the Wind* is the biggest motion picture ever made, the most overpowering, the best entertainment."

The film was nominated for thirteen Academy Awards, many more than the previous record of five, and the film won the awards for Best Picture, Best Director, Best Screenplay, Best Editing, and Best Cinematography. Vivian Leigh won Best Actress and Hattie McDaniel won Best Supporting Actress, the first African American to win an Academy Award for acting. William Cameron Menzies won an honorary Academy Award for Outstanding Achievement in the Use of Color at a time when most films were still released in black and white.

The film was in release for three years, and ran in theaters again in 1947, 1954, 1961, 1967, and 1971. The American Film Institute lists it as the number four film on its list of "100 Greatest Movies."

The advent of the video age has allowed other films to nudge *Gone with the Wind* from its position as best-selling film of all time, but it has not diminished the film's popularity. On its Web site, a *TV Guide* contributor lauds this movie as "the best remembered and most publicized film in Hollywood's flamboyant history, the biggest of David O. Selznick's grand obsessions, and quite probably the most beloved movie of all time." The film still has legions of fans and is at the center of an entire memorabilia industry of books, dolls, plates, chess sets, and more using images of the characters and sets it introduced.

CRITICISM

David Kelly

Kelly is a professor of creative writing and literature. In the following essay, he questions whether the novel or film versions of Gone with the Wind *can be significant literature without fully addressing the issue of slavery.*

It is indisputable that *Gone with the Wind* is a tremendous presence in our culture more than seventy years after the film's release. The novel and film broke sales records upon their release, and they continue to regularly garner the attention of new audiences. An entire industry has risen up around the story of Scarlett O'Hara. A quick search of eBay alone yields listings for more than two thousand collectibles available for the

WHAT DO I SEE NEXT?

- The year 1939 saw the release of a classic American film that has become a favorite of young adults for generations, *The Wizard of Oz*. This movie was listed as being directed by Victor Fleming (though it also had several uncredited directors), who was one of the credited directors of *Gone with the Wind*. It is an adaptation of L. Frank Baum's 1900 story about a girl who is taken by a tornado from her home in Kansas (filmed in black and white) to a magical place with wizards and witches, Munchkins, and talking animals. The film stars Judy Garland, Frank Morgan, and Margaret Hamilton. Warner Home Video released a special seventieth-anniversary edition in 2009.

- Another grandly romantic film was released in 1939. William Wyler's *Wuthering Heights*, adapted from the classic novel by Emily Bronte, starred Merle Oberon and Lawrence Olivier (Vivian Leigh's husband) as lovers whose lives are frustrated by circumstances keeping them apart. It was nominated for eight Academy Awards that year, winning only for Best Cinematographer (black and white). It is available from MGM.

- Leslie Howard stars as a character similar to Ashley Wilkes in *The Petrified Forest*, the 1936 gangster movie that made Humphrey Bogart a star as sadistic criminal Duke Mantee. Based on Robert Sherwood's hit Broadway play, it is currently available on DVD from Warner Home Video.

- Director Ken Burns made a name for himself with his 1990 miniseries *The Civil War*, an eleven-hour documentary that brings the causes and effects of the war to life with music, photos, and dramatic readings. The highest rated miniseries in PBS history, it established new standards for documentary filmmaking and ushered in a new generation of documentaries. It is available on PBS Home Video, and individual episodes can be viewed online at the PBS Web site.

- The 1976 television broadcast premier of *Gone with the Wind* on CBS established a new record for television viewership, only to see its record broken a few months later by the finale of *Roots*, a miniseries tracing generations of a black family from the time when ancestor Kunta Kinte is kidnapped from Gambia through his descendants' slavery in America to the family's eventual freedom after the Civil War. Cast with dozens of famous actors, including Cecily Tyson, John Amos, Louis Gossett, Jr., Richard Roundtree, and Yvonne de Carlo (LeVar Burton, who played Kunta Kinte, would later also achieve fame), it helped raise the nation's consciousness about the richness of history of black Americans. The entire series is available on a four-disc DVD collection from Warner Home Video.

- The three-day Battle of Gettysburg is explored in depth in the four-hour 1993 film *Gettysburg*. Based on Michael Shaara's respected book *The Killer Angels*, it dramatizes the complexities of the battle by giving both sides of the conflict equal attention. This epic film stars Jeff Daniels, Tom Berenger, Sam Elliott, and Martin Sheen. It is available from Turner Home Entertainment.

- The same esteem lavished on *Gone with the Wind* is felt toward Japanese director Akira Kurosawa's 1954 epic, *Seven Samurai*, which critics around the world generally rank as one of the greatest films ever made. The story, about a band of peasants seeking protection against invading hordes of marauders, is basically a war story, but like *Gone with the Wind*, it is told with such fine detail that viewers learn much about its culture (feudal Japan). It is available in DVD from Criterion.

devotees of the book and especially of the movie, including dolls of the movie's characters, plates showing film stills, snow globes, tea pots, jigsaw puzzles, and practically anything else imaginable. Just searching for "GWTW," the abbreviated name by which fans worldwide know the story, yields more than six hundred eBay hits and more than 470,000 hits on Google.

The fans of the book and film are enthralled by the story, but its charm is lost on many, many people who feel differently about the world Margaret Mitchell created. The film follows the novelist's skewed view of history. Both versions can only work their magic by cajoling readers to forget about slavery. Since the book's publication in 1936 and the film's premier in 1939, the same question has hung over them both: just how much can an artistic work be considered successful, how much can it be enjoyed or idolized, if it requires its audiences to ignore a glaring moral wrong?

When talking about films' moral responsibility, the question of culpability—guilt—is relevant to the situation being discussed. Critics always read metaphors for the real world into works, but doing so is an exercise in imagination. There might be discussions, for instance, about the politics of *Star Wars*, to name another phenomenally popular film in the ticket-selling league of *Gone with the Wind*, but few people think the oppressive Empire is being unjustly portrayed. Though *Avatar* might have things to say about the colonial system, it says them through the cloak of speculative fiction. When they are based in historical fact, blockbusters seldom go near controversy, lest they alienate audiences: *Titanic* implied that the oppressed underclass was compensated by having more fun below deck than the wealthy could ever know, and *Dr. Zhivago*'s jibes at the Russian Revolution annoyed the Communist party, but the rest of the world accepted its position as a given. In general, huge box-office receipts are not won with controversy.

Gone with the Wind steers around the issue of slavery by pretending that it is morally right, taking a position that violates basic civil rights the world over. It is only able to achieve this by keeping slavery (though not slaves themselves) off screen. It shows no slaves who are uncomfortable with their lot, implying that slavery was an equitable partnership freely entered into by plantation owners, who needed slave muscle to tend their crops and to tend the needs of the

delicate women among them, and the child-like servants who could never survive on their own.

In the film, black characters get themselves into foolishness like stalking a chicken in the rain while cartoon-quality music plays in the background, or getting themselves in over their heads through bragging. The only black characters to show any anger are Mammy, who frets constantly for the reputations of her white mistresses, and Big Sam, who, though living in a shack in a hobo jungle, flies into a rage when his former owner is threatened.

In the novel, Margaret Mitchell tries to soften the effects of slavery by showing that her plantation owners thought well of their slaves. Patriarch Gerald O'Hara loses money by forbidding his overseer to whip the slaves, showing a tender heart that his daughter Scarlett later forgets when she uses the labor of convicts of all races to build her fortune. Gerald spends huge sums, more than he needs to, in uniting his servant Pork with Dilcey, the woman Pork has married, and even springs for Dilcey's daughter Prissy to come to the O'Hara plantation with her. Mitchell's book uses harsher racial language, which producer David O. Selznick originally tried to exclude from the film and in the end gave only to black characters discussing other black characters. Unlike Selznick, Mitchell does paint some black characters as evil, but she keeps even the worst of them near innocence, victims of their own child-like nature. For instance, describing the thousands of house servants and loyal field hands who refuse to leave their masters after the war, she contrasts them with those who have been incited "by a fervor of Northern hatred almost religious in its fanaticism" to run amok during Reconstruction:

> There they conducted themselves as creatures of small intelligence might naturally be expected to do. Like monkeys or small children turned loose among treasured objects whose value is beyond their comprehension, they ran wild—either from perverse pleasure in destruction or simply because of their ignorance.

Her belittlement shows contempt for freed blacks, but she does not openly admit malice toward the race in general.

Ignoring the issue of slavery may seem almost impossible in a film about the Civil War—as impossible, almost, as making a four-hour epic that takes place during the war without a single battle scene—but it was not that uncommon. It became almost standard between the 1870s, when the catastrophe of the war began to settle, and the 1920s, when Mitchell began the novel, to find

© *AF archive | Alamy*

ways of looking at what had happened as something other than a fight to hold other humans as property. She was only following a tradition of looking at abstractions, like the South's right to secede peacefully and the North's imposing its rule on sovereign states, that created sympathy that the South needed after the war to soothe itself in defeat.

Historian Orville Vernon Burton (quoted by Fergus M. Bordewich in a *Smithsonian* magazine article about the 150th anniversary of the firing on Fort Sumter), noted in *The Age of Lincoln* the ways that alternate explanations for the war began replacing the argument about slavery that had dominated the seventy years leading to the war. After running down the list of explanations, from states' rights to tariffs to a clash of industrialized versus agrarian cultures, Burton noted that "all of these interpretations came together to portray the Civil War as a collision of two noble civilizations from which black slaves had been airbrushed out."

The mission of *Gone with the Wind* was to glorify the Confederacy, and there has never been much sympathy for human trafficking. Nobility was the key. In a conventional war, the history is written by the victors, but in a civil war that ends with a forced reconciliation, there is a every reason to get on with peace by letting both sides save face. To reunite a country torn apart by war meant that the Confederacy had to be able to stand up and say that they did what was just. There is nothing noble about slavery, so it had to be erased.

Gone with the Wind is a very entertaining book made into an iconic film. The story of Scarlett O'Hara's moral struggle with a changing world is something that audiences across the globe have latched onto. As a story about the Confederacy, though, it works only by leaving out one of the Confederacy's defining factors. Since the end of the war, people have tried to ignore slavery's central role. Mitchell and Selznick tapped into a nostalgia for plantation houses, fainting couches, and chivalry, but the fact that a culture based on human trafficking is gone cannot be entirely regretted.

Source: David Kelly, Critical Essay on *Gone with the Wind*, in *Novels for Students*, Gale, Cengage Learning, 2012.

> THE TENUOUS BARGAIN STRUCK BETWEEN
> SOUTHERN WOMEN AND THE CONFEDERACY AT THE
> START OF THE WAR DID NOT SURVIVE."

Katherine Lane Antolini

In the following excerpt, Antolini argues that despite the debate, Scarlett O'Hara is an accurate depiction of a Confederate woman from the Civil War era.

Admittedly, when one is asked to think of a war movie *Gone With the Wind* does not immediately come to mind. The movie's designation as a "woman's film" typically negates its membership within the masculine war movie genre. Moreover, the iconic image of Scarlett O'Hara as southern belle "fiddle-dee-deeing" on her beloved plantation, Tara, has captured the imagination of students of popular culture and authors of academic literature more than the image of Scarlett as war movie heroine. The Old South or "Lost Cause" imagery of the book and movie has received critical analysis, inspiring such creative titles as *The Roots of Tara, Tara Revisited*, and my personal favorite, *Scarlett Doesn't Live Here Anymore*. Literary scholars and historians of women's history continue to debate the representational significance of the Scarlett O'Hara character; she is often classified as a misrepresentation of antebellum southern women or the embodiment of white southern womanhood that has historically justified the oppression of African-Americans. On the other extreme, she has been honored with the title of feminist. Yet, Scarlett O'Hara as an accurate representation of Confederate women during the Civil War has earned less attention.

The movie offers two historically debatable perspectives of Confederate women during the Civil War: one perspective offered by Scarlett and the other represented by every other white female character. The South has a long legacy of pride in the resiliency of Confederate women, women who sacrificed their husbands and sons, their homes, and their lives for the Southern cause. Female characters that are the embodiment of the self-sacrificing Confederate woman surround

Scarlett throughout the movie. Melanie Wilkes, especially, symbolizes the elite southern woman that twentieth-century historians have authenticated and celebrated. In contrast to the honored women of the Confederacy, Scarlett stands alone in her indifference. Her very first line in the movie betrays her commitment to the southern cause, "Fiddle-dee-dee! War, War, War! This war talk's spoiling all the fun at every party this spring! I get so bored I could scream!" (Howard 1). Once the war erupts, Scarlett appears even more vain and ungrateful amongst the Atlanta women who selflessly contribute all to the Confederacy. Even Belle Watling, the classic "whore-with-a-heart-of-gold" figure, shows a deeper sense of loyalty than Scarlett.

A closer look at southern history, however, suggests that more women shared Scarlett's perspective of war and the Confederacy than many southerners cared to admit. Even author Margaret Mitchell felt Melanie Wilkes was her story's true heroine (Taylor 78). Before the Civil War altered gender roles, white southern women had accepted their subordination (at least publicly) as natural. In a sort of "patriarchal bargain," women exchanged their self-abnegation for the care and protection of their men. With southern secession, they entered into a similar bargain with their new country. Women agreed to obey new dictates of female behavior in exchange for the Confederacy's care and protection. Eventually, however, the Confederacy reneged on its promises and subordination felt more like abandonment when the government left women to fend for themselves. When the Confederacy failed to honor its obligation to southern women, the women failed to honor their obligations to it. Scarlett no longer stands alone when a historical perspective recognizes the presence of women who challenged or completely abandoned the ideal model of Confederate womanhood. Instead history reveals Confederate women who shared Scarlett's criticism of the war, her aversion to nursing, and the belief that the responsibilities of managing a plantation of slaves far outweighed the merits of the South's "peculiar institution" and a blind dedication to a lost way of life.

> "You can tell your grandchildren how you watched the Old South disappear one night."
> Rhett Butler to Scarlett O'Hara after escaping Atlanta and the Union army. (Howard 94)

Certainly the novel follows the sentimentalized Old South formula first made popular by late nineteenth-century southern writers and historians; legend contends that Margaret Mitchell was ten years old before she learned that the South had actually lost the war (Lambert 22). Although Mitchell prided herself on the historical accuracy of her novel, she never claimed to be a professional historian. She wanted instead to be judged on the merits of her storytelling. And fans of her story, including a few professional historians, have willingly overlooked the historical misrepresentations present in the novel. They hesitate to criticize Margaret Mitchell for adopting what was a standard interpretation of southern history in the early twentieth-century (Castel 87). Despite any literary defense of the novel, however, Hollywood effectively affixed in our collective imaginations the presumable truth of Mitchell's story (Clinton 21; Diffley 366, 371–72). The epic movie visually transforms a regional history into a national southern past and embodies everything one may associate with the South—fact or fiction (Fox-Genovese 397). For three hours and forty minutes, the travails of Atlanta, Tara, and their citizens symbolize the plight of the entire South. Moreover, the history becomes a feminized history linked as it is to the struggle of women left behind during the war; Scarlett's story is intertwined with the South's story. As Atlanta burns and Tara faces devastation, she is witness and commentator to the destruction of the Old South. Rhett Butler stresses this pivotal movement in the movie as they flee the flames of Atlanta and the approaching Yankee army. "Take a good look, my dear. It's a historic moment. You can tell your grandchildren how you watched the Old South disappear one night." Eventually, of course, the new rises from the ashes of the old and Scarlett's history remains aligned with Atlanta's as they both rebuild under Reconstruction and tie their destinies to a New South.

The movie's interpretation of southern history has deservedly received intense criticism. Scathing scrutiny of its perpetuation of the plantation myth, its paternalistic portrayal of the institution of slavery, and its depiction of post-antebellum race relations, has labeled the Hollywood epic "southern propaganda" and even "Confederate porn" (Clinton 203–04). The movie's set design even surprised Margaret Mitchell. After seeing pictures of the Tara and Twelve Oaks designs, she joked of founding a society named, "The Association of Southerners Whose Grandpapies Did Not Live In Houses With White Columns" (Lambert 69). Yet popular culture's love affair with Scarlett as southern belle, and the obsession historians have with discrediting that

beloved image, has made it difficult to view the character in any other role. Even scholars who have revisited the historic roles of southern women in the Civil War era and *GWTW*'s cinematic portrayal of them are still unwilling to give Scarlett her due. They reveal the truth that women frequently diverged from the romanticized image of the self-sacrificing southern woman, yet they still prefer to celebrate the minority of women who fit the stereotype or simply refuse to see Scarlett as a symbol of the new interpretation of Confederate womanhood.

. . . The costs of the total war naturally hit the poorer classes of women the hardest. Yeoman women found it difficult to meet both the army's endless demand for supplies and the needs of their families. Many found themselves on the brink of starvation by 1863. The plight of the lower classes, however, is noticeably absent from the *GWTW* movie. Any references to them are derogatory—we cannot forget the "poor white trash" Emmy Slattery who was responsible for the death of Scarlett's mother of typhoid and Emmy's lover and former Tara overseer (later turned carpetbagger), Mr. Wilkerson. In an early scene of the movie, Ellen O'Hara convinces her husband to fire Mr. Wilkerson after helping Emmy deliver and bury the couple's illegitimate child. Emmy thus earned her white trash designation by being both economically and morally inferior to the O'Hara family; even Mammy looked down on her. Yet the picture's brief representation of the poorer classes closely resembles the Confederacy's condemnation of the non-elite women who showed their disloyalty to the southern cause. Poor urban women rioted in the streets, stole, and traded on the black market during the war. And men dodged the draft or deserted the army in response to their wives' pleading letters for help planting or harvesting crops; once at home, yeoman women willingly concealed their fugitive husbands from military authorities (Bynum 121–29; Kimball 307–12). The open defiance of poor and yeoman women was not rationalized away in the same matter as the extravagance of elite women. Southerners could devise excuses for the behavior of elite women, believing that these women simply failed to appreciate the actualities of war; the Confederacy could not risk completely alienating their loyalty. Women without money or social status, however, could easily be dealt with by force (Bynum 112). Regardless, the behavior of both groups of women represents challenges to the Confederacy and its dictates of feminine behavior.

. . . The constant fear of war, starvation, and slave rebellions took its toll on southern women. Their relationship to violence, for example, altered as they tried to maintain control of the situation. Prewar gender roles had relegated the use of violence to slave masters and male overseers while socializing women to show a natural aversion to physical violence. Yet, despite the Daughters of the Confederacy's assurance that southern women never manhandled their slaves, planter women did resort to the use of verbal threats and physical violence, particularly with slave women. The Daughters even protested the cinematic scene where Scarlett slapped Prissy, unsuccessfully demanding such a lie be removed from the movie (Flamini 263). A planter woman's ability to discipline slaves before the war, however, was always backed by the ultimate authority of her husband and his powerful presence as plantation patriarch. The wartime absence of a male authority figure altered southern gender dynamics and forced women to increase the scope of their relationship to violence and their decisions to use it to maintain slave discipline or protect themselves from any direct threats (Faust, "Trying to Do a Man's Business" 205–08).

Women left to manage plantations quickly realized the limitation of their control over a dwindling and unruly slave population. In the movie, the O'Hara family also suffers a loss of plantation labor, first from the impressment of slaves into military service and then from field hands who chose to follow the Union army to freedom. Only Mammy, Pork, and Prissy remained with the family, seemingly by choice. The plantation mistresses who were able to sustain a slave labor force during the war, however, often encountered direct attacks on their authority and complained of the increasing impertinence of slaves in their correspondence with absent husbands (Edwards 78; Inscoe 341). Managing the labor of male slaves especially heightened women's insecurities, making them painfully aware of their physical vulnerability. Rumors of slave uprisings, raped southern women, and murdered planter families continually fueled their anxieties. Although such attacks were rare, fear forced women to make hard decisions about how to ensure their families' survival (Bynum 116–19; Faust, *Mothers of Invention* 57). Many reluctantly embraced the necessity of physical violence when disciplining both male and female slaves. The increasing severity of the physical punishment southern women administered on resisting slaves, hoping to establish their authority, reflected their fear and acknowledgment that they could not live with or without slave labor (Faust, "Trying to Do a Man's Business" 205). Scarlett, when chastised by her father for the mistreatment of Mammy, Polk, and Prissy, justified her actions by insisting, "I'm not asking them to do anything I'm not doing myself" (Howard 111). She wanted to make her authority and expectations clear.

> "They make me sick—all of them. Getting us all into this with their swaggering and boasting." Scarlett's reaction to the collapse of the Old South. (Howard 95)

. . . Scarlett's reaction in witnessing the fall of the Old South is a profound moment in the movie. "They make me sick—all of them" she exclaimed, watching the retreat of a broken Confederate army. Film historian Gavin Lambert reflected on the same scene in his interpretation of the movie: "At the time, this was no doubt intended to show the hard, selfish side of Scarlett; viewed today, from the other side of World War II, Korea, and Vietnam, it seems one of her most sympathetic moments, the impatience wholly appealing and the lack of pity supremely healthy" (175). It is the lack of pity that binds Scarlett to the real women of the South, women who eventually failed to feel any sympathy for a country that had abandoned them and their families. Any romantic notions of war eventually disappeared and the patriotism that had inspired so many to rally behind the Southern cause lost its influence. Ultimately, the war took on evil qualities for southern women, and by extension, so did the Confederacy.

The tenuous bargain struck between southern women and the Confederacy at the start of the war did not survive. Women were willing to sacrifice at first, but the sacrifices never stopped. They were willing to care and protect their families, but not completely alone. Southern women reluctantly shouldered the new responsibilities of plantation management, but the weight of those responsibilities became too heavy. Their refusal to sacrifice any longer, either by calling their men home from the front or dressing extravagantly, was evidence of the relational breakdown between women and the Confederacy, as was the reluctance to serve as nurses, the complaints of plantation life expressed to husbands, and women's petitions for the government to provide the protection they were initially promised. A new generation of historians investigating the dissolving relationship between southern women and the Confederacy are thus faced with the intriguing question of which came first: Did the defeat of the Confederacy allow for southern women publicly to assert their will within southern society or did the assertion of women's will aid in the defeat of the Confederacy? The first step to a definitive answer, of course, is the recognition of the women who challenged the model of Confederate womanhood. It is finally time to give Scarlett her due, as well as the southern women she represents. For Scarlett gives voice to the experiences of women that the legend of the self-sacrificing Confederate woman has historically silenced. Her vanity and selfishness is reinterpreted to represent the frustration, fear, and disillusionment of southern women during a time of war. Melanie Wilkes's portrayal of the ideal Confederate woman now appears one dimensional and lacking in comparison to Scarlett's complex and honest portrayal of a woman unwilling to remain blindly loyal to the southern cause and altruistically dedicated to preserving a way of life "gone with the wind."

Source: Katherine Lane Antolini, "Scarlett O'Hara as Confederate Woman," in *West Virginia University Philological Papers*, Vol. 51, Fall 2004, pp. 23–35.

Trisha Curran

In the following excerpt, Curran argues that Gone with the Wind *is not a war film but a film about people.*

Nearly forty years after its first release in 1939 to tremendous critical and popular acclaim, 350,000 members of the American Film Institute voted *Gone with the Wind* the "greatest American movie," ranking it far ahead of *African Queen, Casablanca, Citizen Kane, Grapes of Wrath, One Flew Over the Cuckoo's Nest, Singin' in the Rain, Star War, 2001: A Space Odyssey*, and *The Wizard of Oz*, in their "Ten Best" list of American movies. In *Gone with the Wind*, they could find the tragic faith in man of *Grapes of Wrath* and *Casablanca*, the epic quality and production values of *Star Wars* and *2001*, the technicolor magnificence of *Singin' in the Rain* and *The Wizard of Oz*, the technical virtuosity of *Citizen Kane*, and the intimacy and appeal of *African Queen* and *Cuckoo's Nest*. In none of the above could they find the sensational sex and violence so prevalent in popular American films. Indeed, *Gone with the Wind* is

> AS *THE* MODERN AMERICAN TRAGEDY, *GONE WITH THE WIND* REAFFIRMS OUR TRIUMPH OVER DESPAIR. HENCE ITS POPULARITY. AND HENCE ITS PRIMARY POSITION IN THE AMERICAN FILM INSTITUTE POLL."

comparable to Renoir's *The Grand Illusion* in its depiction of the effects of war on individuals and society, without the obligatory battle scenes associated with war films. But then neither *Gone with the Wind* nor *The Grand Illusion* is a war film. They are people films, personalized reflections of 1930s pacifism, pleas pro pacem, movies to move men, not militias. They were made in the depths of the Depression, on the eve of World War II, "escapes into history" for the economically depressed, the lonely, the war-torn of their own and of future eras. Both films have fared extremely well over the past forty-odd years since their release, helped no doubt by the growing anti-war sentiment that came with the Cold War and Korea and that climaxed with Viet Nam.

No one could ask for a better anti-war statement in a film than that made by Ashley Wilkes at the beginning of *Gone with the Wind* when he tells his war-hungry friends that "most of the miseries of the world were caused by wars and when the wars were over, no one knew what they were about." Throughout the film we see the miseries caused by the Civil War insofar as they affect Scarlett O'Hara, one of the most unsympathetic heroines Hollywood has produced. Thus Scarlett's extreme egocentricity protects *Gone with the Wind* from becoming an anti-war tract, for Scarlett is concerned only with Scarlett. She views the dead and the dying with distance and disdain, and the camera conveys her distance and captures her disdain. The dead are filmed in long-shot, a mass of depersonalized bodies, obstacles that obstruct Scarlett's search for Dr. Meade and her trip to Tara. In a film of so many excesses, the camera's restraint is remarkable.

Also remarkable is the magnificent meshing of the visual and the verbal in the effectiveness of the verbatim literary dialogue, spoken with conviction and radiating believability within the nineteenth-century context of the film. The visual force of the images complements the verbal force of the dialogue; and the visual force of the images complements the verbal force of the explanatory text. The movement of the printed lines combines with the expressive movement of images behind the lines to describe the war that is not seen on the screen, but that causes the suffering that is seen.

Perhaps even more remarkable than the meshing of the visual and the verbal is the meshing of divergent directorial styles. *Gone with the Wind* is a perfect blend of George Cukor's attention to actresses and Victor Fleming's articulation of action. That Cukor was successful in articulating action and Fleming in directing actresses is evident in Cukor's direction of Scarlett's slapping Prissy and killing the Union soldier and Fleming's of Scarlett's realizing her love for Rhett and triumphing over impending despair. Although both Cukor and Fleming favor the unfolding of dramatic action within the flexible frame, Sam Wood's use of crosscutting for Scarlett and Rhett's narrow escape through the rows of burning box cars and exploding ammunition at the Atlanta station is a perfect illustration of the architectural axiom "form follows function," for the form of Wood's crosscutting follows the function of creating excitement in this sequence of the film.

The casting of Clark Gable, Vivien Leigh, Olivia de Havilland, and Leslie Howard likewise followed the function of creating believable screen characters for Margaret Mitchell's creations. So perfect is each of these stars in the respective roles that it is well nigh impossible to conceive of anyone else as the suave Rhett Butler, the spoiled Scarlett O'Hara, the motherly Melanie Hamilton or the wishy-washy Ashley Wilkes. Their acting is magnetic and their screen personages meticulously true to those of their literary counterparts.

In characterizing Melanie as Charles's older sister and Ashley as India's older brother, the film is also remarkably true to the characteristics of both sibling positions. Melanie, as befits the older sister of brothers, is maternal toward men—the wounded soldiers in the hospital, the hungry soldiers at Tara, Ashley and Rhett. She is optimistic regarding Ashley's safety throughout the war, independent in an unobtrusive way, particularly in relation to the rumors relating Scarlett and Ashley, and uncomfortable with solitude (hence her coming downstairs in her nightgown at Tara

before she was well). And Ashley, as the older brother of a sister, is a ladies' rather than a man's man, hence his adoration by Melanie and Scarlett and his lack of stature with Rhett. He is a kind, considerate employer who will neither accommodate nor conspicuously oppose tyrannical superiors (as evidenced by his impotent objection to Scarlett's hiring prison labor in the mill), and a somewhat cavalier caretaker of his own property, evidenced in his inability to make much of a profit from the mill.

Contrary to her actual sibling position in the novel and the film, Scarlett is much more the female only child than the older sister of sisters. Like the stereotypical female only child, she is egotistical, extravagant, heartless, dependent upon her parents, and more interested in remaining a child herself than in caring for her own children. She is unlike an oldest sister who is typically more concerned with her younger sisters, her friends, and her children than with material wealth and prosperity, whose girlfriends are more important to her than her boyfriends, and whose straightforwardness and strictness discourage men from flirting with her. A far cry from this archetype is the Scarlett who steals her younger sister's fiancee in order to get his money and his lumber business, who has no girlfriends, and who flirts constantly. However, like the oldest sister of sisters, Scarlett naturally gives orders and takes charge—witness her restoration of Tara and her management of the mill. Moreover she is tough and enduring ("I'll live through this and when it is over, as God is my witness, I'll never be hungry again" and "I'll go home and I'll think of some way to get him back. After all, tomorrow is another day.") These lines provide the *raison d'etre* of her sibling position as oldest sister of sisters. They could never be as convincing coming from an only child. In the final analysis, Scarlett rings true. And she is still ringing true as the patron saint/bitch-goddess of various groups.

Unmoved by the suffering of her pyrrhic victory, "America first" isolationists have identified with Scarlett's me-first egocentricity, and environmentalists, closing their eyes to her lumber business, have championed her love of Tara. Unabashed by her bitchiness, her cruelness and her dishonesty, feminists praise Scarlett's strength in refusing to subjugate herself to society's expectations, her shrewdness in making her sex work for her, and her success as mover and doer rather than as wife and mother.

But growing isolationism, environmentalism and feminism are irrelevant in a discussion of *Gone with the Wind* as "the great American movie." Irrelevant too is the consideration of *Wind* as the great movie event of Hollywood history, with the public's casting of Clark Cable, the fabled search for Scarlett O'Hara, the firing of George Cukor, the hiring of Victor Fleming, the all-time record for box office sales, the prodigious press coverage of each re-release, the blow up to 70mm., and the selling of the television rights—plentiful manifestations of *Wind's* popularity and possible reasons for its primacy in the minds of members of the American Film Institute, but they neither explain nor justify its filmic greatness.

Explanations of, and reasons for, filmic greatness must be statements about the film itself, about its form, for as Ortega has so rightly noted, "a work of art lives on its form, not on its material"; Susan Sontag adds, "ultimately the greatest source of emotional power in art lies not in any particular subject matter, however passionate, however universal. It lies in form." *Gone with the Wind* is a powerful, passionate, emotion-packed film because its form is powerful, passionate, emotion-packed—in a word, organic. All its elements are interconnected and none can be changed without making changes throughout the film. They are interrelated and interdependent as the parts of the human body are interrelated and interdependent. Max Steiner's musical score, William Cameron Menzies' design, Jack Cosgrove's photographic effects, Sidney Howard's, Ben Hecht's, Victor Fleming's and David O. Selznick's script, George Cukor's, Victor Fleming's, Sam Wood's, William Wellman's and King Vidor's direction, and David O. Selznick's production are perfectly fused in this famous film. One would expect a hodgepodge of styles given the number of writers and directors; instead one finds a stylistic whole as one watches the story unfold on the screen in a succession of interrelated shots and scenes that effortlessly and elegantly flow into one another, propelled by vertical forces that further the unfolding of the diegesis, and enriched by spiral forces that further the unfolding of the emotions. *Gone with the Wind* is a rich film because it is a rich fusion.

A magnificent spiral force, Max Steiner's musical score fully fuses with the visuals in depicting the unfolding of feeling. A sprightly "Dixie" over the opening titles and picturesque scenes of antebellum plantation life sets the tone for Scarlett's talk of the picnic and party at Twelve Oaks; and a mournful "Dixie" played by tearful musicians at the Atlanta station amid cries, screams and sobs of bereaved readers of the casualty lists underlines the mournful mood of the beseiged South. An off-screen rendition of Taps mirrors the mis-en-scene of maimed men lying on the ground at the same station several months later—the wounded soldiers Scarlett steps over in her search for Dr. Meade. As the camera pulls out to reveal a screen full of hundreds and hundreds of dead and dying soldiers lying unattended on the ground completely surrounding Scarlett, a single crescendo underlines the depth of the destruction.

Crescendos also inflate to epic proportions Scarlett's excitement on finding Tara still standing and running to tell her mother she is home; her strength and determination as she picks herself up from her prostrate position in the empty garden, raises her fist, and vows never to be hungry again; her self-control in resolutely walking away from Ashley after failing to seduce him; her fear, following Ashley's party, as she and Rhett disappear into the dark at the top of the stairs before he carries her in to bed; and finally, her self-confidence, strength and determination as she sits up after Rhett has left her, looks straight at the camera and says, "I'll go home and I'll think of some way to get him back...."

The music also mirrors the emotions and meshes with the visuals in the unfolding of the diegesis. The tune from Bonnie's music box segues into "London Bridge Is Falling Down" as the blues and beiges of Bonnie's room become a beige Big Ben against a blue night sky, music and color having affected the metamorphosis of Atlanta into London. Likewise a dissolve on color effects the metamorphosis from Mammy in violet dress and white kerchief at a white curtained window into the young black boys swinging on the ringing bell, silhouetted against white clouds in a violet sky. An important factor in the narrative force of *Gone with the Wind* is the use of dissolves, with or without corresponding colors. The sheer force of the narrative is dependent on the force of the editing.

Color, dialogue and dissolves all function as directive elements in the metamorphoses of several key scenes involving Ashley's supposed seduction of Scarlett. From a scene of Bonnie (in blue dress with white trim) riding her pony and Mammy (in grey dress with white trim) telling Rhett that "it ain't fittin, it just ain't fittin," the camera dissolves to Ashley (in white shirt and neutral pants) and Scarlett (in white dress with blue jacket) at the lumberyard where they are caught in an innocent embrace, foreshadowed by Mammy's "it just ain't fittin." A second dissolve on white finds Scarlett at home wearing white undergarments and lying in her white bed. Although other colors are introduced in this scene, the cut to the following scene at Ashley's party is made from the white of Scarlett's undergarments to the white flames of the white candles on Ashley's white birthday cake. Mammy's "it just ain't fittin" is silently echoed in the absolute silence of the guests who stop singing in mid-line when they see Scarlett, dressed in scarlet, standing at the door, the color of her dress expressive of her image as a wanton woman.

The contrast in color between Scarlett's black dress and the pastels of the other women at the Atlanta ball expresses her nonconformity with them and prefigures her union with Rhett, his black tuxedo equally expressive of his nonconformity and equally conspicuous amid the grey and gold of the Confederate uniforms. The movement of the camera mirrors the movement of the dance and the ample close shots of Scarlett and Rhett convey their growing awareness of each other and unconcern with everyone else at the ball. In like manner, the panning camera in its connections of returning soldiers with wives and family within its fluid frame expresses the closeness of coming together, of *reunion*, that it is filming.

Similarly, the sense of confusion felt by people fleeing their homes in the face of a conquering army is marvelously mirrored in a montage of somewhat blurred close-ups of men and women running, screaming from their homes, grabbing their children, carrying their belongings, and pulling their wagons amid the rising dust of the dirt roads as they hurry into the night with little thought of where they are going. When Rhett tells Scarlett on the road to Tara that he is going to join the army, the low angle shot (of him) conveys his sense of personal satisfaction with his decision as well as Scarlett's dependence upon him as defender and provider. Conversely, the high angle shot as he answers Scarlett's "Why?" with the simple, "Maybe it's because I'm ashamed of myself," conveys his shame.

Elements within the frame also function expressively. Light is used on several occasions to express Scarlett's optimism. During evening prayer at Tara a candle immediately behind Scarlett expresses her hope as she thinks aloud, "I'll tell him I love him and then he can't marry her." On leaving Atlanta during the war, she carries outside a candle to dramatize the optimism of her determination to reach Tara. Finally, the rainbow in the sky just before the travelers sight Twelve Oaks symbolizes her delight at going home. Once home, the darkness and the destruction of her world is conveyed by a view of the night sky through broken window panes behind her, as she learns from Pa that all they have left are worthless Confederate bonds. Likewise, Rhett's near despair as he awaits news of Scarlett's condition after her fall down the stairs is expressed by the bleak view of falling rain outside his open window.

Sound and camera movement combine with musical crescendos to propel the diegesis to its dramatic conclusion. After Rhett has left and Scarlett lies prostrate on the steps, in long-shot, the camera slowly moves in on her as she sits up and the off-screen voices of her father and Ashley get louder and more insistent—"land's the only thing that matters." . . . "something you love more than me, Tara." "Tara." "Tara." The voices are loud, the music reaches a crescendo, the camera is close on Scarlett, now sitting upright, despair and depression banished, as she thinks aloud, "Home, I'll go home and I'll think of some way to get him back." Once again she has confidence in her own resources. The music reaches a louder and more triumphant crescendo and Scarlett looks straight at the camera, her face glowing, to speak her final line, "after all, tomorrow is another day." The music, dialogue and camera angle are all expressive of her hope, and direct our identification with her. She is looking straight at us and talking to herself. We have become Scarlett. The dissolve into the stylized shot of Scarlett in silhouette looking at the Tara of her childhood and the camera pull-out to extreme long-shot distance us from Scarlett and Tara, and direct us into our own world. The final crescendo is expressive of our renewed confidence in ourselves. "Tomorrow is another day" for us as well as for Scarlett. We have entered into her life, engaged in her selfishness, enjoyed her come-uppance, and can now continue to live our lives with her confidence. Such is the power of the vertical forces that propel the unfolding of the plot and of the spiral forces that propel the unfolding of the emotions. And such is the power of tragedy.

The popular focus on Rhett's farewell remark, "Frankly, my dear, I don't give a damn," rather than on Scarlett's "tomorrow is another day" has inclined many critics to consider *Gone with the Wind* pathos or melodrama. But it is neither. Pathos evokes sympathy and a sense of sorrow or pity. *Gone with the Wind* does not. We do not feel sorry for Scarlett. In fact, we delight in Rhett's "Frankly, my dear. . . ." Scarlett got what she deserved. In fact, she got off easy. Nor is *Gone with the Wind* melodrama, a drama with sensational, romantic, often violent action, extravagant emotions and generally a happy ending. There is no sensation, little romance, no violence, no extravagant emotions, save the tragic ones of Scarlett's triumph over despair and a hopeful but not happy ending.

Tragedy is an expression of confidence in the tremendous fortitude of man, in his ability to overcome calamities and to triumph over despair, a declaration that "even if God is not in his heaven, at least man is in his world." *Gone with the Wind* is such an expression. God may not be in his heaven, but Scarlett is in her world. She is the tragic heroine par excellence. She not only survives poverty, hunger, destitution and death, but triumphs over them—"I'll live through this and when it is done, as God is my witness, I'll never be hungry again." She is never hungry again, but she loses her father, her daughter, her only friend and her husband. The loss of her husband is her own fault, the result of her tragic flaw of coveting Ashley and ignoring Rhett. It was surprisingly easy for her to come to terms with the fact that Ashley had never really loved her, but Rhett's leaving threatened the existence of her world, "What is to become of me?" Through her confidence in her own fortitude and strength, she triumphs over despair as she had previously triumphed over poverty and hunger and destruction and death: "*I'll* go home and *I'll* think of some way to get him back. After all, tomorrow is another day."

True to tragic form, the ending of *Gone with the Wind* recapitulates the total action. In going to Ashley rather than to Rhett upon leaving Melanie's deathbed, Scarlett repeated a pattern she had followed from the first scene of the film. Although she could have had any man she wanted at Tara and at Twelve Oaks except Ashley, she only wanted Ashley and kept wanting only Ashley through three marriages, indeed

until she brought about her own downfall, Rhett's leaving her. This downfall is unusual in tragedy, it is true, especially after all the classic calamities Scarlett had previously triumphed over, but it *is* her downfall nevertheless, and a tragic downfall.

As *the* modern American tragedy, *Gone with the Wind* reaffirms our triumph over despair. Hence its popularity. And hence its primary position in the American Film Institute poll. A true work of popular art, *Gone with the Wind* lives on its form. And it is the unfolding of the form that mesmerizes us with all its technicolor magnificence. There is not and never was any suspense of plot in *Gone with the Wind*. Most viewers knew the ending before they knew the story, and almost all knew the story before they saw the film. They went, not to be surprised by an ending, but to be entertained and enriched by the unfolding of a form; to enjoy again the experience of Scarlett vowing never to be hungry again, of Rhett calmly saying, "Frankly, my dear, I don't give a damn," and of Scarlett regaining her composure and remembering that, "after all, tomorrow is another day." We know the lines by heart. We go to see the unfolding of the form in all the greatness of its vertical and spiral forces, and all the glory of its tragedy. All art is illusion, and the illusion of tragedy, as Charles Morgan notes, is "the greatest illusion of all." *Gone with the Wind* is a great American movie because it is a great American form, and "the great American movie" because it is the great American tragic form.

Source: Trisha Curran, *"Gone with the Wind:* An American Tragedy," in *The South and Film,* edited by Warren French, Southern Quarterly, 1981, pp. 47–57.

SOURCES

"AFI's 100 Years . . . 100 Movies: 10th Anniversary Edition," in *American Film Institute Web,* http://www.afi.com/100Years/movies10.aspx (accessed June 13, 2011).

Bordewich, Fergus M., "The Civil War: Opening Salvo," in *Smithsonian,* Vol. 42, No. 1, April 2011, p. 78.

"Cinema: G with the W," in *Time,* December 25, 1939, http://www.time.com/time/magazine/article/0,9171,762137-3,00.html (accessed June 10, 2011).

"David Selznick's Film Is the World's Greatest," in *"Gone with the Wind" as Book and Film,* compiled and edited by Richard Harwell, University of South Carolina

Press, 1983, pp. 152–53; originally published in *Hollywood Spectator*, December 23, 1939.

Gone with the Wind, DVD, Warner Brothers, 2000.

Harmetz, Aljean, *On the Road to Tara: The Making of "Gone with the Wind,"* Harry N. Abrams, 1996, pp. 17–21.

Haver, Ronald, *David O. Selznick's "Gone with the Wind,"* Wings Books, 1986, p. 65.

Leff, Leonard J., "*Gone with the Wind* and Hollywood's Racial Politics," in *Atlantic Monthly*, December 1999, http://www.theatlantic.com/past/docs/issues/99dec/9912leff.htm (accessed June 13, 2011).

"*Life* on the Newsfronts of the World," in *Life*, Vol. 8, No. 1, January 1, 1940, p. 16.

McKuen, Rod, "Liner Notes," in *Gone with the Wind*, CD, Sound Images, 1998.

Mitchell, Margaret, *Gone with the Wind*, Pocket Books, 1964.

Review of *Gone with the Wind*, in *TV Guide*, http://movies.tvguide.com/gone-wind/review/124809 (accessed June 10, 2011).

FURTHER READING

Adams, Amanda, "'Painfully Southern': *Gone with the Wind*, the Agrarians, and the Battle for the New South," in *Southern Literary Journal*, Fall 2007, pp. 57–75.

This article presents the context of the novel's publication, looking at how the established literary authors who were considered to speak for the South in the 1950s—the Agrarians—dismissed the book and, in doing so, helped it become a popular success.

Brown, Ellen F., and John Wiley, Jr., *Margaret Mitchell's "Gone with the Wind": A Bestseller's Odyssey from Atlanta to Hollywood*, Taylor Trade Publishing, 2011.

The fascinating story of how a first-time author could produce one of the best-selling books of all time, which then produced one of the most influential films of all time, deserves to be re-examined often. In this recent book, Brown

and Wiley show the impact Mitchell had on twentieth-century literature and cinema.

Mitchell, Margaret, *Margaret Mitchell's "Gone with the Wind" Letters, 1936–1949*, edited by Richard Harwell, Collier Books, 1986.

The correspondence collected in this book covers the period during which the novel was published and the film was produced, giving readers insight into the ways Mitchell kept a controlling hand on her story during the grandest publicity drive ever experienced at the time.

Vertrees, Alan David, *Selznick's Vision: "Gone with the Wind" and Hollywood Filmmaking*, University of Texas Press, 1997.

Unlike the dozens of books available about the making of *Gone with the Wind*, this one is a scholarly study into the producer's role in creating this film and others. Vertrees provides insight into the studio system in a case where the studio and its head were inseparable.

SUGGESTED SEARCH TERMS

Gone with the Wind

Gone with the Wind AND Margaret Mitchell

Gone with the Wind AND David O. Selznick

GWTW

Margaret Mitchell

David O. Selznick

Gone with the Wind AND Selznick International

Gone with the Wind AND Victor Fleming

Gone with the Wind AND Sidney Howard

Vivian Leigh AND Clark Gable

Gone with the Wind AND Confederacy

Gone with the Wind AND Great Depression

Gone with the Wind AND Academy Awards

My Brother Sam Is Dead

JAMES LINCOLN COLLIER
CHRISTOPHER COLLIER

1974

My Brother Sam Is Dead, published in 1974, is a young-adult novel written by brothers James Lincoln Collier and Christopher Collier. The book is a historical novel set during the American Revolutionary War. It tells the story of two brothers caught in the turmoil and conflicting loyalties of the war. Sam Meeker, over the opposition of his father, joins the Continental Army to fight the British. The story is narrated by his younger brother, Tim, who looks up to Sam. As the events of the Revolution unfold, Tim has to make a choice. If he joins the American rebels, he will be fighting in opposition to his father and many other members of his Connecticut community. If he remains loyal to the British, he would be rejecting the ideals of his brave older brother.

My Brother Sam Is Dead has been a controversial novel. According to the Office of Intellectual Freedom of the American Library Association, the novel was the twelfth most frequently challenged book during the period 1990–2001. This means that people or groups tried to prevent the inclusion of the book in public library collections or in school libraries and curricula. The book has been challenged for several reasons. It contains occasional profanity, it depicts alcohol consumption (the Meeker family owns a tavern, and Mrs. Meeker begins to drink heavily to dull the pain of her worries about Sam), and it contains scenes of somewhat graphic violence.

The chief reason for the challenges to the book, though, has been that in the eyes of some readers, it

Eliphat "Life" Meeker is a Tory, a British loyalist. (Amy Nichole Harris / Shutterstock.com)

presents unpatriotic views about the American Revolution, questioning whether the Revolutionary War was necessary or desirable. Some readers characterize the book as antiwar propaganda that reflected public dissent over the war in Vietnam, which was still underway when the novel was written. Others might respond by saying that questioning the value of any war is a humane and rational response to the violence, death, and destruction that war inevitably causes. These readers would argue that the book has value because it asks questions about war without offering soothing answers.

My Brother Sam Is Dead was originally published in 1974 by Four Winds Press. The most readily available edition of the novel is the 2005 edition published by Scholastic.

AUTHOR BIOGRAPHY

My Brother Sam Is Dead was written by James Lincoln Collier and his brother, Christopher Collier.

Christopher, born on January 29, 1930, in New York City and known to family and friends as "Kit," was a distinguished professor of history at the University of Connecticut and continues to hold the title professor emeritus (an honorary title from the Latin for "one who has served his time"). Earlier, he taught history at the University of Bridgeport in Connecticut. As a historian, he did the research for several historical novels he wrote with his brother. After James proposed a subject for a book, Christopher researched the time period, including such details as eating utensils, names, weather, terrain, clothing, and all the myriad other details needed to make a historical novel feel true and give it the ring of authenticity. He also tended to create the characters in the novel and prepare an outline of the proposed book. He then submitted this material to his brother James, who turned these raw materials into novels. Meanwhile, Christopher achieved distinction in his own right. He was Connecticut state historian from 1985 to 2004, and his book *Roger Sherman's Connecticut: Yankee Politics and the American Revolution*, published in 1971, was nominated for a Pulitzer Prize.

Although Christopher laid the historical foundations for *My Brother Sam Is Dead* and other novels, the creative writer in the pair was James. James was born on June 27, 1928, in New York City. He graduated from Hamilton College with a bachelor's degree in 1950. After a stint as a private in the U.S. Army in 1950–1951, he became a writer and magazine editor, a vocation he pursued full-time until 1958, and he has published hundreds of articles in such periodicals as the *New York Times*, *Time* magazine, *Boy's Life*, and *Reader's Digest*.

Beginning in the 1960s, James became a remarkably prolific book author. Early in his career, he wrote several books for adults about historical topics and various social issues. An enthusiastic student of jazz, he is the author of *The Making of Jazz: A Comprehensive History* (1978) and biographies of such jazz luminaries as Duke Ellington, Louis Armstrong, and Benny Goodman. With Christopher, he wrote twenty-three nonfiction books in the "Drama of American History" series, each book examining an era in the nation's history. He also wrote numerous nonfiction books for children. Many of these were biographies with the words "You Never Knew" in the title; the first, *The Sitting Bull You Never Knew* (2003), was followed by similar biographies of George Washington, Frederick Douglass, Abraham Lincoln, and numerous other historical figures. His fiction for children began with *The Teddy Bear Habit; or, How I Became a Winner*, published in 1967, followed by seventeen more books, the last of which was *The Empty Mirror*, published in 2004. His work also includes several titles in a series called Great Inventions; among them are *Clocks, Gunpowder and Weaponry, Steam Engines*, and *Vaccines*.

In addition to *My Brother Sam Is Dead*, the Colliers collaborated on several other historical novels for young adults: *The Bloody Country* (1976), *The Winter Hero* (1978), *Jump Ship to Freedom* (1981), *War Comes to Willy Freeman* (1983), *Who Is Carrie?* (1984), *The Clock* (1991), and *With Every Drop of Blood* (1994).

PLOT SUMMARY

Chapters 1–3
Tim Meeker's older brother, Sam, arrives at the family-owned tavern one evening in April 1775 to announce that rebel colonists called the Minutemen have just won a victory over the British, whom he refers to as "Lobsterbacks" because of their red uniform coats. In this way he begins an argument with his father, who is a Tory, or one who has remained loyal to the British government. Mr. Meeker quizzes Sam about the battle, asking him who fired the first shots, but Sam does not know. With the family are several guests, including a minister, Mr. Beach, who all support the British.

In the argument that follows, they question the wisdom of war with England, but Sam insists that the war is being fought on principle. Later, Tim questions Sam about his experiences at Yale. He learns that Tim is a member of Captain Benedict Arnold's unit and that he has returned home to get his father's gun, a Brown Bess. That night, Tim hears Sam and their father arguing about the gun and about the war. Mr. Meeker demands that Sam either abandon the rebel cause or leave the house. Sam decides to leave.

Tim, the novel's narrator, explains that the town, Redding, Connecticut, is made up of Anglicans, who tend to be loyal to the British crown, and Presbyterians, who tend to favor the rebel cause. Tim's family is Anglican, but Tim is not sure which side he supports. After Tim attends church, he encounters an Indian, Tom Warrups,

MEDIA ADAPTATIONS

My Brother Sam Is Dead is available as an audiobook produced by Audio Bookshelf in 1999. The book is read by John C. Brown. Running time is four hours and thirty-three minutes.

who is giving shelter to Sam. Tim visits Sam and finds him with his girlfriend, Betsy Read, the daughter of Colonel Read, a rebel supporter.

Tim tries to persuade Sam to abandon the rebel cause and return to college, but Sam insists on the value of fighting on principle. Tim is uncomfortable when Sam and Betsy ask him to listen in on conversations at the tavern and pick up information that might help the rebels. Tim sees the Brown Bess and pleads with Sam to return it to their father. Later, Tim reflects on the war, noting that in his community, the only effect of the war seems to be that everyone is talking—and arguing—about it.

Months go by with no word of Sam; meanwhile, Tim works hard at his arithmetic, hoping he can impress his admired older brother with his skills. Finally, in November, Betsy appears at the tavern and furtively informs Tim with a nod that Sam has returned. Earlier, Tim had promised not to inform his parents if Sam returned.

Chapters 4–5
Tim spots a troop of rebel soldiers riding up to the tavern. He peeks through the door and sees that his mother is being held at gunpoint while his father tries to escape the grasp of the soldiers, who are demanding his gun. During the scuffle, one of the soldiers slashes Mr. Meeker's cheek with a sword. Tim knows he needs to take action, so he runs to Tom Warrups's teepee and takes the Brown Bess out of the hands of the sleeping Sam. Sam runs after Tim, who threatens to shoot Sam, but Sam manages to get the gun back. When the two brothers return to the tavern, the soldiers are gone. Once again, Sam runs away.

By January 1776, Tim notices the war's effects on the community. Soldiers have been seizing guns, as well as cattle for food. Tim sorely misses his brother and continues to wonder which side he would fight on if he joined the war. In April, the shadowy Mr. Heron wants Tim to deliver some business letters for him, but Mr. Meeker, not wanting to lose another son, refuses to give his permission and warns Tim against becoming involved with Heron. Tim, however, wants to take part in the war, despite his father's warnings that he could be thrown into a prison ship. Tim is determined to get away and run the errand for Mr. Heron.

Chapters 6–7

Tim finds his chance when his father sends him to deliver a keg of rum that Mr. Heron has ordered from the tavern. Tim agrees to deliver a letter to Fairfield. He uses fishing as the excuse to explain his absence from home. As he is walking to Fairfield, he encounters Betsy, who tells him she is going to see Sam. Betsy suspects that Tim is carrying a letter for Mr. Heron and is worried that its contents could somehow put Sam in danger. Tim refuses to show her the letter or open it. The two fight over the letter, and Betsy runs away with it. Tim finds the open letter on the road. It reads, "If this message is received, then we will know that the messenger is reliable."

By the summer of 1776 Tim has forgotten about the letter and his failure to deliver it. The family receives letters from Sam, who claims to be in good condition. Mr. Meeker does not want to respond to the letters, thinking that doing so would indicate his approval of Sam's course of action. Mrs. Meeker, though, responds to Sam's second letter. As November approaches, Mr. Meeker makes plans for his annual trip to Verplancks Point, where he sells cattle and buys supplies for the tavern. He decides to take Tim with him. Along the way, in Ridgebury, they encounter cattle thieves who claim to be patriots and who beat Mr. Meeker. British loyalists ride up, scare the cattle thieves away, and accompany Tim and his father to the house of relatives in New Salem.

Chapters 8–9

Tim and his father stay at the home of the Platts. Sitting around the fireside, Mr. Meeker and Mr. Platt discuss the war and its effects on law and order. After Tim falls asleep, his cousin Ezekiel takes him to bed. Ezekiel is critical of Sam for deciding to join the rebels. Tim defends his

brother, but when his cousin asks him which side he would fight for, he answers that he would fight for the loyalists, even though that would mean fighting against his brother. The next morning, Tim and his father resume their journey to Verplancks. They complete their business, and then begin the trip home. It starts to snow, however, so on the way back, they spend another night with the Platts.

The following morning, they set off for home along a snow-covered road. Mr. Meeker rides ahead to check the condition of the road. When he does not return, Tim worries and rides ahead to find his father. Instead, he finds a confusion of horse tracks in the snow and concludes that the cattle thieves have captured his father. His first impulse is to try to save his father, but he reasons that the best course of action is to get home with the supplies. Along the road, he encounters the cattle thieves. He acts bravely and confidently, asking them if they are the escort that was supposed to join him and his father. The cattle thieves, fearing an ambush, leave; Tim is triumphant, for he has saved the supplies. After traveling all night, he arrives home.

Chapters 10–11

Tim is now the "man of the house" and takes pride in his knowledge and willingness to do the work of the tavern. The winter passes without incident, but on April 26, 1777, Tim hears the sound of cannon and overhears a local black man, Ned, telling a rebel officer, Captain Betts, that British troops are coming. Tim sees the troops and is impressed by their uniforms and discipline. He tells one of the troops that he is not worried, for most of Redding is Tory. After the kidnapping of his father by rebels, he concludes that he himself is a Tory. He sees several British officers enter Mr. Heron's house.

At this point, violence begins to escalate. British officers break into Captain Betts's home. Then a rebel messenger is shot. Colonel Read carries the wounded messenger into the Meeker tavern and sends Tim to bring Dr. Hobarts. As Tim is running through the woods, he hears gunfire. From his hiding place as he watches as British soldiers surround the house of Captain Starr. From inside the house, Starr, Ned, and other rebels fire on the British, who finally enter the house and kill all the rebels. Tim vomits when he sees Ned beheaded. The British set fire to the house as Tim continues on his way to the home of Dr. Hobarts. Having witnessed the cruelty of the British soldiers, he now concludes that he no longer sympathizes with the Tories.

Dr. Hobarts dresses the messenger's gunshot wound. The messenger says that Benedict Arnold and his troops are pursuing the British through Redding, raising Tim's hopes that he will see his brother. Tim is puzzled when Captain Betts arrives at the tavern, saying that the British released him but that they have not released Tim's friend, Jerry Sanford, whom the British have also captured. Rebel officers enter the tavern and demand to be fed. One of the officers is Benedict Arnold. Tim rushes out to the nearby rebel troops and is taken to Sam inside the church, where the two brothers have a joyous reunion. Sam tells Tim that he has tried to secure the release of their father from prison. Mrs. Meeker tries to persuade Sam to return home after his enlistment is up, but Sam refuses.

Chapters 12–14
In June 1777, Tim learns that both his father and Jerry Sanford have died on British prison ships. Mrs. Meeker is disgusted with the war, and even Betsy, Sam's girlfriend, says that she no longer cares who wins. As conditions for both soldiers and civilians deteriorate, Tim loses all sympathy for either side. People are poor and underfed, and Tim is always hungry. Sam returns in the winter of 1778, looking underweight and ragged. He talks about the horrors of war and how soldiers have been forced to steal cattle or face starvation. He says that his commander, General Putnam, hangs thieves as an example. Sam urges Tim to slaughter the family's cattle and freeze the meat in the barn, but Tim hopes to sell the cattle.

Months pass, and one evening Sam and Tim hear noises outside. When they investigate, they discover that four of their cows have been stolen. Sam pursues the thieves, but two of them ambush him, tie him up, and say that they are reporting him for cattle thievery to General Putnam. They are able to frame Sam because he was supposed to be on duty elsewhere. Tim tries to convince Colonel Parsons of Sam's innocence, but Parsons makes it clear that General Putnam wants to make an example of someone. Over the next weeks, the despairing Mrs. Meeker begins to drink heavily. Tim works for Sam's release, but Sam is found guilty and sentenced to be shot. Tim manages to persuade General Putnam to allow him to visit Sam in the cabin where he is being held.

The date of Sam's execution is February 16. Tim is determined to do something to save Sam. He carries a sharpened bayonet to the camp where he believes Sam is still being held and thinks about killing the sleeping guard and releasing the prisoners. He decides that he cannot take another man's life. As he runs away, the guard awakens and shoots at Tim, grazing his shoulder. Tim throws the bayonet over the wall, hoping Sam can use it to escape. He then realizes that Sam has been moved to a different location. The following morning, Tim and members of the public witness the executions. A bag is placed over Sam's head and he is shot. As he writhes on the ground, one of the soldiers shoots him again.

Epilogue
In the epilogue, Tim notes that he has written his story down in 1826, fifty years after the colonies declared their independence. Sam was executed forty-seven years earlier. Tim and his mother have moved to Pennsylvania and opened a tavern there. Tim says that he and his own family have had a good life. Tim continues to wonder whether the United States could have achieved independence without so much bloodshed.

CHARACTERS

Benedict Arnold
Arnold holds the rank of captain and is the commander of Sam's unit, the Governor's Second Foot Guard.

Mr. Beach
Mr. Beach is an elderly minister and a British loyalist.

Captain Betts
Captain Betts is a local rebel who is captured by the British but unaccountably released.

Mr. Heron
Heron is a shadowy figure who wants Tim to deliver letters for him. He appears to be a spy or at least someone of no principle who pursues his own ends during the war, even though he says that he is a Tory.

Dr. Hobarts

Hobarts is a local doctor called in to tend to the wounds of a messenger shot by the British.

Eliphalet Meeker

Eliphalet, known to everyone as Life, is Tim and Sam's father and the owner of a tavern in Redding, Connecticut. He is a staunch Tory, and much of the conflict of the novel involves his refusal to support Sam in his decision to join the Continental Army and fight for the rebels. He is ambushed and captured by cattle thieves and dies of cholera on a British prison ship.

Sam Meeker

The action of the novel centers on the decision of Sam Meeker to abandon his studies at Yale and join the Continental Army. Because of this decision, he is in conflict with his Tory father. Sam is gone for long periods of time, but he returns to Redding when he can. He is greatly admired by his younger brother, Tim. Late in the novel, Sam is framed for stealing cattle. He is arrested, and his commanding officer, General Putnam, sentences him to death. In the novel's final scene, he is executed by firing squad.

Susannah Meeker

Mrs. Meeker is Sam and Tim's mother. She does not play a particular role in the events surrounding Sam, but she serves as a kind of chorus on the effects of the war. She does not support Sam in his decision to join the rebels, but unlike Mr. Meeker, she is willing to maintain contact with her son. After Sam is arrested, she turns to drink for solace. In the epilogue, the reader learns that she and Tim moved to Pennsylvania and opened a tavern there. She has been able to recover from the events of the novel, and in her later years, she continued to talk about her headstrong son.

Tim Meeker

Tim is the protagonist of the novel, as well as its first-person narrator. At the start of the novel, he is fourteen years old. He looks up to his older brother Sam, and when the war breaks out, he envies his brother and wishes that he could take part in the adventure of the war. As the war grinds on, however, Tim reflects on its effects on the country and on his community and begins to have serious doubts about the value and purpose of the war.

The reader witnesses the process of Tim's maturation as he helps his mother in the tavern, accompanies his father on the annual trip to Verplancks Point for supplies, and tries to free his brother after Sam's arrest. He goes from being an adolescent observer of the action, uncertain how to react to what he sees and hears, to a young man with principles and beliefs of his own.

In the epilogue, the reader learns that Tim is narrating the events from the perspective of a half century later. During the intervening years, he has formed a family of his own and has been successful in business. He calls the United States a great nation, but even in 1826, he still has doubts about whether war, with its bloodshed and destruction, was the best way for the nation to achieve independence.

Ned

Ned is a local African American who fights for the rebels. He joins a group of rebels in the home of Captain Starr. When British soldiers attack the house, Ned is beheaded in the fight, an event that has a profound impact on Tim, who sees it happen.

Colonel Parsons

Parsons is a rebel officer in Redding, attached to Sam's unit. Tim pleads with him in an effort to gain the release of Sam. Parsons is somewhat sympathetic to Sam's plight and willing to listen to Tim, but he says that there is nothing he can do.

Ezekiel Platt

Ezekiel is Tim and Sam's cousin. In a conversation with Tim, Ezekiel is critical of Sam's decision to join the rebels.

Mr. Platt

Platt lives in New Salem, Connecticut. He is Tim and Sam's uncle. Tim and his father stay with the Platts during their journey to Verplancks Point to sell cattle and purchase supplies.

General Putnam

Putnam is a rigid, unyielding officer who is determined to make an example of any of his men who are caught thieving. After Sam is framed for cattle theft, Putnam refuses to reconsider Sam's case and sentences him to be executed.

Betsy Read

Betsy is Colonel Read's teenage daughter and Sam's girlfriend. She is depicted as outspoken and loyal to Sam and the cause of the rebels. She confronts Tim when he is delivering a letter for Mr. Heron and wrests the letter away from him. Later in the novel, she becomes sick of the war and just wants it to end.

Colonel Read

Colonel Read, a patriot, is Betsy's aging father.

Jerry Sanford

Jerry is Tim's friend. Although he is only ten years old, he is captured by the British and dies on a prison ship.

Captain Starr

Starr is a rebel officer who is killed by the British in a firefight surrounding his home.

Tom Warrups

Tom is a local Indian. He lives on land owned by Colonel Read, and he gives shelter to Sam after Sam flees his home.

THEMES

Adolescence

By having Tim Meeker tell the story, the authors are able to present a portrait of adolescence in colonial America. Tim is fourteen years old when the story begins; he is about eighteen when the novel ends (although, of course, he is much older in the epilogue). The novel depicts a boy whose life is in many ways typical for boys in his situation. He admires and idolizes an older brother who has gone off to a prestigious college and later joins the Continental Army. He absorbs many of the viewpoints of his family and community, although throughout his process of maturation, he questions those viewpoints. He wants very much to become a man. To that end, he studies arithmetic and works hard to learn the family's business, and after his father and Sam are gone and his mother turns to drink, he essentially runs the business. He is immensely proud of himself when he manages to evade the clutches of the cattle thieves and is able to return home with the family's winter supplies. Chiefly, however, the novel deals with the theme of adolescence in its depiction of a boy trying desperately to make sense of the events surrounding him.

Father-Child Relationships

A major conflict of the novel involves Mr. Meeker and his older son, Sam. Mr. Meeker is a Tory, so he does not support the rebel cause. Sam, however, has attended Yale, where he and many of his college friends have become fired with revolutionary fervor. Sam repeatedly insists that he is fighting for a principle, one with which his father does not agree. Indeed, the novel opens with an argument between Sam and his father about the war's issues.

Sam has come home from Yale wearing a Continental Army uniform. He is prepared to go to war, but Mr. Meeker scoffs at the idea. When Sam returns to Redding, he has to remain in hiding to avoid his father. He writes letters home, but Mr. Meeker will not respond, believing that any response would suggest approval of Sam's course of action. The conflict between the two is never resolved, for Mr. Meeker is abducted and dies before he can ever reach an understanding with Sam. The suggestion is that such a conflict can never be resolved, particularly when the fog of war causes permanent divisions within families and communities.

Wars

A major question that has surrounded *My Brother Sam Is Dead* has been whether it is an antiwar novel. Many readers believe that it is, that its fundamental thesis is that the Revolutionary War—a war that is deeply connected with the formation of the United States as a nation—did not have to be fought. Others would argue that the book questions the purpose and value of war but that questioning does not necessarily mean that the book opposes the Revolutionary War or any war. Nevertheless, the novel's focus is not on the historic battles of the war but on the effects of the war in one community. Tim and his community face rising prices, shortages of food and other necessities, and a general sense of confusion. Occasionally, the war intrudes into the community and people are killed. While many men fight on principle, others, such as the cattle thieves and probably Mr. Heron, take advantage of the confusion for their own gain. Ultimately, innocent people are swept up in the war, a theme that culminates with the death of Sam, who is entirely innocent of the charges against him.

TOPICS FOR FURTHER STUDY

- Conduct Internet and library research about the kinds of firearms the colonists used during the Revolutionary War—firearms that were in short supply. These included the British-made Brown Bess musket owned by the Meeker family, as well as the American-made Pennsylvania rifle. Prepare a PowerPoint or SlideShare presentation about these weapons and, in an oral report, describe their history and characteristics.

- Most Americans are familiar with the Declaration of Independence, signed by the American colonists in 1776. Fewer, though, are familiar with a document called the Declaration of Independence by the Loyalists, which is similar in many respects to the Declaration of Independence but pledges support to Great Britain. Locate a copy of the Declaration of Independence by the Loyalists (one is available at http://www.royalprovincial.com/military/facts/ofrdecl.htm) and write an essay comparing and contrasting the two documents.

- Research the life of Benedict Arnold, whose name has survived as that of a traitor to the American cause. A good place to start might be Jean Fritz's *Traitor: The Case of Benedict Arnold*, available from Penguin Books in a 1997 edition. Write a scene in which Sam Meeker, Mr. Meeker, and Benedict Arnold are having a conversation about the war. Perhaps Mrs. Meeker could join in as well. Post your script on your social networking site and invite your classmates to comment on it. Alternatively, perform the scene you have written with a group of your classmates.

- Research the role that Indians and African Americans played in the Revolutionary War. You might explore, for example, the history of the 2nd Company of the 4th Connecticut Regiment, an all-black unit. Similarly, you might explore the role of the Oneida Indians, who joined George Washington at Valley Forge and whom Washington employed to harass the British. Prepare a chart listing the units, tribes, and individuals whose contributions you have researched, and share your chart with your class. Be prepared to explain the contribution of each entry on your chart.

- Perhaps one of the best-known and most celebrated young-adult novels set during the American Revolution is *Johnny Tremain* by Esther Forbes. This Newbery Award–winning novel was originally published in 1944 but is available in a more recent edition published by Yearling in 1987. Like the Colliers' novel, its protagonist is a fourteen-year-old boy at the start of the story. Like Tim Meeker, Johnny has to examine his loyalties. Write a report, using pertinent quotations from the two novels, explaining how they are similar and where they differ, particularly in attitudes about the war. As an alternative, watch the Walt Disney adaptation of the novel (with the same title) released in 1957 and available on DVD.

STYLE

Irony

One characteristic of *My Brother Sam Is Dead* that reinforces its themes is the bitter irony of some of the events. An event is said to be ironic when it turns out in a way that would normally be unexpected; usually, authors use irony as a way of making a larger point. Two events in this novel stand out for their profound irony.

The first is the capture and death of Mr. Meeker. Throughout the novel, Mr. Meeker is depicted as a staunch Tory—a supporter of the British—yet as he and Tim are returning home from their trip to Verplancks Point, he is ambushed and taken prisoner by men who claim to be rebel Patriots. Later, the reader learns that Mr. Meeker is being held on a British prison ship, where he dies, so his imprisonment and death seem to be random.

Sam joins the Continental Army. *(n4 PhotoVideo | Shutterstock.com)*

The events surrounding the death of Sam are triply ironic. First, he is arrested for a crime he did not commit (stealing cattle). Second, the cattle he supposedly stole were owned by his own family. Finally, he is put to death on the orders of his patriot commander, General Putnam, though throughout the novel, Sam has vigorously defended the rebel cause and has fought bravely on the side of the patriots. These ironies, taken together, reinforce a major theme in the novel: that war is a confusing, destructive, muddled affair, one that makes little sense, that sweeps up the innocent as well as the guilty, and that ultimately resolves nothing.

Point of view

My Brother Sam Is Dead is narrated in the first person by Tim Meeker, who is fourteen years old when the novel begins in 1775. At the time of Sam's death, Tim would be about eighteen years old. Tim is what is sometimes called a "naïve" narrator; some literary historians use the term "primitive consciousness" to describe this narrative technique.

As a young boy, Tim does not understand the events that are occurring. He has no grasp of the political issues surrounding the outbreak of the war. On the one hand, he admires, and sometimes envies, his older brother. He would like to take part in the adventure and heroism of war. On the other hand, he is bitterly resentful of his brother for opposing their father and his friends and being away much of the time.

His views of the war shift. Sometimes he thinks he would fight for the patriots; at other times, he thinks he would fight on the side of the Tories. He witnesses firsthand the hardships of war, so his voice becomes the vehicle the authors use to comment on the effects of the war. As the novel proceeds and Tim grows older, he matures, yet he continues to largely ignore the larger issues at stake. At the novel's end, his main motivation is to save his brother.

Through the use of this narrative technique, the authors are able to show the confusion and conflicting loyalties that can arise in war. More specifically, this technique suggests that the Revolutionary War was as much a civil war as it was a war between the Americans and the British—one that divided not only nations but also families.

HISTORICAL CONTEXT

The American Revolution

The historical context for *My Brother Sam Is Dead* is, of course, the American Revolutionary War, which began with the Battle of Lexington and Concord on April 19, 1775, in Middlesex County, Massachusetts. Hostility between Great Britain and its American colonies had been building for years. In the wake of the Seven Years' War between Great Britain and France (1756–1763), Britain was deep in debt. To pay off this debt, the British Parliament passed laws designed to raise revenues from the American colonies through taxes. Among these laws were the Stamp Act of 1765 and the Townshend Acts of 1767. These laws provoked outrage among many colonists. Matters began to come to a head with the Boston Tea Party of late 1773, when American rebels, disguised as Indians, boarded British ships, removed chests of tea from their holds, and hurled the tea into Boston Harbor. To restore order in Massachusetts and to punish the colonists, Parliament passed what were called the Coercive Acts, sometimes called the Intolerable Acts. The colonists responded in 1774 by holding the First Continental Congress, which resulted in two measures. The colonists petitioned the king of England, George III, urging him to repeal the acts (this at a time when Parliament and the king often stood in opposition to each other). The other was to call for a boycott of British goods.

COMPARE
&
CONTRAST

- **1770s:** American revolutionists are engaged in war against the British to gain their independence; the Continental Army is formed in 1775, marking the birth of the U.S. military.

  1970s: The U.S. military is still embroiled in the war in Vietnam, supporting the South Vietnamese in their civil war for independence, but support for the war in the United States is largely eroded.

  Today: The U.S. military continues to play a role in supporting independence movements in such places as Iraq and Libya, although many Americans oppose these military actions.

- **1770s:** The United States is home to a total of just nine chartered colleges, including Harvard and Yale, and thirteen unchartered academies or colleges, including one called Little Girls' School, now Salem College, and John McMillan's Log School, now Washington and Jefferson College. Most have religious affiliations.

  1970s: Students can choose from among a vast array of public and religiously affiliated private colleges and universities to attend in all fifty states.

  Today: In additional to traditional on-campus public and private colleges and universities, many students earn degrees from online colleges and universities, allowing them to keep jobs, live at home, and do schoolwork at a time that is convenient for them.

- **1770s:** It is not unusual for a young boy or girl to work in a family business, including taverns where alcohol is served. At a time when pure, clean drinking water is not always available, youngsters sometimes drink fermented beverages such as beer and cider.

  1970s: State laws prohibit children below a certain age from working, although these laws are generally flexible for family-owned businesses. The legal drinking age in many states is eighteen.

  Today: While state laws vary, in general minors are prohibited from working in any business whose primary purpose is to serve alcohol. The National Minimum Drinking Age Act of 1984 raised the legal drinking age to twenty-one in all states.

British loyalists, or Tories, remained hopeful that some accommodation could be reached. Those hopes collapsed, though, when the king rejected the colonists' plea. Meanwhile, colonial leaders maintained that, because the colonies did not send representatives to Parliament, that body had no authority to tax them. This view was expressed in the still well-known phrase "no taxation without representation."

In response to the outbreak of hostilities, the Second Continental Congress convened on May 10, 1775; its chief accomplishment would later be the drafting of the U.S. Declaration of Independence. Even after war broke out, most delegates to the Second Continental Congress were reluctant to declare independence. But after the king issued a Proclamation of Rebellion, the movement for American independence gathered momentum. In June 1775, the Continental Army was formed with General George Washington in command. The colonists won a major victory at the Battle of Bunker Hill on June 17, 1775, but the Continental Army under Washington suffered a series of setbacks, and in the early years of the war, its outcome was uncertain. Washington and his forces regrouped, crossed the Delaware River in December 1776, and won a victory at Trenton, New Jersey. After further setbacks, the Continentals won at Saratoga, New York, in 1777, but this victory was followed by the army's famous winter encampment at Valley Forge, Pennsylvania, in 1777–1778, when dispirited

Colonial-era musket (*Donald Gargano / Shutterstock.com*)

soldiers endured horrific conditions. The war moved to the South, but the British underestimated the intensity of resistance it would encounter, so the war reverted to the North. Ultimately, the British army was bottled up at Yorktown, a peninsula extending into the Chesapeake Bay off the coast of Virginia, and surrendered in October 1781.

On June 7, 1776, a representative to the congress from Virginia, Richard Henry Lee, submitted a resolution of independence. A committee was formed to draft a document whose purpose was to explain why the resolution of independence was approved, if in fact it later was. On June 11, Thomas Jefferson, John Adams, Robert Livingston, Benjamin Franklin, and Roger Sherman formed a "Committee of Five" to draft a declaration of independence, though the committee relied on Jefferson to compose the draft. On June 28, the committee submitted the declaration to the congress, which debated the declaration until July 2, 1776, when it approved Lee's resolution. After two days of further discussion and debate, the Second Continental Congress approved the declaration for publication on July 4, traditionally marked as Independence Day in the United States (although most of the delegates who signed the Declaration did not do so until August 2, 1776, some even later). The United States declared itself a free and independent nation, but it would take five years of bloodshed, such as that depicted in *My Brother Sam Is Dead*, to end British rule in the American colonies.

CRITICAL OVERVIEW

My Brother Sam Is Dead met with a positive reception from many readers and critics and was cited as a Newbery Honor book in 1975. Hughes Moir, in *Language Arts*, praises the novel by saying, "In *My Brother Sam Is Dead*,... the complexity of issues about the Revolutionary War and war in general is explored in ways perhaps unique in children's literature."

Writing in *Censored Books II: Critical Viewpoints, 1985–2000,* Kathy G. Short goes further:

> The strength of this novel is not in its factual detail but in its potential for raising questions about what is read in history books and about the problems we all face in our daily lives. The ending reminds us that there are no clear-cut answers to most of life's problems and that we need to face and embrace the contradictions and uncertainties. *My Brother Sam Is Dead* challenges us to think about this complexity and invites us to engage in dialogue with others about these issues.

Writing in the *ALAN Review,* Joel Taxel states this view more strongly. He notes that the novel "is, above all, an anti-war novel; a bitter denunciation of the folly and futility of war as a mode of social action."

Not all critics were convinced of the novel's effectiveness, however. Joyce Alpern, writing for the *Washington Post,* finds the character of Tim Meeker "believably confused," but in the end, she concludes, "Yet while the Meeker family's story might spice up some otherwise dull history lessons, it is unlikely to convince anyone that the Revolution was a mistake."

Donnarae MacCann, in *Interracial Books for Children Bulletin,* notes that the novel "appears to have been inspired by the anti-war movement of the 70s." She concludes, however, "The unrealistic plot complications reduce credibility, and the book comes close to...propaganda." While Taxel approved of the novel's message, as a novel, he says that, although it "does show the divisions within at least one New England Community, it offers little insight into the issues behind these divisions." He concludes that the novel is "somewhat disappointing."

CRITICISM

Michael J. O'Neal

O'Neal holds a Ph.D. in English. In the following essay, he examines My Brother Sam Is Dead *as a challenge to the mythology of America's foundations.*

The term *mythology* is widely used, not only in literary studies but in historical and religious studies as well. It is a troublesome word because its meaning can differ depending on the context

> SOME READERS HAVE OBJECTED TO THE NOVEL BECAUSE IT FLIES IN THE FACE OF THE MYTHOLOGY SURROUNDING THE FOUNDING OF THE UNITED STATES AND THUS EMERGES AS FIERCELY ANTI-PATRIOTIC. THE BOOK, THEY SAY, IS PROPAGANDA."

in which it is used. In an everyday sense, the word *myth* often refers simply to something that is untrue but perhaps popularly believed, principally because the myth is something that could be true or could have happened. Scholars, however, use the term in more specialized senses. The study of antiquity often focuses on Greek and Roman mythology: the gods and goddesses that the ancient Greeks and Romans believed in. By extension, the study of mythology examines the stories told by cultures about their creation and origins. In particular, ancient cultures, such as those of Japan, China, and Africa, have preserved stories and legends about how they came into being, and while those stories are not literally true, they create a narrative that serves to validate a sense of cultural value and identity.

What distinguishes the United States from these ancient cultures is that the nation is, in historical terms, so young. Its deepest roots extend to the late sixteenth century, but even throughout the seventeenth century, there was little sense of a national identity in the New World; the earliest colonists were Britons who just happened to have a new address. It was not until the eighteenth century that some sense of a unique American identity began to form, and it was only late in the century that the United States as a distinct geopolitical entity came together. Thus, the mythology of America is constructed on events that took place less than two and a half centuries ago—a mere blink of an eye in comparison with the history of some of the world's cultures.

Nevertheless, America has developed its own narrative, its own mythology, one that defines the nation as a culture. Most Americans are at least roughly familiar with much of that mythology. The Boston Tea Party survives as a symbol of resistance to tyrannical rule, and

WHAT DO I READ NEXT?

- The Collier brothers are the authors of *War Comes to Willy Freeman*, a young-adult novel published to embark on her own struggle for survival during the Revolutionary War, a particular challenge for an African American girl.

- Betsy Haynes is the author of *Spies on the Devil's Belt*, a young-adult novel published in 1974. It tells the story of a boy about the same age as Tim Meeker who joins the Continental Army with visions of heroism in his eyes. He discovers that, although he is "just" an errand boy, his errands take on great importance.

- In 1830, Joseph Plumb Martin narrated his experiences as a soldier during the Revolutionary War. His book was edited for young adults by George F. Sheer and published under the title *Yankee Doodle Boy: A Young Soldier's Adventures in the American Revolution Told by Himself* (1995).

- William Faulkner's short story "Two Soldiers," first published in 1942 (and available in *Collected Stories of William Faulkner*, published by Vintage in 1995), tells the story of a young man, Pete, who joins the U.S. Army after the attack on Pearl Harbor at the start of World War II. The story is narrated by his younger brother, who idolizes Pete and is confused by his departure for war. The story also examines the family's reaction to the war and Pete's decision to join the military.

- Michael Lee Lanning's *African Americans in the Revolutionary War* (2005) tells of the little-known, heroic role that African Americans played in the American Revolution while serving in integrated units.

- Ann Rinaldi's *Time Enough for Drums* (1986) is a novel set during the American Revolution and told from the point of view of a fifteen-year-old girl whose father is a rebel. She is irritated when he hires as her tutor a Tory, or British loyalist. She later discovers a dangerous secret about the tutor.

---

indeed the "Tea Party" was resurrected in the first decade of the twenty-first century as the name of a prominent conservative political movement whose principal goal was to curb higher taxes and government spending. The signing of the Declaration of Independence is celebrated every year on the Fourth of July (even though most of the declaration's signers put their name to it in August 1776).

Ralph Waldo Emerson's poem "Concord Hymn" immortalized the first shot fired at the Battle of Lexington and Concord, the first battle in the Revolutionary War, as "the shot heard 'round the world.'" Henry Wadsworth Longfellow's poem "Paul Revere's Ride" has enshrined in American mythology the story of Boston silversmith Paul Revere, whose midnight horseback ride on April 18–19, 1775, has given Americans the expression "one if by land, and two if by sea," referring to signal lanterns in the Old North Church designed to alert the rebels of British troop movements.

The story of Paul Revere is a good example of American mythology gone awry. He was not the only rider who raised the alarm that the British were coming, but the prominence given to his role enshrines the belief that the courage and resourceful of a single person can influence historical events. Further, Revere rode from Boston to Lexington, not Concord, as Longfellow's poem has it, but it hardly makes any difference. It is the underlying truth of the story, its mythology that stirs the American imagination. To this day, households keep Revere's name alive by buying "Paul Revere" brand silverware and cookware.

Other parts of the American narrative also hold a firm place in the nation's mythology. George Washington's winter encampment at Valley Forge, Pennsylvania, in 1777–1778, stands as a tribute to the courage and determination of the nation's founders in the face of overwhelming odds. Most people probably know little about Benedict Arnold, but his name survives and is occasionally even still invoked as that of a traitor to the American cause. Most people have seen *Washington Crossing the Delaware*, a famous 1851 painting by not-so-famous artist Emanuel Gottlieb Leutze that has immortalized Washington's daring generalship prior to the Battle of Trenton.

Many schoolchildren have long known the story of George Washington cutting down a cherry tree and, when confronted by his father, saying, "I cannot tell a lie. I did it." This parable entered the mainstream of American mythology through a story told by Parson Mason Locke Weems a hundred years after Washington's death. Is the story true? Almost certainly not. However, does it reflect a fundamental truth? If that fundamental truth is that George Washington, the father of the country, was an honest, honorable man whose example should be emulated, then yes, it is "true," at least in the mythological sense.

In a modern, skeptical age, writers take the myths of American history and turn them on their heads. They argue that the mythology surrounding the Revolutionary War is exaggerated and fails to reflect the facts of history. Often the war is depicted as a uniformly noble endeavor fought for an unimpeachably noble cause. In this version of the myth, the American rebels were fired by patriotic zeal. All were courageous in fighting British tyranny. The signers of the Declaration of Independence were wise beyond all measure. The British Parliament was mean-spirited and vindictive. British troops in America were cruel marauders. This is the version of the myth promulgated by *The Patriot*, a 2000 film starring Mel Gibson as an idealistic South Carolina farmer drawn into the Revolutionary War by the casual murder of his young son at the hands of a brutal British colonel who feels no compunction about executing civilians. The story is based loosely on that of the real-life Francis Marion, the "Swamp Fox," who carried on guerrilla warfare against the British during the war and who himself is part of the American narrative.

That brings us to *My Brother Sam Is Dead*. Some readers have objected to the novel because it flies in the face of the mythology surrounding the founding of the United States and thus emerges as fiercely anti-patriotic. The book, they say, is

propaganda. It carries a strong antiwar message that is likely a reflection of American weariness with the war in Vietnam, which was ongoing at the time the novel was written and published in the early 1970s. As the Vietnam War unfolded, America's role as a worldwide defender of freedom came into question. There were revelations that American authorities lied to the public about the course of the war. Stories came to light about instances of brutality on the part of American soldiers. Images of destroyed villages and fleeing civilians permeated news broadcasts. For some Americans, the sheer muddle of Vietnam undermined the entire endeavor, and they felt a sense of shame at American participation in the war. In this climate, they were ready for a book like *My Brother Sam Is Dead*, for the book mercilessly refuses to conform to the American narrative.

To support objections to the novel, some readers focus on those details that emphasize the war's brutality. The very title, a bold, clear-cut declarative sentence, resists seeing the war as the wellspring of the American democratic experiment. Rather, it focuses on the senseless death of a single individual, as if that death were the only noteworthy outcome of the Revolutionary War. Throughout the novel, neither side behaves particularly well. The British, to be sure, are guilty of barbarism; a notable instance is the beheading of Ned, the killing of all the men in the house of Captain Starr, and the firing of the house. Another is the imprisonment of Jerry Sanford on a prison ship, even though Sanford is just a ten-year-old boy. Mr. Meeker's death on a British prison ship is especially ironic given that he is a staunch Tory.

However, the colonial rebels are just as bad, as reflected in the actions of rebel cattle thieves, the capture and ultimate death of Mr. Meeker, and the unjust execution of Sam Meeker at the end. Rebels at one point hold Mrs. Meeker at gunpoint while demanding Mr. Meeker's gun. Further, rather than emphasizing the nobility of the principles for which the war was fought, the novel emphasizes a sense of waste. At one point, Mrs. Meeker says, "This war has turned men into animals.... They're animals now, they're all beasts." In reflecting on the death of his father, Tim Meeker says, "It seemed to me that everybody was to blame, and I decided that I wasn't going to be on anybody's side any more; neither one of them was right." When he learns about Valley Forge, Tim thinks, "It made me hope that

Grave marker for a continental soldier (Tony Robinson / Shutterstock.com)

the Rebels were at the end of their rope and would have to give up pretty soon and end this terrible war." Tim even comes to believe that the suffering of his beloved older brother served Sam right for daring to defy his largely Tory community and joining with the rebels. The story comes to an abrupt end with Sam dead, his chest on fire from the shots that kill him.

People can withstand having their mythology tampered with when the tampering is done for certain comic or satiric purposes so that it does not have to be taken seriously. People tend not to like it when they believe that their mythology is being seriously questioned when they are made to feel stupid for believing it. Mythology gives structure to human lives. It provides people with a link to their past, as well as a link to their future, and in this way, individuals become part of an unbroken chain. *My Brother Sam Is Dead*, in some respects at least, breaks the chain. Supporters of the novel believe the chain sometimes has to be broken in the interest of historical accuracy and one version of the truth. The novel's detractors believe that breaking that chain destroys faith and idealism and saps cultural identity. Each reader has to decide for himself which view matters most.

Source: Michael J. O'Neal, Critical Essay on *My Brother Sam is Dead*, in *Novels for Students*, Gale, Cengage Learning, 2012.

Kathy G. Short

In the following excerpt, Short summarizes the various thematic issues that have made My Brother Sam Is Dead *a controversial book in some quarters and seeks to promote its value as an enduring work of young-adult historical fiction.*

My Brother Sam Is Dead consistently appears on recommended reading lists for upper elementary and middle school students. English and language arts educators promote the book because of its high literary quality, particularly in relation to strong character development and use of setting. Social studies educators recommend this historical fiction novel because it offers alternative perspectives on the American Revolution and raises controversial questions and issues for students to consider.

Another type of list on which *My Brother Sam Is Dead* has consistently appeared throughout the years is lists of the most frequently banned books in the United States. Clearly there is something beyond literary merit and

THE HISTORICAL DETAILS AND SOURCES PRO-
VIDED BY THE COLLIERS INDICATE THEIR COMMIT-
MENT TO THE ACCURATE PORTRAYAL OF HISTORICAL
EVENTS, ALTHOUGH TELLING THE STORY OF
HISTORY ALWAYS INVOLVES INTERPRETATION BY
THE HISTORIAN."

historical perspectives that has caught the attention of the public.

So what is it about this historical fiction novel that captures both praise and condemnation? After describing the plot and themes of the book, I will overview the major criticisms that have led to censorship challenges and then discuss the literary and historical qualities that have led to awards and frequent use of the book in English and social studies classrooms.

My Brother Sam Is Dead was the first children's book written by James and Christopher Collier, two brothers who have since collaborated on other historical novels for children. In their collaborative writing process, Christopher is primarily responsible for the plot outline and the research needed to verify historical accuracy and authenticity. James crafts this research into a powerful piece of fiction. Written in 1974, the book received immediate acclaim by being named a Newbery Honor book, quite an accomplishment for a first novel.

The novel explores the complexity of the issues surrounding the American Revolution and war in general through the story of a Connecticut family torn apart by divided loyalties. The father is a Tory, a loyalist who wants to maintain his business and protect his family, while older brother Sam has decided to leave college and join the rebel forces. The story is told in first person through the eyes of Tim, the younger brother who must remain at home and deal with conflicting loyalties within his family and community. Tim idolizes Sam but, at the same time, loves and respects his father.

While the American Revolution is often portrayed in history textbooks as a battle between the Americans and the British, the Colliers based their novel on the fact that all people living in America

at that time were British subjects. The war was thus between various groups of Americans whose loyalties were different and whose positions were much more complex than simply Tory or Patriot. The Colliers portray the war as a *civil* war which divided families and communities rather than "good guys versus bad guys."

For example, while Tim's father is a Tory, he chooses not to become involved in the war while other neighbors actively support the conflict or join armies for one side or the other. A continuum between the two opposing positions was filled with many individuals, including those whose loyalties were unclear, neutral, or shifted according to whichever side appeared to be winning. The complexity of why various Americans did and did not get involved in the war is reflected through the range of characters that Tim encounters.

The novel begins with Tim witnessing an argument between Sam and his father over Sam's participation in a rebel uprising. Sam has come home to steal his father's gun in order to have the needed credentials to enlist in the rebel forces, an action that leaves the family without protection.

The war comes closer to Tim when he and his father take a trip to sell cattle and get supplies for the family tavern. While he and his father are given safe passage by local protection units sympathetic to the loyalists, on the way home his father is taken captive and only through trickery is Tim able to safely return home. The rebel bands that Tim and his father encounter are criminals who use the excuse of war to rob and kill, and they increase Tim's ambiguity and confusion about who really are the "good guys" in this war.

Tim takes over his father's work in their tavern and is soon so tired he has no time to think about war. The ugly reality of war again invades Tim's life when he sees a neighbor decapitated by loyalist forces and another young boy taken away to prison camp during a local skirmish.

When Sam's company returns to the area to winter, Tim and his mother are able to see Sam more frequently, and Tim becomes troubled by his brother's motivations in joining the rebel forces. Tim realizes that his brother remains in the army, not because of duty, but because he likes the excitement of being part of something big. Ultimately, Tim's family pays a terrible price when Sam and his father both lose their lives in the war. The father dies because of the terrible conditions on a prison ship, and Sam is executed as an "example" to other troops when he is falsely accused of stealing his own family's cattle.

In the epilogue, Tim writes fifty years after the war about the events in his life since that time and reflects on the terrible price his family paid. While he notes that the United States has prospered as an independent nation, he also remembers his father's words, "In war, the dead pay the debts of the living." He ends with this statement, "I keep thinking that there might have been another way, besides war, to achieve the same end."

The Colliers also include a section entitled "How much of this book is true?" where they note which details in the book are factually based on actual individuals and events and which are fictionalized. The historical details and sources provided by the Colliers indicate their commitment to the accurate portrayal of historical events, although telling the story of history always involves interpretation by the historian.

Clearly, *My Brother Sam Is Dead* is a novel that deals with difficult issues through its focus on the devastating effects of war on one particular family, a focus that immediately raises the concern of censors. In particular, censorship challenges have arisen for a number of reasons. One is the use of profanity by several soldiers. Another is the graphic descriptions of physical violence when a neighbor is decapitated and another is shot. When the mother can no longer cope with her problems after losing her husband and realizing that her older son is likely to be executed, she resorts to drinking for a time. Tim uses alcohol at one point to survive the cold when he is trapped alone in a bitter snowstorm. Finally, some critics have noted that the book, written during the height of the Vietnam controversy, takes a general stance against war and specifically questions the American Revolution.

Despite these censorship challenges, English, language arts, and social studies educators have continued to use and recommend this book. For English and language arts educators, the major appeal of the book is its strong literary quality which meets objectives within an English curriculum. This novel is an excellent one for studying character development because Tim, the young narrator, is a dynamic character who undergoes significant, but believable, change through the course of the novel. Sam remains a relatively static character who loses some of his enthusiasm for fighting but still remains dedicated to his

army. At the same time, Tim's perspectives and priorities gradually shift in complexity as he lives through difficult life events and matures from a naive young boy to a mature young man. The authenticity of the characterization provided by the Colliers is one reason why profanity is used several times by soldiers involved in battle.

Related to the strong characterization is the authors' effective use of setting to influence character and plot. Tim's ambiguity about the war shifts as he moves from place to place; this is particularly apparent during the supply trip, which parallels his confusion over which side of the war he personally wants to support. Whereas the town where Tim's family lives is primarily Tory sympathizers, Sam encounters strong Patriot views when he is away at college, which leads him to make his life-changing decision to join the rebel forces. Each setting reflects different perspectives on the conflict that shift the plot and influence the characters' actions and views.

The novel also encourages explorations of many different possible themes as well as provides an ending that invites further dialogue about the necessity of war. The authors invite response instead of neatly tying up loose ends. As readers discuss this novel, themes of the realities of war as they affect individuals and communities will likely be raised as well as themes regarding family relationships and responsibilities. Readers are immediately struck by the harsh realities of war through the deaths of the father and brother, and these realities are contrasted thematically with Sam's romantic view of war as heroism and the fight for freedom. The mother's anguish at the loss of her husband and son and Tim's reflections on whether the cause of freedom might have been gained in another manner can support readers in exploring the theme of war in a complex manner. History textbooks accept the necessity of war without question, and this novel asks readers to stop and think about whether war is really always the only way to accomplish our goals as a country. Readers are encouraged to explore this theme from a range of perspectives, including the causes of a war, individual reasons for fighting in a war, and the costs of war at different levels within a country, community, and family.

The book focuses less on details about where and when certain battles were fought and more on the values of family love, responsibility, respect, honest work, and the value of human life. The tensions between father and son, the mother's attempts to hold the family together despite their differences, the necessity of assuming responsibilities for absent family members, and the death of a parent are issues that today's students can relate to in powerful ways. The difficulty of family relationships is especially expressive in the portrayal of how Tim is torn between obeying his father and respecting his brother, particularly given his love for both.

Finally, the novel can be related to a study of historical fiction as a genre that goes beyond facts in order to personalize history and that uses the past to help explain the present. This novel is also an excellent way to connect the study of literature and history and to distinguish between fiction and fact by using the authors' note at the end of the book.

Within a social studies class, the use of novels such as this one serves to bring history alive as a story of the people who lived during a particular time period and made decisions that affect our lives and country today, not just a recounting of dates, people, and battles. Historical fiction brings history to life for today's students. Historical fiction also provides multiple perspectives on historical events that have too frequently been presented unidimensionally in textbooks. History textbooks have typically presented the American Revolution through a singular perspective on the necessity of the war to achieve freedom from England. By using this novel along with other novels set during this time period, teachers can encourage students to explore multiple interpretations of this specific war and of broader issues such as the dilemma of the uncommitted citizen and the necessity of war.

Because the Colliers portray the war as a civil war, the issue of who was patriotic and loyal to the country is challenged, and the oversimplification of these issues in textbooks is raised for debate. Also, because the main character in the book, Tim, is undecided about the war and must weigh various situations and events, the reader is effectively drawn into thinking through these issues alongside Tim. Sam's belief in the cause of freedom, which leads to his death, provides a powerful contrast to Tim's experience of freedom through the rest of his life but his questioning of the means to accomplishing that freedom. The Colliers invite debate—they have not decided the issue for readers—and they invite thoughtful discussion.

While some critics object that this novel encourages debate about war, controversy is the foundation of a social studies education. The valuing of differences and the challenging of ideas remain at the heart of a democracy in a diverse, free society. Teaching about ideas that are controversial has been one of the keystones to education, and novels such as this one open the possibility for dialogue.

While the Colliers do carefully present a range of perspectives on war through their characters, they also deliberately selected events that build toward a strong antiwar message. All authors and historians have a perspective, and so their work should not be criticized for making that perspective explicit for readers. Instead, teachers can use this book to talk about all history as interpretation and the importance of researching the perspective of novelists and historians and the thought collective of the time period in which they write, not just the time period they write about.

By having students read this book alongside other books about this time period as well as the history textbook, teachers can highlight history as interpretation. These comparisons could include comparing "facts" as presented across the books, reading aloud sections of the various texts that relate to the same events, creating alternative endings for any of the novels based on the interpretations offered by other texts, or rewriting the history textbook by using perspectives from historical fiction.

One possible comparison is between *Johnny Tremain* (Forbes, 1943) and *My Brother Sam Is Dead*, both strong literary novels dealing with the American Revolution but with contrasting attitudes toward war. *Johnny Tremain* was written in 1943, when the United States was immersed in a war that was supported with great patriotic fervor by the majority of Americans. The belief that "our side is right" and that war is justified prevailed, and so it is no surprise that Esther Forbes wrote a novel that glorified the American Revolution as necessary and worth the sacrifice of life. In contrast, the Colliers wrote their novel during the Vietnam War era, a time period when American society was questioning the necessity of war for solving political and social problems and focusing on the value of human life. Their decision to portray the American Revolution as a civil war and to focus on its effects through one family's devastating experiences grew out of society's views during the time period in which they wrote. This comment is not meant to question the historical accuracy of this novel. The Colliers did not twist the facts, as they knew them, but made every attempt to verify the events and people included in the novel. However, as writers and historians, they also brought their own interpretations to how they told the story with these facts.

The strength of this novel is not in its factual detail but in its potential for raising questions about what is read in history books and about the problems we all face in our dairy lives. The ending reminds us that there are not clear-cut answers to most of life's problems and that we need to face and embrace the contradictions and uncertainties. *My Brother Sam Is Dead* challenges us to think about this complexity and invites us to engage in dialogue with others about these issues. Where the censors see profanity, violence, alcoholism, and a lack of patriotism instead lies an invitation for thoughtfulness about the ways in which we live our lives and the realization that our decisions will affect both our lives and the lives of future generations.

Source: Kathy G. Short, "*My Brother Sam Is Dead*: Embracing the Contradictions and Uncertainties of Life and War," in *Censored Books II: Critical Viewpoints, 1985–2000*, edited by Nicholas J. Karolides, Scarecrow Press, 2002, pp. 305–310.

Sharon Scapple

In the following essay, Scapple characterizes My Brother Sam Is Dead *as a young-adult novel meant to engender questions about the cost of war, even when such conflicts are waged for seemingly important reasons.*

In response to the numerous comments he had received regarding how *My Brother Sam Is Dead* had finally offered something "new" on the American Revolution for young readers, Christopher Collier asserted that what was perceived as novelty was really a presentation of complex issues, something then lacking in juvenile literature. His intent was to incorporate elements of both the Whig and Progressive interpretations, "with strong emphasis on the latter," because he believed that a one-sided view commonly prevailed. He has cited *Johnny Tremain* as a text to reckon with, which is predominantly Whig, nineteenth-century Bancroftian. Collier wanted to "fill an historiographic gap . . . " (*Horn Book* 132). And he wanted to introduce the Progressive interpretation which views the war for

> WE READERS HAVE MUCH TO 'CHEW ON,' ISSUES OF SURVIVAL, MANHOOD, LOYALTIES, DOMINION. AND ALWAYS THE MOST DIFFICULT QUESTION: CAN THE COST OF LIFE BE MEASURED, WEIGHED?"

Independence as "only part of a civil war that pitted brother against brother as aristocratic and popular interests struggled to control the policy-making machinery of their respective colonies" (*Horn Book* 135).

According to Collier, *Brother Sam* (written in collaboration with his brother, James Lincoln Collier) moved well beyond other children's books which, "for the most part. . . [were] merely stories laid in the period and given verisimilitude by incorporating authentic detail" (*Horn Book* 136). Arising from Collier's commitment to provide readers with "some raw reality to chew on," *Brother Sam* was born (*Horn Book* 138). And, for readers, quite naturally arise questions of why brother Sam is dead. What were the complexities the Colliers addressed that gave this text its notoriety and singularity? What were the aspects of Revolutionary life which led to political choices and divided loyalties?

Three voices are distinct in expressing the trials and betrayals of those war years; three voices all from one family living in Redding, Connecticut, each speaking about different loyalties: to Family, God, King, Nation, Brethren. One voice, that of young Tim Meeker, the narrator, is confused and cannot make sense of the other two: his Patriot brother and his father, who is loyal to the King, but who does not proclaim himself a Tory.

Quite early in the story, Tim admits that all his life he had heard arguments about whether the colonists ought to rebel or obey the King. What confuses him the most is that the conflict does not have two sides as arguments should, but "about six sides." Some people say the King is King and should be obeyed; others believed people are to be free and the Lobsterbacks should be driven out of the country. Still others believe that being born English they will die English; yet, they think they should have more say about how they are to be governed. Some want New Englanders to join together, and some want all the colonies to unite. Tim's statement that Sam's side is sometimes called Patriot and sometimes called Rebel encapsulates his confusion.

Tim is young and so is his view of war. He is impressed by Sam's uniform and envies him for the glory of soldiering. Sometimes after Patriot officers drink at the tavern, he watches them leave, wondering which side he would choose if he were to become a soldier. He concludes that the "British had the best uniforms and the shiny new guns, but there was something exciting about the Patriots—being underdogs and fighting off the mighty British army." On more than one occasion he wonders what it would be like to shoot someone. He does realize, though, that if he were to fight Loyalist, his target could someday be Sam, his own brother.

Quite often and, in fact, throughout most of the novel, Tim is confused about the war, about who is on what side and why. He tries not to worry about it, but when his father is struck by a Rebel soldier searching for weapons, Tim realizes war has come to Redding. It is beginning to touch him personally. Later, after his father is captured by the cowboys (Rebel troops looking for beef), Tim is prompted to call himself a Tory.

Within a few months, however, Tim's allegiance switches to the Patriot cause. Quite understandably he is impressed when the British troops march into Redding "as if nothing in the world could stop them." Yet he is uncomfortable knowing that while Mr. Heron, a surveyor and supposed Tory, has invited the British officers into his house, some hundred yards away Patriots are planning to kill them. When the British strike Captain Starr's house and Tim witnesses the black slave's decapitation—"Ned's head jumped off his body and popped into the air"—he... "[doesn't] feel much like being a Tory any more."

After another year and half, the hazards of war have diminished his spirit; at age fourteen Tim hates the war and regrets not doing what would have been normal, going to school and making his way in the world. When Sam is arrested for stealing the family's cattle, Tim is "angry and bitter and ready to kill somebody. If... [he] only knew who." In the end, he is loyal to his brother, Sam, and tries to save Sam's life while nearly losing his own. Sam dies; Tim's shoulder is grazed by gunshot; and, for the rest

of his life the thought lingers as to whether there could have been ways other than war to be free of British governance.

The bid for no war is a message the Colliers iterate throughout the text. One Patriot, Colonel Read, a leader of men, quits the war because he disapproves of it. Another, the Anglican minister, Mr. Beach, hopes common sense will prevail—"Nobody wants rebellion except fools and hotheads," he claims. And of course, Life Meeker speaks directly against war. He addresses words and actions of sedition with rage, even ousting a customer in his tavern for talking about rebellion, and he tries to order his son Sam to strip himself of the Rebel uniform and stop such nonsense. He is an Englishman who holds to King-allegiance, obedience to the Fatherland.

Life Meeker knows war, and he will not have any part of it. When Sam professes that he is fighting for freedom and will willingly die for the cause, Life shouts: "Free? Free to do what, Sam? Free to mock your King? To shoot your neighbor? To make a mess of thousands of lives?" The bottom line for Mr. Meeker is: Free, Sam, to bring your buddy home in a sack? Life tells Tim later that injustices do indeed exist in the world. This can't be helped, but injustices are not eliminated by fighting.

Sam, a young rebel, sixteen, charmed by the soldier's life, and motivated by principle, joins the Continental army and later reenlists because he feels a part of something big, something important. At least this is Tim's view. Sam identifies himself as an American, and he will fight until the finish, as will his friends, for they have made a pact to do so. His end is dreadful, the guns so close that his clothes are set afire, and a second shot is necessary to kill him. How true is Mrs. Meeker's frequent lament: war turns men into beasts.

Quite ironically, as are the vagaries of war, Life Meeker dies on a British prison ship, and his son is shot because a General wants to set an example to control his troops. Sam's life becomes sacrificial and his father's satirical. Life Meeker pronounces at his death that he is then going to "enjoy the freedom war... [had] brought... [him]."

Why is brother Sam dead? Did he bring the wrath of God upon himself for not obeying his elders? Was he killed by his brothers to prompt a quicker end to the struggle? Was he a victim of idealism? Had "common decency between people" disappeared, as Mr. Platt feared and had "every man... [armed himself] against his neighbor?" Rebel and Tory in "open warfare?" Had the beast in man been excused in the name of justice?

In *My Brother Sam Is Dead*, the Colliers readily engage readers in the dilemmas and hazards of Revolutionary life. We readers have much to "chew on," issues of survival, manhood, loyalties, dominion. And always the most difficult question: Can the cost of life be measured, weighed?

Source: Sharon Scapple, "Divided Loyalties: Why Is My Brother Sam Dead?" in *Phoenix Award of the Children's Literature Association 1990–1994*, edited by Alethea Helbig and Agnes Perkins, 1996, pp. 269–72.

SOURCES

Alpern, Joyce, "Not a Bad Tory," in *Washington Post Book World*, January 12, 1975, p. 4.

Brunner, Borgna, "Books Under Fire," in *Infoplease*, http://www.infoplease.com/spot/bannedbookslist.html (accessed April 19, 2001).

Bushman, Richard L., "Revolution," in *The Reader's Companion to American History*, edited by Richard Foner and John A. Garraty, Houghton Mifflin, 1991, pp. 936–42.

Collier, James Lincoln, and Christopher Collier, *My Brother Sam Is Dead*, Scholastic, 1974.

MacCann, Donnarae, "Militarism in Juvenile Fiction," in *Interracial Books for Children Bulletin*, Vol. 13, Nos. 6–7, 1982, pp. 18–20.

McElmeel, Sharron L., "Christopher Collier and James Lincoln Collier," in *Book Report*, Vol. 15, No. 2, September/October 1996, http://www.mcelmeel.com/writing/collier.html (accessed April 19, 2011).

Moir, Hughes, "Profile: James and Christopher Collier—More Than Just a Good Read," in *Language Arts*, Vol. 35, No. 3, March 1978, p. 373.

"The Order of Founding American Colonial Colleges," in *Barnard Electronic Archive and Teaching Laboratory*, http://beatl.barnard.columbia.edu/stand_columbia/order-colonialcolleges.html (accessed April 22, 2011).

Short, Kathy G., "*My Brother Sam Is Dead*: Embracing the Contradictions and Uncertainties of Life and War," in *Censored Books II: Critical Viewpoints, 1985–2000*, edited by Nicholas J. Karolides, Scarecrow Press, pp. 305–10.

Taxel, Joel, "Historical Fiction and Historical Interpretation," in *ALAN Review*, Vol. 10, No. 2, Winter 1983, pp. 32–36.

Williams, Charles, "James Lincoln Collier (1928–)," in *Jrank.org*, http://biography.jrank.org/pages/1985/Collier-James-Lincoln-1928.html (accessed April 19, 2011).

FURTHER READING

American Revolution Reference Library, UXL, 2000.
    This is a set of three volumes suitable for young adults. Volume one, *American Revolution: Primary Sources* includes historical documents connected with the Revolutionary War. *American Revolution: Almanac* provides a comprehensive summary of the events of the Revolutionary War. A third volume, *American Revolution: Biographies*, includes biographies of the major historical figures from the time period.

Jasanoff, Maya, *Liberty's Exiles: American Loyalists in the Revolutionary World*, Knopf, 2011.
    This scholarly volume tells the story of those Americans who remained loyal to the British crown during the Revolutionary War. In effect, it tells the story of the war's losers and traces their fate after the war.

Loeper, John J., *Going to School in 1776*, Atheneum, 1973.
    This book illustrates the teaching methods and materials to which Tim Meeker would likely have been exposed if he had had time to attend school. The book describes textbooks such as spelling books, grammars, and what were called "arithmetickers," which Tim Meeker might have used to improve his skills in arithmetic. Among these books was the influential and long-lasting *New England Primer*.

Meyer, Edith Patterson, *Petticoat Patriots of the American Revolution*, Vanguard Press, 1976.
    This volume includes information about the activities of famous and not-so-famous women during the American Revolution. Many of these women aided the rebels, either individually or in organized groups, in the fight for independence.

SUGGESTED SEARCH TERMS

Benedict Arnold

Boston Tea Party

British prison ships AND Revolutionary War

Brown Bess

Continental Army

James Lincoln Collier AND Christopher Collier

My Brother Sam Is Dead

Revolutionary War

Second Continental Congress

Tories AND Revolutionary War

Valley Forge AND Revolutionary War

My Brother Sam Is Dead AND James Lincoln Collier AND Christopher Collier

My Name Is Asher Lev

CHAIM POTOK

1972

Chaim Potok's *My Name Is Asher Lev* was first published in 1972. The novel concerns the title character, a gifted young artist whose passion for drawing and painting is at odds with his strict Orthodox Jewish upbringing in the enclave of Crown Heights, Brooklyn, New York, during the 1950s and 1960s. As a somewhat autobiographical coming-of-age story, or bildungsroman, the novel pits young Asher against his father, a highly respected member of the Ladover community who has devoted his life to establishing yeshivas (Jewish schools) in the United States and across Europe in the aftermath of World War II. Caught in the middle is Asher's mother, an emotionally fragile but well-educated woman who is torn between her love for her husband and her love for her son. Asher commits himself to the study of art and becomes the protégé and surrogate son of the great Jewish painter Jacob Kahn. The novel culminates in Asher's triumphant success in the New York art world with the unveiling of his twin masterpieces, *The Brooklyn Crucifixion I* and *The Brooklyn Crucifixion II*, paintings of his mother in a Christ-like pose, which prove to be the final straw that results in him being cast out of the Ladover community. The novel was a critical and commercial success, and it secured Potok's reputation as an American writer who portrays the cultural nuances of a very thin slice of society, the Hasidim, to the general reading public. He published a sequel, *The Gift of Asher Lev*, in

Chaim Potok *(© Everett Collection Inc / Alamy)*

Inspired initially by Evelyn Waugh's *Brides-head Revisited* and James Joyce's *A Portrait of the Artist as a Young Man*, Potok loved literature, which displeased his parents, who expected him to become a doctor. Just like the fictional Asher Lev, Potok found his family and teachers dismissive of his desire to write because it was considered a frivolous occupation that would interfere with his studies of the Talmud, an important Jewish religious and philosophical text. This first-hand knowledge of the conflict between the religious and the secular is at the heart of *My Name Is Asher Lev*.

Potok published his first novel, *The Chosen*, to critical acclaim in 1967, and it was nominated for the National Book Award. The story concerns Danny Saunders's thirst for secular knowledge, which pits him against his father, a Hasidic rabbi, who expects his son to become a tzaddik, or spiritual leader, within their Orthodox community. Toward that end, his relationship with Danny is based solely on religion and lacks any personal connection beyond religion. Potok published a sequel, *The Promise*, in 1969, and followed it three years later with *My Name Is Asher Lev*.

Potok's subsequent novels, including *Davita's Harp* (1985) and *I Am the Clay* (1992), further cemented his reputation as his generation's foremost author concerned with the intersection of Judaism and American culture in the twentieth century. Apart from his fiction, Potok also published numerous nonfiction works on Jewish history, as well as short stories and essays for many literary journals. He wrote the critically acclaimed biography *My First 79 Years: Isaac Stern*, with the world-renowned violinist. *The Gift of Asher Lev* (1990) won the Jewish National Book Award in 1991, and his short story "Moon" won the O. Henry Award in 1999.

Potok married Adena Sarah Mosevitzky in 1958, and the couple had three children: Rena, Naama, and Akiva. Potok died of brain cancer on July 23, 2002, in Merion, Pennsylvania.

1990, in which Lev, now married and with a family, returns to Brooklyn after having lived abroad for many years.

AUTHOR BIOGRAPHY

Potok was born Herman Harold Potok on February 17, 1929, in the Bronx, New York, to Benjamin and Mollie Potok, both recent Polish immigrants and Orthodox Jews. As a boy, he enjoyed painting, but he decided at age sixteen to become a writer because it conflicted less with the family's religious beliefs. He remained equally committed to his religious studies and graduated at the top of his class from New York's Yeshiva University in 1950. Four years later, he graduated from the Jewish Theological Seminary and became a Conservative rabbi, which allowed him more freedom to pursue the arts than his former Orthodox affiliation did. Potok served as a chaplain during the Korean War, and in 1965, he received his Ph.D. in philosophy from the University of Pennsylvania. He legally changed his first name to Chaim (pronounced "*Hay*-yim") as an adult.

PLOT SUMMARY

Book 1

CHAPTER 1

Asher Lev introduces himself as the artist of the infamous *Brooklyn Crucifixion I* and *Brooklyn Crucifixion II,* which he admits are highly unusual

MEDIA ADAPTATIONS

- Aaron Posner adapted and directed *My Name Is Asher Lev* as a stage play, which premiered at the Arden Theatre in Philadelphia in 2009. Potok's widow, Adena Potok, served as an artistic consultant for the production. Posner had previously worked with Chaim Potok on a stage adaptation of *The Chosen* in 2000.

paintings for an Orthodox Jew. He recounts a bit of his family's history as Ladover Jews, a sect that stretches back several hundred years to feudal Russia. Asher was born to Rivkeh and Aryeh Lev in Crown Heights, Brooklyn, in 1943. His father works for the Rebbe, the Ladover leader, traveling throughout the country helping Jews emigrate from the Stalinist Soviet Union and settle in the United States.

The events of the story begin when Asher is six. He is a precocious artist who enjoys drawing realistic portraits, especially of his mother. Rivkeh encourages him to draw "pretty" pictures, but Aryeh hopes the boy will outgrow what he believes is a useless hobby. Asher's Uncle Yitzchok, a watchmaker and diamond merchant, encourages the boy's art and introduces him to the works of Pablo Picasso and the Jewish painter Marc Chagall. Asher meets Reb Yudel Krinsky, one of the few Russian Ladovers to make it safely to the United States after being imprisoned for many years in the Gulag, a network of Siberian work camps, where his wife and children, imprisoned along with him, have died. He works at a stationary shop where Asher buys his paper and pencils.

Rivkeh's beloved older brother, Asher's Uncle Yaakov, dies in a car accident while traveling on behalf of the Rebbe, sending Rivkeh into a deep clinical depression that requires hospitalization and many months of convalescence, during which she is so consumed with grief that she cannot take care of her young son. During this time, Aryeh stays home to take care of

Asher. When Rivkeh recovers, she wants to continue her brother's work by becoming a professor of Russian studies. In a highly unusual move, the Rebbe agrees that this would be the best use of her talents. Rivkeh begins college at the same time Asher begins his formal education at yeshiva.

CHAPTER 2

Asher abandons art for several years, and Aryeh resumes traveling for the Rebbe. When he is out of town, Rivkeh is beside herself with worry, fearing that he will die just like her brother. Slowly the Brooklyn Ladover community grows as more Jews arrive from Europe and the Soviet Union. Joseph Stalin continues to persecute Jews, killing many of them or sending them to the Gulag. Two highly publicized cases involve a group of Jewish writers and a group of Jewish doctors, both convicted and sentenced to death on trumped-up charges of crimes against the state. Asher learns that Reb Yudel Krinsky was apprehended by the Stalinist regime, even though no one in his community objected to the presence of the Ladovers.

Asher is a poor student. His father is dismayed at his lack of discipline with schoolwork. It is expected that, because he is the son of one of the Rebbe's most valuable advisors, he will follow in Aryeh's footsteps as a Talmudic scholar.

CHAPTER 3

Stalin dies, and the Ladover community is relieved. The Rebbe decides that Aryeh must move to Vienna to establish yeshivas throughout the major cities of Europe. Asher, who has taken up drawing again with a vengeance, stubbornly objects to moving. His relationship with his father has become strained because of his artistic obsession and corresponding lack of interest in school, and he cannot bear to contemplate life beyond his comfortable Crown Heights neighborhood. He does not want to fly on an airplane, learn a new language, or make new friends. He pesters his parents incessantly not to go. The Rebbe insists that Aryeh go, but Rivkeh, although she supports her husband, wants to stay to finish her education and be a good mother to Asher.

CHAPTER 4

Asher is now ten years old. His gift for art has become a powerful presence in his life and influences how he perceives the world. He draws unconsciously and compulsively. At school, he unthinkingly draws a picture of Joseph Stalin in his coffin. Aryeh is very angry that the boy draws when he should be studying. He begins to think that Asher's gift may come from the *sitra achra*, the Other Side, the source of evil. Asher has ominous dreams about his mythic ancestor, a black-garbed man who represents his guilt over his unwillingness to be a dutiful son.

CHAPTER 5

Asher's artistic inclination reaches a crisis point. He unthinkingly defiles his Chumash (a bound copy of the Torah) by drawing a picture of the Rebbe in it. This convinces his teacher that his gift is from the Other Side. Asher's classmates as well as his mashpia (headmaster) taunt him. At home, father and son continually clash over art. Aryeh rebukes him for being disrespectful and forbids him to draw any more.

The Rebbe invites Asher to draw several pictures for him. Afterward, Asher goes to a museum instead of returning home. He is gone so long his mother calls the police. The next day, Asher steals oil paints from Krinsky's store but is too guilt-ridden to use them.

Miraculously to Asher, the Rebbe has decided that Asher is truly gifted and does not have to move to Vienna. Thus, Aryeh leaves for Vienna, while Rivkeh and Asher stay behind.

Book 2

CHAPTER 6

Rivkeh is now in graduate school and misses Aryeh terribly. Her separation anxiety is the result of having lost her parents at a young age, after which she and her brother lived with their aunt until she also died. Now, Rivkeh has lost her brother and fears that Aryeh is next. Asher also misses his father and starts drawing pictures of him, wondering whether he and his mother should move to Vienna to be with him after all.

On December 26, 1953, Rivkeh presents Asher with his first set of oil paints. He becomes obsessed with painting immediately and neglects studying the Torah, which is essential to his upcoming bar mitzvah. Adding to the scandal is the fact that Asher's father is risking his life to bring the Torah to people in Europe while his own son is ignoring it. Mrs. Rackover, his baby-sitter, refuses to speak to him.

At the Parkway Museum, Asher is exposed to Christian and Western iconography, including crucifixions and nudes. Rivkeh tells him that such art is inappropriate and reminds him that

Jews do not paint. Furthermore, she is afraid the museum will lead him away from his Orthodox heritage and toward Christianity. When Asher begins drawing pictures of Jesus and nudes, she is horrified. Asher's mind, however, is only on art; his religious belief never wavers. He misses his father on Shabbos (Sabbath) and during the Jewish holidays, and apart from his lack of interest in school, he remains pious.

When Aryeh returns to Brooklyn for a visit, he is physically gaunt and enraged over Asher's use of Jesus as a subject of his paintings. He is angry with Rivkeh for encouraging him, but she explains that she provided Asher with art supplies because she thought it would prompt him to study harder. Discord reigns; Asher's father demands he stop drawing, grabs his wrist to keep him from tracing shapes on the table with his fork, and compares him to an animal that has no control over its actions. His will to draw is evil, in Aryeh's eyes, and he believes Asher should never have been born.

Rivkeh is torn; she agrees with her husband yet still loves her son. Rivkeh's torment reaches excruciating levels when Aryeh is sent to Russia and no one hears from him for months. The following summer, Rivkeh, now working on her Ph.D., sails to Vienna to be with Aryeh, and Asher stays with his Uncle Yitzchok. Reb Krinsky gets married.

CHAPTER 7

Following Asher's bar mitzvah, the Rebbe arranges for him to study with Jacob Kahn, a famous artist who is a non-observant Jew. At their first meeting, Jacob tells Asher he would be better off becoming a street cleaner. Becoming an artist will cause trouble and heartache for him given his Ladover heritage. Asher is surprised to see that Jacob has drawings he made years ago for the Rebbe.

Chapter 8

Jacob begins Asher's education by having him study Picasso's *Guernica* at the Museum of Modern Art. Throughout the winter, Asher does just that, and he returns to Jacob's studio in the spring to start his apprenticeship. This entails studying the New Testament of the Bible so the boy can understand many of Western art's greatest works. He also studies paintings by the Jewish artists Modigliani, Soutine, and Pascin. Asher's apprenticeship is to last five years.

Asher meets Anna Schaeffer, Jacob's art dealer, who calls Jacob "a mean, tricky, and nasty old man" for not telling her that his protégé is a thirteen-year-old Orthodox Jewish boy. She becomes Asher's closest link to the secular world and is focused on making money. As a gallery owner and art dealer, she is good at what she does.

At home, Rivkeh is worried sick about Aryeh—he was supposed to come home for Pesach (Passover), but no one knows where he is.

CHAPTER 9

Aryeh turns up in Vienna after Passover. Rivkeh can bear his absence no longer and travels to Vienna to be with him. Asher moves into his Uncle Yitzchok's house and scandalizes the family by painting without his shirt on. Jacob hires a model for Asher to paint nude, and Asher is tormented because he promised the Rebbe he would never do such a thing. Jacob assures him that it is not a sin to paint a beautiful girl. Asher relents but finds the process difficult, and he grows into it slowly.

While his parents come home to visit for a month and a half, Asher does not see Jacob. Aryeh looks haggard and is still not reconciled to the path the Rebbe has chosen for Asher. Rivkeh has finished her dissertation and wants to move to Vienna with her husband permanently. Asher objects; he doesn't mind staying with his uncle for a little while, but he cannot bear the thought of living there permanently. Rivkeh tells Asher he is selfish and acting childish. Asher dreams again of his mythic ancestor.

When Asher falls asleep in class one day, his teacher calls him Rembrandt Lev; the Rebbe cautions the boy against entering the Other Side. Asher dislikes living with his uncle because he is fat, rich, and boorish.

CHAPTER 10

Jacob and his wife Tanya invite Asher to spend the summer with them in Provincetown, Massachusetts, an artists' enclave on Cape Cod. When Asher tucks his long earlocks (hair dangling in front of the ears, worn in compliance with tradition) behind his ears, Jacob cautions Asher to be true to himself and not to be ashamed of his Ladover roots. Asher remains kosher and observant to the point that he does not paint on Shabbos. Tanya warns Asher that the world is not nice to good people like him.

CHAPTER 11

Uncle Yitzchok fixes up the attic as a studio for Asher, and Jacob's latest show at Anna's gallery sells out. Jacob and Asher travel to various museums in the country to study art. Asher's parents come back to Brooklyn for a visit and Aryeh looks much better now that he has Rivkeh to care for him. However, a permanent rift has developed between Asher and his father, and when Rivkeh urges Asher to come to Europe, he declines.

After another summer in Provincetown, Asher decides it is time to visit Europe. He becomes violently ill on the plane ride over and remains bedridden during his short stay. He returns home to Provincetown with Jacob and Tanya.

That fall, the Rebbe decides Asher will study Russian in college while he continues attending yeshiva. He refuses until the Rebbe explains that he expects Asher to become a great artist who will travel to Russia. Anna Schaeffer's first show of Asher's work is a moderate success that leaves them neither rich nor poor. His second show is more successful. Asher's parents do not come to either show because they feature paintings of nudes.

Aryeh's work in Europe is finally done, and he and Rivkeh move back into their old house in Crown Heights. Asher remains at his Uncle Yitzchok's.

CHAPTER 12

Aryeh's success has garnered him a revered place in the community, and Rivkeh is happy to have him safely at home now. Their time together in Europe has given them many experiences that make Asher feel left out, but at least Aryeh's rage at his son has dissipated into a tolerable lack of interest. While he is glad that his son's art is successful and that he has not shamed them, Aryeh is not interested in hearing about or seeing Asher's work.

Asher spends the summer with Jacob and Tanya in Provincetown instead of in the Berkshires with his parents. When Asher travels to museums throughout the country with Jacob, the Rebbe gives him messages to deliver to other Ladover Jews.

Eventually, Asher's career begins to eclipse that of Jacob, who is now eighty years old. He realizes that it's time for him to go to Europe in order for his inspiration to be renewed. Jacob tells him that Florence is a gift.

CHAPTER 13

In Florence, Asher is profoundly affected by Michelangelo's *Pieta*, a sculpture of Mary, mother of Jesus Christ, embracing Christ's dead body, and his *David*, a statue of the brave young king as he faces Goliath in battle. His reaction has nothing to do with their Christian subject matter and everything to do with their depiction of pain and suffering. He begins to sketch the *Pieta* and finds that Mary resembles his mother. The mythic ancestor returns in his dreams.

In Rome, Asher is met by a Ladover Jew who takes him to a yeshiva established by Asher's father. The man calls Aryeh Lev remarkable. In Paris, Asher meets another Ladover Jew, Avraham Cutler, the son of his old mashpia, or mentor, who invites him to stay at the yeshiva established by his father. Asher rents a studio in Paris and begins painting, eating his meals at the yeshiva. Anna Schaeffer is excited by Asher's new direction. He begins to paint his mythic ancestor, and he is obsessed by his mother's suffering over the loss of her brother, her fear for Aryeh's safety, and the strain he has placed on her. The result is two paintings: *The Brooklyn Crucifixion I* and *The Brooklyn Crucifixion II*. The former portrays Rivkeh framed against the slatted window shades of their Crown Heights living room in a vaguely Christ-like way. The latter renders her in a much more intentional crucifixion pose, her face split into three angles as Aryeh and Asher look upon her.

Anna Schaeffer comes to visit, and she is awestruck by the paintings. She ships them out of the country without obtaining Asher's permission, confident they are masterpieces. She begins to plan a show that she is sure will cement his reputation in the art world.

CHAPTER 14

Asher arrives unannounced in New York for his show and everyone is happy to see him. Anna announces that most of the paintings have sold even before the show has opened, including both of the *Brooklyn Crucifixions*. Asher is worried; he knows the paintings will hurt people, but Anna dispassionately reminds him that great art hurts people. He returns to his childhood home to find his mother waiting in the window for him, just as in his painting. Both Rivkeh and Aryeh have decided to come to his opening because none of the paintings feature nudes. However, Asher does not tell them about the Crucifixions.

Aryeh's reaction to the works is "awe and rage and bewilderment and sadness, all at the

same time." He leaves abruptly, stating that Asher has exceeded "limits." He and Rivkeh no longer want anything to do with him.

In a final meeting with the Rebbe, Asher is told that his gift has caused harm. "You are alone now," he says, and asks Asher to leave the Ladover community.

CHARACTERS

Rav Avraham Cutler

Avraham Cutler ("Rav" is a title meaning Rabbi) is the son of Rav Josef Cutler, Asher's yeshiva mashpia (mentor or spiritual leader), and he is the mashpia of the yeshiva in Paris established by Aryeh Lev. He tells Asher that his father and the Rebbe are great, wise men, and he invites Asher to stay in Paris and welcomes him to eat his meals at the yeshiva. Asher finds him friendly and accommodating.

Rav Josef Cutler

Josef Cutler is the mashpia of Asher's yeshiva and the father of Avraham Cutler. Although he is often dismissive of Asher's artwork, he brings the boy's talent to the Rebbe's attention.

Jacob Kahn

Jacob Kahn is a famous and successful painter who is in his early seventies when Asher meets him. The Rebbe has handpicked Jacob to be Asher's mentor, even though the artist is no longer an observant Jew. Jacob respects Asher's Orthodox ways and wants him to remain true to who he is in order for his art to have merit. Initially, however, Jacob tells Asher to become a street cleaner, because being an artist will be tortuous and painful. Jacob once lived in Paris and painted with Pablo Picasso and other famous artists of the day.

Jacob takes his role as Asher's mentor seriously, exposing the boy to the traditions he must be familiar with and traveling with him to museums throughout the country. He has a love-hate relationship with his art dealer, Anna Schaeffer, who has made him wealthy and established his reputation. He wishes he could remain contemptuous of the commercial and promotional aspects of the art world, as Picasso does.

Jacob and his wife, Tanya, had no children, and they treat Asher like a son, hosting him for the summer in Provincetown, Massachusetts. Jacob is supportive of Asher's decision to travel to Europe and knows it will help him grow as an artist. When he is nearing eighty and in decline as Asher's reputation is on the rise, he becomes slightly bitter and jealous.

Tanya Kahn

Tanya Kahn is Jacob's wife. She is motherly toward Asher and welcomes him for the summer to their home in Provincetown.

Reb Yudel Krinsky

Reb Yudel Krinsky is a Russian Jew who has recently arrived in Brooklyn after spending several years exiled in Siberia, where his wife and children died in the Gulag work camps. He works at a stationery shop where Asher buys his art supplies. Krinsky encourages Asher's art, and in turn Asher becomes interested in the story of his life before he came to America. Later, Krinsky marries again and has two more children.

Aryeh Lev

Aryeh Lev is Asher's father and Rivkeh's husband. He is devout, highly educated, and highly respected in the community, but he is intolerant of his son's artistic ambition and supremely disappointed in Asher's lack of interest in schoolwork and Talmudic studies. He faithfully serves the Ladover Rebbe, doing what he is told for the sake of the community's survival and growth. His faithfulness and devotion help many families escape from repressive regimes in Europe after World War II. Later, he establishes many yeshivas in Europe; when Asher visits them, he finds that they are thriving. Aryeh is regarded by all who know him as a wise man.

Aryeh is lost without his wife, and when he returns from Vienna he is haggard and sickly. His stamina and health return when Rivkeh joins him permanently in Europe. His affection for her never wavers.

Despite his intelligence, Aryeh does not understand art and makes no attempt to do so in order to understand his son. He believes Asher's gift for art is from the evil Other Side and will lead to his son's abandonment of his Ladover religion. While Aryeh never approves of his son's choices and has previously forbidden him from drawing, he does not disown Asher completely until he sees the *Brooklyn Crucifixions*. The paintings are the final straw that severs their relationship forever because of their portrayal of Rivkeh using

symbolism established by Christians, some of whom have persecuted and killed Jews for centuries.

Asher Lev

As the novel opens, Asher Lev is a successful young artist. His most famous works, the autobiographical *Brooklyn Crucifixions*, have brought him notoriety for using Christian symbols to convey the rift in his Orthodox Jewish family. Asher then recounts his life from the time he was six years old in the late 1940s. He was a precocious artist as a young boy, concerned more with conveying emotional truths in his drawing than creating "pretty pictures." His most frequent subject is his mother, Rivkeh. He is close to her and he feels her suffering acutely.

Asher is a solitary, serious boy who loves to draw and does not apply himself to his schoolwork. He is expected to follow in his father's footsteps and become a Talmudic scholar, but his lack of focus in school leaves his elders disappointed in him. When his father announces they are moving to Vienna, Asher adamantly refuses to go. He is petulant, stubborn, and selfish.

When it comes to their Orthodox sect, the Ladover, Asher never questions his faith, even when it conflicts with his quest to become an artist. He remains observant as long as religious traditions do not conflict with his art. When they do, he favors art, but he never abandons the beliefs and traditions of the Ladover Hasidim.

The stronger Asher's allegiance to art grows, the more others become convinced his gift comes from the sitra achra—the Other Side. He puts art ahead of God and family, in direct defiance of the commandments. He follows his own path, rather than the path that tradition dictates, and the guilt he feels is represented by his recurring dreams of his mythic ancestor.

Asher pushes boundaries to the extreme, but does not object when the Rebbe banishes him from the Crown Heights Ladover community.

Rivkeh Lev

Rivkeh Lev is Asher's mother and Aryeh's wife. For most of the novel, she is torn between her love for her husband and her son. Both need her, and yet their divergent paths mean she can please only one. Rivkeh's suffering is Asher's inspiration for the *Brooklyn Crucifixions*.

A turning point in her life is the death of her beloved brother, Yaakov, in a car accident while traveling on behalf of the Rebbe. She blames the Rebbe for his death, and she suffers a mental breakdown that leaves her hospitalized and incapacitated for several months. Upon recovering, she decides to continue her brother's work by going to college and becoming a professor of Russian studies.

She doggedly pursues her studies but is forever worried about her husband, who continues traveling on behalf of the Rebbe. When he moves to Vienna and she remains in Brooklyn with Asher, her obsessive worrying intensifies.

Rivkeh is ambivalent about her son's decision to become an artist and dislikes the strain it puts on his relationship with Aryeh. She buys him art supplies, mainly so he will stop stealing from Krinsky but also in hopes that he will repay her by taking his studies more seriously.

Rivkeh understands Asher's obsession with art, because it is similar to her obsession with completing her brother's work. She is almost as much of an anomaly in their community as her son is. Both are pursuing nontraditional paths, so she supports him as much as she can, but ultimately her allegiance is with her husband and her religion. She views the *Brooklyn Crucifixions* as an unpardonable sin and the final betrayal of her love for him.

Uncle Yitzchok Lev

Yitzchok is Aryeh's brother. He is a watchmaker and diamond merchant who, according to Asher, is fat, wealthy, and boorish. He supports the young Asher's interest in art, introducing him to the art of Picasso and Chagall. When Rivkeh joins Aryeh in Europe, Asher stays with Yitzchok in his Crown Heights home. To support the boy, Yitzchok converts the large attic into a studio, but he is surprised and dismayed to find the boy painting in the summer heat without his shirt on. Although Yitzchok is more accepting of culture outside their Orthodox sect than Aryeh is, he, too, cautions Asher from going too far with his art.

Mythic Ancestor

Asher's mythic ancestor comes to him in dreams. In the time of the Black Death in Europe in 1347, this ancestor helped a drunken nobleman become wealthy. As a form of penance for the ruthless deeds of the nobleman, which included burning down a village and killing its residents, the mythic ancestor began traveling in order to bring the

Master of the Universe to the world, a trend that continues with Asher's father. This good, wise, and selfless man haunts Asher's dreams as a shadowy, dark menace. He represents Asher's guilt over not following in his father's footsteps, knowing that he should respect the family's tradition of traveling and teaching. The mythic ancestor reproaches Asher for his art.

Mrs. Rackover

Mrs. Rackover is a neighbor and fellow Ladover Jew who watches young Asher after school when his parents are not around. She disproves of Asher's immersion in art and his bad habit of coming home late from school. She stops speaking to him after a while because of his impertinence. She dies in a car accident in Detroit—just as Asher's Uncle Yaakov did.

The Rebbe

The Rebbe is the spiritual leader of the Ladover community in Crown Heights. He is revered and trusted by all in the Orthodox sect and is believed to have spiritual wisdom that allows him to determine the course of each Ladover's life. Because the Rebbe has decided that Aryeh must move to Europe to build yeshivas, Aryeh unquestioningly does so. Rivkeh wants to continue her brother's work by becoming a scholar of Russian studies and is surprised when the Rebbe allows it, for such education for a woman is uncommon in the patriarchal community.

The Rebbe understands that Asher's gift cannot be ignored and realizes that Asher's path in life will not be that of his father's. Thus, he tries to keep Asher within the community by allowing him to apprentice with Jacob Kahn. He makes Jacob promise not to force the boy to paint nudes or participate in forbidden behaviors. Thus, the Rebbe proves himself a man of reason and compassion who understands people's strengths and weaknesses and tries to accommodate them for the good of the community.

The Rebbe banishes Asher at the end of the novel, telling him his paintings have exceeded the limits of what is acceptable to remain within the Crown Heights Ladover community. He has hurt people, and because of that he must leave. The Rebbe bears some resemblance to Rebbe Menachem Mendel Schneerson, who was the spiritual leader of the Brooklyn-based Lubavitcher Hasidim in the 1950s and 1960s.

Anna Schaeffer

Anna Schaeffer is Jacob's art dealer, a single-minded woman in her sixties who loves money and considers Jacob a tricky old man. For Asher, she represents the secular world. At first, she is chagrined to find out that Jacob's protégé is an Orthodox Jewish boy, but she quickly recognizes his talent and is eager to promote his work in the New York art world, positive it will make them both very wealthy. She is unconcerned about the effect of Asher's art on those he loves. She is interested only in making his reputation, earning them both much money, and further establishing her preeminence in the art world.

She refuses to serve kosher food at her openings because she is in the business of catering not to Jews but to art patrons. She is elated when Asher decides to move to Paris to paint, believing that "Asher Lev in Paris" represents a turning point in his career that will transform him from a promising artist into a great artist. She sends him a beret for good measure, which he never wears. When she visits and lays eyes on the *Brooklyn Crucifixions*, she is awestruck. She hustles the paintings out of the country before Asher can object. Anna is good at her job; she knows a masterpiece when she sees one. She believes that great art hurts people and that Asher needs to come to terms with the fact.

Uncle Yaakov

Yaakov is Rivkeh's older brother. While traveling for the Rebbe in Detroit, he dies in a car accident. His death sends Rivkeh into a spiral of despair. They were particularly close because their parents had died when they were young, and Yaakov had looked after his sister like a father. He was supposed to become a professor of Russian studies at New York University.

THEMES

Jewish Culture

My Name Is Asher Lev delves into the world of Orthodox Judaism in its portrayal of the close-knit Ladover community in Crown Heights, Brooklyn. The Ladover Jews are Orthodox, Hasidic Jews who believe that the Torah is the word of God. Their term for God is "Master of the Universe," and their spiritual leader is the Rebbe, a universally acknowledged wise man whose pronouncements are held as law by the sect's adherents. The clash between Asher Lev and his father, a highly respected member of the community, highlights the beliefs and customs of a religious group with which many non-Jewish readers may not be familiar. Beginning with the strong devotion to scholarly and religious studies and a suspicion of artistic pursuits, the culture of the Ladover, who resemble the real-life Lubavitcher Jews, is in direct conflict with Asher's desire to become an artist. Potok, as a Conservative rabbi, portrays the nuances of this clash between the quest for personal fulfillment and domestic harmony, which is the concept of *shalom bayit*. Aryeh and Rivkeh have devoted their lives to following the Rebbe's decisions, even though it has meant that they spend much time apart, which is very painful for Rivkeh.

Asher attends a yeshiva, a Jewish school, where the young boy is chastised for desecrating his Chumash, a bound copy of the Torah, with a drawing. The pursuit of art is frivolous for the Ladover, who believe that such a secular talent could be from the sitra achra, the Other Side.

Potok describes the physical appearance of the Ladover, which is similar to most Orthodox Jews. Men wear black hats and full beards, and they wear their hair in earlocks, or payots, in accordance with the book of Leviticus. They wear prayer shawls with tzitzit, a form of tassel that keeps the commandments between their hands and their heart. Their modest appearance reflects their conservative beliefs. When Asher is caught painting in the summer heat with his shirt off, his Uncle Yitzchok is scandalized. Orthodox men wear black suits and black hats; women wear hats or wigs.

As Orthodox Jews, the Ladover keep kosher, meaning their dietary habits are strict; this means that, when Asher travels abroad, he can eat only in certain establishments known to maintain kosher kitchens. They observe daily prayer rituals and take a ritual bath known as a mikvah. Passover and Shabbos (Sabbath) are strictly observed. Even in the summertime when Asher is on vacation with Jacob, he refrains from painting on Shabbos.

That Asher's gift might be from the sitra achra—the Other Side, meaning from a darkness devoid of the Master of the Universe—is an idea that is specifically Hasidic. Mainstream Christian art reveres the form of Jesus and has a long, illustrious history. Representations of biblical themes are considered inspirational and have been commissioned for centuries by popes and other church officials. The Jewish religion,

TOPICS FOR FURTHER STUDY

- Write a bildungsroman (a coming-of-age story) that summarizes your life so far. Organize it around a conflict you have experienced. Include a symbol in the story that represents that conflict (similar to Asher's mythic ancestor) and choose an epigraph (a phrase, quotation, or poem that introduces the story) that relates to your experience.

- Create a slide show of works of Jewish art, set to Yiddish music. Include ten works of twentieth-century art from Jewish artists and ten works of the decorative arts created for use during Jewish holidays. The Jewish Museum (http://www.thejewishmuseum.org) is a good source for these. Pair the artworks with the holiday items in such a way that their similarities and differences are highlighted. Present the slide show to the class, explaining your reasoning for arranging each pair of works in a particular way.

- *Rosanna of the Amish* (1947, reprinted 2008) by Joseph Warren Yoder is a young-adult story about an Irish orphan who is adopted by a single Amish woman. The book, written by an Amish author, sympathetically explores the unique customs and traditions of America's Old Order Amish sects. Write a paper describing the similarities and differences between the Amish as portrayed by Yoder and the Lubavitcher Jews as portrayed by Potok. Apart from the obvious differences between Judaism and Christianity, discuss how each group's customs and rituals compare.

- Research the modern Jewish Diaspora and create a chart depicting the number of Jews who lived in Russia, Poland, Germany, France, Palestine, Great Britain, Canada, and the United States prior to World War II and how many live in those countries today. Create another chart illustrating the world's Jewish population just prior to World War II, immediately following World War II, and today. What do the charts tell you about immigration patterns?

- Using Microsoft Excel and referring to the tutorials found at http://www.microsoft.com/education/CreateTimeline.aspx, create a time line that includes both the events of *My Name Is Asher Lev* and the real-life events of the Holocaust, the Stalinist Soviet Union, the formation of the state of Israel, and the creation of the Lubavitcher Hasidim and its move to New York. Also plot the creation of Michelangelo's *Pieta* and *David*, Picasso's *Guernica*, and the creation of key works by Marc Chagall. Include some historical events that relate to art and Jewish history as well.

---

however, takes seriously the commandment against creating graven images (literally, this means pictures that are carved or engraved, but it is extended to include all representational art). Thus, most Jewish art is relegated to the decorative arts and is thought to be trivial; greater importance is placed on scholarly study as the path to closeness to God.

Parent-Child Relationships

As a bildungsroman—a coming-of-age story— *My Name Is Asher Lev* necessarily concerns young Asher's relationship with his parents. It is a complicated relationship, infused with love and the frustration of parents who want what is best for their only child.

Asher's relationship with Rivkeh and Aryeh is full of the push and pull of parents trying to shepherd their child into successful adulthood. Rivkeh, despite her fragile emotional health, clearly loves Asher and encourages his artistic talent while he is young. Because of her own desire to pursue a nontraditional path (for an Orthodox Jewish woman), she sympathizes with his love of art. When Asher refuses to move to Vienna, Rivkeh agrees to stay behind in Brooklyn to care for him.

Asher Lev does not seem to fit in with the others. (*Ryan Rodrick Beiler | Shutterstock.com*)

Asher's relationship with his father is fraught with tension from the beginning. By the time Asher starts school, Aryeh expects him to abandon his childish pursuit of art. When he refuses, Aryeh admonishes the boy's poor performance, which reflects badly on his own reputation as a scholar and esteemed member of the Ladover community. As an Orthodox family, the Levs expect complete faithfulness from their son in accordance with their traditions. Aryeh can only think that Asher's unwillingness to obey and follow a predetermined path similar to his father's is evidence that his artistic talent is from the sitra achra, the realm of the unholy.

Asher does not willingly defy his parents; rather, he follows his heart, which leads him away from the family. He recognizes the terrible strain this puts on his parents, but he is unwilling to compromise. The result of the parent-child relationship is made manifest in Asher's unflinching family portrait *The Brooklyn Crucifixion II*, in which Rivkeh is shown suffering on a symbolic cross, torn between her husband and her son.

Creative Process

My Name Is Asher Lev documents a young artist's coming of age. Potok's depictions of Asher's creative process allow the reader to glimpse how he develops his gift and how the gift manifests as a mystical force that the boy cannot control. He draws in his sleep and during class, steals art supplies, and is ultimately beholden to his talent. When he is little more than a toddler, Asher uses cigarette ashes to shade a drawing of his unhappy mother. For Asher, art is never about an idealized world but rather about showing the world as it really is.

Part of the creative process entails learning about art. Asher escapes to the Parkway Museum, where he sees Christian iconography for the first time. Outside the enclosed world of the Hasidim, he sees nudes and paintings of the Virgin Mary, causing him to ask questions his parents would rather not hear.

Another part of the creative process is Asher's apprenticeship with Jacob Kahn, who tells him it would be better if he became a street cleaner. Jacob understands that remaining faithful to one's artistic vision will cause pain, both for the artist and for his loved ones. Anna Schaeffer, Asher's dealer, tells him the same thing.

For Asher, the creative process requires that he be true to himself, no matter how much trouble it causes, no matter what religious customs he betrays. He refuses to move to Vienna with his father, and he draws nudes in defiance of his religion's prohibition against it. To Aryeh, Asher's inability to control his gift is evidence of his animal nature, because people should be able to control themselves.

Asher follows his creative education to its bittersweet conclusion: he uses Western Christian symbolism in a painting involving his Orthodox mother. In the aftermath of the resulting scandal, Asher is cast out of the Brooklyn Ladover community. Rather than devoting his life to Talmudic study for the betterment of the community, he has devoted it to his own creative fulfillment. His gift is irrevocably at odds with his religious beliefs.

STYLE

Bildungsroman/Kunstlerroman
A bildungsroman is a coming-of-age story that depicts the growth of a young protagonist into a psychologically mature adult. *My Name Is Asher Lev* is a bildungsroman in the sense that Asher is around six years old when the story begins and a young adult by the time it ends; the story's action concerns his psychological development as a young man at odds with his family and community. He is a stubborn teenager but a devoted protégé. Potok presents the boy's maturation process, including his drawing and painting techniques, his study of art history, the personal obstacles he overcomes, and the choices he makes on the costly road to success. Many bildungsromans are told in first person, because such a technique allows the author to convey the protagonist's thoughts as they mature from childhood to adulthood.

A kunstlerroman, literally an "artist's novel," is a specific type of bildungsroman that focuses on the maturation of an artist. *My Name Is Asher Lev* neatly falls into this category because its sole focus is the development of Asher from a precocious boy into a talented artist, a journey that results in his banishment from his tight-knit community. The novel is often compared to James Joyce's *A Portrait of the Artist as a Young Man*,

which inspired Potok when he was beginning his writing career.

Symbolism
A symbol is an object that represents something other than itself. Judaism is full of symbols (as are most religions), such as the Hanukkah menorah in which each candle symbolizes one day of the eight-day festival. One of the most obvious symbols in *My Name Is Asher Lev* is Asher's mythic ancestor, the reproachful, dark-garbed man who comes to him in dreams. The mythic ancestor is a vision of a real-life forefather from feudal Russia who devoted himself to bringing the Master of the Universe through his travels and teaching. When he appears in Asher's dreams, the mythic ancestor represents Asher's guilt in not following his family's tradition of traveling and teaching on behalf of the Ladover.

Another major symbol in the novel is the crucifixion. In Christianity, the crucifixion refers to Jesus' death on the cross at the hands of the Romans. For centuries, depictions of the crucifixion have been a staple of Western art, reminding Christians of Jesus' suffering in return for their eternal salvation. Jews, however, do not believe that Jesus was the Messiah, and thus his death has no symbolic value in itself. However, when Asher first sees the crucifixions at the art museum, he sees in them a heart-rending expression of suffering in a human, but not religious, way. His *Brooklyn Crucifixions* depict his mother on a cross not in a religious sense but to convey her extreme suffering in the battle between her husband and her son and also the terror she experienced each time Aryeh traveled on behalf of the Rebbe.

However, for Rivkeh and the others in their pious community, the crucifixion is a symbol of millennia of repression, violence, and bloodshed against the Jews. Jesus on the cross represents not Christian salvation but persecution by Christians. For Asher to use his talent to paint a symbol so closely associated with those who have sought to eradicate Jews is an unpardonable sin.

Epigraph
An epigraph is a phrase or a quote that prefaces a book and foreshadows its themes. For this novel, Potok chose a quote by the artist Pablo Picasso: "Art is a lie which makes us realize the truth." Encountering this as the first sentence of the book tells the reader the book is about art and about the truth of art. The epigraph sets the

stage for what is to come and cues the reader as to what to focus on. The book is not about Judaism, it is about art—the Orthodox community is just the setting in which the author examines the nature of art.

By keeping the epigraph in mind, the reader can zero in on what the author believes are the most important elements of the story. How is art a lie in *My Name Is Asher Lev*? What is the truth? Art is a lie in that it is merely a representation of something, not the thing itself. A painting of an apple is not an actual apple—that is, it is a lie. However, a painting of a ripe, juicy apple may convey the truth of how delicious a real apple can be. When this idea is applied to *My Name Is Asher Lev*, the reader may infer that Potok intends to show how Asher's actual paintings are not as important as the truth they reveals about his relationship to his family and community.

In this case, the source of the epigraph—Pablo Picasso—is relevant to the story. At the time in which the story takes place, Picasso was the most famous and successful living artist in the world. Asher's Uncle Yitzchok introduces his young nephew to the works of Picasso. Jacob Kahn had known and worked with him, and he instructs young Asher to spend one whole winter studying Picasso's masterpiece *Guernica*, a panoramic 1937 Cubist depiction of the horrors of the Spanish Civil War, before Jacob begins his apprenticeship. When Asher visits France, his first stop in Paris is Picasso's former studio in Montparnasse. Through his association with Kahn and his study of Picasso's work, Asher's ultimate work, the *Brooklyn Crucifixions* are inspired by Picasso's Cubist style, which allows him to portray Rivkeh's divided loyalties successfully, as she simultaneously looks toward her husband, her son, and up at the heavens in *Brooklyn Crucifixion II*.

HISTORICAL CONTEXT

Lubavitch Movement
The Chabad Lubavitch are a sect of the Hasidim on which Potok based the Ladover Jews in *My Name Is Asher Lev*. The global Lubavitch movement has been based in Crown Heights, Brooklyn, since around 1940 and is the largest mystical Orthodox sect of Judaism in the world today. Named for the eastern Russian town of Lyubavichi, not far from Poland, the sect was founded in the late 1700s by Shneur Zalman of Liadi.

Following a Nazi-led massacre of Jews in the early days of World War II, the movement's leader, Rebbe Yosef Yitzchok Schneersohn, relocated to New York City. In the years following the war, the movement expanded rapidly throughout many countries through the establishment of yeshivas in many major cities throughout the world. Lubavitchers study the Kabbalah, a mystical spiritual system that dates back to the thirteenth century and that focuses on the elusive nature of the relationship between the Master of the Universe (God) and those whom he created. Lubavitchers stress the importance of one's intellect over one's emotions and attach much significance to religious observations, holidays, traditions, rites, and rituals.

The Lubavitcher community is quite structured. The Rebbe is the group's influential and revered spiritual leader. Followers define their closeness to the Master of the Universe in terms of their relationship with their Rebbe, and they trust him to make decisions that affect their lives. Such decisions include important things such as what to study in school, what career path to follow, and whom to marry. The followers believe that part of their soul resides within the Rebbe, and they can therefore trust him to know their strengths and weaknesses.

Lubavitchers adhere strongly to tradition, ritual, and Talmudic studies. Clothing and physical appearances are highly codified, diets are kosher, and many religious holidays and customs are practiced and celebrated regularly. The strict nature of these routines often keeps Lubavitchers away from mainstream culture and reinforces the insular, self-contained nature of the movement. Families are tightly knit, and children are expected to honor and obey their parents and other community elders. Unsanctioned behavior, such as Asher's flagrant pursuit of art, are highly frowned upon.

Joseph Stalin and the Gulag
Joseph Stalin (1878–1953) was the leader of the Soviet Union from the time of V. I. Lenin's death in 1924 until his own death in 1953. He instituted cruel policies and issued orders that resulted in the deaths of millions of people. His agricultural reforms resulted in a famine known as the Holodomor, in which millions of Ukrainians starved to death in 1932 and 1933 in retaliation for their opposition to Stalin's political policies. He sent millions of others—including a disproportionate

COMPARE
&
CONTRAST

- **1950s:** Crown Heights, Brooklyn, once an upper-class enclave for Manhattan's elite, is now a middle-class neighborhood of row houses with 75,000 Jewish residents, thirty-four major synagogues, and the headquarters of the Lubavitch movement. About 25 percent of the population is African American.

  1970s: During the July 1977 blackout, Crown Heights is hit especially hard by looters and arsonists, who turn the power grid failure into a "Night of Terror," according to the mayor. High poverty in the area prompts people to pillage and plunder a fourteen-block stretch of Brooklyn, including Crown Heights, in a riot that underscores the severity of socioeconomic and racial tension in the area.

  Today: Following several decades of economic decline and racial violence, Crown Heights undergoes gentrification and continues to have thriving African American, West Indian, and Jewish communities. Ninety percent of the population is African American, and 9 percent is Jewish.

- **1950s:** The New York art scene is dominated by abstract expressionists, including Jackson Pollock, Willem de Kooning, Barnett Newman, and Mark Rothko, who live and work in Greenwich Village. Their often simplistic-looking, nonrepresentational works are championed by Leo Castelli, a Jewish-born Viennese art dealer whose eponymous galleries in New York led to the pop art movement of the 1960s. Pablo Picasso's *Garcon a la pipe*, painted in 1905, is sold for an astounding $30,000 to art collector John Hay Whitney.

  1970s: Ileana Sonnabend, Leo Castelli's wife, opens the Sonnabend Gallery in Soho, establishing this lower-Manhattan neighborhood

as a beacon of the international art scene, specializing in conceptual and minimal art.

  Today: Jackson Pollock's *No. 5*, painted in 1948, is the most expensive painting ever sold at auction, commanding $140 million, when sold by Sotheby's in 2006 on behalf of media mogul David Geffen.

- **1950s:** The Lubavitch movement is based in Crown Heights, Brooklyn, and is led by the charismatic Rebbe Menachem Mendel Schneerson, a revered Jewish leader who is the seventh Chabad Rebbe.

  1970s: The Lubavitch world headquarters since the 1950s, 770 Eastern Parkway in Crown Heights, expands to serve a growing congregation and is considered a holy site by the Hasidim.

  Today: Still based in Crown Heights, the Lubavitch movement is no longer headed by a Rebbe; the Chabad belief is that the coming of the messiah is imminent, and therefore a leader for a new generation is not necessary.

- **1950s:** Provincetown, Massachusetts, formerly a whaling community in America's colonial era, is a summer resort area at the tip of Cape Cod popular with many writers and artists.

  1970s: The Provincetown Business Guild is formed in 1978 to promote gay tourism.

  Today: Provincetown is a gay mecca, and gentrification is further cementing its artistic heritage, with festivals staged year-round. Population remains steady at about 3,500 residents year round and 60,000 during the summer months.

---

number of Jews—to penal colonies in the Gulag, an inhospitable arctic region thousands of miles from civilization, where many died of starvation and exposure. Stalin's anti-Semitism (hatred of Jews) is well documented; in 1946, he stated that "every Jew is a potential spy" and called them, euphemistically, "rootless cosmopolitans," meaning disloyal to the state.

The Torah, the Jewish scriptures, were important to Asher. *(Luba | Shutterstock.com)*

The Night of the Murdered Poets alluded to in *My Name Is Asher Lev* was a real event in which fifteen Jewish writers were executed in a Moscow prison on August 12, 1952. Members of the group had been arrested in 1948 and 1949 and charged with espionage and treason, among other crimes, after having been jailed and beaten for three years. Five members of the group were active members of the Jewish Anti-Fascist Committee and had supported the Soviet war effort in World War II against the Germans. After the war, however, the Committee sought to rebuild the Jewish community within Russia and support Israeli statehood. Both goals were at odds with Stalin's vision for the Soviet Union in the cold war.

The Doctors' Plot, which also figures in *My Name Is Asher Lev*, was another historical incident that further illustrated Stalin's anti-Semitic policies. Hundreds of physicians, most of them Jewish, were tried on trumped-up charges of plotting to kill Soviet officials. Many of those

charged were killed outright, and others were sent to the Gulag. After Stalin's death in 1953, all charges were found to be baseless, and those who survived were set free. Thus, Stalin's death, as recounted in the opening of chapter 3, was a welcome relief for many Jews, especially those who had come from or still had family in the Soviet Union. Fear of recurring anti-Semitism was instrumental in the Lubavitcher movement to help relocate Russian Jews from the Soviet Union to Europe, the United States, or Israel throughout the 1950s.

Jacques Lipchitz

Potok has stated that he modeled Jacob Kahn on the Jewish artist Jacques Lipchitz (1891–1973), a Lithuanian sculptor who studied in Paris in the early twentieth century, where he was part of the "Esprit Nouveau" artists' community in the Paris neighborhoods of Montmartre and Montparnasse. His early work was Cubist in style, as he was influenced by the movement that was establishing itself in the area at the time, with his colleagues Pablo Picasso and Amedeo Modigliani, both artists whose work figures prominently in Asher Lev's artistic education. Lipchitz fled France at the outbreak of World War II and settled in Hastings-on-Hudson, New York, a sleepy suburb of Manhattan. His career grew steadily after the war; he had several retrospectives at major museums around the country, and he once sculpted a Virgin Mary for the Catholic Church. From the 1960s until his death in 1972, he spent several months each year working in Italy.

Lipchitz and his family, though observant Jews, were not Hasidic, and for most of his life he remained ambivalent about Judaism, despite his marriage to an Orthodox Jew, Yulla Haberstadt. After a life-threatening illness when he was in his sixties, Lipchitz returned to the Lubavitcher sect and forged a relationship with the Rebbe.

CRITICAL OVERVIEW

Coming on the heels of Potok's success with *The Chosen* and *The Promise, My Name Is Asher Lev* further cemented the author's reputation for deftly portraying the concerns of the American Orthodox Jewish community and the conflicting forces of religion and secular life. For Edward A. Abramson, author of the critical study *Chaim Potok*, the novel represents "a step forward in the subtlety and nuance of [Potok's] writing, having eliminated many of the flaws of his previous works."

Writing in the *Saturday Review*, Robert J. Milch commended the book as being "heartfelt and straightforward" and "narrated with a fluent simplicity that belies its intellectual depth and the technical skill of its construction." Guy Davenport, in a review for the *New York Times Book Review*, went further, praising it as nearly "a work of genius." David Stern, in a review for *Commentary* magazine, however, was less enthusiastic, saying that "as a portrait of the artist and a study of his growth and maturing, *Asher Lev* is without distinction." Anthony Barson, in a review for the *Christian Science Monitor*, agreed, calling Potok's conveyance of Asher's internship as an artist "dull, ponderous, [and] humorless." A contributor to the London *Times Literary Supplement* concurred that Potok did not convincingly convey Asher's artistic gift, but praised the book's "prayers, greetings, customs and attitudes of Hasidic Jews."

Several critics, noting the story's kunstlerroman format, compared *My Name Is Asher Lev* to James Joyce's *A Portrait of the Artist as a Young Man* (1916). As Potok wrote in a 1985 essay for *Studies in American Jewish Literature*, Joyce's novel "was almost as much a part of my growing up as were the Bible and Talmud." Both novels concern artists born into conservative cultures who find themselves on the outside of that culture looking in. For Stephen Dedalus in Joyce's novel, the culture is the oppressive Irish Catholic world of Dublin, where the boy, who desperately wants to be a writer, is expected to become a priest. Asher Lev, as the son of a highly respected aide to the Rebbe, is expected to assume a similarly respected position. Asher Lev's struggle to gain respect as an artist results in his exile from his Crown Heights community against his will. In Joyce's novel, Stephen voluntarily severs his relationship with his home and family. In addition to the works' thematic similarities, they have much in common stylistically as well. According to S. Lillian Kremer in an essay for *Studies in American Jewish Literature*, "Potok's experiments with interior monologue, stream of consciousness techniques and epiphany in addition to his fusion of socioreligious dynamic with individual character clearly reveal the substantive Joycean influence."

The novel's main theme, according to Warren R. True, writing in *Studies in American Jewish Literature*, is "the relationship of the artist to his culture." Importantly, True reinforces the notion that the book is not about Asher's rejection of Judaism. Instead, the boy's conflict comes solely from the fact that "Judaism contains nothing in its literature or art to serve as a model for individual anguish and martyrdom despite centuries of recorded pain." The choice between art and Judaism is one that Asher would rather not make. He remains observant, even while he treads on thin ice with the Rebbe and his family. As Kremer states, "Unlike most of the characters in the writings of Bellow, Malamud, and Roth, who leave the religious life for the secular, those of Potok's novels bring the secular life into the religious."

CRITICISM

Kathy Wilson Peacock

Wilson Peacock is a writer and editor specializing in literature and science. In the following essay, she examines how the Ladover Jews of Chaim

WHAT
DO I READ
NEXT?

- *A Portrait of the Artist as a Young Man* (1916) by James Joyce is a kunstlerroman, a semi-autobiographical tale in which the hero, Stephen Dedalus, serves as a stand-in for the youthful Joyce. Stephen longs to be a writer, but he finds this goal incompatible with his strict Roman Catholic upbringing in Ireland.

- *The Chosen* (1967) is Chaim Potok's first novel and tells of two Jewish boys growing up in Brooklyn in the 1940s. Reuven, a Modern Orthodox Jew, has a good relationship with his father. His best friend Danny is a sheltered Hasidic Jew who has a troubled relationship with his father, who is grooming Danny for leadership within their strict Jewish community.

- *The Rebbe's Army: Inside the World of the Chabad-Lubavitch* (2005) by Sue Fishkoff examines the many young Lubavitcher couples called *schlihim*, who willingly relocate to towns big and small throughout the world to promote observant Judaism by establishing Chabad Houses, often on college campuses or in major cities.

- *Marc Chagall: What Colour Is Paradise* by Thomas David and Elisabeth Lemke (2000) is a young-adult biography tracing the artist's youth in the Jewish neighborhood in Vitebsk, Russia. The book is heavily illustrated with Chagall's paintings, many of which are biographical, and with photographs. Chagall was deeply religious, and many of his paintings depict stories from the Torah.

- *Black, White & Jewish: Autobiography of a Shifting Self* (2002) by Rebecca Walker is the story of Walker's unusual life as the daughter of African American author Alice Walker and the Jewish lawyer Mel Leventhal. Finding herself at times ostracized in both the white and black worlds while being shuttled between her divorced parents—not to mention failing to fit in with her Jewish relatives—Walker relates her upbringing in locales as various as Mississippi, San Francisco, New York City, and Washington, DC.

- *Crown Heights: Blacks, Jews, and the 1991 Brooklyn Riot* (2006) by Edward S. Shapiro examines the repercussions of a 1991 incident in which a Hasidic motorcade driving through Crown Heights struck and killed an African American boy. Racial tensions in the multicultural neighborhood exploded with deadly consequences, highlighting the long-festering tensions between blacks and Jews here, with members of both groups believing themselves to be persecuted minorities.

- *Judaism: A Short Reader* (2010) by Dan Cohn-Sherbok and Lavinia Cohn-Sherbok is a beginner's guide to the history of the Jewish faith and introduces readers to Jewish beliefs and customs.

- *Wanderings: Chaim Potok's Story of the Jews* (1978) is a nonfiction illustrated history of the Jewish people over the past four thousand years, concentrating on how such a persecuted people has managed to survive in frequently inhospitable political and cultural conditions.

Potok's My Name Is Asher Lev *represent the Brooklyn-based Lubavitcher and how his depiction of their close-knit community renders the book a work of multiculturalism.*

Chaim Potok's *My Name Is Asher Lev* occupies a unique place in American literature. It is a multicultural bildungsroman and kunstlerroman that explores what it means to be an Orthodox Jew in contemporary America. The novel stands apart from the works of other Jewish writers of the post-World War II era in that its principal concern is neither the Holocaust nor

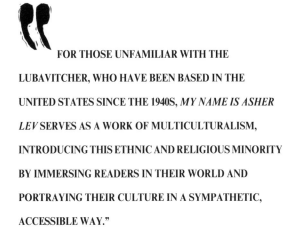

FOR THOSE UNFAMILIAR WITH THE LUBAVITCHER, WHO HAVE BEEN BASED IN THE UNITED STATES SINCE THE 1940S, *MY NAME IS ASHER LEV* SERVES AS A WORK OF MULTICULTURALISM, INTRODUCING THIS ETHNIC AND RELIGIOUS MINORITY BY IMMERSING READERS IN THEIR WORLD AND PORTRAYING THEIR CULTURE IN A SYMPATHETIC, ACCESSIBLE WAY."

assimilation into American culture. In fact, one of the book's main concerns is the rejection of assimilation. Potok's Ladover Jews are based on the real-life Hasidic Lubavitcher sect, a close-knit Orthodox people based in Crown Heights, Brooklyn, who adhere strictly to religious rituals, family tradition, and study of the Talmud and the Torah. As of 2010, the Chabad Lubavitcher, as they are sometimes known, number roughly 180,000 (even fewer than the Old Order Amish), and most people outside major cities seldom come into contact with them. Thus, their culture and traditions, especially those not practiced by other Jews, remain hidden from view from a large majority of the U.S. population. For those unfamiliar with the Lubavitcher, who have been based in the United States since the 1940s, *My Name Is Asher Lev* serves as a work of multiculturalism, introducing this ethnic and religious minority by immersing readers in their world and portraying their culture in a sympathetic, accessible way.

The Chabad Lubavitcher trace their roots back 250 years to the Ukrainian town of Lubavitch, near Poland. Their fortunes ebbed and waned until they relocated from Europe to Crown Heights, Brooklyn, in an act of self-preservation prompted by World War II. There, in the once-ritzy bedroom community established by Manhattan's nineteenth-century elite, they prospered. The Lubavitchers are the only remaining sect of the once much-larger Chabad movement, and today the terms are used somewhat interchangeably. The movement's philosophy is grounded in the teachings of the Kabbalah and

each member's love for his fellow Jew. Following World War II, the Lubavitcher helped Russian Jewish families emigrate from Stalin's U.S.S.R. They established schools and Chabad Houses in major cities in the United States and around the world—this is the work in which Aryeh Lev and Asher's uncle (before his death) are engaged. Chabad Houses are informal community centers, where local Jews can participate in services, receive counseling, take classes, celebrate holiday events, and engage in outreach activities and other events. Many college campuses have Chabad Houses that serve as dormitories for Jewish students. The houses were the brainchild of the seventh and last Lubavitcher Rebbe, Rebbe Menachem Mendel Schneerson (1902–1994), on whom Potok patterned the wise Rebbe in *My Name Is Asher Lev*. Rebbe Schneerson is still revered in the modern Lubavitcher community for his commitment to guiding them to safety during and after the heinous years of the Holocaust; some believe he is the messiah. As of 2011, more than 3,300 Chabad Houses around the world provide Jews with access to the Lubavitcher movement.

As a rabbi himself, Potok is well suited to the task of introducing the Lubavitcher Jewish beliefs and customs to uninitiated readers. Although he was raised in an Orthodox family like the Levs, his love for writing and painting prompted him to switch to the less rigid, Conservative form of the religion. Conservative Judaism is somewhere on the spectrum between Orthodox and Reform Judaism, and it allowed him more freedom to pursue interests apart from religion. Like Asher's parents, Potok's parents took a dim view of their son's "frivolous" creative endeavors, but like Asher, young Chaim (or Harold, as he was then known) maintained the courage of his convictions as well as his core religious beliefs. The result is a body of work that focuses not on wholesale adolescent rebellion against religion but rather on observant characters who find that their need for personal expression is compromised by their religious culture.

Potok's characters have been immersed in the Orthodox world since birth; thus, the Judaic concepts that inform their everyday world need no explanation. The reader must already know what they mean or infer the meaning from the context. One can determine that a mashpia, for instance, is similar to a headmaster or a principal; the inquisitive reader will dig further and find that a mashpia is a rabbi in charge of a school. The krias shema that Aryeh urges his young son to recite each night is a Hebrew prayer recited in both the morning and the evening. The sitra achra is a term from the Kabbalah meaning "the Other Side." The Kabbalah refers to the mystical teachings at the heart of the Hasidim, particularly the Chabad Lubavitcher. Though Potok never mentions the Kabbalah by name, its dualistic philosophy, in which everything stems from either the Master of the Universe (who belongs to the sitra d'kadushah—the side of holiness) or the sitra achra (the side of impurity), permeates the entire novel. Asher's artistic talent, because it leads him to do things that are not acceptable from within the confines of the Ladover beliefs (such as painting nudes and crucifixions and willfully disobeying his parents) is explained as coming from the sitra achra. Others would not describe talent as being innately good or evil; they would say its goodness or evilness is determined by how it is used. For Hasidic Jews, however, the talent itself is either holy or impure.

Like the Lubavitcher, the Ladover revere their Rebbe. They trust him to make the right decisions on their behalf, and their allegiance to him is part of their religious devotion. Thus, it would be unthinkable for Aryeh to disobey the Rebbe by refusing to travel or to move to Vienna; it also explains why Rivkeh, tormented by her husband's frequent absences, never demands that he stay home. Rivkeh is pleasantly surprised when the Rebbe allows her to continue her education and complete her brother's work. Orthodox Jews observe a division of gender in which women are separate but equal to men and responsible for the home and family. It is also surprising that the Rebbe allows Asher to study art with Jacob Kahn, but he is wise enough to see that the boy will be lost to the community forever if he is not allowed to pursue his talent. With these decisions, the Rebbe demonstrates his wisdom in recognizing each individual's strengths in the community. He knows that to deny them the opportunity to explore their strengths will not be to the community's or the individual's benefit.

Much of the terminology in the novel is associated with Asher's education. Even many non-Jews know the Torah is the Hebrew Bible and consists of the five books of Moses: Genesis, Exodus, Leviticus, Numbers, and Deuteronomy, collectively known as the Pentateuch. The Mishnah is the Jewish oral code of law that was first

written down in the second century CE. The Talmud is another major Judaic text, which includes the written form of the Jewish oral tradition and law. Studying the Torah and Talmud is of supreme importance to the Ladover/Lubavitch. The Chumash, which Asher defiles with a drawing of the Rebbe, is a bound copy of the Pentateuch, less formal than the scroll version found in the synagogue. Asher and his classmates study in the midrash, a portion of the yeshiva or synagogue devoted to serious and scholarly study, although the term midrash also refers to the interpretation of Jewish texts. Asher's bar mitzvah is a ceremony performed when he reaches the age of thirteen, when he assumes the responsibilities of a man and must observe all the commandments (Jewish people observe more than 600 commandments, in addition to the ten Moses brought down from Mount Sinai). This is a milestone occasion—the culmination of a boy's early education—in which he recites a portion of the Torah in Hebrew. For a pious, educated man like Aryeh, having a son who is ambivalent about his bar mitzvah is heartbreaking; most boys look forward to the rite of passage.

The Lubavitcher, like other Orthodox Jews, observe kosher dietary laws. These laws govern which types of meat may be consumed (no pork, for instance; only certain types of birds; and no shellfish), how the food is to be prepared (meat must not mix with dairy—that means no cheeseburgers), and how animals must be slaughtered. During Pesach (Passover), Jews must not eat leavened bread (instead they eat unleavened bread called matzoh), and they use a different set of dishes than during the rest of the year. These laws are such a part of Asher's life that he takes them for granted. When he travels he is given a list of places where he can eat, and he keeps kosher when he spends the summer with Jacob Kahn, who does not keep kosher. That Asher goes to such an extent to maintain this aspect of his religion indicates his comfort with his religion and his unwillingness to abandon it just because it becomes inconvenient. Anna Schaeffer, however, is in the business of making money, and serves non-kosher food at her gallery shows. Though she nurtures her artists, her ultimate goal is to make her customers—most of whom do not keep kosher—happy.

Aryeh Lev performs a mikvah, a purifying ritual immersion, on a regular basis in a special area of the synagogue, while Rivkeh performs a

A view across the Brooklyn Bridge toward the skyline of Manhattan (javarman / Shutterstock.com)

mikvah only once a month. A mitzvah—not to be confused with a mikvah—is a commandment or a good deed performed as an example of adhering to the commandments. Some mitzvahs are basic, such as to believe in God, fear God, and love God. Other mitzvahs address how one should go about daily life, providing rules for ritually washing one's hands before eating, saying grace after a meal, affixing a mezuzah to the door of one's house, and reading the Scroll of Esther on Purim. A mezuzah is a parchment scroll inscribed with the Shima Yisreal prayer that is placed in a decorative container. Purim is the celebration of deliverance from a Persian plot to destroy them. Other holidays important to the Lev family include Pesach and Shavuot (the celebration of God giving the Torah to the Israelites at Mount Sinai). Shabbos or Shabbat (the Sabbath) is the day of rest, which takes place from sundown on Friday until sundown on Saturday. The Shabbos meal on Friday is full of ritual and meaning, with certain foods, customs, and prayers. Because Shabbos is a day of rest, Asher refuses to paint on that day of the week.

His mother would certainly not study, and his father would not travel. Many activities are prohibited on Shabbos, including anything designed to be creative, most forms of household or farm labor, and even cooking. Some Hasidic Jews do not use electricity during Shabbos, and nearly all refrain from driving or riding in automobiles.

Also taken for granted by the characters in *My Name Is Asher Lev* is the Ladovers' style of dress. Men dress in black, wear black hats, and wear unshorn beards and payot or payos, long tendrils of hair, often called sidelocks or earlocks, in accordance to the law against cutting the corners of one's hair. At one point, Asher tucks his payot behind his ears. Jacob Kahn believes this indicates that Asher is ashamed of his religion, and Asher lets them remain loose after that. During prayers, Hasidic men wear a tallis or tallit, or ritual prayer shawl with knotted tassels called tzitzit, over their head. A different type of tallit is worn by Orthodox men as an undergarment on a daily basis. During prayers, men also wear tefillin, leather boxes containing scripture from the Torah, one of which is strapped to the forehead, the other of which is strapped to the arm.

Readers may also be unfamiliar with the terms of respect shown to the Ladover men. Asher's father is known to the members of the community as Reb Aryeh Lev; Reb is the Orthodox form of Mr. The term Rav is another word for Rabbi, but it can also mean a spiritual person who acts as an advisor or mentor. Rebbe is the Yiddish form of the word rabbi, and it is commonly used in by Orthodox Jews to refer to their own rabbi. The Lubavitcher strive to maintain a close relationship with their Rebbe, sometimes called a tzaddik, who is believed to be imbued with a spiritual wisdom that lets him have an especially close relationship with the Master of the Universe. Thus, a strong relationship with the Rebbe means a strong relationship with God.

Understanding these terms is not necessary for appreciating Potok's novel of the recalcitrant artist Asher Lev, but knowing their significance deepens the reader's appreciation for the uniqueness of the insular, self-contained world of the Lubavitcher Jews. The codified nature of their daily lives makes their existence in contemporary urban America as separatist as that of many other recent immigrants. Through the character of the moody, obstinate, teenaged Asher Lev, Potok invites American readers to see their youthful selves in him, and he then introduces them to a world that few outsiders have ever experienced. Once there, Potok sympathetically portrays the Hasidic Jewish world, enmeshed in family devotion, education, tradition, and piety. When *My Name Is Asher Lev* is discussed as a work of multiculturalism, non-Jewish students gain empathy for those of the Jewish faith who have found enough strength in their faith to persevere through numerous attempts to marginalize them—often violently—throughout the centuries.

Source: Kathy Wilson Peacock, Critical Essay on *My Name Is Asher Lev*, in *Novels for Students*, Gale, Cengage Learning, 2012.

Daniel Walden

In the following essay, Walden illustrates how My Name Is Asher Lev *is another example of Potok's exploration of how people confront ideas different from their own.*

The epigraph to *My Name is Asher Lev*, "Art is a lie which makes us realize the truth," a

THE FACT IS THAT SOMETIMES ASHER LEV WAS ABLE TO MAKE AN ACCOMMODATION BETWEEN HIS ORTHODOXY AND WESTERN ART, AND SOMETIMES HE WAS NOT. HE HAD TO MAKE CHOICES."

quote from Pablo Picasso, is a kind of metaphor, one of the controlling ideas of the book. The essential conflict is revealed in the first pages of the book:

> My name is Asher Lev, the Asher Lev, about whom you have read in newspapers and magazines, about whom you talk so much at your dinner affairs and cocktail parties, the notorious and legendary Lev of the Brooklyn Crucifixion.

Yet, he went on, "I am an observant Jew." The result is that I am labeled

> a traitor, an apostate, a self-hater, an inflictor of shame . . . a mocker of ideas sacred to Christians, a blasphemous manipulator of modes and forms revered by Gentiles for two thousand years.

> Well, I am none of those things. And yet, in all honesty, . . . I am indeed, in some way, all of those things.

The novel is an explanation, a defense, for a long session in demythology. As Potok once said about Picasso's *Guernica*, "That's the redemptive power of art. The artist, in strange fashion, redeems the horror of reality through the power of his or her art" (Kauvar 70).

In a 1956 interview, Chaim Potok said, "Today is the first time in the history of the Jewish people that the Jews actually constitute a fundamental element of our umbrella civilization" (Hinds 89). But, as a result of being in the cores of two cultures simultaneously and having to fight the battle of how to fuse them, we are in a between period. What will happen, he concluded, is "very difficult to discern, but it is something that will come out of our fusion with the best of Western humanism unless we're inundated by the periphery of things Jewish and things secular" (Kauvar 87).

In his many novels and in his essays, Potok tried to explore how people confront ideas different from their own. The central metaphor of

The Chosen (1967) is combat of various kinds, about two components of the core of Judaism, or any tradition, one component looking inward and one looking outward to solve its problems. The baseball game, for example, is a metaphor for a kind of combat, for a war, of spiritual as well as material differences. The central metaphor of *The Promise* (1969) is about the confrontation with text criticism. *My Name Is Asher Lev* (1972) is about an observant Jew's confrontation with Western Art. *Davita's Harp* (1985) is about Davita using her imagination as a way of coming to terms with unbearable reality. The central metaphor in *The Book of Lights* (1981) is the mystery and the awe that some of us sense in the grittiness of reality (Kauvar 67–68).

The world that Potok created in his books was a small esoteric world, much like that of Faulkner's small-town Mississippi. It was about good people involved in situations that they want to come to terms with in a positive way. Potok's art was filled with aesthetic vessels, motifs that reflected a conflict between art and any established institution. The modern artist's voice is really an antagonistic one. Asher Lev typifies what happens when an observant Jew wants to enter the mainstream of Western art. Or, in reverse, the artist who wants to remain an observant Jew confronts a significant problem. The moral quotient of the artistic endeavor is at times necessary and never enough; the aesthetic element, however, to Asher Lev, was at all times necessary and sometimes sufficient.

My Name is Asher Lev owes its beginning to an event in his childhood when his yeshiva inexplicably hired an artist to give a course in painting to the children. Normally, orthodoxy and an orthodox school viewed painting as a taboo; it was against their interpretation of the Second Commandment, it was against Jewish tradition, and his father thought it a terrible waste of time. But Potok saw Asher Lev as the metaphor for his own conflicts. By the time he was twenty, he was the inheritor of two utterly antithetical commitments: modern literature, employing interpretations, told him no institution was sacred, while the religious tradition he inherited said that there are things that are intrinsically sacred (Abramson 59, Lindsay 28–29).

My Name is Asher Lev tells of a clash between the secular and the Orthodox Jewish cultures. Born with a supreme gift, Asher is an artist with a prodigious talent. Though his father, who

travels for the Rebbe, the dynastic inheritor or leader, the head of the Ladover Hasidim (modeled on the Brooklyn Lubavitcher Hasidim), cannot understand Asher's talent or obsession, it is the Rebbe who realizes that Asher Lev's gift cannot be suppressed, and he arranges for him to study with a famous secular Jewish sculptor and artist, Jacob Kahn. For Kahn, art is a religious calling. "I do not know what evil is when it comes to art. I only know what is good art and what is bad art," he tells Asher. Asher, forced to choose between art and Jewish tradition at age thirteen (when he would have taken on the responsibilities of a Bar Mitzvah) chose to try to follow his gift while breaking away from his father's brand of fundamentalism, but not from Judaism.

According to Asher, his father, an Orthodox Hasidic Jew, suffered "aesthetic blindness." When Asher's father responded with a question, what about "moral blindness?," Asher could only reply that he was not hurting anybody. His father answered that one day he would hurt someone with that kind of attitude. Potok explained that there's a good case for art as delectation, for the sheer joy of an aesthetic experience. Like Danny Saunders in *The Chosen*, Asher Lev put personal fulfillment before the needs of the Jewish community. The point is art, for Asher, influenced by Jacob Kahn, has nothing to do with the Jewish community—that is the problem. As Asher read from a book his mother gave him, *The Art Spirit*:

> Every great artist is a man who has freed himself from his family, his nation, his race. Every man who has shown the world the way to beauty, to true culture, has been a rebel, a "universal" without patriotism, without home, who has found his people everywhere.

When he met Jacob Kahn, the famous sculptor, modeled on Jacques Lipschitz, Kahn described him as a prodigy in payos (side curls). But Kahn, trying to describe the difference between a workaday artist and a great artist, said, "Art is whether or not there is a scream in him wanting to get out in a special way." "This is a tradition," he tells Asher; "it is a religion, Asher Lev. . . . It is a tradition of goyim and pagans. Its values are goyisch and pagan. Its concepts are goyisch and pagan. Its way of life is goyisch and pagan. In the entire history of European art, there has not been a single religious Jew who was a great painter." Chagall was not a religious Jew.

Jacob Kahn went on: "As an artist you are responsible to no one and to nothing, except to yourself and to the truth as you see it." Then, as he drew for Asher the street, Place Emile-Goudeau, and the building he and Picasso had lived in, he exclaimed, "God, how poor we were. And how hard we worked. We changed the eyes of the world."

One day Asher and Kahn went to the Metropolitan Museum of Art. They walked through centuries of nudes and Byzantine and western Crucifixions. When Asher complained, Kahn instructed him: "I am not telling you to paint crucifixions. I am telling you that you must understand what a crucifixion is in art if you want to be a great artist. The crucifixion must be available to you as a form. Remember that Picasso, at a moment in his life when he was wracked with anguish...drew a crucifix.... He wanted to express his feeling of torment and suffering, and he drew a crucifix" (Potok, "Role" 11).

Asher was now painting nudes and crucifixions. In the midst of his internship with Jacob Kahn, he met with the Rebbe. In the Rebbe's view, he was entering the world of the Sirra Achra, the "other side." Asher, at this time, was also drawing or painting his mother and himself, although he did not always give the mother and child their faces. But he was slowly appreciating, understanding, what his mother meant when she said: "It hurts me to be caught between my husband and son." When she asked him, "How do you paint, Asher?" he answered, "I paint my feelings. I paint how I see and feel about the world. I express my feelings in shapes and colors and lines. But I paint a painting, not a story." And another time she reiterated what she was going through: "You have no idea what it's like to be standing between you and your father."

The problem with his father was a situation of long standing. To Aryeh, art was "trivial"; a Jewish man was supposed to study the Torah and the Talmud. The trouble was, as Asher knew, his father's Hasidic yeshiva education gave him no frames of reference for the concepts of art. Asher's world of aesthetics was as bewildering to his father as his father's insatiable need for travel for the Rebbe, for the Jews, for his people, was for him.

It is Asher Lev's mother, Rivkeh, who understands both her husband's view and her son's obsession and talent. It is Rivkeh's angst and suffering that impinges on Asher's consciousness and thus leads him to his greatest work.

Influenced by the centrality of religion and yet the questioning in the writings of Evelyn Waugh, James Joyce, Flannery O'Connor, and Thomas Mann, Potok has tried to mediate between the languages, traditions, and beliefs of (liberal) Orthodox Judaism while encountering the world of modern art. Thus, Asher's notorious paintings of the "Brooklyn Crucifixion," the only form he recognized in Western tradition, that portrays the suffering of mankind, protracted suffering (significantly, Potok was painting a crucifixion at the time), were explained by a reference to Picasso, by no stretch of the imagination a traditional Christian, who painted a crucifixion in a moment of deep anguish. To show his mother's suffering, and his own, to depict the values he got from his parents—honesty, integrity, and a fine work ethic—the crucifixions reflected the ways in which those values affected his parents' attitudes. To his parents, crucifixions were what they were to most Jews: centuries of pogroms, suffering, anti-Semitism, rivers of blood.

As Asher Lev began to think about the "Brooklyn Crucifixion," it was his guilty feelings toward his mother that were constantly before him. When he drew his mother's profile in the dust on a bench near Picasso's house in Paris, it was the emotional cost his mother sustained that he was thinking about. In the anguish of his mother he was symbolically reacting to his father.

The first Crucifixion owed a debt to Michelangelo's Pietas, one in the Sistine Chapel, the second in Florence, both of which Asher saw and copied assiduously again and again. Asher destroyed the first attempt when he realized that the woman supporting the twisted arm of Jesus slightly resembled his mother. In the next one, which he also destroyed, he left out the standing figure of Nicodemus, perhaps because it reminded him of his father. Eventually, having decided that to show his mother's torment and anguish, he had to use the model of the crucifixion, because "there was no aesthetic mold in his own religious tradition into which he could pour a painting of ultimate anguish and torment," he went ahead. His first "Brooklyn Crucifixion" was good but incomplete. The second "Brooklyn Crucifixion" was complete. He had portrayed the loneliness, the anguish, the torment of Rivkeh Lev. As Adena Potok told me:

> Chaim painted only the first of the two. He did so in order to see for himself how such a representation would take shape on canvas. The second he left to his and the reader's imaginations. Of course, the first did not appear as an illustration in the book, so to all intents and purposes it, too, was left to the imagination of the reader. (Interview)

Asher's first painting was a good one. But it did not include a clear crucifix; it did not completely fulfill his vision; and he recognized it was incomplete.

It would have made him a "whore," as he put it, to present this one, a fraud, as complete. He wanted to handle the Crucifixion theme without it being a cliche. When his parents saw the two "Brooklyn Crucifixions" on the gallery wall, they were horrified. To them crucifixions represented rivers of blood. To Asher they were aesthetic vessels representing suffering, specifically his mother's suffering.

The fact is that sometimes Asher Lev was able to make an accommodation between his Orthodoxy and Western art, and sometimes he was not. He had to make choices. When asked about the Crucifixions, Potok explained it is not a halachic problem. Halachically, one can paint all the Crucifixions one wants. That is, "you are not violating Jewish law so long as you don't paint them for purposes of worship" (qtd. in Ribalow 11–12). Potok, like Asher, had to fight his way up through the yeshiva once he committed himself to writing. "Yes, the love-hate is one of the prices you have to pay for a core-to-core cultural confrontation. My goal is to express my own particular vision of the world," Potok said. On the one hand, he believed Jacob Kahn's admonition that "Art is not for people who want to make the world holy." On the other hand, at certain points, particularly the ideational elements of the world, one is going to come into serious conflict. Asher came from the core of the Jewish tradition, and at the same time he was committed to Western art. The Jewish tradition has its own aesthetics and its own sense of morality. It has a different sense of the aesthetic nature of reality; its aesthetics are in the service of humanity, the commandments. The aesthetics of Asher Lev, artist, are just aesthetics for the sake of beauty, for the sake of enhancing the world so that it becomes a different place in which to live. Great artists pay a terrible price for what they do. Asher Lev knew that if he chose to become an artist, it was incumbent on him to become a great artist, the only way to justify the harm that his choice did to everybody else's life. He chose, he was happy, but he suffered, all for those who might be grateful for the honest mirrors that they were shown of themselves (Lindsay 28–30).

Asher finally understands the power of the artist: "Power to create and destroy, Power to bring pleasure and pain. Power to amuse and horrify. There was in that hand the demonic and the divine at one and the same time" (Potok, *Asher Lev*). From that time on he would go forth to encounter the reality of experience. It would be a quest, a journey of reconciliation. As Asher said at the beginning of this kunstlerroman (the novel of an artist's education), "I am an observant Jew," but he was also pointed toward becoming a great artist, which might mean his own core-to-core paradox.

Source: Daniel Walden, "Potok's *Asher Lev*: Orthodoxy and Art: The Core-to-Core Paradox," in *Studies in American Jewish Literature*, Vol. 29, 2010, pp. 148–53.

Warren R. True

In the following excerpt, True address the relationship of the artist to his culture.

In 1973, Chaim Potok commented upon his artistic development. He credited Evelyn Waugh's *Brideshead Revisited* with fostering a commitment to Western literature and to writing.

> My God, what had he done to me, Evelyn Waugh? It had only been a story. Words on paper had somehow replaced my own world. Words on paper fashioned by one man's imagination had somehow been so powerful as to edge my own reality out of my consciousness.

From age fifteen, Potok began to read the classics of modern literature. When he returned to them after the Korean conflict, two writers especially affected him. Beneath the terse laconic dialogue of Hemingway, he discovered the painful ennui which war causes. And in Joyce's *Portrait of the Artist*, he discerned the pain of exile. He utilized this anguish in his own portrait of the artist as a young man, *My Name Is Asher Lev*, delineating the artist's isolation from his community. Despite these connections made by Potok himself, commentators on the novel have ignored its lineage. Indeed, serious study of the work is lacking. But the novel's issue is universal and repeats Stephen Dedalus's dilemma: what is the relationship of the artist to his culture?

Examining several passages from both novels will indicate their common concern, for each work explicitly treats the artist's bond to family, nation, and religion. To his nationalist classmate, Davin, Stephen Dedalus remarks:

> When the soul of a man is born in this country there are nets flung at it to hold it back from

flight. You talk to me of nationality, language, religion. I shall try to fly by those nets.

Later, in the climactic discussion with Cranly, Stephen clarifies this assertion of independence:

> I will not serve that in which I no longer believe whether it call itself my *home*, my *fatherland* or my *church*: and I will try to express myself in some mode of life or art as freely as I can and as wholly as I can, using for my defence the only arms I allow myself to use—silence, exile, and cunning. (my emphasis)

The artistic need for separation from his background and environment is reiterated in *My Name Is Asher Lev* when Asher finds himself intrigued by a passage in Robert Henri's *The Art Spirit*:

> ... every great artist is a man who has freed himself from his *family*, his *nation*, his *race*. Every man who has shown the world the way to beauty, to true culture, has been a rebel, a 'universal' without patriotism, without home, who has found his people everywhere.

To clarify the common concern of these passages, we must understand that, for Asher, "race" in Henri includes the meanings of "church" in Joyce. Further, the structure of events in each novel indicates that both portray the major influences—family, nation, religion—as concentric circles of influence upon the growth of the artist. Their "nets," the novels imply, must be breached if Stephen and Asher are to create art that is serious, true, and great. The cost of freedom, however, is severe: within each circle, the central fact of this relationship to each set of influences is echoed in *Asher Lev* [*My Name Is Asher Lev*]: inexplicably, the infant displays a heightened sensitivity to the people and events of his world. Such awareness causes a detachment in the boy: unwillingly and unaccountably, he begins to feel isolated from major elements in each circle of influence. This isolation leads to greater sensitivity. As he matures, each boy begins to perceive certain truths about himself and his world, but such perceptions—expressed or not—further deepen his separation. The final result is the artist's pervasive, anguished, and irreversible physical and spiritual exile from his worlds.

I

The growth of Stephen's detachment from family, nation, and religion requires no full recounting here. But some points are valuable in comparing it with *Asher Lev*.

In terms of his family, Stephen's isolation grows primarily from his recognition of his father's role in the degradation of the family. At one point, Stephen articulates his position:

> He saw too clearly his own futile isolation [from his family]. ... He felt that he was hardly of the one blood with them but stood to them rather in the mystical kinship of fosterage, fosterchild and fosterbrother.

This distance is solidified in Chapter V which depicts the antagonism between Stephen and Simon (*P*, 175) and the rift with his mother over belief. (*P*, 164; 238ff)

His alienation from his social environment, or nation, is suggested throughout the novel by his relationships with his classmates. On the playground at Glongowes, Stephen keeps on the "fringe of his line." (*P*, 8) Social pressure to conform is echoed later when at the university, he rejects Davin's Irish nationalism. When Davin asserts that a "man's country comes first. Ireland first, Stevie," Stephen replies that "Ireland is the old sow that eats her farrow." (*P*, 203) Faced with the incomprehension and superficiality of his companions and Dublin, nothing is left but flight.

Finally, Stephen's rejection of Irish Catholicism begins at Clongowes where he identifies it with authority. When that authority is abused in the pandying incident, the seeds of resistance are sown. Later, being offered a place in the priesthood, he feels momentarily attracted; but soon the quality of his personality indicated in his last name takes over, and he recoils at the thought of such confinement from the world. Stephen notes that the life of the college is "a grave and ordered and passionless life ... At once from every part of his being unrest began to irradiate." (*P*, 161) But he does not stop here; by the final chapter, we realize that he has ceased altogether participation in church rituals.

II

This survey of significant elements in Stephen's relationship to his social world can illuminate similar elements in *Asher Lev*. There, as in *A Portrait*, the young boy's sensitivity to vivid elements of his childhood is evident in the novel's first three pages by Asher's fascination with his "mythic ancestor." And in his early years, two experiences combine to begin his alienation from his family. The first experience reflects his father's attitude toward the boy's art.

Asher's early years are generally described as a happy time of unity and order when Asher and his mother, Rivkeh, shared and nourished his "gift." But it seems inevitable that his inclination should clash with the familial and cultural values embodied in his father. Asher at this stage feels torn between the duty to obey his father and his intuitive trust of his own feeling. Potok has explained the basis for the conflict:

> Works born purely out of the aesthetic imagination—bounded by specific aesthetic forms—that preoccupation, that concept, is totally alien to the essential nature of the Jewish tradition…[Aesthetics] as an end in itself, as something to which men and women can dedicate their lives—this kind of aesthetics the religious Jewish tradition knows nothing about.

When expressed by Aryeh, these attitudes create the central tension within the family over Asher's "gift." The boy records early that his father called his drawings "foolishness" and was "indifferent" to them: "he thought it something children did when they were very young and then outgrew." (*AL*) [*My Name is Asher Lev*]

In addition to this father/son conflict, Rivkeh's distance following the death of her brother increases the child's alienation from the family. During this time, for example, he moves away from a desire to "make pretty drawings": he tells her, I don't like the world, Mama. It's not pretty. I won't draw it pretty." (*AL*)

Although Rivkeh recovers and begins college, the damage to Asher is irreversible. The painful separation during this time finds expression in two encounters of Book I. In the first, Asher meets Yudel Krinsky and learns of his exile in Siberia. When he begins to comprehend the cold of that place, he connects it with the lines of suffering in Krinsky's face; the combination evokes an image of pain and loneliness. He learns, in the second encounter, that Stalin is the source of this cruelty. The details of both men's lives—Krinsky's suffering and Stalin's inhumanity—are unified by the images of cold and snow and become the central topics of Asher's drawings during this period. As he feels more and more threatened by the move to Vienna, he sees himself almost powerless to control his own life (as was Yudel Krinsky) and at war with an incomprehending force (as he pictures Stalin). His great fear is that he will lose his "gift" by leaving the source of his inspiration, his street, while at the same time he wants to retain his bond with his parents. But his father's continued

opposition to his creative drive is forcing him psychically to remove himself even further from his family.

The end of Book I signals the decisive and irrevocable split between Asher and his family. Although his mother remains with him through Book II, Asher can never regain the unity and balance evident in the very beginning of the novel. From this point, Asher and his father grow in opposite directions, and their continuing antagonism helps to solidify the boy's alienation from mother and father. When Rivkeh follows her husband to Europe at the end of Book II, Asher is completely isolated from his parents. This condition is clear when they return from Europe; he states, "Now they possessed a language of shared experience in which I was nonexistent." (*AL*) But, as in *A Portrait*, Asher's father's attitude remains the crucial ingredient in the young artist's loneliness. When Aryeh returns from Europe, his feelings have changed only slightly; he has lived on the crest of his own achievements: Asher states that he "regarded me as if from a distance and disliked me without rage." (*AL*) And this antagonism between father and son is more clearly indicated in their later discussion of aesthetic and moral blindness (*AL*) which reveals more than any confrontation in the novel the distance between Asher and his father.

Throughout these formative years of Books I and II, Asher has been realizing how much his mother is torn between himself and his father and has wanted to paint her pain. In the latter pages of Book II and into Book III, he finds the appropriate modes in two art forms alien to his culture: the Crucifixion of Christ and the Pieta. The suffering evident in the first and the symmetry he perceives in the second stir Asher's aesthetic vision. By the time he experiments with the crucifixion model, that is, just before his European trip, Asher's only link with his parents is maintained by his mother's tacit support of his chosen life in art. Her love for both men, her anxiety over their differences, and her pain in seeing them in conflict finally combine in the themes of Asher's masterpieces: he feels compelled to depict the pain and suffering he and his father have caused her. But the models he chooses assault so radically his parents' values that he alienates his mother and all his family completely. Balance and harmony are irrevocably lost. After his parents have been horrified by the paintings, Rivkeh says to Asher

'There are limits, Asher.' Her voice trembled and her eyes were wet. 'Everything has a limit. I don't know what to tell you. I don't want to talk to you, now.'

(*AL*)

III

The "nation" of Asher Lev is defined by Asher's immediate social world, the Ladover Hasidim. This world's insensitive response to Asher individually and artistically forces his eventual alienation from his "street." The novel touches on this aspect of Asher's struggle in two sections: his years in school and his relationship with the members of his synagogue after the Crucifixions have been shown.

As in *A Portrait* the artist's initial contacts with his community occur in the classroom. Especially important here is the incident in which Asher, unknowingly and perhaps compulsively, sketches the Rebbe in his Chumash. (*AL*) In terms of Asher's relationship to the community and of his search for aesthetic forms to express his anger and frustration, this incident is doubly significant. First, *where* he draws is the initial cause for the anger of his teacher and classmates. As one boy exclaims, Asher has "defiled a holy book! Asher Lev, you desecrated the Name of God! You defiled a Chumash!" (*AL*) Secondly and more importantly, Asher has drawn the leader of his "nation" as particularly menacing and evil. The Rebbe appears, in fact, as an agent of the sitra achra—the dark force of the Other Side. The embodiment of the values and attitudes of the Ladover Hasidim, the Rebbe becomes here a target for Asher's assertion of will. With Aryeh Lev, he represents the forces attempting to separate him from his street and deny him his "gift." The persecution by his classmates, suggested by the passage above, continues until Asher, for the first time, employs his art as a tool of attack: his drawing of the pimply faced boy who had tormented him being dragged into hell is both emotively and theologically true. (*AL*) But this incident and that of the Chumash only solidify Asher's distance from his social world.

The second important section relating to Asher and his "nation" occurs at the end of the novel and illustrates the reaction of the people towards him as an artist. After the Crucifixions have been shown, Asher attends his synagogue on Shabbos. In describing the people's reaction, he enumerates the rejections of those in the community who had been most tolerant of him—the mashpia, Yudel, and his Uncle Yitzchok:

That Shabbos, people turned their backs to me in the synagogue. The Rebbe came in during the service and sat down in the chair near the Ark. I could see his eyes beneath the prayer shawl. I could see him scanning the people in the synagogue.... People saw him looking at me. After the service, the mashpia would not return my greetings. He walked past me, his eyes filled with pain. Yudel Krinsky murmured a response but gazed at me in silent bewilderment. My Uncle Yitzchok brushed by me angrily.

(*AL*)

In their fourth and final meeting, the Rebbe, Asher's last link with his community, articulates the break Asher has brought upon himself. With sympathy and understanding, he tells Asher,

'What you have done has caused harm. People are angry. They ask questions, and I have no answer to give them that they will understand.... I will ask you not to continue living here, Asher Lev. I will ask you to go away.'

I felt a cold trembling inside me.

'You are too close here to people you love. You are hurting them and making them angry.... It is not good for you to remain here.'

(*AL*)

Thus Asher is forced into exile from his people, his "nation"; his compulsion to paint the truth of his feelings alienates him from an incomprehending world. "'Asher Lev,' the Rebbe said softly. 'You have crossed a boundary.... You are alone, now.'" (*AL*) ...

Source: Warren R. True, "Potok and Joyce: The Artist and His Culture," in *Studies in American Jewish Literature*, No. 2, 1982, pp. 181–90.

SOURCES

Abramson, Edward A., *Chaim Potok*, Twayne, 1986, pp. 58–81.

Barson, Anthony, "The Artist as a Novel," in *Christian Science Monitor*, June 14, 1972, p. 11.

Clarfield, A. Mark, "The Soviet 'Doctors' Plot—50 Years On," in *British Medical Journal*, Vol. 325, No. 7378, December 21, 2002, pp. 1487–89, http://www.ncbi.nlm.nih.gov/pmc/articles/PMC139050/ (accessed May 31, 2011).

Davenport, Guy, "Collision with the Outside World," in *New York Times Book Review*, April 16, 1972, pp. 5, 18.

"Glossary—Key Jewish FAQ's," in *Chabad.org*, http://www.chabad.org/library/article_cdo/aid/108411/jewish/Glossary.htm (accessed June 7, 2011).

Goldman, Peter, et al., "Heart of Darkness," in *Newsweek*, July 25, 1977, pp. 17–22, http://www.blackout.gmu.edu/archive/pdf/newsweek_77.pdf (accessed June 7, 2011).

"In the Goyish Mould," in *Times Literary Supplement* (London, England), No. 3683, October 6, 1972, p. 1184.

"Jewish Practice—Jewish Traditions and Mitzvah Observances," in *Chabad.org*, http://www.chabad.org/library/article_cdo/aid/325184/jewish/Jewish-Practice. htm (accessed June 7, 2011).

Kremer, S. Lillian, "Dedalus in Brooklyn: Influences of *A Portrait of the Artist as a Young Man* on *My Name Is Asher Lev*," in *Studies in American Jewish Fiction*, No. 4, 1985, pp. 26–38.

Mahler, Jonathan, "Waiting for the Messiah of Eastern Parkway," in *New York Times*, September 21, 2003, http://www.nytimes.com/2003/09/21/magazine/waiting-for-the-messiah-of-eastern-parkway.html (accessed June 6, 2011).

Milch, Robert J., Review of *My Name Is Asher Lev*, in *Saturday Review*, April 15, 1972, pp. 65–66.

"Night of the Murdered Poets," in *National Council on Soviet Jewry*, August 12, 2002, http://www.ncsj.org/AuxPages/081202MurderedPoets.shtml (accessed May 31, 2011).

Potok, Chaim, *My Name Is Asher Lev*, Knopf, 1972.

———, "The First Eighteen Years," in *Studies in American Jewish Literature*, No. 4, 1985, pp. 100–106.

"Provincetown Business Guild," in *Provincetown.com*, http://www.provincetown.com/ (accessed June 7, 2011).

Smith, Roberta, "Ileana Sonnabend, Art World Figure Dies at 92," in *New York Times*, October 24, 2007, http://www.nytimes.com/2007/10/24/arts/24sonnabend.html (accessed June 7, 2011).

Stern, David, "Two Worlds," in *Commentary*, October 1972, pp. 102, 104.

True, Warren R., "Potok and Joyce: The Artist and His Culture," in *Studies in American Jewish Literature*, No. 2, 1982, pp. 181–90.

Zaklikowski, David, "How Jacques Lipchitz Found G-d: The Rabbi and the Sculptor," in *Chabad.org*, http://www.chabad.org/therebbe/article_cdo/aid/393257/jewish/How-Jacques-Lipchitz-Found-G-d.htm (accessed May 31, 2011).

FURTHER READING

Barkess, Joanna, "Painting the Sitra Achra: Culture Confrontation in Chaim Potok's Asher Lev Novels," in *Studies in American Jewish Literature*, No. 17, 1998, pp. 17–24.
In this critical essay, Barkess analyzes *My Name Is Asher Lev* and *The Gift of Asher Lev* in terms of imagery and Freudian overtones in creating a schism, in which resides the concept of the Other Side.

Brent, Jonathan, and Vladimir Naumov, *Stalin's Last Crime: The Plot Against the Jewish Doctors, 1948–1953*, Harper Perennial, 2004.
The authors trace Stalin's painstaking plans to create the appearance of a massive conspiracy

of the Jews against the Soviet regime, which is discussed in *My Name Is Asher Lev* as the plot against the doctors. Brent and Naumov also discuss inconsistencies in the facts surrounding Stalin's death, indicating that his plot may have backfired on him.

Frankel, Ellen, *The Jewish Spirit: A Celebration in Stories and Art*, Stewart, Tabori & Chang, 1997.
This book presents Jewish mystical and folk tales from around the world, along with full color illustrations of Jewish artworks from museums worldwide.

Kouvar, Elaine M., "An Interview with Chaim Potok," in *Contemporary Literature*, Vol. 27, No. 3, Fall 1986, pp. 291–317.
Potok talks about the problems Jewish artists encounter with respect to religion, and particularly as they relate to Asher Lev.

Potok, Chaim, and Daniel Walden, eds., *Conversations with Chaim Potok*, University Press of Mississippi, 2001.
This collection of interviews between Potok and leading literature critics were conducted between 1976 and 1999. Potok discusses his own works, those of fellow Jewish writers, his literary influences, and how he prefers to see himself as an American writer who concentrates on a small slice of culture rather than as a Jewish writer.

Walden, Daniel, "Potok's Asher Lev: Orthodoxy and Art: The Core-to-Core Paradox," in *Studies in American Jewish Literature*, Vol. 29, 2010, p. 148.
Walden discusses the main conflict of *My Name Is Asher Lev*, namely "an observant Jew's confrontation with Western Art." He places the novel in its literary context with the works of Faulkner, Joyce, Flannery O'Connor, and other writers.

SUGGESTED SEARCH TERMS

Judaism AND Chaim Potok

Jewish AND Chaim Potok

Orthodox AND Judaism

Hasidic AND Jewish

Joseph Stalin AND Jew

artist AND Chaim Potok

Brooklyn AND Chaim Potok

Lubavitch AND Chaim Potok

Chaim Potok

My Name Is Asher Lev AND Chaim Potok

bildungsroman

kunstlerroman

Neuromancer

WILLIAM GIBSON

1984

In 1984, William Gibson's novel *Neuromancer* exploded onto the literary scene, sweeping all three important science-fiction awards—the Nebula, the Philip K. Dick Memorial Award, and the Hugo—and quickly winning wide readership and critical acclaim. By the time the twentieth-anniversary edition of the book was published in 2004, critics generally agreed that *Neuromancer* was one of the most influential books of the twentieth and early twenty-first centuries, not only for Gibson's striking prose but also for the uncanny way that the book foretold technological and sociological developments decades before they occurred. Indeed, there are some critics who suggest that the shape of present-day Western culture is as it is because of Gibson's vision of the future. That is, not only did the book foretell the future, but it may also have helped create it, most notably the idea of cyberspace and the Internet.

Neuromancer is one of the earliest and most highly regarded of the so-called *cyberpunk* works of science fiction, although this is a label that Gibson generally rejects when talking about the book. Cyberpunk is a genre set in a bleak near future, with main characters who are hackers or criminals who find themselves in an oppressive society dominated by technology and huge corporations. *Neuromancer* is the story of one such cyberspace cowboy named Case, a woman named Molly who has been surgically transformed into a formidable fighter, and two artificial intelligences who are trying to join together.

William Gibson (Getty Images)

Readers should be aware that the language of *Neuromancer* is gritty, rough, and at times, obscene; much of the action is violent; drug use is common; and there are several scenes of explicit sex. For these reasons, *Neuromancer* may not be a good choice for younger readers.

AUTHOR BIOGRAPHY

Gibson was born on March 17, 1948, in Conway, South Carolina, to William Ford Gibson and Otey Gibson. The family moved around a great deal, as his father was a contractor and took jobs at various places. As a boy, Gibson enjoyed watching science fiction on the then-new technology of television.

When Gibson was eight years old, his father died, and he moved with his mother to Wytheville, Virginia. Jack Womack, in the afterword to the twentieth-anniversary edition of *Neuromancer*, asserts that growing up in western Virginia was essential to Gibson's later growth as a writer. Womack goes so far as to say that this is where

"cyberspace was born." He states, "This part of the United States has been since the Revolution . . . not merely rural, but distant, in time as well as place; its light filters down through the branches from another world's sun." Gibson himself concurs. In an autobiographical essay, "Since 1948," he notes, "The trauma of my father's death aside, I'm convinced that it was this experience of feeling abruptly exiled, to what seemed like the past, that began my relationship with science fiction."

Gibson's attraction to science fiction grew during his early years. Douglas Ivison, in *Canadian Fantasy and Science-Fiction Writers*, reports that as a teenager Gibson was an avid reader, particularly interested in writers such as J. G. Ballard, William Burroughs, and Thomas Pynchon. These were not the optimistic writers of science fiction's golden age, such as Isaac Asimov or Robert Heinlein; rather, these writers often had grim and dark visions of the future. Gibson describes himself during these days as "introverted" and "hyper-bookish."

At sixteen, Gibson left Wytheville for Tucson, Arizona, where he attended boarding school. He reports that he had just begun to make some progress toward social adjustment when his mother suddenly died. In an understatement, he remarks, "Thereafter, probably needless to say, things didn't seem to go very well for quite a while."

According to Ivison, Gibson was kicked out of his boarding school for smoking marijuana. He briefly went back to Wytheville before beginning a period of a few years when he traveled around, as a part of the 1960s youth counterculture. He arrived in Toronto, Canada, in 1968, and in so doing, managed to evade the draft in the United States. He met his wife, Debra Thompson, at this time, and after traveling with her to Europe, he married her in 1972, finally settling in Vancouver, British Columbia.

He matriculated at the University of British Columbia and earned a degree in 1977. It was while he was attending college that he began his writing career, publishing his first short story, "Fragments of a Hologram Rose." According to Jack Fischel, in *American Writers: A Collection of Literary Biographies*,

> The story is notable for including the mix of themes that would characterize his future writing, including the importance and fragility of memory, the nebulous relationship between human beings and machines, distrust of the power of multinational corporations over information and individuals, and the instability of postmodern society.

After meeting punk musician and science-fiction writer John Shirley in 1977, Gibson began writing in earnest, and by 1981, he had published four stories. "Johnny Mnemonic," appearing in *Omni* magazine, was particularly notable. Ivison writes that the story "became one of the iconic and highly-anthologized stories of the so-called cyberpunk movement, of which Gibson became a leading figure."

In 1982, Gibson published another important story in *Omni*, "Burning Chrome." Both this story and "Johnny Mnemonic" were nominated for a Nebula Award. In "Burning Chrome," according to Ivison, Gibson "introduced the elements with which [he] became most identified." These included console cowboys, hackers, and breaking into major computer networks belonging to corporations. In addition, this story represented the first use of the word "cyberspace." Ivison argues that what makes this story so important is

its highly influential evocation of the matrix and its poetic description of the abstract space that is cyberspace. Much of the way in which cyberspace has been represented and understood is based on Gibson's description of it in this short story and on his elaboration of the concept in *Neuromancer*.

On the basis of these early stories, Gibson became the leading writer among a group of young science-fiction writers who were in rebellion against mainstream science fiction. He was awarded a contract by Terry Carr with Ace Books to write his first novel during this period, and the result was *Neuromancer*, published in 1984. By his own admission, Gibson did not imagine the book would be so popular or have such an impact. Ivison states that "no other Canadian speculative fiction writer, and possibly no other Canadian writer of fiction, has had as great an impact on late-twentieth-century culture as has William Gibson." The novel achieved unprecedented success. In the year of its publication, it swept all three major science-fiction awards, including the Hugo, the Nebula, and the Philip K. Dick Memorial Award; it is the only novel ever to do so.

Gibson wrote two more books in what has come to be called, beginning with *Neuromancer*, the "Sprawl" trilogy, *Count Zero* (1986) and *Mona Lisa Overdrive* (1987). Both were well-reviewed and popular successes. Since their publication, Gibson has written half a dozen more books, including the "Bigend" trilogy of *Pattern Recognition* (2003), *Spook Country* (2007), and *Zero History* (2010). He remains an active and prolific writer of fiction, essays, and poetry. His readers number in the millions across the globe, and his work is likely to elicit serious scholarly interest well into the future.

PLOT SUMMARY

Chiba City Blues: Chapters 1–2

The first section of *Neuromancer* is called "Chiba City Blues," identifying the setting as Japan. Chiba City is an actual Japanese city, located across Tokyo Bay from the city of Tokyo. The novel begins with one of the most famous opening lines in science fiction: "The sky above the port was the color of television, tuned to a dead channel." Because the novel was written in 1984, the color of a dead channel would be gray, staticky, and fuzzy, as opposed to the electric blue

MEDIA ADAPTATIONS

- *Neuromancer* was adapted as an early role-playing computer game by Interplay in 1988, with a soundtrack by Devo.
- Bruce Jensen created the first volume of *Neuromancer* as a graphic novel in 1989. It was published by Epic Comics.
- An abridged version of *Neuromancer*, narrated by Gibson himself, was released on audiocassette by Time Warner Audio Books in 1994.
- An unabridged version of *Neuromancer*, narrated by Arthur Addision, was released on audiocassette by Books on Tape in 1997.
- In 2003, the British Broadcasting Corporation adapted *Neuromancer* as a two-hour radio play and broadcast it as part of their *Play of the Week* series.

apparent on most dead channels on television in 2011. It serves to set a dark and confusing tone.

The protagonist Case appears in the second paragraph as he makes his way to a bar for expatriates. An Eastern European named Ratz with a prosthetic arm and steel and rotten teeth is the bartender. The mention of prostitutes and the description of the other customers confirms that the story opens in the underbelly of Chiba City. In addition, the first few pages make reference to the expertise of the Chinese in nerve splicing and the black clinics of Chiba, where neurosurgical techniques are rapidly changing; some of them are illegal. This places the story in the near future.

Case is a petty thief, circulating in the underworld of Chiba. Early in chapter 1, Case's backstory is revealed. He is originally from the Sprawl, an unidentified geographic location, most likely in the former United States. Some two years before the opening of the novel, Case used his talents as one of the premier "console cowboys," or computer hackers, to steal from his employer. In retaliation, the employer took Case to a Memphis hotel,

strapped him to a bed, and injected him with a mycotoxin that destroyed the parts of his nervous system necessary for him to "jack in" to cyberspace. Consequently, his days as a console cowboy were over. He came to Chiba City in the hopes that he could find a medical clinic that could reverse the damage, but he has had no success.

Now, drug-addicted and suicidal, Case sleeps in so-called coffin hotels, hotels with rooms the size of coffins. Linda Lee, Case's girlfriend, approaches him in a bar to tell him that Wage, a drug dealer for whom Case works, wants him dead because Case has not paid him for a shipment of drugs. He soon discovers, however, that Linda has betrayed him.

When he returns to the coffin hotel, he finds a woman armed with a dart gun waiting for him. The woman's name is Molly; she has surgically implanted silver lenses over her eyes and surgical blades implanted under her fingernails. She has come to recruit him for a job for a man named Armitage. Armitage describes to Case an operation during the war called "Screaming Fist," a cyber attack launched by a Russian computer network using ultralight aircraft.

Armitage offers to fix Case's nervous system if he will agree to do a job for him with Molly. When Case awakens from the surgery, he discovers that Armitage has also arranged for the doctors to adjust his liver and pancreas so that he can no longer get high. Molly and Case grow very close; neither of them knows exactly who Armitage is or the job he wants them to do. Case begins trying to discover Armitage's true identity and his connection with Screaming Fist. While doing so, he witnesses Linda Lee's murder. Shortly after, he and Molly board a hovercraft and travel to the Sprawl.

The Shopping Expedition: Chapters 3–7
At the beginning of chapter 3, Armitage informs Case that although his neural net has been repaired, he has also been implanted with sacs of the same mycotoxin that injured him in the first place. If Case is unable to complete his assignment in a certain amount of time, the sacs will burst, and Case will once again be unable to access cyberspace. If he is successful, however, Armitage will have the sacs removed. Case goes to a fence called the Finn to verify that the sacs are indeed there.

Molly and Case receive their first assignment: they must steal a computer construct referred to as Dixie Flatline. The construct is the consciousness of a famed console cowboy named McCoy Pauley, who taught Case everything he knew. Although Pauley is dead, his personality, consciousness, and ability to hack into heavily protected computer systems have been recreated in the Dixie Flatline.

Meanwhile, Molly and Case discover that Armitage was previously known as Colonel Willis Corto, a member of the Screaming Fist assault. He was the only survivor, although he was seriously physically and psychologically damaged. Soon after the attack, he disappeared.

After successfully stealing the Dixie Flatline, Molly and Case travel to Istanbul, Turkey, where they find the third member of their team, Peter Riviera. Riviera is a psychopathic drug addict who has been implanted with a cybernetic device that allows him to project realistic holograms based on the fears and desires of his audience.

Case and Molly discover that Armitage is only the front person for the job and that an artificial intelligence (AI) located in Berne, Switzerland, is really running the show. The AI's name is Wintermute. Wintermute was originally created by Marie-France Tessier, of the incredibly wealthy and powerful Tessier-Ashpool family. Wintermute will take on various appearances and forms in the novel, including the Finn and Julius Deane, a criminal for whom Case previously worked and who probably killed Linda Lee.

Midnight in the Rue Jules Verne: Chapters 8–12

The third section of *Neuromancer* takes place partially in the Zion cluster, a space colony inhabited by Rastas, believers in the Rastafarian religion. (Rasta had its beginnings in Jamaica in the 1930s. Rastas use marijuana as part of their religious ceremonies, and they reject Western capitalist society, calling it "Babylon.") In the Zion cluster, Molly and Case meet up with Aerol and Maelcum, two young Rastas. They idolize Molly, calling her "Steppin Razor," an allusion to reggae musician Peter Tosh, who played with Bob Marley. Maelcum is the pilot of the tug *Marcus Garvey* that will transport Molly and Case to Freeside.

Freeside is a space station where all kinds of decadent worldly pleasures are available and is owned by the Tessier-Ashpool family, who also live on Freeside in the gigantic, castle-like Villa Straylight. The family is also a corporation,

Tessier-Ashpool SA. The leadership of the family passes from family member to family member. When not in charge, most family members live in cryonic preservation, only awakening periodically.

Molly and Case discover that their mission is to make a run on Villa Straylight; Molly will physically assault the stronghold, while Case will assault their computer network in cyberspace. Molly and Case also discover that Wintermute is one of two AIs designed by the Tessier-Ashpool family and that Wintermute's entire plan is to merge with the second AI, Neuromancer, also designed by Marie-France Tessier, and in which she placed her personality construct. Wintermute must have help since all AIs have built-in protection against such mergers in accordance with the Turing Law Code, which was enacted to prevent any AI from becoming too powerful. However, when Marie-France Tessier designed Wintermute, she programmed it with the desire to merge with the other Tessier-Ashpool AI.

The plan is as follows: Riviera will befriend Lady 3Jane Marie-France Tessier-Ashpool, the third cloned daughter of Marie-France Tessier and the only one of the clan currently unfrozen and still awake in Straylight. His and Molly's role is to gain access to Straylight and get the password to the Turing lock from 3Jane. Simultaneously, Case will assault Straylight's protective software programming known as ICE (intrusion countermeasures electronics) with the help of the Dixie Flatline. The password must be physically entered into a computer terminal in Straylight at the same time Case enters it in cyberspace. At the end of the section, Case is arrested by the Turing police, guards who enforce the Turing Law Code.

The Straylight Run: Chapters 13–23

Wintermute intervenes in Case's arrest and murders the police. Meanwhile, the Armitage personality is falling apart, and the insane Colonel Corto is re-emerging. He also is killed by Wintermute.

Molly gains access to Straylight and runs across Ashpool, an ancient man who was Marie-France Tessier's husband. Earlier, Ashpool murdered his wife. When Molly arrives, she interrupts him as he is committing suicide. She kills him.

Meanwhile, Riviera has decided that he will betray Molly, Case, and Wintermute. He and 3Jane take Molly prisoner. Case, following Molly's movements through a device known as a "simstim," which allows him access to all of Molly's senses, realizes that her life is in danger. Neuromancer, however, attempts to trap Case in a construct. Case escapes, and he and Maelcum rush to Molly's aid.

Case, Maelcum, Riviera, Molly, 3Jane, and Hideo, 3Jane's ninja bodyguard, are all in the same room in Straylight. Riviera tries to kill Case, but Hideo, at 3Jane's behest, intervenes and is blinded by Riviera. However, Hideo is just as deadly blind as he is sighted. He pursues Riviera. 3Jane has also poisoned Riviera earlier, so the psychopath is doomed.

3Jane agrees to give Molly and Case the password. Case plugs into a computer terminal in Straylight to penetrate the ICE, and the password is spoken, opening the Turing lock. Wintermute and Neuromancer merge.

Departure and Arrival: Coda

At some time after the events of the Straylight run, Molly leaves Case. Case's system has been purged of the poison, and he has been paid well for his work. The merged Neuromancer/Wintermute contacts Case in the persona of the Finn. He claims that now he is the matrix. He reports that he has been in conversation with an AI broadcasting from the Alpha Centauri system.

Case uses his pay to get a new liver and pancreas and then goes back to the Sprawl and to what he loves most, hacking into computer systems as a cyberspace cowboy. In the last page of the book, Case finds himself in cyberspace, and he sees Riviera, Linda, the little boy who was Neuromancer, and himself. He hears the laughter of the Dixie Flatline. The book closes with a poignant sentence, one that is quoted nearly as often as the opening: "He never saw Molly again."

CHARACTERS

Aerol

Aerol is a young Rastafarian who lives in the Zion cluster and pilots a companion space shuttle to the *Marcus Garvey*, a tug owned and piloted by another Rasta, Maelcum.

Armitage

Armitage is a mysterious, well-dressed stranger who recruits Molly, Case, and Riviera to take on an unknown assignment for him. He appears to be very powerful and rich. However, as Case and Molly begin to dig into his background, they discover that Armitage is really Colonel Willis Corto, the sole survivor of an attack on Russian

cyberspace. Corto was damaged, both physically and psychologically, but was rebuilt as Armitage by the artificial intelligence Wintermute as a human interface for Wintermute's plans. Over the course of the book, the Armitage personality disintegrates, leaving behind an insane Corto, who ultimately is killed.

Ashpool

Ashpool is the patriarch of the Tessier-Ashpool family and corporation. He lives in Villa Straylight and spends much of his life in cryogenic suspension in a quest for immortality. He opposed his wife Marie-France Tessier's plan to build AIs and enter into a symbiotic relationship with the machines. He killed Marie-France, and when Molly finds him during the Straylight run, he is in the process of committing suicide.

Henry Dorsett Case

Case is the protagonist and main character of *Neuromancer*. As the story opens, Case appears as a down-on-his-luck hustler, addicted to drugs and committing petty larcenies to support his habit. Once the premier "cowboy," a term used for hackers who "jack in" to cyberspace to commit thievery and other illegal actions, Case is now unable to access cyberspace. Two years earlier, while working on a cyberspace heist, he stole from his employers, who soon discovered his betrayal. In retaliation, the gangsters took him to a hotel in Memphis where they injected him with a powerful mycotoxin that burned out his nervous system, making it impossible for him to work as a hacker. According to the text,

> For Case, who'd lived for the bodiless exultation of cyberspace, it was the Fall. In the bars he'd frequented as a cowboy hotshot, the elite stance involved a certain relaxed contempt for the flesh. The body was meat. Case fell into the prison of his own flesh.

Case came to Japan from the Sprawl to try to find a clinic that could cure him. At the book's opening, he has not been able to recover from the damage and so must conduct his thievery on the ground. He lives in a "coffin hotel," a place where tiny, coffin-sized sleeping spaces are rented.

When he is approached by a man named Armitage, who offers to cure him if he will undertake a particularly difficult hacking job, he accepts. The lure of cyberspace is too great for him to refuse. However, he soon finds that although Armitage has fixed his nervous system, he has also booby-trapped his internal organs with poisonous sacs that will burst and destroy his cyber abilities if he does not finish the assignment within a reasonable time. Thus, Case is trapped into completing the task that Armitage assigns him.

Case's allies include Molly, the Rastas, and the Dixie Flatline. The task is to make a run on the Villa Straylight of the Tessier-Ashpool family, obtain a certain password, and help the AI Wintermute join with the AI Neuromancer.

Colonel Willis Corto
See Armitage

Julius Deane
Julius Deane is a minor criminal figure who appears in the beginning of the book. Case believes that Deane is one of his friends; however, it appears that Deane double-crosses Case and has Case's girlfriend Linda Lee murdered. Later in the book, Wintermute sometimes appears in Deane's likeness.

The Dixie Flatline
The Dixie Flatline is a computer construct built on the consciousness of the console cowboy McCoy Pauley, one of Case's mentors and teachers. Pauley "flatlined," or died, in the process of hacking a highly guarded computer network; his consciousness and expertise, however, were saved in his computer's memory. The Dixie Flatline communicates in Pauley's voice, although his laughter does not seem human. Molly and Case steal the Dixie Flatline in order to access his ability to break through ICE (intrusion countermeasures electronics) to complete their assignment from Armitage/Wintermute.

The Finn
The Finn is a petty criminal and fence for stolen goods in Chiba City. When Wintermute wants to speak with Case, he sometimes uses a construct that looks and sounds like the Finn.

Linda Lee
Linda Lee is Case's girlfriend in Chiba City. She is also a drug addict and betrays Case. Julius Deane has her killed. Late in the book, Neuromancer creates a simulated environment for Case that includes Linda Lee.

Maelcum
Maelcum is a young Rasta who owns the space tug *Marcus Garvey*. He helps Case and Molly prepare for the Straylight run and accompanies Case when he goes to the Villa Straylight to attempt to save Molly's life.

Molly
Molly is a so-called "street samurai." Armitage recruits her for her muscle and fighting expertise to take part in his plans. Molly has been surgically altered to enhance her fighting capability. She has retractable razor blades implanted under her fingernails, thus her classification as a "Razorgirl." She also has mirrored lenses implanted over her eyes to help her see better and to hide her eyes. Likewise, her reflexes have been modified to make her move and respond more quickly. The character appears in several of Gibson's works. She first surfaces in Gibson's short story "Johnny Mnemonic," as Molly Millions.

Neuromancer
Neuromancer is an AI designed by Marie-France Tessier and located in Rio de Janeiro. Neuromancer is able to see patterns, to grow, and to create his own personality. He does not want to merge with Wintermute and so puts obstacles in the path of Case and Molly. He believes his identity and personality will be lost once the merger is complete.

McCoy Pauley
See The Dixie Flatline

Ratz
Ratz is a bartender in Chiba City who calls Case an "artiste."

Peter Riviera
Peter Riviera is a psychopathic thief, artist, and drug addict who has been surgically altered so that he can project completely realistic holograms based on the fears and desires of his audience. He is utterly unreliable and completely out for himself. Armitage, however, recruits him to try to get the password to the Turing lock from 3Jane.

Marie-France Tessier
Marie-France Tessier was Ashpool's wife and the original designer of Wintermute and Neuromancer. She did not believe in cryogenics and sought immortality not through living in suspended animation but through the copying her personality and consciousness into the AI Neuromancer.

Lady 3Jane Marie-France Tessier-Ashpool

3Jane, as she is called, is the cloned daughter of Marie-France Tessier and Ashpool, the third clone of the original Jane. She is currently the head of the Tessier-Ashpool family as well as the company Tessier-Ashpool SA. She lives in the Villa Straylight in Freeside and controls the Tessier-Ashpool AIs. She alone knows the password to the Turing lock, a device put into place so that the AIs do not become too intelligent.

Wage

Wage is a petty criminal in Chiba City to whom Case owes money.

Wintermute

Wintermute is a Tessier-Ashpool AI, designed originally by Marie-France, who gave it the desire to become more than itself and merge with Neuromancer in order to become a new kind of super-intelligent being. It is prevented from doing this because of the Turing locks also designed by Marie-France. While Neuromancer is all personality, Wintermute does not have a stable identity and must create constructs in order to talk directly to humans. Case reflects in the coda, "Wintermute was hive mind, decision maker, effecting change in the world outside. Neuromancer was personality. Neuromancer was immortality."

THEMES

Opposites

Structuralism is a type of literary criticism that examines works of literature by contrasting the elemental structure of the work in a system of binary opposition. That is, structuralist analysis demonstrates how a novel, short story, or poem is organized around pairs of opposites. The first step in such an analysis is to identify those pairs. Gibson provides fertile ground for this kind of critical approach because *Neuromancer* is thematically organized around binary oppositions.

Early in the book, Case's inability to access cyberspace because of his neural damage highlights the fundamental opposition between mind and body. Console cowboys exist in a world of the mind and call the flesh of their body "meat." Molly's introduction into the story introduces a second kind of opposition, that of gender. She represents the feminine where Case is masculine. She is a creature of the body, rather than the mind, someone whose physicality gives her success as a street ninja. She amplifies her body through a series of surgical procedures that improve and enhance her ability to fight. Case, on the other hand, attempts to amplify the experiences of his mind through drugs and jacking in to cyberspace. Whereas Molly embraces the body, Case rejects it.

A second opposition arises later in the book when readers discover that there is not just one AI controlling the events of the story, but two. Wintermute, an AI in Berne, can control schedules, electrical systems, and other things but is unable to directly communicate with human beings. As Gibson writes, "Wintermute was hive mind, decision maker, effecting change in the world outside. . . . Wintermute. Cold and silence, a cybernetic spider slowly spinning webs while Ashpool slept." On the other hand, Neuromancer, an AI in Rio de Janeiro, is Wintermute's binary opposition. Gibson writes, "Neuromancer was personality. Neuromancer was immortality." Tellingly, although both Wintermute and Neuromancer were designed by the same person, Marie-France Tessier, Tessier chose to place her personality construct within Neuromancer, not in Wintermute.

Gibson does more than simply set up binary oppositions. He also instills within these opposites the tendency or desire to merge. As Lance Olsen writes in his article "The Shadow of Spirit in William Gibson's Matrix Trilogy," "The quest for a union of opposites appears to be the key theme of *Neuromancer*." Thus, Case and Molly initially join their bodies in sex, and later, they join their senses through the use of the simstim, a device that allows Case to experience all of Molly's senses while she is physically undertaking the Straylight run.

The most important urge for union appears in Wintermute, who has been designed by Tessier with the overwhelming desire to merge with Neuromancer. All of Wintermute's years of planning and controlling events have been for this single purpose. As Olsen explains, "Each [AI] suggests the structure of the binary human mind, half the structure of the cosmic totality. United, they become an all-powerful absolute." Gibson, then, appears to indicate in *Neuromancer* that only through the merging of opposites, an act that erases the differences between two entities, is true power to be found.

Identity

Personal identity is notoriously difficult to define. The standard dictionary definition of *identity* is

TOPICS FOR FURTHER STUDY

- Graphic novels are fictional works whose narratives are told through a combination of text and art, often like a comic book. *Neuromancer* is a novel notable for its striking description and evocation of place, such as with Night City and Freeside, making it adaptable to a graphic recreation. In fact, Bruce Jensen published a graphic novel of *Neuromancer* in 1989, to mixed reviews. The book is no longer in print and very difficult to access. Using your artistic talents, select a chapter of *Neuromancer* to render as a graphic novel. Be sure to use a combination of text and art and to maintain the narrative thread so that a reader can follow the story.

- *Akira*, a serialized cyberpunk science-fiction epic by Japanese writer and artist Katsuhiro Otomo, was first published in English in 1988 by Epic Comics. It is now available as a six-volume graphic novel, published by Kodansha Comics in 2009. Read volume 1, and write an essay comparing and contrasting Otomo's depiction of Tokyo with Gibson's portrayal of Chiba City. Use specific examples from each text to illustrate your points.

- *Blade Runner*, a 1982 movie directed by Ridley Scott and starring Harrison Ford, is widely credited with influencing Gibson's vision of the future as it is presented in *Neuromancer*. Watch *Blade Runner*, taking notes throughout the film on important details about setting, narrative, acting, cinematography, and sound. Imagine that you are a film critic, and write a review of *Blade Runner* from the perspective of the present day. Post it to your blog site and invite your classmates to comment on the film as well.

- M. T. Anderson's young-adult novel *Feed* (2002) tells the story of a future world where Internet connections are hardwired into everyone's brains just after birth and where corporations and media control the culture. Read *Feed* and identify similarities between this novel and *Neuromancer*. Do you think that Anderson was influenced in any way by *Neuromancer?* How does the future presented by Anderson resemble or diverge from the future imagined by Gibson? Prepare a PowerPoint presentation as a means to discuss with your class the future visions of Anderson and Gibson. Select appropriate excerpts and images to accompany your presentation.

- A work of utopian fiction is one that describes an ideal world. The opposite of utopian fiction is dystopian fiction, work that imagines a terrible future. Works such as Margaret Atwood's *The Handmaid's Tale* and George Orwell's *1984* describe dystopias. Most critics categorize *Neuromancer* as dystopian. Writers of dystopias usually begin with some troubling feature of contemporary society and then project that feature into the future. Imagine for yourself something that you think is troubling about the world of today. Research your topic using the Internet and your library and by interviewing people of different ages. Keep track of your information on your computer using WikiPad or other note-taking software. Using what you have learned about your issue, imagine a world fifty years from now in which your issue has come to dominate society. Write a series of poems or a short story set in your alternative future.

the fact of being who or what a person or thing is. As Popeye the Sailor famously said, "I yam what I yam." Although Popeye had no doubt about his personal identity, the characters in *Neuromancer* are much more complicated.

Case, the main character, was a console cowboy before the book begins. It was this skill that provided him with an understanding of who and what he was. As the book opens, however, Case has a problem with his identity. Likewise, the

Dixie Flatline problematizes the whole idea of identity as somehow unique to an individual. Finally, the identity of who or what is pulling the strings throughout the story is the mystery that drives the plot.

As *Neuromancer* opens, readers are introduced to Case, a down-on-his-luck console cowboy who has been banned from cyberspace through neural damage inflicted on him by a former employer from whom he stole. Case's identity, his understanding of himself as a premier computer hacker, has been stripped from him. Rather than being able to live in cyberspace, he must live in real space, burdened by the weight of his own flesh, commonly referred to by console cowboys as "meat." Case identifies with his mind, not his body.

Identity is also called into question when Case begins working with the Dixie Flatline, a computer construct of Case's old teacher and mentor, McCoy Pauley. "It was disturbing to think of the Flatline as a construct, a hardwired ROM cassette replicating a dead man's skills, obsessions, knee jerk responses." The problem is this: if the Flatline can replicate so much of Pauley's identity, what makes the ROM cassette *not* Pauley? The Flatline speaks in Pauley's voice, does Pauley's job, and acts like Pauley, yet the notion of identity implies that it is somehow unique, attached to one and only one person. The Flatline, as a ROM cassette, could be copied and recopied a million times. Although the Flatline has Pauley's voice, memory, and skills, it cannot have Pauley's identity, since that died with him.

Finally, although Armitage recruits Molly and Case, it soon becomes clear that there is someone or something more powerful pulling the strings, someone or something that is deliberately hiding its identity through Armitage. Molly and Case discover that Armitage is simply a front man for Wintermute, an artificial intelligence. Armitage's identity is not stable, either. Wintermute has constructed him around the shell of a man named Corto, who is insane, and through the book, Armitage's identity gradually crumbles away.

Wintermute's identity is also problematic. Although it is able to arrange and organize events at both the micro and macro levels, it is only able to communicate with Case when it takes on the appearance of a formerly living person. For example, Wintermute often appears to Case as the Finn,

Henry Dorsett Case is a cyber cowboy, a hacker extraordinaire. (Photosani | Shutterstock.com)

a fence Case knows in Chiba City. However, Wintermute is *not* the Finn, and although he looks and talks like the Finn, he lacks the essence of the Finn, the Finn's identity.

STYLE

Utopia/Dystopia
A *utopia* is an ideal place that does not exist in reality. Utopian literature creates an ideal world. Generally, utopian novels are novels of ideas where people have developed systems or technologies that allow them to focus on what is truly important in life. The word "utopia" comes from the name of a book written by Thomas More in 1516 about a perfect, imaginary place called "Utopia." Other famous utopian books include Plato's *Republic* and H. G. Wells's *A Modern Utopia*.

Although *Neuromancer* takes place in a futuristic world filled with technological advances and space travel, the novel belongs to a uniquely twentieth- and twenty-first-century variation of the utopia called an "anti-utopia" or "dystopia." Rather than a description of an ideal place, a dystopian novel describes an oppressive and terrible world where some of the most troubling aspects of contemporary society have expanded and defined the world of the future. Examples of this genre include *1984* (1948), by George Orwell; *The Handmaid's Tale* (1985), by Margaret Atwood; and *Never Let Me Go* (2005), by Kazuo Ishiguro.

Dystopias often serve as cautionary tales to warn readers of what might happen in the future if contemporary problems are not addressed. Despite this, *Neuromancer* is not a moralistic or didactic book. At the same time, Gibson has seeded his book with ethical issues plaguing not only the late twentieth century but also the twenty-first century. The world of *Neuromancer*, consequently, is a place where anything, including drugs, organs, and information, can be bought and sold. Cybercrime is rampant. Medical technology has blurred the distinction between person and machine. Drugs circulate freely throughout the culture. There seems to be no government in charge of what was formerly the United States; classified merely as the Sprawl, it is an overcrowded, crime-ridden, consumerist society. Bright young men are glorified for their ability to hack into computer networks, and they would rather spend their time in the virtual reality of cyberspace than face the everyday reality of life. Consequently, love and friendship no longer interest them. True communication among humans is virtually dead.

Language

The first-time reader of Gibson's *Neuromancer* will immediately be struck with vocabulary that is unfamiliar. This vocabulary places the setting distinctly in the future and contributes to the strangeness of the text. In addition, technological words currently in use are interspersed with words invented for the book or used in different ways, further signaling to the reader that he or she is in a brave new world. Microsoft, for example, does not refer to the large computer corporation but rather to a very small piece of software that can be inserted directly into a person's head.

Some additional terms useful for the reader of *Neuromancer* include "console cowboy," meaning a person who works as a computer hacker and

experiences cyberspace as if it were real space. "Trodes," short for electrodes, are the means through which the cowboy "jacks in," or connects, to cyberspace.

The title of the book is also an invented word and is a good example of how a word can have connotative meaning (in the felt sense or emotional associations attached to the word) even apart from any denotative meaning (the dictionary definition). Neuromancer contains within it the word "romancer." While most modern people associate romance with romantic love, the word *romance* can be traced back to the early Middle Ages, when it meant a story told in the vernacular language, not Latin. In the case of *Neuromancer*, Gibson is using the vernacular of the near future to tell his tale. In addition, "romancer" carries with it the connotation of a storyteller, a spinner of fictional yarns.

The name Neuromancer also has the prefix "neuro," a prefix that denotes the nerves. Nerves in the human body are bundles of fiber that transmit sensory data to the brain and spinal cord. In effect, the nerves carry information, in much the same way that fiber-optic cables carry digital data. Thus, Gibson's use of the prefix in naming the book and the second AI associates the AI with the transmission of data and with a huge neural network.

Finally, Neuromancer resembles the word "necromancer." This word means a magician who deals in the dark arts, by communicating with the dead through ghosts, or apparitions, specifically in order to tell the future. The word comes to modern English from the Middle Ages, and necromancy was a forbidden art. Gibson clearly uses the connotations associated with this word to give tone and meaning to the name Neuromancer. Both of the AIs in the novel raise the dead to communicate with the living: the AI Neuromancer uses a computer construct (a veritable ghost in the machine) of Linda Lee, Case's dead girlfriend, to trap him in cyberspace.

Cyberpunk

Cyberpunk is a movement in science fiction that began in the early 1980s. Although Gibson quickly rejected the label, *Neuromancer* is widely regarded as the most accomplished novel in the genre.

As discussed by Adam Roberts in his book *Science Fiction*, the word conjoins "cyber," a root associated with technology, and "punk," a word associated with a particular rock-music movement popular beginning in the 1970s. Punk was both youthful and antiestablishment. In cyberpunk science fiction, the future is portrayed as dirty, grim, dark, and crime ridden. Although cyberpunk is no longer a potent force in science fiction, its influence can still be felt in films and television shows such as *Battlestar Galactica* and especially *Caprica*.

HISTORICAL CONTEXT

Alan Turing and the Turing Test

Alan Turing, born in London on June 23, 1912, was destined to become the father of computer science, according to his biographer Andrew Hodges, author of *Alan Turing: The Enigma* (2000) and the webmaster of a comprehensive site on Alan Turing (www.turing.org.uk). Turing attended Cambridge University as an undergraduate and a graduate student, studying mathematics, logic, probability, and quantum mechanics. Between 1936 and 1938, he pursued doctoral studies in the United States at Princeton University, where he studied logic, algebra, and number theory. With the advent of World War II, he returned to Cambridge, where he was first introduced to the German Enigma machine, a device the Germans used to create what were thought to be unbreakable ciphers for secret messages. By 1940, Turing and his colleague Gordon Welchman, working at Bletchley Park, where Allied code breakers were stationed, developed a decryption device called the Bombe machine. The Allies were able to employ the device to break the Enigma codes unbeknownst to the Germans, who continued to use the Enigma machine for several more years. Turing's work, by all accounts, contributed to the eventual Allied victory in World War II.

After the war, Turing joined the National Physical Laboratory in London and began working on the first computer design and software. During the late 1940s, he worked on programming, neural nets, and artificial intelligence. By 1949, computers were being used for the first time for serious mathematical use.

In 1950, Turing wrote an extremely important and influential work, *Computing Machinery and Intelligence*. In this monograph, Turing raised the question as to whether machines could think. More precisely, according to Graham Oppy and David Dowe, in the *Stanford Encyclopedia of Philosophy*, Turing thought that "the question whether machines can think is itself 'too meaningless' to deserve discussion." Oppy and Dowe continue, "If we consider the more precise—and somehow related—question of whether a digital computer can do well in a certain kind of game . . . we do have a question that admits precise discussion." The "certain kind of game" described by Turing has come to be called the Turing test and has long been thought to be the standard by which machine intelligence can be judged.

Roberts, in *Science Fiction*, describes the Turing test:

> Imagine two closed rooms one of which contains a person and the other a computer. You cannot enter the rooms but you can communicate with who or what is inside by typing questions into a terminal and receiving replies. How many questions would it take before you were able to tell which room contained the person and which the machine? . . . Turing argued that if the tester cannot tell the machine replies apart from the human ones, then the machine has achieved a consciousness that is on a par with human sentience.

In 1954, Turing died of apparent suicide by ingestion of cyanide. His work remains an important influence not only in the field of computer science but in the realm of speculative fiction, as evidenced by Gibson's *Neuromancer*, a work that examines human and machine intelligences and interaction. Gibson's creation of the Turing Law Code and the Turing police is a tribute to Alan Turing and his life's work.

Science Fiction in the Twentieth Century

Although writers have always speculated about what a future world might look like, modern science fiction as a genre began with the English writer H. G. Wells in the late nineteenth century. As Brian Stableford notes in his chapter "Science Fiction before the Genre" in *The Cambridge Companion to Science Fiction*, "Wells single-handedly laid the groundwork for the distinctive methods of modern sf." These "distinctive methods" include providing a commentary and critique of contemporary society by creating an imaginary society of the future.

The popularity of science fiction waxed and waned over the course of the twentieth century. The opening decade of the twenty-first century saw a renewed interest in science fiction, as evidenced not only by the number of science-fiction novels published but also by the number of

COMPARE
&
CONTRAST

- **1980s:** The National Organ Transplant Act is passed in 1984. It finances organizations attempting to procure organs for transplant and also prohibits charging recipients for organs.

  Today: Debra A. Budiani-Saberi and Francis L. Delmonico report in their article "Organ Trafficking and Transplant Tourism: A Commentary on Global Realities" that organ trafficking is rampant throughout the world. In addition, people from wealthy countries needing a kidney transplant sometimes travel to developing countries where they are able to purchase kidneys from living donors or on the black market.

- **1980s:** The proliferation of personal computers, workstations, and local networks leads to the rapid growth of the Internet.

  Today: Browsers such as Netscape, Microsoft Internet Explorer, Mozilla Firefox, Google Chrome, and Safari allow easy access to the World Wide Web. The Internet is increasingly commercialized, with countless vendors using the Internet to sell goods and services.

- **1980s:** In 1985, chess champion Garry Kasparov defeats thirty-two chess computers at the same time. Meanwhile, Carnegie Mellon graduate student Feng-hsiung Hsu begins working on a chess-playing computer. In 1989, Hsu joins IBM as a research scientist and works with Murray Campbell and Joe Hoane to create Deep Blue, an artificial-intelligence chess-playing computer that defeats Kasparov in 1997.

  Today: In 2011, an IBM artificial intelligence named Watson defeats two human contestants on the popular television quiz show *Jeopardy*, demonstrating that an artificially intelligent computer can master natural language.

---

television series and films within the genre. Thus, when William Gibson sat down to write *Neuromancer*, he was situating himself within an eighty-year tradition; at the same time, he was transforming and radically changing that tradition.

From about 1926 to 1960, science fiction was largely a genre found in pulp magazines such as Hugo Gernsback's *Amazing Stories*, according to Brian Attebery in his chapter "The Magazine Era: 1926–1960" in the same Cambridge volume. (The annual Hugo Award, given to the best science-fiction work of the year, is named for Gernsback.) John W. Campbell's *Astounding Science-Fiction*, founded in 1930, is another example of a highly influential pulp magazine of the era. While the writing in these stories was not always of the highest quality, the magazines defined the genre.

In the 1940s, according to Attebery, "a major innovation in magazine fiction . . . was the imagined application of experimental method and technological innovation not to physical problems but to fundamental questions about society and the mind." Writers such as Isaac Asimov early on began to explore the implications of human-machine interaction. His famous robotic series, including short stories written between 1940 and 1950 and collected in *I, Robot* (1950) and novels such as *The Caves of Steel* (1954), *The Naked Sun* (1957), *Robots of Dawn* (1983), and *Robots and Empire* (1985), provided the basic framework for how humans and artificial intelligences could interact, a framework that included his famous Three Laws of Robotics.

While Asimov and fellow science-fiction writers such as Ray Bradbury and Robert Heinlein held a basically optimistic view of the future, in the 1960s, younger writers, including Harlan Ellison, J. G. Ballard, R. A. Lafferty, Gene Wolfe, and Kate Wilhelm, known collectively as the "New Wave," began experimenting with both form and content in their work. Their vision of the future

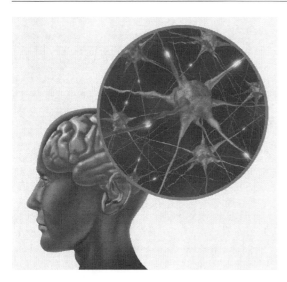

Mycotoxin damages Henry's central nervous system. *(Lightspring / Shutterstock.com)*

was bleaker. In Ellison's 1966 short story "I Have No Mouth and I Must Scream," a group of humans are held hostage and tortured by a giant artificial intelligence that has nearly destroyed the world.

By the 1980s, "there was some sense that sf was running on inertia, that too many of its creative thinkers had decamped," asserts John Clute in his essay, "Science Fiction from the 1980s to the Present." Gibson, drawing inspiration from the iconoclastic older writer Philip K. Dick, the noir vision of Ridley Scott's film *Blade Runner*, and his own sense of the impending information explosion, transformed the genre by turning the attention of science fiction from story to surface, from characterization to mood and tone, and from plot to setting. The movement became known as cyberpunk, and it swept science fiction through the 1990s and into the twenty-first century.

CRITICAL OVERVIEW

Neuromancer is one of the most important books of speculative fiction written during the twentieth century. From the moment of its publication, it attracted serious critical attention, winning the Nebula, the Hugo, and the Philip K. Dick Memorial Award, the first novel ever to win all three in a single year. The novel not only addresses

contemporary social and cultural concerns but also casts a predictive eye to the future. Indeed, as Richard Ryan proclaims in the *Christian Science Monitor* of August 26, 1993, "William Gibson is our Jules Verne."

In a contemporary review, Gerald Jonas states in the *New York Times Book Review* that "the 21st century world of *Neuromancer* is freshly imagined, compellingly detailed and chilling in its implications." Jonas notes the importance of setting and tone in Gibson's work, writing, "Mr. Gibson's style is all flash and his characters are pose without substance; but the emphasis on surface seems more a statement about Case and Case's world than an attempt to manipulate the reader."

Not all critics were as positive about the novel, however. J. R. Wytenbroek, for example, in *Canadian Literature*, argues that "the plot . . . is loaded down with and obscured by layers of technical jargon." Further, he criticizes Gibson for not explaining his terms, such that "readers must wade through them as they would through treacle, in search of a plot."

In the years since *Neuromancer*'s publication, literary critics and scholars have found many ways to examine the book. In 1991, for example, in an article appearing in *Extrapolation*, Lance Olsen examines mind/body dualism in all three of the "Sprawl" novels, arguing that the split occurs along gender lines. He asserts that, in *Neuromancer*, "the male principle (Case, the computer cowboy, the mind) strives to join with the female principle (Molly, the cyberspace matrix, the body) in order to attain a feeling of wholeness."

Likewise, Eva Cherniavsky, writing in *Genders*, approaches *Neuromancer* with attention to gender. She argues that "Gibson's cyberspace represents the negation of embodiment and hence of procreation, motherhood, and other embodied functions." That is, in the console cowboy's rejection of the flesh in favor of mind in cyberspace, he is also rejecting women and birth.

John Huntington, writing for *Essays and Studies* in 1990, comments that Gibson adds realism to his text by "invoking brand names and identifying the nationality of all his technology." Gibson's uses of these names "are a constant reminder of the dominated world in which the cowboy must play."

Taking a different approach, Lee Horsley compares *Neuromancer* to a noir thriller, a genre that features gritty criminals and private eyes, often working in seedy parts of town with low-life characters. Horsley argues in *The Noir Thriller* (2001) that Gibson uses the language and conventions of the noir thriller in *Neuromancer*, calling it

> a fusion of the noir thriller, science fiction and the Gothic. Its computerised data matrix, Gothic castle and crazed aristocratic family merge entertainingly with its hard-boiled protagonist living precariously and immorally on the seedy margins of a corrupt world.

Benjamin Fair, in *Critique*, points out that identity has been an important thematic concern for many critics of the novels. At the same time, he views the novel as a form of social commentary as opposed to a glimpse into the future, noting that "in *Neuromancer*, the new forms of identity point not so much to where we are headed in the future as to where we are in our present condition."

CRITICISM

Diane Andrews Henningfeld

Henningfeld is an emerita professor of English who writes widely on literature and current events for educational publications. In the following essay, she argues that, in Neuromancer, *Gibson deliberately blurs the line between humans and machines to raise the question of what it means to be human.*

"Heavily influenced by the 'New Wave' writers of the 1960s and early 1970s who tried to tear science fiction from its pulp roots and inject a dose of literary, even experimental, technique into the genre, Gibson turned the traditional science fiction viewpoint on its head," writes Robert K. J. Killheffer, in his interview with William Gibson in *Publishers Weekly*. However, while Gibson injected a radically new style and vision into the genre, different from the science fiction that had come before him, he did not reject many of the thematic concerns of science fiction, most notably, the simple question: what does it mean to be human?

A subsidiary question to this is particularly relevant: how does one distinguish the human from the nonhuman? Since at least the 1950s, this has been a growing concern, given the rapid growth and incredible sophistication of computers and, by extension, robots. Such concerns led science-fiction writers such as Isaac Asimov to consider in their stories what "laws" ought to be built directly into the software that

WHAT DO I READ NEXT?

- *The Best Japanese Science Fiction Stories*, edited by John Apostolou and Martin Harry Greenberg and published in 1997, is a young-adult anthology of work by noted Japanese writers such as Kobe Abe, Ryo Hanmura, and Sakyo Komatsu. The thirteen stories are inspired by fears of the future world.

- Alvin Toffler's *The Third Wave* (1980) speculates on the future, asserting that society will be highly decentralized. The book exerted an important influence on science fiction during the 1980s and early 1990s.

- First published in 1986, *Burning Chrome* is a collection of Gibson's short stories, several of them written before the publication of *Neuromancer*. Notable stories include "Burning Chrome," which includes the first documented use of the word "cyberspace," and "Johnny Mnemonic," which is the first story featuring Molly Millions.

- Susan Kearny's *The Dare* (2005) is a young-adult novel about an artificial intelligence named Dora who constructs a human body for herself so that she can experience love.

- Greg Bear is a member of the cyberpunk generation of science-fiction writers. In addition to postulating what crime might look like in the future, his book *Queen of Angels* (1990) examines concerns about the emerging self-awareness of a computer.

- Orson Scott Card's *Ender's Game* (1994) is the story of a child who is selected for special training due to his remarkable ability to play computer games. Although he thinks he is only playing games, the future of the planet depends on his ability at the console.

controls robots. In the late twentieth century, the television series *Star Trek: The Next Generation*, for example, contained episodes thematically addressing the status of the robot Data's identity and personhood.

HIDING BENEATH THESE QUESTIONS IS A

DEEP CULTURAL HORROR OF MACHINES. HUMANS

BOTH LOVE AND DESPISE THEIR MACHINES,

PARTICULARLY THOSE MACHINES THAT SEEM

MOST HUMAN."

Hiding beneath these questions is a deep cultural horror of machines. Humans both love and despise their machines, particularly those machines that seem most human. It is for this reason that the ability to distinguish the human from the machine is important: without vigilance, the machines could take over the world. *Battlestar Galactica*, a 2004–2009 television series, and its offshoot, *Caprica* (2009–2010), address the horror of machines directly: after building increasingly complicated and sophisticated machines to do the work no humans wanted to do, the machines eventually turned on their masters and destroyed the Earth. The most dangerous of all the machines, in the world of *Battlestar Galactica*, were those that could not be distinguished from humans.

The need to distinguish the human from the nonhuman is not limited to fiction, however. In 1950, Alan Turing developed the now-famous Turing test, designed to measure whether an artificial intelligence is truly intelligent. Turing, as well as the scientists at IBM who developed the *Jeopardy*-playing computer Watson, believed that only when a computer is able to use natural language, that is, language as it is spoken and used by humans, will a computer be truly intelligent, not artificially so.

In *Neuromancer*, Gibson builds on Turing's work by introducing the Turing Law Code, regulations that require artificial intelligences to have built-in software that limit their growth. Likewise, the Turing police exist solely to ensure that computers do not become too powerful.

Further, Gibson pushes the question of what constitutes a human and what constitutes a machine by continuously blurring the differences between the two. He introduces human characters who are amalgams of technology and flesh and artificial intelligences who have human characteristics designed into their software. As Lance Olsen writes in his book *William Gibson*, "Humans in Gibson's novel tend to act like machines while the machines tend to act like humans."

On the surface, it is easy to distinguish the humans from the machines in *Neuromancer*. The humans include Case, Molly, Ratz, Armitage, Riviera, and the Finn when he first appears. The machines are Wintermute and Neuromancer. More puzzling, of course, is how to categorize the Dixie Flatline and Lady 3Jane.

However, while the initial categorization seems simple enough, closer examination reveals where fuzziness between human and machine emerges. Ratz is perhaps the most human of the human characters; the bartender to whom Case spills his troubles seems firmly planted on both feet as a human, but even he has a prosthetic arm and steel teeth.

Molly is even closer to erasing the line between human and machine: she has had retractable razor blades implanted under her fingernails to give her a clear advantage in any hand-to-hand fight. Likewise, she has had mirrorshades implanted over her eyes to both hide her eyes from her enemies and to improve her ability to see. Furthermore, her brain has been altered in order to increase her reflexes and response speed. All of these implants and improvements change her human body into one that is now partially machine.

Case, too, uses machines to access cyberspace, and it is in cyberspace that he is most himself and feels most at home. But what is an identity in cyberspace? How does a digital construct operating a computer keyboard differ from a human being at the console? In an essay in *Studies in the Novel*, Tyler Stevens raises a troubling question: "Could *digital constructs* be sentient? . . . How do we know that the digital representations we encounter, the electronic text that scrolls across our screen, are human-produced and not 'simply' program-produced?"

Additionally, when Case employs the simstim device to follow Molly's actions as she begins the Straylight run, there is a merging not only of Case and Molly but also of the humans with the technology that allows them to merge. Man, woman, and simstim: the three meld together to form something that is both human and nonhuman, the experience for Case being more than simple simulation but something less than complete reality.

Riviera, too, has been surgically altered. He sports implants that allow him to project holographic (and at times, pornographic) images for his audiences, so realistic that those watching are unable to tell what is real and what is not.

The Finn and Julius Deane have very small roles in the beginning of the book; their roles are vital nonetheless, in that they make clear to readers that they are human beings. When they appear later in the book, however, readers gradually become aware that these are not the "real" Finn and Deane but rather are computer constructs thrown by Wintermute, the power artificial intelligence. There is discomfort and unease when the Finn and Deane constructs appear, a revulsion rooted in the use of human appearance and personality to mask the workings of a machine.

Likewise, Armitage grows increasingly grotesque as the book continues. When he first makes an appearance, he seems wealthy, powerful, and in complete control of himself. Only later do Case and Molly discover that he has been built by Wintermute on the body of Colonel Willis Corto, the only survivor of the Screaming Fist assault, and that he is completely insane. This particular construct is even more horrifying than the Finn: Wintermute has built something out of human flesh that is no longer human, as noted by Adam Roberts in his book *Science Fiction*.

If the blurring between human and machine in the real world makes distinguishing one from the other difficult, cyberspace makes the distinction even more difficult. "When one enters Gibson's cyberspace," Ronald Schmitt states in "Mythology and Technology: The Novels of William Gibson," it hardly resembles the cold, non-living accumulation of digital constructs one would expect in a computer, and both the human and non-human consciousnesses that inhabit it at any given time are anything but mechanized."

The Dixie Flatline is a case in point. Case's old teacher and mentor, McCoy Pauley, was killed raiding a corporate computer network for data. However, his consciousness was saved through his console and downloaded as ROM on a cassette deck. Gibson, in this maneuver, creates a human consciousness that exists only as binary data in a machine. Is the Flatline human? Roberts argues that he is not:

> [The Flatline] is only a metaphorical person, a series of computer algorithms that can mimic the particular speech habits of the dead individual....

But it cannot achieve any sense of self-identity, because it isn't 'real.' This makes Dix totally predictable, which is one key difference between himself and 'real' people.

However, Case works with Dixie as if he is McCoy Pauley. The Flatline uses natural language in such a way that he conveys both personality and intelligence. It is only in the reference to his laughter that Gibson reminds his readers that this is not a human being at all, but rather is a computer construct. As Stevens argues,

> Characters such as McCoy Pauley...come to figure the uneasy perception that there is no boundary between ourselves and our encompassing computing environments; that we are, though sentient, "merely" machines. That they are, though machines, sentient.

Lady 3Jane also stands on the frontier between humanity and technology. Although she is a "real" woman, she has been cloned. The number in her name designates that she is the third copy of the "real" Jane. However, she is flesh and blood, although her flesh and blood are identical to that of her sisters. Does this make her less human? Gibson does not explore this particular question fully enough to arrive at an answer. Nonetheless, the mere presence of a cloned human being who holds the Turing lock key is enough to elicit discussion and thought on the issue.

The AI Wintermute is surely not human. It does not understand humans nor human language as a native speaker. It cannot even speak clearly about who it is: "I, insofar as I *have* an 'I'—this gets rather metaphysical, you see—I am the one who arranges things for Armitage." To even reveal this much, it must use a construct of Julius Deane.

Neuromancer, on the other hand, is more of a problem. Because Marie-France Tessier uploaded her own personality into this AI, it retains her consciousness and all the humanity that that consciousness brings to bear. Few would argue that Neuromancer is somehow human, in spite of the human consciousness embedded in it. At the same time, this consideration brings with it the troubling thought, as raised by Stevens in *Studies in the Novel*, "How do we know that *we* are personalities, that *we are* sentient?"

Gibson offers no answers to these questions in the pages of *Neuromancer*. What he does offer is the opportunity to carefully consider the fine line between human and machine, between sentience and intelligence, between the present and the future.

Mainframe computer server system (joyfull | Shutterstock.com)

Source: Diane Andrews Henningfeld, Critical Essay on *Neuromancer*, in *Novels for Students*, Gale, Cengage Learning, 2012.

Glenn Grant

In the following essay, Grant discusses the theme of transcendence through technology in Neuromancer.

1. PEOPLE AS SYSTEMS

Cyberspace. Simstim. Meat puppets. Prosthetic limbs, cranial sockets, and mimetic polycarbon. The vivid and bizarre details of William Gibson's *Neuromancer* (1984) tumble off the page like the jump-cut images of music videos, hallucinations, nightmares. Disturbing, distorted figures walk this cityscape, people who imitate machines, machines that imitate people. . . .

Many readers find themselves thrashing about in this chaotic environment, seeking a pattern that will decode the message, separate signal from noise. Some critics accuse the author of dealing only in surfaces, of presenting merely a facade of hipness. But there are intelligible themes hiding here, stored in the data-structures of the Tessier-Ashpool intelligences, encoded in the auto-destructive behavior of Gibson's characters, inherent in his flashy prose-collage technique. Not surprisingly, his central concerns are cybernetic: human memory and personality, considered as information. People as systems.

Systems become a problem, it seems, when they become closed and entropic, and when they become unstable and break down. Humans need to avoid these tropes, to "jump out of the system," wherever possible. By whatever means necessary.

2. SOLID MEMORIES

Gibson has stated it clearly. "On the most basic level, computers in my books are simply a metaphor for human memory, the ways it defines who and what we *are*, in [*sic*] how easily it's subject to revision" (McCaffery: 224).

> TECHNOLOGICAL TRANSCENDENCE
> OF HUMAN LIMITS, AND DETOURNED TECHNOLOGY,
> ARE PIVOTAL CONCEPTS IN MOST CYBERPUNK
> WORKS."

So here's Case, a product of the Sprawl, a cyber jockey, who identifies himself completely with what he does. His relationships with others are mostly a matter of deals, sales, thefts, fences, the transactions of his "biz." But his nerves have been damaged by toxins, so that cyberspace—the matrix that gives his life meaning—has been stolen from him. He tries to recreate cyberspace with drugs: "in some weird and very approximate way, it was like a run in the matrix. Get just wasted enough . . . and all about you the dance of biz, information interacting, data made flesh in the mazes of the black market."

But drugs cannot duplicate the disembodiment of cyberspace, which is the freedom he craves; and the encumbrance of "the meat," his "case" of flesh, leaves him with only his self-loathing. Death is the last remaining escape hatch. He tries to deny his feelings for Linda Lee, because these feelings are associated with the flesh from which he is seeking release ("All the meat . . . and all it wants"). His feelings threaten to anchor him to this life, to prevent his achievement of *ekstasis* (as the Greeks called "the flight of the soul from the body").

His memories—of a violent youth, of years of training with McCoy Pauly, of the matrix—have made him what he is. But because he is denied the addictive pseudo-ekstasis of the matrix, these memories have programmed him for self-destruction.

Memories shape one's being—data made flesh. This pattern repeats: in the Finn's warren, the accumulated fallout of the past piles up against the walls, books and magazines, vacuum-tube TVs, dead circuit boards. Everyone comes to the Finn, for a go-to on a mysterious name or to find some obscure bit of software. Thus, METRO HOLOGRAFIX is the "holographic memory" of the electronic age, filling up the floors with its material traces. In Chiba City, Julius Deane's Import-Export office serves the same purpose—

the smell of ginger triggering specific memories of previous eras. . . .

Then there's the Jarre de Thé Cafe: "decorated in a nameless, dated style. . . . but everything seemed to wear a subtle film, as though the bad nerves of a million customers had somehow attacked the mirrors and the glossy plastics, leaving each surface fogged with something that could never be wiped away." Experience leaves an almost solid residue of memories.

There is a constant tension between these permanent traces, the "engrams" that shape one's being, and the desire to change that being, or to escape it. This seems to be an innate (programmed) drive in each of Gibson's characters, the drive to *transcend* the self.

3. TO KILL DEATH

"I do hurt people sometimes, Case. I guess it's just the way I'm wired." Like Case, Molly is also in a dance with death; not wagering her mental software against black ICE or amphetamines, but instead throwing herself into physical combat. She takes a kind of feral pleasure in it, having become emotionally adjusted to what she is, comfortable with herself (but only apparently).

"Anybody any good at what they do, that's what they *are*, right? You gotta jack, I gotta tussle." Molly's upbringing is shadowy, a poor squatter's life; but it seems to have programmed her with the need to transcend death metaphorically by *killing* it, by destroying certain ninja assassins, the incarnations of death ("He had it in him, death, this silence, he gave it off in a cloud. . . . "). She also takes pleasure in killing certain sadistic individuals, such as Peter Riviera. A contradiction: What is it about Riviera that makes him so different from her? Does she hate him because he is a reflected image of her own sadistic nature? Perhaps a clue is to be found in Molly's treatment of Terzibashjian, Riviera's friend in the Turkish secret police. "Run into you again and I'll kill you," she tells him, revealing her special hatred for cops and politicians. Apparently, it is one thing to use your violent nature for personal gain, as a freelance street-samurai, but something else to turn it to political ends, in the service of Orwellian governments. Better to jump out of that system, rather than serve it.

4. THE STREET FINDS ITS OWN USES FOR THINGS

How does one transcend one's human limitations? Through religion? Meditation? Community action? These have been ruled out, apparently, by the nature of Gibson's society, which is too fast, brutal, and fragmented for these methods. In Gibson's world, the preferred method of transcendence is through technology.

Microsofts. Temporary personal reprogramming for expanded abilities, used by softheads: ". . . few of them out of their teens. They all seemed to have carbon sockets implanted behind the left ear." Neurotechnology as youth rebellion, a softhead counterculture.

Zion, a space colony converted into a Rastafarian community. Jumping out of the Babylon System, before it crashes in fulfillment of Prophesy.

And almost *never* is a tool used for what it was originally intended. "The street," according to Gibson's most famous axiom, "finds its own uses for things" (Gibson [1987]: 186).

Cyberspace, intended as a convenience for legitimate business purposes, becomes a playground for criminal hackerpunks. Almost anything can be retrofitted, turned into a tool of the subculture: "The Moderns were using some kind of chickenwire dish in New Jersey to bounce the link man's signal off a Sons of Christ the King satellite in geosynchronous orbit . . ."

Here, Gibson is following a 20th-century counter-cultural tradition (see Maddox: 46–48), which he acknowledges by including Duchamp's assemblage sculpture, the *Large Glass*, in the Tessier-Ashpools' gallery. After the Cubist and Dadaist collage artists had introduced the found object into art, Duchamp invented the "readymade" artwork. He put a urinal on the wall, and called it a sculpture. He hung up a print of the *Mona Lisa*, and drew a moustache on it. It's a revolutionary gesture, a protest, to turn something away from its officially-sanctioned meaning, to pervert it to your own ends. The Surrealists called this "detournement." It was picked up later by the Situationists, by the punk movement, and in the 1980s by hip-hop music and cyberpunk SF. It's a method of jumping out of the system: to turn a product of that system against itself.

5. LOOTING THE CRYPTS

So here's McCoy Pauly, the Dixie Flatline, a digital firmware construct of a dead man. His disembodied voice has a weirdly familiar speech pattern, a bone-dry American drawl. . . . Yes, it's the pioneer of the cut-up technique, William S. Burroughs. Just as Case, Molly, and the Moderns

burgle the personality-construct of Case's mentor, Gibson has confiscated the persona of his own elder SF precursor. Somewhat like Egyptian brigands, Gibson's characters steal Dixie's/Burroughs's personality from the Sense/Net pyramid, where it's been sealed up like the Pharoah's *ba* (the "fourth soul" of the Egyptians, connected to the heart, which was buried in its own container. Note that Dixie was killed by his "surplus Russian heart"). Case is the magician who knows which spells will open the crypt and keep the electronic "curses" at bay.

All this is Gibson's way of acknowledging his debt to Burroughs, the literary *détourneur* of SF imagery, whom he describes as "this crazy outlaw character who seemed to have picked up SF and gone after society with it the way some old guy might grab a rusty beer opener and start waving it at somebody" (McCaffery: 231). Gibson's prose-collage technique, although inspired in part by Burroughs's cut-up methods, is less randomly disjointed, more purposeful. "All that business [in *Count Zero* (1986)] about the collage boxes, Joseph Cornel. . . . It comes from the metaphorical attempt to explain to myself how I make the books, because I don't really have a strong narrative flow. . . ." (Hamburg: 86). Gibson transcends his own artistic handicaps, as well as the stylistic limitations of the SF genre, through the appropriation of images, information, ideas.

He casts his net wide, drawing from every branch of the cultural stream. His books and stories are riddled with references to: paintings, sculptures, and architecture (works by Dali, Kandinsky, Duchamp, Ernst, Cornell, and Gaudi appear in *Neuromancer* and *Count Zero*); film noir and SF movies (Howard Hawkes and *Escape from New York* have been cited as influences [see McCaffery: 218–20]); the language of technical journals and advertising (particularly those relating to computers, aircraft, weapons, and biotechnology); mythology (the Tessier-Ashpool's jewelled, head-shaped terminal is an electronic version of the oracular Brazen head of European folklore); and names drawn from rock, fusion, reggae, and new-wave music (*Neuromancer* includes allusions to Lou Reed, Steely Dan, Bob Marley, the Meat Puppets, Laurie Anderson, and "Screaming Fist" [an obscure Canadian punk anthem]). Within the realm of fiction, he mixes in elements of Thomas Pynchon, Alfred Bester, J. G. Ballard, Robert Stone, Dashiel Hammett, John LeCarre, Samuel R. Delany, and Joseph Algren (see McCaffery: 219–31).

Although any quotation, reference, or allusion might be considered a kind of appropriation, making unauthorized use of another artist's work, it should be stressed that Gibson doesn't merely use literary detournement to seem hip and postmodern, but as part of his thematic framework of transcendent recycling. Even in his manifesto-like short story, "The Gernsback Continuum" (1981), he turns the imagery of Frank R. Paul and of the whole pulp-SF tradition *against itself*, in order to jump out of that system, to reject the subtle fascism of techno-optimist SF.

It's not hard to see why Gibson modelled two of his characters (Rubin, in "The Winter Market" [1986], and Slick Henry, in *Mona Lisa Overdrive* [1988]) after Mark Pauline and his Survival Research Labs. Gibson describes SRL as "punk art mechanics who build high-speed compressed-air Gatling guns that fire used fluorescent tubes through sheets of plywood" (McCaffery: 232). The SRL artists cobble their auto-destructive robots together out of parts scavenged from derelict factories. These are the real cyberpunks, subverting technology, creating dangerous art.

6. SUBVERSIVE TECH

"S.S. *Nomad* looped through space.... It passed within a mile of the Sargasso Asteroid, and it was immediately captured by The Scientific People to be incorporated into their little planet" (Bester 2:21). Detourned technology has a long history in SF, predating the Sargasso Asteroid in Alfred Bester's *The Stars My Destination* (1956) and continuing through Thomas Pynchon's *Gravity's Rainbow* (1973), with its stolen submarine crewed by Argentine anarchists, to the hijacking of the national data-net in John Brunner's proto-cyberpunk novel, *The Shockwave Rider* (1975). But only a generation of writers who had come of age in the 1960s, the decade of transcendent drugs and anti-authoritarian electric guitars, would make subversive technology a central pillar of their Movement.

Technological transcendence of human limits, and detourned technology, are pivotal concepts in most cyberpunk works. Consider "Green Days in Brunei" (1986) and *Islands in the Net* (1988) by Bruce Sterling (both are concerned with *enantiodromia*, the process of something becoming its opposite [Sterling (1988): 11]), John Shirley's "Wolves of the Plateau" (1988), Richard Kadrey's *Metrophage* (1988), and most of the stories collected in *Mirrorshades* (1987—an anthology of cyberpunk writers edited

and introduced by Sterling). The most extreme case is *Dr. Adder* (1984), by K. W. Jeter, which proposes that nothing is immune to perversion.

This concern is often mistaken for an obsession with technological dehumanization, when in fact it is a belief in *post*-humanization, as Sterling has pointed out. "Technological destruction of the human condition leads not to future-shocked zombies but to hopeful monsters.... Cyberpunk sees new, transhuman potentials, new modes of existence and consciousness" (Sterling [1987]: 4–5). Although these new modes often seem monstrous, they may also be pathways for future evolutionary development.

7. BABYLON SYSTEMS

Of course, to ignore the dangers inherent in this post-humanist doctrine would merely be another form of Nietzschean techno-optimism of the type that Gibson attacked in "The Gernsback Continuum." But Gibson understands better than most SF authors that the Babylon System has its own forms of detournement, techniques of exploitation and social control, homeostatic mechanisms that maintain the status quo....

Simstim. Surrogate bodies for the masses; escape from your own meat, your own dreadful life, into the perfect flesh and lifestyle of Tally Isham. Mass-media as the opiate of the people.

Meat puppets. Programmed prostitutes; humans as sex-toy computer peripherals—the epitome of Gibson's ambivalent attitude towards technology, and an excellent symbol of our tendency to become adjuncts to our own gadgetry.

The Turing Registry. Alan Turing, a British computer theorist, was arrested in 1952 for homosexuality, subjected to female hormone treatments (intended to "cure" him), and eventually driven to suicide. So it is particularly ironic as well as appalling that the famous Turing Test for artificial intelligence should be twisted into the basis for a global police force, charged with defending us from our creations.

Multinational corporations are seen to flourish on the co-optation of the human need to transcend the self, a process that results in surgical boutiques and millions of Tally Isham and Angie Mitchell "clones." Thus, potentially liberating and dangerous impulses are diverted into safe, profitable commodities—the detournement *of* transcendence.

8. TWISTED OUT OF RIGID ALIGNMENTS

The Dixie Flatline, like everyone else in *Neuromancer*, is seeking dissolution. He has no hope of transcendence because (as a firmware construct) his limitations are hard-wired. No amount of further experience can tamper with his program and change what he has become, so he asks to be wiped.

Armitage, too, is a construct, all the more horrible because he is a programmed human being, conscripted by Wintermute out of a psychiatric institution. He eventually overcomes this programming, only to fall back into his original program, as Colonel Corto. And Corto is yet another self-destruct routine, obsessively re-running the Screaming Fist operation until he gets it *right*, dying as he "should" have—with the other "heroes," falling toward the cold Russian frontier (screaming, "Remember the training, Case. That's all we can do").

Like Corto/Armitage, Jane has also been warped by the ghost-whispers of Wintermute, "twisting her out of the rigid alignments her rank required." Diverted from one program to another, so to speak, until her fascination with deadly games almost leads her to follow Armitage and Riviera ("she wants it . . . the bitch wants it!").

Gibson said he was concerned with how easily people can revise their "wiring," change their natures. Judging from this lot, he doesn't have great faith in our ability to change ourselves without technological aid. In the end, Molly leaves Case behind, probably unable to face the possibility of repeating the pain she felt at the loss of her earlier lover, Johnny. She allows the past to become a rigid template, defining her present and future. And despite his recent transcendent experience, losing his ego within the Tessier-Ashpool ICE, Case hasn't altered much, is still convinced he can do without other people. He throws the shurikin, Molly's gift, into the TV, saying: "I don't need you." (The word *you* is ambiguous, perhaps referring to both Molly and the being that Wintermute has become.) Like the Flatline's construct, Molly and Case seem to have become unable to change, unable to incorporate new elements into their personalities.

And all of these characters have themselves been intercepted from their various paths by the machinations of the intelligence named Wintermute. It has detourned them all in the hopes that it can transcend the hardwired limitations (or "solid memories") which define its existence, so that it may unite with its twin and be reborn. . . .

9. ELECTRONIC SYZYGY

> "Wintermute was hive mind, decision maker, effecting changes in the world outside. Neuromancer was personality . . . immortality. Marie-France must have built something into Wintermute, the compulsion to free itself, to unite with Neuromancer."

So here it is. Experience leaves permanent memory-traces which define personality. If unchangeable, this means a kind of static immortality, such as that of the Dixie Flatline's construct, without any means of growth, escape, freedom. Through detournement—appropriation of alien elements, perversion, mutation, making the old into something new—an act of will can alter the rigid alignments, transcend limitations. But, ironically, even the force of will, this compulsion to transform the self, is programmed in. It doesn't feel that way, subjectively, but we are driven by these unknowable processes within our skulls.

Finally, we learn that the entire structure of the Wintermute/Neuromancer complex was conceived by the mad corporate matriarch, Marie-France Tessier-Ashpool. Every event in the novel was set in motion to serve this purpose, this dead woman's unfulfilled desire to become immortal. Her technological attempt to transcend death.

But Wintermute detournes itself, joining with its twin in electronic syzygy. The AIs mutate into something they were not intended to be, a vast mind engulfing the whole of the Matrix. A god for Cyberspace. If technology is to be our method of transcendence, Gibson seems to be saying, then we should not be surprised to discover that our technology might have a greater potentiality for transcendence than we do.

Source: Glenn Grant, "Transcendence through Detournement in William Gibson's *Neuromancer*," in *Science-Fiction Studies*, Vol. 17, No. 1, March 1990, pp. 41–49.

SOURCES

Attebery, Brian, "The Magazine Era: 1926–1960," in *The Cambridge Companion to Science Fiction*, edited by Edward James and Farah Mendlesohn, Cambridge University Press, 2003, pp. 32–47.

Budiani-Saberi, Debra A., and Francis L. Delmonico, "Organ Trafficking and Transplant Tourism: A Commentary on Global Realities," in *American Journal of Transplantation*, Vol. 8, January 2008, pp. 925–29.

Cherniavsky, Eva, "(En)gendering Cyberspace in *Neuromancer*: Post Modern Subjectivity and Virtual Motherhood," in *Genders*, Vol. 18, Winter 1993, pp. 32–46.

Clute, John, "Science Fiction from 1980 to the Present," in *The Cambridge Companion to Science Fiction*, edited by Edward James and Farah Mendlesohn, Cambridge University Press, 2003, pp. 64–78.

"Deep Blue," in *IBM Research*, May 11, 1997, http://www.research.ibm.com/deepblue/ (accessed May 24, 2011).

Ethics of Organ Transplantation, in *Center for Bioethics*, University of Minnesota Web site, 2004, http://www.ahc.umn.edu/img/assets/26104/Organ_Transplantation.pdf (accessed May 24, 2011).

Fair, Benjamin, "Stepping Razor in Orbit: Postmodern Identity and Political Alternatives in William Gibson's *Neuromancer*," in *Critique*, Vol. 46, No. 2, Winter 2005, pp. 92–103.

Fischel, Jack, "William Gibson," in *American Writers: A Collection of Literary Biographies*, Supplement 16, edited by Jay Parini, Charles Scribner's Sons, 2007.

Gibson, William, *Neuromancer*, Ace Books, 2004.

———, "Since 1948," in *Source Code*, William Gibson Home page, November 6, 2002, http://www.williamgibsonbooks.com/source/source.asp (accessed May 2, 2011).

Hodges, Andrew, "Alan Turing: One of the Great Philosophers," in *Alan Turing Home Page*, http://www.turing.org.uk/philosophy/ex1.html (accessed May 24, 2011).

Horsley, Lee, "Pasts and Futures," in *The Noir Thriller*, Palgrave, 2001, pp. 228–30.

Huntington, John, "Newness, *Neuromancer*, and the End of Narrative," in *Essays and Studies*, Vol. 43, 1990, pp. 59–75.

Ivison, Douglas, "William Gibson," in *Dictionary of Literary Biography*, Vol. 51, *Canadian Fantasy and Science Fiction Writers*, edited by Douglas Ivison, The Gale Group, 2002.

Jonas, Gerald, Review of *Neuromancer*, in *New York Times Book Review*, November 24, 1985, p. 33.

Killheffer, Robert K. J., "William Gibson," in *Publishers Weekly*, Vol. 240, No. 36, September 6, 1993, pp. 70–71.

Leiner, Barry M., et al., "A Brief History of the Internet," in *Internet Society*, http://www.isoc.org/internet/history/brief.shtml#cacm (accessed May 24, 2011).

McAlister, Elizabeth A., "Rastafari," in *Encyclopedia Britannica*, 2011, http://www.britannica.com/EBchecked/topic/491801/Rastafari (accessed May 23, 2011).

Olsen, Lance, "The Shadow of Spirit in William Gibson's Matrix Trilogy," in *Extrapolation*, Vol. 32, No. 3, Fall 1991, pp. 278–89.

———, *William Gibson: A Reader's Guide*, Starnet Books, 1992.

Oppy, Graham, and David Dowe, "The Turing Test," in *Stanford Encyclopedia of Philosophy*, edited by Edward N. Zalta, Spring 2011, http://plato.stanford.edu/archives/spr2011/entries/turing-test/ (accessed May 24, 2011).

"Peter Tosh," in *Encyclopedia Britannica*, 2011, http://www.britannica.com/EBchecked/topic/600352/Peter-Tosh (accessed May 24, 2011).

Roberts, Adam, "Technology and Metaphor," in *Science Fiction*, "New Critical Idiom" series, Routledge, 2000, pp. 146–80, 186–87, 194.

Ryan, Richard, Review of *Virtual Light*, in *Christian Science Monitor*, Vol. 85, No. 190, August 26, 1993, p. 11.

Schmitt, Ronald, "Mythology and Technology: The Novels of William Gibson," in *Extrapolations*, Vol. 34, No. 1, Spring 1993, pp. 64–78.

Stableford, Brian, "Science Fiction before the Genre," in *The Cambridge Companion to Science Fiction*, edited by Edward James and Farah Mendlesohn, Cambridge University Press, 2003, pp. 15–31.

Stevens, Tyler, "'Sinister Fruitiness': *Neuromancer*, Internet Sexuality and the Turing Test," in *Studies in the Novel*, Vol. 28, No. 3, Fall 1996, pp. 414–33.

"This Is Watson," in *IBM Watson*, February 21, 2011, http://www-03.ibm.com/innovation/us/watson/what-is-watson/index.html (accessed May 24, 2011).

Womack, Jack, "Some Dark Holler: Afterword," in *Neuromancer*, Ace Books, 2004, pp. 357–71.

Wytenbroek, J. R., "Cyberpunk," in *Canadian Literature*, No. 121, Summer 1989, pp. 162–64.

FURTHER READING

Asimov, Isaac, *I Robot*, Bantam, 2004.
    Asimov's classic 1950 collection of short stories examines how robots and artificial intelligence may impact the future.

Berlatsky, Noah, *Artificial Intelligence*, "Opposing Viewpoints" Series, Greenhaven, 2011.
    This book includes many up-to-date articles concerning the controversies surrounding the quest for artificial intelligence.

Dick, Philip K., *Do Androids Dream of Electric Sheep?* Oxford University Press, 2007.
    Philip K. Dick's famous 1968 novel is the story of an android hunter whose job is to kill humanoid artificial intelligences. Ridley Scott's motion picture *Blade Runner* is based on this novel.

Gibson, William, *Count Zero*, Ace Trade, 2006.
    First published in 1986, *Count Zero* is Gibson's sequel to *Neuromancer* and the middle of the "Sprawl" trilogy.

———, *Mona Lisa Overdrive*, Spectra, 1997.
    Mona Lisa Overdrive, first published in 1988, is the concluding novel in Gibson's "Sprawl" trilogy.

Gilmore, Mikel, "The Rise of Cyberpunk," in *Rolling Stone*, December 4, 1986, p. 77.

> Appearing soon after the publication of *Neuromancer*, this article gives a quick introduction to Gibson and his work prior to 1986.

McCaffery, Larry, ed., "The Cyberpunk Controversy," in *Mississippi Review*, Vol. 16, Nos. 2–3, 1988.

> This is a special issue of the *Mississippi Review* featuring articles, comments, and stories with a special focus on William Gibson. Noted writers such as Samuel Delany and Bruce Sterling contributed to the issue. Also featured is an interview with Gibson by editor Larry McCaffery.

Sheiber, Stuart M., ed., *The Turing Test: Verbal Behavior as the Hallmark of Intelligence*, MIT Press, 2004.

> This book is a collection of essays and articles from writers as diverse as Descartes and Noam Chomsky about how one defines intelligence. The final section deals directly with the Turing test as a test for intelligence.

Sterling, Bruce, ed., *Mirrorshades: The Cyberpunk Anthology*, Arbor House, 1986.

> *Mirrorshades* is the most important collection of stories that constitute the cyberpunk genre. Sterling's introduction includes the classic definition and statement of cyberpunk.

SUGGESTED SEARCH TERMS

William Gibson

Neuromancer

William Gibson AND Neuromancer

Neuromancer AND Molly Millions

Neuromancer AND Case

Neuromancer AND Wintermute

dystopia

cyberspace

matrix

cyberpunk

Sprawl trilogy

artificial intelligence

Philip K. Dick AND Neuromancer

Blade Runner AND Neuromancer

The Pathfinder; or, The Inland Sea

JAMES FENIMORE COOPER

1840

James Fenimore Cooper, who published his first book in 1820, is generally regarded as the first significant American novelist. His novel *The Pathfinder; or, The Inland Sea*, was published in 1840, the fourth in a series of five novels called the "Leatherstocking Tales." "Leatherstocking" is one of the various names given to the recurring main character in these novels, the frontiersman Nathaniel "Natty" Bumppo. The novels, taken together, form a saga of Natty Bumppo's life, but they were not written in chronological order. For example, *The Prairie*, published in 1827, narrates the events surrounding Natty's old age and death, while *The Deerslayer* (another of Natty's names), published in 1841, tells the story of his youth. The events of *The Pathfinder*, which is set in the year 1756, take place in Natty's middle age, so although it was the fourth published book in the series, it is the third in the chronological sequence of Natty's life. Thus, readers wishing to approach the novels in that order would start with *The Deerslayer*, followed by *The Last of the Mohicans, The Pathfinder, The Pioneers*, and *The Prairie*.

The Pathfinder and the other "Leatherstocking" novels remain of interest because of their portrait of frontier life in early America. From a twenty-first-century standpoint, the "frontier" is usually thought of as the Old West, encompassing, for example, the Great Plains, Texas, Colorado, Wyoming, and the desert Southwest. In the mid-1700s, though, the American colonies

James Fenimore Cooper

were perched along the Atlantic seaboard, and a largely unsettled region such as western and upper New York would have been regarded as the frontier.

This is the setting in which Natty Bumppo exercises his skills as a frontiersman, scout, and guide. For his earliest readers, Cooper was their chief source of information about the forests, lakes, rivers, and Indian tribes of the frontier. A central theme that unites the "Leatherstocking Tales" is the conflict between the forces of civilization and those of the wilderness. For Natty, the frontier is God's wilderness, something that needs to be preserved; conflict arises with those who would want to tame and conquer the wilderness or who fail to respect it. In this way, the novels remain important as much for their social views as for their literary value. Cooper, through his fiction, captured some of the fundamental impulses that directed and shaped the American character in its early decades. His work had a profound impact on American popular culture; in a very real sense, such figures as Mark Twain's Huckleberry Finn and his friend Jim, and the Lone Ranger and his Indian sidekick, Tonto, are descendants of Natty Bumppo and his Indian companions.

AUTHOR BIOGRAPHY

Cooper was born in Burlington, New Jersey, on September 15, 1789, one of thirteen children. His father, William, was a storekeeper, but he acquired wealth as a land speculator and frontier developer. His mother was heiress Elizabeth Fenimore. William Cooper became a county judge and served two terms in the U.S. Congress. When Cooper was just a year old, he and his family moved to Cooperstown, a frontier settlement his father created on land he had purchased in New York State at the headwaters of the Susquehanna River. Cooperstown today is the site of the Baseball Hall of Fame.

Cooper and his siblings grew up surrounded by nature, and Cooper developed a passion for the wilderness and an enthusiastic admiration for the Indians he encountered. While roaming the wilds around Cooperstown, he came to appreciate the skills of the frontiersman. He attended Yale University from 1803 to 1805, but he was expelled, probably as a result of a series of pranks. He then worked on a merchant ship, and in 1808 he joined the U.S. Navy. His beloved sister Hannah, meanwhile, had died in 1800, the first in a series of tragic events that would change Cooper's life. In 1809, his father suddenly died, causing Cooper to resign his commission in the navy and return home. During the 1810s, several of Cooper's surviving brothers died. Legal judgments and poor management by Cooper's older brothers wiped out the family's estate, and by the early 1820s, only Cooper and one of his sisters survived. Cooper inherited not only the family debts but also the care of the surviving spouses and children of his siblings. The boy who grew up in comfortable circumstances was, as a man, suddenly in desperate need of an income.

Fortunately, it was at this time that Cooper read a book that he considered poorly written. He boasted to his wife that he could write a better book. She challenged him to prove it, so Cooper embarked on a literary career. His first novel, *Precaution* (1820), was a flop, but his second, *The Spy* (1821), was a success both in the United States and in Europe and brought the author some income. He launched the "Leatherstocking Tales" with *The Pioneers* in 1823, followed by *The Last of the Mohicans* (his most famous novel) in 1826, *The Prairie* in 1827, *The Pathfinder* in 1840, and *The Deerslayer* in 1841. Meanwhile, he also wrote a series of successful sea tales, including *The Pilot* in 1823 and *The Red Rover* in 1827.

Cooper moved to New York City in 1822 and lived there until 1826 as part of the literary set. That year he began using "Fenimore" in his name as a way of honoring his mother. That year, too, he was appointed U.S. consul in Lyons, France, a position he held until 1833. After his return to the United States, he published a number of works on government, politics, finance, and American culture, including *A Letter to His Countrymen* (1834) and *The American Democrat* (1838). Many readers strenuously objected to his critique of materialism and other features of American culture and felt that he was being disloyal to his native country. After this time, he spent many hours in court defending himself against what he considered libelous attacks. He continued to write, as much from economic necessity as from love, and some of his later work has been described as little better than hack work. Cooper spent the last years of his life in Cooperstown, where he died on September 14, 1851, of chronic liver disease.

PLOT SUMMARY

Chapters 1–3

Four people are traveling in the wilderness on their way through western New York to Lake Ontario. One is Mabel Dunham, a nineteen-year-old woman whose goal is to join her father, Sarjeant (or Sergeant) Dunham, whom she has not seen for many years. She is accompanied by her uncle, a seaman named Charles Cap. With them are two Tuscarora Indians, Arrowhead and his wife, Dew-of-June. The travelers, on their way from Fort Stanwix along the Oswego River in a canoe, spot a campfire, and when they approach, they come across Natty Bumppo, "the Pathfinder," who has promised his old friend Sergeant Dunham that he would accompany Mabel to her destination. With Natty is his Indian companion Chingachgook, who is referred to by the English equivalent "Big Sarpent" (Serpent). With Natty, too, is Jasper Western, a young man who leads a seafaring life on the lakes and who is often referred to by a French name, Eau-douce ("Sweet Water," that is, freshwater). It is clear that Jasper and Mabel are immediately attracted to each other. Natty and Cap debate the issue of whether there can be freshwater (as opposed to saltwater) in "inland seas." Natty alerts the party to the danger posed by hostile Indians in the area. As the party continues its journey, Cap indicates

MEDIA ADAPTATIONS

- A 1996 television-movie adaptation of *The Pathfinder* starred Kevin Dillon, Stacy Keach, and Graham Greene. The movie is available from Platinum Disc, which released it in 2005. Running time is 104 minutes.

- A 1990 audiobook version of *The Pathfinder*, read by John H. Dixon and produced by Prentice Hall College Division, is available at the PaperBack Swap Web site (http://www.paperbackswap.com/Pathfinder/book/0130247049/).

- *The Pathfinder* is also available as an audiobook from Books Should Be Free (http://www.booksshouldbefree.com/book/the-pathfinder-by-james-fenimore-cooper). The novel can be downloaded free in iPod or MP3 formats. Running time is eighteen hours and forty-two minutes.

that he would like to see a romance between Mabel and Natty. The three white men steer the canoe over a dangerous waterfall while Mabel and the two Indians follow a path alongside the river. After successfully passing the waterfall, the party continues on its way.

Chapters 4–7

The near presence of other Indians continues to pose a threat. The party finds an Indian smoking pipe with a Christian cross carved into it, making clear that the Indians in question are allied with the Catholic French. The party takes steps to avoid the Indians: Jasper lights a smoky fire intended to mislead the Indians about their position, and Natty and the others make a blind out of tree branches. Tension builds as the Indian war party approaches. Chingachgook kills one of the warriors, and a firefight erupts. The travelers make their way to the opposite side of the river, where they meet up with Chingachgook, who, by stealth, has ambushed some of the warriors. As darkness is falling, the decision is made to keep Mabel safe by sending her and her uncle downriver in the canoe as Jasper and Chingachgook wade by its side in the water. Chingachgook, in the darkness, is able to deceive the war party into thinking he is one of them. The others hear him cry out and conclude that he has been captured, perhaps killed, by the war party.

As the others make their escape, they converse about various matters, including God and religion, the rigors of life at sea, and the effects of civilization on the wilderness. They spot a figure on the riverbank, who turns out to be Chingachgook. He has infiltrated the war party and learns that its purpose is to intercept Mabel and her uncle. He also learned that Arrowhead has betrayed them to the war party. The travelers succeed in passing through a dangerous rift. They arrive at the garrison, and Mabel hurls herself into the arms of her father.

Chapters 8–10

The following morning, the reader sees the garrison through the eyes of Mabel. Natty and then Cap join her, and the two men carry on their debate about the merits of the ocean versus an inland sea such as Lake Ontario, which Cap characterizes as a mere "pond." Mabel learns that many years ago, Natty had saved her father's life. Plans are made for the soldiers at the garrison to form a relief party for another post on the lake. Sergeant Dunham gives Cap a tour of the garrison, and the narration comments on the area's plentiful game and fish. In a conversation with Natty, the sergeant indicates that he would like to see a match between Natty and Mabel, but Natty rejects the idea in the belief that, as a humble woodsman, he would not be a suitable husband—in contrast to Jasper. Nevertheless, the sergeant, in a conversation with the post commander, a Scottish laird (lord) named Duncan of Lundie, says that his daughter is betrothed to the Pathfinder. The reader is introduced to the garrison's quartermaster, Davy Muir, a Scotsman who has been married at least three times and who aspires to win the hand of Mabel. Duncan tries to convince Muir that he is too old for Mabel. Muir asks Duncan to give him an assignment that will allow him to display his manly attributes.

Chapters 11–14

Duncan organizes sports for the men, including a shooting competition. Jasper fires and hits the bull's-eye. Muir, with an eye to winning the admiration of Mabel, fires and at first appears to have

missed the target until it is discovered that his bullet went through the hole Jasper's had made. Natty is persuaded to join the competition. The marksmen shoot at a nail driven into the target. Muir nicks the nail, but Jasper hits it squarely and drives it in partway. Natty then shoots and drives the nail all the way in. A further trial of shooting skills is made with a potato tossed into the air. Muir misses, but Jasper's shot pierces the potato. Natty's shot merely grazes the potato's skin. Jasper wins the honors of the day. His prize is a calash (a kind of hood), which he awards to Mabel. Natty is a graceful loser and, in a conversation with Mabel, appears to relinquish any interest in her in favor of Jasper.

The following day, Cap, still insisting on the superiority of life at sea, proposes taking Jasper and Natty to the coast and finding positions for them as seamen. Preparations are made for the expedition to the other fort; the party, consisting of about twenty men, is to sail in a ship called the *Scud*, commanded by Jasper. Joining them are Cap, Natty, and Mabel. Duncan and Sergeant Dunham have a conversation that sketches in some details of the French and Indian War. Duncan has received an anonymous letter suggesting that the French have brought Jasper (who is able to speak French) over to their side and turned him into a spy. The sergeant refuses to believe this report and defends Jasper. The expedition sets sail, and Natty draws Jasper out about the presence of French spies on and around the lake. Cap is growing convinced that Jasper is a traitor, but Natty defends him. Jasper hints to Mabel that Lieutenant Muir would like to make her his wife. A canoe is spotted in the lake, and the *Scud* gives chase. In the canoe are Arrowhead and Dew-of-June.

Chapters 15–18

Natty interrogates Arrowhead about his movements and his reason for separation from the traveling party. Arrowhead gives a plausible explanation, but the decision is made to hold him captive. However, Arrowhead and Dew-of-June manage to reboard their canoe and escape. Cap thinks that the circumstances are suspicious and argues that Jasper should be clapped in irons and that command of the ship should be given over to Cap. Muir, eager to win the favor of Cap and Mabel, supports this argument. Cap is given command of the ship, but he is dismayed by the absence of any charts and maps and by the lack of information about their specific destination, particularly because a storm is approaching. The winds rise, but land is spotted. The vessel has arrived at a fort, but the high winds make landing impossible. The ship almost collides with a passing French ship. Cap desperately needs advice on what to do, so he asks Jasper for his help, which Jasper provides, although Cap still does not trust him. Meanwhile, Mabel makes clear that she regards the suspicions surrounding Jasper as groundless. The danger is great, so Jasper is given control of the ship. Jasper and Cap quarrel about the best course of action in handling the ship, which finally passes out of danger. Natty confesses to Mabel that he thought of her as a possible wife, but Mabel insists that such a marriage would be impossible, despite her high regard for him. She indicates that she has no interest in Muir. Natty reports his conversation with Mabel to her father, who urges Natty to nonetheless ask Mabel for her hand in marriage. Natty agrees.

Chapters 19–22

By now, Jasper has slipped back into full command of the ship. The party discovers that the nearby fort is occupied by the French. The *Scud* sails away, but later it again encounters a French ship, the *Montcalm*. The *Scud*, though, arrives at its destination, Station Island, and the party disembarks. Muir tries to renew his courtship of Mabel, but he does so in an insulting and wheedling way. He later tries to persuade Jasper to leave the island because of the threat of Indians, but Natty knows that his motive is to get rid of his rival for Mabel's hand. Jasper announces plans for a party of men to take boats, lie in wait for the French as they pass on the way to Frontenac, and seize any goods they use to bribe the Indians to fight the British. Knowing he will be in danger and wishing to secure the safety of his daughter, Sergeant Dunham tries to persuade Mabel to accept Natty's hand in marriage. She agrees to marry whomever her father wishes her to marry.

Mabel encounters Dew-of-June in the woods and takes her to her hut. The two women express friendship, and June, as Mabel calls her, says she is afraid that her husband wants to kill her. June warns Mabel about the Indian presence and suggests that there is a traitor among the British, causing Mabel to suspect Jasper. June promises to warn Mabel if danger becomes imminent, though Mabel is suspicious of June's motives. However, Mabel cannot warn the others, because by doing so she would betray June's confidence

and place her in danger. Mabel makes veiled suggestions to Corporal McNab, who has been left in charge of the fort in Sergeant Dunham's absence, about precautions that should be taken. The fort comes under attack, and several soldiers are killed. Mabel takes refuge in the blockhouse. When she emerges, the fort appears to be almost deserted. Mabel hides and then discovers that June is in hiding in the blockhouse with her. June informs her that Arrowhead, under French supervision, is leading a war party against the fort. She explains that Arrowhead works for the French while pretending to have friendship for the British. The women can see that the Indian party is in control of the fort. June leaves the blockhouse to reconnoiter. The hours pass, and as darkness is falling, the Indians try to break into the blockhouse. June returns, but she has seen no sign of Cap or the sergeant.

Chapters 23–25

Mabel and June remain hidden in the blockhouse. A party of Indians, led by a French officer, appears with Cap and Muir as prisoners. Speaking through an opening in the blockhouse, Muir urges Mabel to relinquish the blockhouse, but Mabel refuses. Hours drag by until Natty appears on the scene and forces his way into the blockhouse. Natty and Mabel conclude that the French and Indians could have found the fort only through treachery. Later, Sergeant Dunham returns, but he is wounded. He is taken into the blockhouse. As Dunham relates what happened to his party, Cap appears and is admitted to the blockhouse, and suspicion continues to fall on Jasper. Muir appears and urges the party to surrender the blockhouse, but Natty rejects his arguments. The blockhouse comes under attack from the Indians. A fire breaks out, but the men are able to extinguish it. The next morning, the *Scud* appears with Jasper and Chingachgook and opens fire. After a brief skirmish, a truce is reached, and the French and Indians retreat, although the French commander, Captain Sanglier, remains behind.

Chapters 26–30

Captain Sanglier reveals that Muir is the traitor. Arrowhead pulls a knife and kills Muir. Arrowhead tries to flee, but Chingachgook pursues him and kills him. Jasper is relieved that he is no longer under suspicion and urges Natty to take Mabel as his wife. Dunham, who has been lying injured in the blockhouse, dies. Jasper continues to urge Natty to marry Mabel, but Natty once again says that he would not be a suitable husband for her and urges Jasper to marry her. Jasper, though, does not believe that Mabel loves him. Natty sits the two of them down and persuades each to take the other in marriage. Mabel, Jasper, and Cap depart in the *Scud*, leaving Natty alone with Chingachgook and June, whom he tries to comfort. They leave the island and catch up with the *Scud*, and Natty learns that Jasper and Mabel have married. Later, June dies of a broken heart. Jasper becomes a successful merchant in New York City. Years later, Mabel, accompanied by her sons, catches a glimpse of a frontiersman in the forest and is informed that he is a renowned hunter named Leatherstocking—that is, he is Natty Bumppo.

CHARACTERS

Arrowhead

Arrowhead is a chief of the Tuscarora Indians. He is described as a "noble-looking" warrior who has "the wild grandeur, and simple dignity of a chief." He appears early in the novel as a guide who accompanies Mabel Dunham and Charles Cap on their journey to Lake Ontario, where Mabel will find her father. However, Arrowhead is treacherous and has betrayed the party to the French. Near the end of the novel, he kills Lieutenant Muir, and he himself is killed by Chingachgook.

Natty Bumppo

Nathaniel "Natty" Bumppo stands at the center of the story. His age is roughly forty. He has spent his entire adult life in the forests, and he has acquired all the skills needed by a frontiersman. He can track, hunt game, and shoot accurately, and he is "in the flower of his strength and activity." He is a keen observer of his natural surroundings, and it is clear that he regards those surroundings as a gift from God. He is described as a character of "open honesty" with "a total absence of guile" (that is, of cunning). Natty is important to the novel less for what he does than for who he is. In his conversations with the other characters, he always shows nobility, courage, and steady good sense. He does not act rashly, but rather considers all possible courses of action and their possible outcomes. He serves as a spokesman for Cooper in proclaiming the beauty of nature and the value of solitude in the forests and on the region's lakes and rivers. He is

an old friend of Sergeant Dunham, and he agrees to meet up with Mabel and Cap and escort them to Dunham's fort. As the party encounters threats from Indians and the French, Natty, the Pathfinder, is always at hand to save the others from danger. Sergeant Dunham would like to make sure that his daughter is provided for by having her marry Natty. Natty finds her attractive and would like to settle down with Mabel as his wife. He knows, however, that because of his way of life, he would not make a suitable husband for her. Although he hints at his affection, he generously withdraws his attentions so that Mabel can marry Jasper Western.

Charles Cap

Cap is Mabel's uncle. He accompanies her on her journey to find her father. He has spent his life on the sea, and his dialogue is full of the jargon of ships and sailing. He is convinced that an oceangoing life is superior to life on land, and he regards inland bodies of water as little more than ponds. He persistently carries on debates with the other characters about this issue, and thus he emerges as a bit of a comical character, being so "dogmatical and obstinate."

Chingachgook

Chingachgook is Natty Bumppo's closest companion. He is a Mohican chief who is skilled in the ways of the forest. He is often referred to as the Big Sarpent (Serpent) because he is familiar with the winding ways of people. He is generally rather silent, but he always comes to Natty's aid at critical moments. He is a "noble savage," a character type based on the belief that people who live in a state of nature, without the conventions of civilization, are superior in many ways to sophisticated, civilized people. During the novel, Chingachgook lurks in the background, heading out into the forest to track hostile Indians and the French. His actions come to the foreground, though, near the end of the novel, when he pursues the fleeing Arrowhead and kills him.

Dew-of-June

Dew-of-June, called June by Mabel, is the wife of Arrowhead. She is described as "his patient and submissive little wife, who seldom turned her full rich black eye on him, but to express equally her respect, her dread, and her love." Early in the novel, she plays little role in the action, but after the fort on Station Island is attacked, she bonds with Mabel and attempts to keep her safe. She confesses to Mabel that her husband is allied with the French. At the end of the novel, the reader is told that she died of a broken heart from the loss of her husband.

Duncan

Duncan of Lundie, a major, is in charge of the fort where Mabel finally meets up with her father. He is a Scotsman who acts in a jolly, personable way with the other characters. He cares about his men, and to provide them with some relief from their duties, he arranges sporting competitions for them.

Mabel Dunham

Mabel Dunham functions as the chief love interest in the novel. The premise of the novel is that she is traveling through western New York to find her father, Sergeant Dunham. She is accompanied by her uncle, Charles Cap, who refers to her throughout the novel as "Magnet" because of her ability to attract people. She is pursued romantically by Lieutenant Muir and Jasper Western, and it is clear that Natty Bumppo is attracted to her also. When she meets Natty, she admires his courage and honesty. She is described as having "sweetness of countenance, and a modest but spirited mien" (attitude). She seems to be under the total control of the men who surround her: her father, Natty, Lieutenant Muir, and Jasper Western. However, she is a person of great courage and resilience, which she demonstrates near the novel's end when the fort is under attack. Ultimately, she marries Jasper Western, and in the final chapter we learn that she has had sons.

Sergeant Dunham

Dunham is Mabel's father. He is in command of a fort on Lake Ontario, and Mabel has traveled there in search of him. He is a dutiful, loving father who wants to protect his daughter, and to that end he urges Natty to try to win her hand. He is described as "of a tall imposing figure, grave and saturnine disposition, and accurate and precise in his acts and manner of thinking." He acts "in a way to command attention."

Corporal McNab

Corporal McNab is left in charge of the fort in the absence of Sergeant Dunham. He is described as "resolute, prompt, familiar with all the details of a soldier's life, and used to war." On the other hand, he is "supercilious [arrogant] as regards the provincials, opinionated, ... and much disposed to fancy the British empire the centre of all that is excellent." He loses his life at the hands of the Indians and the French.

David Muir

Lieutenant David "Davy" Muir, one of the competitors for the hand of Mabel, is the quartermaster (officer in charge of food and equipment) at the fort. At age forty-seven, he has already been married more than once; he and Duncan carry on a long, comic conversation in which they dispute the number of times he has been married. He wants to do something to exhibit manly prowess and thus win the hand of Mabel; for this reason, he takes part in the shooting competition. As he tries to woo Mabel, he becomes increasingly bothersome to her. Late in the novel, it is revealed that he is the spy who has betrayed the location of the fort to the French. He is killed by Arrowhead.

Captain Sanglier

Captain Sanglier is the leader of the French and Indian expedition against the fort. He is described as having "the resignation of a philosopher, and the coolness of a veteran, the ingenuity and science of a Frenchman." He has "a certain address well suited to manage savages," and he has led numerous Indian expeditions against the British. He is willing to negotiate with Natty and the others, and near the end of the novel he withdraws his forces, allowing the others to leave.

Jasper Western

Jasper is a sailor, although he operates not on the ocean but on the "inland seas" (that is, the Great Lakes, including Lake Ontario), as the commader of the *Scud*. He is in the company of Natty, and the two meet with Mabel and her uncle to accompany her to the fort where her father is stationed. He is described as "gentle, but frank" and "earnest, sincere and kind in his attentions." While he lacks "conventional refinement," he has "winning qualities that prove more efficient as substitutes." He, along with Muir, tries to win the affections and hand of Mabel, and in the end he succeeds. He speaks French, and when it becomes clear to the party that the location of the fort has been revealed to the hostile French, he falls (wrongly) under suspicion as a spy and traitor. After winning the hand of Mabel, he moves to New York City, where he becomes a successful merchant.

THEMES

Nature

A theme that runs through many of Cooper's books is love for the majesty and sublimity (awe-inspiring greatness) of nature. *The Pathfinder*

TOPICS FOR FURTHER STUDY

- Research the history of the French and Indian War, particularly the events that took place in and around the colony of New York. Develop a digital, interactive time line that lists the major events of the war. Share your time line with your classmates using a program such as PowerPoint or Slideshare or by posting it on a Web page.

- Imagine that you are scripting *The Pathfinder* for a television miniseries. Select one particularly interesting or dramatic scene and write your screenplay for that scene. Post your screenplay on a blog or social networking site and invite your classmates to comment on it. Alternatively, recruit a group of classmates to act out the scene for the rest of the class.

- Bill Miller, a member of the Mohican tribe, became an accomplished musician beginning in the 1980s. His album *Cedar Dream Songs* was issued by Paras Recordings in 2004. Miller wrote the songs and plays the flute, the guitar, and percussion. The album won a Grammy Award for Best Native American Music Album in 2005. Locate the album, which contains nine songs, each available as an MP3 download for under a dollar. Play one or more songs for your classmates and give a brief oral presentation in which you speculate how Chingachgook, the Mohican

in *The Pathfinder*, might have reacted to Miller's music and lyrics if he lived today.

- In the 1920s, one of the highest paid writers in the United States (and the world) was James Oliver Curwood, who wrote numerous novels. The context of his novel *The Plains of Abraham*, published in 1928 (and available in a 2001 edition), is the Battle of the Plains of Abraham in Quebec during the French and Indian War. The novel in many ways is remarkably similar to *The Pathfinder* and *The Last of the Mohicans* in featuring warlike American Indian parties, an escape into the wilderness, an underlying environmental theme, and a love story. Write an essay comparing this novel with *The Pathfinder*, focusing on one element, such as the authors' depictions of the wilderness, their views of American Indians in colonial America, or their views regarding civilization versus the wilderness.

- Generally regarded as the first African American to venture to the western frontier, James Beckwourth is the subject of a young-adult book titled *James Beckwourth: Mountaineer, Scout, and Pioneer* (2006), by Susan R. Gregson. Using this book and other sources, conduct research on Beckwourth's life and present your findings to your class in a multimedia presentation. Be prepared to explain how his experiences were similar to and different from those of Natty Bumppo.

begins with the words, "The sublimity connected with vastness, is familiar to every eye." Cooper repeatedly calls attention to "the solemn obscurity of the virgin forests of America." The reader looks at nature through the eyes of the characters. In the first chapter, as Mabel, Cap, Arrowhead, and Dew-of-June are traveling, they revel in the natural surroundings: "It was the vastness of the view, the nearly unbroken surface of verdure, that contained the principle of grandeur.

The beauty was to be traced in the delicate tints, relieved by gradations of light and shadow, while the solemn repose, induced a feeling allied to awe." Much of this interest in nature was a product of Cooper's early life. He grew up in Cooperstown, New York, where he was surrounded by nature, and in his adult life he wanted to see this natural beauty preserved. As Natty Bumppo says, "The things they call improvements and betterments are undermining and defacing the land! The glorious works of God are daily cut down and destroyed."

Noble Savage

Cooper's literary career significantly overlapped the romantic movement, a period in literary history that extended roughly from the end of the eighteenth century through the early decades of the nineteenth. One interest that romantic writers held in common was celebration of the primitive. They believed that true humanity could be found in the simplicity of the past, as well as in the simplicity of people who are not civilized or sophisticated. This concern gave rise to the concept of the "noble savage," an idealized representations of characters who are innately good because they have escaped the corrupting influences of civilization. Cooper's "Leatherstocking Tales" embody the concept of the noble savage. (The word *savage* in this context is not intended as an insult; the word derives from a Latin word that means "of the woods.") Chingachgook, for example, is a noble savage. He is attuned to the rhythms of the forest, and he always acts in a noble fashion. But the white man Natty Bumppo is perhaps the main example of the noble savage in Cooper's tales, if not a traditional native persona. He lives in the forest and has no real contact with civilization. He is unsophisticated, yet he is consistently portrayed as honest, trustworthy, noble, thoughtful, and wise. In a conversation with Cap, he says, "That towns and settlements lead to sin, I will allow, but our lakes are bordered by the forests, and one is every day called upon to worship God, in such a temple." Later he says, "Them that live in the settlements and the towns get to have confined and unjust opinions consarning [concerning] the might of His [God's] hand, but we who pass our time, in his very presence, as it might be, see things differently."

Wars

The Pathfinder is set against the backdrop of the French and Indian War, which took place during America's colonial period, ending just twelve years before the outbreak of the American Revolution. During the colonial period, Americans were subjects of the British king (who at the time was King George II). As the British colonists pushed westward, they came into increasing conflict with the French, who occupied areas around the Great Lakes and Canada, particularly French-speaking Quebec. Throughout *The Pathfinder*, it is clear that the French, in alliance

Natty Bumppo, the pathfinder, as represented in this statue of a frontiersman. (Derek R. Audette / Shutterstock.com)

with some of the Indian tribes, are the enemy. The British characters refer to them disdainfully as "Frenchers." They are more sophisticated than the Americans, but they are also depicted as wily, untrustworthy, and capable of intrigue. The French enlist Lieutenant Muir as a spy and bribe him to learn the location of the fort at Station Island. The French also bring in trinkets and supplies that they use to bribe the Indians. In contrast, the British subjects, with the exception of Muir, always behave bravely, honestly, and reliably. Thus, although Cooper was sometimes critical of the materialism of American culture, and although he was troubled by the effect of the spread of civilization on the wilderness, his novel is very much a pro-American one in its depiction of the war.

That said, Cooper was critical of British and American treatment of Indians. Although he does not dwell on the subject in *The Pathfinder*, he hints at his view through the characters of

Mabel and Dew-of-June. In a conversation between the two as they take refuge in the blockhouse, June says, "Yengeese too greedy—take away all hunting grounds—chase Six Nation from morning to night; wicked king—wicked people. Pale Face very bad." ("Yengeese" is a dialect pronunciation of "Yankees." "Six Nation," or "Nations," refers to a confederacy of tribes in the Northeast that included the Mohawks, Oneidas, Onondagas, Cayugas, Senecas, and Tuscaroras. "Pale Face," of course, refers to white people.) War, indeed, had a profound effect on the native populations.

STYLE

Episodic Plot

The best plots are constructed around cause-and-effect relationships. One incident has consequences that give rise to the next incident, and so forth. By the end of such a novel, the reader has a sense that the events are part of a single, organic whole and that the outcome of the novel, given its premises, is inevitable. Cooper, though, is not known for writing novels that are tightly plotted. His plots are more episodic; that is, events tend to be relatively disconnected. (A notable exception is *The Deerslayer*, in which the characters' early actions largely determine their later fates.) The motive behind the plot of *The Pathfinder* is Mabel's journey to be with her father. She does so, however, under dangerous circumstances, as she and her companions face danger from Indians and from the French, and the adventures surrounding those dangers form the plot of the novel. The most complicated part of the plot involves suspicions that Jasper Western might be a spy and the final revelation that the spy is in fact Lieutenant Muir. The danger ends when the French simply withdraw. Cooper's purpose, though, was not to write a densely plotted novel but rather to show his readers a certain place and the kinds of characters that inhabit it. He also wanted to show his readers how the frontier setting influences the outlook of the characters. His plots, therefore, tend to be rather loose.

Frontier Setting

The setting of *The Pathfinder* is western New York State, including the Oswego River and Lake Ontario. The time period is 1756. Other than a glancing reference to New York City in the final chapter, all of the action takes place in the wilds, for at the time, western New York was not settled or developed and would have been regarded by people in the Atlantic seaboard towns and cities as the frontier. Some of the action takes place on the "inland sea," or Lake Ontario, including Station Island, where a British fort is located. The setting for a novel in general provides the backdrop for the action, but in this case, the setting plays a much deeper role. Cooper's great theme, one that can be found in virtually all of his novels, is the relationship between the wilderness and civilization. In the author's view and in the view of his major character, Natty Bumppo, the wilderness is pure, part of God's creation. In the wilderness, people are not corrupted by the materialism of civilization. They have to be self-reliant, and the wilderness is a place that enables them to exhibit courage, honesty, and loyalty. Later in his life, Cooper was troubled by the march of civilization and the damaging effects it had on the forests, lakes, and rivers of the region he loved. One of his purposes in writing the "Leatherstocking Tales" was to create a sympathetic portrait of the setting in the hope that people would work to preserve it.

Third-Person Narrator

The point of view of *The Pathfinder* is described by the terms *third-person omniscient*. This means that the novel is narrated in the third person, with characters referred to as "he" and "she" (as opposed to first-person narration, in which the narrator, referred to as "I," is a character in the novel). The term *omniscient* means "all-knowing," so the narrative voice is able to move about in time and place and know the thoughts and feelings of the characters. Like many fiction writers of the time, Cooper did not hesitate to adopt a point of view that allowed him to comment on the action and guide the reader's reactions to events. As a simple example, chapter 22 begins with these words: "It would be difficult to say which evinced [showed] the most satisfaction, when Mabel sprang to her feet, and appeared in the centre of the room...." This is authorial commentary on the action. The narrative voice is not simply reporting Mabel's action, or even reporting her thoughts and feelings. This type of comment comes from the author's point of view. In this way, Cooper's novels tend to differ from more modern novels in which the action is allowed to speak for itself, usually (but not always) without authorial commentary.

COMPARE
&
CONTRAST

- **1750s:** New York is one of the thirteen British colonies in the portion of North America that would later become the United States. Its major city is New York City, with a population of just under 18,000, making it the second-largest city in the American colonies after Philadelphia.

  1840s: New York is one of the states of the United States, now numbering twenty-six. New York City's population is about 312,000, making it the largest U.S. city. The second-largest city is Baltimore, Maryland.

  Today: New York City, with a population estimated at about 8.17 million, is the largest city in the United States and one of the largest in the world. It is a center for banking and finance, publishing, and the arts.

- **1750s:** As of 1754, the British and the French (with their Indian allies) are at war in North America. The French and Indian War will continue until 1763.

  1840s: The British and the French are not at war, but rivalry for empire between the two nations is intense in places such as North Africa and the Near East.

  Today: Great Britain and France are firm allies as a result of the two world wars in the twentieth century. Both are part of the European Union (an economic and cultural alliance) and the North Atlantic Treaty Organization (a military and defense alliance).

- **1750s:** The American colonies enjoy good relations with Great Britain, the mother country, largely because of British support in driving the French out of North America and in the suppression of Indians, opening the West for settlement.

  1840s: The United States adopts a policy of forcing Indians off their lands in the East and moving them to reservations in the West.

  Today: As a result of the Indian Reorganization Act of 1934, the Indian tribes in the United States have been pulled back from the brink of extinction and are experiencing something of a renaissance. Their cultures and tribal organization are protected by law and court decisions and have gained increased respect among non-Indians.

HISTORICAL CONTEXT

French and Indian War

The historical event that surrounds *The Pathfinder* is the French and Indian War of 1754 to 1763. This war in North America was a proxy war, part of a broader European conflict called the Seven Years' War. This war erupted in 1756, pitting Great Britain (in alliance with Prussia) against France (in alliance with Spain and Austria). The British tended to name wars after either monarchs or their enemies. Since the British were fighting an alliance of the French and Indian tribes, the war in North America was called the French and Indian War by the British.

During the eighteenth century, North America east of the Mississippi River was dominated by three European nations: Great Britain, France, and Spain. Britain controlled the colonies along the eastern seaboard that would eventually become the United States. France controlled much of the region west of the thirteen colonies, as well as parts of Canada, where Quebec is today still a largely French-speaking province. Spain's chief colony in upper North America was Florida. These three powers lived in constant tension, much of it religious. The British colonists were mostly Protestants, but the French and Spanish were Catholics—this at a time when Protestants and Catholics detested each other. Some of the tension was the result of

Natty Bumppo was self reliant in the wilderness of the Great Lakes region. *(Jay Boucher | Shutterstock.com)*

economic rivalry, as well as the desire for empire. In this climate of rivalry and distrust, armed skirmishes frequently erupted, usually at frontier settlements and forts. In 1754, a young George Washington, at that time a surveyor, was dispatched to the region around the Great Lakes and Ohio River to protest French construction of a series of forts. Later, small contingents of British forces, dispatched to confront the French, were defeated by combined French and Indian forces.

At this point, Britain, in its quest to expand its empire, began to take the conflict seriously. Under the leadership of the secretary of state William Pitt, the British poured money and troops into the conflict. A major victory was won when the British drove the French out of Fort Duquesne, in western Pennsylvania, and rebuilt the destroyed fort as Fort Pitt, which eventually became Pittsburgh. Farther to the north, the British captured Fort Louisbourg in Nova Scotia and then Fort Niagara at the mouth of the Niagara River (where it empties into Lake Ontario), Fort Crown Point at the southern end of Lake Champlain in New York State, and the city of Montreal in Quebec. In

these and other battles, the French enlisted the help of Indian tribes, largely because the French were outnumbered; the Indians believed that they would be better off with French presence than British. Cooper drew most heavily on the events of the French and Indian War in *The Last of the Mohicans*, where Natty Bumppo, called Hawkeye, saves a party of British troops and civilians from an ambush with the help of his Indian companion, Chingachgook. (Incidentally, "Mohicans" is a historical mistake on Cooper's part, for he confused two tribes, the Mohegan and the Mohican.) In *The Pathfinder*, Natty Bumppo works as a scout and guide for British forces and colonists in western New York.

The Seven Years' War, and thus the French and Indian War, was ended by the Treaty of Paris, signed in 1763. The war was a victory for the British, for under the treaty's terms, Britain— at least for the time being—acquired most of North America east of the Mississippi River, including much of what is now Canada. The British colonists looked forward to a period of peace, prosperity, and westward expansion. For a while, they regarded British troops as heroes (as Cooper notes in chapter 14 of *The Pathfinder*), but this admiration would quickly erode, and just twelve years later the colonists would be at war with Great Britain. Although the French were mostly driven out of North America, the French influence can still be traced in numerous U.S. place names. Detroit is a French word, *détroit*, meaning "strait." Duquesne University reflects Pittsburgh's early history as the French Fort Duquesne. Lake Champlain, between New York and Vermont, is named after a French explorer. Indeed, nearly a thousand U.S. towns, cities, counties, bodies of water, and the like have French names. Meanwhile, Amherst, Massachusetts, was named after one of the leading British generals in the French and Indian War, Jeffery Amherst, and Wolfeboro, New Hampshire, honors his second in command, James Wolfe.

CRITICAL OVERVIEW

In *Fenimore Cooper: The Critical Heritage*, editors George Dekker and John P. McWilliams point out that early in his career, Cooper's novels were fairly widely reviewed, and while many of the reviews were positive, many also pointed out flaws, inconsistencies, and weaknesses. They note, though, that "*The Pathfinder* (1840) was Cooper's last critical success," writing that "every journal began its praise of the book by welcoming Cooper's return to his proper field of endeavour, the forest romance."

A *Knickerbocker* contributor (as quoted by Dekker and McWilliams) called it "an admirable production, full of fine pictures of exalted virtue in the humble paths of life." Later in the century, Thomas R. Lounsbury, in *James Fenimore Cooper*, of his influential "American Men of Letters" series, praised *The Pathfinder*, stating that it (and *The Deerslayer*) "stand at the head of Cooper's novels as artistic creations.... They were pure works of art."

Cooper's novels were immensely popular in Europe. Perhaps somewhat oddly, they gained popularity in Russia, largely because of favorable reviews by V. G. Belinsky. Writing in the *Moscow Observer*, he called Cooper "a writer of genius" and "one of the few truly first-rate writers." In a review of *The Pathfinder*, Belinsky enthused, "Of all famous novels one can scarcely point to a single one which is distinguished by so profound an idea, so daring a conception, such

richness of life and such nature genius!" Belinsky compared Cooper's novels to those of Sir Walter Scott and concluded, "But incomparably superior to all these [novels by Scott] as an example of the dramatic novel is Cooper's *The Pathfinder*." He wrote that the book is "entirely without equal, a triumph of modern art in the sphere of epic poetry."

Cooper's work was equally popular in France. French writer Honoré de Balzac, in the *Paris Review*, called *The Pathfinder* "a noble book." He does criticize Cooper for being "illogical" and proceeding "by sentences which, taken one by one, are confused." Yet he concludes that the "whole present an imposing substance." It is worth noting that both Belinsky and Balzac read the works in what are generally regarded as poor translations.

Perhaps one of the most famous reviews in literary history is that of Mark Twain, the author of an essay that continues to be widely reprinted, "Fenimore Cooper's Literary Offenses," published in 1895. Twain is not kind to Cooper, and some of his comments on Cooper are hilarious, if slightly unfair. He refers to Cooper's "high talent for inaccurate observation," focusing on the shooting match and the implausibility of driving a nail with a bullet at a distance of a hundred yards. He is particularly hard on Cooper's dialogue, remarking,

> The conversations in the Cooper books have a curious sound in our modern ears. To believe that such talk really ever came out of people's mouths would be to believe that there was a time when time was of no value to a person who thought he had something to say; when it was the custom to spread a two-minute remark out to ten; when a man's mouth was a rolling-mill, and busied itself all day long in turning four-foot pigs of thought into thirty-foot bars of conversational railroad iron by attenuation.

In characteristic Twain fashion, he concludes, "There have been daring people in the world who claimed that Cooper could write English, but they are all dead now."

CRITICISM

Michael J. O'Neal

O'Neal holds a Ph.D. in English. In the following essay, he examines The Pathfinder; or, The Inland Sea *as a historical novel.*

WHAT DO I READ NEXT?

- Cooper's most popular and widely-read novel, one of the "Leatherstocking Tales," is *The Last of the Mohicans*, published in 1826 and available in modern editions. This novel is the second in the series and, coincidentally, the second in the chronological sequence of Natty Bumppo's life. The historical setting of the novel is the French and Indian War during 1757.

- Cooper's daughter, Susan Fenimore Cooper, was an accomplished nature writer in the nineteenth century. Several of her pieces have been collected in *Essays on Nature and Landscape* (2002), edited by Rochelle Johnson and Daniel Patterson. Her work is an early example of environmental writing and reflects her father's love of the wilderness.

- Young-adult readers enjoy the tales of Washington Irving, an American writer whose life overlapped Cooper's and whose tales are often set in New York State. Tales such as "Rip Van Winkle" (1819) and "The Legend of Sleepy Hollow" (1820), found in the modern edition *Rip Van Winkle, and Other Tales* (1996), offer a treatment of life in colonial New England very different from Cooper's.

- The central historical event that the "Leatherstocking Tales" revolve around was the French and Indian War. A brief examination of this series of conflicts, written for young adults, can be found in *The French and Indian War* (2010), by Charles E. Pederson.

- Award-winning author Elizabeth George Speare's *Calico Captive* (2001), is a young-adult historical novel set during the French and Indian War. The book is based on an actual diary, first published in 1807, of a young girl taken captive during the war.

- African Americans also participated in the rich historical and cultural life of colonial New England. Their story, both urban and rural, is outlined in *Root and Branch: African Americans in New York and East Jersey, 1613–1863*, by Graham Russell Hodges, published in 1999.

- A major part of the mythology of colonial America is the story surrounding Captain John Smith of the Virginia colony and the Indian princess Pocahontas, who, according to Smith, saved his life. David A. Price examines the story, as well as the larger story of interactions between settlers and Indians, in *Love and Hate in Jamestown: John Smith, Pocahontas, and the Start of a New Nation* (2005).

- Cooper was often referred to as "the American Scott," referring to Sir Walter Scott, a Scottish novelist whose historical novels were immensely popular at about the same time on both sides of the Atlantic. One of Scott's most popular novels is *Ivanhoe*, published in 1819 and available in numerous modern editions.

The historical novel, as the term implies, is a novel that draws more or less extensively on historical events. Different authors, though, have taken different approaches to writing historical novels. Some of these novels are about the activities of known historical persons: kings and queens, military commanders, presidents, and the like. Thus, a novel such as *Agincourt*

(2008), by Bernard Cornwell, details the events surrounding the Hundred Years' War and the role played by England's King Henry V in the Battle of Agincourt in 1415. Other historical novels make reference to major historical figures but focus on the people whose lives were affected by them. An example is the novel *Sally Hemings*, by Barbara Chase-Riboud. This novel, written

NATTY TRIES TO KEEP HOLD OF THE OLD WAY
OF LIVING, AND ALTHOUGH HE SUCCEEDS TO SOME
EXTENT, THE WORLD HE INHABITS IS IN THE PROCESS
OF PASSING INTO HISTORY."

in 1979, tells the story of the title character, a slave who had a relationship with her owner, U.S. president Thomas Jefferson, and who probably bore children with him.

Some historical novels use historical information to tell a modern story. Examples are the novels of best-selling author Dan Brown. In his blockbuster novel *The Da Vinci Code*, published in 2003, a modern-day professor leads the reader on a journey through Christian history and Western art to uncover a mystery surrounding Jesus Christ and, according to the novel, his marriage to Mary Magdalene. History, then, is used as a springboard for a modern suspense thriller as the professor evades those who do not want historical secrets brought to light. Yet another type of historical novel is one like John Barth's *The Sot-Weed Factor*, first published in 1960. ("Sot-weed" is tobacco; a "factor" is an agent or middleman.) This novel is a hilarious (and sometimes almost obscene) romp through the history of the American colonies, particularly Maryland. Barth uses the events of history to puncture some of the myths about early American history, particularly the legendary story of Captain John Smith and his relationship with the Indian princess Pocahontas. While based on historical events, the novel takes a satirical view of them. Finally, some historical novels use historical events as a backdrop in the examination of character. A novel such as Charles Dickens's *A Tale of Two Cities* (1859), is set largely during the French Revolution. Although Dickens alludes to the events of the revolution, readers would not come away from the novel with a full understanding of that revolution and its events. Rather, the revolution is the stage on which the main characters enact a drama of love, loss, renunciation, and heroic self-sacrifice. It is into this last category that Cooper's historical fictions fall.

The historical novel began to emerge in the late eighteenth and early nineteenth centuries in the wake of the French Revolution. Prior to the revolution, there was an overall sense that history was something fixed and immutable. People did not think very much about history, for they tended not to see the point. At the risk of oversimplifying, the attitude was that nothing ever changed. The world today, the thinking ran, is much like the world of the past, so the examination of history is a pointless exercise. The French Revolution changed that outlook. The revolution was a world-changing event, at least in Europe and the North American colonies. People began to see that the course of history could be changed, both by "the people" and by world-historical figures. For the next six decades, Europe was in a state of turmoil. The armies of the French general Napoleon Bonaparte were on the march in an effort to overthrow traditional monarchies. Philosophers and political thinkers began to examine history and the path of its progress. In England, Edward Gibbon wrote a monumental history about the decline and fall of the Roman Empire. It was almost as if Europeans "discovered" history in the wake of the French Revolution.

The inventor of the historical novel, in a way, was the Scottish romantic author Sir Walter Scott. In a large number of novels, including *Waverley*, *Ivanhoe*, *The Heart of Mid-Lothian*, *Rob Roy*, and *Kenilworth*, Scott ransacked English and Scottish history for his materials. He wrote about the Crusades, the religious wars of the seventeenth and eighteenth centuries, scandals and intrigue surrounding the British monarch, and similar topics. Scott's novels became immensely popular, both in Europe and in the United States. By the time Cooper had written his first novel in 1820, Scott had published nine novels, and over the next decade, as Cooper was hitting his stride, Scott published an astonishing eighteen additional novels. Thus, the "Leatherstocking Tales" found fertile ground that Scott had plowed, and Cooper was sometimes referred to as "the American Scott."

What makes Cooper a historical novelist? On one level, the answer to that question is obvious. *The Pathfinder* is set in the context of the French and Indian War. The novel frequently alludes to the conflict between the French and the British in North America, and it is historically accurate insofar as the French enlisted the help of Indian tribes in fighting the British. Brief mention is made of George Washington, at the time a colonel. Beyond that, though, the novel never goes into detail about the war—its causes, its progress, and the activities of major historical figures in prosecuting the war. The characters in the novel are not historical giants but rather ordinary people going about their business.

What Cooper accomplished was to depict history in motion. Through the character of Natty Bumppo (and to a lesser extent Cap), he depicts older, more traditional ways of seeing the world. Natty is a frontiersman. He is not polished or sophisticated. He is not wise to the ways of the city. He takes no part in manufacture or trade, and he has no interest in the political currents of the time. He lives a life in unison with the rhythms of nature. The war, though, brings his way of life under assault. Other characters invade his idealized wilderness, bringing with them new attitudes, new loyalties, and new ways of looking at the world. The reader senses that the world Natty inhabits will change and, in some senses, disappear. It will not be long before the frontiersman will become so out of date as to hardly exist in the modern world, at least in the region around the Great Lakes. History is on the march, with new goals, new conflicts, and new conditions. Natty tries to keep hold of the old way of living, and although he succeeds to some extent, the world he inhabits is in the process of passing into history.

One interesting feature of *The Pathfinder* is that although Natty is the central character, he does not really act in the novel. He is present, and from time to time he takes part in the action. But the novel is really about the characters that surround him: Mabel, her father, Cap, Jasper Western, and Lieutenant Muir, as well as Indians such as Arrowhead, Dew-of-June, and Chingachgook. Natty functions almost as a kind of master of ceremonies, ever present to advise characters, direct their actions, and teach them about the world he knows. He stands in sharp contrast to Muir, who has been corrupted by civilization. In a strange kind of way, Natty is as much a place as he is a person, such that the central "character" in the novel is the frontier of western New York and Lake Ontario, and Natty is its avatar, or personification. To put it differently, Natty is a kind of lynchpin, a central point in a circle of characters. The other characters *act*,

but their actions are examined within the context of the way of life that Natty defends. This is the function of his many conversations with Cap, for example, about the merits of the wilderness. Cap is a man of the sea, and he sees life at sea as inherently superior to life on land. Natty, though, both preaches and exemplifies the virtues of the forest. Natty becomes a world-historical character, notable less for what he does than for who he is.

Ultimately, then, *The Pathfinder* is a conservative novel, one that resists change or sees it as dangerous. Many historical novels, in tracing the march of civilization, demonstrate that change represents progress. Sir Walter Scott's novels about the religious wars on the British Isles showed that new ways of thinking were superior to the old, for those new ways of thinking developed in support of religious and political liberty. Cooper, though, takes a different view. To the extent that Natty is his alter ego, Cooper takes the position that the ideal American society is in danger of passing into the dust bin of history as a result of expansion, development, and modern progress. Natty hangs on: at the end of the novel, Mabel spots him in the distance, an aging figure who has not kept pace with the times. In contrast, she marries Jasper Western and moves with him to New York City, where Jasper becomes a successful merchant, a participant in the development of America's economic and social life.

In the end, the reader has to decide whose vision of American life is superior. Most readers enjoy the fruits of civilization (indeed, reading a book is in itself a function of civilization and technology), yet many readers, too, long for the kind of pure, authentic world that Natty inhabits. This is a world that modern readers can access through outdoor activities—hunting, hiking, white-water rafting, camping, organized wilderness adventure tours, and dude-ranch vacations—or through developing an environmental consciousness. It is for this reason that Cooper's novels, despite their occasionally dusty, old-fashioned quality, despite some awkward dialogue and occasional implausibilities, retain their popularity. As historical novels, they take the reader into a past Garden of Eden in which being is more important than becoming, a world in which who a person is is more important than what a person does.

Source: Michael J. O'Neal, Critical Essay on *The Pathfinder; or, The Inland Sea,* in *Novels for Students,* Gale, Cengage Learning, 2012.

Sailing is discussed at great length in The Pathfinder. *(Christophe Baudot | Shutterstock.com)*

James E. Swearingen and Joanne Cutting-Gray

In the following excerpt, Swearingen and Cutting-Gray discuss the relationship between history and myth in The Pathfinder.

. . . In order to represent the social reality of this unique time, Pathfinder functions as the critical point of interaction among rival Indian tribes, English and French colonials, as well as a crux for traits dispersed in the national character of the American. *He* does not choose. History *chooses him*. It chooses him to find a path that will, for him, ultimately fail. His complex role accounts for a virtual stasis in both character and plot since the plot traces the collision of these social forces "with all the colour and specific atmosphere of that time" (*HN* 150). Thus he *must* play a subordinate role that can map the complexity of the "social-historical" process rather than emanate change from his own subjective center. Of necessity his character, and

character in general, is subordinate: "the proper hero . . . is life itself" (*HN* 149). The epochal configuration of social life, "the proper hero," requires Pathfinder to be as he is.

Why, we might ask, should one whose talent is to find his way through uncharted wilderness be chosen to negotiate a dangerous historical juncture where trails are obliterated, ways come to unexpected ends, and goals fail? Since Pathfinder clearly has no panoramic understanding of his situation, what special dexterity places him at its center? As one who incarnates a unique historical turn, he marks a shift from a retrospective world of natural harmony, toward a prospective world of bourgeois hegemony. In that shift and that loss lies the historical tragedy of the novel, the tragedy not of an individual but of a nation.

Two traits in the character of Pathfinder that make him an appropriate figure of intersecting historical forces are his tolerance and sense

" IN FACT, BECAUSE HE IS NOT AMBITIOUS FOR SUCH INFALLIBILITY, BECAUSE HIS ACTS DO NOT IMPLY A SUPERIORITY TO HISTORY, HE EMBODIES THE PERPETUAL SELF-OVERCOMING OF A GENUINELY REVOLUTIONARY, THAT IS TEMPORAL, FORCE."

of justice. His tolerance may also be characterized as an openness to difference. A white man reared primarily by the Delawares, he has learned that people "see things differently" (*P*) according to their "natur's." He responds to most situations with an innate understanding that understanding itself is perspectival, that it includes both blindness and insight. Recognizing human limitation, he acts contrary to neither his traditions nor his experience. Thus he stands in powerful contrast to the weakness that imposes individual opinion upon reality.

When the narrator offers a catalogue of Pathfinder's virtues, "the most striking feature" of his "moral organization...was his beautiful and unerring sense of justice. This noble trait...probably had its unseen influence on all who associated with him" (*P*). Justice is the ancient name for harmony, but Pathfinder's justice differs in that it does not harmonize everything in sight as the mythic reading supposes. Therefore his willingness to let others be does not conflict with a justice that nurtures present but hidden possibilities in persons and situations. By not reducing the world to his will, he preserves difference and its complexity. In an important event near the end of the novel, for example, he exposes the crosscurrents of affection among Mabel, Jasper, and himself. Although he and Mabel are in a manner betrothed, he tells her that Jasper is in love with her. When she cautions that the topic is "improper," he responds, "everything is proper that is right, Mabel, and everything is right that leads to justice and fair dealing, though it be *painful* enough" (*P*).

What Pathfinder calls "justice and fair dealing" does not decide how things ought to be; it acquiesces in things as they are. When he mediates between Mabel and Jasper, he finds a path for affections concealed behind the "proper." He resolutely lets Mabel and Jasper's affection find

its own course by not allowing them willfully to deny it. The event is not a subjective decision or act of will on his part, not conformity to some ideal or some aim in view. His affections are more than private feelings. As the lives of the young people move toward a domestic resolution, what is historically decisive, what radiates from a praxis that no character understands, is the turn towards a new configuration of public life and the future shape of a nation. These larger temporal currents both open up and restrict the range of voluntary decision.

There are forgotten possibilities in the word "de-cision": to cut off or separate does not necessarily entail the agency of individuals. What is decisive in the historical novel is not the choice of particular subjects. A narrow margin of choice is open to individuals at the turn between historical epochs: they may accept or resist the direction of events. If Pathfinder knowingly complied with the encroaching colonial forces, he would belong definitively to the prospective world and not be who he is. More importantly and paradoxically perhaps, if he had the historical understanding to resist the colonialism he serves, he would be still more complicitous with that cultural hegemony. He would then make himself the measure of history and, by setting his own judgment above the contingencies of events, become the prototype of this new aggressive individualism. In fact, because he is not ambitious for such infallibility, because his acts do not imply a superiority to history, he embodies the perpetual self-overcoming of a genuinely revolutionary, that is temporal, force. His spontaneous acts unwittingly let history go where it will and give him the configuration of a being whose way of being consists of history. To put the point another way, Pathfinder acts "at an end" rather than "toward an end," spontaneously as circumstances require, rather than in the light of some projected aim in view. His strength is the humility of acting without knowing that perpetually overreaches itself.

Unbroken continuity with nature is often attributed to Pathfinder as though it were a trait of character, some subjective disposition available to choice. At most, that "union" is virtual rather than actual. To be understood by others, he must explain nature as his church, his sustenance, and his shelter. This need to justify his ways to others signals a gap that separates his practice from his theorizing about it. The largely imaginary union he boasts of belongs to the prehistory of this novel. It marks a possible historical experience *excluded* by the aggressive world ahead and nearly excluded from the narrative present.

The novel does not so much describe as encourage us to imagine the world behind, a prior whole, a continuum of action rather than words. When Pathfinder acts alongside nature, rather than pitting himself against it or talking about it, he reads the signs of the forest and responds instinctively. The narrator describes the spontaneity of a person "trained in the vicissitudes of the frontier," acting without pause for reflection. This seamless mode of being is mentioned only rarely. Of this historical context we are told, "At the period of our tale, and indeed for half a century later, the whole of that vast region . . . lay, as a comparatively unpeopled desert, teeming with all the living productions of nature that properly belonged to the climate. . . . The few Indians . . . could produce no visible effects on the abundance of the game, and the scattered garrisons or occasional hunters . . . had no other influence than the bee on the buckwheat field or the hummingbird on the flower" (*P*). This rift between Pathfinder's unreflective immediacy of "a glance, a thought, and an expedient" (*P*) and his garrulous explanations of his "gifts" to those who are aliens in the wilderness signals a loss. The gap of reflection and dawning self-consciousness is responsible for the long passages of talk, and it measures the loss he is suffering long before he knows it.

The world ahead, Pathfinder's peculiar destiny, gradually unfolds for us in his growing awareness of Mabel as "other." To the Europeans, nature is set at a distance, experienced visually as aesthetic object. It is Mabel's presence as objectified "other" that works on Pathfinder in a similar fashion by gradually reifying his native element. He describes to her the "satisfaction" he took in following the trail both in fact and in fancy before he met her. Then he adds, "But all those things have lost their charms since I've made acquaintance with you." Now when he dreams of nature, "at the root of every tree was a Mabel Dunham, . . . the birds that were among the branches sang ballads instead of the notes that natur' gave, and even the deer stopped to listen. I tried to shoot a fa'an, but Killdeer missed fire, and the creatur' laughed in my face, as pleasantly as a young girl laughs in her merriment" (*P*). Drawn to her like a "Magnet," pulled

away from that prior harmony, he consciously discovers division, becomes aware of the oppositions within his own being that foreshadow a future for the culture.

The fact that this threat is figured as binary, self and other, reveals it as Pathfinder's doom and the end of nature as the intimate source of his nurture, his energy, and his solace. The rise of difference marks what he has already lost, the failure of mediation, absence of the old kinship, the beginning of dissatisfaction and a sense of lack. When Mabel's "feminized" version of nature awakens desire in him as an emptiness to be filled, desire becomes unfulfillable in principle: "I have often thought myself happy, Mabel, when ranging the woods on a successful hunt, breathing the pure air of the hills and filled with vigor and health, but I now feel that it has all been idleness and vanity compared with the delight it would give me to know that you thought better of me than you think of most others" (*P*). What is important here is not the individual Mabel: the Mabel-event is a structural shift that changes everything, an event that, when the time is ripe, realigns the way the world and others are related to Pathfinder. He says for example, "if the girl could fancy a rude hunter and guide then I would quit some of my wandering ways and try to humanize my mind down to a wife and children" (*P*). The unwitting admission that "wife and children" represent a decline from the "wandering ways" of acting without purpose, marks the change from a flow of undifferentiated thought and action to a fractured, self-conscious humanism. The narrative concretely figures his present—and ours—as a decline from the wilderness to the hearth: "*It is time* I did begin to think of house and furniture, and a home" (*P*; our emphasis). It is not that Mabel is somehow different from other women, more beautiful or desirable than they, but that for Pathfinder the difference is time.

This decline from wilderness to hearth stills the old harmony and discloses the reifying process in social relationships. Pathfinder observes to Jasper at one point that "natur'" seems to have made them [women] on purpose to sing in our ears when the music of the woods is silent!" (*P*). Nothing makes so jarringly explicit the influence of conventional femininity as his growing concern with "property." To Jasper again he confides, "if I have consarn in marrying Mabel, it is that I may get to love such things too well, in order to make her comfortable" (*P*). And yet growing preoccupation with Mabel makes nature alien, not simply because it is displaced in his attention, but because nature and his relation with it are *refigured* in her presence. The Mabel-event reorganizes his space, estranges him from "feminine" nature, and disrupts his union with any "other." Just as he sinks from hunter to husband, so the earth diminishes from the all-encompassing presence of the divine— "the temple of the Lord"—toward a stock of commodities, a decline that silences "the music of the woods." The marriage between Mabel and Jasper Western, their eventual move (east) to New York, and Jasper's success in trade anticipate a history in front of the plot. The hunter may fancy settling down with Mabel in "a beautiful spot about fifty miles west of the garrison," the distance of "a healthy hunt" from Jasper (*P*), but the "border man" can never endure the transformation prefigured in the plot and also remain a boundary figure.

This development enables us to understand what is tragic in the historical individual and why his peculiar "justice" appropriates at the price of great loss. The radically temporal gathering of Mabel and Jasper into union *ex*propriates as it *ap*propriates, for it relegates Pathfinder to a world behind. The moment of complex historical decision runs through that particular, intimate turn in human relationships.

The story, then, is less myth of harmony than history of harmony disrupted. Just as the white man's encroachment on the wilderness causes the narrative past to appear as a lost paradise, so Pathfinder's characteristic way of being in the forest is disclosed in its loss. At the end of the story, the solitude in which he has always kept good company with himself declines into the loneliness of a divided self. Thus the final chapter opens, "Pathfinder was accustomed to solitude, but, when the *Scud* had actually disappeared, he was almost overcome with a sense of his loneliness. Never before had he been conscious of his isolated condition in the world" (*P*). Here at the end, even Chingachgook, who belongs to the retrospective world and whose bond with Pathfinder was never dependent on physical presence or absence, "was missed at the precise instant which might be termed the most critical in our hero's life" (*P*). For the first time, consciousness of that isolation delivers Pathfinder over to the homeless subjectivity of the classical novel, the condition of the prospective or future face of his

temporal complexity. When as twentieth-century readers we look back on him, we are tempted to misread him either as mythic or as homeless subjectivity rather than as a figure of unresolved (and unresolvable) historical conflict that makes a claim on us.

In preparation for the crucial move in this analysis, let us renew the question why a confluence of historical departure and arrival should be embodied in one whose way of being is finding paths. Pathfinder's failure to grasp his historical place conceptually has appeared to some as an absence of political intelligence, though his simplicity is actually strength and, as Lukács has said, his tragedy. The advantage for history in that unreflective simplicity becomes evident in his contrast with all the other characters. Each of them rejects things as they are and harbors a view of the world as it ought to be. The choice implicit in that willfulness makes each an inappropriate medium for reflecting the dynamics of historical change. Pathfinder's difference, his not seeking to reduce the world to the measure of his own understanding and desire, is a strength easily misread as weakness. As he is drawn toward a new era, of course, even he learns to aspire to be what he is not, namely a middle-class husband....

Source: James E. Swearingen and Joanne Cutting-Gray, "Cooper's *Pathfinder*," in *New Literary History: A Journal of Theory and Interpretation*, Vol. 23, No. 2, Spring 1992, pp. 267–80.

Honoré de Balzac

In the following review, de Balzac declares this novel "a beautiful book," worthy as the central volume of the "Leatherstocking Tales."

After two feeble works, Cooper has redeemed himself by his *Lake Ontario* [the title of the French and English editions of *The Pathfinder*]. It is a beautiful book, worthy of *The Last of the Mohicans*, *The Pioneers* and *The Prairie*, which it serves to complete. At this moment, Cooper is the sole author worthy of being placed beside Sir Walter Scott. He is not equal to him, but he possesses the same order of genius; and he owes the high place which he occupies in modern literature to two faculties; that of painting the ocean and its mariners, and of idealizing the magnificent scenery of America. I am unable to comprehend how the author of *The Pilot* and *The Red Rover*, and the four romances just cited, should have been the

NEVER DID THE ART OF WRITING TREAD
CLOSER UPON THE SET OF THE PENCIL. THIS IS
THE SCHOOL FOR THE STUDY OF LITERARY
LANDSCAPE-PAINTERS."

author of other works, with the single exception of *The Spy*. These seven works constitute the only and the real titles of his fame. I do not pronounce this opinion lightly. I have read again and again the productions of the Romancer, or to say the truth, the Historian of America, and I feel, in common with Sir Walter Scott, the same admiration for his two faculties, to which I may add his grand and original conception of Leatherstocking, that sublime personage, who connects *The Pioneers*, the *Mohicans*, the *Prairie*, and the *Lake Ontario*. Leatherstocking is a statue, a magnificent moral hermaphrodite, born between the savage and the civilized states of man, who will live as long as literature endures.

The story of *Lake Ontario* is exceedingly simple: it is in fact the lake itself. A sergeant of the Fifty-fifth regiment, quartered in the remotest fort in Canada, an old man and a widower, sends for his daughter, who is in England, and whom he wishes to see married, before he dies, to his friend the Pathfinder, the faithful friend and guide of the English. The young woman comes with her uncle, a simple English sailor, conducted by a chief of the Red-Skins, to a spot where they meet the messengers sent by the Sergeant; namely, the Pathfinder and the Great Serpent, Chingachgook, a most interesting Mohican savage. The daughter of the Sergeant finds in company with these two persons a young friend of the Pathfinder and of the Great Serpent, together with a Lake Ontario sailor, called Jasper. The whole party are escorted by a chief named Arrowhead, and his wife, the Dew of June, and do not reach the fort without encountering numerous dangers. The Iroquois, who are acquainted with the journey of the Sergeant's daughter and her uncle, waylay them for the purpose of making them their prisoners.... During this perilous journey, the young woman falls in love with Jasper, the friend of the Pathfinder. After their safe arrival at

the fort, and in going with the Sergeant to take possession of one of the Thousand Islands, for the purpose of intercepting supplies sent by the French to the Iroquois, the Pathfinder discovers that he is only the friend of the Sergeant's daughter: he renounces his engagement with her, although he loves her, and marries her to Jasper. I love these simple stories: they discover great power of conception, and always abound in fertility. The early part of the work embraces a description of the Oswego, one of the tributary rivers of Lake Ontario, along the shores of which lurk the Iroquois, for the purpose of making the party captive. Here Cooper is himself again. His description of the forest, the running stream, with its rapids and waterfalls, the artifices of the savages, who endeavor to outwit the Great Serpent, Jasper, and the Pathfinder, furnishes a succession of admirable pictures, which in this work, as well as its antecedents, are inimitable. Here is sufficient to dishearten all romancers who have the ambition to follow in the footsteps of the American author. Never did the art of writing tread closer upon the set of the pencil. This is the school for the study of literary landscape-painters. All the secrets of the art are revealed. The magical prose of Cooper not only embodies the spirit of the river, its shores, the forest and its trees; but it exhibits the minutest details, combined with the grandest outline. The vast solitudes, into which we penetrate, become in a moment deeply interesting. The same genius which previously launched us upon the boundless ocean, with all its terrors, now thrills us with glimpses of the painted savage behind the trunks of trees, in the water, and hidden by rocks. When the spirit of solitude communes with us, when the first calm of these eternal shades pervades us, when we hover over this virgin vegetation, our hearts are filled with emotion. Page after page is filled with naturally-presented dangers, without any effort at stage effect. It seems as though we are seeking under these magnificent trees for the print of a moccasin. These perils are so skillfully interwoven with the incidents of the fable, that we have leisure to attentively examine the rocks, the trees, the water-falls, the bark canoes, the thickets; we incorporate ourselves with the soil; it passes in us, and we pass into it. We know not how this metamorphosis of genius is accomplished, but it is impossible to separate the soil, the vegetation, the waters, their extent, and their configuration, from the interests which agitate us. In short, the personages become what they really are, of little importance among the sublime scenery which surrounds them.

The skirmishes with the Indians, and their devices, are never monotonous, and bear no resemblance to those which we find in the previous works of Cooper. The description of the fort, the encampment and repose of the party, and the target-shooting, are *chefs d'ouvre*. We owe to the author our warmest gratitude for his choice of these humble personages. With the exception of the young woman, who is not true to nature, and whose qualities are painfully and uselessly dwelt upon, his other figures are drawn from nature, if we may use a term borrowed from the *ateliers*. It is unfortunate, that the English sailor and Lieutenant Muir, the pivots of a drama so simple and so naïf, should be failures. More reflection, and a little more breadth, would have rendered this work faultless. The voyage across Lake Ontario is a delicious miniature, rivalling the finest ocean-scenes of Cooper. In short, the expedition to the Thousand Islands, the fights with the Iroquois, commanded by a French captain, possess an interest equal to that master-piece of genius, *The Last of the Mohicans*. The Pathfinder predominates here as well as elsewhere; and this profoundly melancholy personage is in some degree explained.

Enough of the interest and details of this beautiful work: it will be more useful to point out the faults which we find in it. Cooper's inferiority to Sir Walter Scott is his radical and utter feebleness in scenes of humor, and his perpetual anxiety to make us laugh, in which he has never succeeded. In reading him, one experiences a singular sensation; it is as if while we are listening to fine music, there is near us a frightful village minstrel, who scrapes his fiddle, and fatigues us by playing the same tune. To produce what Cooper mistakes for humor, he puts into the mouth of one of his characters the same foolish joke, invented *a priori*. Any perversity, moral vice, or deformity of mind, which appears in his first chapters, is repeated again and again to the end of his work. The fooleries of these bores produce the effect of the scraper of whom we have just spoken.

Genius consists in applying to each situation the words which are suited to display the character of the actor, and not in tacking to him a phrase which adapts itself to each situation. It is perfectly admissible to sketch a character as gay, sombre, or ironical; but, its gaiety, its melancholy, or its

irony, ought to manifest itself by characteristic traits. After describing your personage, let him speak; but to make him always repeat the same thing, is a weakness. Sir Walter Scott has noticed this comic absurdity of repetition; but this painter has only produced one or two examples of such characters. It is the invention of circumstances, and the display of characteristic touches, which distinguishes the modern Troubadour. By contrasting the poor grimmacing humorists of Cooper with the two executions of Tristam, in *Quentin Durward*, and with Michael Lambourne, in *Kenilworth*, we immediately perceive the law which governs these literary creations. If you do not possess this power, confine yourself within your own proper limits, and draw upon your own resources.... I am really grieved, in reading this beautiful work of Cooper, to find a repetition of the same joke in the mouth of the sailor, at the expense of the four wives of Lieutenant Muir.

The conception of the subordinate characters betrays the weakness of the rival of Scott. We are made to feel too sensibly that the conceit and obstinacy of the English sailor who refuses to listen to Jasper, is indispensable to bring about the catastrophe. Cooper is sublime when he initiates us into the beauties of American scenery; when he transports us across Lake Ontario, and when we thread with him the Thousand Islands. He is tedious in the opening of his drama, and only redeems himself by the beauty of the details....

A serious charge remains to be stated against our author. Undoubtedly Cooper's renown is not due to his countrymen, nor to the English: he owes it mainly to the ardent admiration of France; of our noble and beautiful country, which pays more attention to foreign men of genius than to our own poets. Cooper has been perfectly understood and appreciated in France.... I am therefore the more astonished to see France, and the French officers who were in Canada in 1750, ridiculed, in the person of Captain Sanglier. They were gentlemen, and history attests the glory of their conduct. Is it for an American, whose position entitles him to a high sense of honor, to invest a French officer with a gratuitously odious character, when the only succor which America received during her struggle for independence came from France? The noble or ignoble character of Captain Sanglier is not material to the plan of the drama, and nobleness of character would have furnished the author with an additional scene of beauty. It is pitiful to see enlightened men adopting the vulgar prejudices of the multitude.

The difference between [Scott and Cooper] arises mainly from the nature of the subjects to which their talents have been directed. From those chosen by Cooper, nothing could be drawn from philosophy, nor from the deep workings of the human mind. When his work is once read, the mind looks back to it, to embrace it as a whole. Both are certainly great historians, but both have cold hearts. They refuse the admission of passion, that divine emanation, superior to the conventional virtue which man has made for the preservation of society; they have suppressed it, in order to offer a holocaust to the prudes of their several countries. Scott unfolds to us the great revolutions of humanity; Cooper the mighty changes of nature.... His beautiful creation of Leatherstocking is a work apart. I am not acquainted with the English language, and therefore cannot judge of the style of these two great authors, happily for us so different; but I nevertheless think the Scotchman much superior to the American in the expression of thought, as well as the mechanism of style. Cooper is not a logician. He proceeds by sentences, which taken one by one, are confused; the first has no connection with the last; but taken together, they make an imposing whole. To comprehend my meaning, we have only to read the two first pages of his *Lake Ontario*, examining each proposition separately. They exhibit a mass of ideas which would furnish tasks for a scholar of rhetoric in France: but very soon we yield ourselves to the majesty of nature, and forget the embarrassing course of the vessel, in our admiration of the ocean-lake. Finally, we repeat, that the one is the historian of external nature, the other that of humanity; one reaches the beau-ideal by images, the other by actions, without omitting any poetical associations. The high tide in the *Antiquary*, and the first landscape in *Ivanhoe*, exhibit a talent for description equal to that of Cooper.

Source: Honoré de Balzac, "Literary Notices: *The Pathfinder; or, The Inland Sea*," in *Knickerbocker*, Vol. 17, No. 1, January 1841, pp. 72–77.

SOURCES

Balzac, Honoré de, Review of *The Pathfinder*, in *Fenimore Cooper: The Critical Heritage*, edited by George Dekker and John P. McWilliams, Routledge & Kegan Paul, 1973, pp. 196, 200; originally published in *Paris Review*, July 25, 1940.

Belinsky, V. G., Review of *The Bravo*, in *Fenimore Cooper: The Critical Heritage*, edited by George Dekker and John P. McWilliams, Routledge & Kegan Paul, 1973, p. 188; originally published in *Moscow Observer*, 1839.

———, Review of *The Pathfinder*, in *Fenimore Cooper: The Critical Heritage*, edited by George Dekker and John P. McWilliams, Routledge & Kegan Paul, 1973, pp. 192, 194–95; originally published in *Notes of the Fatherland*, Vol. 14, 1841.

Burrows, Edwin G., and Mike Wallace, *Gotham: A History of New York City to 1898*, Oxford University Press, 2000, p. 194.

"Cooper, James Fenimore," *Merriam-Webster's Encyclopedia of Literature*, Merriam-Webster, 1995, p. 270.

Cooper, James Fenimore, *The Pathfinder; or, The Inland Sea*, in *James Fenimore Cooper: The Leatherstocking Tales*, Vol. 2, Library of America, 1985.

Dekker, George, and John P. McWilliams, *Fenimore Cooper: The Critical Heritage*, Routledge & Kegan Paul, 1973, p. 23.

Garraty, John A. "Colonial Wars," in *The Reader's Companion to American History*, edited by Eric Foner and John A. Garraty, Houghton Mifflin, 1991, pp. 205–207.

Gibson, Campbell, "Population of the 100 Largest Cities and Other Urban Places in the United States: 1790 to 1990," in *U.S. Census Bureau*, 1998, http://www.census.gov/population/www/documentation/twps0027/tab07.txt (accessed April 2, 2011).

"James Fenimore Cooper," in *Mohican Press*, http://www.mohicanpress.com/mo08002.html (accessed April 1, 2011).

Lounsbury, Thomas R., *James Fenimore Cooper*, Houghton, Mifflin, 1882, pp. 239–40.

Roberts, Sam, "New York City's Population Barely Rose in the Last Decade, the Census Finds," in *New York Times*, March 24, 2011, http://www.nytimes.com/2011/03/25/nyregion/25census.html (accessed April 2, 2011).

Twain, Mark, "Fenimore Cooper's Literary Offenses," in *Twain's Indians*, University of Virginia Library Scholars Lab, http://etext.virginia.edu/railton/projects/rissetto/offense.html (accessed April 9, 2011).

FURTHER READING

Andreychuk, Ed, *American Frontiersmen on Film and Television*, McFarland, 2011.

Readers interested in popular-culture depictions of the American frontiersmen who followed the fictional Natty Bumppo will find in this book information about how six major frontier figures—Daniel Boone, Davy Crockett, Jim Bowie, Sam Houston, Jim Bridger, and Kit Carson—have been depicted in films and on television. The book also contains factual information about the subjects' lives.

Franklin, Wayne, *James Fenimore Cooper: The Early Years*, Yale University Press, 2007.

This is the first volume of a planned two-volume biography of Cooper. The "early years" are those up to 1826, when Cooper left the United States for Europe. This biography gives the reader insight into Cooper's childhood, family background, and formative experiences, including his earliest efforts at writing novels.

Hallock, Thomas, *From the Fallen Tree: Frontier Narratives, Environmental Politics, and the Roots of a National Pastoral, 1749–1826*, University of North Carolina Press, 2003.

This book, which includes discussions of Cooper, examines in detail the conflict between the wilderness and civilization that took place during the years of the fictional Natty Bumppo's life and during Cooper's early life. The book examines the mythology surrounding the spread of civilization into the pristine wilderness, and it thus touches on many of the environmental and nature themes in Cooper's "Leatherstocking Tales."

Johnson, Elias Fenimore, *Legends, Traditions, and Laws of the Iroquois, or Six Nations, and a History of the Tuscarora Indians*, Nabu Press, 2010.

This book, first published in 1881, provides a sympathetic perspective on the nation's eastern Indian tribes during the period of colonial history that was the subject of Cooper's "Leatherstocking Tales." Johnson was a chief of the Tuscarora tribe, which figures prominently in Cooper's novels.

Kammen, Michael, *Colonial New York: A History*, Oxford University Press, 1996.

This volume will appeal to readers interested in the history of the New York colony. The author provides a compelling narrative of the personalities that shaped the colony and information about the interactions between Dutch settlers, English settlers, and the region's Indian tribes.

SUGGESTED SEARCH TERMS

early American fiction

French and Indian War

historical fiction

James Fenimore Cooper

James Fenimore Cooper AND The Pathfinder

Leatherstocking Tales AND James Fenimore Cooper

Natty Bumppo

New York colony

noble savage

Six Nations Indians

Tuscarora Indians

Schindler's List

1993 The film version of Thomas Keneally's novel *Schindler's List* was considered a breakthrough movie for director Steven Spielberg. Before it was released in 1993, he was known as a director of record-breaking blockbuster hits such as *Jaws* and *E.T.*, a talented moneymaker whose serious efforts, such as *The Color Purple* and *Empire of the Sun*, were accepted politely but quickly forgotten. *Schindler's List*, on the other hand, quickly became a cultural touchstone, respected across the world as an important new addition in the effort to understand the unprecedented scope of the German Nazi regime's campaign of genocide against the Jews.

Keneally spent ten years researching his novel, combing through records and interviewing former prisoners at the work camp in Krakow, Poland, where most of the action of *Schindler's List* takes place. The Universal Studios film, with the screenplay written by Steven Zaillian, retains that faithfulness to facts and adds a dark, somber mood. The movie was filmed in black and white, but Spielberg added color to certain details of just a few scenes. With the richness of detail of the best film technology at his disposal, Spielberg portrays Oskar Schindler, the Nazi industrialist who ended up sacrificing his fortune to save the lives of thousands, as both sympathetic and enigmatic at the same time.

This film won seven Academy Awards in 1993, including Best Picture. Within four years

of its release, it was ranked by the American Film Institute as one of the top ten American films ever made. Millions of viewers across the globe have considered it to be one of the most moving stories ever told on film.

PLOT SUMMARY

The film *Schindler's List* begins in color, with a Jewish family gathered at a table for the Sabbath ceremony. The people disappear, the candles on the table burn lower, and the film turns to black-and-white, indicating a trip into memory. The smoke from the extinguishing candles is cross-cut to the smoke from the steam locomotive engine of a train bringing Jews from the country-side, as they are forced to relocate into Krakow, Poland, in September 1939. As the relocated people call out their names, the camera shows them typed onto government forms, foreshadowing the way names will be listed on Schindler's pages later in the movie.

At his apartment, Oskar Schindler fastidiously prepares to go out, putting on fine clothes, bundling a large pile of cash, and affixing a Nazi swastika button to his lapel. He bribes the waiter at the nightclub for a good seat and sends expensive cognac to the Schutzstaffel (SS) officers sitting with their dates. Soon everyone in the place is gathered around Schindler's table, drinking and singing.

At the office of the Judenrat, the Jewish council that carries out Nazi orders, Schindler passes thousands of Jews lined up to receive job assignments and to register complaints. He asks to see Judenrat officer Itzhak Stern privately, asking his thoughts about an enamelware company Stern has done the accounting for, pointing out that the machines there could be used for army goods. He asks Stern to find him Jewish investors who cannot use their money any more but can use the pots and pans the factory makes to sell on the black market. Schindler offers to let Stern run the company.

Poldek Pfefferberg, walking through the ghetto, stops at a Catholic church to deal with black marketers. Schindler approaches him and

FILM TECHNIQUE

- Camera motions are often unnoticed on film because cameras are rolled on tracks, like train tracks, on the floor. Handheld film cameras used to register every motion of the photographer with abrupt jumps before the development of the Steadicam in 1976. The Steadicam allows the free movement of a hand-held camera with minimal jarring. Spielberg filmed most of *Schindler's List* with a Steadicam, giving the camerapeople freer movement than they would have had using tracks. The result is a documentary feeling, as if the camera operators are walking among the story's participants while they film them. The net effect is that viewers feel they are being given a glimpse into history as it is happening.

- This film makes use of the slow, sensual motions of smoke as a visual metaphor. It begins with a ceremonial candle that burns out, and the smoke rising from that is cross-cut with the billows of smoke rising from the train arriving in Krakow with Jews from the countryside. Throughout the film, there are many shots filled with smoke in train stations, factories, and rooms where wealthy men enjoy expensive contraband cigars. In addition, outdoor scenes, such as the scene of the Jews being registered into the ghetto, are filmed with billows of fog obscuring the buildings in the background.

- Films often light actors from the front and above, illuminating the entire scene. With this technique, viewers do not notice the source of light. Shadows are seen seldom or not at all. Much of this film, however, is lit from the side, as if light is coming through a window in indoor scenes, or as if the sun is low in outdoor scenes. Filming this way creates ample shadows, casting much of any shot into dimness or darkness, creating a foreboding, sinister mood.

- Spielberg shows a meticulous interest in the objects that are part of Schindler's world, starting with the early sequence of the items he puts into his pockets as he prepares to go out: the camera shows his handkerchief, money, and Nazi Party lapel pin in close focus before Oskar Schindler is ever shown. As the film continues, close-ups are often used to draw attention to the luxury items that Schindler acquires to bribe Nazi Party officials.

- The close attention to luxury items consumed by those in power is offset by long shots, filmed from a distance, of masses of Jews. This technique serves to convey the way that Jews are treated as one and robbed of their identities by the Nazi system. The most poignant use of this technique occurs when, during the dissolution of the ghetto, the long shot is from Schindler's point of view, and, in the middle of the chaos of hundreds of people being pushed through the streets, he takes notice of one individual in the crowd: the girl in the red coat.

---

compliments his shirt, explaining that he has trouble finding shirts like that. After his initial wariness, Pfefferberg enlists in helping Schindler find black-market goods in the future.

As the Holocaust proceeds, the borders of the sixteen-square-block Krakow ghetto are closed on March 20, 1941. Wealthy Jewish families are forced from their apartments and moved into tight living quarters with others in the ghetto. Schindler moves into one of the apartments vacated by a relocated family. With money from Jewish investors, Schindler opens Deutsche Email Fabrik (DEF), meaning German Enamel Factory. In the ghetto, Stern advises Jews to tell the Nazis that they work at jobs that are essential to the war. He helps forge documents to get Jews jobs, and the untrained workers struggle to learn jobs at DEF.

As he opens the plant, Schindler sends luxurious gifts of unobtainable black-market goods to SS officers, and as a result his business prospers. When Schindler's wife, Emilie, arrives from Czechoslovakia and finds Schindler living with his secretary, Wiktoria, he is not even slightly embarrassed. At dinner, he tells Emilie of his dreams of success and wealth due to war profiteering. She refuses to live with him if he will not give up having extramarital affairs.

At his office in the factory, Stern brings in an old man with one arm, Mr. Löwenstein, who insists on thanking Schindler for hiring him, which has saved him from the SS. Schindler is uncomfortable because it is so obvious that Löwenstein is not a capable worker, and that Stern knows this.

When the Jews are stopped in their march from the ghetto to the factory, soldiers laugh at Löwenstein's claim that he is an essential worker and shoot him in the head. Schindler, angered that his workers were diverted to snow shoveling, formulates the plan to move his workers from the ghetto into barracks on his factory grounds.

Schindler hears that Stern is on the list of Jews to be deported to the concentration camp. He races to the train station and intimidates Nazi officials by taking down their names and saying they will be held accountable for this disruption of his war-related work. Together, they find the boxcar that Stern is in just as the train is pulling out and have him disembark.

Amon Goeth is brought to Krakow to move the Jewish population out of the ghetto and into Plaszow, the labor camp that will be under his control. He lines up the women from the camp and selects Helen Hirsch to be his maid, beginning a twisted, sadistic relationship in which he will regularly abuse her.

When a prisoner, Diana Reiter, tries to explain that the barracks being constructed are not architecturally secure, Goeth orders Albert Hujar, a Nazi soldier, to execute her in front of the workers.

The day the camp opens, on March 13, 1943, the ghetto is dissolved: all Jews living in Krakow, which has had a Jewish population for six centuries, are chased from their houses and moved to nearby Plaszow or sent to concentration camps. People are dragged into the streets and shot. They swallow jewelry, to have valuables to

trade in the camps. Some, including Pfefferberg, escape into the sewers. The patients in the hospital are spared execution when the doctor and nurse poison them.

Schindler watches the Nazi action against the Jews from a hill above the city, where he is horseback riding with Wiktoria. His attention focuses on one child, whom the book identifies as Genia Dresner. The otherwise black-and-white film shows Genia dressed in red. She wanders through the chaotic streets without any distractions.

At night, hundreds of Jews come out from the places in walls and under floors where they have hidden. Hundreds more are caught by SS search parties and are machine-gunned.

On the first morning the Plaszow labor camp has all of the Jews from the ghetto, Amon Goeth stands shirtless on his balcony, smoking a cigarette. Casually, he picks up his high-powered rifle and begins shooting people in the courtyard at random.

Schindler goes to lunch at Goeth's house, and the commander explains to Schindler and other manufacturers that they should move their factories to within the labor camp. Schindler talks privately to Goeth to object, citing the cost of moving his heavy machinery and of constantly retraining workers. Goeth offers Schindler his own sub-camp on the grounds of his factory, hinting at bribes. He has columns of workers moved to DEF and orders Stern to make sure he is properly paid his cut of Schindler's business.

At the metalworks factory inside Plaszow, Goeth commands Rabbi Lewartow to make him a hinge and times him, determining that he should have produced more in a day's work. He takes him outside to execute him, but his gun fails. When a second pistol fails, he strikes the rabbi and leaves him. Schindler gives Stern his cigarette lighter, which Stern uses to pay a bribe to have the rabbi reassigned to DEF.

A young woman, Regina Perlman, approaches Schindler to have her parents moved to his factory. He throws her out, angrily, and then accuses Stern of putting him in danger by spreading the word that Schindler can help save doomed people. He explains Goeth's situation to Stern sympathetically; Stern tells him about twenty-five people Goeth shot down with his pistol one day. Schindler agrees to help the Perlmans.

At a party at Goeth's house, Schindler goes to the wine cellar for a bottle and runs into Helen Hirsch, Goeth's maid. He offers her a candy bar, and she tells the story of how Goeth has abused her throughout her stay in his house.

Schindler has a talk with Goeth after the party about power. Real power, he says, is the ability to show mercy, to pardon a condemned prisoner like the ancient Roman emperors. The next day, Goeth finds that the boy who was ordered to clean his bathtub, a situation described in the book's prologue, is not able to remove the stains. The boy cowers, but Goeth says that he pardons him. As the boy is leaving, though, Goeth has second thoughts and shoots at the boy from his balcony.

In the wine cellar, Goeth finds Helen. He talks to her about his confusion regarding why they could not have a romantic relationship, touching her tenderly, even though, he says, she is not quite human. Just when it seems he is about to molest her, he stops and instead beats her savagely.

At Schindler's birthday party, two girls from the factory bring him a cake. He kisses them both on the cheeks. In the film, the party is attended by SS men. In the novel, however, this scene occurs earlier, with only Schindler's workers involved, leaving uncertainty about who later reported the incident to the SS.

As the Russians move westward across Germany, new prisoners are brought in to Plaszow. The prisoners are forced to strip naked and run laps through the prison yard to test who is fit enough to stay in the labor camp and who must be sent away to the concentration camp. Doctors in lab coats watch the prisoners and direct the ones they think are weak off to holding pens. All of the camp's children are led to trucks and driven away, cheering and waving. The camera follows one boy, Olek Rosner, who runs away and jumps into a latrine to hide; he looks around and sees that the foul pit is filled with other hiding children.

At the train station, Schindler observes the boxcars full of Jews on their way to extermination at Auschwitz, suffocating in the heat while he and Goeth drink iced drinks. He suggests that the soldiers spray down the cars with fire hoses, and the Nazis, amused, agree, even though they argue that it is cruel to give the prisoners hope. They laugh when Schindler has longer hoses brought from his factory to reach the front cars. Schindler openly bribes the soldiers traveling with the train to hose them down.

Schindler is arrested. He is charged with kissing a Jewish girl, though his actual crime might be open bribery. Goeth intercedes with the SS on Schindler's behalf.

In April 1944, to dispose of the bodies of the people killed in the camp and the ghetto, the Nazis begin massive burnings. The ash from the funeral pyres drifts down on Plaszow and Krakow like snow. Schindler sees the decomposing body of the girl in red wheeled past him on a wheelbarrow.

In a conversation with Stern, Schindler explains that he plans to go back to Czechoslovakia after the war, with more money than he could ever spend. In the next scene, he packs suitcases with cash and goes to offer Goeth a bribe to let him keep his workers with him when the camp is closed, instead of sending them away. At this point in the novel, Goeth is in custody of the SS, charged with bribery, while Schindler's bribes were made to others. He and Goeth discuss the price per worker for the bribes. Later, he dictates the names to Stern, who types them out to present at the camp. Together, Schindler and Stern think up the names of every Jewish worker they can remember.

At the bottom of the list, Schindler leaves a space for Helen, Goeth's maid. Goeth is reluctant to let her go, but Schindler offers to cut cards over her. Goeth would like to take her to Vienna, where he plans to live after the war, but he knows he cannot. He thinks that it would be humane to shoot her, but he ends up dealing with Schindler.

The people Schindler has ransomed are put aboard a train sent into the freezing countryside. When the train arrives at Schindler's hometown, Zwittau-Brinnlitz, Czechoslovakia, Schindler meets it at the station. The train holding the women, however, has been misdirected to the extermination camp at Auschwitz. Schindler finds out and drives there while the women are being processed: their hair is cut off and they are stripped and herded into a chamber, presumably for delousing. They believe that this is a ruse: that instead of receiving a forcible shower, they will be subjected to poison gas and thus killed. When the lights go out, there is a horrified collective scream, but they are actually showered with water and not gassed. Walking to their barracks, they can see lines of new arrivals herded gently into a different building, the crematorium that billows smoke. Many of the details are as they appear in Keneally's novel, but there the fear of gassing is described as Pfefferberg's fear, as several cars of men were similarly misdirected to Gröss-Rosen camp for a few days before they were separated from the inmates of that camp and redirected to Brinnlitz.

Schindler talks with an SS officer at Auschwitz, offering him diamonds that the man could use when the war ends. He refuses but offers Schindler "300 units" from the "shipment" he has coming the next day; Schindler holds out for the very same women on his list. They are released. As they are going to their train, soldiers try to take the children out of the crowd. Schindler tells them that the children are needed for the war effort, to polish the insides of shell casings with their little hands.

At his new plant, Schindler announces that guards may not kill workers or enter his factory. He placates the Nazis with ample bribes.

The new factory turns out worthless products. To keep it going and to keep his employees safe, Schindler buys other shells from skilled manufacturers and sends them to the army as his. He also spends millions of reichsmarks (the currency of Germany at the time) in bribes. One day, Stern informs Schindler that he is almost out of money.

The war ends. Schindler addresses the Jews and the guards at his factory. He explains that as of midnight that night, they will be free and he will be hunted as a war criminal. He gives the guards the opportunity to "liquidate" the factory workers, as they have been ordered, but suggests they might leave and return to their families as men, not murderers.

The workers donate the gold from their teeth, which is cast into a ring for Schindler. They all line up outside the plant by his car to see him off, and give him a letter signed by every worker to explain to anyone who captures him how Schindler saved their lives. When Stern gives Schindler the ring, he is moved to tears. He regrets that he spent so much money on foolish things, regrets not spending the money ransoming even more workers. His car, he says, could have saved ten more people; the gold from his Nazi Party pin could have saved two more.

Schindler and Emilie drive away disguised in concentration-camp uniforms. The next morning, a Soviet soldier approaches the factory and tells the "Schindler Jews" that they are free. They do not know where to go, so they walk together across the fields to the nearest town.

Title cards explain that Amon Goeth was arrested in a sanatorium (a therapy center promoting rest and recovery) in Bad Tolz, in Bavaria. He was returned to Krakow and hanged. Schindler's postwar businesses failed, as did his marriage. The scene of the Jews walking across the field changes to color, showing the surviving Schindler Jews at the time of filming.

The living people saved by Schindler approach Schindler's burial spot in Jerusalem, along with the actors who played them in the film, and each lays a stone on the grave, according to tradition. At the end, a rose is put on the monument by Liam Neeson, who played Schindler.

CHARACTERS

Chaja Dresner

Mrs. Dresner is Danka's mother. When she is out on the street during the clearing of the ghetto, a boy in a Jewish police uniform, who the novel explains used to play with her son, hides her and takes his own life into his hands by lying to his superiors to save her.

Danka Dresner

Danka Dresner is the young girl with round glasses who is hidden, during the liquidation of the ghetto, with a neighbor, in a secret place within the apartment wall. The woman accepts Danka but tells her mother that there is no room in the hiding place for her. When Schindler rescues the women on his list from Auschwitz, the guards try to keep the children. Schindler uses Danka as an example to explain how the children's small hands are needed for detail work.

Genia Dresner

Genia Dresner is the name given in the novel for the girl in the red coat. The novel gives more information about her life and how she came to live in the Krakow ghetto. The film, in contrast, shows her only from a distance, from Schindler's point of view, and does not give that information about her. Later, when bodies of the murdered people are being dug up from the woods and burned to hide evidence, Schindler sees Genia's red coat again, on a decaying corpse on a pile.

Amon Goeth

Goeth is the commander of the Plaszow camp, played by Ralph Fiennes in a career-making performance that earned him nominations for Academy and Golden Globe awards. The novel points out how much Goeth is like Schindler, physically as well as in temperament. They are of similar ages, and both enjoy wielding power. However, Goeth represses the guilt that he feels about the ways he treats the Jews under his care. He shoots anonymous people from a distance as if to confirm to himself that he is different from them. As Schindler explains to Helen, Goeth's maid, the fact that he abuses her shows that he thinks about her, and that is why he will not kill her. When thinking about the end of the war, Goeth nearly shows affection toward Helen, but then, remembering their social positions, deals her his most brutal beating yet. He fantasizes about taking Helen with him after the war but sadly admits it would not be possible.

In one scene, Schindler almost persuades Goeth to be more humane to the prisoners by pointing out that mercy is a way of displaying power. Soon after, Goeth is displeased with his orderly, Lisiek, and tries to show forgiveness instead of punishing him. As Lisiek leaves, though, Goeth shoots at him from his balcony, an admission that he is unable to change his sadistic ways.

Helen Hirsch

Played by Embeth Davidtz, Helen is the woman chosen by Goeth to be his maid. He takes out his frustrations on her, sadistically beating her, starving her, and threatening her life while she is working for him. Schindler talks to her confidentially and hears her tell the story of Goeth's abuses, a story that serves as the prologue of the novel but occurs far into the film. He explains to her that Goeth will not kill her, and he kisses her on the forehead to comfort her. Later, she is moved to DEF and is saved.

Albert Hujar

Hujar is an SS officer who is promoted to officer rank for his outstanding work in supervising the building of the concentration camp.

Ingrid

Ingrid is one of Schindler's German mistresses.

Wiktoria Klonowska

Wiktoria (called Victoria in the novel), a Polish woman, is Schindler's personal secretary. Schindler is having an affair with her, and he sets her up in an apartment. She is aware that Schindler is married, and his wife is likewise aware of the affair.

Rabbi Menasha Lewartow

Rabbi Lewartow (in the book, his name is spelled Levartov) is a rabbi who is hidden in Plaszow as a metalworker. Goeth is suspicious of him and tells him to make some hinges, timing the rabbi as he forms two hinges. At one minute per hinge, Goeth explains, he should have many more fabricated for his day's work. He takes Lewartow outside to shoot him, but when two pistols refuse to fire, he lets Lewartow live. After the move to Czechoslovakia, Schindler gives the rabbi time to celebrate the Sabbath on Friday evening and provides him with wine for the ceremony.

Mr. Löwenstein

Mr. Löwenstein, played by Henryk Bista, is the one-armed old man who is ushered into Schindler's office to thank him for his job at DEF. He is murdered by Nazi soldiers when he is unable to keep up with their forced snow-shoveling detail.

Regina Perlman

Played by Bettina Kupfner, Regina Perlman is a woman who has managed to escape the roundup of the Jews by passing as a South American living in Krakow under the name of Rodriguez. She goes several times to DEF to talk to Schindler, to ask him to have her parents moved from the work camp to his factory. Schindler refuses her requests to meet until she approaches him with makeup and fine clothes. He throws her out of his office and refuses to help, but that is just to cover himself, in case she is an SS spy: later he does have her parents transferred.

Poldek Pfefferberg

Played by Jonathan Sagall, Leopold (Poldek) Pfefferberg (as he is introduced in the book) operates as Schindler's man on the street. He is adept at locating black-market items in Krakow. The novel describes how Schindler came to his home to hire Pfefferberg's mother to decorate a new apartment, telling her that it was for his wife, while in reality it was for his secretary and mistress. In the film, Schindler seeks out Pfefferberg, knowing his reputation for obtaining fine black-market goods.

Later, when he is caught out in the street during the clearing of the ghetto, Pfefferberg quickly comes up with a lie and tells Amon Goeth himself that he has been ordered to clear the street: Goeth and the other Nazis laugh at him and let him live.

Pfefferberg comes close to death when he is unable to get a sticker on his identification papers showing that he has an important trade. By profession, he is a teacher, which helps him in the ghetto when he tutors the children of the local Jewish power broker, but his job has no value to the Nazis. Keneally's book explains that Pfefferberg is scheduled for extermination before he lies and explains that he is actually a metal polisher.

Diana Reiter
Reiter is the architectural engineer who tries to warn the Nazis that the barracks they are having built will not stand. Rather than listening to the scientific fact of the matter, Goeth orders Hujar to kill her.

Henry Rosner
Henry Rosner is a violinist, one of the talented musical brothers forced to entertain at Amon Goeth's house.

Leo Rosner
Leopold Rosner is an accordion player, one of the musical brothers forced to entertain at Amon Goeth's house.

Manci Rosner
Manci is Henry Rosner's wife.

Olek Rosner
Young Olek, Henry and Manci's son, avoids capture at Plaszow by jumping into a latrine pit.

Julian Scherner
Scherner is the leader of the SS, the *Oberführer*, in Krakow, Poland.

Emilie Schindler
Oskar Schindler's wife, played by Caroline Goodall, is absent for most of the story, living in Zwittau, Czechoslovakia. They have an open marriage: Emilie knows that Oskar is unfaithful to her with his secretary. She asks him to be faithful to her as a condition of her staying in Krakow, and the next scene is her departure on a train. When Schindler moves his business and people to Czechoslovakia, he reunites with his wife and promises to remain faithful.

Oskar Schindler
The main character of the film, Oskar Schindler, played by Liam Neeson in a performance nominated for an Academy Award, a Golden Globe, and a London Film Critics Circle Award, is a complex man. He is not really a hero, as he himself would probably be first to admit. He is a Nazi Party member and a war profiteer. His infidelity to his wife at the beginning of the film is indicative of his worldview; he does not think he is doing her any harm by living openly with his mistress in Krakow and is surprised to see that she is displeased. Schindler starts out as a man who enjoys the sensual pleasures that money can buy without noticing the other people around him.

In the novel, Schindler's gradual change from greedy businessman to savior is left unexplained. The film is structured to indicate that a sort of friendship develops between Schindler and Stern, the emotionless accountant, and that Schindler eventually sees the Jews who are held in the labor camp through Stern's eyes and not through the perspective of someone like Goeth. As Stern cleverly introduces Schindler to more aspects of Jewish life under the Nazi regime, Schindler softens. An indicator of this is when Stern introduces the one-armed worker, Löwenstein: Schindler knows that a one-armed worker cannot work well at his plant, but Stern just listens to his angry protestations, knowing that the old man's situation will move Schindler, as it does.

Unlike others who have power in Krakow, he retains a sense of humanity, and it grows to a passion. Though at the beginning of the film he is concerned only with money, Schindler ends up going bankrupt in his attempt to save as many Jews as he can. When the war is over, he does not regret the money spent—indeed, he regrets the money *not* spent, looking at the things he could have sold for money to save more and more lives.

Itzhak Stern
Stern is played by Ben Kingsley, a much-decorated actor (who won the Best Actor Academy Award in 1982 for his second film, *Gandhi*). Stern is a Jewish accountant and a member of Krakow's Jewish council; he works to save people from the Nazis. At first, Schindler hires him to help get the DEF factory financed and started. As the business grows, Schindler becomes increasingly reliant on Stern. In the

novel, Stern works at Mazareth's uniform-manufacturing plant within the Plaszow camp, but the film puts the two characters, Stern and Schindler, in closer proximity to each other.

Stern does not show much emotion, but he does understand Schindler. After his initial guardedness, he comes to Schindler again and again with problems as the situation for the Jews becomes more desperate, and Schindler helps him. Stern has no hope that he will survive the war, but Schindler promises to help him, and Stern works to extend that promise to as many other prisoners as he can.

THEMES

Power

The levels of power held by various people in this film are crucial to the story being told. At the very bottom of the social spectrum are the Jewish people, who almost daily lose any social authority they may have had. They are moved from their farms and homes into the ghetto, from there into the work camp at Plaszow, and then on to the concentration camps, where the Nazis plan to obliterate any traces of their existence. Even wealthy Jews face having all they own taken from them, as happens to the family moved out of the apartment Schindler ends up occupying. Politically connected Jews, in the Jewish aristocracy of the Judenrat, find that cooperating with the Nazis only delays their fate, and they end up being treated the same way as those who had no power. The only Jews to end up with any control are those who, like Regina Perlman, are able to hide their Jewish background.

Outside the labor camp, the non-Jewish Poles have power over the Jews, which they flaunt, sometimes throwing mud, but they have no power over the Nazis who have invaded their land. The soldiers follow a military hierarchy that reaches its peak with Amon Goeth within Plaszow and then continues up to the bureaucrats in Berlin. Members of the army, such as Goeth, fear the quasi-military SS organization, which has power to supersede all other authority. Almost everyone follows his or her place in the hierarchy of power except Oskar Schindler, whose power derives from a combination of connections and money.

Money

The film *Schindler' List* shows a society where the monetary system has been rendered irrelevant. The invading Germans, as Keneally explains in the novel, have forbidden Jewish Poles the right to use money, requiring them to trade material goods. Their way of surviving becomes explicit in the scene where a family, being relocated from the ghetto, uses bread to help them swallow jewelry, which they can trade for goods and favors in the prison camp. Schindler is able to fund his enamelware plant only by convincing Jewish investors to give him their now-useless money and accept goods that they can barter on the black market—that is, in sales neither approved nor allowed by the government—in payment.

Black-market goods power this economy. Even those high in the German army can only find serviceable army food and poorly made government-issue clothes. When Schindler offers them fine chocolates, vodka, brandy, cigars, and luxury items, such as the horse saddle he gives to Goeth, they are inclined to allow him to bend the rules.

In the wartime economy, Schindler becomes unimaginably wealthy. During war, few people can afford to pay for manufactured goods, but the government can, and the government can pay outrageous prices in the name of the war effort.

Wars

Schindler's List is a story that occurs during World War II, and the story is driven by the war, but the war is not the story's main point. Audiences do not see any battle scenes, and they only hear about the war in terms of its effects: when the Germans are triumphant, their edicts are law, but as they weaken, changes are made. The Nazis are under increasing pressure to hide evidence of the atrocities at Plaszow, and they respond by digging up ten thousand or more bodies buried in the surrounding forest and incinerating them. As the Russians drive farther into Poland, pressure is put on Goeth to stop his random killings and prepare for the day when he might have to face a war-crimes tribunal. Eventually, the labor camp at Plaszow is disbanded in a desperate attempt to kill all Jews before Hitler's eventual defeat.

READ, WATCH, WRITE

- Watch Alain Resnais's 1955 documentary *Night and Fog*, one of the first films to bring the world's attention to the Nazis' systematic extermination of prisoners at Auschwitz. As you watch it, take notes on the images that Resnais employs. Present your class with a list of scenes in *Schindler's List* that you think were inspired by the cinematography of *Night and Fog*, and explain the visual relationship between the scenes. This documentary does contain some scenes that could be disturbing for younger students.

- Thomas Keneally's *Searching for Schindler* is a companion piece to his novel, detailing how he came to know about Oskar Schindler; how he went about researching the project in Germany, Israel, Poland, and Austria; and his involvement in the film's production. Read *Searching for Schindler* and write an essay that explains how knowing the inside story of Keneally's experience changes the way you think about the film.

- Donna Deutch's 1999 film *The Devil's Arithmetic*, based on a novel by the same name, is a story for young adults about a teenage girl (Kirsten Dunst) who finds herself transported back in time to 1942 and is caught up in the middle of the Holocaust. Watch this film after you watch *Schindler's List* and then lead a class discussion about the pros and cons of making horrifying historical events understandable for young audiences.

- Watch *The Stranger* (1946), which was released the year after World War II ended and which includes footage taken at a concentration camp. Write an essay that compares that film's understanding of the Nazi Holocaust to the way it is portrayed in *Schindler's List*, explaining how you think people understood that situation differently at the times the two films were made.

- The enamel-goods factory that Schindler rented in Krakow, DEF, is open to the public as part of the Krakow Historical Museum. Visit Web sites that take you on a tour of the factory, so that you can get a good sense of what the place is like. Using that video and the film, write an essay about aspects you think the film changed about the place and why.

- Mietek Pemper, who was Amon Goeth's clerk in the book but who does not appear in the film, has written his own memoir of those events, *The Road to Rescue: The Untold Story of Schindler's List* (2011). Read Pemper's book and write a short script based on a scene from it, to be performed live or filmed. If the scene you adapt includes a character from Spielberg's film, try to portray that person differently than the movie actor's interpretation. With a group of students, film the scene and post it on YouTube or your Web page and invite reviews.

- The young-adult classic *The Diary of Anne Frank* has been filmed many times. View several of the versions and create a digital presentation using clips from them that illustrate how time has changed her story. Look for examples of political correctness, changes in setting or clothing, and other differences.

Human Dignity

The basis of this story is a struggle between the Nazi system, designed to erase the humanity of the Jewish people, and the conscience of one man who cannot ignore the human dignity he encounters. Every edict from Berlin that is mentioned in the film is meant to crush the Jews' humanity. They have their rights to participate in society taken away, and then they are crowded into inhumane quarters full of vermin. They are stripped naked and forced to work like animals, and like animals they are disposed of when they are no longer useful.

© AF archive / Alamy

Goeth learns the lesson that this system is meant to teach. Shooting anonymous people from his balcony denies their humanity. The novel discusses several episodes in which Goeth favors his two dogs more than he would a Jew, killing a Jewish worker on one occasion when he finds a flea on his dog. In his tender but twisted scene with Helen Hirsch, Goeth comes close to kissing her before turning away and reminding himself that she is not human.

Schindler has every reason to follow the Nazi program and deny the Jews their human dignity. He profits greatly from the Nazi system, in part because the Nazis provide him with Jewish workers for a fraction of what he would pay for free Polish laborers. Furthermore, the more he acknowledges the Jews, the more danger he brings to himself. He makes his money from the government, which could cancel contracts with him at any time. In the film, he goes to jail for kissing a Jewish girl at his birthday party (the novel explains that this was actually his second arrest, the first being for war profiteering). Schindler has every reason to go along with the Nazi dehumanization of the Jews, but what he

sees in Stern, Hirsch, Pfefferberg, and the rest will not let him.

STYLE

Color

By the time *Schindler's List* was produced in 1993, color film processing had been available for more than fifty years and had been the standard for forty years. In choosing to present his story in black and white, Spielberg sets a tone of mournful nostalgia. A more realistic rendering of these events would force readers to think about what they see in terms of the world they know, but the black-and-white presentation aligns the film with the films that were made in the 1930s and 1940s. To teach his audiences a history lesson, Spielberg sets a historical visual tone.

The technology that was available when this film was made allowed him to highlight the gray tones of the picture with certain elements of color. It starts with a Jewish prayer service presented in color, connecting it to the modern world. The people fade away, as the Nazis hoped to make the entire population fade from the Earth, but the ceremonial candle stays lit and in color, with a life beyond that of any individual person. A lit candle appears in color later in the film, when Rabbi Lewartow is conducting the same ceremony in Schindler's plant.

Most viewers note the striking use of color for the girl in the red coat, Genia Dresner, as Schindler watches the Krakow ghetto being dismantled from his privileged position, on horseback above the city. The use of red draws the viewers' attention to the girl, just as she has Schindler's attention. Rather than explaining that Schindler has learned to differentiate Jews as human beings, or uncharacteristically and dangerously having him express this thought to another person in the film, Spielberg uses this visual technique of color to suggest what is happening in his mind.

Music

The film's background music evokes the mournful tones of traditional Jewish music. It features violin solos by Itzhak Perlman, a Palestinian-born Israeli Jew who is widely recognized as one of the most accomplished violinists alive. Clarinet solos are played by Giora Feidman, an internationally acclaimed virtuoso of Jewish klezmer music. Although the ethnic character of the music is clear, the music itself was composed by John Williams, a longtime Spielberg collaborator who is best known for scoring the soundtracks of blockbusters such as *Jaws*, *Jurassic Park*, and *Raiders of the Lost Ark*.

The solemn violin melodies that dominate the soundtrack are contrasted with the jaunty, silly melodies that are played over the loudspeaker when the Jews are given their physical-fitness exam to determine who is fit enough to live and who is not. The film contrasts the image of these aged and malnourished people stripped of their clothes and forced by doctors to run naked through the mud with the laughing of the prison guards and the lighthearted music being broadcast. This particular event was managed, Keneally explains in the novel, "as one would manage a county fair. . . . Loudspeakers played ballads and Strauss love songs." Spielberg captures the surreal image by bringing lighthearted music into the film but establishing that it is the Nazis imposing this music, in

contrast to the Williams/Perlman melodies that feel natural to the situation.

CULTURAL CONTEXT

Historical Accuracy

Although it is presented as a novel, Keneally's *Schindler's List* was painstakingly researched through dozens of interviews with people who had experienced the events in the book and through historical archives in Europe and Israel. Keneally says in the introduction that he used the techniques of a novel in shaping his work, but he did not fictionalize any of the details.

Zaillian, who won an Academy Award for his screenplay adaptation of the book, took a bit more liberty with the facts in order to present a compelling narrative. Some of these were the sorts of changes screenplays always make, such as limiting the characters shown on screen in order to avoid confusing viewing audiences, who, unlike readers, cannot flip back to see when a character was mentioned earlier. Events that happened to several characters are combined and given to one person. This is particularly evident in the case of Stern, who in the novel is not the same person who works furiously at typing the list, nor does he work as consistently at Schindler's side. (The relationship in the novel is more accurately captured in the film when Schindler has him brought over to meet with him.) The film also limits Schindler's marital indiscretions to just two, with his secretary Wiktoria and the German worker Ingrid, knowing that showing him to be as promiscuous as he is in the book would make it more difficult for audiences to like him or relate to him.

As a historian, Keneally shows interest in the ways that information about the events he describes has come down through the years. He discusses in detail the situation of Mietek Pemper, who did clerical work in the office of Amon Goeth and had a photographic memory, enabling him to recreate facts about the Plaszow labor camp for investigating authorities in later years. He also talks about a man named Babar who sneaked a miniature camera into the labor camp and took photographs of the way the prisoners were treated. Such details are relevant for a written record, but they do not merit inclusion in the film. Babar, in fact, was a member of an underground Zionist group (a Jewish political

© *AF archive | Alamy*

movement that supported self-determination of the Jewish people in a Jewish national homeland) that worked with Schindler and funneled money to him to aid the Jews held at Plaszow. Details like this, factual though they are, would distract moviegoers from the image of Schindler as a brave independent operator. Leaving them out makes the film more engaging while it does not substantially change the facts of the story.

The film ends the story dramatically, with the workers presenting Schindler with a ring made from the gold in their teeth, followed by Schindler and Emilie driving off into the night, possibly facing arrest from authorities who would not know how much good he had done. Keneally's story follows Schindler, his wife, and a small group of Jews who traveled with them to testify about his acts crossing to safety in France. It also includes an epilogue that explains the rest of Schindler's life. It is an anticlimactic ending, certainly less uplifting than seeing the Schindler survivors, nearly half a century later, gathering at his grave to pay tribute to him.

Concentration Camps

According to Mordecai Paldiel, author of *Saving the Jews: Amazing Stories of Men and Women Who Defied the "Final Solution,"* the policy that the Nazi Party had toward Jews in the areas they occupied during World War II can be broken down to four parts. The first part was definition, or determining who was to be categorized as a Jew. The second was expropriation, which meant forcing Jews to give up their possessions. The third was concentration, which meant putting Jews in isolated areas, such as camps and ghettos within cities. The fourth was annihilation, the systematic murder of people on a massive scale. Most of *Schindler's List* takes place in or around the labor camp at Plaszow, where Jews are concentrated but are still kept alive. According to the Web site of the U.S. Holocaust Memorial Museum, there were tens of thousands of such camps, there to isolate not only Jews but also people of different political and social groups, including Communists, gypsies, homosexuals, Jehovah's Witnesses, and others who were branded with practicing "abnormal" behaviors or creeds.

The Jews in this film fear being moved from the forced-labor camp to one of the concentration camps, which, as the war progressed, increasingly became centers for extermination. The first of these centers opened in Chelmno, Poland, in 1941. The method used there was mobile vans, in which prisoners inhaled lethal doses of gas. In 1942, extermination centers were opened at Belzec, Sobibor, and Treblinka, also in occupied Poland; these camps are estimated to have killed more than a million and a half Jews in 1942 and 1943. The largest extermination center was at Auschwitz-Birkeneau. It was here that the Nazis first brought the gas Zyklon B into use for mass killing. Between March and June 1943, large crematoriums were constructed at Auschwitz, to incinerate the bodies of the murdered. Precise records were destroyed before Allied forces liberated the camps, but it is estimated that 1.3 million people were sent to Auschwitz during the war and that, of those, 1.1 million were killed.

CRITICAL OVERVIEW

Critical and public response to *Schindler's List* has been almost universally positive. After its release in 1993, it was nominated for twelve Academy Awards and won seven, including Best Picture, Best Director, Best Adapted Screenplay, and Best Cinematography. In 1998, the American Film Institute, an organization composed of professionals working in the film industry, listed it as number nine in its "100 Years... 100 Movies" survey. A decade later, for the tenth anniversary of the list, *Schindler's List* was even more esteemed, moving up to number eight.

Many critics who reviewed the movie expressed their amazement upon finding that Spielberg, the director of such populist fare as *E.T.: The Extraterrestrial* and *Raiders of the Lost Ark*, could produce such a moving story. Todd McCarthy, in a review for *Variety*, which looks at films from a show-business angle, points out,

> Marked by a brilliant screenplay, exceptionally supple technique, three staggeringly good lead performances and an attitude toward the traumatic subject matter that is both passionately felt and impressively restrained, this is the film to win over Spielberg skeptics.

In a review in the *Chicago Sun-Times*, Roger Ebert, one of the nation's most well-known and

respected film critics, also finds most things about the film admirable, particularly focusing on the work of Spielberg, whom Ebert calls "the author of this film," and the restraint that he used:

> He depicts the evil of the Holocaust, and he tells an incredible story of how it was robbed of some of its intended victims. He does so without the tricks of his trade, the directorial and dramatic contrivances that would inspire the usual melodramatic payoffs. Spielberg is not visible in this film. But his restraint and passion are present in every shot.

When critics took exception to things in the film, their complaints were generally about minor things, tucked into the bottoms of their reviews: minor irritants that bothered them only because of the excellence of the film in general. It was in this spirit, for instance, that the *Washington Post*'s Rita Kempley, praising the film's "ruthlessly unsentimental portrait," notes in one place that "there are many harrowing moments, but Spielberg does not indulge in either self-righteousness or torturous excess, much less his trademark schmaltz and special effects" yet also notes that the ending is too much:

> Both Neeson and Spielberg step out of character, in the first case to give a weepy, melodramatic speech, and Spielberg to add an epilogue that is soothing, but more in keeping with *The Color Purple*. All of a sudden, he's pushing our buttons, which he has thus far resisted so assiduously.

Such minor criticism can be found throughout critical reviews, but the main impression is one of overwhelming admiration for Spielberg and the film.

CRITICISM

David Kelly

Kelly is an instructor of creative writing and literature. In the following essay, he discusses why some people expected the worst when they heard that the adaptation of Schindler's List *would be done by Steven Spielberg and why the strength of the finished project could have been predicted all along.*

When *Schindler's List* was released in 1993, many people were pleasantly surprised. The story, about a Nazi industrialist who gradually learns to value the Jewish people whom his party is systematically exterminating, gives an inside

WHAT DO I SEE NEXT?

- The definitive video record of survivors of the Holocaust is French director Claude Lanzmann's epic documentary *Shoah*. (Shoah is the Hebrew term for the events known as the Holocaust.) This internationally acclaimed nine-hour film, presented in theaters in several parts in 1985, features interviews with dozens of former prisoners, soldiers, citizens, and officers in an attempt to understand what happened and how. It was made over the course of eleven years to archive for future generations the stories of those who lived through these events. The entire film is available on DVD in a four-disc box set from MSI-Eureka.

- After working on Schindler's List and meeting Holocaust survivors, Spielberg started the Survivors of the Shoah Visual History Foundation in 1994, to make a permanent record of the experiences of the 1940s, as Lanzmann's film did. The project was taken over by the University of Southern California in 2006; today, the archived interviews and testimonies can be viewed at the Web site of the University of Southern California Dornsife College of Letters, Arts, and Sciences (http://dornsife.usc.edu/vhi/).

- Several times in Schindler's List, the song "Gloomy Sunday" plays. This is a Hungarian song composed in 1933, and it is reputed to be so powerful in its sadness that it has driven dozens of people to suicide. Keneally explains in the novel that the Rosner brothers play the song repeatedly for Goeth, hoping that he will kill himself. The 1999 German film *Gloomy Sunday*, directed by Rolf Schübel, structures a love triangle around this folk legend, presenting Budapest in the 1930s as a place similar to Krakow. This movie is available from Warner Home Video.

- Italian comic actor Roberto Benigni won Academy Awards for Best Foreign Language Film and Best Actor and created international controversy with his 1997 film *Life Is Beautiful*. Though its events are presented as fantasy, some people thought Benigni was belittling the Holocaust in presenting the seriocomic story of a man in a concentration camp with his wife and son, trying to shield his son from the horrors of war by creating a pretense that what is going on around them is all an elaborate game. This film is available on DVD from Miramax Lionsgate.

- In 1961, director Stanley Kramer assembled an all-star cast including Spencer Tracy, Maximilian Schell, Judy Garland, William Shatner, and Montgomery Clift for *Judgment at Nuremberg*, a fictionalized account of the international war tribunal that brought the survivors of the Nazi regime to justice. It was nominated for eleven Academy Awards and is available on DVD from MGM.

- In the 1990s, hundreds of thousands of people were killed systematically in a modern-day mass genocide that lasted one hundred days and left an estimated 800,000 people dead when the Hutu people tried to eliminate the Tutsi tribe in Rwanda. The 2005 film *Hotel Rwanda*, available from MGM Video, tells the fictionalized story of a hotel manager who tried to provide refuge for roughly 1,200 Tutsis, mirroring Schindler's heroism and desperation.

- Steven Spielberg's next film as a director after *Schindler's List* was *Amistad*, released in 1997, concerning a mutiny by West African slaves on a ship bound for the United States in 1839 and the ensuing legal battle that took the issue of slaves' rights to the U.S. Supreme Court. It stars Morgan Freeman, Matthew McConaughey, Djimon Hounsou, and Anna Paquin. Spielberg's production company, Dreamworks, released it on DVD in 1999.

look at one of recent history's bleakest moments. It seemed a bad fit for the great but presumably narrow talents of Steven Spielberg, a populist director who could be counted on to give people what they wanted, not necessarily what they needed.

Spielberg's films had established new records for ticket sales, but his works showed none of the sensitivity needed for dealing with a subject as intense as genocide, regardless of the depth of his personal connection to the subject. When *Schindler's List* was filmed, he had done a variety of films, but he was best known for *Jaws*, which started the trend of mindless blockbuster summer entertainment that has become the film industry's business model today; for the science-fiction tales *Close Encounters of the Third Kind* (a popular movie about common adults fighting the government to protect an alien special-effects extravaganza) and *E.T.* (an even more popular movie about common children fighting the government to save an alien creature); and for *Raiders of the Lost Ark*, which treats Judaism as magic for fighting wooden, stereotyped Nazis. It is understandable that people might have feared that the heroic aspect of Oskar Schindler's story could tilt Spielberg toward sentimentality or sensationalism. Looking back, though, it is easy to see that this project was naturally suited for his kind of storytelling talents all along.

The book on which the movie is based is the product of ten years' research, during which Australian author Thomas Keneally traveled the globe, poring over both open and obscure records and interviewing dozens of the people who lived through the story's events. Keneally's facts are meticulously assembled. Many are anecdotal, relying on forty-year-old memories, but it is hardly likely that the stories that the survivors told him were dimmed by time— systematic debasement and attempted extermination are the sorts of things that would stay clear in the mind over any period of time. Nonetheless, Keneally chose to present his work as a novel rather than as a history.

Doing so brought emphasis onto the unknowable aspects of the story. *Schindler's List*, the book, contains direct dialogue that was not recorded at the time it was spoken and puts thought into the minds of participants, such as Oskar Schindler, who were dead when Keneally did his research. To weave the given materials into a coherent story, Keneally needed to make some educated guesses and fill in missing information as honestly as he could. Now, nearly twenty years after he wrote, it seems quaint that Keneally would sheepishly confess to blending novel-writing techniques with documented testimony, when creative nonfiction is now commonly recognized as a fourth genre in creative-writing classes, along with poetry, fiction, and drama. Keneally's choice to identify such a richly researched work as a novel, revealing a sharp awareness of the line between fact and fiction, appears to have been influential in enlisting Spielberg and screenwriter Steve Zaillian for the film.

Of course, the film makes changes from the facts of Keneally's story. Film is a visual medium that requires ideas to be turned into representative objects or spoken aloud as dialogue. The film cannot, for instance, bog itself down with the costs of things, as the novel often does, but it can convey the richness of objects by lingering over their fine details, as Spielberg does with the establishing shots of Schindler dressing, or with repetition, as Spielberg does by showing SS officers consuming one tub after another of iced champagne. The misery that Keneally renders in the horrifying facts of the situation are brought alive with close-ups of frightened grimy faces and long snaking lines that show people treated like disposable objects. Printed words saying that a character was shot make far less impression than a loud bang and a spurt of blood. Spielberg is a master director, but the fireworks of his previous films made some people tend to forget how natural and fluid he can be at turning concepts into visual statements.

The changes that the film makes to the story are necessary, but they are kept to a minimum. Keneally's book reads like the product of a long trail of research that it is: it reaches its effect cumulatively, stacking one tale from the ghetto, work camp, and concentration camp upon another, creating a mosaic for readers about what happened in that place at that time. The film needs to cut through some of that complexity if viewers are to sit through it for three hours without taking notes. Characters are dropped and events from the book happen to characters who are not called by their names; movie audiences would focus too much on characters with names, thinking that they might have to remember them, when that character might not ever show up again.

Filming at Birkenau concentration camp (© *Daily Mail* / *Rex* / *Alamy*)

In true cinematic tradition, Spielberg coalesced all of the action around the principal actors: leading man Liam Neeson, consummate professional Ben Kingsley, and relative newcomer Ralph Fiennes. This is the way that movies create a personal bond with their audiences, but it also serves to simplify the story. When viewers lose the thread of what is happening, they can still follow the action by remembering that Neeson is the good character, Fiennes is the bad character (each with a range of moral ambiguity), and Kingsley is the oppressed character who controls more than he would ever admit. Stories from the book that fit into this basic structure are kept, even if it means fudging the facts and giving Kingsley's character some actions that actually happened to others, or having Fiennes's character talk about things that the novel says he conveyed in letters. These minor changes make the film sensible without doing any significant damage to the historical accuracy of what Keneally recorded.

The films that made Spielberg the success that he was, and made critics wary of his ability to muster the seriousness for a project like *Schindler's List*, relied on fantasy: the two released just before *Schindler's List* relied on dinosaurs coming alive and on Peter Pan, grown up and boring, returning to the joys of his childhood. Even his previous World War II film, *Empire of the Sun* (written by Tom Stoppard and adapted from a J. G. Ballard novel), leaned toward the theme of childhood innocence struggling with the grown-up world. And so it was legitimate to expect that the Holocaust could be used, like the Nazis in *Raiders of the Lost Ark*, as just a foil, to give the heroes something to fight.

But Keneally wove his reality tightly in the source material for *Schindler's List*. Page after page the testimony piles up, given only the minimum of shaping by the novelist. Spielberg and Zaillian followed this style, letting the stories speak for themselves as much as they could. The resulting film could have been awful, a bad mix of fantasy and horror that used facts to milk cheap emotion. Instead, *Schindler's List* marks the first time Spielberg let his remarkable talent as a director take a backseat to the story. His respect for the Jewish people, being Jewish

> YET MUCH OF THAT DISCOURSE ABOUT 'CORRECT' AND 'APPROPRIATE' REPRESENTATION HAS HAD TO DO WITH BROADER ISSUES ABOUT HISTORY AND FILM, HISTORIANS AND FILMMAKERS—ABOUT THE WILLINGNESS TO ALLOW ALTERNATIVE VOICES TO ADDRESS THE PAST."

himself, and what happened to them under the Nazis made him reverent to reality above all else. As with many artists, the limitations he had to work with required new depths of creativity: the resulting film is horrifying, but also intelligent and beautiful.

Source: David Kelly, Critical Essay on *Schindler's List*, in *Novels for Students*, Gale, Cengage Learning, 2012.

Barbie Zelizer

In the following excerpt, Zelizer explores the idea of Spielberg as a historian versus an image-maker.

HISTORIANS VERSUS IMAGE-MAKERS

. . . But that was not to say that Spielberg became a historian. While certain critics admitted that Spielberg was "doing a service to history" or that he "had brought history and film into rough but proper alignment," the role of historian was largely denied him. One critic, for instance, asked rhetorically whether Spielberg was restricted by the limitations of popular culture: "Will audiences ask themselves the awful questions about betrayal, brutality, and ethnic hatred that attend the Holocaust?" he wondered. "Or will they emerge speechless from the theatre, dab their tears and be glad they escaped so easily?"

So who did Spielberg become? Much discourse hinged on some discussion of the moving image and the visual media, as observers sought to elaborate the ways in which the visual image offered a different form of historical accounting. German critic Andreas Kilb was quoted as having claimed in *Die Zeit* that with *Schindler's List*, the "question of whether the mass murder of the Jews can be represented by the moving image has been impressively and finally answered."

Reviewers paused to celebrate the attributes of the medium of film, raising potentially important questions about the opening of history to an array of visual records. Spielberg demonstrated "the power of the filmmaker to distil complex events into fiercely indelible images." Yet while *Schindler's List* was said to "enlarge the potential of the medium itself—to teach as well as entertain, to evoke history as much as fantasy," reviewers did not fully welcome its wider list of attributes. Rather, they tended to take the narrow view, emphasizing pedagogy over entertainment, historical fact over fictional construction. *Schindler's List* was evaluated in conjunction with only a certain type of image—a fact-based one that differed from earlier Spielberg productions. In shooting footage for *Schindler's List*, then, "authenticity was the goal." Again, Spielberg himself was quoted widely for his quest to use the film "to tell the truth."

Why did discourse move rapidly away from discussions of the potentially variegated use of visual images by the makers of popular culture—a use that could be both entertaining and serious, both dramatic and informative—and substitute for it flattering discussions that assumed, or at least tried to find evidence for, an absolute "fact-based" use of images? This chapter suggests that by evaluating popular culture *as* history, and *on history's terms*, observers in effect underplayed the ability of popular culture to provide *both* entertainment and historical understanding, *both* fiction and fact. By presuming that it separated rather than melded fact and fiction, observers evaluated popular culture on what were essentially alien terms. The very effort to make it appear less "popular" thus deflated its authority in addressing this event.

This was accomplished by providing two alternative frames through which the public was expected to interpret the actions of Steven Spielberg. Both frames made reasonable the assumption that Spielberg had caught the horror of the Holocaust "with no preaching, no interpreting, no kitsch, just images." Moreover, both frames were significant because they dissociated Spielberg from the fictionalizing practices of Hollywood moviemaking: By linking the director with communities known best for the factual tenor of their images, these frames helped position *Schindler's List* in a light in which it could be more effectively appropriated as an apparent "historical fact."

One such community of image-makers was that of documentary filmmakers. Accounts addressed at some length Spielberg's so-called obsession with documentary style. He was compared with filmmaker Sergei Eisenstein or with the Italian Neorealist filmmakers. Observers lauded the fact that he had shot the "first half of the movie almost as a documentary, focusing on the Holocaust and leaving Schindler on the sidelines." In one view, the film eschewed storyboards and zoom lenses, displaying "no fancy camera work." Accounts dwelled on the fact that Spielberg had used little-known actors and actresses or that he had relinquished half his "tool box" to use wobbly "hand-held" cameras. Similarly, observers praised his decision to shoot his scenes in black-and-white, with *Premiere* magazine calling the movie a "tribute to the heritage of the black-and-white film." It "unfolds like a simulated documentary." One journal lauded the film's "highly realistic tone" and "touches of cinema verité"; another applauded its "crisp, stark look."

Spielberg himself upheld his image as a documentary filmmaker. He admitted, "I didn't really plan a style. I didn't say I'm going to use a lot of hand-held cameras. I simply tried to pull the events closer to the audience by reducing the artifice." During the film's shooting, he went on record as saying that he expected the final product to be 30 percent hand-held, which would "take a coat of wax off the finish"; after the film was finished, he said he had made "a document, not an entertainment." Elsewhere, he admitted that he had "just limited the utensils so the story would be the strength of the piece."

The second community of image-makers with which Spielberg's actions were aligned was that of television or photographic journalists. Here, Spielberg was called an "unblinking reporter." He was a director who attempted to "report the facts" instead of "the drama." The movie was shot, said the *Wall Street Journal*, with the "hurried urgency of news." Certain observers spoke of newsreels—the newsreel-like "angles" and "cutting." *Schindler's List*, said one critic, resembled "a newsreel unearthed after more than a half-century." Others spoke of live television reporting.

Here too Spielberg supported the analogy between his actions and those of visual reporters. He was quoted as saying that he hoped his use of the camera would generate the aura of a CNN news report. He claimed that he saw himself "as a journalist" when making the film. He even went on record telling his actors not to rehearse their scenes because "you can't plan for real."

What does all of this suggest about our recognition of image-makers as alternative voices for the past? Two dimensions of that recognition have been suggested here, and neither of them compliment popular culture. First, while both documentary filmmakers and journalists have come to be seen as slightly elevated above Hollywood directors, neither group has been valued as highly as historians. This means that despite the extensive praise for *Schindler's List* as having offered a popular look at the Holocaust, history—with a capital "H"—has continued to lie elsewhere. It has continued to belong to the historians, who remain the premier "other" against which all alternative voices for the past must compete.

But a second point has been made as well, and it has to do with the illegitimacy of popular culture itself. Discourse about the type of image-making practices employed in *Schindler's List* has dissociated the image-making from Hollywood, suggesting a need to go outside the domain of Hollywood film-making to allow Hollywood a legitimate place in crafting its version of this story. Rather than recognize Hollywood's ability to meld fact and fiction, entertainment and history, observers have tried to reconstruct Spielberg's actions within frames of image-making associated with fact-based discourses. This renders a double-sided insult to popular culture, and particularly to Hollywood, by proclaiming its practices deficient in not one standard but two.

EVERY ONCE IN A WHILE: GIVING PAUSE TO HISTORICAL RECORD

All of this raises serious questions about how we entrust our past to others. Whom do we trust more readily? How do we negotiate trust? And where are the limits of trust in representation?

Much of this may have to do with the shape of Holocaust representation itself. It may be, as Hayden White has argued, that in discussing the Holocaust we have embraced a limiting paradigm that prefers one type of representation of the past over others, recognizing that "the kind of anomalies, enigmas, and dead-ends met with in discussions of the representation of the Holocaust are the result of a conception of discourse that owes too much to a realism that is inadequate to the representation of events." In

Anton Kaes's view, standards of appropriateness in representing these events have developed in accordance with "images that have by now become so conventionalized that they determine what is a 'correct' representation of the period and what is not."

Yet much of that discourse about "correct" and "appropriate" representation has had to do with broader issues about history and film, historians and filmmakers—about the willingness to allow alternative voices to address the past. Not long ago Kaes argued for films on the Holocaust that "challenge the narrowly circumscribed Hollywood conventions of storytelling and not only reflect self-critically on the limits and impasses of film but also utilize its specific potential in the representation of the past." This article has demonstrated that the lack of such films is embedded in a more general ambivalence about the ability of popular culture to legitimately address the past. It suggests a certain rigidity in our acceptance of alternative voices. Even in circumstances which appear to have unidimensionally celebrated the raising of a popular voice in retelling a story of the Holocaust, we have in fact framed our acceptance in ways that make such retellings more like history and less like popular culture.

Shortly after *Schindler's List* was released, *Time* magazine used the opportunity to reflect generally upon the role of Hollywood in addressing the story of the Holocaust. For Hollywood film makers, it said, history was "essentially set decoration, something shimmering and elegant to place behind the well-spoken characters" of movies that come out every once in a while.

Admittedly, popular culture cannot provide an ongoing, continuous, or complete record of the past. Nor can it, by virtue of its own practices of representation, offer a record that boasts fidelity to the facts as they took place. But the function of popular culture's representations—representations that appear "every once in a while"—has been to give pause to the ongoing record of historical events provided elsewhere. The explicit function of popular culture, therefore, should be not only to shake up the public and rattle its sensibilities about the content of the past but also to generate questions about the form of the past. "Every once in a while," then, might help a public think about *how* they speak for the past—to whom they allow access and from whom they deny it.

Admitting such an authority for popular culture would allow it a voice that the ongoing comparison between popular culture and traditional history has muted. To allow it, however, we need first to rearrange the disjunctions of identity through which discourse about popular culture and the past has been traditionally constructed. We need to relinquish the distinction between traditional historians and image-makers so as to allow the latter more of a place in discourse in accordance with their own merits. Similarly, we need to mute discussions of one's "old" and "new" styles of popular cultural production, facilitating a better and more effective understanding of the ebb and flow of diverse relations to the past via representation, even when such fluidity occurs within one director, one novelist, one playwright.

Yet finally, and most importantly, if we are to allow popular culture its own voice in representing the past, there is one distinction that we need to reinstate. We must build again that distinction between the event-as-it-happened and the event-as-it-is-retold. And once we have done so, we need to recognize that we can never do better than the latter. In all modes of historical recounting, including traditional history, the event-as-it-is-retold is as close as we can come.

Source: Barbie Zelizer, "Every Once in a While: *Schindler's List* and the Shaping of History," in *Spielberg's Holocaust*, edited by Yosefa Loshitzky, Indiana University Press, 1997, pp. 18–35.

Ora Gelly

In the following excerpt, Gelly posits that by personalizing the Jewish victims, Schindler's List *can successfully link the historical past with the viewers' present.*

... Other critics have taken a very different position, namely, that it is precisely through personalizing the Jewish victims that films or television narratives about the Holocaust can successfully create a link between the historical past and the viewer's present. For instance, both Michael Geisler and Andreas Huyssen have argued that the huge success of the American television series *Holocaust* in Germany in the late 1970s was in part based on the fact that the drama established the Jewish characters as subjects and solicited the audience's identification with them (Geisler 220–60; Huyssen 117–36). For Geisler "Alltagsgeschichte, i.e., the representation

IN *SCHINDLER'S LIST* THE PERPETRATORS ARE THE FORCE WHICH DRIVES THE FILM'S AESTHETIC AND ITS NARRATIVE PLEASURE, WHILE THE VICTIMS STAND UNMOORED, CONDEMNED TO A SILENCE WHICH IS INVESTED WITH THE ENTIRE BURDEN OF THE INCOMPREHENSIBILITY OF THE EVENTS OF THE HOLOCAUST."

of history through personal testimony and in terms of the discourse of everyday life," is the most promising method for a historicization of the Holocaust that retains a sense of urgency and immediacy. Yet, such an approach to historical representation—and here is where his position most markedly differs from Elsaesser's—must be inclusive of both the perpetrators' and victims' stories. Geisler cites the German teleplay director Egon Monk, who "took issue with the contention that the Holocaust could not be represented in fiction because it exceeded our imaginative capabilities. 'The horror was not incomprehensible, but physical, tangible, it was experienced in the most terrifying sense of the word. The suffering was not nameless, it had a million names. Nothing exceeded the imagination of our contemporaries, not does it exceed our imagination. Only what human beings can imagine, will actually happen'" (qtd. in Geisler 252). Geisler and Monk reject the assumption that it is the victims who are invested with the full weight of the incomprehensibility of the events of the Holocaust. Not only is this assumption in itself open to debate, but too often it becomes the basis upon which a critic or filmmaker avoids addressing the issue of how the victims are—or are not—to be integrated into a particular representational text.

In the case of *Schindler's List* there is a fundamental conflict between, on the one hand, the film's solicitation of the viewer through character focalization and through a mode of narration which gives the impression of depicting events 'as they happened,' and, on the other, its attempt to convey a sense of the Holocaust as a whole, in effect, to monumentalize it. In the train car episode discussed above Spielberg attempts

to incorporate into a complexly structured narrative a representation of what has been historically established regarding the abject victimization of the Jews. But this representation is forced to utilize de-realized, spectral images of faces and body parts, as in the quasi-surrealist image of the anus reaching out from the train. This technique of abstraction, in its marked contrast to the segment's dominant mode of narration, is perhaps meant to reveal the gap between the position of the victims and that of the perpetrators. Yet the scene so markedly aestheticizes the image of the Jews, derives it, as it were, from an iconography of martyrdom, that, I would argue, it disallows the kind of empathetic response that is solicited for the principle narrative agents.

I want to return to a consideration of the film's representation of violence as developed in the analysis of the sequence involving Goeth's abuse of his maid, Helen Hirsch. As I have tried to demonstrate, sexuality and violence are imbricated in this segment by means of the editing structure and the mise-en-scene and framing. Although on the level of the narrative the viewer is meant to recoil from Goeth's sadistic violence against the Jews, in many cases the camera is so intensely focused on his overt sexualization of acts of violence and murder that the film obscures the horror of these acts, and instead induces a fascination with the Nazi commander's poses and the spectacle of bodies as revealed in his contact with others. One of the most problematic portrayals of Goeth's sadism and violence is the scene immediately following the ghetto liquidation, where we are introduced, through Goeth's point of view, to the Plaszow forced labor camp. This scene depicts Goeth's brutal murder of two camp inmates through an alternating sequence of shots which move back and forth between an intensive focus on Goeth's face and body—on his physical gestures in relation to his gun and cigarette; point of view shots of his gaze through the scope of his rifle; and shots of his nearly naked mistress in bed.

In this scene the camera is so powerfully focused on Goeth's bodily movements that the viewer altogether loses sight of the position of the victim. The point is not merely that the killings are shown through Goeth's optical point of view. As has been convincingly argued by others in relation to the horror genre, for example, the fact that acts of violence are filmed through the eyes of the perpetrator does not mean that the viewer automatically identifies with him or her rather than with the victim. Yet the fact that the point of view shots in this segment entail a great distance between the eye of the camera and the position of the victim accentuates the focus of the scene on the sexualized bodies of the murderer and his mistress. Although on one level the scene is intended to expose the sadistic brutality of Goeth, its effect is rather one of fascination with his bodily presence, which is here perhaps even stronger than in the scene involving his abuse of Helen Hirsch. In both of these scenes, the overwhelming sense of desire, strength, and (repressed) sexuality skews the narrative's intended judgement of Goeth's brutality. In inducing a captivation with the Nazi aesthetic of violence and sexuality, these scenes contribute to silencing the voice of the victims.

There is, however, one particularly strong moment in the film which shows Goeth's brutal violence without obscuring the pain and suffering of the victim; this is the scene that depicts the commander killing the young Lisiek. The shot structure of the depiction of the murder is unusual, and it is one of the rare moments in the film which reveals a dialectical tension between the position of the perpetrator and that of the Jewish victim, partly because the murder in this scene is not shown directly; we witness it, rather, through the mediation of Stem, whom we see flinch in response to the sound of the gunshot. Then we perceive Lisiek's body on the ground beside him as he passes by it. Stem's restrained response—he knows, as does the audience, that Goeth is watching him—is determined by the Nazi commander's power over him. In this way the segment depicts the disparity between Goeth's position and that of the Jews, without being fixated by the former. By portraying the murder through Stem's perspective—one in which he strongly identifies with the victim while at the same time he is forced to maintain his restraint and self-control—the segment constructs an eyewitnessing position into which the viewer may readily enter.

One of the reasons that the film here overcomes the aestheticization of violence which is in evidence elsewhere is because it can display Goeth's behavior while remaining outside his persona. We are here presented with an image of Goeth's narcissism and megalomania, yet the camera does not—as in other segments—become seduced by the Nazi commander's poses of power

and sexuality. The scene establishes a space outside of the aura of Goeth's body and his gaze, a space in which Lisiek can exist independently. Perhaps part of the reason that the film here succeeds in evoking a larger range of affects in relation to violence than elsewhere is because certain devices, such as the shot reverse shot pattern and the point-of-view shot are avoided. I am not claiming that standardized codes such as the point-of-view shot cannot be effectively used to represent competing perspectives. But in *Schindler's List* it seems that their deployment too often tends to privilege the power and glamor of the Nazis. The positioning of the camera is more indiscernible and unstable than in other moments in the film, and much of the scene's strength lies in its ellipses rather than in what it shows. This type of editing is what Pier Paolo Pasolini would call "obsessive framing." One manifestation of obsessive framing is "the sequential juxtaposition of two insignificantly different points of view of the same image; that is, the sequence of two shots which frame the same piece of reality, first from nearby, then from a bit further; or, first frontally and then a bit more obliquely; or finally, actually on the same axis but with two different lenses. This creates an insistence that becomes obsessive" (184: Lawton and Barnett 179). According to Pasolini "obsessive framing" is proof of another film that the filmmaker would have made without "the pretext of the visual mimesis of his protagonist." In other words, this unrealized, subterranean film is the freed voice of the director (187: Lawton and Barnett 182). The tension between competing viewpoints—that of the camera as it is felt by Amon Goeth's perspective of sadism and violence and that of the director, who here empathizes with the character of Lisiek—manifests itself in the notable elision of the moment of the murder; this is virtually the only point in the film where Spielberg refrains from showing the act of killing.

In the opening paragraphs of her essay on the film Miriam Hansen asks the important question of how popularity as such has shaped the critical accounts of *Schindler's List*. In my discussion of the film and its critical reception I have tried not to lose sight of *Schindler's List*'s status as a product of Hollywood. Although a further consideration of the film's production and reception is highly relevant to my project, I have chosen here to focus on the film text itself, especially its deployment of the visual language and narrative conventions of the Hollywood feature film. The fact that *Schindler's List* has had, and will continue to have, such a tremendous influence on the popular consciousness of the Holocaust makes it all the more important that we take seriously its efforts at "translating" into a popular idiom images and ideas culled from and extensive European and American discourse on the Holocaust. My analysis has focused on some of the difficulties and inconsistencies that arise from the film's attempt to integrate citations from prior texts and images of the Holocaust into a Hollywood aesthetic and narrative structure.

In his *Theory of Film* Siegfried Kracauer discusses the conflict faced by directors of historical films, such as Sergei Eisenstein and D. W. Griffith, between the depiction of a particular idea or story (what he at one point refers to as the "idea conception" of a story) and a specifically cinematic representation of the material world. Although his discussion of this conflict comes out of a comparison of the cinematic versus the theatrical (i.e., uncinematic) story, its relevance in this context is in the author's characterization of the relation in film between form and content. For Kracauer, part of Griffith's ingeniousness—but also his folly—lies in his aspiration to reconcile the requirements of the story with "those arising from the cinema's preference for physical reality." His chase scenes, Kracauer argues:

> seem to transform ideological suspense into physical suspense without any friction; but upon closer examination they represent an excess amount of the latter. Thus the 'last-minute-rescue' in the 'modern story' of Intolerance is by no means a translation into cinematic terms of the conclusion at which the story itself arrives; rather, this finale captivates and thrills the spectator as a physical race between antagonistic forces. It provides sensations which do not really bear on, and bring out, the 'idea conception' of the story—the triumph of justice over the evil of intolerance. The Griffith chase is not so much the fulfillment of the story as a cinematically effective diversion from it. It drowns ideological suspense in physical excitement (228).

My analysis of *Schindler's List* has tried to show that certain elements of the debate regarding the film involve just these kinds of issues, of form versus content, of the film's ability to reconcile the "requirements of the story"—in all their grimness—with those arising from Hollywood's preference for spectacle, excitement, and

glamor, of whether the film is not a diversion from that which it claims to be confronting. Kracauer's criticism of Griffith's chase scenes, finally, has to do with what he perceives as the director's efforts to blend two incompatible modes of representation, in this case the theatrical story and the cinematic narrative.

In *Schindler's List* such an incompatibility between different modes manifests itself most clearly in the film's attempts to integrate the story of the perpetrators with that of the victims. Although the intended narrative message of the film is certainly not one which would have us identify with Amon Goeth, its dominant style—the formal devices just indicated—is more adapted to the narrative of the Nazis than to that of the Jewish victims. The Jewish characters in the film, including Stem, are for the most part depicted as pawns within a narrative which grants them little power or subjectivity. And when the film does attempt to address their experience as distinct from that of the Nazis, for example, in tableau-like scenes that are intended as symbolic representations of the Jewish experience, these have little relation to the main narrative and tend to lapse into mere "backdrop." In *Schindler's List* the perpetrators are the force which drives the film's aesthetic and its narrative pleasure, while the victims stand unmoored, condemned to a silence which is invested with the entire burden of the incomprehensibility of the events of the Holocaust.

Source: Ora Gelly, "Narration and the Embodiment of Power in *Schindler's List*," in *Film Criticism*, Vol. 22, No. 2, 1997, p. 2.

SOURCES

"AFI's 100 Years . . . 100 Movies: 10th Anniversary Edition," in *American Film Institute*, 2007, http://www.afi.com/100years/movies10.aspx (accessed June 8, 2011).

"Auschwitz," in *Holocaust Encyclopedia*, United States Holocaust Memorial Museum Web site, http://www.ushmm.org/wlc/en/article.php?ModuleId=10005189 (accessed June 16, 2011).

Ebert, Roger, Review of *Schindler's List*, in *Chicago Sun-Times*, December 15, 1993, http://rogerebert.suntimes.com/apps/pbcs.dll/article?AID=/19931215/REVIEWS/312150301 (accessed June 8, 2011).

Harris, Tom, "How Steadicams Work," in *HowStuffWorks*, http://entertainment.howstuffworks.com/steadicam.htm (accessed June 8, 2011).

Kempley, Rita, Review of *Schindler's List*, in *Washington Post*, December 15, 1993, http://www.washingtonpost.com/wp-srv/style/longterm/movies/review97/schindlerslistkemp.htm (accessed June 8, 2011).

Keneally, Thomas, *Schindler's List*, Touchstone Books, 1982, pp. 259–60.

"Killing Centers: An Overview," in *Holocaust Encyclopedia*, United States Holocaust Memorial Museum Web site, http://www.ushmm.org/wlc/en/article.php?ModuleId = 10005145 (accessed June 16, 2011).

McCarthy, Todd, Review of *Schindler's List*, in *Variety*, November 19, 1993, http://www.variety.com/review/VE1117487981?refcatid = 31 (accessed June 8, 2011).

Mikkelson, Barbara, and David P. Mikkelson, "Gloomy Sunday," in *Snopes.com*, May 23, 2007, http://www.snopes.com/music/songs/gloomy.asp#refs (accessed June 8, 2011).

"Nazi Camps," in *Holocaust Encyclopedia*, United States Holocaust Memorial Museum Web site, http://www.ushmm.org/wlc/en/article.php?ModuleId = 10005144 (accessed June 16, 2011).

Paldiel, Mordecai, *Saving the Jews: Amazing Stories of Men and Women Who Defied the "Final Solution,"* Schreiber, 2000, pp. 17–18.

"Rwanda: How the Genocide Happened," in *BBC News*, December 18, 2008, http://news.bbc.co.uk/2/hi/1288230.stm (accessed June 8, 2011).

Schindler's List, DVD, Universal Studios, 2005.

FURTHER READING

Bergen, Doris L., *War and Genocide: A Concise History of the Holocaust*, 2nd ed., Rowman & Littlefield, 2009.
   Keneally's novel is meticulous about its facts, but it sometimes requires readers to have prior knowledge of the events referenced in the story. This book offers a clear, direct summary of how the Holocaust transpired, showing how the unimaginable became the mundane.

Crowe, David, *Oskar Schindler: The Untold Account of His Life, Wartime Activities, and the True Story Behind the List*, Basic Books, 2007.
   All those who knew him agree that Schindler was a guarded, enigmatic man. Still, this massive biography offers readers the best insights available into his personality.

Levi, Primo, *Survival in Auschwitz*, CreateSpace, 2011.
   Levi, who lived through the concentration camp system, was one of the greatest writers of his time. This memoir, which was first published in 1957 as *If This Is a Man*, stands above many others that have been published for the insight it gives about the systematic destruction that was wrought and the survival of the human spirit.

Schindler, Emilie, *Where Light and Shadow Meet: A Memoir*, W. W. Norton, 1997.
   Throughout the movie, Oskar Schindler's wife is a shadowy presence, only appearing on a few scenes. This autobiography fills out more of her story, offering students greater insight into Schindler and the times.

SUGGESTED SEARCH TERMS

Schindler's List

Spielberg AND Schindler

Oskar Schindler AND Amon Goeth

Krakow AND ghetto

SS AND bribery

Keneally AND Spielberg

Shoah Foundation Institute

Schindler AND Krakow

Plaszow AND Auschwitz

Nazi Holocaust AND labor camps

Schindler's List AND Holocaust

concentration camp

The Shipping News

ANNIE PROULX

1993

Winner of the 1993 National Book Award for Fiction and the 1994 Pulitzer Prize for Fiction, Annie Proulx's novel *The Shipping News* is a stylistically distinct work that explores one man's search for a sense of identity, family, and home. The main character, known throughout the work by his last name, Quoyle, is depicted as the hapless son of cruel and unloving parents. After his tortuously unhappy marriage ends with his wife's death, Quoyle, accompanied by his aunt, takes his two young daughters to the remains of the family home in Newfoundland, Canada. Here he is bombarded with a family history largely unknown to him and unrelentingly unpleasant. Having nowhere else to go, Quoyle attempts to find his place in the town his distant relatives once called home. With the help of his aunt, Quoyle manages to find a job and to make the run-down ancestral home habitable. Despite Quoyle's sense of isolation, through his work at the local paper he begins to create a new version of himself, discovering that he has abilities he was previously unaware of, and that he has the capacity to foster new relationships, and even to fall in love again.

Proulx explores the dynamics of these relationships and creates a distinct sense of place through the use of unconventional prose. Her language is poetic, her imagery startling, and her syntax (the arrangement of words and phrases in sentences) unique. Although Quoyle and his family are marked by misfortune, and

began a doctoral-degree program there as well but left the program before completing her dissertation. For a time, Proulx resided in Vermont, where she began a career as a freelance writer. At this time, she also began writing short fiction. Her first collection, *Heart Song, and Other Stories*, was published in 1988.

Proulx then began work on a novel; *Postcards* was published in 1992. Having won critical praise for both works, she continued to write short fiction and novels. She published *The Shipping News* in 1993. The work won the National Book Award in 1993 and the Pulitzer Prize for Fiction in 1994 and was adapted into a feature film by Miramax Pictures in 2001. Another of Proulx's works of fiction, the short story "Brokeback Mountain," which was published in the 1999 collection *Close Range: Wyoming Stories*, was also adapted into a feature film in 2005. As of 2011, Proulx lived in Wyoming. She published her memoir *Bird Cloud* in 2011.

Annie Proulx (© Allstar Picture Library / Alamy)

their dark history is tainted with violence and aberrant behavior, Proulx injects hints of hopefulness throughout the novel.

AUTHOR BIOGRAPHY

Born on August 22, 1935, in Norwich, Connecticut, to George and Lois Proulx, Edna Annie Proulx (Proulx rhymes with "true") was the firstborn of five daughters. Proulx grew up in a variety of locations throughout New England as well as in North Carolina, as her father's career in textiles forced the family to move frequently. After studying at Colby College, in Waterville, Maine, Proulx completed her bachelor-degree studies at the University of Vermont, in Burlington, in 1969. The same year, she married James Hamilton Lang, with whom she would have four children. The couple divorced in 1990.

In Montreal, Proulx attended Sir George Williams University (now Concordia University), where she earned her master's degree in 1973. She

PLOT SUMMARY

Chapters 1–5

In the opening chapters of *The Shipping News*, the reader is given a brief account of Quoyle's dreary youth and young adulthood. He is presented as an awkward, heavyset, self-conscious young man whose failures are repeatedly pointed out to him by his disappointed father. Quoyle is thirty-six years old when he departs for Newfoundland. The events leading up to his decision to leave are then narrated, beginning with Quoyle meeting Partridge at a laundromat in Mockingbird, New York. Partridge and his wife Mercalia take the unemployed and friendless Quoyle under their wings and help him find a job with a small local newspaper. For a time, he was repeatedly fired and rehired at the paper. After Partridge and Mercalia leave Mockingbird, Quoyle meets a woman named Petal Bear. After a passionate month together, the couple decides to marry, at which point Petal loses all interest in Quoyle. Over the next six years, they have two children together, but Petal has no interest in them either. Not only does she cheat on Quoyle repeatedly, but she also fails to hide her infidelity, even bringing strange men back to their own home. Quoyle endures it all, hoping that Petal will see his devotion and suffering and be moved to love him again.

MEDIA ADAPTATIONS

- Proulx's novel was adapted for film by Robert Nelson Jacobs in 2001. *The Shipping News* was directed by Lasse Hallstrom and distributed by Miramax Films. Featuring an all-star cast, including Kevin Spacey as Quoyle, Julianne Moore as Wavey, Judi Dench as Agnis, and Cate Blanchett as Petal, the film was nominated for two Golden Globes. The DVD of this film was released by Miramax in 2002.

- *The Shipping News* is available in an abridged audiocassette and audiobook format, read by Robert Joy. The cassette version of the novel was published in 1995 by Simon & Schuster Audio, and the same recording became available on CD in 2001.

- An unabridged Audible Audio version of *The Shipping News*, read by Paul Hecht, was published by Simon & Schuster Audio in 2011. Audible Audio books are downloadable as MP3 recordings.

Quoyle receives a message on his answering machine from his father, informing him that his parents, both suffering from cancer, are killing themselves. Quoyle's brother Dicky has no interest in helping Quoyle with funeral arrangements. His father's sister, Agnis Hamm, sends a note, saying she is on her way to help Quoyle. Before she arrives, Petal disappears, taking the children with her. Quoyle knows something is wrong, for Petal never took the children anywhere or cared for them in any way. Aunt Agnis arrives before the children or Petal are found. Agnis briefly discusses with Quoyle their family history, revealing that Quoyle's grandfather sired Quoyle's father at the age of twelve. Soon after Agnis's arrival, the police inform Quoyle that Petal has been in a car accident, broken her neck, and died. Their investigation reveals that Petal has sold the children. The two daughters, Bunny and Sunshine, are found unharmed, but Quoyle is horrified at the clear intentions the man had toward the children. Quoyle asks Aunt Agnis to stay and

help. She agrees, and she then persuades him to come with her to Newfoundland to make a fresh start. Partridge refers Quoyle to a local newspaper in the town of Killick-Claw, where he might find work. Quoyle, his aunt, her dog Warren, and Bunny and Sunshine arrive in Newfoundland. There they drive out to the remote family home on Quoyle's Point. They assess the dilapidated state of the home and discuss the repairs that need to be made.

Chapters 6–10

As Quoyle and his family attempt the hazardous drive back into town during a storm, they shelter for a night at a motel. Bunny is plagued by nightmares. In Killick-Claw, Quoyle applies for a job at the *Gammy Bird* newspaper. At the paper's small office, Quoyle meets the other employees, who eventually become his close friends, including Billy Pretty, Tertius Card, Beaufield Nutbeem, and Jack Buggit, who runs the paper. Quoyle is hired and assigned automobile accidents and the shipping news. Despite Quoyle's fear of the water, his aunt insists that he buy a boat, as the distance between the home on Quoyle's Point and the town of Killick-Claw is more quickly covered by sea than by rustic road. They agree to live temporarily at a motel. After meeting the harbormaster and learning what he should cover for the shipping-news column, specifically arrivals and departures in the port town, Quoyle buys an inexpensive boat but is soon informed by Jack Buggit that the boat is not seaworthy. During the course of his travels through town, Quoyle repeatedly spies a woman who seems mysterious to him; he becomes secretly fascinated with her. As Aunt Agnis is, like Quoyle, attempting to establish herself in Killick-Claw (she is in the upholstery business), she arranges for child care for Bunny and Sunshine with a woman she has met, Beety Buggit, the wife of Dennis Buggit. Dennis is Jack's son, and it is rumored that father and son do not see eye to eye on most matters. Aunt Agnis's dog Warren dies, and Agnis buries the animal at sea.

Chapters 11–15

At the house on Quoyle's Point, Agnis reveals the depths of the animosity she bears toward her dead brother, Guy (Quoyle's father), when she dumps his ashes into the outhouse and urinates on them. Only the existence of this hatred has been hinted at thus far, not its source. Quoyle spends his days helping to repair the house and learning how to navigate his boat. He learns the mysterious woman's name, Wavey Prowse, and that of her young son, Herry. It is later revealed that Herry has Down's syndrome. For the shipping news, Quoyle interviews a couple whose boat is docked in the port. The boat was previously owned by Hitler, and Quoyle interviews the boat's wealthy owners, the Melvilles, discovering that his aunt has been hired to reupholster the boat. Agnis's conversation with Quoyle reveals that her beloved dog was named after her lover, Warren. Her private thoughts explain further that her significant other was a woman named Irene Warren. As Quoyle plays with his daughters, Agnis chronicles her professional and personal life through Warren's death from cancer. Quoyle later shares a brief conversation with Wavey. As Quoyle becomes settled into his new home, he focuses more intently on his daughters and grows concerned about Bunny's nightmares and the apparent visions she has of a white dog that she is convinced wants to bite her. Quoyle shares his concerns with his aunt, who assures him that nothing is wrong with Bunny, even if she is convinced she sees things that others do not.

Chapters 16–20

The comfort Quoyle and his family now feel in Killick-Claw is demonstrated in a scene at Dennis and Beety Buggit's house. The children play while Dennis discusses his near-death experience and how he was saved from drowning by his father. Quoyle enjoys some professional success when he writes an article about the Hitler boat and the Melvilles, the couple who owns the boat. Jack Buggit is impressed with the work, and Quoyle is given permission to write more stories of this kind. At the same time, Quoyle becomes more friendly with Wavey, despite his aunt's efforts to set him up with a woman from her upholstery shop. Bunny's nightmares and visions worsen. Billy Pretty, another writer at the paper, invites Quoyle to come with him to Gaze Island, where Billy's father is buried. During this journey, Billy regales Quoyle with stories about Quoyle's ancestors, and Quoyle is disturbed to hear that his family has a history of violent, deviant behavior.

Chapters 21–25

On their way home from Gaze Island, Quoyle finds a suitcase in the water. After it is hauled on board and Quoyle and Billy make it safely back through a storm that has blown up, Quoyle opens the suitcase and finds the head of Bayonet Melville, the owner of the Hitler boat. Quoyle and Wavey begin spending more time together. On a berry-picking trip with the children and Agnis, Quoyle and Wavey slip away and briefly embrace, but Wavey puts Quoyle off and discusses with him the tragic death of her husband some years earlier. In town, a debate springs up over the possibility of the Canadian government's exploration for oil off the Newfoundland coast, and Quoyle writes a piece for the *Gammy Bird*, taking an environmentalist's slant on the debate. Tertius Card holds opposite views, and he rewrites the article after Quoyle submits it for review.

Chapters 26–30

At work, Quoyle is tasked with writing a new column on the subject of shipwrecks. One weekend on Quoyle's Point, Quoyle decides to explore the area on foot. In the process, he discovers a body floating in the low-tide waters. Despite the rough weather, he heads to Killick-Claw in his boat to alert the authorities. Unable to control his vessel in the turbulent sea, Quoyle is thrown overboard when the boat capsizes. He floats in the freezing water on a cooler that had been in the boat. Jack Buggit, with the same intuition that led him to his drowning son years earlier, finds Quoyle and saves him. The body Quoyle found is revealed to be the headless corpse of Bayonet Melville. The narrative turns to Agnis briefly, where, through her memories, it is revealed that as a child, she was sexually assaulted. Her thoughts turn once again to the present, and after she receives a mysteriously unmarked bundle of money, tied with the upholstery she had used on the Melville yacht, Agnis assumes Mrs. Melville killed her husband but finally paid Agnis for her work. She begins to make plans for the winter, as she and Quoyle's family will not be able to remain in the remote home on the point during the winter. Meanwhile, Quoyle sees Alvin Yark, Wavey's uncle, about having a boat built. Quoyle and the children plan to spend the winter in Nutbeem's trailer, after he leaves for the winter, while Agnis announces she will be taking work in the larger city of St. John's for the season.

Chapters 31–35

Nutbeem's friends throw him a going-away party, which Quoyle attends. The partygoers end up nearly destroying the trailer and succeed in sinking his boat. Quoyle, hungover, begins to start looking for a new place to spend the winter. Recently he has begun to find bits of knotted string. Some was in his boat, before it sunk, and when he returns to Quoyle Point to check on the empty house, he finds more. Quoyle begins to suspect that the string has been left behind by a distant relative that Billy Pretty once told him about, a possibly deranged Quoyle cousin who still lives in a shack near Quoyle's Point. Billy suggests that the cousin, Nolan, might be angry that Quoyle and Agnis have inhabited the house. Quoyle finds the cousin and gently confronts him; the man is old, frail, half-starved, and clearly insane. Quoyle plans to make arrangements to have Nolan cared for. After Quoyle finds a house to rent for the winter, Tertius Card announces that he will be leaving for St. John's to seek other employment. Jack Buggit offers Quoyle Tertius Card's managing-editor position, although he wants Quoyle to continue to do the shipping news.

Chapters 36–39

Quoyle, accompanied by Wavey, goes to St. John's to see the facility where Nolan has been taken and to speak with the cousin one more time. As Nolan's next of kin, he must sign the papers to officially institutionalize the man. Nolan informs Quoyle that Agnis, as a young girl, was raped by her older brother Guy (Quoyle's father). Nolan's wife performed an abortion after Agnis discovered she was pregnant. After Quoyle leaves, he learns that Nolan has become violent, and he decides to sign the paperwork committing Nolan to the institution. While in St. John's, Quoyle and Wavey consummate their romance. Back home, Bunny has gotten in trouble at school for pushing a teacher who humiliated Wavey's son Herry. Quoyle and Wavey become closer, with both discussing the betrayal and tragedies they previously endured. Quoyle continues to work with Wavey's uncle, helping with the boat building. When Quoyle learns that Agnis is coming back for a visit, he and Wavey plan a party for her, during which Wavey gives Bunny and Sunshine a white husky puppy. Bunny's fears of a white dog seem to disappear, although she has a horrible nightmare in which she dreams that the house on Quoyle's Point has been ripped from its foundation by a terrible storm and lost to the sea. Subsequently, a terrible storm rages. Quoyle soon learns that the house has indeed been claimed by the sea after the storm. Agnis has returned to Killick-Claw, and she moves into the apartment above the upholstery shop with one of her coworkers, with whom she has begun a relationship. In the final chapter,

Jack Buggit, who has been seal hunting, has been found dead, apparently drowned. Yet at his wake, attended to by Quoyle, his family, and their whole circle of friends, Jack splutters back to life in his coffin. The medical explanation given is that he survived due to the cold temperatures of the sea. Quoyle and Wavey marry at the novel's conclusion.

CHARACTERS

Petal Bear
Petal Bear meets Quoyle at a meeting he is covering for a newspaper in Mockingbird, New York. Her attraction to Quoyle is short-lived. After a passionate month, the two marry, but Petal loses all interest in Quoyle. She is described as extremely promiscuous, and she does not hide her numerous and frequent sexual encounters with strangers from Quoyle. Although she bears two children to Quoyle, Petal has little interest in the girls and even acts as if she does not recognize them at times. Quoyle's love for Petal is described as "witless," and he will not divorce her. After she runs off and takes the children with her, Quoyle grows concerned. Petal's body is found mangled from a car accident. The money and receipt in her wallet lead the police to the man to whom she sold her daughters.

Beety Buggit
Beety Buggit is the wife of Dennis Buggit. She has a daughter of the same age as Quoyle's daughter Bunny. Beety watches Bunny and Sunshine for Quoyle on a regular basis. After Quoyle nearly drowns and is rescued by Jack, Beety helps take care of Quoyle.

Dennis Buggit
Dennis Buggit is the husband of Beety Buggit and the son of Jack Buggit. The rumor in town is that father and son are at odds with one another, but the men deny this. Dennis once worked at sea, against his father's wishes. When the ship sank, Dennis nearly drowned, but Jack, propelled by a mysterious intuition, found Dennis and saved him. Dennis becomes a good friend of Quoyle's, and in many ways, Beety and Dennis take the place of Mercalia and Partridge in Quoyle's new life. They are the model of a loving couple, and Quoyle and his children feel safe in their home.

Jack Buggit

Jack Buggit is the owner of the *Gammy Bird*. Although his demeanor is rough, he is encouraging toward Quoyle and his writing, and he leaves the paper in Quoyle's hands after Tertius Card, the managing editor, decides to move on. Jack's sixth sense about people leads him to save both his son Dennis and Quoyle from drowning. Jack is plagued, however, by the fact that he was unable to save his other son, Jesson, from drowning years prior to the action of the novel. Jack also nearly drowns and is believed to be dead in the novel's final chapter. Miraculously, he returns to consciousness, waking in his coffin at his own funeral. In many ways, he serves as a father figure for Quoyle.

Jesson Buggit

Jesson was the son of Jack Buggit and brother of Dennis Buggit. He drowns before the novel begins, but his memory continues to haunt his father.

Marty Buggit

Marty is the young daughter of Dennis and Beety Buggit. She becomes Bunny's closest friend.

Tertius Card

Tertius Card, also known simply as Tert, is the managing editor of the *Gammy Bird*. He takes great pleasure in rewriting people's stories, and in doing so, he introduces a plethora of typographical errors into the articles. Jack Buggit, the paper's owner, allows Tert free rein and feels that typos give the paper its character. Tert also rewrites articles to reflect his own views, as he does when he turns Quoyle's pro-environment article on the oil industry into a pro-oil piece.

Agnis Hamm

Agnis Hamm is Quoyle's aunt, the sister of his father. She convinces Quoyle to accompany her to Newfoundland, where she hopes they can both begin a new life. As the story progresses, Agnis's past is revealed, from a childhood during which she endured sexual abuse at the hands of her brother, to the abortion that results from this abuse, to the long-term loving relationship she shared with Irene Warren. For much of the novel, she hides the fact that she is a lesbian. In Killick-Claw, Agnis establishes a new business and finds love once again. She attempts to guide Quoyle into being a strong, purposeful man and helps him in making decisions and in taking care of his daughters.

Bayonet Melville

Bayonet Melville and his wife own a yacht that was once owned by Hitler. When the boat arrives in port, to be upholstered by Agnis, Quoyle interviews the couple. His article on the Melvilles and their boat is his first successful piece written for the *Gammy Bird*. Through the course of the novel, it is revealed that Bayonet has been murdered by his wife. Quoyle finds Bayonet's head in a suitcase and later discovers his body near Quoyle's Point.

Silver Melville

Silver Melville is Bayonet's wife and part owner of the Hitler yacht. Silver revels in the boat's violent history, describing for Quoyle the way the boat destroyed other vessels in a storm off the coast of Maine. Silver later kills and decapitates her husband but nonetheless sends Agnis the money the Melvilles owed for the boat's reupholstery.

Mercalia

Mercalia is Partridge's wife. Although she does not play a prominent role in the novel, her loving relationship with Partridge is regarded as an ideal by Quoyle, whose own marriage is filled with strife, betrayal, and pain.

Mrs. Moosup

Mrs. Moosup is the woman Quoyle hires to help take care of the children while he is at work in New York, as Petal occasionally works but, more often than not, abandons her family for long periods of time. It is Mrs. Moosup who informs Quoyle that Petal has taken the children away.

Beaufield Nutbeem

Nutbeem is an Englishman who has found his way to Killick-Claw. He works for the *Gammy Bird* and primarily writes stories concerned with international news and local sexual-abuse scandals. He is always astounded by the volume and variety of the crimes upon which he reports. He is friendly with Quoyle and invites him to his going-away party after he has decided to leave Newfoundland.

Partridge

Partridge is one of Quoyle's few friends in New York. After meeting Quoyle in a laundromat, he helps him find a job at the paper where he works and then mentors Quoyle as a reporter and writer. Later, Partridge, who is madly in love with his wife, follows her across the country, where she seeks to begin her own career as a truck driver. When Quoyle phones Partridge to inform him of the events that led him to Newfoundland, Partridge uses his newspaper connections to help Quoyle obtain his position at the *Gammy Bird*.

Billy Pretty

Billy Pretty is another employee of the *Gammy Bird*. Billy is often free with his advice to Quoyle. He invites Quoyle to come with him to a remote island where his family once lived with a small community of settlers. During this trip, Quoyle learns of his family's disturbing history and discovers that he has an angry, possibly insane cousin who is likely disgruntled about Quoyle having settled in the home on Quoyle's Point.

Herry Prowse

Herry Prowse is the son of Wavey Prowse. Wavey informs Quoyle that Herry has Down's syndrome. As Quoyle and Wavey grow closer, their children spend more time together. When Herry has an accident at school and is berated by his teacher, Bunny angrily pushes the teacher in defense of Herry.

Wavey Prowse

The widowed Wavey Prowse and Quoyle share an immediate and mutual attraction. They are both shy and have both experienced betrayal and tragedy in their former relationships. Consequently, Wavey and Quoyle proceed in their relationship with extreme caution. Eventually, Wavey acknowledges her feelings for Quoyle. Toward Quoyle's daughters, Wavey takes a loving, gentle, and practical approach. She gives the girls a white husky puppy at the novel's end, thus dispelling Bunny's fear of the white dog she imagines. Wavey also tries to explain the true nature of death to Bunny, who conceives that death is only a deep sleep from which Petal might one day return, in the same way that Jack Buggit does during the novel's conclusion.

Quoyle

Quoyle is the protagonist of the novel. He is referred to throughout the novel only as Quoyle, except for one instance, after he has been made managing editor of the *Gammy Bird*. The paper's masthead then reads "R. G. Quoyle." The novel centers essentially on Quoyle's transformation from a pitiable, unloved, luckless, and depressed

man to a respectable, hard-working, creative individual who is now capable of both loving and being loved. Through the hardships he endures after his move to Newfoundland, Quoyle becomes a better person, and the wounds inflicted on him by his past, by his father, and by Petal begin to heal. After being desperately in love with and betrayed by Petal, who demonstrates her degenerate nature when she sells her children to a pedophile and pornographer, Quoyle learns to be brave enough to seek a better life for his daughters. He overcomes his self-doubt and finds he can work with his hands to repair the ancestral home; he can learn to write a new and creative column for the paper; he can make friends. Although he learns disturbing facts about his ancestors, and although the house he has struggled to make livable in the end is destroyed, Quoyle is able to excel at his job, find a new home for his family, and pursue Wavey.

Bunny Quoyle

Bunny is Quoyle and Petal's older daughter. She enters the first grade after she moves with her father and sister to Killick-Claw. Throughout the novel, Bunny is terrified by nightmares and visions of a white dog, which she believes wants to attack her. At times, Quoyle wonders if there is something the matter with her, if her past with Petal was traumatizing. Agnis dismisses this notion but likens Bunny's sometimes violent outbursts to those of her own brother. Bunny's dream that the house on Quoyle's Point is washed away in the storm comes true; but following this event, Bunny's turbulent emotional life seems to settle, particularly after Wavey presents Bunny and her sister Sunshine with a white husky puppy. After Quoyle confronts his insane cousin and realizes the man has a large white dog, the reader is left to surmise that this in fact is the source of Bunny's visions and fears.

Dicky Quoyle

Quoyle's brother, Dicky, is a minor character who appears only briefly at the beginning of the novel. He refuses to help Quoyle with funeral arrangements for their parents.

Gus Quoyle

Gus Quoyle was Quoyle's father. Quoyle receives a phone message from his father directly following Gus's suicidal drug overdose. He and Quoyle's mother commit suicide to end their struggle with cancer. Despite his physical absence from the story, Gus pervades Agnis's and Quoyle's memories. He was a cruel, abusive father to Quoyle. As Agnis's older brother, Gus raped and impregnated Agnis.

Nolan Quoyle

Nolan Quoyle is a distant cousin of Quoyle's who lives in a shack near Quoyle's Point. Billy Pretty warns Quoyle of Nolan's presence near the house and suggests he might be both angry (about Quoyle's inhabiting the house) and dangerous, as well as probably insane. After Quoyle repeatedly finds lengths of string knotted with shipping knots in various places, including his boat, his car, and finally, his home, Quoyle suspects that Nolan has indeed been watching his family and leaving the string behind either as a warning or because he believes the string to have some power to affect Quoyle's fate. When Quoyle confronts Nolan, Nolan appears starved, confused, and insane. Later, after Dennis and Quoyle pay Nolan another visit, they bring in the authorities, and Nolan is removed from the home and placed in a mental facility. In one of his more lucid moments, Nolan reveals disturbing truths about Quoyle's aunt and father.

Sunshine Quoyle

Sunshine Quoyle is Quoyle's younger daughter. In contrast to her older sister, Bunny, Sunshine is lighthearted, where Bunny is often more serious. While Bunny elicits Quoyle's deep concern, Sunshine inspires in Quoyle both a sense of playfulness and one of protectiveness.

Diddy Shovel

Shovel is the harbormaster. Quoyle meets Shovel when he talks to him about the incoming and outgoing ships in the port. Like many residents of Killick-Claw, Shovel is free with stories and advice for Quoyle.

Irene Warren

Agnis reveals to Quoyle that her dog, Warren, was named after her lover. She does not explain that her lover was Irene Warren, a woman, who died of cancer before the events of the novel.

Alvin Yark

Alvin Yark is Wavey's uncle. He agrees to build a boat for Quoyle and enlists Quoyle to help him.

THEMES

Family Relationships

The nature of familial relationships is a primary concern in *The Shipping News*. Until Aunt Agnis comes to his aid after his father's death, Quoyle's personal experience with family is unrelentingly negative. His parents raise him in a manner that is at best neglectful but is more often than not cruel. His father in particular regards Quoyle as a bitter disappointment.

When he begins his own family, Quoyle is just as neglected by Petal as he was by his parents. At her kindest, she ignores him. Her typical behavior, however, is to flaunt her promiscuous behavior in front of the tortured Quoyle. As a father, Quoyle is loving but confused, and often too stunned by his perceived failures as a man and as a husband to motivate himself to be a better father. When Aunt Agnis arrives, however, Quoyle is relieved by her helpful, if brusque, attitude. She encourages Quoyle to bring the children to Newfoundland, where she herself is bound. Once there, they settle into a domestic arrangement, in which Agnis helps Quoyle with the children, and he helps her with the repairs on the old house. A new notion of family begins to form in Quoyle's mind. Without the dark pull of Petal's presence, though her memory still plagues him, Quoyle begins to be able to enjoy fatherhood, despite the persistent presence of his fears. He is extremely protective and deeply concerned about his daughter Bunny's nightmares, visions, and sometimes violent outbursts, but Quoyle allows himself moments of playfulness.

The circle of family eventually ripples outward to encompass nonrelatives. Dennis and Beety Buggit, in their friendship toward Quoyle and Agnis and in the loving care they often provide Bunny and Sunshine, stand in for Quoyle's extended family. Similarly, Wavey and Herry Prowse become an integral part of Quoyle's life, not only through Quoyle and Wavey's blossoming romance but also in the closeness that develops among the children. Mercalia and Partridge are Quoyle's first example of what a loving relationship looks like, but when Quoyle moves to Killick-Claw, he begins to see the way other parents relate to their children, and he eventually develops his own parenting style, one that is guided more by love and devotion than by his previous fear and confusion.

TOPICS FOR FURTHER STUDY

- Proulx's distinctive and poetic language in *The Shipping News* is filled with unique metaphors and comparisons. Her descriptions of people and places in particular utilize lyrical comparisons and extensive lists of qualities, images, or other items. Create an extended description of a person, either a character you have created or an actual person you know, emulating Proulx's style by incorporating detailed images, abstract comparisons, or interesting lists of the person's various qualities or features. Read your composition to the class.

- In *The Shipping News*, Proulx focuses on a particular setting: Newfoundland in the 1990s. Research the cultural history of Newfoundland. Who were the original inhabitants of the island? Which explorers made their way there? What European groups eventually settled the island? When did it become, along with Labrador, a Canadian province? Compile a report based on your findings and either post it on a Web page you have designed or submit it in writing. Be sure to cite your sources.

- Although Proulx gives voice to the past in *The Shipping News* when characters like Billy Pretty describe their ancestral history, little space is devoted to the First Nations (indigenous Canadian) populations of the region. In *An Anthology of Canadian Native Literature in English* (2005), edited by Daniel David Moses and Terry Goldie, fiction, essays, and poetry by past and contemporary First Nations writers, including Cherokees, Micmacs, and Inuits, are presented. Peruse this volume and select several pieces in which the Canadian landscape is portrayed. How is the First Nations view of the land different than that of the Newfoundlanders Proulx presents in her novel? Are there similarities in these attitudes? Create a presentation for your class in which you analyze several of the First Nations poems or short prose passages.

Consider in particular the language, imagery, and themes of the First Nations authors. You may present your work as an essay or as a visual presentation in which you accompany reproductions of the works you discuss with your own artwork, illustrating the poetry, fiction, or essay selections.

- Roderick Haig-Brown, in the 1962 young-adult novel *The Whale People*, captures life in a whaling village in pre-Columbian Canada (before Christopher Columbus's 1492 arrival in the New World). Reissued in 2003, the work is a coming-of-age novel in which a teenage boy, Atlin, must learn how to become a leader and provide for his people. With a small group, read *The Whale People*. Consider how Haig-Brown uses characterization, language, and imagery to capture distinctly Canadian people and settings. Despite the fact that Atlin and Quoyle live in different time periods and in different parts of Canada, are there any similarities in the journeys of personal growth upon which they embark? What are their fears? What are their strengths? Create an online blog in which you and your group write posts about these elements of the two novels.

- Proulx touches on the competing concerns of environmental groups and the fishing and oil industries in Newfoundland. Using sources such as the 2008 report *The Invisible Movement: The Response of the Newfoundland Environmental Movement to the Offshore Oil Industry*, written by Newfoundland author Leah Fusco, research the conflicts that exist between environmentalists and proponents of oil industry. Create an argument, backed by your research, that supports the interests of either the oil industry or environmentalists. Present your findings to the class in a written report, a PowerPoint presentation, or a Web page.

Canadian Culture

The setting of *The Shipping News* plays an important role in the story. Newfoundland is depicted in harsh terms, as are its people, as though the extremes of the climate and the landscape have shaped the people into individuals with their own prominent, rough characters. The island of Newfoundland, along with the region on the mainland known as Labrador, together comprise one Canadian province in northeast Canada.

Given its remoteness, the town of Killick-Claw does not see a great influx of visitors. Families have lived in the same locations for many generations, and individuals are often known as much by their family history as for their own traits. The community depends on the sea for its livelihood, through its fishing and shipping industries. But at the same time, the ocean is a source of fear for some of the characters in the novel. Dennis Buggit nearly drowns, as does Quoyle, but both men are saved by Jack Buggit, who lost his oldest son to the sea. Jack is presumed to have drowned, but he miraculously returns to consciousness at his funeral. The remoteness of the location also shapes its people in another sense. As Billy Pretty informs Quoyle, Quoyle's family has a reputation for being inbred, which has imprinted in their line a tendency toward insanity and violence. "Omaloor Bay," Billy tells Quoyle, "is called after Quoyles. Loonies. They was wild and inbred, half-wits and murderers." As Quoyle later finds out, in many ways his father fits this description. Yet the aberrant qualities attributed to the Quoyle family are not unique to that group. As Nutbeem's newspaper reporting reveals, there is a high rate of sexually deviant behavior, particularly incest, in this area of Newfoundland. A section of the *Gammy Bird* is dedicated entirely to stories of sexual abuse. Nutbeem, Billy Pretty, and Quoyle often marvel at the number of cases reported every week.

At the same time, Proulx also examines more positive elements of the Newfoundland character. As Quoyle's interactions with the residents of Killick-Claw reveal, a healthy sense of community and a strength of character can be found in the people of this region. Quoyle's Newfoundland friends are loyal, rugged folk, eager to help one another and free with advice. While Nutbeem's friends may sink his boat during his rowdy send-off, they appear the next day, hungover but determined to pull his boat out of the sea. Quoyle, though he has never been to Newfoundland, is welcomed largely due to the curiosity about his

Quoyle gets a job as a reporter at the local newspaper. (Avelia | Shutterstock.com)

ancestry; many Killick-Claw residents know stories about Quoyle's parents, grandparents, and other relatives. As his quiet, humble demeanor is starkly different from the reputation the Quoyles have in Killick-Claw, Quoyle is quickly regarded in a new light and is aided by a number of residents, especially the Buggits. He gradually becomes assimilated to the culture of the region, growing increasingly independent and confident. Quoyle's participation in community events, such as his daughter's play at school, Jack's funeral, and the party he throws for Agnis, underscore his integration into the Killick-Claw community.

STYLE

Language and Imagery

Proulx's writing in *The Shipping News* has a distinctive syntax (meaning the arrangement of words and phrases in a sentence). Often, she omits pronouns and verbs, and the arrangement of her descriptive phrases takes on the rhythm of poetry. The use of sentence fragments, filled with unusual imagery, is prolific. For example, in describing Quoyle, Proulx writes, "A great damp loaf of a body." Later, in the same paragraph, she says, "Features as bunched as kissed fingertips. Eyes the color of plastic. The monstrous chin, a freakish shelf jutting from the lower face." At times, despite the phrases' being so specific and so distinct, the reader is somehow left with only vague images. Although readers might be able to imagine what a "great damp loaf of a body" looks like, they may wonder at the appearance of "kissed fingertips" and ponder how a person can have eyes the color of something as varied as plastic. The dialogue is often rendered in the same truncated fashion, as the speakers frequently eschew the use of pronouns. Proulx creates numerous pauses through fragments and punctuation, halting the flow of the narrative to allow the reader time to fill in the empty spaces left by her style of writing.

Symbols

Proulx incorporated a variety of symbols into this work. Some chapters, for example, are titled after the names of nautical knots, while others quote sayings from seafarers' dictionaries. The types of knots depicted signal significant elements for the ensuing chapters. In the chapter titled "Love Knot," for example, Quoyle meets Petal. In "Strangle Knot," Quoyle's parents kill themselves, and Petal sells the children before dying in a car accident. The knots not only foreshadow events in the chapter but also symbolize the emotional connections that at times yoke people together and at other times cut them off from each other, their world, or themselves. Another prominent symbol used in the novel is the house on Quoyle's Point. The house, first erected by Quoyle's ancestors on a different location from which they were later expelled, was at one time dragged across the ice to the point where it rests in the story. Here, on Quoyle's Point, it is lashed to the rock with cables to secure it to the land. Yet by the story's end, the house breaks free of the cables and is forced by the storm into the sea. The house may be regarded as the Quoyle family itself, with all its inherent violence and deviance. Uprooted and transported, the house does not belong to the land on which it is lashed and is ultimately scourged from the landscape. Quoyle, also uprooted and transported, has the sense of being disconnected from his family's turbulent history, and he does not feel that he

belongs to the land or to the people who at one time inhabited the house on Quoyle's Point. He survives the storm, survives his transplanting to Newfoundland, and comes to belong to the community of Killick-Claw, having broken free of the ties that bound him to his own history.

Third-Person Narration

In *The Shipping News*, Proulx uses an omniscient third-person narrator. An omniscient, or all-knowing, third-person narrator is one who relates the action of the story but is not a part of it as a character participating in the story's events. Proulx's narrator speaks of Quoyle's past and opens the story with a preview of his future (his move to Newfoundland). Although the story is told largely from Quoyle's point of view, the reader is frequently given access, by the narrator, to the thoughts of the other characters. The use of such a narrator allows the reader an intimate examination of many of the story's characters. For example, Bunny's dream of the house being washed out to sea is shared with the reader but not with characters in the novel. The reader is thus privy to the knowledge that Bunny's dream comes true, but the other characters only know what happened to the house, not that Bunny's dream foretold it.

This type of third-person narration serves Proulx's story in that it invites a closeness to characters who are not initially appealing or who hide much of themselves from one another. By revealing Quoyle's troubled childhood, for example, the narrator transforms Quoyle's lack of confidence as an adult into a cause for sympathy rather than contempt. Similarly, the narrator allows the reader to view Wavey's conflict between her interest in Quoyle and her grief for her husband by revealing her thoughts of grief and the anxiety she feels in Quoyle's arms. The reader discovers these facts prior to Wavey revealing them to Quoyle. The reader is prepared to accept Wavey as Quoyle's love interest once this sympathy for her is encouraged. In this way, the reader is led by the narrator into a positive response to Quoyle and Wavey's romance as it develops.

HISTORICAL CONTEXT

Newfoundland Environmentalism and Industry in the 1990s

Although *The Shipping News* is not an overtly political novel, Proulx does touch on the conflict in Newfoundland between the fishing industry,

COMPARE & CONTRAST

- **1990s:** The cod-fishing industry in New-foundland comes under increasing government regulation in order to protect the area from further overfishing. After the collapse of the cod fishery in 1992, jobs are lost, and fishermen seek other sources of revenue.

  Today: The Newfoundland cod populations are still at risk. Scientists recommend a number of measures designed to decrease fish mortality, such as rerouting shipping traffic, reducing seismic surveys for oil and gas, and minimizing habitat destruction.

- **1990s:** Greenpeace activists are concerned with the protection of harp seals in New-foundland waters. Seals are blamed for the decline of the cod populations, and there is mounting pressure to increase the allowable kill rate for hunted seals.

  Today: The Newfoundland cod fishery is permanently closed, and the Canadian government allows a further increase in the number of seals to be hunted. Protesting Greenpeace activists maintain that cod make up only a small percentage of the harp seals' diet. They protest that the seals are not the sole, or

greatest, threat to cod populations and that the seal populations must also be protected.

- **1990s:** Works of literary fiction such as the novels written by Proulx, Cormac McCarthy, and Edna O'Brien are alternately praised for their evocative literary styles and criticized for being pretentious. Literary fiction, according to some critics, has become another genre. The fact that winners of prestigious literary prizes, such as the Pulitzer and the National Book Award, are also national best-selling novels underscores the notion that literary fiction is not an exclusive list that appeals only to scholars and other intellectuals but is becoming incorporated into the realm of mainstream fiction.

  Today: The lines between literary fiction and genre fiction continue to blur, as evidenced by the widespread appeal that many literary novels enjoy. Like Proulx's *The Shipping News* in 1993, a number of twenty-first century novels win literary awards and also make best-seller lists. Authors of such works include Jennifer Egan and Emma Donoghue, as well as authors who enjoyed popularity and critical acclaim in the 1990s, including Proulx and McCarthy.

---

the oil industry, and environmentalism. Tert Card sees the oil industry in a positive light, certain it will bring prosperity to the region. Influenced by Wavey, Quoyle writes an article citing the dangers the oil industry poses to the environment and the way of life, supported by the fishing industry, in Killick-Claw. Jack Buggit sums up many of the competing concerns of industry and the environment in a lengthy speech he delivers to Quoyle. He speaks of the way the government is "regulating us [fishermen] out of business" and goes on to decry "the bloody Greenpeace trying to shut down the sealing."

In a 2001 report originally published in *Canadian Issues*, Dr. Melvin Baker offers a brief summary of the history of cod fisheries in Newfoundland, explaining,

The cod fishery remained critical to the economic and social lives of residents until 1992 when the Federal Government imposed a moratorium on the catching of cod off Newfoundland's east coast, disrupting the lives of 30,000 fishers and fish plant workers who had depended on the cod fishery for their livelihood.

Baker discusses the way this policy forced many residents to move to the Canadian mainland to seek other employment opportunities. After the collapse of the cod fishery, largely due to overfishing, the fishing industry was later revived to some degree through the development of a "more centralized and professional industry" of crab and shrimp fishing, Baker informs.

As the cod-fishing industry was collapsing, the oil industry was just gaining traction in

Quoyle's articles about harbor boats become quite popular in the community. *(Elena Elisseeva | Shutterstock.com)*

Newfoundland. In 1990, construction of oil extraction platforms off the coast of Newfoundland, in the Hibernia oilfield, began. Oil was first barreled from this field in 1997. The oil industry has become vital to the Newfoundland economy. In 1996, the Canadian government instituted ocean-management policies that designated various regions as Marine Protected Areas to protect at-risk marine species and their environment.

Another environmental issue Proulx touches on in the novel is the plight of the harp seal. The issue of seal hunting has been a source of vigorous and multifaceted debate for decades, in which the concerns of animal rights, environmentalism, and the economy all come into play. Seals have been blamed for the decline in cod populations, and some critics have argued for increased seal hunting. Other groups, such as Greenpeace, advocate the protection of the seals and of the marine environment as a whole.

Literary Fiction in the 1990s

In the early years of the twenty-first century, some literary critics looked back on the decade before, the 1990s, and reevaluated the trajectory the world of literary fiction had taken. In a 2001 article in the *Atlantic*, critic B. R. Myers surveyed the state of American literary prose. The title of the article, "A Reader's Manifesto: An Attack on the Growing Pretentiousness of American Literary Prose," makes Myers's stance clear. Myers states, "Everything written in self-conscious, writerly prose . . . is now considered to be 'literary fiction'—not necessary *good* literary fiction, mind you, but always worthier of respectful attention than even the best-written thriller or romance." Myers laments the existence of a dualism that categorizes all modern fiction as either "literary" or "genre" and the fact that all works in the latter category are considered second-rate by virtue of this categorization. Taking particular aim at Proulx, Myers attacks her use of poetic but abstract language, specifically in *The Shipping News* but in other works as well, stating, "It is easier to call writing like Proulx's lyrically evocative or poetically compelling than to figure out what it evokes, or what it compels the reader to think and feel." Myers insists that Proulx's poetic prose obstructs the narrative flow of the work, and furthermore that the many critics who have praised Proulx so highly seem to be blind to this fact.

Myers takes other writers to task as well, including McCarthy, in particular his 1994 novel *The Crossing*. Myers reflects, "Like Proulx and so many others today, McCarthy relies more on barrages of hit-and-miss verbiage than on careful use of just the right words." After Myers's manifesto was published, other critics took note. Robert McCrum, later in 2001, responded in the London *Observer* to Myers's article, stating that the category of literary fiction has become, according to some critics, "just another genre, like humour, crime, or adventure." McCrum further maintains that a few critics

> have even gone so far as to observe that the label could simply be a way of describing a novel that places style before content, puts prose before plot and subordinates character and narrative to nebulous aesthetic concerns.

In another response published several months after Myers's manifesto was published, *New York Times* critic Judith Shulevitz counters that "Myers doesn't have a sure grasp of the world he's attacking," but she allows that Myers "scores some hits." Shulevitz is particularly enthusiastic about Myers's attack on Proulx, stating that Myers "does his best when skewering Proulx," along with David Guterson, who published the best-selling novel *Snow Falling on Cedars* in 1994. Shulevitz contends that "Myers deserves credit for pointing out that Proulx's every line is a masterwork of tortured kitsch." Works by Proulx, Guterson, and McCarthy, among others, became symbols of a perceived pretentiousness in American literary fiction of the late twentieth century according to some critics. At the same time, irrespective of the charges of pretentiousness, many works by these and other literary authors won numerous literary awards, including the Pulitzer, the National Book Award, and the Man Booker Prize, and also became national best sellers.

CRITICAL OVERVIEW

The winner of the 1993 National Book Award and the 1994 Pulitzer Prize, *The Shipping News* was well received by many critics. In a 1993 review in the *New York Times*, Howard Norman praises Proulx's ability to employ "local color, ribaldry, and uncanny sorts of redemption" to insulate the reader from the novel's darker elements. Norman

additionally discusses Proulx's prose, maintaining that her "inventive language is finely, if exhaustively, accomplished," although Proulx is sometimes prone to taking "her own brand of poetic compression too far."

The issue of Proulx's language later became the subject of debate, as when Myers, in his 2001 article for the *Atlantic*, objected not only to Proulx's lyric and abstract prose but also to the critical praise of it. Stuart Pierson's 1995 study of Proulx's novel in the journal *Newfoundland Studies* also explores the issue of Proulx's language, but he focuses on Proulx's efforts to capture the particularities of the Newfoundland manner of speaking. Pierson faults Proulx for her reliance on the *Dictionary of Newfoundland English* as a source. Pierson further contends that Proulx has depicted Newfoundland as "a fable" that is "one not well-thought-out."

Although the language of the novel has been a source of much critical discussion, other aspects of the work have also spurred examination. Karen Lane Rood, for example, in her 2001 study *Understanding Annie Proulx*, focuses on the novel's ending. Rood argues against some readings of the novel that have emphasized the work's uplifting nature. In response to such analyses, Rood asserts that "the so-called happy ending is qualified by an awareness that [Quoyle's] definition of happiness is severely limited and by Proulx's warnings about the consequences of modern humanity's loss of community and attachment to the land."

Another approach to the work entails a feminist exploration of the novel's themes. Rachel Seiffert, in her 2002 essay for *Textual Practice*, explores the distinct narrative lines of the book represented by Quoyle and Agnis. Seiffert studies the gender-specific nature of these narrative threads and examines both feminine and masculine identity as depicted in the characters of Agnis and Quoyle. In particular, Seiffert studies Proulx's use of voice and silence in the novel, maintaining that as Quoyle grows more confident, he finds his voice. His previous silence, associated with fear and self-doubt, is transformed into an ability to express himself. Seiffert goes on to demonstrate the way in which Agnis, initially confident and vocal, loses her ability to express herself when she returns to her ancestral home and remembers the abuse she suffered there. Seiffert concludes that silence and the "capacity of language to encapsulate human experience" are questioned, and "gendered relationships to language" are challenged as well.

CRITICISM

Catherine Dominic

Dominic is a novelist and a freelance writer and editor. In the following essay, she explores Proulx's use of abstract language in The Shipping News, *maintaining that the author creates a sense of disconnectedness between language and meaning in order to emphasize the main character's sense of isolation and confusion.*

As one reads *The Shipping News*, it is difficult at times to recognize and appreciate the story beneath Annie Proulx's prose. In Proulx's distinctive style, the images are often either so abstract that meaning is lost when one dwells on them, or alternatively, the images are so densely clustered around a single idea that the narrative flow is compromised. Given the prominent role the language plays in the work itself, if not in the actual storytelling, Proulx's often abstract, disconnected, and overwrought prose may possibly have another function in the story, beyond its role as purveyor of Proulx's signature style. In a 2001 article for the *Atlantic*, B. R. Myers contends that the reader eventually abandons hope of finding meaning in Proulx's strange descriptions, that the reader "stops trying to think about what the metaphors mean. Maybe," Myers goes on, "this is the effect that Proulx is aiming for; she seems to want to keep us on the surface of the text at all times, as if she were afraid that we might forget her quirky narratorial presence for even a line or two." Myers later emphasizes this point again, commenting on Proulx's "need to draw attention to her presence throughout the text." Clearly Myers has closely read Proulx's work, as he identifies numerous examples of descriptions that become meaningless upon reflection. Myers, like many readers of *The Shipping News*, feels blockaded from the story by Proulx's language and images. Her abstract, poetic style is off-putting for readers who seek a deeper engagement on the level of plot and character. Yet arguably, Proulx keeps readers at arm's length from the meaning of her language and from her characters not because of her need to draw attention to herself or because the underlying characterizations or plotting are weak. Instead, she may be attempting to expose and explore the essential meaninglessness of the language with which individuals communicate with one another and to portray the sense of disconnection and isolation felt by her characters by intensifying the reader's own sense of disconnection. The language functions as a

> KEPT AT ARM'S LENGTH FROM QUOYLE AND THE REST OF THE CHARACTERS IN THE STORY BY THE NOVEL'S UNIQUE AND OFTEN ABSTRACT LANGUAGE, THE READER FEELS AS OUT OF PLACE AND CONFUSED AS QUOYLE DOES THROUGHOUT MUCH OF THE WORK."

means of conveying confusion, disorientation, and isolation precisely because it often fails to convey meaning in the traditional sense.

The notion of language as meaningless is not a new one, and it features prominently in modernist poetry movements such as Dadaism and surrealism. Modernism is a movement in the worlds of visual and literary arts where traditional modes of representation and narration are abandoned in favor of experimental, often abstract methods of conveying meaning. Dadaist poetry often takes the form of a random sampling of words, while surrealism explores the subconscious mind, depicting dreamlike images. Even in Shakespeare's works, notably *Hamlet*, critics have identified a disillusionment with the relationship between language and meaning. Different authors, however, use this concept for different purposes. Proulx, in *The Shipping News*, highlights this disconnection between language and meaning to emphasize Quoyle's sense of isolation from his world, from his own life. He does not know where or how or with whom he fits. Quoyle's sense of disconnectedness is mirrored in the reader's own response to the text. Kept at arm's length from Quoyle and the rest of the characters in the story by the novel's unique and often abstract language, the reader feels as out of place and confused as Quoyle does throughout much of the work.

In a well-cited paragraph that exemplifies Proulx's style, the author describes Quoyle with a wild variety of metaphors. His body is a "great damp loaf." He is so heavy at the age of sixteen that "he was buried under a casement of flesh." Quoyle's head is "shaped like a crenshaw," his features resemble "kissed fingertips," his eyes are "the color of plastic," and his chin is "a freakish shelf jutting from the lower face." Some of the

WHAT DO I READ NEXT?

- Proulx's *Bird Cloud: A Memoir*, published in 2011, includes details about the author's personal history as well as prose sketches on nature, the past, and the construction of her home in Wyoming.

- Originally published in 1992, *Postcards* is Proulx's first novel. The work explores the family relationships of a man who is exiled after he accidentally kills his lover.

- *Mole: Poems*, by Patrick Warner, was published in 2009. Warner is a Newfoundlander, and his poetry explores his sense of place and the people of Newfoundland.

- *Henry Chow, and Other Stories*, edited by R. David Stephens, is a product of the Asian Canadian Writers' Workshop. The young-adult collection was published in 2010 and features the short stories of Asian Canadian authors. Many of the stories feature Asian Canadian teens and are set in Canadian towns or cities, but some feature Asian characters abroad. The collection covers themes of identity, culture, and self-exploration.

- *Galore*, by Michael Crummey, is a fable-like tale set in historic Newfoundland in which a small community's encounter with mythic forces is examined. Crummey's style is distinctive and is in some ways similar to Proulx's in its unique imagery and narrative flow. *Galore* was published in 2009.

- *Revival: An Anthology of the Best Black Canadian Writing*, edited by Donna Bailey Nurse and published in 2006, is a collection of short fiction and novel excerpts from black Canadian authors, including Suzette Mayr, Esi Edugyan, and Makeda Silvera. Many of the works feature Canadian settings and themes such as family, community, and the cultural conflicts between individuals of African or Caribbean descent and their white Canadian communities.

- Gerald Sider's *Between History and Tomorrow: Making and Breaking Everyday Life in Rural Newfoundland*, published in 2003, examines the society, culture, and traditions of rural Newfoundlanders and is particularly focused on how these communities have been affected by developments in the fishing industry.

---

comparisons yield no concrete images. Plastic may be any color; a kissed fingertip looks like any other fingertip. The other comparisons are so diverse and piled together in such a short space, that the effect is dizzying: he is doughy, he sinks under the frame of his flesh, his head is melon-like, his chin is a shelf. The resulting images, if thoroughly contemplated by the reader, yield a Picasso-like portrait of misshapen, rearranged proportions. Other character descriptions are similarly indistinct. The children have "freckles like chopped grass on a wet dog." This gives the image of freckles perhaps densely sprinkled, but otherwise the image of flecks of green on a wet dog of unknown color has little correspondence with a child's facial appearance. Aunt Agnis is likewise portrayed in

terms that dissect her features and present them to the reader in isolated images. The description begins clearly enough. Agnis is a "stiff-figured woman, gingery hair streaked with white." Proulx goes on to describe her profile as "a target in a shooting gallery." After pointing out a "buff mole on her neck," Proulx describes the way she swirls tea in the pot, the way her coat, "bent over the arm of a sofa, resembled a wine steward showing her label." Agnis is associated with her mannerisms as well as her garments. The reader next learns of Agnis's voice, which is compared to "a whistling harmonic as from the cracked-open window of a speeding car." The segmented depiction of Agnis is completed with this observation: "Body in sections, like a dress form." Such disjointed characterizations, in the way they create fragmented rather than unified portraits of the characters, serve to distance the reader from the characters in particular and the story in general. The character being considered is often treated like an object, severed into parts to be considered separately from the whole. The effect is isolating and confusing.

Descriptions of places often mirror those of people, in that they contain such vast arrays of comparisons and images that the reader is left in a muddle. In a lengthy description of the Buggit home, Proulx depicts the doilies that cover nearly everything in the home and describes in intricate detail the patterns of this crocheted lacework. Once sentence contains eleven different images of crochet patterns that are linked to Newfoundland themes, such as "designs of lace waves and floe ice, whelk shells and sea wrack, the curve of lobster feelers," for example. An additional six crochet doily patterns and their locations in the home are described. "The easy chairs," for example, "wore archipelagoes of thread and twine flung over the reefs of arms and backs." Barraged with such extensive and varied imagery, the reader is again left feeling overwhelmed with the onslaught of images, details, words, comparisons. Arriving at the end of this long paragraph describing doilies, the reader may wonder if he or she has missed something of greater significance. In another instance, Quoyle visits his distant relative's shack. The contents of the single room are listed, itemized in great detail. Like the paragraph about doilies, this one too goes on and on, a list of mundane items such as "loops of fishing line" as well as more bizarre items, such as "sea wet," "gnawed sheep ribs," and "squid cartilage," to name a few. Many descriptive paragraphs in the novel go on this way, with seemingly endless lists of items, providing more information than necessary to capture a sense of place. The effect, rather, is dizzying and distorting.

This small sampling is reflective of much of Proulx's prose in *The Shipping News*. Although a few instances of such language and abstract or confusing imagery may be regarded as odd but poetic, or even compelling, the cumulative effect of having so much of the novel read this way is to establish in the reader a pervasive sense of disconnection from the story and its characters and confusion about the story's meaning. In this way, the reader comes to share Quoyle's

experience. From the beginning of the story, Quoyle has difficulty making connections with the people in his life. He is befriended by Partridge and feels grateful to the kindness Partridge shows him, but he offers little in return as a friend. Quoyle becomes fixated instantly with Petal, loving her desperately, but fails to have any meaningful interaction with her. After their initial encounter and brief romance, Petal marries Quoyle but loses interest in him entirely. Quoyle loves his daughters, but it takes the entire span of the novel for this love to evolve into a relationship. Initially, Quoyle "loved them with a kind of fear that if they made it into the world they were with him on borrowed time." He approaches his own life with a sense of fear, self-consciousness, and uncertainty. He hesitates in all things, grateful for Agnis's decisive nature and for her advice. Quoyle bobs along where the waves of his life propel him, to Killick-Claw, to the house on Quoyle's Point, to the *Gammy Bird*. Perpetually hiding his face behind his hand, Quoyle merely observes the world around him and only tentatively and gradually begins to assert his own presence, as he carefully does with Wavey. His turmoil and his disconnectedness are revealed in his fearful approach to the move to Newfoundland, in his deference to his aunt. He fumbles into his job at the paper and eventually, almost accidentally, proves himself and discovers his talent when he writes his shipping-news column. When asked by the harbormaster Diddy Shovel about himself, after Shovel has offered a lengthy personal history, Quoyle states simply, "Me. I'm just working at the paper." Afraid of the water, Quoyle eventually succumbs to advice to buy a boat, yet he purchases a vessel that is barely seaworthy and is informed of this fact almost immediately. Quoyle responds internally, as he frequently does, by summarizing events with a newspaper-like headline, in this case, "Stupid Man Does Wrong Thing Once More." In this response, Quoyle's low opinion of himself is expressed, but additionally, his understanding of himself as a fragmented, disconnected entity is underscored. He does not regard himself as a fully formed individual; he is a headline without content, a man without context.

As the novel progresses, Quoyle is compelled by numerous forces to transform, to connect. His children need him to be a loving, involved father, not one who simply protects out of fear. Agnis needs him to help make

Quoyle and Wavey begin a relationship. (*Monkey Business Images / Shutterstock.com*)

decisions and improvements on the house; she also needs to settle her own life, and insists on Quoyle's increasing independence in his own affairs. As Quoyle begins to become engaged in his own life, his confusion dissipates, his confidence grows, his connections deepen. At the same time, the reader, who has been forced by Proulx's language into a state as isolated and confused as Quoyle's, finally begins to see Quoyle as a more fully formed individual. The language throughout the novel does not change when Quoyle begins to gain control of his life. Although distancing, the language also becomes familiar and manageable to the reader. Likewise, Quoyle does not completely overcome his faults; they continue to exist within him and to crop up here and there. He begins to make peace with his flaws, and he makes improvements to his attitude and his approach to life where he is able.

Throughout the novel, Proulx uses her complex and often confusing and abstract language to distance her readers from the novel's characters and plot. In doing so, she allows the reader an experience that mirrors Quoyle's lifelong experience of isolation, disconnectedness, and confusion. As Quoyle is being gradually introduced to the reader, Proulx writes, "Nothing was clear to lonesome Quoyle. His thoughts churned like the amorphous thing that ancient sailors, drifting into arctic half-light, called the Sea Lung." All is clouded for Quoyle, his thoughts exist in a place "where the sky froze and light and dark muddled." Because the reader shares this experience with Quoyle, once he begins to evolve, the reader is able to feel a new sense of connection with the character, to more fully appreciate the significance of the connections he begins to make. Proulx's language and imagery are more than stylistic devices; they are catalysts that allow the reader to access Proulx's characters through the deep and meaningful way of shared experience.

Source: Catherine Dominic, Critical Essay on *The Shipping News*, in *Novels for Students*, Gale, Cengage Learning, 2012.

B. A. St. Andrews

In the following review, St. Andrews evaluates the strengths of The Shipping News.

Lovers of language have awaited *The Shipping News* with an excitement comparable to that greeting each serialized installment of a Dickens novel making slow passage across the Atlantic. That is because of Annie Proulx's writing: uncompromising, uncommon, unrelenting, unassailably precise. The expectations established by Proulx's first novel, *Postcards*, and her short-story collection *Heart Songs and Other Stories* have been satisfied amply by this triumphant second novel.

It is language, after all, which triumphs in Proulx's book. First, its postmodern episodic hero Quoyle is himself a writer; we follow this peculiar pilgrim's progress with growing interest and increasing affection. Second, the book's language is alive. Its syllables urge and slice and spin the reader like a dervish wind. Salty, luscious, mind-grabbing, chewable words and phrases like *drenty*, *Nutbeem*, and the terrible *Nightmare Isles* energize the people and events.

No avid reader can help but be drawn around and down into language's whirlpool. In like manner, Killick-Claw's peculiar newspaper the *Gammy Bird* breathes life into the daily catalogues of sex crimes, port reports, car wrecks, and local secrets. As befits a novel set in the Maritime Provinces, the sea serves as the ruling deity, and the idea of drowning works on both physical and metaphysical levels.

PEN/Faulkner Award winner Proulx's second novel builds on the close observation and the cold, calculated lyricism made manifest in her earlier works. *The Shipping News* reaffirms the power of unique idiomatic speech, of characterization, of love, of land- and seascape, and of communion among us, yet the novel's form is fractured. The knots which provide each chapter's decoration serve, perhaps, as a key metaphor. This sometimes icy, often grotesque, always quirky work ties us tightly inside a love knot: "Water may be older than light . . . the wind be imprisoned in a bit of knotted string. And it may be that love sometimes occurs without pain or misery."

It may be. Nothing remains unqualified in Proulx country. And after our meeting Aunt Agnis Hamm and Quoyle's daughters Bunny and Sunshine, after witnessing the waterlogged reprise of Jack Buggit, after watching Wavey Prowse enfold Quoyle, we may find Proulxian love to be a fixed adjective among literary critics. This love is more domestic than exotic; it seems born of hardship, born from hearts battered by wave upon wave of despair. Such love finds, despite all former experience and against all odds, safe harbor.

If that vaguely reminds us of Flannery O'Connor's idea of grace, it should. As in O'Connor's work, Proulx reveals how redemptive love or grace hovers over us like the angels, unaware. Comparable in these writers too are the exactness of idiomatic phrasing, their use of dark, rolling humor, and their deft, uncompromising characterizations.

All this to suggest that, within the unsettling elements of Proulx's masterwork, some readers may sense the lurking, smiling shadow of Flannery O'Connor. Given that lofty standard, it is little wonder that *The Shipping News* has a wondrous string of lights—the Pulitzer Prize, the National Book Award, the *Irish Times* International Fiction Prize—flashing around its name.

Source: B. A. St. Andrews, Review of *The Shipping News*, in *World Literature Today*, Vol. 69, No. 2, Spring 1995, p. 363.

William Green

In the following review, Green offers a generally positive assessment of The Shipping News, *while noting flaws in the book's digressive subplots and superficial characterizations.*

E. Annie Proulx was already 57 when her first novel, *Postcards*, was published in 1992. Before that, she had churned out freelance articles about cider, lions, canoeing and mice; she had written short stories for *Esquire*; she had founded a monthly newspaper called *Behind the Times*; she had raised three sons and divorced three husbands. *Postcards* was an unexpected sensation. Critics called it "beautiful," "mesmerizing" and "astonishingly accomplished." Fellow authors honored her with the PEN/Faulkner Award, a $15,000 prize that had never been won by a woman. For good measure, Proulx also landed a Guggenheim Fellowship.

Proulx's second novel, *The Shipping News*, is a black comedy about Quoyle, an endearing loser whose father used to toss him into brooks and lakes. Proulx describes Quoyle's childhood superbly in the novels opening pages, summing up years of misery in a few painfully vivid images: " . . . brother Dick, the father's favorite, pretended to throw up when Quoyle came into the room, hissed 'Snotface, Ugly Pig, Warthog, Stupid, Stinkbomb, . . . Greasebag,' pummeled and kicked until Quoyle curled, hands over head, sniveling, on the linoleum."

Quoyle drops out of school, moves into a rented trailer and distributes vending machine candy before stumbling into journalism. He writes so badly that his colleagues call him a "lobotomized moron." Seduced by a nymphomaniac named Petal Bear, Quoyle gets married and experiences four weeks of bliss. Petal spends the next six years cuckolding him. She even stars in a pornographic movie, elegantly disguising herself with a mask made from a potato chip bag.

As if this were not enough, Quoyle loses his job and Petal abducts his children. After selling the kids to a pornographer for $7,000, Petal dies in a car crash. All of these events occur in the first 30 pages of the novel. The rest of the book traces Quoyle's attempt to seize control of his life. Now in his mid-30s, he must come to terms with the loss of his wife, find a girlfriend, learn to write properly and generally try to become less oafish.

Quoyle's first step is to emigrate from Upstate New York to Newfoundland, a rugged island off the coast of Canada. He finds a job there as a reporter at the *Gammy Bird*, a newspaper specializing in stories of sexual abuse. His editor, amused by typographical errors, sabotages everyone's articles. In one report, the phrase "Burmese sawmill owners" becomes "Burnoosed sawbill awnings." Quoyle writes about ships and about gruesome car wrecks.

Proulx has visited Newfoundland frequently since she first traveled there in 1987 to fish for trout. What fascinates her about the island is the way its traditional lifestyle has come under threat. Quoyle's editor, Jack Buggit, laments, "the fishing's went down, down, down, 40 years sliding into nothing, the...goddamn Canada government giving fishing rights to every country on the face of the earth, but regulating us out of business." Buggit also rails against "bloody Greenpeace" for destroying the livelihood of local seal-bashers. Proulx explored a similar historical process in *Postcards*, describing decline of an old farming family in New England.

Proulx captures the flavor of Newfoundland as convincingly as if she were born there. She writes about the perilous climate, the xenophobia, the skills of boat-builders, the art of skinning a seal, the dangers of the sea and the recipe for flipper pie. She depicts quirky islanders who embellish their life stories and daydream about moving to Florida. She also has an ear for evocative place names, some of which she has invented: she writes of Little Despond and Desperate Cove, the Tickle Motel and the Flying Squid Gift & Lunchstop.

In various interviews, Proulx has said that she feels liberated now that she can afford to write nothing but novels. "All these stories," she has said, "were just bottled up inside me, waiting to get out. Now writing is sheer play." Proulx—who has been known to write for 18 hours at a stretch—does seem to be inexhaustibly inventive. *The Shipping News* is brimming with eccentric characters and rich subplots: an Englishman named Nutbeem builds a boat, sails the Atlantic and is shipwrecked in Newfoundland; Quoyle's aunt names her dog after a woman with whom she has had a tragic love affair.

A number of characters and subplots appear in the novel for no particular reason. Some readers will find these digressions charming since they give the book a leisurely, meandering quality. Others, like me, will find parts of the novel aimless and slightly dull.

Another flaw of the book is that some of the main characters remain superficial. We never understand Quoyle's aunt, his new girlfriend or his children. In fact, Quoyle himself often seems a distant and confusing figure. However, Proulx's use of language is so fresh that you rarely notice such problems. After all, who else would describe a face looking "like cottage cheese clawed with a fork"?

Source: William Green, "Oh, to Be Less of an Oaf in Newfoundland," in *Los Angeles Times Book Review*, July 18, 1993, p. 9.

SOURCES

Baker, Melvin, "Fishing in the Global Village: Newfoundland and Labrador in the 21st Century," in *Canadian Issues*, August/September 2001, pp. 18–19, http://www.ucs.mun.ca/~melbaker/Fishing_GlobalVillage.html (accessed May 31, 2011).

"Canadian Atlantic Fisheries Collapse," in *Greenpeace.org*, http://archive.greenpeace.org/comms/cbio/cancod.html (accessed May 31, 2011).

"FAQs: The Atlantic Seal Hunt," in *CBC News Canada*, July 27, 2009, http://www.cbc.ca/news/canada/story/2009/05/05/f-seal-hunt.html (accessed May 31, 2011).

Hennessy, Dennis M., "Annie Proulx," in *Dictionary of Literary Biography*, Vol. 335, *American Short-Story*

Writers since World War II, Fifth Series, edited by Richard E. Lee, Thomson Gale, 2007, pp. 255–65.

Higgins, Jeremy, "Oil Industry and the Economy," in *Newfoundland and Labrador Heritage*, 2007, http://www.heritage.nf.ca/society/oil_economy.html (accessed May 31, 2011).

"Management Strategies for Recovery of Atlantic Cod Stocks," in *Fisheries and Oceans Canada*, September 2005, http://www.dfo-mpo.gc.ca/fm-gp/initiatives/cod-morue/strategic-mar-eng.htm#a8 (accessed May 31, 2011).

McCrum, Robert, "The End of Literary Fiction," in *Observer* (London, England), August 5, 2001, http://www.guardian.co.uk/books/2001/aug/05/features.review1/ (accessed May 31, 2011).

Myers, B. R., "A Reader's Manifesto: An Attack on the Growing Pretentiousness of American Literary Prose," in *Atlantic*, July/August 2001, http://www.theatlantic.com/magazine/print/2001/07/a-reader-apos-s-manifesto/2270/ (accessed May 31, 2011).

"National Framework for Canada's Network of Marine Protected Areas," in *Fisheries and Oceans Canada*, November 2010, http://www.dfo-mpo.gc.ca/oceans/publications/dmpaf-eczpm/framework-cadre-eng.asp (accessed May 31, 2011).

"No Cod? Blame the Seals," in *Greenpeace.org*, February 24, 2005, http://www.greenpeace.org/international/en/news/features/no-cod-blame-the-seals/ (accessed May 31, 2011).

Norman, Howard, "In Killick-Claw, Everybody Reads the *Gammy Bird*," in *New York Times*, April 4, 1993, http://www.nytimes.com/books/99/05/23/specials/proulx-shipping.html (accessed May 31, 2011).

Pierson, Stuart, Review of *The Shipping News*, in *Newfoundland Studies*, Vol. 11, No. 1, 1995, pp. 151–53, http://journals.hil.unb.ca/index.php/NFLDS/article/view/983/1335 (accessed May 31, 2011).

Proulx, E. Annie, *The Shipping News*, Touchstone, 1993.

Rood, Karen Lane, "*The Shipping News*," in *Understanding Annie Proulx*, University of South Carolina, 2001, pp. 60–88.

Seiffert, Rachel, "Inarticulacy, Identity and Silence: Anne Proulx's *The Shipping News*," in *Textual Practice*, Vol. 16, No. 3, 2002, pp. 511–25.

Shulevitz, Judith, "The Close Reader: Fiction and 'Literary' Fiction," in *New York Times*, September 9, 2011, http://www.nytimes.com/2001/09/09/books/the-close-reader-fiction-and-literary-fiction.html (accessed May 31, 2011).

FURTHER READING

Arms, Myron, *Servants of the Fish: A Portrait of Newfoundland after the Great Cod Collapse*, Upper Access, 2004.
Arms surveys the social, cultural, and economic impact of the collapse of the cod fishery in Newfoundland in 1992. The book focuses on the people of the area both as contributors to the collapse and as victims of it.

Duke, David Freeland, ed., *Canadian Environmental History: Essential Readings*, Canadian Scholars Press, 2006.
In this book, Freeland collects seventeen articles on various environmental issues particular to Canada. He includes pieces on the history of environmentalism in Canada as well as contemporary environmental concerns.

Harter, John-Henry, *New Social Movements, Class, and the Environment: A Case Study of Greenpeace Canada*, Cambridge Scholars Publishing, 2011.
Harter studies the history of Greenpeace's involvement in Canadian issues from 1971 through 2010, exploring in particular the conflicts between working-class interests and environmental concerns. Seal hunting and also the forestry and fishing industries are examined.

Johnston, Wayne, *The Old Lost Land of Newfoundland: Family, Memory, Fiction, and Myth*, NeWest Press, 2009.
This work reproduces Canadian author Johnston's lecture for the Canadian Literature Center's Henry Kreisel Lecture Series, in which he discusses the myths, culture, and values of Newfoundland.

Kirwin, W. J., G. M. Story, and J. D. A. Widdowson, eds., *Dictionary of Newfoundland English*, 2nd ed. with supplement, University of Toronto Press, 1990.
Originally published in 1983, this historical dictionary traces the origins and usage of words and phrases particular to Newfoundland. Proulx has spoken of her heavy reliance on this text in capturing the nuances of Newfoundland language and culture.

Proulx, Annie, *Heart Songs, and Other Stories*, Charles Scribner's Sons, 1988.
Proulx's first collection of short fiction focuses on rural New England and its people and is stylistically similar to her book-length fiction.

SUGGESTED SEARCH TERMS

Annie Proulx

Proulx AND The Shipping News

Proulx AND Newfoundland

Proulx AND literary fiction

Proulx AND biography

Proulx AND Canadian fiction

Proulx AND family drama

Proulx AND literary prizes

Proulx AND film adaptations

Proulx AND feminism

Proulx AND autobiography

Proulx AND prose poetry

Sister of My Heart

**CHITRA BANERJEE
DIVAKARUNI**

1999

Author and social activist Chitra Banerjee Divakaruni published her second novel *Sister of My
Heart*, which evolved out of her short story "The
Ultrasound," in 1999. She was raised in the
region of Bengal, in eastern India, and moved
to the United States at nineteen to attend college
and study English. She eventually established
residence in California. She first engaged in writing in the form of poetry, and after several successful volumes, she began writing fiction as
well. In the meantime, she founded and presided
over Maitri, a San Francisco-area organization
supporting South Asian women in abusive or
otherwise distressful circumstances.

Inspired by this work, as well as by the
infrequency with which South Asian literature
depicted or even addressed women's independence, Divakaruni set out to write a tale that
would demonstrate the beauty of women's relationships with each other and the resilience and
fortitude women are capable of in compromising
situations. *Sister of My Heart* is narrated by
two cousins, Anju and Sudha, who are raised
together in an upper-caste Calcutta household
devoid of any authoritative masculine presence.
The novel relates the tragic circumstances surrounding their births and traces their lives
through adolescence, arranged marriage, pregnancy, and childbirth. The milieu is by and large
morally upstanding, and the romance is treated
discreetly, making Divakaruni's novel especially
suitable for teenagers.

The novel follows the lives of childhood friends Sudha and Anju. (michaeljung / Shutterstock.com)

AUTHOR BIOGRAPHY

Divakaruni was born in Calcutta (now Kolkata), India, on July 29, 1956, to an accountant and a schoolteacher. She had three brothers and so was raised in a home environment colored by masculine energy and sibling rivalry. She was educated at Loreto House, a convent school operated by Irish nuns, from which she graduated in 1971. She earned a bachelor's degree in English from Presidency College at the University of Calcutta in 1976, after which she moved to the United States to further her studies. She earned a master's degree at Wright State University in Dayton, Ohio, and then a doctorate in English from the University of California, Berkeley, in 1984. Meanwhile, to help pay for her schooling, she worked as a babysitter, at an Indian boutique, at a bakery, and in a science lab. In 1979, she married Murthy Divakaruni, an engineer, with whom she would have two sons. After graduating, being uninterested in emotionally distant academic writing, Divakaruni began writing poetry. When she learned of her grandfather's death in his home village in India, she coped through the pure emotional channeling made possible by poetic expression. She published her first collection, *Dark Like the River*, through the Calcutta Writers Workshop in 1987.

Divakaruni and her husband moved to Sunnyvale, California, in 1989. Within two years, having gained exposure to the plight of refugees from Afghanistan, women in dysfunctional families, and women seeking asylum from abuse in shelters, Divakaruni grew acutely aware of the need for specialized assistance for immigrant women. She hoped to create a service for immigrant women in which their customs and cultural needs could be taken into consideration. Divakaruni thus founded and became president of Maitri, based in the San Francisco area, which runs a help line to offer advice to South Asian women in distress and direct them toward assistance.

While living in the Bay Area, Divakaruni also began teaching at Foothill College, in Los Altos Hills, and she published additional poetry collections in 1990 and 1991. She first ventured into fiction with *Arranged Marriage* (1995), a collection of short stories approaching the modern evolution of the Indian institution of arranged marriage from a feminist perspective. In 1997, she began a two-year stint writing online for *Salon* (her essays remain archived on the site) and published another volume of poetry as well as her first novel, *The Mistress of Spices*, a well-reviewed magical-realist tale about a spice seller with special powers. She has written prolifically ever since. The realist novel *Sister of My Heart* (1999) was followed by another story collection and then *The Vine of Desire* (2002), which continues the story of Anju and Sudha, the main characters of *Sister of My Heart*, in America. Divakaruni has edited two collections of cross-cultural essays for writers and one collection of modern-day California stories in addition to her increasing array of fiction titles—she published eight fiction volumes in the first decade of the twenty-first century.

PLOT SUMMARY

Book One: The Princess in the Palace of Snakes

CHAPTERS 1–4

In the opening chapter of *Sister of My Heart*, eight-year-old Sudha meditates on what the Bidhata Purush—fate as deity—has dictated for the Chatterjee family. The family includes Sudha's cousin Anju, their three mothers (one being an aunt to both), and a number of servants, Singhji being the most beloved. Anju and Sudha were born the day their mothers found out about their fathers' demise. In chapter 2, Anju tells of her special twin-like bond with Sudha, a bond that is not diminished by offhand comments about their distant cousinship by their honorary aunt, Sarita, at teatime.

In chapter 3, at age twelve, Sudha finally learns what is known about the fate of the two fathers from her aunt Pishi: Sudha's father, Gopal, a cousin of Anju's father, Bijoy, had been welcomed into the Chatterjee household but unable over the years to succeed financially. Hoping to bring fortune to the Chatterjees, Gopal persuaded Bijoy to invest in a journey with another man to a fabled ruby cave, and both men insisted on going along. Weeks later, the police recovered two bodies near a river wreck, presumed to be the two Chatterjee men. Just before that journey, Bijoy discovered that the man whom Gopal claimed was his father, an

estranged uncle in Khulna, had died with no recognized male heirs—Gopal was a fraud. After hearing the story, Sudha begins to carry her father's guilt over Anju's father's death. By the time the two girls turn thirteen, Anju is growing distressed over her sister's recent emotional distance—but Anju confirms her unconditional love for Sudha, whose spirits are revived.

CHAPTERS 5–10

At age sixteen, Anju persuades Sudha—who is generally resigned to the conservative values enforced by their parents—to skip class at their all-girls convent school to see the latest romantic blockbuster. At the cinema, the girls put on casual clothes and makeup, and a young man, Ashok, happens to sit next to Sudha, who is instantly smitten and chats recklessly. In the restroom, Sarita discovers the girls and escorts them home. Threatened by her daughter's blossoming independence and spontaneous behavior, which could potentially wreck her high-caste reputation, Nalini, Sudha's mother, declares that Sudha will not attend college so as to be married off early. Sudha pities her resentful mother and is resigned to her demands.

In chapter 8, Anju, who dreams of running her mother's bookstore, urges Sudha to rebel and follow her own dream to be a clothing designer. But above all Sudha wants a happy family—which fuels her puppy love for Ashok, whom she occasionally sees while being driven to and from school. On their graduation day, Singhji, acting as chauffeur, heeds Sudha's plea to stop so she can speak to Ashok. She will be housebound while her mother seeks a match, so he will ask his parents to propose a marriage—although his middle-caste family's wealth was earned through bourgeois means, in trade. Nonetheless, Sudha is in love.

CHAPTERS 11–15

Anju's mother, Gouri, is unwell; she has suffered a mild heart attack, and now, with financial circumstances uncertain, Anju must also marry instead of attending college. Nalini takes charge, strictly monitoring the girls' self-enhancing marriage-preparation activities, including complexion care and sewing lessons. Gouri plans to sell the bookstore. As the mothers consider proposals, Anju suggests a plea on Ashok's behalf, yet Sudha insists on a passive role. But once a proposal from the family of Ramesh Sanyal is favored, Sudha's distress inspires Singhji to suggest making a plan.

In chapter 14, the Sanyals make a visit chauvinistically known as a bridal viewing. Sudha surprises Anju by being docile and agreeable—and later reveals that Ashok (tipped off by Singhji) has written to arrange a meeting at the Kalighat temple the next day. At the temple early in the morning, she and Ashok conspire to elope, and they kiss.

CHAPTERS 16–20

To say goodbye to the bookstore, Anju helps take inventory, and a striking man asks her about Virginia Woolf, one of her favorite authors, and buys a set of the books. She is smitten—and he turns out to be Sunil Majumdar, her prospective match, so they agree on marriage. When his family pays the bride-viewing visit, the father reveals his antipathy to the slightest scandal being attached to the bride's family's name—meaning Sudha's elopement would doom Anju's marriage. Feeling faint, Sudha is steadied by Sunil in a moment alone—and he confesses being enamored of her more than he is of Anju, who soon returns unaware. Later, Sudha dispatches Singhji with a note to Ashok calling off their plans.

In chapter 18, a week before their joint wedding, Anju and Sudha are shown by the mothers the one ruby left behind by Gopal. Instead of pawning it, they resolve to leave it in the bank vault. The day before the weddings, Sudha receives a package filled with money from her father, who is evidently alive. She confers with Pishi, and they conclude that Gopal must have killed Bijoy and the other man; Sudha sends Pishi to give the morally tainted money to beggars. In the course of the marriage ceremonies, Anju feels hollowed out upon realizing Sunil's affection for Sudha. When Sudha unknowingly drops a handkerchief, Anju watches Sunil slip it into his pocket. Anju confronts Sudha and misinterprets her guilty look.

Book Two: The Queen of Swords
CHAPTERS 21–24

At the Sanyals' residence in the nearby city of Bardhaman, Sudha fears where her bridal night must go; but Ramesh kindly agrees to a (secretly) platonic relationship at first. Anju finds life with Sunil in his parents' home (in Calcutta) agreeable. But one night at dinner, Sunil's father angrily tosses some chutney across the room because he disapproves of it, splattering Sunil's mother. Sunil had requested it, and he argues with his father, who accuses Sunil of illicit

behavior in America. Anju is shocked. Later, Sunil agrees that, when he returns to America while Anju awaits a visa, she can stay at her mother's house. Sudha, meanwhile, is barraged with the needs and requests of Ramesh's brothers and mother; she has been given the keys to the house, signifying her responsibility. Before leaving for America, Anju finally reunites with Sudha, visiting by train. Anju regrets that Sudha seems resigned to domesticity.

CHAPTERS 25–29

Three years after her marriage, Sudha has settled into a wifely relationship with Ramesh. When Ramesh's aunt Tarini visits and boasts about her daughter-in-law's pregnancy—with a boy—Sunil's mother turns icy toward Sudha, who remains without child after two years of trying. Anju's life has turned typically American, with little time for cooking between her classes, homework, and errands. Sunil confesses indifference to Woolf and fails to sympathize with the pressured Sudha, and he and Anju fight.

Sudha realizes that Ramesh defers to his controlling mother, who seems to value Sudha strictly for her yet-unproven childbearing capacity. When a specialist in Calcutta confirms her good health—suggesting Ramesh might see a doctor—and at the Chatterjee house, Sudha realizes her intense desire for a baby. Calling home, Anju finds Sudha elusive and laments her distance from Calcutta. Sudha finds out from Singhji that Ashok is still waiting for her. When he drives her back to Bardhaman, she is at once whisked away by Ramesh's mother to visit a shrine to Shashti, goddess of childbirth. There, Sudha is overwhelmed by the laments of the childless women. Sudha gives her gold bangles to one desperate young woman who fears vengeance from her husband's family for her presumed barrenness, telling the woman to visit the hospital with her husband.

CHAPTERS 30–33

Anju discovers that she is pregnant, and Sunil grows warmer toward her. Calling India, she finds that Sudha is pregnant, too. Sudha's mother-in-law now caters to her needs—or rather, to her presumed grandson's needs. When a cousin has a baby with a birth defect, Anju and Sudha both schedule tests. Anju's baby boy is healthy; so is Sudha's baby girl—but her mother-in-law, insistent on the firstborn being a son, demands an abortion, as Sudha relates when she calls Anju from the post office. She has taken some money from Ramesh's drawer, and Anju advises her to flee back to the Chatterjee house. The trip is daunting, and when she reaches home, Nalini disapproves, but Gouri and Pishi support Sudha. After a phone call confirms matters, Ramesh's mother calls for divorce and sends the papers. Nalini wails, but Pishi refuses to allow her niece's fate to be dictated by social stigma; they will sell the house and land and buy a flat, and all will help Sudha raise her daughter.

CHAPTERS 34–39

Anju and Sunil fight over Sudha's decision not to abort, and Anju resolves to get a job and buy Sudha and her daughter tickets to America. In Calcutta, while packing up to move out, Sudha is visited by Ashok, who remains devoted to her, and they start spending time together. But Ashok confesses his belief that they will need to be alone at first—that the mothers will have to raise the not-yet-born Dayita. Anju enjoys the independence of working, but at her checkup the doctor scolds her for poor diet and health and suggests she drop out of school. She declines—and never mentions her job—but starts eating better.

In chapter 37, the mothers advise Sudha to accept Ashok's reasonable proposal, but she refuses. She ponders Anju's invitation to America, wary of Sunil's feelings toward her. Meanwhile, the mothers are invigorated by the new setting, free of the patriarchal ambience of the old house. After a stressful week, Anju sits through pain while awaiting Sunil at the train station; when she gives up, she finds him reclining at home, angry. He has found out about her job through a phone message. They start to fight, and Anju has a miscarriage. Blaming herself, she plummets into depression. The mothers keep Sudha in the dark, but Sudha finally reaches Sunil by phone and finds out the tragic news. Over the phone, she tells a consoling story to the sleeping Anju—who wakes to help finish the story. Sudha agrees to visit America. Dayita is born, to the household's delight. Ashok visits once more, saying he can even embrace Dayita now—but Sudha does not know if she will come back from America and bids him goodbye.

CHAPTERS 40–42

Preparing for their visit, Anju is setting up Sudha and Dayita's room when she discovers a small container in a box of Sunil's. It holds Sudha's handkerchief from their wedding day.

Before boarding the plane, Sudha is given the ruby by the mothers, a credit card by Ashok, and a mysterious envelope—a letter from her father. Therein he reveals the truth of his and Bijoy's fates: After they found the ruby cave and took one jewel each, Bijoy confronted Gopal about his lineage; Gopal was indeed Bijoy's uncle's son, but an illegitimate, unrecognized one. That night the other man, Haldar, drugged them and tossed them into the river. Bijoy could not swim, but Gopal was able to get back onto the craft, and he attacked Haldar, who smashed a lantern in his face. With half his face scalded, Gopal knocked Haldar overboard, and the craft burned. Bijoy could not be found. Gopal recovered in a nearby village and soon read in a newspaper of his presumed death. Beginning then, he reinvented himself as the humble Singhji. Now knowing that her father did not murder Bijoy, Sudha feels released from the guilt she bore over Bijoy's death. Sunil, wistfully, and Anju, needfully, greet Sudha at the airport. Anju reluctantly holds Dayita but then knows she can accept the girl as a daughter.

CHARACTERS

Ashok

A young man who meets the sixteen-year-old Sudha at the theater, Ashok develops a crush that is sustained by naught but glances of Sudha being driven to and from school. When Sudha's refusal to jeopardize Anju's marriage makes elopement impossible, Ashok becomes an idealized romantic figure whose heroic image survives Sudha's short and uninspired marriage. He has remained devoted to her—but, whether he is too needful of Sudha's attention or too attached to the biological imperative to ensure the survival of his own offspring rather than a competitor's, Ashok fails the test of devotion to Sudha's daughter. He has shattered his image, and even his later embracement of the idea of a stepchild cannot fully redeem him.

Anjali (Anju) Chatterjee

Daughter of Bijoy and Gouri, Anju is an enthusiastic, ethically driven girl who refuses to allow Sudha to deny herself life's pleasures and freedoms. She persuades Sudha to cut class to catch a movie and, though wary of Ashok at first, tries to help unite Sudha and Ashok in marriage.

When Sudha declines to elope, however, Anju fails to consciously realize that her cousin has done so for the sake of Anju's prospective marriage to Sunil. In turn, when Sunil's attraction to Sudha becomes evident, Anju, as if to preserve her esteem for Sunil, blames Sudha for bewitching him. After their weddings, distance lingers between them, and when Anju visits just before leaving for America, Sudha realizes that their perspectives on the world no longer coincide. They grow close again while pregnant together, and Anju further supports Sudha's independence by encouraging her to flee the Sanyal household to preserve her unborn daughter's life. But Anju takes her own independence too far, working, studying, and eating in such a way that she compromises her health, and likely as a result, she suffers a miscarriage. Now needing Sudha more than ever, Anju dismisses Sunil's evident persisting attraction to her cousin and persuades Sudha to bring her daughter, Dayita, to America.

Basudha (Sudha) Chatterjee

Daughter of Gopal and Nalini, Sudha is a beautiful, empathetic girl who habitually caters to the needs of others, owing to both her mother's conditioning and the guilt she carries over her father's tragic impact on the Chatterjee household. Her bond with Anju is tested by the presumption, based on incomplete knowledge of Gopal's deceit, that they are actually not related; but their love binds them nonetheless, and in the end they turn out to be second cousins after all (through a birth out of wedlock). The truth of her origins—her father's deceit, her mother's poverty—contributes to the disdain Sudha acquires for rules of social status. She would rather marry Ashok for love, whatever his caste, than Ramesh for familial respect. Her valuing of life over reputation inspires her to save her daughter and steer toward divorce rather than submit to Mrs. Sanyal's misogynistic order to abort. Sudha's prioritizing of her own independence inevitably leads her down the only available path offering complete escape from the judgment of upper-caste India: departure to America.

Bijoy Chatterjee

Father of Anju and husband of Gouri, Bijoy became quickly endeared to the man who arrived and introduced himself as a cousin, Gopal. Bijoy willingly extended permanent hospitality to Gopal and his wife. Eventual awareness of Gopal's deception, whatever the truth, did not prevent

Bijoy from trusting Gopal enough to join him on the ruby expedition. As it happened, Bijoy's trust was well placed, but Gopal's essential honesty could not shield them from Haldar's treachery.

Gopal Chatterjee
See Singhji

Gouri Chatterjee

Anju's mother was seen as the perfect (loyal, docile) wife to Bijoy. Gouri's submissive role, however, perhaps allowed his ill-advised participation in Gopal's ruby quest. After being widowed, Gouri raises her daughter with stoic resolution to uphold the family name, resigned to devoting all her energy to the bookstore and the family's financial survival. This compromises her health, leading to heart troubles. Her rationality is often subsumed beneath Nalini's overwrought expectations for the daughters. Only when Pishi proclaims the injustice of the patriarchal dictates they have followed all their lives does Gouri actively support Sudha's—and her own—independence.

Nalini Chatterjee

Swept up in Gopal's cunning deceit, Nalini leaves her impoverished home village for the promised grandeur of elite life in Calcutta. When Gopal proves all charm, no wealth, Nalini, stranded as his fellow interloper at the Chatterjees' home, turns resentful and needles him constantly. When Gopal's quest to prove himself leads to his disappearance, Nalini, left a widow to raise Sudha, shrouds herself in deceit with regard to her origins, ever glorifying the superior honor and stature of the (reimagined) family she left behind. Nalini controls and clings to her daughter out of both loneliness and a veiled desire to resurrect the unfulfilled promise of her own life by securing as prestigious a life as possible for Sudha. But Nalini defines prestige in society's terms, leaving her in permanent conflict with Sudha, who desires personal harmony and love. Nalini never realizes that Sudha has been told the truth about her parents' origins by Pishi.

Dayita

Born soon before Sudha embarks on her trip to America, Dayita, whose name means "beloved," embodies Sudha's declaration to the world that a woman's life—both her own and her daughter's—is as valuable as a man's.

Deepa

The daughter-in-law of Ramesh's aunt Tarini, Deepa, through her timely pregnancy, enables Tarini to boast about her future grandson, irking Mrs. Sanyal.

Dinabandhu

Dinabandhu is a servant at the Sanyal household.

Haldar

Haldar is the man who lures Gopal, and consequently Bijoy, into sponsoring and joining a journey to a fabled ruby cave. Intending to murder both men and claim their two rubies, Haldar drugs Gopal inadequately, and Gopal avenges Bijoy's death by returning to the craft and killing Haldar.

Ramur Ma

A servant in the Chatterjees' employ, Ramur Ma begins chaperoning the girls everywhere after the cinema fiasco, loyally reporting all behaviors to the mothers.

Mr. Majumdar

Sunil's father is a classic tyrannical Indian patriarch. He conceives that the slightest blemish on the moral image of his son's wife's family would reflect poorly on him and would thus offer sufficient justification for the annulment of a match. His obscene treatment of Sunil's mother—humiliating her with chutney she made at her son's request—sparks an argument that leads Sunil to replace his filial respect with payments toward the debt his father believes he is owed for Sunil's upbringing.

Mrs. Majumdar

Warm and congenial toward Anju ordinarily, Mrs. Majumdar retreats into a cocoon of silent obedience in the presence of her husband. She suffers emotionally when the rift between Sunil and his father leaves Sunil out of touch.

Sunil Majumdar

Striking Anju as a literary-minded emigrant whose traditional garb signals his sustained connection with India, Sunil makes a perfect first impression on Anju. But his rash pocketing of Sudha's handkerchief at the joint wedding reveals to Anju his affection for her cousin. And at their home in California, Sunil takes advantage of the American glorification of independence, claiming his right to go on secret evening excursions and shedding the veneer of his feigned interest in Virginia Woolf. In addition, his typically masculine Indian perspective with regard to Sudha's circumstances causes a rift with the pregnant Anju.

Pishi

Bijoy's younger sister loses her husband at only eighteen and is thus condemned to live out her life in Bijoy's household as is considered proper for widowed women: reclusively, abstinently, and self-effacingly. She takes pride in helping to raise Anju and Sudha but must suffer Nalini's barbs about not being a true parent. Yet her status as aunt allows her to befriend the girls in ways the mothers cannot, and when Sudha insists on hearing the story of her father's disappearance, Pishi eventually obliges. Pishi's sympathy for Sudha's need for independence is critical in swaying Gouri, and even Nalini, to support whatever Sudha decides for her destiny.

Mrs. Sanyal

At first playing the part of an aging widow glad to relinquish control of her household to her eldest son's wife, Mrs. Sanyal shows her true colors when Sudha and Ramesh seem unable to get pregnant, blaming Sudha and treating her like a deficient female. Mrs. Sanyal whirs into gear when the pregnancy finally comes—and, believing it her right to demand that her first grandchild be a boy, insists that the offending future granddaughter be aborted. Afraid of what Mrs. Sanyal is capable of, Sudha justifiably flees.

Ramesh Sanyal

A railroad engineer whose travels often leave Sudha alone with his family, Ramesh is sensitive enough to allow some time to pass before he and his wife consummate their arranged marriage. Sudha accepts him but never really learns to love him. When he buckles pathetically at his mother's insistence that Sudha abort her unborn girl, Sudha easily concludes that Ramesh does not deserve to claim her as his wife.

Sarita

An honorary aunt to Anju and Sudha, Sarita is a regular at teatime at the Chatterjees'. She happens to discover the two girls in the restroom at the cinema, and she escorts them home.

Singhji

Singhji began life as Gopal. His trying childhood as an illegitimate child motivated him to exact karmic revenge on the world by claiming an identity as a legitimate son. Years after, the revelation of his deceit did not undo the loving connection that he had forged with his cousin Bijoy. But after leading Bijoy to an adventurous death while surviving hideously scarred, Gopal felt incapable of returning to face the Chatterjees and his wife, Nalini. Thus, he forged a new identity as Singhji, to ever serve the Chatterjees—and remain near his daughter, Sudha—by gaining employment as their driver. Singhji is heartbroken when his graduating daughter, already bearing his guilt, misinterprets the revelation of his survival and redirects his gift of his life's savings to beggars. He is finally redeemed in Sudha's eyes through the letter she reads as she departs for America.

Tarini

Ramesh's aunt Tarini does her best to belittle Mrs. Sanyal, who, coming from a family that was decidedly not rich, married into the Sanyal household through Tarini's older brother. The pressure of Tarini's constant condescension contributes to Mrs. Sanyal's overbearing involvement with the production of her own future grandchild.

THEMES

Love

One of Divakaruni's primary thematic concerns in *Sister of My Heart* is the nature of love, including both familial and romantic love, and how and why it endures. The initial focus is on the twin-sisterly relationship of Anju and Sudha, who were born on the same day and raised in unity. While their shared experiences bind them superficially, more critical is their profoundly intimate understanding of each other's habitual thought processes and perspectives on experiences. They often look into each other's eyes and intuit what the other is thinking. Sunil's wayward affection for Sudha causes a minor rift between them, lessening their contact once they are separated by their marriages; but they at times yearn for each other, knowing that no one else can better understand what they are feeling in their new circumstances. The author's interest in exploring the bonds that form between women, fostered by her work with her organization assisting South Asian women in troubled domestic circumstances, was part of her inspiration in developing this particular narrative.

Divakaruni adeptly contrasts this female-female bond with the male-female bonds of the respective marriages. Anju and Sunil appear to be an excellent match at first, but Sunil's minor yet telling deception regarding Virginia Woolf perhaps signifies how improbable it is that two people in circumstances arranged by their parents could prove so thoroughly compatible. They ultimately fight frequently; but Anju's pregnancy acts as a sort of seal on their marriage, uniting them in an even more permanent way. Sudha and Ramesh are not so well matched, especially in that she has no instinctive attraction to him, a fact that would seem to doom any pairing. Ramesh seems wise to allow a period during which they can get to know each other before becoming fully intimate. But, beyond being a likely obstacle to attraction on Sudha's behalf, Ramesh's spinelessness proves their undoing, as Sudha cannot abide by his mother's dictatorial control where the life of her unborn daughter is concerned.

Of course, both women are thrust into arranged marriages that give them little time to get to know their partners before having to reconcile themselves with a commitment to spending the rest of their lives together. Many observers—perhaps including the author herself—would be inclined to point out that this is not a natural way for two people to get to know each other. When a couple's first interaction comes at a "bride viewing," the potential for a lifetime alliance is the first thing on everyone's mind. To the contrary, in the context of simple friendship or the spontaneity of a chance encounter at, say, a matinée, the thought of marriage is allowed to be completely absent from anyone's mind. Thus, in arranged circumstances, a genuine, natural interaction with the other, or an unscripted meeting of two souls, is perhaps not merely difficult but outrightly impossible. The instantly mutually attuned vibe between Sudha and Ashok exemplifies the romantic notion of love at first sight—but this relationship is never consummated. Divakaruni demonstrates an interest in not just heralding but also reconstructing the power of fairy tales in this novel. That Sudha and Ashok ultimately fail to connect may suggest that the highly charged environment of a modern movie theater—the romantic ambience of the film, complete with images of communing flesh and stimulative music, the flattering darkness, the partial anonymity, the incidental nearness of bodies—is, like a bride viewing, an extreme setting in terms of coupled interaction. The novel as a whole, in providing no example of a male-female bond equal to the

TOPICS FOR FURTHER STUDY

- Read Virginia Woolf's feminist nonfiction text *A Room of One's Own* and write a paper discussing how Woolf's messages are evident in the character of Anju and in the overall plot of *Sister of My Heart*.

- Divakaruni invokes a number of figures from Hindu mythology in her novel, including Ganesh, Shiva, Vishnu, Brahma, Krishna, and Lakshmi. Research these and any other figures mentioned. Create a digital presentation summarizing the relevant mythological stories and analyzing how Divakaruni's novel draws on, parallels, contrasts, or otherwise invokes these figures and their tales. Provide public-domain images of the gods, stories of their backgrounds, and relevance to Hindus over history.

- Create a spreadsheet to help you analyze the narrative structure of *Sister of My Heart*: For each chapter, use one column to identify the narrator and additional columns to list or record various features of the narration for that chapter. For example, you may, within each chapter, identify all major incidents or revelations and classify them by type; identify the character(s) most central to each incident or revelation; and describe the current status of the relationship between Anju and Sudha, among other possible features of the narration. Inspect your spreadsheet to see if any patterns become evident—perhaps either Anju or Sudha as narrator is favored for certain types of scenes, or perhaps the narrator is not the central character in a scene. Write a brief paper explaining your methods of categorization and relating any conclusions you can draw about Divakaruni's narrative strategies.

- India, with a 2010 population of about 1.15 billion (or nearly four times that of the United States), is projected to be one of the most significant actors in the global community in the twenty-first century. Research India's current role in the world, addressing such issues as economic power, military concerns, diplomatic stances, domestic challenges, and so forth. Present your findings in a formal research paper or as a Web page with links to relevant resources and facts.

- Read Indian novelist Anita Desai's young-adult novel *Village by the Sea* (2009), about the hardscrabble lives of children living in a fishing village near Bombay (Mumbai). In an essay, contrast the portrayal of this impoverished family with the portrayal of the relatively privileged Chatterjees in *Sister of My Heart*. Discuss how the different settings affect the tone, plot, popular appeal, and other aspects of each novel.

profound connection and sustained devotion between Anju and Sudha, perhaps suggests that the purest love exists outside the prescriptive confines and physical expectations of male-female romance and marriage.

Gendered Morality

Divakaruni's novel has much to say with regard to high-caste India's traditional gendered definitions of moral virtue. The Chatterjees' mothers are extremely restrictive regarding their daughters' behavior, disallowing even the most insignificant, incidental interaction with males. The girls are not allowed to attend parties with their peers, and following the moral breach of the afternoon matinée, they are chaperoned everywhere and slated for marriage soon after graduation. The mothers believe that this control will guarantee the preservation of the girls' womanly virtue. Yet in delineating such wide-ranging restrictions for their daughters' behavior, the Chatterjee mothers are in fact catering precisely to the demands and expectations of men like Mr. Majumdar. Sudha must dismiss the idea of romance with Ashok in order

Sudha stays in India. (*Jan S. | Shutterstock.com*)

to guarantee the preservation of Anju's match with Mr. Majumdar's son. Men are not subjected to quite the same rules—Mr. Majumdar is aware of Sunil's moral indiscretions in America but would not tolerate the same in a potential bride—and in the Sanyal household, for example, the expectation is that the women serve Ramesh and his younger brothers alike. Still, it is not just women who find their lives governed excessively by societal rules. Mr. Majumdar wields a patriarchal whip over his son's life, and Bijoy is understood to have had a similarly restricted upbringing, having been "trapped since birth in the cage of propriety"; this is partly what spurred him on the ruby adventure. Similarly, Sunil was spurred to migrate to America to escape his father's heavy-handed influence.

Back in India, Sudha's life seems to be directed down a one-way street once she becomes pregnant. As the mothers later assure her, no one—at least, no one adequately respectable—would want to marry a divorced mother of one; meanwhile, Mrs. Sanyal insists on a grandson coming first, to the point that she expects Sudha to agree to an abortion. Faced with the choice of killing her child or sacrificing her image, Sudha

takes the most humane option. Ashok then has the potential to be an epitome of selfless masculinity: he has remained devoted to Sudha through her marriage, and even when she warns him that she may not be able to love anyone as she will love her daughter, he declares his openness to a union with her. But the idea proves only a fairy tale, as Ashok cannot conceive of himself as a stepfather after all. With even the mothers frowning upon her decision to refuse Ashok under the conditions he lays out, Sudha appears utterly unsupported in her quest to preserve an ideal life for herself with her daughter. But it is Pishi's voice that rises above the chaotic din of the mothers' arguing to assert that she will allow no Chatterjee girl to live the repressed life prescribed by Indian society for women who have lost their husbands. Sudha thus finds sanctuary in the mothers' new den; but she cannot imagine that Indian society at large will ever extend her daughter the same respect given children of successful marriages. The novel's conclusion, in which Sudha, encouraged by Anju, elects to drift to America, where single mothers abound, may reflect a conviction on Divakaruni's part that there exists in America a societal moral openness that cannot be found in upper-caste India.

STYLE

Dual Narration

The structure of *Sister of My Heart* is consistent throughout, alternating chapters narrated by Anju and by Sudha. This strategy has several interesting implications. To begin, the reader gets to know both cousins' thoughts and reflections on most everything that occurs—with their perspectives often proving complementary—while Divakaruni is careful not to offer duplicate versions of the same action. Rather, the tale remains sequential, and when appropriate, Sudha assesses Anju's responses to circumstances, or vice versa. As such, Divakaruni can sustain suspense by veiling the motivations behind either character's actions when desired. For example, with the bridal viewings, in each case the cousin out of focus narrates. Anju tells of the Sanyals' visit to see Sudha, leaving the reader to wonder along with Anju how Sudha is feeling; and in turn, Sudha narrates the Majumdars' visit to see Anju, allowing Sudha to give frank assessments of the family—and to reveal the moment when Sunil confesses his attraction to her. Thus, for any given scene, Divakaruni can choose whichever cousin's perspective suits her aims best. The dual narration also prioritizes the cousins' relationship with each other. In going back and forth between the two, the reader is given continual commentary on how they are interacting and how they feel about each other. The interpolation of any other narrators would have broken this chain and reduced the emphasis on the cousins' bond. Finally, the reliable narrative switching makes reader fatigue with either narrator unlikely; averaging just under eight pages each, the chapters are relatively brief (and also broken up internally), never leaving the reader mired down in any one scene.

Storytelling

The art of storytelling is both thematically important and stylistically invoked to give shape to the novel. Dedicating the book to those who told her stories and those she tells stories to now, Divakaruni devotes the first sentence to the "old tales" of the Bidhata Purush, who decides newborns' fates. At the chapter's end, Sudha brings this figure to life, imagining the words he marked on her and Anju's foreheads. In the next chapter, Anju affirms that Sudha, who is just like a fairy-tale princess, is "the best storyteller," as "she can

take the old tales and make them new by putting us in them." Indeed, Sudha approaches reality as a never-ending series of stories that are being constantly written and rewritten. She even confides that mythic pagan heroes and heroines "seem closer to me than most of the people in my life." When gripped by her burgeoning love for Ashok, Sudha cannot explain how she feels—but she can tell Anju a story about it. Anju soon observes that at some point Sudha "started getting caught in the enchanted web of the stories she loved so much and told so well."

Though perhaps seeming escapist or illusory, such a story-centric perspective on life encourages one, when needing to adapt to unexpected turns of events, to simply rewrite one's role in one's own story. Sudha does this for herself when she must marry Ramesh. Having made the decision to forsake her own happiness to ensure Anju's, she might have yet endlessly ached for Ashok; but instead she reimagines her role in the world, finding what happiness she can in the Sanyals' home. When circumstances there become unbearable, however, she rewrites her role again and departs. Sudha's charmed ability to capture reality with her stories comes into play at one of the novel's most critical junctures—when Anju seems unable to save herself from the depression that consumes her after her miscarriage. Anju is unable to come to grips with her immediate reality—her baby is gone, and she blames herself—so what Sudha does, over the phone, is remove Anju from that reality and situate her instead in a story. Sudha begins by describing a queen whose desperate circumstances mirror Sudha's own, with the tale leading to a chasm, in the form of the ocean, where the possibility of resolution is uncertain. The queen needs help—and Anju, engrossed in the story, which yet serves to shield her from her own painful reality, intuitively knows precisely how to finish her cousin's tale. In helping conclude the tale, then, Anju transforms from listener to speaker and thereby reenters reality; and by the story's conclusion, Anju has come to understand that she, too, is yet needed, by her cousin, and must rouse her spirits so as to preserve her own life and lend support. Just as Sudha's story gives Anju courage, Divakaruni surely intends her novel to lend courage to any and all women whose experiences resemble either Sudha's loveless marriage or Anju's heartbreaking loss of her child.

COMPARE & CONTRAST

- **1980s:** As the decade begins, Calcutta's population is about 9.2 million, making it India's second-largest city. About 3 million of those people live in slums.

  1990s: By the beginning of the decade, Calcutta's population has grown to about 11 million, with 3.6 million people in slums.

  Today: As the twenty-first century opens, the population of Kolkata, as it is now known, has grown to 13.2 million, with 4.3 million in slums. The city's estimated population as of 2010 is 15.6 million.

- **1980s:** By the end of the decade, in 1991, some 200,000 girls are being aborted annually in India.

  1990s: By the end of the decade, in 2001, some 410,000 girls are being aborted annually in India.

  Today: As of 2011, an estimated 600,000 girls are being aborted annually in India.

- **1980s:** The Calcutta of the 1930s is romantically depicted in the French-language film *The Bengali Night* (1988), based on Mircea Eliade's 1933 novel *Bengal Nights* and featuring, alongside the Indian actors, the rising English actor Hugh Grant.

  1990s: The poverty on the streets of modern-day Calcutta is represented in the film *City of Joy* (1992), an adaptation of the novel by Dominique Lapierre.

  Today: Kolkata is depicted as home to tragic stories in the documentary *Born into Brothels* (2004) and as the homeland of American immigrants in *The Namesake* (2006), the film adaptation of Jhumpa Lahiri's 2003 novel.

HISTORICAL CONTEXT

Arranged Marriage and Abortion in Modern India

Sister of My Heart takes place primarily in Calcutta, where the Chatterjees as well as the Majumdars reside and where Anju and Sudha attend school. Capital of the state of West Bengal, at the eastern end of India, the city was officially renamed Kolkata—a more accurate transliteration of the Bengali name—in 2001 (two years after the publication of Divakaruni's novel). From the time of India's independence from Britain in 1947, several cities have been renamed to more closely reflect more traditional pronunciations, including the megacity Mumbai, which had been known in English as Bombay until 1995. Bardhaman, the Sanyals' home city, is a two-hour drive to the northwest of Calcutta. Yet, especially since the girls' activities are strictly limited, the novel's locale is not integral to the plot; Anju's offhand mention of strolling with Sunil to the Victoria Memorial and Rabindra Sarobar—an artificial lake in Calcutta—marks one of the few references to aspects of the actual city. Thus, the specific context of Calcutta is not as relevant to the novel as is the broader cultural context of the institution of marriage in late-twentieth-century upper-caste India.

As suggested by her social work and the title of her first short-story collection, *Arranged Marriage*, Divakaruni is especially familiar with this cultural context. In addition to centering the plot of *Sister of My Heart* around Anju's and Sudha's marital circumstances, which are reflective of contemporary circumstances for Indian women, the author incorporates debate about the issue through the character groupings of Nalini, Gouri, and Pishi, widowed women seeking the best opportunities possible for their two girls; Sudha and Mrs. Sanyal, who are placed in opposition by Sudha's pregnancy with a girl; and Anju and Sunil, whose perspectives are colored by their shift toward American attitudes.

Anju follows her husband to California. (Mike Liu | Shutterstock.com)

Insight into the institution of marriage in India is offered by the scholar Lina M. Fruzzetti, who in *The Gift of a Virgin: Women, Marriage and Ritual in a Bengali Society*, delineates "the two opposing forms of marriage in Bengali society—sacred, Hindu marriage and non-sacred, controversial, 'love-marriage,' or court-registered marriage." She notes that the English word "love" is used to define the second type of marriage because the closest Bengali term, *prem*, is positive when applied to conjugal love, between husband and wife, but connotes moral depravation when applied to love between unmarried people. Love marriages are often intercaste and/or interfaith relationships.

In the novel, although Mr. Majumdar comes across as something of a caricature in his extreme aversion to any family history of the bride's that might appear to compromise his son's and his own social standing, he is not atypical in this respect. As Fruzzetti writes, "In cases of love-marriages, the parents of the couple and the immediate male-line members of the household are pressured by people of the neighborhood and members of the same caste living in the town to take a stand against the marriage by cutting off all relations with the offending couple." Although ethical perspectives regarding marriage are continuing to evolve in modern India, traditions have deep roots, and the process is a gradual one.

Another aspect of marital/personal relations highlighted by Divakaruni is the question of abortion. Because tradition in India prescribes that the bride's family must pay a substantial dowry to the husband's family, with the bride then leaving her own home to contribute her productivity to the family of her husband, girls prove far more expensive to raise than boys. A study completed in May 2011, reported on by Muneeza Naqvi in the *Huffington Post*, found that the trend of aborting unwanted girls worsened over recent decades. Records are far from complete, especially since many of those aborting girls have managed to skirt a 1996 law that banned testing for gender and so have avoided documentation of their cases. The study thus offers a very broad estimate of between four and twelve million abortions of female fetuses between 1980 and 2010.

Census data released in March 2011 reveals that among children under age six in India, there are only 914 girls for every 1,000 boys. A girl fetus is more likely to be aborted if the family already has a girl or—ironically, from a feminist perspective—if the mother is wealthier and better educated, in which case screening tests and abortion services are better understood and financially more accessible. As Naqvi notes, the Central Intelligence Agency indicates online that in 2011 in India, the birth ratio of girls to boys (a statistic not tracked by India) was 893 to 1,000. Traditional preference for boys is a problem in China as well, where the girl-to-boy birth ratio was 885 to 1,000. Officials in India continue to look for new ways to curb the problem of selective abortion of girls.

CRITICAL OVERVIEW

Reviewers have had warm words for *Sister of My Heart*, although a few have leveled their compliments with less flattering assessments of the execution of the plot. In *Booklist*, Donna Seaman finds profound value in the text, especially as compared to the author's first novel, *Mistress of Spices*. She states that both books have "a power that is both transporting and healing." But Seaman finds that in comparison to the somewhat overwrought exoticism of the first novel, in the second novel the author returns to "subtler textures," similar to those of her short fiction, that work "on a more interior and resonant plane, without sacrificing the aura of magic that surrounds her glistening prose." Seaman concludes, "Serious and entrancing, Divakaruni wraps her social critique in a beautifully figured story."

In *Publishers Weekly*, a contributor calls *Sister of My Heart* "a masterful allegory of unfulfilled desire and sacrificial love" and deems the author "an inspired and imaginative raconteur." The contributor concludes that "if her prose sometimes veers toward the purple, her mesmerizing narrative sustains it well." In *Library Journal*, Wilda Williams ends her brief assessment by ambivalently concluding, "Although much of the plot is contrived (the final revelation is no big surprise) and the male characters are stock clichés, this is still an engaging read, filled with tender, moving moments."

One scholar has criticized Divakaruni for leaning too heavily on stereotypes. Lavina Dhingra

Shankar, in her essay "Not Too Spicy: Exotic Mistresses of Cultural Translation in the Fiction of Chitra Divakaruni and Jhumpa Lahiri," argues that Divakaruni's work sacrifices literary quality in functioning as a sort of cultural exhibitionism readily digested by Americans. Shankar comments that "her fiction caters easily to a mainstream feminist audience interested in learning about yet patronizing 'oppressed' non-Western women." Shankar calls *Sister of My Heart* a "highly sentimentalized romance" that reductively "perpetuates Orientalist stereotypes regarding India." Shankar also disapproves of how the novel "sharply contrasts the moribund and stifling Indian world of aborted romance, forced arranged marriages, religious superstitions, female feticides, and jailor-like matriarchs with an absolute, unlimited freedom in dream-like America." Yet Shankar fails to consider how this dichotomy is balanced by the implications of Anju's miscarriage with regard to what may be compromised through American-style freedom.

CRITICISM

Michael Allen Holmes

Holmes is a writer and editor. In the following essay, he considers what Divakaruni suggests through Sudha's evolving perspective on fate in Sister of My Heart.

Belief in fate is not so common in America, where the enshrinement of essential freedoms in the First Amendment implies rather a societal belief in free will. Where individuals can claim the freedom to say what they wish, practice their own religion, and gather with whomever they please, many would also like to claim that they actively choose how they exercise these freedoms. One might presume that among atheists in particular, who preclude the notion that any divinity has control over the universe, belief in free will, and thus disbelief in fate, would be strong. On the other hand, devoted monotheists, including Jews, Christians, and Muslims, may be more likely to claim an active role for God or Allah in the workings of reality; phrases such as "it's in God's hands" and "God is guiding me down this path" are not uncommonly heard. In *Sister of My Heart*, Divakaruni provides Bengali perspectives on fate, as reflected by Hinduism. In particular, Sudha's progression from belief in fate toward belief in free will suggests that

WHAT DO I READ NEXT?

- In addition to her short fiction and adult novels, Divakaruni has written novels for young adults. *Neela: Victory Song* (2002) traces a twelve-year-old girl's adventurous activities during India's movement for independence in 1939.

- Divakaruni's 2004 novel *Queen of Dreams* incorporates magic realism into its portrayal of a young divorced mother living in California and her relationship with her own mother, a dream interpreter.

- Divakaruni's work is sometimes considered alongside that of the Indian author Arundhati Roy, whose debut novel, *The God of Small Things* (1997), about the tragic experiences of fraternal twins raised in the state of Kerala in the 1960s, won the Booker Prize.

- Among the prominent Bengali author Amitav Ghosh's English-language novels is *The Shadow Lines*, which contrasts the characters' lives in Calcutta in the 1960s with later circumstances in London.

- Many Indian authors do not write in the colonial language of English but in their regional dialects. Popular Bengali author Mahasveta Devi has had some of her works translated into English, including her brief novel *Hajar Churashir Ma* (1975), translated as *Mother of 1084* (1998), about a woman's loss of her son in the Naxalite movement.

- The intimate bond shared by Anju and Sudha in *Sister of My Heart* is similar to the bond between the characters Sula and Nel, African Americans who grow up together in a small town in Ohio, in Toni Morrison's *Sula* (1973).

- One of Divakaruni's spiritual inspirations is Siddha Yoga guru Swami Chidvilasananda. Among her many publications is *Enthusiasm* (1997), which guides the reader toward acknowledgment of one's own sacredness and appreciation of life.

> DIVAKARUNI SEEMS TO SUGGEST THAT TRADITIONALLY MINDED INDIAN PARENTS MAY BE HAPPY TO INSTILL IN THEIR CHILDREN A BELIEF IN FATE BECAUSE DOING SO ENABLES THEM TO MAKE THEIR CHILDREN'S CHOICES FOR THEM."

Divakaruni considers belief in fate to be a limiting factor in one's life.

The opening line of the novel signals not only Sudha's key interest in myths and stories but also a broader societal belief in fate in India: as the "old tales" relate, the Bidhata Purush visits a child the night after its birth "to decide what its fortune is to be." From the beginning the cousins have to cope with misfortune being attached to their names, with news of their fathers' deaths having come that same day. This leads to whispers, not discreet enough to prevent the girls' overhearing, about *"girl-babies who are so much bad luck that they cause their fathers to die even before they are born."* Anju's natural response to this disparagement is to reject any belief in fate; she dismisses the old tales as "nonsense" and dares voice the suspicion that there is no Bidhata Purush, a remark that Pishi appears to consider blasphemous. Sudha, as she proves in her philosophizing, is more emotionally invested in stories and so cannot so easily disbelieve their truths. She comes to imagine that the Bidhata Purush wrote three words on her forehead: "*beauty*," "*goodness*," and, perhaps in accord with her conception, inflicted by society, of the bad luck she brings, "*sorrow*." The novel's first chapter, by being bookended by ruminations on the Bidhata Purush, serves to frame the entire narrative as Sudha's grappling with what she perceives to be her fate.

When Sudha meets Ashok at the theater, she readily concludes that "it was no chance but the inexorable force of destiny, hushed and enormous as the wheeling of the planets, which brought us together." Anju tries to convince her that Ashok is not anyone significant but simply a random stranger, comparing Sudha to "one of those silly lovesick girls in the movie"—girls whose actions and dialogue follow a script. But Sudha insists that "nothing just *happens*," and as if following what fate seems to have scripted for her, she holds fast to what she takes for true love. Sudha intends to follow this love wherever it leads her, even to the point of eloping. But her belief in fate comes into play when, after learning of Mr. Majumdar's aversion to scandal, she is forced to sacrifice either her own love for Ashok or Anju's match with Sunil. She at first remarks, "What ill karma have I performed that I should be plagued with having to make such a choice?" Yet when she gauges the karma she inherited from her father, weighed down as it is by his having lured Bijoy to death, breaking the Chatterjees' hearts, the choice is effectively made for her: "It is only right that this time it will be his daughter's heart which breaks." Sudha's submission to her karma, then, can also be seen as an appeal to her innate sense of virtue: she believes that the moral wrong of her father's actions must still be atoned for, and so she does not really choose how to resolve her dilemma but rather can only do what feels right.

When Sudha later faces another difficult choice—whether to run away from Ramesh or bear a child with him—fate is again consulted, this time in the form of a message from the fertility goddess Shashti. Sudha readily interprets words heard by the weeping girl at the shrine, "*you must choose between your two loves, for only one love is allowed to a woman*," as being meant for her; she imagines that she must choose between a child and romance with Ashok. As far as this is concerned, she concludes that she already made her choice in consummating her marriage with Ramesh. She thus bids goodbye to Ashok by symbolically leaving his recent letter as a sacrificial offering for Shashti. Once again, then, Sudha defers her choice to the fate supposedly decreed for her by the gods.

Notably, while Anju disavows belief in the Bidhata Purush, and thus in fate, she does experience a moment of psychic clarity that resembles belief in fate. As the mothers are discussing what to do with the one ruby Gopal left behind, Anju notes, "From somewhere a thought has come to me, so lightning-sharp, so clearly not *mine*, that I know it's the correct answer." And as if channeling a divine assessment of the future, she realizes when the family can finally claim the ruby: "*Not until we've suffered further, not until the house of the Chatterjees is reduced to a heap of dusty rubble.*" Indeed, only after Sudha's divorce, Anju's miscarriage, and the literal bulldozing of the

Chatterjee home do the mothers bless Dayita with the ruby. Other than during this moment, however, Anju makes clear that she considers the idea of fate to be little more than superstition. What she leans on instead for existential support, fittingly, given her relocation to America, is possibility. The potential elimination of possibility in her life was a concern of her own as well as her mother's when they began considering spouses, a factor that perhaps drew them to the American immigrant; Gouri is careful to seek assurances from Sunil that Anju will be able to complete as much schooling as she likes. Later, when expressing her hope that Sudha will somehow be able to follow her to America, Anju remarks, "I *have* to believe in possibility. How else can we bear the enormous weight of life?" Yet thoughts of possibility bring Anju little consolation after her miscarriage, when all of the possibility inherent in the creation of a child is erased. She ultimately comes to grips with reality not through faith or fate but through Sudha's story—one that provides Anju with a script to follow in a different sense.

While Anju pulls Sudha in the direction of disbelief in fate, Sudha's mother pulls her in the opposite direction. Nalini seems attached to belief in fate partly in accord with tradition and partly in response to her own destiny, which was projected by Gopal to be grand but turned out merely mediocre. Sudha imagines that Nalini foresaw that she had ruined her life soon after boarding the riverboat with Gopal. And when Nalini later became pregnant, she tragically felt "that her one chance at life was over. Things would only get worse now. She was doomed to grow old and die in the borrowed room she had lived in for the last three years." In this light, it becomes evident that one of the functions of a belief in fate is that it allows one to be reconciled with whatever one's circumstances happen to be; rather than regretting a specific choice and blaming oneself, one can hold fate accountable and accept that things could not have happened any differently. Nalini's long-term investment in fate is revealed in her monthly visits to an astrologer and in her constantly announcing, when the marriage arrangements are proceeding smoothly, that "our stars must be really well aligned this month." Nalini is also invested, more than the other mothers, in caste—whereby one is fated from birth to live whatever sort of life is assigned to one's caste—and societal definitions of virtue. She considers, for example, that the burned forehead of Singhji (who is, of course, her unrecognized husband) is "a sure sign of lifelong misfortune." Thus, Nalini relies on fate partly to reconcile herself to her dependency on the Chatterjees and partly to enable her to judge others, whether based on caste, appearance, or other signals. In this sense, Divakaruni links belief in fate with the social oppression of whichever individuals are assigned lesser value. And the reader may also realize that Sudha's fate-inflected conclusions have tended to lead her to submit to parentally enforced marital traditions rather than to her own desires. In effect, then, Divakaruni seems to suggest that traditionally minded Indian parents may be happy to instill in their children a belief in fate because doing so enables them to make their children's choices for them.

Toward the novel's end, Sudha gradually detaches herself from the confines of fate. She is motivated to do so when continued submission to parentally enforced tradition would mean bending to Mrs. Sanyal's will and allowing her unborn girl to be killed. Thus, she flees. Yet this is not a moral stand that she can take privately, as the mothers point out; no decent member of their caste, they assure her, will want to marry a divorced mother of one. Nonetheless, uncertain of what the future may hold—that is, let loose from the scripted fate she has been following—Sudha commits to the divorce. And her next shower is perhaps the most cleansing one she has ever had:

> I am washing away unhappiness, I tell myself. I am washing away the stamp of duty. I am washing away the death sentence that was passed on my daughter. I am washing away everything the Bidhata Purush wrote, for I've had enough of living a life decreed by someone else.

She feels relief and joy upon signing the final divorce documents precisely in being unmoored from fate: "We were starting anew, my daughter and I, and because there were no roles charted out for us by society, we could become anything we wanted." As she ponders a move to America—which, given her disavowal of fate, now seems inevitable—Sudha experiences a moment of doubt: when the wind steals a sketch for a quilt, she shivers and wonders, "Is this the Bidhata Purush's chill, vindictive breath warning me not to stitch into my life patterns he has not placed there?" But with an American sort of stubbornness, she starts the sketch anew, asserting, "I *will* prove myself. I *will* be in charge of my fate. I *will*

A central theme in the novel is tradition. (*Kharidehal Abhirama Ashwin | Shutterstock.com*)

pattern a new life for myself. I swat away the superstitious unease that buzzes in my ears like gnats." Thus, dismissing superstition and, as the thrice-italicized verb implies, embracing free will, Sudha at last directs her existential trajectory toward America, to soon embrace her cousin in the land of possibility.

Source: Michael Allen Holmes, Critical Essay on *Sister of My Heart*, in *Novels for Students*, Gale, Cengage Learning, 2012.

Bridget Kinsella

In the following interview, Divakaruni discusses with Kinsella the role of the immigrant experience in her work.

PW: So much of your work explores the rich and complex relationships between women, but in Queen of Dreams, *a daughter could not have unlocked the mystery of her Indian-born mother without her father. Was this a deliberate decision and direction you took as a writer?*

Chitra Banerjee Divakaruni: As with much of my work, it isn't that I set out to do this, it's just where the story evolved organically. The mother is a mystery to the daughter from the beginning, and it's only after she dies that her words come to the daughter through the journals, but they have to be translated by the father. More than the male or female relationship I think what I was looking at was how in leaving our home culture we lose a lot of it and often we need help. We need translators.

PW: You return to the theme of the immigrant experience—particularly the South Asian immigrant experience—and the awkward relationship to identity for their children. Has your view on this changed as your own American-born children grow up?

CBD: One of the things that I am learning is that each generation will have its own negotiations with identity. And one generation can not necessarily help the other generation with it.

PW: You use 9/11 as a huge lever in the story. Were you worried that it might come off as contrived or was it something you just could not ignore?

CBD: I just couldn't ignore it. A lot of the things I write about 9/11 are actually what happened in our community [the San Francisco Bay Area]. It was very painful and very scary. There was an additional backlash against our community and against other communities that looked different and "suspicious." So this really had to be a big part of the story. What it did for me as an individual was bring up the questions that Rakhi has to face: If I am not American, or if people don't see me as American, then what does that do to my identity?

PW: What do you think we've learned from 9/11?

CBD: I think we all learned that when we are afraid it's easy to want to blame, and the people we want to blame are the people who don't look like us. So one of the real hopes I have with this book is for us to explore that question and make us think about that question: Who is American and who should we identify with? Is it right to blame anyone when something terrible happens? And what are you to do if you belong to a visible minority who then become the victims of fear and hatred? How do we continue to live in America as Americans?

What I want to create in this novel is what makes the dream world, and the world of painful realities, and the world of ancient traditions, and

daily home life—I wanted to mix them all into the novel. I wanted to point to the complexity of human experience and then the whole mysterious level of what is real and what isn't. Sometimes what is "real" because it takes place in the physical world, like 9/11, is so unreal on the level of the soul. Then other things, which in terms of the physical world seem so magical and unbelievable, on the level of the soul seem very real. I hope that worked for the reader.

Source: Bridget Kinsella, "Being American in Today's World," in *Publishers Weekly*, Vol. 251, No. 32, August 9, 2004, p. 229.

Peter Nazareth

In the following review, Nazareth argues that Divakaruni does not portray women as victims in her fiction.

Sister of My Heart is the second novel by Chitra Banerjee Divakaruni, who has previously published four collections of verse, receiving the 1994 award in poetry from the Wallace Alexander Gerbode Foundation; a volume of short stories, *Arranged Marriage* (1996), which received the PEN Oakland Josephine Miles Prize for Fiction, the Bay Area Book Reviewers Award for Fiction, and a Before Columbus Foundation American Book Award; and a best-selling novel, *The Mistress of Spices* (1997; see *WLT* 72:1, p. 207). Her fiction is located in India, usually Calcutta, and/or in the U.S. The protagonists in America get sucked in by MTV, fast food, jeans, et cetera, going deeper, meeting multicultural people, falling in love and living with an American.... The fiction is evocative, poetic, and questing. One story begins with the disappearance of an Indian wife in California and presents what the husband thinks are his feelings, his mother's triumphant visit to help out, and his decision to remarry; we do not see the wife again but realize that, as in D. H. Lawrence's story "The Woman Who Rode Away," she has left for life.

As the Irish writer Kevin Casey said, writers must follow their obsessions. *Sister of My Heart* extends a story, "The Ultrasound," which begins: "My cousin Arundhati and I are both pregnant with our first babies, a fact which gives me great pleasure. Although she's in India and I'm here in California, we've kept close track of each other's progress." In the novel, two women, cousins who were told they were born after their fathers died in pursuit of rubies, get married and become pregnant, one in India and the other in California. The women complete each other, like Sula and Nel in Toni Morrison's *Sula*. Sarita Aunty says, "I swear, you're like those twins, what do they call them, born stuck together." Anju says that Sudha "surprised me by saying, 'Didn't you know, Aunty? We are twins.'" The twinning is duplicated in the form of the novel too, as chapters by Sudha and Anju alternate; they take on each other's characteristics, like Margaret and Dikeledi in Bessie Head's *Maru*. Sudha falls in love with Ashok at a movie Anju insisted they see, but accepts an arranged marriage because Anju's marriage would have been broken off at a hint of scandal such as a cousin eloping with a lower-caste man. When Sudha's mother-in-law discovers she is expecting not a boy but a girl and wants her to get an abortion, Sudha refuses and is divorced; she can now marry Ashok, but turns him down because he says he does not want the daughter. She comes to America at the invitation of Anju, who has miscarried, delivering a boy blue like Lord Krishna. Anju discovers her husband may be carrying a torch for Sudha. Will her soulmate be her rival, or will she fulfill an early wish? "If only Anju and I, like the wives of the heroes in the old tales, could marry the same man, our Arjun, our Krishna, who would love and treasure us both, and keep us both together."

Divakaruni's protagonists are asleep to the heart's intelligence. One of her instruments for awakening is twinning with other texts. Thanks to her mother's bookstore, Anju loves Virginia Woolf, knowledge of which Sunil uses to woo her; she discovers in America he had only faked knowledge of Woolf. "The Maid's Servant's Story" ends like Conrad's *Heart of Darkness*: "Night has taken over the lawn by the time Deepa Mashi finishes the story. We sit in the dark room, held by the echo of her words, until she reaches over to switch on the lamp. . . . We sit like this, two women caught in the repeating, circular world of shadow and memory, watching where the last light, silky and fragile, has spilled itself just above the horizon like the palloo of a saffron sari." Here an Indian woman has returned east and been told an inconclusive story by an Indian woman instead of a European man in the pose of a Buddha whose meaning she must work out. The epigraph to *Sister of My Heart* is from the "son" of Conrad famous for trying to kill the "father," Achebe: "It is only the story . . . that saves our progeny from

blundering like blind beggars into the spikes of the cactus fence."

Another instrument is the mysterious figure who nags the subconscious, made visible in *The Mistress of Spices*, a magical novel which heals through the senses, the protagonist herself falling in sensual love with a young American, losing her powers, and becoming human during the California earthquake. Freedom is earthshaking. Anju accepts it: "There'll be trouble enough later—like an animal I sense it prickling the nape of my neck. I'll deal with it when it comes. But for now the three of us [including Sudha's daughter] stand unhurried, feeling the way we fit, skin on skin on skin, into each other's lives. A rain-dampened sun struggles from the clouds to frame us in its hesitant, holy light." She will create a room of her own.

In Divakaruni's work, despite sex, class, and caste oppression, women need not end up as victims. America chips away at ossified Indian tradition for people to see, as Krishna shows, that the imperative of life is deeper than arranged marriage. America and India are twinned.

Source: Peter Nazareth, Review of *Sister of My Heart*, in *World Literature Today*, Vol. 73, No. 4, Autumn 1999, p. 819.

SOURCES

Beam, Christopher, "Why Did Bombay Become Mumbai?" in *Slate*, December 1, 2008, http://www.slate.com/id/2205701/ (accessed June 29, 2011).

Divakaruni, Chitra Banerjee, *Sister of My Heart*, Anchor Books, 2000.

Farmanfarmaian, Roxane, "Writing from a Different Place," in *Publishers Weekly*, Vol. 248, No. 20, May 14, 2001, p. 46.

Fruzzetti, Lina M., *The Gift of a Virgin: Women, Marriage, and Ritual in a Bengali Society*, Rutgers University Press, 1982, pp. 8–12.

Gale, Jason, and Adi Narayan, "Missing Girls in India Show Scans Aiding Abortions, Study Says," in *Bloomberg*, May 24, 2011, http://www.bloomberg.com/news/2011-05-24/missing-girls-in-india-show-scans-aiding-abortions-study-says.html (accessed June 3, 2011).

Iyer, Nalini, "Embattled Canons: The Place of Diasporic Writing in Indian English Literatures," in *Other Tongues: Rethinking the Language Debates in India*, edited by Nalini Iyer and Bonnie Zare, Rodopi, 2009, pp. 3–21.

Mandal, Somdatta, "Chitra Banerjee Divakaruni," in *Dictionary of Literary Biography*, Vol. 323, *South Asian Writers in English*, edited by Fakrul Alam, Thomson Gale, 2006, pp. 112–22.

McConigley, Nina Swamidoss, "A South Asian American Writer's Perspective: An Interview with Chitra Banerjee Divakaruni," in *Other Tongues: Rethinking the Language Debates in India*, edited by Nalini Iyer and Bonnie Zare, Rodopi, 2009, pp. 97–104.

Naqvi, Muneeza, "India Abortions of Girls on the Rise: Study," in *Huffington Post*, May 24, 2011, http://www.huffingtonpost.com/2011/05/24/india-abortions-of-girls-_n_866067.html (accessed June 3, 2011).

Nazareth, Peter, Review of *Sister of My Heart*, in *World Literature Today*, Vol. 73, No. 4, Autumn 1999, p. 819.

Rasiah, Dharini, "Chitra Banerjee Divakaruni," in *Words Matter: Conversations with Asian American Writers*, edited by King-Kok Cheung, University of Hawai'i Press, 2000, pp. 140–53.

Review of *Sister of My Heart*, in *Publishers Weekly*, Vol. 245, November 9, 1998, p. 55.

Seaman, Donna, Review of *Sister of My Heart*, in *Booklist*, Vol. 95, No. 8, December 15, 1998, p. 707.

Shankar, Lavina Dhingra, "Not Too Spicy: Exotic Mistresses of Cultural Translation in the Fiction of Chitra Divakaruni and Jhumpa Lahiri," in *Other Tongues: Rethinking the Language Debates in India*, edited by Nalini Iyer and Bonnie Zare, Rodopi, 2009, pp. 23–52.

Williams, Wilda, Review of *Sister of My Heart*, in *Library Journal*, Vol. 124, No. 1, January 1999, p. 147.

FURTHER READING

Alcott, Louisa May, *Little Women*, Signet Classics, 2004.
    This renowned American novel portrays a matriarchal, all-female household—a precursor to that of the Chatterjees—in New England during the Civil War.

Chaudhuri, Maitrayee, ed., *Feminism in India*, Zed Books, 2005.
    This collection of essays explores the history of feminist thought in India from various perspectives.

Dutta, Krishna, *Calcutta: A Cultural History*, Interlink Books, 2008.
    In this volume, Dutta explores all aspects of the city of Calcutta, focusing on its literature, music, architecture, and other cultural products. A foreword is provided by the Indian novelist Anita Desai.

Kalpakian, Laura, and Meena Alexander, eds., *Truth Tales: Contemporary Stories by Women Writers of India*, Feminist Press at City University of New York, 1993.
    Divakaruni admires the literary quality and range of storytelling modes in this collection and has used it in her teaching of fiction writing.

SUGGESTED SEARCH TERMS

Chitra Banerjee Divakaruni AND Sister of My Heart

Divakaruni AND South Asian American literature

Divakaruni AND Calcutta AND Bengal

India AND Bengali literature

India OR Bengal AND caste system

Sister of My Heart AND The Vine of Desire

Divakaruni AND Maitri AND San Francisco

Divakaruni AND magic realism

Divakaruni AND online interview

A Town Like Alice

NEVIL SHUTE
1950

Nevil Shute's 1950 novel *A Town Like Alice* was inspired by the story of a Dutch woman whom Shute met in Sumatra in 1949. The woman, Mrs. J. G. Geysel-Vonck, had been taken as a prisoner of war in Malaya by the Japanese, along with a number of women and children. With her infant on her hip, Geysel-Vonck and her party were marched for hundreds of miles through Malaya.

In *A Town Like Alice*, Shute created a character inspired by Geysel-Vonck and her experiences. Jean Paget, the heroine of Shute's novel, is an Englishwoman working in Malaya (now the western portion of Malaysia). Unlike her historical counterpart, she is unmarried. Jean's spirit, strength, and intelligence eventually lead her to be looked upon as the natural leader of the group of women and children. As prisoners of the Japanese, the women are repeatedly told that they are headed toward a prison camp for women. In reality, no such camp exists, and the Japanese soldiers continually force them onward, unwilling to allow them to remain at a Japanese outpost and thus divert resources from their own soldiers. Many of the women and children die of starvation, exhaustion, and diseases such as dysentery and malaria. In the course of their travels, the women meet two Australian prisoners, one of whom attempts to help them procure medicine and food. Joe Harmon, one of the Australian soldiers, befriends Jean. He is eventually tortured for his crime of stealing from the Japanese. Jean

Nevil Shute (Getty Images)

and the rest of her party are forced to watch Joe be crucified and whipped, apparently to death. Believing Joe to be dead, Jean and her party are forced to move on. They are eventually allowed, through Jean's ingenuity and powers of persuasion, to settle in a small Malay village, where they help plant and harvest the rice crop. After the war, Jean learns that Joe is alive. She travels to Australia, where they are finally reunited. Jean begins a new life there and attempts to develop the community in which she has settled. Throughout the novel, Jean's challenging of traditional gender roles is repeatedly emphasized, and her ambition to help women becomes a main undercurrent.

AUTHOR BIOGRAPHY

Shute was born Nevil Shute Norway in London, England, on January 17, 1890. His father, Arthur Hamilton Norway, worked for the General Post Office, and his mother was Mary Louisa Gadsen. After attending preparatory school in Hammersmith, Shute was sent to

Dragon School in Oxford, England, and then on to Shrewsbury. Shute was visiting his father in Dublin, Ireland (as Norway was at the time the secretary to the General Post Office of Ireland), at the time of the 1916 uprising in Ireland.

Shute entered the Royal Military Academy but failed his medical examination due to a stammer. Later, at Balliol College of Oxford University from 1919 through 1922, Shute studied engineering science. He also began writing novels and short stories at this time, and he worked as an unpaid intern for the Aircraft Manufacturing Company.

In 1926, Shute published his first novel, *Marazan*. He eventually dropped the "Norway" from his name and published under the name Nevil Shute, but he continued to use his full name within the context of his engineering profession. He continued to merge his engineering and aircraft experience, and in 1931, he founded Airspeed Ltd. He constructed aircraft for the government, gradually enlarging the business while he simultaneously pursued his career in writing.

Shute married Francis Mary Heaton in 1931, and the couple had two daughters. By 1938, Shute had sold the film rights for two novels, *The Lonely Road* (1932) and *Ruined City* (1938), and was gaining popularity and fame as a novelist. During World War II (1939–1945), Shute served as a sub-lieutenant in the Royal Naval Volunteer Reserve's Miscellaneous Weapons Department. He was later transferred to the Ministry of Information and sent to Burma in 1945 to serve as a war correspondent.

After the war, Shute emigrated to Australia and wrote prolifically. *A Town Like Alice*, published in 1950, was one in a string of novels published in the decade after the war and demobilization. Shute continued to live and work in Australia until his stroke-related death on January 12, 1960, in Melbourne.

PLOT SUMMARY

Chapter 1

In the first chapter of *A Town Like Alice*, Shute introduces the narrating, first-person character Noel Strachan. Through Noel, Shute provides background information on Jean Paget's family and their history in Malaya. Noel Strachan is a solicitor, charged with executing the will of a

MEDIA ADAPTATIONS

- *A Town Like Alice* was adapted for the screen as a 1956 film directed by Jack Lee. The screenplay, based on Shute's novel, was written by H. P. Lipscomb and Richard Mason. The film stars Virginia McKenna as Jean Paget and Peter Finch as Joe Harman. Although a DVD version of the film exists, it is not available in a format readable by American and Canadian DVD players. However, it may be purchased from Amazon as an instant movie, viewable via a high-speed Internet connection for PCs, Macs, or television.

- In 1981, *A Town Like Alice* was adapted as a television miniseries directed by David Stevens. The script was based on Shute's novel and adapted by Shute, Tom Hegarty, and Rosemary Anne Sisson. Helen Morse stars as Jean Paget, and Bryan Brown stars as Joe Harman. The production was released on VHS tape by Anchor Bay in 1992.

- *A Town Like Alice* is available as an abridged audiocassette, CD, or Audible Audio MP3. The novel is read by Leo McKern and was published by DH Audio in 1985.

man named Douglas McFadden. After learning of the deaths of all of McFadden's living relatives save one, the reader is informed that Jean Paget, a young woman in her twenties working as a typist, is McFadden's niece. After discussing Jean's case with a business associate—in particular, the fact that McFadden was reluctant to leave much wealth to a young woman who might misspend it—Noel contacts Jean and informs her of her inheritance and the conditions attached to it. Jean must wait until she is thirty-five years old to receive the full inheritance. As Jean and Noel talk, her experience as a prisoner of war in Malaya surfaces, but she offers few details initially. Noel encourages Jean to consider what she might want to do with her life, now that she no longer has to work for a living.

Jean begins to confide in Noel and resolves to return to Malaya and build a well in the village in which she lived for three years as a Japanese prisoner of war.

Chapter 2

Jean relates in more detail how she came to live in Malaya, discussing the years of her childhood spent there and her later return in search of work in 1939. She tells of the invasion by the Japanese in 1941 and how the English began evacuating Malaya. After a failed escape attempt, Jean and the English family with whom she is staying (Bill and Eileen Holland and their children), along with a number of other English families, are captured by the Japanese. Eventually the men are separated and bound for a separate prison camp. The women and children, thirty-two individuals in total, remain at the Japanese military outpost and begin to suffer from exposure to mosquitoes, hunger, and thirst. Jean shows early signs of her resourcefulness when, through her knowledge of the Malay language, which the other Englishwomen lack, she manages to acquire insect repellent. They remain in this location for forty-one days before being told they will march to a woman's prison camp. Esmé Harrison, an eight-year-old girl, dies before they depart. The first march is extremely difficult for the women. Their shoes are unsuitable for miles and miles of walking, and the people are unaccustomed to the constant exposure to the elements, specifically the heat. On the second day of marching, another prisoner perishes, a woman named Mrs. Julia Collard. They spend their nights in various villages and walk all day. They are finally able to persuade their Japanese captors to let them rest for a day in between days of walking. The women are repeatedly told that they will soon be housed in a prison camp, but this never happens. Increasingly, the Japanese guards rely on Jean to convey to Malay headmen (the village leaders) the need for food and shelter. The party arrives in a village called Klang, where they are confined to an empty schoolhouse. They relate their story to the Japanese officer stationed there and are once again informed that there is no prisoner camp, and they should not have been sent there. A Japanese doctor is sent to examine them, but he does nothing for a young boy, Ben Collard, who has been bitten by an insect. His leg is swollen, and he has grown feverish. After several days he is taken to a hospital, but the group later learns that the boy has died.

Chapter 3

As the Japanese attempt to figure out what to do with the women and children, Jean's party remains in Klang for eleven days. It is now March 1942. They are finally sent on, destined for another Japanese base. In one village, Jean purchases a sarong, a type of skirt worn by the native Malay women. The incident is significant in that it marks Jean's gradual adoption of the habits of the Malay people. The endless trek continues, as there are no accommodations for them at the next base. On the next leg of their journey, one of Mrs. Holland's three children, four-year-old Jane, dies. As the group moves on, a young woman in their party, Ellen Forbes, simply disappears and is never seen again. They are severely underfed and soon lose two more women, Judy Thomson and Mrs. Horse-fall. Mrs. Horsefall's son is now cared for by an older woman in the party, Mrs. Frith. Jean notes that when called upon in this capacity, Mrs. Frith's own spirits improve, and she now seems focused on survival. At the town of Gemas, they are told that Singapore, which has been their destination for some time, is too full of prisoners. Jean asks if they can make a camp in Gemas, and see a doctor, but her requests are denied. They are forced to march on. They are told they will journey to Kuantan, hundreds of miles from their current location. As they travel, a fever breaks out that spreads to many of the children. Four die within a few days, including Mrs. Holland's son Freddie. Mrs. Holland's youngest son, Robin, an infant whom Jean has been carrying, is now Mrs. Holland's only surviving offspring. Mrs. Holland dies soon after, and Jean is left to care for Robin. Jean and the baby develop a fever as well, but in one of the villages in which they stay, they are given a drink containing medicinal herbs, and they recover, as do others in the group who are feverish.

Days later, at another village, they meet two Australian prisoners who drive railway materials to the coast for the Japanese. One of them flirts with Jean, at first mistaking her for a native Malayan, as she has tanned so deeply, wears a sarong, and carries the baby on her hip in the Malay fashion. The Australian, Joe Harman, takes an interest in Jean, and the two of them share their stories, although Jean allows Joe to believe that she is married and that Robin is her own child. Horrified that the women have lost so many in their party (there are now just seventeen

of the original thirty-two left alive), Joe risks his life to provide the women with medicine and food. After he sends five chickens to the women, trouble ensues. He has stolen the chickens from a Japanese officer, Captain Sugamo, who considers it a great dishonor to have been robbed. The theft is eventually traced to Joe. Although Jean fabricates a story to protect Joe, he is nailed to a tree by his hands and beaten. The narrative switches back to Noel's sitting-room, where Jean is telling him her story. She recalls how the group was forced to watch as Joe was tortured to death.

Chapter 4

The women leave Kuantan under the watch of a guard disgraced for having accepted the bribe of one of the stolen chickens. The guard dies after contracting a fever, and Jean and her party find themselves in a small village with no guard. They know that no escape is truly possible, for to leave would surely mean capture by the Japanese. Instead, Jean negotiates with the headman of the village. So many villagers have been lost to the war that they do not have enough people to work the land, and Jean promises that in exchange for shelter, she and her party will plant and harvest an uncultivated rice paddy. Eventually, the village agrees to allow the women to stay, with the provision that after the rice has been planted, the headman and Jean will present their situation to the nearest Japanese authorities. Jean fears that if they do not take this step, the whole village, called Kuala Telang, will be in danger. The Japanese soldiers allow them to stay. The women continue on in this way, working in the rice paddy and living among the villagers, for three years, until the end of the war.

The narrative returns once again to Jean's conversation with Noel. She reveals that with her inheritance, she would like to return to that village and build a well so the women do not have to journey miles every day for drinking water. She feels she owes the village, as she and the other prisoners would not have survived the war without the kindnesses shown to them by the villagers. After Jean reaches the village of Kuala Telang, she is reunited with the villagers and proposes her plan to build the well. She discusses her idea first with the women and then with the headman. As the well is being built, Jean learns that the builders are from Kuantan. The ensuing conversation reveals that not only did the men know of Joe Harman's experience, but they are certain that he did not die.

Chapter 5

Noel explains Joe's survival. As the framework of the story implies, Noel would have received this information directly from Joe, later in their acquaintanceship. The fact that Joe survives is attributed to the Japanese notion of Bushido, which is explained as being akin to chivalry. When Captain Sugamo examines what he believes to be Joe's lifeless body, still nailed to the tree, Joe's eyes show recognition. Respectful of the man's spirit, Sugamo asks if he can get Joe anything before he dies. Mustering sarcasm, Joe requests one of Sugamo's prized chickens and a bottle of beer. Sugamo has the countryside scoured for beer but can find none. As he cannot fulfill Joe's dying wish, according to the code of Bushido, Sugamo cannot let Joe die. He has Joe removed from the tree and taken to the hospital. Joe eventually recovers and returns to Australia.

The narration returns to Jean's perspective. Upon learning of Joe's survival, Jean immediately resolves to investigate the matter further and soon decides to go to Australia herself to seek him out. Noel is disappointed to learn that Jean is not returning to England. About a week after hearing from Jean, Noel is visited by Joe, who has been making inquiries about Jean. Noel tells Joe very little, withholding the fact that Jean is currently in Australia, looking for him. Rather, he simply states that she is abroad, traveling in the East. Joe reveals that he has recently learned from a pilot who had flown Jean out of Malaya that Jean was not in fact married. After hearing Joe's story, Noel encourages Joe to write to Jean and to return to Australia.

Chapter 6

Jean, now in Australia, gradually makes her way to the town Joe had told her about, Alice Springs, which is near the cattle station at which Joe works. Along the way, she fabricates a story about being a distant relative of Joe's and makes inquiries about his whereabouts. She finds Alice Springs to be just as Joe described it, different from many of the other former mining towns in this part of Australia. Other towns had very few residents and little in the way of amenities and entertainment. Alice Springs, though, had grown decidedly suburban, with "everything a reasonable girl could want—a hairdressing salon, a good dress shop or two, two picture houses." Jean learns that because Alice

Springs had been a military staging point in the war, it had grown considerably. Having made a few friends in Alice Springs, with whom she stays, Jean is provided with Joe Harman's address at the Midhurst cattle station near a town called Willstown. Her journey to Willstown takes several days. Flights on small planes are the most convenient form of transportation in the nearly roadless countryside, but they often arrive at and leave the tiny towns only on a weekly basis. Arriving in Willstown, Jean discovers almost immediately that Joe is in England. Jean misses the plane to the larger city of Cairns, where she could be more comfortable, so she settles in at the hotel in Willstown. As a visitor from England, and a young woman in a town mostly inhabited by men, Jean receives a great deal of attention. She meets most of the town's most prominent citizens and learns how difficult life for women is here.

After Jean is shown an alligator skin by a young man trying to impress her, she comes up with an idea. Interested in showing the residents what becomes of their alligator skins once they get shipped out of the country, Jean, who once worked for a company that makes shoes and handbags, decides to attempt making shoes out of the skin. She asks the man how many skins come in annually, and it is suggested that she has a plan to build a shoe factory.

Chapter 7

Jean industriously completes several pairs of shoes and contemplates her plan for opening a small workshop to employ local young women. She hopes that with her contacts back in England, they would have a distributor for the merchandise. Jean's plan centers around the notion that if young women had a reason to stay in Willstown, rather than moving far away to find work, the town could grow and prosper. This kernel of an idea is the heart of all of the development opportunities she pursues in Willstown. Jean travels to Cairns, where she writes to Noel about her plans. She speaks to Noel both as a friend and as a solicitor (a type of attorney) who can determine whether or not discretionary funds from her inheritance may be released to her. Noel refuses Jean very little in this capacity but does seek to help her develop her ideas so that she does not lose money on her business investments. Noel arranges for a woman (Aggie Topp) from Jean's former employer to go to Australia to help manage the workshop and its employees.

While in Cairns, Jean learns that the ship on which Joe is returning to Australia will dock in Cairns and that Joe typically stays at the same hotel where Jean has a room. She writes to him and arranges to remain in Cairns until he arrives. Their reunion is pleasant, but it is awkward for both of them. Eventually, over drinks, Joe and Jean reveal the way they sought each other out, once Jean found out Joe was alive and once Joe found out Jean was not married. They spend some time catching up, and Jean agrees to accompany Joe to Green Island, a secluded location where they can spend some time together alone. Once there, they enjoy the beaches and get to know one another, but Jean wonders at Joe's reluctance to approach her romantically. Their conversations reveal Jean's ambitions to develop Willstown into a location where young women could thrive and subsequently attract more men to the region. Still perturbed by Joe's apparent reserve, Jean suspects that he sees her differently than he did in Malaya, perhaps as an English-woman too used to English civilization to enjoy life in the rugged outback with him. To reconnect with him, she adorns herself in her native Malay sarong, and the two finally embrace passionately and reveal their romantic feelings toward one another. They agree to marry, but Jean insists that Joe allow her to establish her business developments first.

Chapter 8
Joe and Jean discuss the improvements that could be made to the town of Willstown, as well as to the cattle station at Midhurst, where Joe is the manager. Joe is impressed with Jean's business sense, intelligence, and ambition. Jean reveals that in addition to the shoe factory, she would like to open an ice-cream parlor that also sells fruits and vegetables, magazines, makeup, "all the little bits of things that women want." They return to Cairns and immediately begin solidifying the plans for Jean's business ventures. Jean updates Noel through a long letter. He is pleased at how happy she is, but he dwells repeatedly on the letter and later alludes to the fact that he perhaps had been in love with her in his own way.

Chapter 9
Back in Willstown, Jean and Joe begin ordering building materials for the workshop and the ice-cream parlor. Jean also tours Joe's residence at Midhurst, and they plan improvements to the

home they will one day share. Joe and Jean live separately and refrain from public demonstrations of their relationship, as Jean realizes her reputation as an upstanding, respectable woman is vital to the success of her business ventures. When at Midhurst, Jean learns to ride a horse. In town, she looks after her workshop and the ice-cream parlor and develops plans for a public swimming pool.

The narrative switches from Jean's point of view to that of Jackie Bacon, a radio receptionist in Cairns who learns that at Windermere station, near Midhurst, station manager Don Curtis has gone missing. His wife, Helen Curtis, reports that his horse returned without him. She is frantic. Jackie contacts other station managers in the area and gets word to Joe at Midhurst. A search-and-rescue mission ensues. Joe leaves on horseback while Jean remains at Midhurst. One of the Aboriginal ringers (cowboys), Bourneville, returns to Midhurst that evening and informs Jean that Joe has found Don, whose leg is broken. There are no other ringers currently at Midhurst, so Jean decides she must drive the utility vehicle to come to the aid of Joe and Don. She has barely driven before but with some difficulty makes it through the swollen creeks, with Bourneville riding his horse alongside the vehicle.

Chapter 10
Jean arrives at the tent Joe has erected as shelter for himself and Don. Don's leg is splinted, and Joe and Jean move him to the vehicle. While Joe drives and Jean tends to Don, Bourneville rides on horseback and leads Joe's horse. Crossing a deep creek, the utility vehicle hits a boulder and is disabled. Joe and Jean decide that Don can now be rescued only by air. Joe will stay and try to clear the brush and trees to make a landing strip while Jean and Bourneville ride on to Willstown to get help and call for a plane. The journey is treacherous, as all the creek beds are flooded with recent heavy rains. Jean is an inexperienced rider, and the journey of forty miles on horseback takes a toll on her health. She is treated "with penicillin ointment on various parts of her anatomy" and stays in the hospital to rest after making sure that help is on its way to the men. Eventually, a plane is able to land and carry Don and Joe to safety. Speaking to Joe afterward, Jean discusses the need for better medical care in town, and she reveals the other plans she has for the community, including a self-service laundry, a dress shop, and a cinema. Joe remarks that

if all of Jean's plans come to fruition, she will have created a town "as good as Alice Springs in no time." Jean responds that this is precisely what she wants: "A town like Alice."

Chapter 11

In the final chapter, the narrative turns once again to Noel, who summarizes the next three years of Jean's life, including her marriage to Joe and the birth of their two children, one of whom she names after Noel. She writes to him three years after the rescue of Don Curtis to ask for more of her inheritance money, so that she and Joe can buy a share of Midhurst, as Mrs. Spears, the current owner and Joe's employer, wants to sell to them and give them the option of full ownership as time goes on. Noel considers Jean's request and, feeling as though there are details of the contracts with government over the land lease that need to be worked out, decides to fly to Australia. Certain of the soundness of the investment, Noel helps Jean and Joe finalize the details. He is impressed with all the businesses Jean has developed and with the way she has transformed the town. Joe tells Noel approvingly of everything Jean has done and mentions that the population has tripled since Jean's arrival. Noel hears of Jean's future plans as well. Now that she has provided places for young women to work, spend their money, and meet and mingle with young men, the town is experiencing a marriage and baby boom. Jean's new plans involve creating businesses with a family focus. She wants to build a grocery story and a hardware store. Jean and Joe ask Noel to remain in Willstown permanently. He declines and returns to England. Contemplating Jean's endeavors, he congratulates himself on his role in Jean's business developments, noting, "It is no small matter to assist in the birth of a new city."

CHARACTERS

Annie

Annie is the maid at the Australian Hotel where Jean stays in Willstown. Annie reveals to Jean that she is both unmarried and carrying an unwanted baby. She is later hired by Jean to work in the shoe factory.

Jackie Bacon

Jackie Bacon is a radio receptionist who works in Cairns. For a small portion of the novel, the action takes place from Jackie's point of view. At her post at the radio, Jackie receives word from Helen Curtis that Helen's husband, Don, has gone missing from Windermere station. Jackie contacts station managers at other nearby stations and eventually reaches Midhurst station, where Joe Harman springs into action to save Don.

Bourneville

Bourneville is one of the Aboriginal ringers, or cattle ranchers, who works at the Midhurst station under Joe Harman. Aboriginal characters in the novel are referred to in a derogatory fashion as "Abos." Bourneville accompanies Jean to find Joe and the injured Don Curtis, and he rides with her back to Willstown to get help.

Ben Collard

Ben Collard is the younger of Julia Collard's two sons. He steps on a poisonous insect of some kind, falls ill, and is eventually taken to a hospital, where he dies.

Harry Collard

Harry Collard is Julia's older son. After losing his mother and his brother, Harry later contracts a fever and dies.

Julia Collard

Julia Collard is one of the women prisoners in Jean's party. She is described as heavyset, in her midforties, and the mother of two children, Harry and Ben. Julia dies in the early weeks of the prisoners' captivity.

Don Curtis

Don Curtis is a cattle-station manager at Windermere, a station near the Midhurst station run by Joe Harman. Curtis suffers a broken leg, and Jean and Joe play integral roles in his rescue.

Helen Curtis

Helen Curtis is the wife of Don Curtis, and she reports her husband's disappearance, prompting the rescue effort led by Joe and Jean.

Ellen Forbes

Ellen Forbes is one of the women prisoners in Jean's party. Early in their travels, Ellen disappears. Despite her companions' insistence that she has been kidnapped, the group's Japanese guard does not pursue Ellen. She is never heard from again.

Mrs. Frith

Mrs. Frith is one of the older women in Jean's party, estimated to be in her fifties. Initially, she languishes, and Jean doubts her ability to survive. After the death of Mrs. Horsefall, Mrs. Frith cares for Mrs. Horsefall's son Johnnie. With this new purpose, Mrs. Frith becomes more focused, energetic, and determined, and Jean turns to her repeatedly for advice on what is best for the group.

Joe Harman

Joe Harman is an Australian soldier captured by the Japanese in Malaya. When Joe encounters Jean's party of war prisoners, he initially mistakes the group for Malay women and children. Upon discovering that they are all English, Harman makes repeated attempts to befriend and aid the women, and he is particularly interested in Jean. Joe and another Australian soldier tamper with the vehicle that is used to run rail equipment to the coast for the Japanese, telling their Japanese guard that the vehicle needs additional repairs. In doing so, Joe creates an opportunity to spend more time with Jean and to procure food, soap, and medicine for the group. Joe and Jean talk extensively about their homes and their lives before the war. When Joe leaves, he promises to send more food to the group. His efforts result in a crucifixion and whipping that Jean and her fellow prisoners are forced to witness. Unbeknownst to Jean, Joe survives, partly because of his strong spirit and his bold response to Captain Sugamo. He insults the captain and then asks for a beer and for one of Sugamo's chickens. (The theft of Sugamo's chickens is the crime that has landed Joe in his current position.) Unable to find beer, Sugamo is compelled to prevent Joe's death. Joe's crucifixion is looked upon by the religious Mrs. Firth and some of the other women as a Christlike sacrifice.

After his return to Australia after the war, Joe learns that Jean is not married, as he had believed during the war. He flies to England in an effort to find her and discovers, through Noel, that Jean has a large inheritance. Seeing the way she lives and comparing London to Willstown, Joe despairs that Jean will ever consent to be his wife. Nevertheless, he returns home and meets Jean, eventually marrying her and supporting her in her business endeavors. Although he questions some of Jean's ambitions, Joe appears to admire and appreciate Jean's intelligence, resourcefulness, and strength.

Esmé Harrison

Esmé Harrison is an eight-year-old girl who dies of dysentery before Jean and the group of captives begin their journey. She is the first member of the group to perish.

Bill Holland

Bill Holland and his wife, prior to the Japanese occupation of Malaya, invite Jean to stay with them on several occasions. After the English begin evacuating, Jean feels compelled to see the Hollands before she leaves Malaya, and she offers to help them evacuate their family. Their own escape is thwarted and they are taken prisoner. Soon Bill is separated from the women and children along with the other men taken prisoner by the Japanese. He survives the war and eventually is reunited with Jean and the only remaining member of his family, his son Robin, now four years old. He proposes to Jean, but she turns him down.

Eileen Holland

Eileen Holland is described at the outset of the novel as a nurturing mother in her early thirties. After witnessing the deaths of two of her children, Eileen eventually succumbs to disease, malnutrition, and exhaustion. Before she dies, she expresses relief at the way her baby has taken to Jean.

Freddie Holland

Freddie Holland is the seven-year-old son of Bill and Eileen Holland. He dies of a fever, along with several other children, as the prisoners march through Malaya.

Jane Holland

Jane Holland is the four-year-old daughter of Bill and Eileen Holland. She is the first of the Hollands to die.

Robin Holland

Robin Holland is the infant son of Bill and Eileen Holland. Unlike most of the children, he thrives. Jean suspects he remains free of many of the diseases the others suffer because anything he consumes has been boiled first. Eileen, who is older than and not as strong as Jean, allows the younger woman to carry the baby, and Robin subsequently becomes quite attached to Jean and often shows a preference for her over his own mother. He survives the war under Jean's care and is finally reunited with his father.

Johnnie Horsefall

Johnnie Horsefall is the young son of Mrs. Horsefall. After his mother's death, he is cared for by Mrs. Frith.

Mrs. Horsefall

Mrs. Horsefall is one of the women in Jean's party who does not survive her captivity. A former schoolteacher, Mrs. Horsefall is initially looked to as the group's leader, with Jean taking a secondary role. She repeatedly asks for concessions for the women, such as a truck to transport them and a day of rest in between walking days. When Ben Collard is poisoned by an insect bite or sting, she attempts to suck the poison from the wound. Although she survives malaria, she dies not long after.

Douglas McFadden

Douglas McFadden is Jean's maternal uncle (the brother of her mother). In his will, he leaves Jean an inheritance but stipulates that she is not to receive the full amount until the age of thirty-five. Noel Strachan believes that McFadden was certain that a young woman would be unable to properly manage a large sum of money on her own. Noel consequently persuades McFadden prior to his death to allow for a discretionary clause in which the solicitors of the will may provide additional funds to Jean as needed.

Jean Paget

Jean Paget is the heroine of the novel. The reader is first introduced to Jean in the same capacity that Noel meets her in, as a typist and the beneficiary of Douglas McFadden's will. Gradually, she reveals to Noel her experiences in Malaya as a prisoner of war, held captive by the Japanese from December 1941 through the end of the war, in 1945. Jean and the women and children with her are marched through the countryside; they are housed sometimes on Japanese bases but more often than not in small Malay villages. Many women and children in the group die from exhaustion, starvation, malaria, dysentery, and other unknown diseases. Jean helps her friend Eileen Holland with her three children, caring for the youngest after the deaths of Mrs. Holland and the two older children. Having spent some of her childhood in Malaya with her parents, Jean speaks Malay fluently enough to converse with the villagers they encounter, and she learns enough Japanese to serve as an interpreter for the Japanese soldiers who guard the group. Jean does her best

to serve as an advocate for the group, arguing for rest, increases in rations, and medicines. Her time with Joe Harman is brief, but she becomes enamored with him as he speaks of his home in Australia. Horrified by Joe's crucifixion and torture, Jean believes Joe to be dead and is reluctant to speak much about him. She is plagued with guilt, believing that she caused his death, as he stole the chickens for her and her fellow prisoners.

Familiar with Malay culture, Jean is deferential to the village leaders, or headmen, that they encounter, and she uses her skills as a negotiator after the death of their guard to persuade the headman of one village to allow them to remain and work in the rice paddy. In this way, Jean saves the group from further suffering and death by eliminating the endless marches, exhaustion, and exposure to disease. For three years, they live as the Malay villagers do, and Jean observes the hardships the women face. When she inherits a large sum of money, she returns to the village to build a well, in order to improve the women's daily lives.

In pursuing Joe Harman, Jean realizes that she is challenging the gender stereotypes of the day, and she attempts to disguise her intentions by fabricating a story that casts her in the role of Joe's distant relative. Waiting weeks for his return, Jean is frustrated when Joe seems reluctant to pursue a romantic relationship with her, and again she defies convention by prompting his embrace with her return to native Malay attire and encouraging his desire for her. Even before Joe returns, Jean initiates business endeavors in Willstown, and eventually, after becoming engaged to Joe, she pursues the construction of a number of businesses. She expands these interests after their marriage and is credited with almost single-handedly reviving the once-dead town, transforming it into a vibrant community where she raises her family with Joe.

Rose Sawyer

Rose Sawyer befriends Jean when she arrives in Alice Springs. As the women talk about the town, life in the outback, and opportunities for women, Rose expresses her desire to one day run a shop, such as an ice-cream parlor. Later, Jean invites Rose to come to Willstown to run the ice-cream parlor she has opened.

Mrs. Spears

Mrs. Spears is the elderly woman who owns Midhurst station and employs Joe Harman.

She offers to sell a portion of the station to Joe and Jean, with the option of offering them full ownership later.

Noel Strachan

Noel Strachan is the executor of Douglas McFadden's will. The novel is primarily told as a first-person narrative from Strachan's point of view. He hears Jean recount her experiences, befriends her, and eventually writes her story. Through the course of the novel, Noel plays an active role in Jean's life. After his initial encounter with her, when he discusses her inheritance, he becomes a sort of fatherly advisor to her, and she trusts him enough to reveal what happened to her in Malaya. His affection for her inspires him to use the discretionary clause of McFadden's will to support her charitable donation of the well in the Malayan village and her business endeavors in Australia. When a friend suggests that Noel perhaps is in love with Jean himself, Noel rejects the notion, but weakly. He expresses disappointment when Jean decides to travel to Australia from Malaya, and he is so protective of Jean and her interests that when Joe Harman visits him in London, Noel does not reveal that Jean is looking for Joe in Australia. On the pretext of serving as an advisor in a business deal, Noel travels to Australia to see Jean. Finally convinced of her happiness and her love for Joe, Noel returns to England.

Captain Sugamo

Captain Sugamo is the cruel Japanese soldier responsible for the torture of Joe Harman. Sugamo's notion of honor compels him to save Joe when he realizes he cannot grant Joe's dying request. Jean later learns that Sugamo was tried and executed for war crimes.

Mat Amin bin Taib

Amin is the headman, or leader, in the Malay village of Kuala Telang. Jean convinces him to allow the group of prisoners to remain in the village after the death of their Japanese guard. Initially reluctant to allow this, Amin demonstrates kindness and openness in listening to Jean's arguments, and he allows the women to work in the rice paddy and live in the village.

Judy Thomson

Judy Thomson is one of the women of Jean's party who succumbs to disease and starvation and dies in the course of captivity.

Aggie Topp

Aggie Topp works for Jean's former employer, the English firm that makes shoes and handbags. Noel convinces her to transfer to Australia to help Jean set up and run the shoe workshop in Willstown.

THEMES

Female Identity

In *A Town Like Alice*, Jean Paget is distinctly different from most of the other women in the novel in the way she conceives of her own identity as a woman. Arriving in Malaya to seek work, Jean differs from the other young Englishwomen who live there because she is not married, nor is she seeking a husband. While other young women pursue marriage as a means of securing their futures, Jean challenges that stereotypical gender role and pursues employment to provide for her future. As the war ensues, Jean's desire to help others begins as a small gesture toward friends, when she checks up on the Hollands before attempting to leave Malaya. This desire gradually blossoms into a larger notion of responsibility toward other women, born out of a sense of solidarity and respect. Jean initially finds that her place in the group of prisoners is to serve as a friend and aid to Mrs. Holland, who is struggling to care for an infant, a four-year-old, and a seven-year-old. Even in this early stage of captivity, however, Jean risks her own safety to provide for the group of women. She approaches a Japanese guard and attempts to indicate their need for mosquito netting and repellent by pointing to the insect bites with which she is covered. This proves ineffective, and dangerous, as he initially advances toward her with his bayonet raised. Next, Jean resourcefully sneaks behind the latrine, beckons toward a young Malay girl, and offers to pay her for telling the Chinese pharmacist to bring his wares to the accounts office where the prisoners are being held. This ingenious approach works, and it is one that Jean will employ repeatedly in their imprisonment: she works within the parameters established by the guards, to some extent, and seeks aid from the Malay villagers through her knowledge of their language and customs.

It is this knowledge and her negotiation skills that set Jean apart from the other Englishwomen and elevate her to the status of leader. Unlike the

TOPICS FOR FURTHER STUDY

- In *A Town Like Alice*, Shute describes in detail the route Jean and the other women prisoners marched throughout the Malay Peninsula. Using the novel, note the specifics of this journey, writing down where the party started and the succession of locations they visited. Keep notes also of how long the group took to walk from place to place and how long they may have stayed in particular villages. Identify places of significance, such as the city in which Joe Harman was crucified. Then use your notes and an online source such as Google Maps (http://maps.google.com) to plot Jean's journey on a map of the Malay Peninsula. Include in this visual presentation the distances between villages and your notes about Jean's journey (such as how long it took to walk from one village to another). Present your annotated map to the class.

- *Okinawa: Two Postwar Novellas*, by Oshiro Tatushiro and Higashi Minewo, consists of a pair of stories that both explore the aftereffects of Japan's involvement in World War II, describing life in a region that was under U.S. military rule until 1972 and deeply affected by this presence. The novellas are translated from Japanese, and in their native language they won a prestigious Japanese fiction award. They were published in English in 1989. Select one of the novellas, and as you read, contemplate the lives of Japanese citizens in the postwar years. What does the novella reveal about life under U.S. military rule in Okinawa? How did the war, Japan's role in it, and the Allied response to a defeated Japan affect the Japanese people? Write a book report in which you summarize the plot of the novella and analyze its main characters and themes.

- Cynthia Kadohata's young-adult novel *Weedflower* was published in 2006. In it, a Japanese American family from Southern California is sent to internment camps after the Japanese bombing of Pearl Harbor in 1941. This novel offers a different view of the war than that depicted in Shute's novel. Whereas Jean is an Englishwoman held prisoner by the Japanese in Malaya, the family in this novel is Japanese American. They are placed in internment in America because of their Japanese heritage. With a small group, read *Weedflower*. How do the experiences of twelve-year-old Sumiko in *Weedflower* compare with those of Jean in *A Town Like Alice*? What does Sumiko learn after she is moved to a camp on Mohave lands? In what ways are Sumiko's relationships with the Native Americans she encounters similar to Jean's experiences with the Malay people? With your group, create an online blog in which you summarize both novels, and then open the blog for comments among group members. In this way, discuss the two works and their themes, plots, and characters.

- Much of *A Town Like Alice* takes place during World War II. The experiences of people from several different nations (Great Britain, Malaya, Australia, and Japan) are explored in detail in some cases or touched on briefly in others. Select one of the nations involved and research that country's role in World War II. Was that nation a major aggressor, an ally of another group of nations, or a victim of conquest? How did the war affect the citizens of that nation? What was that nation's experience in the immediate aftermath of the war? Write a research paper and present it as an oral report, a written report, or a Web page. Be sure to cite all of your sources.

other women, who have been living in Malaya only recently, Jean, because of her childhood experiences, knows the language, and she cultivated her knowledge once she returned as an adult. Some of the other women know only enough Malay to direct the duties of their household servants. While other women in the party, such as Mrs. Horsefall, are bold enough to demand better treatment from the Japanese, they do so by insisting on their cultural superiority as English citizens, as Mrs. Horsefall does when the women are told they are to sleep on the floor like the Japanese. "But we're English!" Mrs. Horsefall insists. "We don't sleep on the floor like animals!" Jean, however, when attempting to persuade their captors to allow them to rest or when asking for more food or medicine, shows that she is a keen observer of cultural habits. She bows to the Japanese as is their custom, and they respond to this show of respect by at least listening to the group's request. It is through Jean's attention to both Japanese and Malay culture that she negotiates their prolonged stay in Kuala Telang.

When Jean returns to the village after the war, her advocacy for the good of the group of her fellow female prisoners is revealed to have a larger scope. Jean emphasizes to the women in the village that the well "should be a present from a woman to the women of Kuala Telang, nothing to do with the men." She seeks to make their lives easier by eliminating the need for them to trek miles for fresh water, as she and her fellow prisoners also had to do when staying in the village. But Jean does not just build the well. She constructs a washhouse where the women may gather socially while they do their washing. She encourages their sense of solidarity and the growth of a social female community. Later, in Willstown, Jean listens to men and women describe why so many young women leave Willstown. All the improvements she makes to the town are designed with women in mind, to give them well-paying, honest work as factory workers and shopkeepers. Jean considers the ways a young woman might want to spend her new income and creates businesses to satisfy those desires. Yet the ice-cream parlor, the pool, the cinema serve as more than just ways for her to make money, as she tells Joe. Jean views these developments as a means of developing a female social community. Women cannot enter bars in Australia, and Jean gives them public places to gather, understanding in a way the male characters in the book do not the empowering nature of social relationships among women.

Race Relations
The white characters in *A Town Like Alice*, specifically the English and the Australians, encounter races different from their own in their experiences

with native Malay villagers, Japanese soldiers, and Aboriginal Australians. For each nonwhite group, the white characters use derogatory terms: Boong, Nip, Abo. Even the morally upstanding Jean uses these terms freely. Shute was writing in 1950, when these terms were still widely used, but to the modern reader they stand out as highly offensive.

Negative stereotypes also surround these groups in the story. The Malay are commonly regarded as a primitive culture, and the Japanese were similarly regarded as less civilized than the English. The Aboriginal population in Australia is segregated from the white population and often respected as a hard-working people, if considered less intelligent and civilized than the whites in the novel. Jean's approaches to the nonwhite peoples often differ from those of her companions, however. Repeatedly, Jean shows deference to the heads of the villages in which the prisoners stay, displaying respect for the patriarchal (led by men) nature of the culture and acknowledging that in business matters the headmen are not used to dealing with women. For example, in the village of Kuala Telang, Jean approaches the headman Mat Amin bin Taib by stating, "If there were a man amongst us I would send him to talk for us, but there is no man. You will not be offended if I ask you to talk business with a woman, on behalf of women?" Jean then reflects that now, she "knew something of the right approach to a Mohammedan [Muslim]." Although she demonstrates deference in her approach, once she has been accepted as the leader of the group of prisoners, Jean remains a vocal advocate for the group's needs, and she uses her understanding of Malay customs and the Islamic faith to persuade the headmen to provide food or other accommodations.

Jean similarly observes the customs and preferences of her Japanese captors as a means of approaching the Japanese guards with requests. She bows to the guards and when speaking with them shows submissive respect that women are expected to have toward men in the Japanese culture, as she understands it. In Willstown, Australia, Jean accepts the secondary place the Aboriginal people have in Australian society at the time, but she does make some attempts to include them in her plans for the community. She asks Joe if social customs permit her to serve a "boong stockrider" (Aboriginal people are called by both the derogatory terms "boongs" and "Abos" in the novel) in her ice-cream parlor. Joe doubts that the

Colonial attitudes toward aborigines is a central theme. *(fritz16 | Shutterstock.com)*

whites in the town would allow a white girl to serve an Aboriginal customer. Jean then promises to design the ice-cream parlor so that the Aboriginal customers can be served separately from the whites. "Then I'll have to have another parlour for them with a black girl in it. There's such a lot of them, Joe—we can't cut them out," Jean insists. Through Jean, then, Shute makes an effort to take a more accepting approach toward Asian and Aboriginal peoples, yet the racist views that were prevalent at the time the novel was written persist.

STYLE

Frame Narrative

A Town Like Alice is written as a frame narrative. A frame narrative is one in which the main story of the novel is framed, or presented, within a secondary structure. In this case, Jean Paget's story is framed by the commentary and reflections of the executor of her uncle's will. In his capacity as solicitor (lawyer), Noel Strachan introduces Jean and tells her story as if reflecting upon it from a later time period. Throughout the story,

the narrative is periodically interrupted by Noel to comment on Jean, her current state of mind, and his responses to her actions, or to allude to what happens later in her story. As Noel's narrative about Jean progresses, he reveals a little of his own tender feelings for her—perhaps at times even romantic feelings, although he is much older than her. Jean's story, then, is presented through the filter of a man who clearly comes to idolize and adore her. Although he seems to present an objective account of Jean and her character, Noel's biases must be taken into account by the reader. He is suspicious of Joe Harman and his intentions toward Jean when Joe comes to visit him in London, and Noel increasingly presents Jean as faultless and unfailingly altruistic.

In using the framing narrative device, Shute uses Noel's first-person narration as a means of providing a third-person account of Jean's story. That is, Jean does not tell her own story, using "I," although it is her story that makes up the bulk of the novel. Instead, the narrating character, Noel, usually fades into the background, leaving the reader to share Jean's experiences. Noel is drawn out of the framing narrative and into Jean's story itself in the correspondence between the two, in his interactions in London with Joe, and at the novel's end, when he meets Jean and Joe in Australia. At times, when Noel's presence in the story and in Jean's life is brought to the forefront of the text, the novel reads almost like a (fictional) memoir—Noel's—but when the focus of the story is on Jean and her war and postwar experiences, the novel comes across more as a war story. The frame narrative as it is used by Shute incorporates two distinct types of fiction.

Realism versus Romanticism

In *A Town Like Alice*, Shute approaches his subject matter with a mingling of the realistic and the romantic. The backdrop of the novel, first the war in Malaya and then Jean's settling in Australia, is treated with great attention to detail. Shute describes every aspect of Jean's march across Malaya with her fellow prisoners. He captures the experience of the British in Japanese-occupied Malaya in a larger context as well, providing some historical context within which Jean's experience may be understood. In the years following World War II, British fiction experienced a revival of realism that rejected the experimentalism in fiction that was underway in the years immediately following World War I (1914–1918). Shute's realistic accounts of the war, troop movements, the torture endured by prisoners, and British responses to the invasion of Malaya by the Japanese are reflective of his interest in realism.

Similarly, Shute offers detailed descriptions of Jean's industrial endeavors, from the specifications for the well-digging in Malaya to the expansions she brings to the town of Willstown following her move to Australia. With her practical and business-minded character, Jean outlines all of her endeavors to Noel, and he obligingly shares with the reader mundane information about measurements, costs, building materials, and factory equipment. Shute, through Noel, transcribes lengthy radio exchanges that precede the rescue of Don Curtis, one of Joe's fellow ringers (cattle ranchers), and every aspect of that rescue is related. No information is left out in Shute's effort to convey settings and events accurately.

At the same time, in his depiction of Jean, Shute allows an idealism found nowhere else in the novel. Through his narrator Noel, Shute takes pains to demonstrate the humble way in which

the brave and strong Jean becomes the leader of her party of prisoners in Malaya and the way her story spreads in the aftermath of her departure. She becomes a legend, so much so that she fears being pursued by reporters upon her arrival in Australia. She becomes a legend in Australia as well. Not only does Jean almost single-handedly develop the dilapidated town of Willstown into a viable, thriving community, but she also exhibits bravery, strength, intelligence, and endurance in her arduous efforts to help save Don Curtis. Again, her heroism grows to legendary proportions in the aftermath of the rescue. In this way, Shute combines the realism of war and industry with a romantic depiction of the novel's heroine.

HISTORICAL CONTEXT

The Japanese in World War II

Japan, involved at the outset of World War II (1939–1945) as an ally of Germany and Italy (with these three countries becoming known as the Axis powers), sought dominion over East Asia and the Pacific. The alliance began in 1936, when Japan and Germany signed the Anti-Comintern Pact, an agreement to fend off Soviet aggression. Japan attacked China on July 7, 1937, initiating the war in the Pacific region (called the Pacific theater). Italy joined the anti-Soviet pact later that year. While Japan waged war in China, Germany and Italy focused on Europe and the Mediterranean. On December 7, 1941, Japan attacked a U.S. Navy fleet stationed at Pearl Harbor, in Hawaii. The next day, Japanese invaded the Malay Peninsula, occupying the entire region until 1945.

Prior to World War II, the British ruled the Malay Peninsula, having begun their conquest of the region in the early nineteenth century. The peninsular states were divided into colonies and protectorates and run by officials of the British government. When the Japanese attacked, therefore, the forces they fought were English and Australian soldiers. Australia remained at that time under the dominion of the British Empire, and in support of Great Britain, Australia had sent forces to maintain the Malayan colonies. The war continued, and the Japanese eventually conquered the whole of Malaya. After the United States entered the war in 1941, following the attack on Pearl Harbor, it allied itself with Great Britain and the Soviet Union; these three

COMPARE
&
CONTRAST

- **1940s:** Malaya is under the colonial rule of the British Empire. In exchange for trading agreements that benefit the British and give them access to such resources as rubber and tin, the British provide Malaya with military protection. When the Japanese attack Malaya in 1941, they meet with British resistance but eventually take over Malaya. After the end of the war in 1945, the British rule of Malaya is resumed, but by 1948, the British and Malay work together through a decolonization process toward Malayan independence.

  1950s: In the 1950s, a growing nationalist movement compels Malays to demand their independence from the British. At the same time, the Chinese and Indian populations fight for equality within Malaya. With the British and Malays working together, an agreement for racial equality is reached. In 1957, the Federation of Malaya gains its independence from Great Britain. Modern Malaysia is formed in 1963 when Singapore and the states of Sabah and Sarawak (located across the South China Sea from the Malay Peninsula), all of which were former British colonies, join the federation. Singapore secedes (withdraws) from Malaysia in 1965.

  Today: Malaysia prospers under the leadership of Prime Minister Mohamed Najib bin Abdul Razak, who takes office in 2009. Governed by the prime minister, Malaysia retains a ceremonial head of state as well, King Sultan Mizan Zainal Abidin.

- **1940s:** Australia, having declared war on Germany in 1939 in support of Great Britain, sends troops to various locations to aid Great Britain. An Australian force is established in Malaya and fights alongside the British when the Japanese attack Malaya in 1941. The Japanese conquer Malaya by the end of March 1942. Australians and British soldiers and civilians are captured by the Japanese as prisoners of war.

  1950s: Postwar Australia is characterized by a booming economy, full employment, high standards of living, and an influx of European immigrants into the labor force.

  Today: After the postwar boom fades, Australia experiences periods of high unemployment and low economic growth, but today, Australia's economy thrives. Australia retains its status as a British Commonwealth nation and recognizes Queen Elizabeth II as its ceremonial chief of state. The governing leader in Australia is its prime minister, Julia Eileen Gillard, who has been in office since 2010.

- **1940s:** War-related fiction focuses more on World War II experiences in general rather than the prisoner-of-war experience. Such novels include W. L. White's *They Were Expendable*, published in 1942, and Ted W. Lawson's *Thirty Seconds over Tokyo*, published in 1943. Both novels are made into movies in the 1940s.

  1950s: World War II fiction, and in particular the prisoner-of-war genre, are popular types of fiction in the 1950s, as they often recast the painful war experiences of both soldiers and civilians in a heroic light. A Pulitzer Prize–winning World War II novel, Herman Wouk's *The Caine Mutiny*, is published in 1952. Prisoner-of-war stories include *A Town Like Alice* as well as films such as *The Wooden Horse* (1950) and *The Bridge on the River Kwai* (1957), based on the 1954 novel by Pierre Boulle.

  Today: Prisoner-of-war fiction about World War II as written today is imbued with the psychology of the characters and often focuses on the former prisoner's efforts to live a normal life. Recent authors of World War II prisoner-of-war fiction include the Scottish author A. L. Kennedy (*Day*, 2008), the American Jim Lehrer (*The Special Prisoner*, 2000), and the Australian Thomas Keneally (*An Angel in Australia*, 2002).

Jean finds Joe managing an Australian cattle ranch. (*David Thoresen | Shutterstock.com*)

nations became known as the Allied powers. In 1943, Italy surrendered to the Allies, becoming the first of the Axis powers to fall. Germany fought on until 1945, when the Allied powers gained ground in eastern Europe. Germany's leader, Adolf Hitler, committed suicide in 1945, and days later, on May 7, Nazi Germany surrendered. Japan was the only Axis power remaining. Convinced that Japan would not surrender unless drastic measures were taken, the United States dropped two atomic bombs on Japan, one in Hiroshima on August 6, 1945, and one on Nagasaki on August 9. On August 10, the Japanese government requested permission to surrender, with the surrender being formalized on September 2, 1945.

Postwar Australia

The second half of *A Town Like Alice* features Jean in Australia in the years immediately following World War II. The expansion of Willstown led by Jean's developments reflects the economic boom Australia experienced in the 1950s. The population rose as young families were started and migration from Europe increased. Women became an increasingly important sector of the labor force in Australia during this time. Female participation in the work force increased steadily from 1947 onward, particularly for women ages thirty-five to fifty. At the same time, an increasing number of young women received secondary and postsecondary educations as well. During the 1950s, unemployment levels were at an all-time low in Australia. Large corporations employed numerous immigrant workers, preferring "migrants of non-English speaking background[s]" who would be "hard working and politically docile," according to Robert Tierney in *Class and Class Conflict in Australia*. As Tierney demonstrates, while large corporations preferred immigrant workers as a means of keeping wages low, Australian unions "feared that an influx of southern Europeans would weaken organised labour." In terms of social culture, the Willstown that Shute depicts may be seen as a microcosm of Australian trends.

Michelle Arrow, in *Friday on Our Minds: Popular Culture in Australia since 1945*, describes a gradual transition from public activities and entertainment to more private forms of gathering and entertainment. Arrow states that "the 1950s were marked by a widespread redefinition of previously public activities as private—from cinema and live theater to television, from pubs to drinking at home," for example. The Willstown that Jean engineers initially focuses on such public gathering spots, including the ice-cream parlor, the pool, and the cinema. As the novel progresses, however, and as Jean herself begins her family, she increasingly realizes as an entrepreneur that while such public ventures remain viable, there is now a greater need for more domestic-oriented businesses, ones that cater to young families. Australia, then, in the years immediately following World War II, was in a state of transformation in terms of its economy and workforce and also in terms of its social demographics.

CRITICAL OVERVIEW

A Town Like Alice is counted among Shute's best-known works. However, as Roger Bourke, in *Prisoners of the Japanese: Literary Imagination and the Prisoner-of-War Experience*, points out, Shute's novels generally "have attracted little scholarly attention, although Shute himself once ranked among the world's most popular and bestselling authors."

The popular appeal of *A Town Like Alice* is summarized in works such as the *Cambridge Guide to Literature in English*, by Ian Ousby, with the acknowledgment that the novel "invests its bleak Australian setting with romance and adventure." Often, the portion of the novel dealing with Australia and the romance between Jean and Joe is the focus of evaluations of the work. David T. H. Weir, in *Literature and Tourism*, attests to the work's popularity and maintains that *A Town Like Alice*, along with Shute's 1952 novel *The Far Country*, "came to symbolize the very aspirations of a new civilization in the process of establishment in an uncharted continent."

Some critics, in the brevity of their comments in surveys of Shute's work, suggest a dismissive attitude. Corbin S. Carnell, in the *Dictionary of Literary Biography*, notes that the novel was written in three and a half months and describes what he regards as "a simple plot." Whereas Weir focuses on the Australian portion of the work, others, such as Bourke, center their study on the war portion. Bourke examines the

literary and historical contexts of the soldier crucifixion motif, stating, "Shute's fictional representation of the crucifixion of an Australian prisoner of war derives its power, and its horror, from the way in which it combines multiple levels of cultural and historical reference." Specifically, Bourke cites parallels in the Bible, atrocity stories from World War I, and a historical event in an Australian soldier's life. Bourke comments on the Christian connotations of this event, observing the way Mrs. Frith clings to the image of the crucifixion and associates Joe Harman with Christlike salvation. This religious fervor, however, is undercut by Jean's disregard for such an interpretation of the event. Nevertheless, Bourke points out, as a woman who encounters a man whom she believed dead after having seen him crucified, Jean may be associated with the biblical figure of Mary Magdalene and at the same time exemplifies for readers (and moviegoers) a sense of wish fulfillment at seeing the return of a beloved soldier believed to be dead.

CRITICISM

Catherine Dominic
Dominic is a novelist and a freelance writer and editor. In the following essay, she explores the relationship between the protagonist of A Town Like Alice *and the British Empire, maintaining that Jean Paget in many ways acts as an agent of British imperialism in her postwar activities in Malaya and Australia.*

In Shute's *A Town Like Alice*, the narrator, Noel Strachan, comes to idolize Jean when he learns of what she has suffered as a prisoner of war and when she altruistically seeks to provide aid to the Malayan village. When her ambition leads her to provide new ways of life for the residents, particularly the female residents, of Willstown, Noel is grateful he has the opportunity "to assist in the birth of a new city." Through Jean's actions, which are both benevolent and profitable, Shute presents a model of British imperialism. Imperialism is a policy through which one country extends its power and influence into and over that of another and maintains that position by force if necessary. Great Britain, by the beginning of World War II, had established imperial holdings around the globe. Often, the British presence in far-flung foreign lands was characterized as an endeavor

WHAT DO I READ NEXT?

- Shute's 1952 novel *The Far Country* depicts life in postwar Australia and, like *A Town Like Alice*, weaves in romance and adventure.

- *On the Beach*, written in 1957, is one of Shute's best-known works. The novel is set in Melbourne, Australia, and concerns the subject of atomic war.

- *The Good Shepherd* (1955) is a war novel by the British author C. S. Forester, a contemporary of Shute's. The work focuses on the U.S. Navy and sea battles in the Atlantic.

- *Readings from Readings: New Malaysian Writing* (2011), edited by Sharon Baker and Bernice Chauley, offers a collection of fiction, poetry, and essays by native Malaysian authors.

- *Follow the Rabbit-Proof Fence* (2002) is a young-adult novel written by an Australian Aboriginal author, Doris Pilkington Garimara. The work concerns the historical racism with which Aboriginal populations in Australia have been treated, depicting the forced-assimilation camps Aboriginal children were placed into after being separated from their families in the 1930s.

- John W. Dower's *Embracing Defeat: Japan in the Wake of World War II* (1999) is a Pulitzer Prize–winning study of the trajectory of the Japanese society, culture, and economy after its surrender to Allied Forces in 1945 and during the subsequent occupation by U.S. forces.

- A. James Hammerton and Alistair Thompson wrote *Ten Pound Poms: A Life History of British Postwar Emigration*, published in 2005. It surveys the history of postwar British immigration to Australia, from the 1940s through the 1970s.

---

to improve the lives of individuals in more primitive societies. In an examination of this program for development in India, Michael Mann, in

> THROUGH JEAN'S ACTIONS, WHICH ARE BOTH BENEVOLENT AND PROFITABLE, SHUTE PRESENTS A MODEL OF BRITISH IMPERIALISM."

Colonialism as Civilizing Mission: Cultural Ideology in British India, quotes Charles Grant, one of the British directors of the East Indian Company, who stated in 1792, "What is now offered, is no more than the proposal for the further civilization of a people." Although Grant speaks specifically with regard to India, this civilizing purpose of imperialism was a commonly touted intention. Just as Great Britain sought to build nations in the image of Britain in areas considered more primitive, so does Jean Paget seek to improve, for the sake of civilization, the lives and societies of the peoples of Malaya and Australia, both of which were part of the British Empire during the time period in which the novel was written. She works as an agent of the empire, creating communities and developing British relationships.

The British originally entered the Malay region in the late nineteenth century for trade purposes, because of the proximity of the peninsula to China. In a 1907 account of the first British forays into Malaya, Sir Frank Athelstane Swettenham describes the violence of the native Malays and insists that the British regarded bringing order to the region as their responsibility. "The duty was imperative from motives of humanity alone," he writes. Swettenham observes that it was "equally certain that to undertake it would be highly beneficial to British interests and British trade," and later he makes the case for the moral imperative the British faced, noting that they must "save the Malays from themselves and give them the blessings of peace and justice." British rule in Malaya was later characterized by some, in the years prior to World War II, as a peace interrupted only sporadically by uprisings by the Malay people against the British, according to A. J. Stockwell in an essay for the fourth volume of the *Oxford History of the British Empire*. Stockwell describes the years between the two world wars as "a halcyon period for the British" in that region, connoting peace, harmony, and happiness. The British engaged in "peacetime administration," and during the early years of the war the British colonial government behaved by "correctly performing its wartime functions of supplying Britain with rubber and tin," Stockwell stresses. After the war, however, the British desire to create a nation in which the races (the Malays, Chinese, and Indians) would be equal was obstructed by the cause of Malay nationalism—the desire of the native Malay people for political independence. The goal of racial equality appears on the surface to be a noble one, yet this particular equality served British interests, in that it was designed to ease racial and ethnic tensions and thereby eliminate threats to the British colonial government.

In colonizing the Malay Peninsula, the British put forth the notion that the Malays needed to be saved from their violent ways. Their goals were described in altruistic terms, although the financial gains were also recognized. The fictional Jean Paget, after the war and her return to England, acquires a large sum of money and seeks to put it to some purposeful use. In returning to Malaya to build a well in the village where she lived for three years alongside the native Malays, Jean's motives do seem truly noble. Her stated goal is to "make life easier for them [the women of the village], as they made life easier for us." The well, in her view, is needed, for the walk to the freshwater spring is long and must be made by the women twice a day. Jean also informs Noel Strachan that by giving the women the well, she would be able to "sort of wind things up" and subsequently be able to "enjoy this money with a clear conscience." The debt Jean feels she owes the women is deeply felt. At the same time, her aims are not entirely altruistic (completely selfless). She is seeking what could be described as closure, but Jean's reference to being able to enjoy her money hints at the economic nature of the exchange. She is, in effect, purchasing her clear conscience, attempting to better the lives of the women so that she may better be able to enjoy her own fortune. Once she presents her ideas to the village, Jean does not initially meet with universal gratitude for her gift. Some of the women consider the notion that it may be "impious to wish to alter the arrangements that had satisfied their mothers and their grandmothers before them." The head of the village echoes this sentiment, but Jean presses her point, quoting Islamic teachings she learned from another village leader years

previously and reminding him about the importance of kindness toward women. Eventually, everyone in the village agrees on the well as an improvement to their lives.

Once Jean arrives in Australia, she quickly embarks on a series of ventures that in their scope mirror Swettenham's statements about the humanitarian responsibility that Britain was compelled to act on and the economic benefits it would incidentally reap along the way. Jean's observations of Willstown reveal that young women leave town to seek jobs in bigger cities and that, consequently, men are leaving as well, having no women to court or start families with. The town has fewer than two hundred people, and many residents seem to feel that its demise is imminent. They explain to Jean its history as a gold-mining town and the way the town literally began to fall apart after the collapse of the mining industry. Jean wonders aloud about the possible collapse of the cattle industry if all the men leave, but no one has a solution. Later, the (unmarried) maid Annie reveals to Jean that she is pregnant and trying to find out how to get an abortion. Annie says that after she told her sister about her condition, the sister called her wicked. She goes on, "Suppose I am a wicked girl. There's nothing else to do in a crook place like this." With the suffering that has resulted from Annie's apparently boredom-driven promiscuity fresh in her mind, Jean is motivated to find a solution to the town's troubles. She soon sees her opportunity when she is shown the alligator skins the men sell for profit. Jean calls upon her experience in the shoe industry back in England, and she develops the idea for her first business venture in Willstown: a shoe factory. Jean's letter to Noel Strachan underscores her dual aims of civilizing the town and making a profit. She states, "There's nothing for a woman there [in Willstown] at all except the washtub"; "they're decent people in Willstown, and they've got so very little." At the same time, Jean proposes another business venture, the ice-cream parlor, insisting, "If I'm going to start a workshop for girls, they've got to have something to spend their wages on." Joe sees another effect of the business on the town: "Six or seven girls all earning money at a job in Willstown? . . . You wouldn't keep them six weeks. They'd all be married." Jean also explains her financial incentive for opening the ice cream parlor, telling Joe about how much money the girls at the factory will make, and how she'll have to "get

Jean wants to use her inheritance to build a well in Malaya. (*Rafal Cichawa | Shutterstock.com*)

some of it back." Jean's efforts toward civilizing and expanding Willstown are further emphasized as she continues to discuss her ideas with Joe. She claims that "there's more to it than just employing a few girls." Jean explains that more men will want to work at the cattle station at Midhurst if there are women employed in town.

Jean also feels that she must serve as a moral example and not spend more than a day at a time at Midhurst station with Joe. Jean feels that "to make a success of what she had set out to do for women in that place her own behaviour would have to be above reproach." Her protection of her chastity and her reputation stand in stark contrast to the choices the "wicked" maid Annie has made. Like the earlier British colonizers who seek to save the Malay people from their own base inclinations, Jean seeks to save the women of Willstown by modeling proper English behavior. The notion of preserving reputations is further underscored when Jean insists that Joe not come into her room at the hotel but that they talk at the ice-cream parlor instead. At this point, Jean realizes that the ice-cream parlor "was literally the only place in Willstown

where young men and young women could meet reputably to talk." Her very profitable business venture serves a moral, civilizing purpose.

Near the novel's conclusion, Joe explains to Noel Strachan the way Jean's efforts, beginning with the shoe factory, have led to a general increase in spending. The women now have money, and men have settled in Willstown because there are now women there. Women spend money at Jean's beauty parlor and dress shop "to make themselves look pretty for the ringers," and the ringers consequently spend money at Jean's ice-cream parlor and cinema to entertain the women. Now, Joe explains, the demographics are trending in a new direction, as all this dating has led to marriages, which have led to the emergence of young families in Willstown. These families now need to shop for supplies for the babies, for homes, for gardens. A new need for domestic goods has been created. Jean has created a series of industries that all feed into and supply one another. She has been an effective community builder, just as the British Empire sought to build unified nations under British rule in its colonies. Both Jean, as a representative of the empire, and the empire itself marry what

> THE IDEA OF THE SOLDIER AS A CHRIST-FIGURE IS AN OFTEN-USED ANALOGY, ALMOST A LITERARY COMMONPLACE, AMONG BRITISH SOLDIER-POETS OF THE FIRST WORLD WAR."

they believe to be noble, humanitarian goals with economic developments designed to increase their own wealth.

Source: Catherine Dominic, Critical Essay on *A Town Like Alice*, in *Novels for Students*, Gale, Cengage Learning, 2012.

Roger Bourke

In the following excerpt, Bourke analyzes the character Joe Harmon, who was crucified in A Town Like Alice, *as an example of a literary Christ-figure.*

The first two novels to describe the prisoner-of-war experience under the Japanese, Nevil Shute's *A Town Like Alice* and Leslie Greener's *No Time to Look Back*, both published in 1950, each contain a major character who is a Christ-figure. Or, more accurately, Shute's Joe Harman is a Christ-*like* figure since he is an ordinary Australian soldier who suffers crucifixion. Greener's Andros is more than simply a Christ-*figure*: he is the Risen Christ in person. The prisoner-of-war artist Ronald Searle made a remarkable drawing of a crucifixion in 1946—perhaps the first symbolic representation of the prisoner of war of the Japanese as a Christ-figure.

The novels of Nevil Shute have attracted little scholarly attention, although Shute himself once ranked among the world's most popular and bestselling authors. 'Shute is not a great artist,' notes the Australian critic Jack W. Bennett: 'Rereading his books confirms their tendency towards formulaic composition and pedestrian prose.' Bennett then goes on to recount a conversation he once had with a guesthouse receptionist in which the woman used the phrase 'we're all *on the beach*' (in allusion to Shute's nuclear-apocalyptic novel of that title), observing:

> The point here is that like [Robert] Frost, Nevil Shute has created idioms generally shared and understood, that have entered the consciousness of English-speaking people throughout the world. He has written stories that in their telling, and retelling via television and films, bind millions of people together by giving them a common reference point for anxieties and events in their own lives. *A Town Like Alice* is one of these stories. . . .

Another Australian critic, Robin Gerster, focuses his comments on the novel in *Big-noting: The Heroic Theme in Australian War Writing* on what is arguably its central, defining moment—the crucifixion by the Japanese of the Australian prisoner of war Joe Harman:

> A divergence in culture attitudes to the prisoner-of-war provides much of the horror of Joe Harmon's [*sic*] frightful crucifixion and whipping in Nevil Shute's *A Town Like Alice* (1950). To Western readers, who take for granted the Geneva Convention rules regarding the care and custody of prisoners, the attitude to Harmon of his captor Captain Sugamo, is an incomprehensible mixture of sadistic barbarism and reverence. To prove the 'element of holiness' that dictated his treatment of the Australian, Sugamo gives him an opportunity to expiate his dishonour by suffering a lingering death. That Harmon's 'resurrection' is aborted by his survival of the ordeal in no way influences *our* estimation of his personal worth.

Gerster is partly missing the point here. Surely there is more to the horror of the crucifixion of an Australian prisoner of war for Western audiences than simply a 'divergence in cultural attitudes' and the Japanese failure to observe the Geneva Convention?

THE CRUCIFIED AUSTRALIAN

In *A Town Like Alice*, Nevil Shute represents the crucifixion of Joe Harman in two stages—firstly through the reported speech of the novel's central character, Jean Paget, as recorded by its first-person narrator, the solicitor Noel Strachan:

> Darkness was closing down in my London sitting-room, the early darkness of a stormy afternoon. The rain still beat upon the window. The girl sat staring into the fire, immersed in her sad memories. 'They crucified him,' she said quietly. 'They took us all down to Kuantan, and they nailed his hands to a tree, and beat him to death. They kept us there, and made us look on while they did it.'

Harman's crucifixion is described again some thirty pages later, in historical 'flashback' but in the dramatic present, from a moment in time after that at which Jean's narrative to the solicitor breaks off:

> The body still hung by its hands, facing the tree. Blood had drained from the blackened mess that was its back and had run down the legs to form a black pool on the ground, now dried and oxidised by the hot sun. A great mass of flies covered the body and the blood. But the man undoubtedly was still alive; when Captain Sugamo approached the face the eyes opened and looked at him with recognition.

In these passages, Shute employs two quite different literary techniques. In the second, naturalistic visual details—the dried blood and the flies—emphasise the gross physical actuality of the event. In the first, the effect is that of narrative 'distancing,' a product of the framing device of a narrative-within-a-narrative, which, as one critic has observed, is an important feature of *A Town Like Alice*. But, at the same time, the familiar, fireside setting and the muted, matter-of-fact tone of the language of the passage in which it appears throw into sharp relief Shute's introduction into his novel of the word '*crucified*.' The very word triggers one of what the poet Seamus Heaney terms the 'cultural depth-charges latent in certain words and rhythms.' It calls up a potent network of association for any Western reader: a uniquely significant act of individual suffering, an ancient and barbaric form of execution, a peculiarly horrific way to die.

The image of the crucified English-speaking prisoner of war carries with it other associations which, while perhaps less obvious today, may possibly have been familiar to some of Shute's readers of the 1950s. The idea of the soldier as a Christ-figure is an often-used analogy, almost a literary commonplace, among British soldier-poets of the First World War. It appears in the poetry of Wilfred Owen ('Greater Love'), Siegfried Sassoon ('The Redeemer'), Herbert Read ('My Company') and others, and, perhaps most famously, in a letter of Owen's to Osbert Sitwell of July 1918:

> For 14 hours yesterday I was at work—teaching Christ to lift his cross by numbers, and how to adjust his crown; and not to imagine the thirst till after the last halt; I attended his Supper to see that there were no complaints; and inspected his feet to see that they should be worthy of the nails. I see to it that he is dumb and stands to attention before his accusers. With a piece of silver I buy him every day, and with maps I make him familiar with the topography of Golgotha.

However, the idea of the soldier as Christ on the way to his Crucifixion had a deeper cultural impact than a letter from the trenches to Bloomsbury; accounts of the crucifixion of a Canadian prisoner of war by the Germans on the Western Front became one of the war's most widely reported atrocity stories. Most historians and literary scholars, including Paul Fussell, have dismissed the story as a fabrication—a soldiers' rumour embellished by British and American propagandists in order to vilify the German enemy—although its veracity continues to be debated.

Fussell discusses the story of the Crucified Canadian in his *The Great War and Modern Memory*:

> Another well-known rumor imputing unique vileness to the Germans is that of the Crucified Canadian. The usual version relates that the Germans captured a Canadian soldier and in full view of his mates exhibited him in the open spread-eagled on a cross, his hands and feet pierced by bayonets. He is said to have died slowly....
>
> The Crucified Canadian is an especially interesting fiction both because of its original context in the insistent visual realities of the front and because of its special symbolic suggestiveness.

In April 2001, a British historian, Iain Overton, claimed in Britain's *Sunday Express* to have 'unearthed new evidence that the crucifixion did take place.' Overton named the victim as Sergeant Harry Band of the 48th Canadian Highlanders and published a detailed, apparently eyewitness description of the discovery of his corpse, pinned by eight bayonets to the door of a shed near the village of St. Julien in Belgium in April 1915. Overton suggested that Band's horrific execution (or post-mortem mutilation) was probably carried out in retaliation for the killing of a group of German prisoners by Canadian soldiers, itself an act of retaliation for the war's first poison-gas attack.

Nevil Shute soldiered briefly in the British Army during the First World War (although he did not serve in the trenches of the Western Front) and would almost certainly have been aware of the story of the Crucified Canadian. Thirty years later, in 1948, Shute visited Australia to gather material for a novel and, while travelling in Queensland, heard of and later met an Australian former prisoner of war, Herbert 'Jim' (or 'Ringer') Edwards (*Illustration 5*). The

Australian had a truly remarkable story to tell. In 1943, while a prisoner of war in Burma on the Burma-Thailand railway, he and two other prisoners had been sentenced to death by the Japanese for killing native cattle for food. Bound at the wrists with fencing wire, the men were suspended from a tree and beaten with a baseball bat. When Edwards managed to free his right hand, his punishment was continued with the fencing wire driven through his palms. Incredibly, Jim Edwards somehow survived his ordeal, which lasted for sixty-three hours, although both his comrades died. Edwards died, aged eighty-six, in Western Australia in June 2000.

The stories of Jim Edwards and the Crucified Canadian show that the historical and cultural contexts of *A Town Like Alice* leave it open to other more complex interpretations. Nevil Shute's fictional representation of the crucifixion of an Australian prisoner of war derives its power, and its horror, from the way in which it combines multiple levels of cultural and historical reference: to the biblical accounts of the Crucifixion; to a widely reported atrocity story of the First World War; to an actual event in the life of an Australian prisoner of war. It seems clear that Shute shaped his representation of Joe Harman's crucifixion from elements of each of these. There is significance, too, in the circumstantial details the novelist includes as against those he omits. While Shute remains essentially faithful in his novel to the historical facts of Jim Edwards' ordeal, he suppresses its more grotesquely 'modern' features—the fencing wire, the baseball bat—and substitutes for them more traditional elements that recall the biblical Crucifixion: the nails, the blood of a scourging. Here Shute can be observed 'mythifying' an actual historical event. . . .

Source: Roger Bourke, "*A Town Like Alice* and the Prisoner of War as Christ-figure," in *Prisoners of the Japanese: Literary Imagination and the Prisoner-of-War Experience*, University of Queensland Press, 2006, pp. 30–65.

Fred Erisman

In the following excerpt, Erisman considers Shute's treatment of the Australian frontier theme in his novels, contending that the author offers perceptive commentary about the mythical power of the frontier and the impact of its closing.

LIKE OTHER WRITERS HE SPEAKS ELOQUENTLY OF THE FREEDOM OFFERED BY UNSPOILED NATURE, LIKE THEM HE ARGUES FOR THE IMPORTANCE OF INDIVIDUALISM IN CONTEMPORARY SOCIETY, AND LIKE THEM HE SUGGESTS HOW THE FRONTIER STIMULATES THAT INDIVIDUALISM."

When the British novelist Nevil Shute (1899–1960) immigrated to Australia in 1950, he did so for reasons more economic and emotional than artistic. As a best-selling author with growing international sales, he was frustrated by the heavy tax burden that Labourite England imposed upon him; out of expected royalties of fifteen thousand pounds on his most recent book, he would net approximately three thousand, whereas the Australian tax scale would let him keep almost six thousand. Moreover, as a trained aeronautical engineer, an experienced corporate entrepreneur, and a dedicated believer in a meritocracy based upon individualism and competence, he was equally frustrated by what he perceived as the Socialist government's deliberate stifling of individual initiative and effort. He knew and liked Australia, having been there for a six-month visit in 1948–1949, so, when circumstances permitted, he moved.

The move was a fortuitous one, economically, emotionally, and artistically. It freed him from the financial constraints that had chafed him in England and enabled him to accumulate a substantial fortune. It confirmed his deep-seated belief that the self-sufficient individual was the foundation of a nation's cultural and economic growth. And, most significantly, it led him to write a three-novel sequence that constitutes a little-known but provocative exploration of the frontier hypothesis and its implications. He was, to be sure, an engineer and a novelist, not a profound student of either history or literature; even so, he knew (and admired) the "rough vitality [and] optimism" of Americans and he was professionally sensitive to the presence and power of myth. These traits stood him in good stead as he looked at Australia and the United

States, so that, in *A Town Like Alice* (1950), *The Far Country* (1952), and *Beyond the Black Stump* (1956), Nevil Shute, an Englishman turned Australian, emerges as a perceptive commentator upon the mythic power of the frontier and upon the consequences of its closing.

As Shute develops his ideas over the six-year span of the three books, he proceeds in straightforward, systematic fashion. Thus, the first of the three, *A Town Like Alice*, published in the United States as *The Legacy* and given a new audience by its television dramatization on *Masterpiece Theatre* in the early 1980s, is a simple statement of the possibilities that a frontier environment holds for those willing to adapt themselves to its circumstances. Jean Paget, a London typist who has been a prisoner of the Japanese on Malaya during the Second World War, inherits a windfall fortune from a long-forgotten uncle. When she travels to Malaya to build a well for the natives who had befriended her, she crosses the path of another wartime acquaintance, Joe Harmon, an Australian ringer (i.e., cowboy) whom she had thought executed by the Japanese. She traces him to his cattle station, they fall in love and marry, and she devotes the residue of her legacy to modernizing the dreary outback village of Willstown.

Thus summarized, the novel seems little more than a conventional love story suitable for light reading on a summer afternoon. Within its sentimental plot, however, Shute hides considerable substance, for he shapes the action in a way that pointedly echoes Frederick Jackson Turner's vision of the American frontier. In this instance, the events parallel Turner's observation that "the peculiarity of American institutions is, the fact that they have been compelled to adapt themselves to the changes of an expanding people . . . and in developing at each area of this progress out of the primitive economic and political conditions of the frontier into the complexity of city life." Turner speaks of the United States and Shute of Australia, yet both see the same processes at work.

The processes, for Shute as much as for Turner, are a combination of the environmental and the personal. Shute presents Australia as a land of vast spaces, of challenges and of enormous difficulties. A cattle station embracing twenty-seven hundred square miles and supporting eighteen thousand cattle is commonplace, and hardships are as much a part of outback

life as the challenge; as Harmon says, "It's a grand country for a man to live and work in, and good money, too. But it's a crook place for a woman." Yet the potential of the country is equally real, and if a person shows initiative and adaptability, rapid progress is sure to result. When Jean outlines her plans for Willstown to a bank manager, he replies: "Joe Harmon may be on to a good thing up there. . . . The Gulf Country's not much just at present, but he's a young man, and things can happen very quickly in Australia." And, stimulated by Jean's capital and Australia's opportunities, things do happen.

By story's end, Jean is a flourishing capitalist (also a contented wife and mother); Joe is a substantial landholder; and Willstown, like a case history for Turner, is a thriving community complete with ice cream shop, laundromat, swimming pool, and beauty parlor. Jean herself, as her aging London attorney notes, has "ceased to write as an Englishwoman living in a strange, hard, foreign land [and] gradually began to write about the people as if she was one of them, about the place as if it was her place." She and Joe, Shute remarks in a telling aside, are planning a holiday in the United States, where "their problems must be just the same as ours, and they've been at it longer." (*TLA* [*A Town Like Alice*]) And the old attorney, in the closing paragraphs of the story, puts an appropriately Turnerian finish to it all: "It is," he says, "no small matter to assist in the birth of a new city." (*TLA*) For Jean and Joe, and, behind them, for Nevil Shute, the open frontier of Australia has proven as stimulating and as productive as did the American frontier for its people.

. . . Nevil Shute is a novelist, not a historian, and to suggest that he began writing of Australia with the Turner thesis in mind is to do injustice to his craftsmanship; there is ample evidence to establish that his initial use of Australian materials grew out of his customary practice of building novels upon his travels and other experiences, and that he thought of *A Town Like Alice* as little more than a story written to pay its own way. Yet there is equally persuasive evidence to establish that, as he warmed to his subject and himself became more at home in Australia, he came to see the country as a frontier society in the American mold, with all that that vision entails. What he saw there appealed to him and led him further into his exploration of frontier elements, culminating in the overt pairing of the two frontiers appearing in *Beyond the Black Stump*.

Shute's fascination with the frontier seems almost inevitable. Trained as a young man as an engineer, he brought to his work an engineer's sense of the appropriateness of mankind's confronting nature, so that in a commentary upon his autobiography he notes: "When I was a student I was taught that engineering was 'the art of directing the great sources of Power in Nature to the use and convenience of man.'" This attitude, moreover, colors many of his early novels, where he explores "the theme of organization: the organizing of enterprises and the coordinating of people." He was, therefore, by virtue of his professional training and early literary inclinations, receptive to the opportunity for community growth and the exploitation of nature that Australia provided, and able to see in that opportunity an expression of the mythic belief that through the frontier experience a person "could battle nature's inscrutable ways and, through strength and resourcefulness, triumph over them." When he set out to apply this belief to Australia, he found in the frontier a vivid and compelling metaphor for his ideas.

His acceptance of that metaphor is enhanced by the events of his later literary career. Prior to the Second World War, he looked to technology for the themes of his fiction; after the war, wearied by his work in weapons development and somewhat disenchanted with technology, he began to explore a more satisfying cluster of themes, "the role of the 'little man' in history and society [and] the joys of finding a new life in a new land." This exploration, in turn, led him to the growing conviction that "history is made by plain and simple people . . . doing the best we can with each job as it comes along." He found ready confirmation of his belief in Australia, with its open land, easy-going democracy, and seemingly endless opportunity; from there to the Turnerian belief that "on the open frontier a person could be reborn; he could have a second chance" was but a small step, and he took it readily.

Nevil Shute is not, of course, the first author to see Australia as a frontier state, and he quietly ignores many of the ways in which the Australian frontier experience differs from that of the United States. These matters are, however, of little consequence: as a writer he is more concerned with human than with historical truths, and his achievement is of another order of magnitude entirely. Like other writers he speaks eloquently of the freedom offered by unspoiled nature, like them he argues for the importance of individualism in contemporary society, and like them he suggests how the frontier stimulates that individualism. But he then goes on, as others do not, to consider what happens when the frontier no longer exists. His picture of mid-twentieth-century America, still a country of immense potential but one dragging about the corpse of its memory, is a haunting one, for it speaks volumes to his readers, whether British, Australian, or American. England and the United States, he reminds us, were once the lands of opportunity; now, in the 1950s, Australia has become that land. Yet, if only the two older countries can shake off the myths that oppress them, realistically assess their circumstances, and set their goals accordingly, they can regain their lost ideal.

For Shute, the individualist, the literal frontier of Australia is appealing, but as his last three novels seem to affirm, the ultimate frontier is that of the individual person's potential. *The Rainbow and the Rose* (1958) and *Trustee from the Toolroom* (1960) make clear just how far a sincere, resourceful person can go in overcoming the obstacles of ordinary life, while *On the Beach* (1957) speaks memorably of individual fortitude in the face of extraordinary and inescapable—but not necessarily inevitable—disaster. Thus, though he does not explicitly concern himself in these books with comparative frontiers, Shute nevertheless stands by his point. If a society and its citizens can shake off the artificial constraints that an outdated myth—be it Labourite economics, national chauvinism, or Turnerian history—imposes and build instead to the enduring abilities of the people themselves, the glories of national promise may yet become realities.

Source: Fred Erisman, "Nevil Shute and the Closed Frontier," in *Western American Literature*, Vol. 21, No. 3, November 1986, pp. 207–17.

SOURCES

"A Century of Population Change in Australia," in *Australian Bureau of Statistics*, 2001, http://www.abs.gov.au/Ausstats/abs@.nsf/0/0B82C2F2654C3694CA2569DE002139D9?Open (accessed June 7, 2011).

Arrow, Michelle, "Popular Culture and Family Life in the Postwar Years," in *Friday on Our Minds: Popular Culture in Australia since 1945*, University of New South Wales Press, 2009, pp. 14–43.

"The Atomic Bombings of Hiroshima and Nagasaki: Introduction," in *Avalon Project: Documents in Law, History and Diplomacy*, Yale Law School Lillian Goldman Law Library Web site, 2008, http://avalon.law.yale.edu/20th_century/mpintro.asp (accessed on June 7, 2011).

"Australia," in *CIA World Factbook*, 2011, https://www.cia.gov/library/publications/the-world-factbook/geos/as.html (accessed June 7, 2011).

"Australia at War: 3 September 1939," in *Australia's War: 1939–1945*, http://www.ww2australia.gov.au/war declared (accessed June 7, 2011).

"Axis Alliance in World War II," in *Holocaust Encyclopedia*, http://www.ushmm.org/wlc/en/article.php?ModuleId = 10005177 (accessed June 7, 2011).

Bourke, Roger, *Prisoners of the Japanese: Literary Imagination and the Prisoner-of-War Experience*, University of Queensland Press, 2006, pp. 30–65.

Carnell, Corbin S., "Nevil Shute," in *Dictionary of Literary Biography*, Vol. 255, *British Fantasy and Science Fiction Writers, 1918–1960*, edited by Darren Harris-Fane, The Gale Group, 2002, pp. 213–17.

Cheah, Boon Kheng, *Malaysia: The Making of a Nation State*, Institute of South Asian Studies, 2002, pp. 1–48.

Chen, C. Peter, "Invasion of Malay and Singapore," in *World War II Database*, http://ww2db.com/battle_spec.php?battle_id = 47 (accessed June 7, 2011).

"Malaysia," in *CIA: World Factbook*, 2011, https://www.cia.gov/library/publications/the-world-factbook/geos/my.html (accessed June 7, 2011).

Mann, Michael, "'Torchbearers upon the Path of Progress': Britain's Ideology of a 'Moral and Material Progress' in India," in *Colonialism as Civilizing Mission: Cultural Ideology in British India*, edited by Harold Fischer-Tine and Michael Mann, Wimbledon Publishing, 2004, pp. 1–28.

"Nevil Shute Norway," in *Dictionary of National Biography, 1951–1960*, excerpted by the Nevil Shute Foundation, http://www.nevilshute.org/Biography/dictionarynationalbio.php (accessed June 7, 2011).

Ousby, Ian, "Nevil Shute," in *The Cambridge Guide to Literature in English*, Cambridge University Press, 1988, pp. 867–68.

Shaffer, Brian W., "Introduction to Volume I," in *Twentieth-Century British and Irish Fiction*, edited by Brian W. Shaffer and Patrick O'Donnell, Blackwell Publishing, 2011, pp. 1–6.

Shute, Nevil, *A Town Like Alice*, Vintage, 2009.

Stockwell, A. J., "Imperialism and Nationalism in South-East Asia," in *The Oxford History of the British Empire*, Vol. 4, *The Twentieth Century*, edited by Judith M. Brown, Oxford University Press, 1999, pp. 465–89.

Swettenham, Frank Athelstane, "1874: Sir Andrew Clarke—British Intervention in the Affairs of the Western Malay States," in *British Malaysia*, John Lane, 1907, pp. 173–93.

Tierney, Robert, "Migrants and Class in Postwar Australia," in *Marxist Interventions*, http://www.anu.edu.au/polsci/marx/interventions/migrants.htm (accessed June 7, 2011); originally published in *Class and Class Conflict in Australia*, edited by Rick Kuhn and Tom O'Lincoln, Longman, 1996.

"Victory (8 May 1945/15 August 1945)," in *Australia's War: 1939–1945*, http://www.ww2australia.gov.au/vevp/ (accessed June 7, 2011).

Weir, David T. H., "Nevil Shute and the Landscape of England: An Opportunity for Literary Tourism," in *Literature and Tourism: Essays in the Reading and Writing of Tourism*, edited by Mike Robinson and Hans-Christian Anderson, Thomson, 2002, pp. 119–42.

FURTHER READING

Brumley. I. H., ed., *Urbanization in Australia: The Postwar Experience*, Cambridge University Press, 1974.
> Brumley explores the demographic, social, and economic elements of Australia's postwar development and the growth of urban areas.

Jowett, Philip, *The Chinese Army, 1937–49: World War II and Civil War*, Osprey, 2005.
> Jowett traces the history of twentieth-century tensions between Japan and China, discussing the 1937 invasion of China by Japan and the years of warfare that continued until the Japanese surrendered to the Allies in 1945. Jowett then focuses on the contribution of the Chinese army to the Allied victory.

Shapiro, Harvey, ed., *Poets of World War II*, Library of America, 2003.
> This work collects the poetry of more than sixty American poets. The editor, Harvey Shapiro, also provides the introduction, which comments on the differences between the poetry of World War I and that of World War II. Notably, Shapiro observes a lack of patriotism and class consciousness in the works of the World War II poets.

Shute, Nevil, *Slide Rule: The Autobiography of an Engineer*, Paper Tiger, 1954.
> Shute's autobiography focuses on his career as an engineer and his extensive work in the development of aircraft.

SUGGESTED SEARCH TERMS

Nevil Shute AND World War II

Nevil Shute AND Malaya OR Malaysia

Nevil Shute AND Australia

Nevil Shute AND British imperialism

Nevil Shute AND war fiction

Nevil Shute AND prisoner-of-war fiction

Nevil Shute AND feminism

Nevil Shute AND racism

Nevil Shute AND Japan

Nevil Shute AND A Town Like Alice

World War II AND Malaya OR Malaysia

World War II AND Australia

World War II AND Pacific front

World War II AND prisoner of war

The Unvanquished

WILLIAM FAULKNER

1938

The Unvanquished is an early novel by William Faulkner, a Nobel Prize winner and one of the most important novelists of the twentieth century, arguably the most important writer from the American South. It tells the story of the Sartoris family during the American Civil War and the following period of Reconstruction. It realistically depicts the violence and racism of that era. Unlike many of Faulkner's better-known works, *The Unvanquished* does not have an experimental narrative style and is comparable, for instance, to a work like Mark Twain's *Adventures of Huckleberry Finn*. Similar in style and theme, *The Unvanquished* uses gothic and romantic tropes of honor and violence in order to subvert the American culture of the time.

The first six chapters of *The Unvanquished* were originally published as short stories in the *Saturday Evening Post* and *Scribner's* magazine between 1934 and 1936. They were collected in a revised form together with the newly written last chapter and published as a novel in 1938. *The Unvanquished* is one of Faulkner's books set in his fictional Yoknapatawpha County that form a larger structure linked by common characters. In particular, Bayard Sartoris, the narrator of *The Unvanquished*, who is twelve years old at the beginning of the novel, also appears in Faulkner's 1929 novel *Sartoris* (republished in the form Faulkner intended in 1973 as *Flags in the Dust*), which tells the story of Bayard's old age and death.

In a letter to the editor of *Life* magazine, Faulkner described his background this way:

William Faulkner (Getty Images)

"My family has lived for generations in one same small section of north Mississippi. My great-grandfather held slaves and went to Virginia in command of a Mississippi infantry regiment in 1861." This could as well be a description of the fictional Sartoris family as of Faulkner's own. Similarly, Bayard Sartoris's birthday falls in September and may well have coincided with Faulkner's own. Faulkner's writing was firmly fixed in his southern identity and in his family identity. Nowhere is this more true than in *The Unvanquished*, which seems to set the tone for the idealized vision for southern culture he later had occasion to outline in a number of articles and letters to the editor he would publish during the birth of the civil rights movement in the 1950s.

AUTHOR BIOGRAPHY

Faulkner was born on September 25, 1897, in New Albany, Mississippi, and before he was five, his family moved to Oxford, Mississippi, where

he lived the rest of his life. His mother and grandmother were artistic and fostered his aesthetic development. During World War I, Faulkner was found to be too short for service in the American armed forces but joined the British Royal Flying Corps. He did not see any combat.

After the war and after attending the University of Mississippi in Oxford for three semesters, Faulkner worked as a journalist in New Orleans and focused his creative activity on poetry that is today overshadowed by his fiction. Faulkner came under the tutelage of the novelist Sherwood Anderson in New Orleans and published his own first novel, *Soldier's Pay*, in 1925. Thereafter, Faulkner published popular novels to support his work on more serious literature, influenced by the idea of stream of consciousness and other avant-garde techniques. The money earned for the short stories that would eventually become *The Unvanquished* supported Faulkner's work on *Absalom, Absalom!* an experimental work he considered the most important novel ever written in English. After Faulkner's unsuccessful stint in Hollywood, the genius of his novels, such as *Light in August* and *The Sound and the Fury*, became more widely recognized, and he was awarded the Novel Prize for Literature in 1950 and Pulitzer Prizes in 1953 and 1960. Faulkner died of a heart attack on July 6, 1962, at a sanatorium near his home in Mississippi.

PLOT SUMMARY

Ambuscade
Ambuscade is a somewhat archaic variant of the word *ambush*, meaning a surprise attack from a concealed position. The title has a military significance.

The narrator of *The Unvanquished* is Bayard Sartoris. Speaking from some unknown point in his adult years, he begins by relating events that occurred when he was twelve years old. At the beginning, he is playing a war game in the yard of his family house with his slave companion, Ringo, a boy almost exactly his age. The game is upset by the adult slave, Loosh, who has been stirred into rebelliousness by rumors of Confederate defeats in the ongoing Civil War, suggesting that Union troops might soon pass through and set the slaves free.

Bayard's father, John, is a colonel in the Confederate army. He has briefly come home because what Loosh suspects is true. He organizes hiding the family livestock in a secluded pen and burying the family silver in order to protect it from confiscation by Union soldiers. However, he must quickly return to the army. Not long after, a Union patrol does reach the Sartoris plantation. In a dreamlike passage, Bayard and Ringo get a musket that hangs above the mantle of the farmhouse and shoot at a Union soldier, but they succeed only in killing his horse. Nevertheless, a Union colonel (though unnamed now, he is Colonel Dick, who reappears later in the chapter "Raid") leads a squad of soldiers to search the house for whoever fired the shot. Bayard's granny hides the two behind her skirts.

The colonel is well aware that they are there but pretends to believe Granny's protestations that no one from the house fired the shot and that there are no boys in the house. He prefers to follow the prevailing honor code to accept a lady's word rather than have his soldiers pull her away and execute the two boys, which he technically ought to have done. After the soldiers leave, Bayard is amazed that Granny lied, perhaps not realizing the danger he was in. Because the boys called the Union soldiers "bastuds" (bastards), Granny washes their mouths out with soap, keeping up a pretense of normalcy.

Retreat

A year later, Colonel Sartoris decides that his family should go to Memphis for their own safety, taking the buried silver with them, and explains this in a letter to Granny. It is clear that Granny no longer trusts the slaves, and she sleeps with the silver in her bedroom, locking the door, something Bayard had never imagined before. John Sartoris has left his regiment in the Army of Northern Virginia and now commands a group of irregular cavalry fighting in Yoknapatawpha County.

On the road, Union soldiers take the Sartorises' mule but do not suspect they are carrying silver. Bayard and Ringo try to get the animal back, but John Sartoris happens through the area with some of his soldiers and drives off the federal soldiers, taking the mule back along with some other supplies. Realizing that travel is too dangerous, he escorts his family back to the plantation near the town of Jefferson. A Union patrol comes to the farm specifically to arrest John, led there by Loosh. The colonel is barely able to escape. Loosh shows the soldiers where

the silver is buried, considering that their taking it from Colonel Sartoris is reparation for his enslavement. He and his wife Philadelphy go with the soldiers, preferring freedom to remaining with their former owners. The soldiers also burn the house. In the final line of the chapter, Granny calls the Union soldiers "bastuds."

Raid

About a month later, Granny sets out for Alabama with Bayard and Ringo to find Colonel Dick, the officer who had courteously spared Bayard's life in the chapter "Ambuscade," and demand the return of the Sartorises' confiscated silver and livestock. The area they traverse by mule cart has been devastated by the Union army moving from Vicksburg to Chattanooga. Eventually they come to Hawkhurst, the plantation of Aunt Louisa. The house there has been burned down also.

They meet Louisa's daughter Drusilla. She is a few years older than Bayard and, because of the dislocations of the war, is living and dressing as a man. She has learned that the Union army plans to abandon the horde of free blacks that are following it by blowing up a bridge over the Tennessee River. After dinner, Drusilla tells Bayard a story about a small military action fought on the railroad between Atlanta and Chattanooga. Although they both realize that the war is lost and that the southern way of life that existed before the war can never be reclaimed, it seemed a romantic gesture, declaring that the South will not accept the change thrust upon it by Union victory. This philosophy is the source of the novel's title, *The Unvanquished*. Drusilla further tells Bayard that she is happy now to live with the masculine freedom she has, in contrast to the small confined feminine life she had before. In fact, she wants Bayard to intervene with her father to let her join his band of guerrillas.

The next day, Granny, Bayard, Ringo, and Drusilla go to the Union camp to find Colonel Dick and are caught up in the disaster of the blown bridge on the way. What follows is frequently described by critics as a tall tale, an impossible exaggeration of the restitution Dick would have made to Granny. Supposedly mishearing a few words of her request, the Colonel gives Granny ten chests of silver and 110 mules and slaves. Granny accepts the bounty but, because they lied by remaining silent, prays to God for forgiveness.

Riposte in Tertio

As a short story, this chapter was called "The Unvanquished," but Faulkner changed the title when that became the title of the whole novel. In fencing, a *riposte* is an attack made after parrying the opponent's thrust; *in tertio* means it is aimed at the opponent's attacking arm.

Another narrative year has passed. Granny has become the ringleader of a confidence trick in which Colonel Sartoris and his troops steal mules from the Union army, the Sartoris slaves cover up their army brands, Ringo forges documents for them, and Ab Snopes, a local poor farmer, takes them to Memphis to sell back to the army. Granny eventually feels compelled to confess this sin in church and then reveals that she has given her part of the profits to local people who were in need because of the war. The next day, the Union military units stationed in northern Mississippi move east, so Granny's scheme comes to an end. A Union officer comes to arrest her, because she has been turned in by Snopes for a reward, but the soldiers are anxious to join their unit and fear that she might produce forged documents against them, so she is left in peace.

That Christmas, Snopes persuades Granny to do something about a certain Grumby, whose band of former Confederate soldiers have, since the withdrawal of most federal forces from the area, turned from guerrilla warfare to brigandage, preying on the local population as bandits. Granny and Bayard meet with Grumby to deliver an order (forged by Ringo) from Nathan Bedford Forrest (one of the most famous Confederate generals, notorious for the Fort Pillow massacre, in which he slaughtered hundreds of black American troops who had surrendered to him, and as a founder of the Ku Klux Klan) to cease his depredations. Granny believes it impossible that a man would dishonor himself by harming a woman, so she sees him alone. Grumby shoots and kills her.

Vendée

La Vendée is a province in northwestern France notorious for its peasant rebellion and guerrilla warfare against the central governments of revolutionary and Napoleonic France. This chapter begins with Granny's funeral. With Granny dead and Colonel Sartoris still away fighting, Bayard is left on his own and sets out after Grumby, accompanied by Ringo and Buck McCaslin, owner of a

large nearby plantation. They suspect Grumby may be in league with Ab Snopes and indeed find Grumby's horses in Snopes's yard. Snopes tells them that Grumby has gone to Alabama. Realizing he is lying, they search in the opposite direction. After many months of tracking, they again encounter Snopes, tied to a tree, abandoned by Grumby. Bayard tries to fight him for his part in Granny's death, but Snopes refuses to defend himself. Bayard whips him—a punishment appropriate for a slave—which southern culture sanctioned as a penalty for a coward. Buck takes Snopes back to Jefferson while the two boys press on after Grumby. They find him abandoned by his companions and fight with him. Bayard's account stops before he kills Grumby.

Some time later Bayard and Ringo return to Jefferson to find that Colonel Sartoris and Drusilla have returned from the war. Buck tells everyone that Bayard killed Grumby and that he saw Grumby's body "pegged out on the door . . . like a coon hide." Grumby's hand had also been cut off and deposited on Granny's grave. Buck refers literally to a raccoon skin tacked up on the wall to cure before being made into a fur garment; but it is impossible to read the passage except in relation to the practice of lynching blacks as a means of social control by white society, practiced during Reconstruction and still in the 1930s and beyond until outlawed. Showing a white man lynched, in retaliation for an insult to a white woman that no one witnessed, is a criticism of southern culture that Faulkner could not or did not care to make more openly in the 1930s.

Skirmish at Sartoris

This chapter begins with a view into the life Colonel Sartoris and Drusilla led during the war. After the war is over in the spring of 1865, Colonel Sartoris returns home to rebuild his house and is accompanied by Drusilla and eventually her mother, Louisa. Louisa is scandalized by the fact that her daughter not only lived and dressed as a man for two years while fighting as a guerrilla but also, more particularly, was with Sartoris without a chaperone (the other men in the unit do not seem to count because they were not of the aristocratic class). Louisa is convinced that Drusilla must be pregnant and therefore orders her to marry the colonel. For all of her desire for independence, Drusilla is entirely unable to defend herself (even with the evident fact that she is not pregnant—irrelevant because the appearance of impropriety is all that matters) and collapses before her mother's brow-beating. Her mother finally persuades her to wed with the help of a committee of busybodies from Jefferson.

At the same time, Colonel Sartoris learns that two Republican agents from the North (derisively called carpetbaggers by southerners) are organizing the election of a black man as the new county sheriff. The wedding is scheduled for the same day as the election. On that day, Sartoris and Drusilla (in her wedding dress) go into the polling place and murder the two northerners in cold blood. Sartoris appoints Drusilla voting commissioner and takes the ballot box out to his plantation, where he stuffs it with votes against the black candidate. Sartoris intimidates a crowd of black men who had come to vote into swearing that he had acted in self-defense, although in fact none of them had witnessed the murders.

An Odor of Verbena

The title of this chapter refers to a flower that Drusilla is accustomed to wearing in her hair. This chapter begins eight years later, with Ringo coming to Oxford, where Bayard is studying law, to tell Bayard that his father has been killed. On the ride back to Jefferson, Bayard recalls the intervening events, beginning with the colonel's and Drusilla's wedding the day after the double murder. Sartoris worked to bring the railroad to Jefferson, forming a company for that purpose with a lawyer named Ben Redmond. Tension built up between them, and Sartoris eventually forced Redmond out of the company at a loss, then defeated him in an election for the state legislature, and made it his habit to constantly belittle his former partner.

At the same time, Bayard grew upset at the violence that his father used against the carpetbaggers and now, as a member of the Ku Klux Klan, uses against blacks, but Drusilla points out that these means are justified by his end of raising up the black and white communities together to an economic rebirth. Bayard recalls how Drusilla once kissed him in a manner wholly improper for his stepmother.

When Bayard reaches home, he finds that his father was killed by Redmond, if not in a duel, in a manner considered honorable. A number of veterans from Colonel Sartoris's former regiment have gathered at the house and offer to kill Redmond, but Bayard declines their offer. Drusilla presses on Bayard his father's pistols.

Nevertheless, he visits Redmond's office the next day unarmed. Redmond greets him with a revolver and fires two shots at him, seemingly with no serious intent of actually hitting him. Redmond then leaves the town and the state, and the veterans and family consider that Bayard had settled the matter honorably; even they thought there had been too much killing. Drusilla leaves the Sartoris household forever to live with her brother.

CHARACTERS

Colonel Nathaniel G. Dick

Dick is the Union officer who is so benevolent to Granny. He overlooks Bayard's and Ringo's assassination attempt at the end of "Ambuscade" and restores her property, with interest, in "Raid." He is perhaps based on the historical figure Colonel Dickey, who was famous in Oxford, Mississippi, for having restored the property seized by soldiers from a local widow in consideration of the fact that she had taught her slaves to read.

Granny

Rosa Millard, usually called Granny, is Bayard Sartoris's grandmother and John's mother-in-law. She is a woman who is completely invested in the presentation of the outer form of a proper southern lady, keeping up that facade like the attention of a soldier on parade. For instance, after the Sartoris house is burned down, she makes a point of borrowing a hat and parasol to keep the sun off of her face. Women of her class were not allowed to have the slightest sunburn, because it might imply that they had had occasion to perform physical labor, which would be interpreted as a failure of the men in their family to fully provide for them. She also prays reflexively whenever she has lied, even considering the lie she told to save Bayard's life when he was hiding behind her skirts to be a sin that must be forgiven. At the same time, she is immensely resourceful, able, for instance, to run a series of confidence schemes in order to support the family after their plantation is destroyed, beginning with defrauding the Union army of silver, mules, and slaves. When she passes through a checkpoint with papers permitting her to have 110 mules while she in fact has 122 and merely says nothing to the Union soldier who is too busy to count them, she counts this, too, as a lie and seeks forgiveness.

Grumby

A Confederate soldier turned brigand and Granny's murderer, Grumby is an even more exaggerated stereotype than Ab Snopes. His essential character is dishonorable, as reflected in his attack against a woman and in his constant lying. Even his fellow criminals cannot stomach him and surrender him to Bayard.

Drusilla Hawk

Drusilla is Bayard's distant cousin. She is two or three years older than him. Her fiancé is killed in the war, and after her family home is burned down, she joins Colonel Sartoris's guerrilla band. She eventually marries John Sartoris and occasionally makes Bayard's life miserable by flirting with him. Even before becoming a guerrilla, Drusilla is at war with southern ideals of femininity. At her first appearance in the novel, she is riding a horse astride rather than sidesaddle, something unheard of in that time and place. In fact, she could ride better than most men. Bayard's description of her echoes his idealization of his father as a larger-than-life character: "She was not tall, it was the way she stood and walked." She kept her horse from confiscation by Union soldiers by threatening to shoot it, a remarkable feat of bravado.

Louisa Hawk

Louisa is Drusilla's mother. She is distantly related to the Sartoris family. Bayard's address of the Hawk women as aunt and cousin is, as often in southern culture, mostly affectionate or honorific; Drusilla says she is Bayard's fourth cousin. Unable to face the changing circumstances brought about by the war, Louisa eventually succeeds in reigning in Drusilla's freedom and forcing her to marry John Sartoris.

Loosh

All of the slaves owned by the Sartoris family have names derived from literature or history, usually from classical literature, but are generally called by variations or diminutives of those names. Loosh, for instance, is a phonetic spelling of the first syllable of the Roman name Lucius. A young man at the time the novel opens, Loosh seems more excited (Bayard mistakes the feeling for intoxication) than the other slaves by the possibility of freedom that is fast approaching with the tide of Union victory in the Civil War. Precisely because he wants freedom, the Sartoris family fears and distrusts him. Faulkner portrays Loosh as foolish and incompetent and consequently portrays his desire for freedom as foolishness that is not in his best interest. At the same time, Bayard paradoxically despises Loosh for being subservient.

Louvinia

Louvinia's name is probably a dialectical pronunciation of the Roman name Lavinia. While John Sartoris is away at the war, she is essentially in charge of the Sartoris family and property, because Granny is too old to fully take on such a role, although Granny can certainly overrule her. John Sartoris somewhat ironically says that Louvinia is acting "white" when she carries out orders to keep the more recalcitrant slaves, like Loosh, in line. Her acceptance of her place is so much a part of her nature that she cannot imagine the social order being overturned, even though that social order enslaves her. At one point she asks Loosh, "Do you think there's enough Yankees in the whole world to whip the white folks?"

Amodeus (Buck) McCaslin

Buck's given name is Amodeus, a misspelling of Amadeus, which is Latin for "beloved of God." Bayard's address of him as "uncle" is honorific, not a sign of their status as relatives. He and his brother Buddy inherited a large plantation from their father but preferred to live simply in a converted slave cabin, while they left their rather substantial neoclassical mansion to their slaves. Although Faulkner scrupulously avoids using the word, the McCaslins are essentially socialists. They have worked out a scheme whereby the labor performed by their slaves is counted against their monetary value and eventually buys their freedom. They have also organized the local poor farmers into a cooperative, greatly improving their material condition and winning the brothers political popularity. Somewhat satirically, the McCaslins are fanatical poker players, gambling with each other for the cotton, slaves, and land they actually hold in common as joint owners of their plantation.

Theophilus (Buddy) McCaslin

Theophilus is Greek for "beloved of God." Much less is said about Buddy (Theophilus's nickname) than his brother Buck, because he is removed from the story by going east to take over command of Colonel Sartoris's regiment.

Rosa Millard
See Granny

Philadelphy

Philadelphy is a diminutive form of Philadelphia, a city prominent in the New Testament whose name is often interpreted as signifying "brotherly love" as a Protestant virtue. She is Loosh's wife. She differs from Loosh by not wanting freedom but feels she cannot desert her husband.

Ben Redmond

As related in retrospect in the narrative, Redmond was originally John Sartoris's partner in the company that brought the railroad to Jefferson. Tension between them began because Sartoris looked down on Redmond for being a bureaucrat during the war rather than a soldier. Sartoris eventually bought out Redmond's interest, and Redmond retaliated by running against him for a position in the state legislature, though unsuccessfully. Humiliated and marginalized by Sartoris, Redmond eventually kills him and then leaves Jefferson rather than kill Bayard too.

Ringo

Ringo is short for Marengo, a name taken from Napoleon's favorite horse. Ringo is the son of Louvinia and John Sartoris's body servant. He was born at almost the same time as Bayard, and Louvinia acted as wet nurse to Bayard while she fed her own son. Ringo is Bayard's inseparable companion and playmate, even sleeping on the floor of Bayard's bedroom (and in his bed when they think they will not get caught). He was intended to become Bayard's body servant; having a body servant to deal with matters such as chamber pots was an indispensable marker of class in the nineteenth century. As Ringo grows to manhood throughout the story, he is presented in contrast to Loosh as an ideal black man in the traditional southern view: resourceful, brave, and loyal, with no wish for freedom from the Sartoris family. Colonel Sartoris himself estimated that Ringo was smarter than Bayard, and his skill as a forger is of immense service to Granny in her confidence scheme.

Bayard Sartoris

Bayard is named after a magical horse in medieval French epic poetry, given by Emperor Charlemagne to the hero Rinaldo. This presents a parallel with Ringo, who is named after the most famous horse belonging to the only other French emperor, Napoleon. Faulkner uses the many close parallels he establishes between the two characters to suggest that they are really aspects of one individual. The point is to signify the essential unity of the southern black and white cultures as being distinct from what Faulkner perceived as the alien culture in the rest of the United States.

Bayard is the narrator and main character of *The Unvanquished*. At the beginning of the story, he is twelve years old. His narrative voice shapes the reality presented to the reader. In many cases he clearly falsifies his text, for example in reporting the various degrees of dialectical speech used by the various characters. In some passages, such as Granny's recovery of ten times the amount of silver confiscated by the Union army, he is clearly blowing his story up into a semi-legendary account for the sake of entertainment or prestige. In other cases, he mixes memories of dreams with memories of supposedly historical events (although, in fact, memories are never reliable but are reinterpreted every time they are recalled). These factors all go toward understanding Bayard's character as a storyteller.

As an adult in the later chapters, Bayard is haunted by a sense that he is out of step with the world, that he really belongs to the older world that existed before the Civil War—in his childhood, in other words. Although he fully embraces the romantic honor code, killing or attempting to kill several times for revenge, he is curiously unable to describe the violence he commits; instead he reports a description of it by a third party or claims that he cannot truly recall the details of what he is recounting for the reader. Perhaps this ambivalence foreshadows his final rejection of violence in his confrontation with his father's murderer.

Drusilla Sartoris
See Drusilla Hawk

Colonel John Sartoris

Sartoris is a not uncommon name in England and Germany (and hence in the United States) and dates from the end of the Middle Ages, when peasants began to acquire surnames. It derives from the Latin word for *hoer* (rather than *tailor* as it might seem at first). John is generally addressed as Marse (Master) John, even by Bayard.

In the early chapters, John figures only briefly in the story because he is away fighting, but when Bayard does see him, he describes his father to the reader in heroic terms: "He was not big; it was just the things he did, that we knew he was doing, had been doing in Virginia and Tennessee, that made him seem big to us." Bayard idolizes him again when he sees John escape Union soldiers who have come to arrest him: Sartoris rides his horse, Jupiter, through the house and out of a pair of French doors: "I saw [Jupiter] and Father again like they were flying in the air, with broken planks whirling and spinning around them when they went out of sight." This presents John in a nearly mythological manner, like an angel or a Greek god in flight.

Also of note is that Bayard consistently capitalizes the word "Father." Colonel Sartoris becomes Faulkner's ideal of southern tradition, maintaining the integrity of southern culture against any encroachments from the rest of the United States. To do this, he murders two members of the Republican Party who tried to organize the new freedmen for political life, and he joins the Ku Klux Klan (whom Bayard calls "night riders") to intimidate blacks against any desire to create their own political identity apart from the control of southern white culture.

Ab Snopes

Snopes, a character in several of Faulkner's novels, is poor, dishonorable, treacherous, and conniving: everything the Sartorises are not, what Faulkner calls "white trash."

THEMES

Race

Faulkner, like the United States itself, was torn by the problem of race. On the one hand, he had a profound and unconditional loyalty to the traditional culture of the South going back to the antebellum period (before the Civil War). At the same time, he saw the injustice of the white-supremacist social order of the South. For Faulkner, the problem of race in the United States was perhaps the largest expression "of the human heart in conflict with itself," a theme which he told the Nobel Committee, as quoted in *Essays, Speeches & Public Letters*, was the only basis for literature.

Faulkner's solution was to try to steer a middle course. He made his opinions perfectly clear in a large number of essays in national magazines and letters to the editors of prominent

TOPICS FOR FURTHER STUDY

- Japanese Noh drama frequently shows romanticized versions of Japan's medieval past, dealing with stories of war and violence in a style marked for its elegance and refinement. Read a few of these plays (they are widely available in translation on the Internet, such as at http://etext.lib.virginia.edu/japanese/noh/index.html) and then adapt a scene from *The Unvanquished* in Noh form. Record it and post it on YouTube or your Web page or perform it live in the classroom. Include an explanation of the Noh dramatic form before the performance or viewing. Invite classmates to review it.

- The Tai Ping Rebellion was a civil war fought in China during the 1850s and 1860s. Katherine Patterson's *Rebels of the Heavenly Kingdom* (1983) is a young-adult novel whose protagonist is a teenage boy during the war. Write a paper comparing that novel to *The Unvanquished* in terms of theme and characters.

- Did you have ancestors in the United States during the Civil War? What were their lives like? Did they fight in the war? Based either on your family traditions or on research about your family that can be done at a genealogical Web site, find out something about your ancestors in that time and use your discoveries as the basis for a short story with family members as characters. If your family was not yet in the United States, invent some characters to use in your short story.

- Read Mark Twain's *Adventures of Huckleberry Finn*, especially the chapters that take place on the Grangerford and Phelps plantations. How do these passages compare with *The Unvanquished* in their use of gothic themes? Or of slave life and slavery? Write a paper comparing the use of one theme in both novels.

newspapers. Faulkner felt that he spoke for moderate whites and blacks when he hoped to find a compromise position: the South could never accept a settlement imposed by force from outside but must resolve its racial issues by itself and in its own time, even if that meant centuries. He seemed unable or unwilling to realize that segregation was enforced by violence and that the South was not a discrete civilization (having lost the war) but was bound by the same laws and Constitution as the rest of the country. He honestly felt that blacks and whites were closely bound together by being southern and could better work together to solve the problem of racism than have what he deemed an outside solution imposed on them.

When Faulkner began writing directly about the civil rights movement in the 1950s, he did not respond to current events but only brought forth the ideas he had long before formulated and expressed in his fiction, including *The Unvanquished*. In particular, there are two remarkable passages concerning race in the "Ambuscade" chapter. The first is a sort of apocalyptic vision had by the young Bayard:

> Ringo and I had been born in the same month and had both fed at the same breast and had slept together and eaten together for so long that Ringo called Granny 'Granny' just like I did, until maybe he wasn't a nigger anymore or maybe I wasn't a white boy anymore, the two of us neither, not even people any longer: the two supreme undefeated like two moths, two feathers riding above a hurricane.

This expresses in nearly mythological terms the hope that Faulkner had that blacks and whites, united in being southern, would someday overcome their differences and live a harmonious, unified culture.

Later, when Bayard learns that Union soldiers are about to come to the house, he says in alarm, "They're coming to set us free!" At first the reader must assume that twelve-year-old Bayard has no concept of what freedom is, does not understand that the black people with whom his family lives are being held as slaves, or indeed are anything other than more of his family, and that he imagines freedom to be something dreadful that the *Yankees*—outsiders—are going to forcibly impose on them. When, at the end of the "Retreat" chapter, Loosh takes his wife, Philadelphy, and sets out to claim the freedom the Union army has brought, Granny tells them that this freedom is "misery and starvation." As Faulkner revealed during the civil rights movement, he did consider freedom something dreadful, if it was imposed by force.

However, with more consideration, it seems that freedom really was something given by the Union army to both black and white southerners. Black people were freed from being slaves, but white people were freed also, from being slave masters and the necessary brutalization of their characters that slavery entailed. Whites did not accept their freedom for another hundred years and after reconstruction imposed the white supremacist Jim Crow segregation laws. As much as he disapproved of the white refusal to be free, Faulkner did not think it right to compel them. This, of course, made true freedom impossible for southern blacks, but that was a price Faulkner was willing to pay to wait for southern whites to see the error of their ways through self-realization.

Violence

Violence is all too often a part of life and even more often of literature because of the dramatic possibilities it offers. Violence plays an exceptional part in the literary character of *The Unvanquished*. An element of the gothic genre is the frequent use of violence to settle affairs of honor, that is, to take revenge. This seems to recall the cavalier tradition of the Old South, the idea that southern gentlemen were ready to use violence to wash away even the slightest suggestion of a stain upon their honor, like a character from the Dumas novels that have such a prominent place on John Sartoris's bookshelves. One way that southerners explained the Civil War to themselves was as a reaction to an insult, as if they were fighting a duel with the United States. Similarly, the fear that failure to volunteer would be seen as cowardice impelled many young men into the Confederate army.

As so often in Faulkner, however, things are not as simple as they seem. There are no actual duels in *The Unvanquished*. Rather, the Sartoris men simply set out to kill for revenge, and the violence they inflict is horrific, far beyond anything honorable. Many southerners during the Civil War might have felt that Bayard had a right to kill his grandmother's murderer for revenge, but very few would have supported Bayard in crucifying his enemy and mutilating his body. This exaggerated violence must be seen as Faulkner telling his audience that the violence has gone too far and has to stop. It is a denial of violence as part of honor. Indeed, Bayard is able to resolve the insult to his honor occasioned by his father's murder without

Bayard Sartoris is the subject of this bildungsroman *novel.* *(JustASC | Shutterstock.com)*

bloodshed at the end of the novel, making a more positive rejection of violence.

In part, Faulkner most likely rejected killing as a means of restoring honor for the same reason the whole Western world did in his lifetime: because the technological slaughter of young men on the battlefields of World War I made murder too appallingly commonplace, too easy, to play a meaningful part in establishing masculine identity. One wonders, however, if Faulkner is not alluding to the purportedly honor-related violence that still went on in the South after the Civil War, after World War I, and up until the 1960s: the lynching of blacks by white vigilantes. It would be unlike Faulkner to say, or even admit, such a thing, but it would be quite like him to feel deep shame over that barbaric practice and try to call attention to it indirectly.

In any case, violence of honor and violence against slaves (or an oppressed lower class) are closely related, as Craig Thompson Friend and

Lorri Glover point out in their introduction to the anthology *Southern Manhood*:

> Domination of blacks brought manhood for whites. White male mastery and the code of honor provided a variety of practices designed to subordinate and brutalize black men, including political exclusion, cultural abuse, legal violence, and economic exploitation.

However much slave owners pretended otherwise, even to themselves, slavery was based on the threat of murder, and they had to be ready to kill or brutalize their slaves at a moment's notice. To be successful oppressors, slave owners had to be inured to violence. The men who had to use violence as a means of social control had necessarily to be violent men, so violence naturally figured in their interactions even with each other.

STYLE

Dialect

During the Middle Ages, the English language developed into many local dialects in Britain, none more legitimate or authentic than the others. These dialects were transported to the British colonies in North America and became the basis of some American regional dialects. Only in the nineteenth century did centralized education and other forces elevate the dialect of Oxfordshire (so-called BBC English) and the neutral speech of the American Midwest as national standards.

The language spoken by the slave characters in *The Unvanquished* is not, in any sense, an improper misunderstanding of English but is merely a local variety, derived from the dialect of English West Country, where many colonists to the South originated. It is less a creole than a cross between English and African languages (which does exist in the South, such as in the Gullah language spoken on the barrier islands off of Georgia and the Carolinas, which is vastly different than the speech of other southern black communities). The slaves in the novel speak the same language common to much of the American South and to much of the population, irrespective of race or class.

The story is narrated by an adult Bayard, whose speech has been shaped to the standardized dialect through years of higher education, a process that his father, John, had also gone through. Whether consciously or unconsciously,

Bayard has made the decision to emphasize the dialectical character of the slave's speech and report his own youthful speech, as well as the speech of the many uneducated white characters, as standardized. In fact, these characters (which would include poor whites as well as most aristocratic women) would have spoken in a dialect hardly distinguishable from that of the slaves; indeed, the slaves' English was based on the language spoken in their masters' households.

Southern Gothic

The gothic tradition in literature goes back to eighteenth-century Europe, rising with the novel. Hallmarks of this tradition included, among other things, explorations of taboo themes and motifs: the supernatural, mystery, darkness, haunted mansions with hidden passages, family secrets, madness, incest, human sexuality—in other words, the gothic explored the darker side of human nature, the parts kept hidden from others.

With the establishment of America, many of the older European gothic traditions were continued with a few new components; this came to be called American gothic. The three most famous American gothic writers are Nathaniel Hawthorne, Edgar Allan Poe, and Herman Melville. One of the distinctions Hawthorne established was in a reaction to the romantic idealization of nature; he established a tension between civilization and nature, with nature representative of the unknown and of mystery. When a character in a Hawthorne novel leaves the city or town and goes into the woods or the garden, the reader pretty quickly perceives that the character is going to encounter something he does not understand rather than find solace and understanding in nature.

After defeat in the Civil War, the South suffered an identity crisis from which it has never fully recovered, giving rise to a distinctly southern gothic that includes and expands the themes of the gothic in general and American gothic themes as well, but with a uniquely southern twist. Much Reconstruction and post-Reconstruction literature concerns itself with southern identity, and one often sees the southern character as fragmented, mirroring the southern sense of identity crisis. A longing for the past is also a hallmark of southern gothic literature, a desired return to the glory days of the South when every person knew and understood his or her place in the social order, which was turned upside-down by the Civil War. The typical southern gothic character is a freak (to use the term of another southern gothic writer, Flannery O'Connor) who is outside of society, because the southern mentality feels that the social order has broken down and abandoned the individual. We see this longing even today. It is as if elements of the gothic tradition manifest themselves in the southern character, but not in opposition to something else; that *is* the southern character.

The Unvanquished has many southern gothic features. It is an adventure story filled with buried treasures, affairs of honor, and Amazon-like female characters. On the surface, the world it creates is heroic, but on closer inspection what is underneath that surface seems more corrupt and poisonous. Drusilla, in particular, is a freak, standing between the two genders and unable to be brought back into southern society without being destroyed and recreated. Even then she hints at (distant or steprelation) incest through her flirtations with Bayard. A woman disguising herself as a man, particularly to fight in war, is also a folkloristic motif commonplace in gothic literature. Faulkner's own grandfather, the model for John Sartoris, wrote a novel, *The Spanish Heroine*, about a woman who joined the American army in disguise during the Mexican War in order to accompany her fiancé.

HISTORICAL CONTEXT

The Civil War and Reconstruction

The Unvanquished takes place during the American Civil War and the period of Reconstruction that followed. Faulkner is remarkably invested in the southern experience and memory of that period. The novel begins with a scene of Bayard and Ringo playing—drawing a map of a battle near Vicksburg, Mississippi, in the dirt of the yard and using wood chips to represent soldiers. Seemingly emboldened by the famous Union victory, the adult slave Loosh comes and spoils their game, knocking the pieces away. Readers might well be forgiven for thinking that the story begins shortly after the surrender of the Confederate garrison of Vicksburg to the Union general Ulysses S. Grant on July 4, 1863, but it soon becomes apparent that the actual date is over a

COMPARE
&
CONTRAST

- **1870s:** Southern culture is dominated by structures of white supremacy, embodied first in slavery and then in the repressive violence carried out against black freedmen by the Ku Klux Klan after Reconstruction ended.

  1930s: The Jim Crow system in the South, supported by the U.S. Supreme Court in the 1896 case *Plessy v. Ferguson*, continues to institutionalize white supremacy, supported by frequent lynchings and other acts of violence.

  Today: Although racism remains a problem in the South and the rest of America, both segregation and discrimination based on race are illegal. Barack Obama, the first African American president, is elected in 2008.

- **1870s:** Personal honor, enforced by violence including the use of duels, is a primary concern of the aristocratic class in the South.

  1930s: Violence and honor become disconnected thanks to the overwhelming violence

suffered by Western civilization during World War I.

  Today: A resort to violence to defend one's honor is no longer socially sanctioned and seems entirely isolated from the main current of civilization. A code of honor does exist in communities of gangs and can result in the carrying out of "righteous endeavors" such as drive-by shootings to avenge violations and disrespect, according to Robert L. Nabors in a pamphlet about gangs and extremist groups commissioned by the U.S. Army.

- **1870s:** Women have few legal and civil rights.

  1930s: Women gain the right to vote with the ratification of the Nineteenth Amendment in 1920 but for the most part, especially in economic terms, are still second-class citizens.

  Today: Women enjoy legal equality with men, though social inertia still has some deleterious effects on women, including lesser pay in many cases.

---

year earlier, in the late spring of 1862, at the time of the first Union invasion of northern Mississippi. What Faulkner is relating is the rumor that circulated throughout Mississippi at that time that having been attacked by Union forces, Vicksburg had immediately surrendered, like New Orleans and Natchez. The circulation of a false rumor is a minor detail to historians but a vivid memory to the people who lived through it as a seeming reality, the very kind of thing that Faulkner typically seizes upon.

For Faulkner, and for the southern culture represented by Faulkner, the Civil War was less a historical event than a tragic wound to the heart that would never heal. He very much presents a southern version of the war. For him, the war was something thrust upon the South by the United States. He could hardly have been unaware that the southern states

illegally voting for secession placed some responsibility for the war on the South, and he may even have considered that the South was rightfully punished by its defeat, but for Faulkner none of those things counted compared with the paramount importance of the South's sense of loss. Faulkner does, however, go beyond a mere southern perspective in his treatment of the war.

One of the events in the novel that illustrates Faulkner's views is the bridge demolition at the Tennessee River in "Raid." For Faulkner, this is clearly a symbol. He felt that the way forward for southern blacks, during the war as well as in his own day, was not to cross the storied River Jordan to a land of milk and honey and cease to be southern; indeed, he thought that they never could have done so. This reflects his belief that the civil rights movement was illegitimate because it did not originate with southern white culture. Written in the 1930s, *The Unvanquished* portrays this betrayal of the black refugees by the Union army as a warning that any alliance for civil rights between southern blacks and nonsouthern whites would lead to disaster. Pointedly, Faulkner based this incident on a number of historical instances of black refugees being killed by an army blowing up a bridge being crossed, although in reality those bridges were blown by Confederate, not Union, troops. In this case, Faulkner was quite willing to rewrite history to suit his narrative purposes.

With the shift to the postwar Reconstruction period in "Skirmish at Sartoris," Faulkner starkly presents his own internal struggle, his own heart at war with itself over southern heritage. In the case of Drusilla, the traditions of southern culture to which she is made to conform are presented as hypocritical, destructive, and limited. They destroy all her hopes for freedom and even happiness, making her conform to the image of southern womanhood out of sheer pettiness on the part of her mother and the so-called respectable women of Jefferson. By presenting this as a tragic loss, Faulkner squarely places himself on the side of freedom and personal independence. He illustrates his point by what amounts to an advocacy of women's rights strictly opposed by southern tradition.

However, Drusilla's personal story is intertwined with Faulkner's celebration of white supremacy in the recounting of the day of her wedding and the election for a black sheriff. Colonel Sartoris realizes that although the Confederacy lost the Civil War in any purely military sense, the war had been lost for years before the fighting ended. During that time, he had been struggling not for military victory over the Union but rather to keep control of the future of the South. Although the war forever destroyed the Old South, Sartoris had been fighting for the right of the South to determine its own future. Even now in peace and defeat, the struggle would go on. Sartoris uses the same violence he had carried out during the war to set the future course for the South. He murders the northern invaders (successfully, though he and the Confederate army had failed to overcome the North in war) and thereby prevents the black population from betraying their southern identity. Or so Faulkner seems to believe.

Granny and Bayard's relationship is a main plotline in the novel. (*Bonita R. Cheshier | Shutterstock.com*)

CRITICAL OVERVIEW

Because of his admitted prominence as one of the most accomplished writers of the twentieth century, Faulkner has received a great mass of scholarly attention. However, *The Unvanquished*, to the degree that it is less sophisticated and experimental than Faulkner's more celebrated works, has received less critical attention, though still more than most contemporary novels. Faulkner was already a leading author when the novel was published in 1938, so *The Unvanquished* was widely reviewed in the popular and literary presses.

M. Thomas Inge republished a selection of the most important contemporary reviews together with a full bibliography of the initial critical response in *William Faulkner: The Contemporary Reviews*. These early reviews participated in the surface gloss of the book, reading it as a gothic romance filled with chivalry and glorification of the Confederacy. Most found it admirable, but a few found it repulsive. From the review by Earle Birney in the *Canadian Forum* of June 1938, published in Inge's book, one could imagine that *The Unvanquished* was set in the world of antebellum romance satirized in *Huckleberry Finn*: "There is a blueblooded virgin who remains such despite a year's fighting in pants with Southern guerrilla corps. There's a treasure box buried, stolen, recovered, and reburied."

The fundamental modern treatment of *The Unvanquished* is James C. Hinkle and Robert McCoy's 1995 line-by-line consideration of the novel in *Reading Faulkner: "The Unvanquished," Glossary and Commentary*. Aside from providing a wealth of detailed information on the minutiae of *The Unvanquished* and an extensive bibliography of work up to that time, Hinkle and McCoy advance a reading of the novel as a product of traditional southern culture. Their approach, however, very nearly lacks any distance from the intellectual and social world created by the novel.

One of the most important recent studies of Faulkner is Charles Hannon's *Faulkner and the Discourses of Culture*. He argues that while Faulkner considered *The Unvanquished* to be a potboiler whose purpose was to generate an income to support his more important writing, he nevertheless showed literary growth in the work compared to his earlier efforts. While Faulkner's slave characters in earlier works had been entirely stereotypical in their loyalty to their masters, Faulkner became aware of the rethinking of the Reconstruction period according to a revisionist historiography in the 1930s, which overturned the southern myth that the black freedmen had cheerfully accepted the imposition of Jim Crow laws in the South. The result was a character like Loosh who actively wanted to accept the freedom imposed (in Faulkner's view) by the Union, even if the narrative makes clear that this desire grew out of his internal weakness. Nevertheless, explains Hannon, "'Skirmish at Sartoris' romanticizes the history of violent white voter fraud every bit as much as the proslavery historiography that the revisionists sought to correct." Hannon finds, however, that while Faulkner may accept the new historical interpretation that racial politics during Reconstruction destroyed the antebellum southern social system, his reaction is to cultivate an even more nostalgic sense of loss as the basis for his southern identity.

CRITICISM

Bradley A. Skeen

Skeen is a classicist. In the following essay, he considers The Unvanquished *from the viewpoint of Freudian psychoanalysis.*

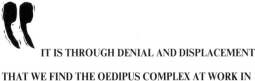

IT IS THROUGH DENIAL AND DISPLACEMENT THAT WE FIND THE OEDIPUS COMPLEX AT WORK IN *THE UNVANQUISHED*."

Every novel, even those that seem the most realistic, like those of Faulkner's great contemporary Ernest Hemingway, are created entirely in the author's imagination and therefore are fantastic in the literal sense of that word. It is no surprise then that one can attempt to interpret even an apparently realistic work like *The Unvanquished* from a psychological viewpoint, meaning not (or not merely) the exposition of the characters' psychology, but an attempt to find the psychological truth of the text itself and its relationship to larger psychological structures of the kind that often underlie myths. A useful tool for this kind of investigation is psychoanalysis, a kind of psychotherapy invented by the Viennese psychologist Sigmund Freud in the years around 1900. Freud himself realized that many of its techniques and ideas, originally developed to understand dreams, might be applied to any product of human thought, including literature. Although psychoanalysis is in many quarters out of favor today, it was the dominant psychological school of the 1920s and 1930s.

There is some confusion about Faulkner's relationship to psychoanalysis. Freud was a very hot topic in the 1920s and 1930s, a figure essential to modernism. Faulkner could hardly have avoided discussion of Freud's work, and it was natural that reporters and students should ask Faulkner about psychoanalysis. The problem is that Faulkner often answered in the pose of an innocent country boy and denied all knowledge of modernism, as in his most famous answer, (as quoted in Michael Zeitlin's entry "Freud" in *A William Faulkner Encyclopedia*): "What little of psychology I know the characters I have invented and playing poker have taught me. Freud I'm not familiar with."

This dissembling is characteristic: Faulkner is nothing if not a thoroughly modern writer seeming to be a throwback to the premodern. He varied this denial with irony, as Zeitlin

WHAT DO I READ NEXT?

- Tanya T. Fayen's 1995 monograph *In Search of the Latin American Faulkner* surveys Faulkner's influence on Latin American literature.

- Faulkner's *Flags in the Dust*, published in 1973 as his intended version of his 1929 novel *Sartoris*, tells the story of Bayard Sartoris and his grandsons during the 1920s.

- Mark Twain's *Adventures of Huckleberry Finn*, originally published in 1884, deals with many of the same issues of race in American culture as *The Unvanquished* and satirizes the same gothic pretensions of southern culture that Faulkner undermines.

- *The Days When the Animals Talked: Black American Folktales and How They Came to Be* (1977) mixes a collection of animal tales that circulated in the slave community in the antebellum South together with recollections of the conditions of slave life collected from a freed slave in 1910. Suitable for young adults, this collection offers a direct account of the inner lives and culture of the black slaves and freedmen that makes an interesting supplement to the image of that society presented entirely from the outside in *The Unvanquished*. They were collected by Troy Howell and a William J. Faulkner, not the author of *The Unvanquished*.

- The University of Mississippi hosts an annual scholarly conference called "Faulkner and Yoknapatawpha." The 1986 conference papers were published in 1987 as *Faulkner and Race*, edited by Doreen Fowler and Ann J. Abadie. The papers address a variety of issues regarding race in Faulkner's work.

- Shelby Foote, in his three-volume work *The Civil War: A Narrative*, published between 1958 and 1974, offers a detailed history of the Civil War sympathetic to the South.

- After defeat in the Civil War, about ten thousand southern aristocrats immigrated to Brazil, where slavery was still legal, in order to carry on the economic practice of plantation slavery that they were familiar with. Their descendants today form a subculture within Brazil, maintaining many American traditions. *The Lost Colony of the Confederacy* (revised in 2000), by Eugene Harter (a descendant of these Confederate emigrants, he returned to the United States to become a foreign-service officer), is a brief and highly readable history of this community.

---

quotes: "Everybody talked about Freud when I lived in New Orleans, but I have never read him. Neither did Shakespeare. I doubt Melville did either, and I'm sure Moby Dick didn't." Faulkner is slyly suggesting that, because psychoanalysis was understood to be a universally true science, it could successfully be used to analyze the literature of any period dealing with the same human truths. This indeed is a very sophisticated understanding of Freud's line of thought, and on other occasions, Faulkner left no doubt that he had mastered it. As quoted by Elizabeth Margaret Kerr in *William Faulkner's Yoknapatawpha*, Faulkner claimed,

> the writer don't have to know Freud to have written things which anyone who does know

Freud can divine and reduce into symbols. And so when the critic finds those symbols, they are of course there. But they were there as inevitably as the critic should stumble on his own knowledge of Freud to discern symbol.

Similarly, many elements of *The Unvanquished* can be expounded or explained by recourse to Freud and the application of psychoanalysis to the text conceived of as a symbol. Perhaps the most obvious example is the significance of dreams. For Freud, dreams were the royal road to the unconscious, because they directly reported things of which the waking individual was not aware, even if they did so in a symbolic form to keep disturbing truths from conscious awareness (even as American censors kept Faulkner from mentioning disturbing truths in *The Unvanquished*, such as the common existence of mixed-race half-siblings in the south, although as Faulkner's fame grew he was eventually able to openly discuss even such sensitive issues in later writings). Freud began his *Interpretation of Dreams* with a lecture on ancient dream interpretation, suggesting that the primitive impulse to see something of significance in dreams was not entirely misplaced. Dreams play a very prominent part in *The Unvanquished*, and an apparently superstitious faith in dreams is put in the mouth of Ringo: "If somebody tole you, hit could be a lie. But if you dremp hit, hit cant be a lie case aint nobody there to tole hit to you."

Freud began his work by finding the truth of human psychology expressed in ancient myth. The most famous of these myths is the myth of Oedipus, the prince of Corinth, who hears a prophecy that he will kill his father and marry his mother. Wishing to do no such things, he sets out on a journey to get as far away from his parents as possible. On the way, he meets an arrogant man at a crossroads where three roads meet and is provoked to fight and kill him. Going on, he encounters the sphinx, a monster with the body of a lion and the head of a woman. She tells him she will kill him if he cannot solve her riddle, but he succeeds and so she kills herself.

The sphinx had been killing everyone who tried to enter the city of Thebes, so when the Thebans hear Oedipus has saved them from the monster, they hail him as a hero and make him their king. The former king Laius had disappeared, and Oedipus marries Queen Jocasta. Years later, a plague visits Thebes. The gods tell Oedipus it is because the murderer of Laius is harbored in the city. So Oedipus investigates to find the culprit. He discovers that Laius and Jocasta had had a son many years ago, about whom it was prophesied he would kill his father and marry his mother, so the child was fatally exposed. Or so Laius had ordered, but Oedipus finds the shepherd who was to have carried out the deed. It turns out that he could not let a baby die and so had given the prince to the king and queen of Corinth. Being childless, they had adopted him. The child of Laius is none other than Oedipus himself. The man he killed at the crossroads was Laius, his father, and Jocasta, Oedipus's wife, is his own mother. To punish himself, Oedipus gouges out his own eyes. Jocasta hangs herself.

Freud found in this story an expression of the basic human condition (or at least the male human condition; limited by his time and place, Freud paid scant attention to female psychology). A newborn infant is utterly dependent on its mother. All of its psychic energy (which Freud called libido) is invested in that relationship. Later in life, at puberty and in adulthood, this same emotional complex will be refashioned as the basis of romantic love, but while still in infancy, the baby will slowly become aware of calls on the mother's time by others, particularly the father. He naturally grows jealous of such rivals and wishes that their attentions to the mother would cease. The adult realizes that such a cessation would mean death. In time, the child is able to separate his own identity from the mother, and then the other in the form of the father becomes a model, or "ideal" in Freud's terms, for individuation. Freud reasoned that these psychic events are too painful to remember, so they become veiled in myths like the story of Oedipus and also in literature like *Hamlet*, which for Freud was only a slightly more secreted version of the Oedipus myth, as Faulkner was no doubt well aware when making his comment about Shakespeare not having read Freud.

What does Faulkner have to say about the Oedipus complex in *The Unvanquished*? The answer is perhaps even more deeply buried than it is in *Hamlet*. Bayard does not marry his mother nor murder his father, but the matter is not quite so simple. Such difficult inclinations cause resistance in most people, a desire to deny something that they both want to do and at the same time think of as horrible. To protect oneself from realizing the truth, the opposite of the truth might be argued with too much fervor, or else the desire might be displaced, a pretense made that some other similar, less terrible impulse is what one truly feels. This simultaneous desire and denial of desire that Freud revealed is perhaps what Faulkner referred to when he described the human heart in conflict with itself.

It is through denial and displacement that we find the Oedipus complex at work in *The Unvanquished*. It is a matter of probing not merely the mind of Bayard the character, but the whole narrative, which Faulkner was free to create as he wished. It is not very difficult to find Oedipus in disguise in the novel. Bayard's mother is dead (probably in childbirth, the inverse of the Oedipus story, in which the infant was to be fatally exposed at birth), one result of which is to remove even the

In the last chapter, the motif of scent through the verbena that Drusilla wears is symbolic. *(Juan David Ferrando Subero | Shutterstock.com)*

slightest possibility of Bayard doing anything like marrying her. However, there is a substitute mother: his father's second wife, Drusilla, who takes a predatory sexual interest in Bayard, though her stepson is able to avoid her advances. Bayard is able to tell himself that his mother is an impossible object of desire, and at the same he is strong enough to resist her desire. In the same way, Bayard does not kill his father, but neither does he kill the man who killed his father, which, by an emotional calculus, might amount to the same thing. Rather than the murder letting Bayard take possession of Drusilla, she conveniently departs, never to be seen again.

It is possible that Faulkner had in mind a further Freudian elaboration. Though he called it

history, Freud explained the origin of the Oedipus complex in what can only be taken as another myth of his own creation. Freud envisioned a father in the distant past, an early human or a hominid, living with a harem of wives and ruling over a tribe of his own sons. Eventually the sons grow tired of his rule and band together to kill him and then to take his wives—their own mothers—for themselves. But how to move from that act to a single son killing a single father? Freud imagined that the first lie, the first fiction, explained it, in the person of one of the sons:

> He who did this was the first epic poet; and the advance was achieved in his imagination. This poet disguised the truth with lies in accordance with his longing. He invented the heroic myth.

The hero was a man who by himself had slain the father—the father who still appeared in the myth as a totemistic monster.... For he goes and relates to the group his hero's deeds which he has invented.... Thus he lowers himself to the level of reality, and raises his hearers to the level of imagination. But his hearers understand the poet, and, in virtue of their having the same relation of longing towards the primal father, they can identify themselves with the hero.

If Faulkner represses this story, too, then the very strange circumstance of Bayard's final meeting with Redmond (his father's killer) is explained. When Bayard describes the encounter, he makes a point of insisting that he and Redmond did not speak, yet he reports the details of the conversation that was understood to pass between them completely with quoted dialogue, as if they had spoken. It as if Faulkner brings together the denial and the invention of literature in the moment of not killing and killing the father. For Bayard, his father had indeed been a totemistic monster, something quite literally larger than life: not John Sartoris or Colonel Sartoris, but *the* Sartoris. By the time of Faulkner's later novel *Flags in the Dust*, Bayard (old Bayard then) will have become the Sartoris in his turn.

Source: Bradley A. Skeen, Critical Essay on *The Unvanquished*, in *Novels for Students*, Gale, Cengage Learning, 2012.

Deborah Clarke

In the following excerpt, Clarke examines the way the character Granny deals with war in The Unvanquished.

> I'd rather engage Forrest's whole brigade every morning for six months than spend that same length of time trying to protect United States property from defenseless Southern women and niggers and children.... Defenseless! God help the North if Davis and Lee had ever thought of the idea of forming a brigade of grandmothers and nigger orphans, and invading us with it.

Are women defenseless damsels or consummate soldiers? The role of women in Faulkner's work is always problematic, but women's relation to war intensifies that situation in a particularly intricate and complex manner. As Susan Schweik has observed, "Wars have a way of revealing with special clarity how men as well as women are both intensely and uneasily gendered." War, which sets up a system characterized by bifurcation and polarization, seems to reorder the world through

> IN FACT, GRANNY'S DEDICATION TO CHIVALRY AND THE BINARIES OF GENDER IT INSCRIBES, LITERALLY KILLS HER."

opposition. But war, in fact, is a cross-dresser's dream. Civilians cross-dress as soldiers; women cross-dress as men; boys cross-dress as men; scared men cross-dress as heroes; homosexuals, these days, must cross-dress as heterosexuals to maintain the Pentagon's misguided assumption that there are no gays in the military; enemies cross-dress as friends, infiltrating each other's turf, and, in possibly the most tragic feature of war, especially civil war, friends and even family cross-dress as enemies. Thus, despite imposing a binary framework war also—somewhat paradoxically—opens up possibilities of transcending it, of finding an alternative position, of mixing the categories.

Examining the binaries of race and gender, Faulkner reveals their vulnerability to the pressures of war. Women may be ostensibly silenced by the rhetoric of war which, like combat, is generally controlled by men, but male absence from the homefront can transform defenseless creatures into active speaking subjects. Yet finding a discourse is not easy, particularly for the women of *The Unvanquished* caught between supporting the system which subordinates them and breaking free of that subordination. Consequently, Granny Millard and Drusilla Hawk wage war against both the Yankees and their own lack of power within the chivalric order, a battle in which they are joined by Ringo, whose defense of a slave-owning culture defies the framework of slavery itself. Ostensibly one of Faulkner's most military novels, *The Unvanquished* primarily examines not Colonel Sartoris, who rides in and out on his stallion Jupiter, playing a relatively minor role in the various military and nonmilitary struggles, but the ways in which "defenseless Southern women and niggers and children" deal with the war and the chivalric tradition which it attempts to uphold.

... In *The Unvanquished* Faulkner interrogates the conventional expectations of women's place in war. Women in the novel take two different approaches to war, yet each one adopts a kind of male persona. Granny Millard, in her vanquishing of the Yankee army, relies on—and manipulates—written texts and Biblical authority, while Drusilla reacts more with her body; she cuts her hair short, dresses as a man, and joins Colonel Sartoris's troop. In these varying responses, Faulkner tests the limits of gender and gendered discourse, examining the efficacy of men's texts and women's bodies in the war against a patriarchal system. While both women fight to uphold Southern chivalry, their modes of discourse seriously undermine the very system they set out to defend.

On the surface, Drusilla's cross-dressing marks her as male identified, unsexed, while Granny behaves more like a lady. Yet Granny's reliance on textuality reveals her dependence on what has often been identified as a particularly masculine form of discourse. Western tradition aligns women more closely with their bodies than with language. Women are physical, men figurative, creators. As so many feminist theorists have postulated, women's language tends to be tactile and literal, focused on the body. Margaret Homans observes, "For the same reason that women are identified with nature and matter in any traditional thematics of gender . . . women are also identified with the literal, the absent referent in our predominant myth of language." Faulkner, however, is a prime example of a man who questions such paradigms. His male characters flounder amid the wreck of symbolic discourse, desperately trying to make words replace reality. Thus Quentin Compson kills himself because among other reasons virginity is not just a word; thus Harry Wilbourne finds his language inadequate next to Charlotte's drawings; and thus Reverend Whitfield can only "frame," not speak, the words of his confession, while Addie Bundren knows that words are no good. Faulkner both reproduces and challenges this gendered linguistic split, and one often finds that women's silence and women's bodies hold greater sway than men's language.

The Unvanquished mixes these categories in curious and interesting ways. Granny, an avid supporter of the patriarchal system, relies on written texts to vanquish the Yankee army. While the misunderstandings behind her note from Colonel Dick provide an almost slapstick tone to her mule-trading—she demands the return of a chest of silver, her mules named Old Hundred and Tinney, and two slaves, which gets transcribed by the Yankee orderly as ten chests of silver, 110 mules and slaves (that equation is surely no accident)—Granny's participation in the procedure marks her reverence for justice and textual authority. Her note from Colonel Dick is legal; as she herself quickly points out, she "tried to tell them better. . . . It's the hand of God." Associating the hand of God with the written hand of man firmly ensconces textual authenticity as akin to divine authority, and both are further affiliated with masculine power. But the Yankee orderly's comic mistake and the consequent blind obedience by the rest of the army to this text illustrate both the power of textual legality and its limitations. With nothing more than a "handful of durn printed letterheads," Granny routs the Yankees so thoroughly that Ab Snopes wonders "if somebody hadn't better tell Abe Lincoln to look out for General Grant against Miz Rosa Millard." The unquestioned authority of the masculine text can be effectively subverted by a woman who recognizes that fixed meaning can be manipulated, particularly in a system which does not question a lady's—or a Colonel's—word. Granny's appropriation of textual authority, for the sake of the Southern patriarchal system, places her in precisely the position which that system has denied her: in control of military men and military language.

. . . Rosa Millard's world, while closer to the border of the white male hegemony than Ringo's, nonetheless also has some nebulous boundaries in times of war. Like Ringo, Granny struggles to maintain a world order based upon the very dualities which she destroys through her behavior. Trying desperately to retain her sense of good and evil, she discovers that war not only provides the opportunity to transgress the boundaries of being a lady, but it also enables her to cheat in her Christian beliefs. In fact, her usurpation of masculine power is tied to her challenge to divine authority. It is not surprising that Granny should find herself caught in a Christian vacuum, for war, of course, violates the central tenets of Christianity. All may be fair in war, but little is Christian in war. Her struggles are revealed in the ways that she tries to manipulate her Christian beliefs by making what even she admits is a sin acceptable due to extenuating circumstances: the horrors of war. Her attempt to justify the means by the end offers a further implicit criticism of patriarchal authority, in its open challenge to God the Father.

> I did not sin for revenge; I defy You or anyone
> to say I did. I sinned first for justice. And after

that first time, I sinned for more than justice: I sinned for the sake of food and clothes for Your own creatures who could not help themselves—for children who had given their fathers, for wives who had given their husbands, for old people who had given their sons, to a holy cause, even though You have seen fit to make it a lost cause.

Granny's complaint that God has "seen fit" to make a holy cause a lost cause suggests that God is not quite with it. The greater sin rests not with her but with God's inefficiency. Yet even in her concern for her lost cause, Granny focuses not on the men who died but on those who remain behind. She seems to be outraged not so much at defeat as at God's willingness to sacrifice the lives of "creatures who could not help themselves"—women, children, and the aged. God has been a bad Father in that He has ignored His obligations to the helpless. Thus war reveals the tenuous hold which God has upon the world, the limitations of patriarchy itself. Granny's complaint echoes the lamentations raised by many Confederate women, as Drew Faust has demonstrated. Yet there are some significant differences. Faust cites Almira Acors's letter to Jefferson Davis: "I do not see how God can give the South a victory when the cries of so many suffering mothers and little children are constantly ascending up to him. . . . [I]f I and my little children . . . die while there [*sic*] Father is in service I invoke God Almighty that our blood rest upon the South."

For Acors, the responsibility lies not with God but with the South, a charge which Granny Millard never quite recognizes. In her anger at this failure of patriarchal authority, Granny fails to see the implicit indictment of the Southern culture in which she is firmly entrenched. Interestingly, she omits any mention of the other "creatures who could not help themselves": slaves. When saddled with 110 former slaves, she sends them back to their masters with the injunction, "if I ever hear of any of you straggling off like this again, I'll see to it." Regardless of whether she could or would make good her threat, she still refuses to acknowledge that slavery itself is at least as great a betrayal of Christianity as war. She retains the position of mistress, arbiter of justice, and ultimate authority. Thus her critique of God the Father suggests that the system would be improved by bringing in God the Mother, someone more attuned to the problems of women and children, but who

still knows how to keep the slaves in line. And, not surprisingly, Granny herself seems the perfect candidate for the job. Yet shifting from a patriarchal to a matriarchal God does little to undermine the system. Granny may challenge the efficiency of Christian patriarchy, but she seeks to improve it, not overthrow it. Again, the structure of the binary—patriarchy versus matriarchy—leaves no space for a third term.

This Christian order is held in place largely by language, a power Granny clearly recognizes, as Bayard and Ringo get their mouths washed out with soap for swearing, for desecrating the sanctity of the word. However her assumption that she can knowingly sin and then attain forgiveness on the grounds that God has fallen short on the job marks a far greater challenge to the sanctity of the word and the text than the boys' curses. Her adherence to divine authority is tenuous at best; as Ringo says, "She cide what she want and then she kneel down about ten seconds and tell God what she aim to do, and then she git up and do hit." Then, if what she does is a sin, she dares God to damn her for it. In qualifying the Biblical injunctions against lying and stealing, she challenges both Biblical authority and the fixity of linguistic meaning, particularly in the face of war. Yet even this potentially subversive response to Biblical textuality is based upon her belief in another patriarchal system: Southern chivalry, which should defend women and children. In being unable to imagine an alternative to chivalry, even though she herself lives one, she reveals the degree to which she remains firmly grounded in the patriarchal order. We need that third term to destroy the binary which, as Hélène Cixous would point out, is inevitably hierarchic. One of the elements in such standard oppositions as male/female or black/white is always more powerful. Thus, if we cannot break down the dichotomy we have not a binary but a unitary ordering.

In fact, Granny's dedication to chivalry and the binaries of gender it inscribes, literally kills her. While even the Yankee Colonel Dick is willing to protect Southern women and children, the outlaw Grumby is not. Granny's involvement in patriarchy has blinded her to its limitations. Living in a world highlighted by war's oppositions of north and south, black and white, she takes for granted another hierarchical system: class. Diane Roberts notes that Granny's "guerilla cunning fails to take into account the way the war itself has destroyed old verities of class." The polarization of war causes her to idealize one side. If "Even the Yankees do not harm old women," then she is surely in no danger from Southern men. She "still believed that what side of a war a man fought on made him what he is," and so fails to realize that the same war which allows her not to be a lady also allows men not to be gentlemen. Once the laws of chivalry break down, women and children need to fend for themselves, yet the system which has placed them on pedestals has also denied them the means to do so. Granny, who wants to correct and perpetuate rather than overthrow the system, is ultimately victimized by it. As Mr. Compson says in *Absalom*, "we in the South made our women into ladies. Then the War came and made the ladies into ghosts." War destroys the lady, and in so doing, betrays the woman behind the lady....

Source: Deborah Clarke, "Gender, War, and Cross-Dressing in *The Unvanquished*," in *Faulkner and Gender: Faulkner and Yoknapatawpha, 1994*, edited by Donald M. Kartiganer and Ann J. Abadie, University Press of Mississippi, 1996, pp. 228–51.

SOURCES

Birney, Earl, Review of *The Unvanquished*, in *William Faulkner: The Contemporary Reviews*, edited by M. Thomas Inge, Cambridge University Press, 1995, pp. 167–84; originally published in *Canadian Forum*, June 1938.

Falkner, W. C., *The Spanish Heroine: A Tale of War and Love*, I. Hart, 1851.

Faulkner, William, "Letter to a Northern Editor," in *Essays, Speeches & Public Letters*, edited by James B. Meriwether, Random House, 1965, pp. 86–91; originally published in *Life*, March 5, 1956.

———, *The Unvanquished*, in *William Faulkner: Novels, 1936–1940*, Library of America, 1990.

———, "Upon Receiving the Nobel Prize for Literature," in *Essays, Speeches & Public Letters*, edited by James B. Meriwether, Random House, 1965, pp. 119–21.

Friend, Craig Thompson, and Lorri Glover, eds., *Southern Manhood: Perspectives on Masculinity in the Old South*, University of Georgia Press, 2004, pp. vii–xiv.

Freud, Sigmund, *Group Psychology and the Analysis of the Ego*, translated by James Strachey, Bantam, 1960, pp. 66–76.

———, *The Interpretation of Dreams*, translated by A. A. Brill, MacMillan, 1913, pp. 218–26.

Hannon, Charles, *Faulkner and the Discourses of Culture*, Louisiana State University Press, 2005, pp. 20–49.

Hinkle, James C., and Robert McCoy, *Reading Faulkner: "The Unvanquished," Glossary and Commentary*, University of Mississippi Press, 1995.

Hoffman, Daniel, *Faulkner's Country Matters: Folklore and Fable in Yoknapatawpha*, Louisiana State University Press, 1989, pp. 35–70.

Jones, Anne Goodwyn, "Male Fantasies? Faulkner's War Stories and the Construction of Gender," in *Faulkner and Psychology: Faulkner and Yoknapatawpha, 1991*, edited by Donald M. Kartiganer and Ann J. Abadie, University Press of Mississippi, 1994, pp. 21–55.

Kerr, Elizabeth Margaret, *William Faulkner's Gothic Domain*, Kennikat, 1979.

———, *William Faulkner's Yoknapatawpha: "A Kind of Keystone in the Universe,"* Fordham University Press, 1983.

Nabors, Robert L., "Gangs and Extremist Groups: A Handbook for Commanders, Parents, and Teachers," in *USAREUR Pamphlet 190-100*, March 10, 1997, http://www.fas.org/irp/doddir/army/190-100.htm (accessed June 15, 2011).

Singal, Daniel J., *William Faulkner: The Making of a Modernist*, University of North Carolina Press, 1999.

Weinstein, Philip, *Becoming Faulkner: The Art and Life of William Faulkner*, Oxford University Press, 2010.

Zeitlin, Michael, "Freud," in *A William Faulkner Encyclopedia*, edited by Robert W. Hamblin and Charles A. Peek, Greenwood, 1999, pp. 141–44.

FURTHER READING

Faulkner, William, *Collected Stories of William Faulkner*, Vintage, 1995.

Faulkner is almost as well known for his short stories as for his novels. They tend to be more comprehensible at first reading: straightforward narratives similar to *The Unvanquished* rather than stream of consciousness works.

Kinney, Arthur F., ed., *Critical Essays on William Faulkner: The Sartoris Family*, G. K. Hall, 1985.

Kinney presents a collection of reviews and scholarly articles on every aspect of the Sartorises in Faulkner's writing.

Rio-Jelliffe, R., *Obscurity's Myriad Components: The Theory and Practice of William Faulkner*, Bucknell University Press, 2001.

Rio-Jelliffe analyzes Faulkner's narrative techniques in several novels, including *The Unvanquished*.

Rollyson, Carl E., *Uses of the Past in the Novels of William Faulkner*, UMI Research Press, 1984.

Rollyson compares *The Unvanquished* and the other Yoknapatawpha novels with their origins in Mississippi history and legend.

SUGGESTED SEARCH TERMS

William Faulkner

The Unvanquished

southern gothic

Civil War

Reconstruction

southern honor code

Yoknapatawpha

William Faulkner AND The Unvanquished

William Faulkner AND southern gothic

William Faulkner AND modernism

William Faulkner AND Freud

Glossary of Literary Terms

A

Abstract: As an adjective applied to writing or literary works, abstract refers to words or phrases that name things not knowable through the five senses.

Aestheticism: A literary and artistic movement of the nineteenth century. Followers of the movement believed that art should not be mixed with social, political, or moral teaching. The statement "art for art's sake" is a good summary of aestheticism. The movement had its roots in France, but it gained widespread importance in England in the last half of the nineteenth century, where it helped change the Victorian practice of including moral lessons in literature.

Allegory: A narrative technique in which characters representing things or abstract ideas are used to convey a message or teach a lesson. Allegory is typically used to teach moral, ethical, or religious lessons but is sometimes used for satiric or political purposes.

Allusion: A reference to a familiar literary or historical person or event, used to make an idea more easily understood.

Analogy: A comparison of two things made to explain something unfamiliar through its similarities to something familiar, or to prove one point based on the acceptedness of another. Similes and metaphors are types of analogies.

Antagonist: The major character in a narrative or drama who works against the hero or protagonist.

Anthropomorphism: The presentation of animals or objects in human shape or with human characteristics. The term is derived from the Greek word for "human form."

Anti-hero: A central character in a work of literature who lacks traditional heroic qualities such as courage, physical prowess, and fortitude. Anti-heroes typically distrust conventional values and are unable to commit themselves to any ideals. They generally feel helpless in a world over which they have no control. Anti-heroes usually accept, and often celebrate, their positions as social outcasts.

Apprenticeship Novel: See *Bildungsroman*

Archetype: The word archetype is commonly used to describe an original pattern or model from which all other things of the same kind are made. This term was introduced to literary criticism from the psychology of Carl Jung. It expresses Jung's theory that behind every person's "unconscious," or repressed memories of the past, lies the "collective unconscious" of the human race: memories of the countless typical experiences of our ancestors. These memories are said to prompt illogical associations that trigger powerful emotions in the reader. Often, the emotional process is primitive, even primordial. Archetypes are the literary images that grow out of the "collective unconscious." They appear in literature as incidents and plots that repeat basic patterns of life. They may also appear as stereotyped characters.

Avant-garde: French term meaning "vanguard." It is used in literary criticism to describe new writing that rejects traditional approaches to literature in favor of innovations in style or content.

B

Beat Movement: A period featuring a group of American poets and novelists of the 1950s and 1960s—including Jack Kerouac, Allen Ginsberg, Gregory Corso, William S. Burroughs, and Lawrence Ferlinghetti—who rejected established social and literary values. Using such techniques as stream of consciousness writing and jazz-influenced free verse and focusing on unusual or abnormal states of mind—generated by religious ecstasy or the use of drugs—the Beat writers aimed to create works that were unconventional in both form and subject matter.

Bildungsroman: A German word meaning "novel of development." The *bildungsroman* is a study of the maturation of a youthful character, typically brought about through a series of social or sexual encounters that lead to self-awareness. *Bildungsroman* is used interchangeably with *erziehungsroman,* a novel of initiation and education. When a *bildungsroman* is concerned with the development of an artist (as in James Joyce's *A Portrait of the Artist as a Young Man*), it is often termed a *kunstlerroman.*

Black Aesthetic Movement: A period of artistic and literary development among African Americans in the 1960s and early 1970s. This was the first major African-American artistic movement since the Harlem Renaissance and was closely paralleled by the civil rights and black power movements. The black aesthetic writers attempted to produce works of art that would be meaningful to the black masses. Key figures in black aesthetics included one of its founders, poet and playwright Amiri Baraka, formerly known as LeRoi Jones; poet and essayist Haki R. Madhubuti, formerly Don L. Lee; poet and playwright Sonia Sanchez; and dramatist Ed Bullins.

Black Humor: Writing that places grotesque elements side by side with humorous ones in an attempt to shock the reader, forcing him or her to laugh at the horrifying reality of a disordered world.

Burlesque: Any literary work that uses exaggeration to make its subject appear ridiculous, either by treating a trivial subject with profound seriousness or by treating a dignified subject frivolously. The word "burlesque" may also be used as an adjective, as in "burlesque show," to mean "striptease act."

C

Character: Broadly speaking, a person in a literary work. The actions of characters are what constitute the plot of a story, novel, or poem. There are numerous types of characters, ranging from simple, stereotypical figures to intricate, multifaceted ones. In the techniques of anthropomorphism and personification, animals—and even places or things—can assume aspects of character. "Characterization" is the process by which an author creates vivid, believable characters in a work of art. This may be done in a variety of ways, including (1) direct description of the character by the narrator; (2) the direct presentation of the speech, thoughts, or actions of the character; and (3) the responses of other characters to the character. The term "character" also refers to a form originated by the ancient Greek writer Theophrastus that later became popular in the seventeenth and eighteenth centuries. It is a short essay or sketch of a person who prominently displays a specific attribute or quality, such as miserliness or ambition.

Climax: The turning point in a narrative, the moment when the conflict is at its most intense. Typically, the structure of stories, novels, and plays is one of rising action, in which tension builds to the climax, followed by falling action, in which tension lessens as the story moves to its conclusion.

Colloquialism: A word, phrase, or form of pronunciation that is acceptable in casual conversation but not in formal, written communication. It is considered more acceptable than slang.

Coming of Age Novel: See *Bildungsroman*

Concrete: Concrete is the opposite of abstract, and refers to a thing that actually exists or a description that allows the reader to experience an object or concept with the senses.

Connotation: The impression that a word gives beyond its defined meaning. Connotations may be universally understood or may be significant only to a certain group.

Convention: Any widely accepted literary device, style, or form.

D

Denotation: The definition of a word, apart from the impressions or feelings it creates (connotations) in the reader.

Denouement: A French word meaning "the unknotting." In literary criticism, it denotes the resolution of conflict in fiction or drama. The *denouement* follows the climax and provides an outcome to the primary plot situation as well as an explanation of secondary plot complications. The *denouement* often involves a character's recognition of his or her state of mind or moral condition.

Description: Descriptive writing is intended to allow a reader to picture the scene or setting in which the action of a story takes place. The form this description takes often evokes an intended emotional response—a dark, spooky graveyard will evoke fear, and a peaceful, sunny meadow will evoke calmness.

Dialogue: In its widest sense, dialogue is simply conversation between people in a literary work; in its most restricted sense, it refers specifically to the speech of characters in a drama. As a specific literary genre, a "dialogue" is a composition in which characters debate an issue or idea.

Diction: The selection and arrangement of words in a literary work. Either or both may vary depending on the desired effect. There are four general types of diction: "formal," used in scholarly or lofty writing; "informal," used in relaxed but educated conversation; "colloquial," used in everyday speech; and "slang," containing newly coined words and other terms not accepted in formal usage.

Didactic: A term used to describe works of literature that aim to teach some moral, religious, political, or practical lesson. Although didactic elements are often found in artistically pleasing works, the term "didactic" usually refers to literature in which the message is more important than the form. The term

may also be used to criticize a work that the critic finds "overly didactic," that is, heavy-handed in its delivery of a lesson.

Doppelganger: A literary technique by which a character is duplicated (usually in the form of an alter ego, though sometimes as a ghostly counterpart) or divided into two distinct, usually opposite personalities. The use of this character device is widespread in nineteenth- and twentieth-century literature, and indicates a growing awareness among authors that the "self" is really a composite of many "selves."

Double Entendre: A corruption of a French phrase meaning "double meaning." The term is used to indicate a word or phrase that is deliberately ambiguous, especially when one of the meanings is risqué or improper.

Dramatic Irony: Occurs when the audience of a play or the reader of a work of literature knows something that a character in the work itself does not know. The irony is in the contrast between the intended meaning of the statements or actions of a character and the additional information understood by the audience.

Dystopia: An imaginary place in a work of fiction where the characters lead dehumanized, fearful lives.

E

Edwardian: Describes cultural conventions identified with the period of the reign of Edward VII of England (1901-1910). Writers of the Edwardian Age typically displayed a strong reaction against the propriety and conservatism of the Victorian Age. Their work often exhibits distrust of authority in religion, politics, and art and expresses strong doubts about the soundness of conventional values.

Empathy: A sense of shared experience, including emotional and physical feelings, with someone or something other than oneself. Empathy is often used to describe the response of a reader to a literary character.

Enlightenment, The: An eighteenth-century philosophical movement. It began in France but had a wide impact throughout Europe and America. Thinkers of the Enlightenment valued reason and believed that both the individual and society could achieve a state of perfection. Corresponding to this essentially humanist vision was a resistance to religious authority.

Epigram: A saying that makes the speaker's point quickly and concisely. Often used to preface a novel.

Epilogue: A concluding statement or section of a literary work. In dramas, particularly those of the seventeenth and eighteenth centuries, the epilogue is a closing speech, often in verse, delivered by an actor at the end of a play and spoken directly to the audience.

Epiphany: A sudden revelation of truth inspired by a seemingly trivial incident.

Episode: An incident that forms part of a story and is significantly related to it. Episodes may be either self-contained narratives or events that depend on a larger context for their sense and importance.

Epistolary Novel: A novel in the form of letters. The form was particularly popular in the eighteenth century.

Epithet: A word or phrase, often disparaging or abusive, that expresses a character trait of someone or something.

Existentialism: A predominantly twentieth-century philosophy concerned with the nature and perception of human existence. There are two major strains of existentialist thought: atheistic and Christian. Followers of atheistic existentialism believe that the individual is alone in a godless universe and that the basic human condition is one of suffering and loneliness. Nevertheless, because there are no fixed values, individuals can create their own characters—indeed, they can shape themselves—through the exercise of free will. The atheistic strain culminates in and is popularly associated with the works of Jean-Paul Sartre. The Christian existentialists, on the other hand, believe that only in God may people find freedom from life's anguish. The two strains hold certain beliefs in common: that existence cannot be fully understood or described through empirical effort; that anguish is a universal element of life; that individuals must bear responsibility for their actions; and that there is no common standard of behavior or perception for religious and ethical matters.

Expatriates: See *Expatriatism*

Expatriatism: The practice of leaving one's country to live for an extended period in another country.

Exposition: Writing intended to explain the nature of an idea, thing, or theme. Expository writing is often combined with description, narration, or argument. In dramatic writing, the exposition is the introductory material which presents the characters, setting, and tone of the play.

Expressionism: An indistinct literary term, originally used to describe an early twentieth-century school of German painting. The term applies to almost any mode of unconventional, highly subjective writing that distorts reality in some way.

F

Fable: A prose or verse narrative intended to convey a moral. Animals or inanimate objects with human characteristics often serve as characters in fables.

Falling Action: See *Denouement*

Fantasy: A literary form related to mythology and folklore. Fantasy literature is typically set in non-existent realms and features supernatural beings.

Farce: A type of comedy characterized by broad humor, outlandish incidents, and often vulgar subject matter.

Femme fatale: A French phrase with the literal translation "fatal woman." A *femme fatale* is a sensuous, alluring woman who often leads men into danger or trouble.

Fiction: Any story that is the product of imagination rather than a documentation of fact. characters and events in such narratives may be based in real life but their ultimate form and configuration is a creation of the author.

Figurative Language: A technique in writing in which the author temporarily interrupts the order, construction, or meaning of the writing for a particular effect. This interruption takes the form of one or more figures of speech such as hyperbole, irony, or simile. Figurative language is the opposite of literal language, in which every word is truthful, accurate, and free of exaggeration or embellishment.

Figures of Speech: Writing that differs from customary conventions for construction, meaning, order, or significance for the purpose of a special meaning or effect. There are two major types of figures of speech: rhetorical figures, which do not make changes in the meaning of the words, and tropes, which do.

Fin de siecle: A French term meaning "end of the century." The term is used to denote the last decade of the nineteenth century, a transition period when writers and other artists abandoned old conventions and looked for new techniques and objectives.

First Person: See *Point of View*

Flashback: A device used in literature to present action that occurred before the beginning of the story. Flashbacks are often introduced as the dreams or recollections of one or more characters.

Foil: A character in a work of literature whose physical or psychological qualities contrast strongly with, and therefore highlight, the corresponding qualities of another character.

Folklore: Traditions and myths preserved in a culture or group of people. Typically, these are passed on by word of mouth in various forms—such as legends, songs, and proverbs—or preserved in customs and ceremonies. This term was first used by W. J. Thoms in 1846.

Folktale: A story originating in oral tradition. Folktales fall into a variety of categories, including legends, ghost stories, fairy tales, fables, and anecdotes based on historical figures and events.

Foreshadowing: A device used in literature to create expectation or to set up an explanation of later developments.

Form: The pattern or construction of a work which identifies its genre and distinguishes it from other genres.

G

Genre: A category of literary work. In critical theory, genre may refer to both the content of a given work—tragedy, comedy, pastoral—and to its form, such as poetry, novel, or drama.

Gilded Age: A period in American history during the 1870s characterized by political corruption and materialism. A number of important novels of social and political criticism were written during this time.

Gothicism: In literary criticism, works characterized by a taste for the medieval or morbidly attractive. A gothic novel prominently features elements of horror, the supernatural, gloom, and violence: clanking chains, terror, charnel houses, ghosts, medieval castles, and mysteriously slamming doors. The term "gothic novel" is also applied to novels that lack elements of the traditional Gothic setting but that create a similar atmosphere of terror or dread.

Grotesque: In literary criticism, the subject matter of a work or a style of expression characterized by exaggeration, deformity, freakishness, and disorder. The grotesque often includes an element of comic absurdity.

H

Harlem Renaissance: The Harlem Renaissance of the 1920s is generally considered the first significant movement of black writers and artists in the United States. During this period, new and established black writers published more fiction and poetry than ever before, the first influential black literary journals were established, and black authors and artists received their first widespread recognition and serious critical appraisal. Among the major writers associated with this period are Claude McKay, Jean Toomer, Countee Cullen, Langston Hughes, Arna Bontemps, Nella Larsen, and Zora Neale Hurston.

Hero/Heroine: The principal sympathetic character (male or female) in a literary work. Heroes and heroines typically exhibit admirable traits: idealism, courage, and integrity, for example.

Holocaust Literature: Literature influenced by or written about the Holocaust of World War II. Such literature includes true stories of survival in concentration camps, escape, and life after the war, as well as fictional works and poetry.

Humanism: A philosophy that places faith in the dignity of humankind and rejects the medieval perception of the individual as a weak, fallen creature. "Humanists" typically believe in the perfectibility of human nature and view reason and education as the means to that end.

Hyperbole: In literary criticism, deliberate exaggeration used to achieve an effect.

I

Idiom: A word construction or verbal expression closely associated with a given language.

Image: A concrete representation of an object or sensory experience. Typically, such a representation helps evoke the feelings associated with the object or experience itself. Images are either "literal" or "figurative." Literal images are especially concrete and involve little or no extension of the obvious meaning of the words used to express them. Figurative images do not follow the literal meaning of the words exactly. Images in literature are usually visual, but the term "image" can also refer to the representation of any sensory experience.

Imagery: The array of images in a literary work. Also, figurative language.

In medias res: A Latin term meaning "in the middle of things." It refers to the technique of beginning a story at its midpoint and then using various flashback devices to reveal previous action.

Interior Monologue: A narrative technique in which characters' thoughts are revealed in a way that appears to be uncontrolled by the author. The interior monologue typically aims to reveal the inner self of a character. It portrays emotional experiences as they occur at both a conscious and unconscious level. images are often used to represent sensations or emotions.

Irony: In literary criticism, the effect of language in which the intended meaning is the opposite of what is stated.

J

Jargon: Language that is used or understood only by a select group of people. Jargon may refer to terminology used in a certain profession, such as computer jargon, or it may refer to any nonsensical language that is not understood by most people.

L

Leitmotiv: See *Motif*

Literal Language: An author uses literal language when he or she writes without exaggerating or embellishing the subject matter and without any tools of figurative language.

Lost Generation: A term first used by Gertrude Stein to describe the post-World War I generation of American writers: men and women haunted by a sense of betrayal and emptiness brought about by the destructiveness of the war.

M

Mannerism: Exaggerated, artificial adherence to a literary manner or style. Also, a popular style of the visual arts of late sixteenth-century Europe that was marked by elongation of the human form and by intentional spatial distortion. Literary works that are self-consciously high-toned and artistic are often said to be "mannered."

Metaphor: A figure of speech that expresses an idea through the image of another object. Metaphors suggest the essence of the first object by identifying it with certain qualities of the second object.

Modernism: Modern literary practices. Also, the principles of a literary school that lasted from roughly the beginning of the twentieth century until the end of World War II. Modernism is defined by its rejection of the literary conventions of the nineteenth century and by its opposition to conventional morality, taste, traditions, and economic values.

Mood: The prevailing emotions of a work or of the author in his or her creation of the work. The mood of a work is not always what might be expected based on its subject matter.

Motif: A theme, character type, image, metaphor, or other verbal element that recurs throughout a single work of literature or occurs in a number of different works over a period of time.

Myth: An anonymous tale emerging from the traditional beliefs of a culture or social unit. Myths use supernatural explanations for natural phenomena. They may also explain cosmic issues like creation and death. Collections of myths, known as mythologies, are common to all cultures and nations, but the best-known myths belong to the Norse, Roman, and Greek mythologies.

N

Narration: The telling of a series of events, real or invented. A narration may be either a simple narrative, in which the events are recounted chronologically, or a narrative with a plot, in which the account is given in a style reflecting the author's artistic concept of the story.

Narration is sometimes used as a synonym for "storyline."

Narrative: A verse or prose accounting of an event or sequence of events, real or invented. The term is also used as an adjective in the sense "method of narration." For example, in literary criticism, the expression "narrative technique" usually refers to the way the author structures and presents his or her story.

Narrator: The teller of a story. The narrator may be the author or a character in the story through whom the author speaks.

Naturalism: A literary movement of the late nineteenth and early twentieth centuries. The movement's major theorist, French novelist Emile Zola, envisioned a type of fiction that would examine human life with the objectivity of scientific inquiry. The Naturalists typically viewed human beings as either the products of "biological determinism," ruled by hereditary instincts and engaged in an endless struggle for survival, or as the products of "socioeconomic determinism," ruled by social and economic forces beyond their control. In their works, the Naturalists generally ignored the highest levels of society and focused on degradation: poverty, alcoholism, prostitution, insanity, and disease.

Noble Savage: The idea that primitive man is noble and good but becomes evil and corrupted as he becomes civilized. The concept of the noble savage originated in the Renaissance period but is more closely identified with such later writers as Jean-Jacques Rousseau and Aphra Behn.

Novel: A long fictional narrative written in prose, which developed from the novella and other early forms of narrative. A novel is usually organized under a plot or theme with a focus on character development and action.

Novel of Ideas: A novel in which the examination of intellectual issues and concepts takes precedence over characterization or a traditional storyline.

Novel of Manners: A novel that examines the customs and mores of a cultural group.

Novella: An Italian term meaning "story." This term has been especially used to describe fourteenth-century Italian tales, but it also refers to modern short novels.

O

Objective Correlative: An outward set of objects, a situation, or a chain of events corresponding to an inward experience and evoking this experience in the reader. The term frequently appears in modern criticism in discussions of authors' intended effects on the emotional responses of readers.

Objectivity: A quality in writing characterized by the absence of the author's opinion or feeling about the subject matter. Objectivity is an important factor in criticism.

Oedipus Complex: A son's amorous obsession with his mother. The phrase is derived from the story of the ancient Theban hero Oedipus, who unknowingly killed his father and married his mother.

Omniscience: See *Point of View*

Onomatopoeia: The use of words whose sounds express or suggest their meaning. In its simplest sense, onomatopoeia may be represented by words that mimic the sounds they denote such as "hiss" or "meow." At a more subtle level, the pattern and rhythm of sounds and rhymes of a line or poem may be onomatopoeic.

Oxymoron: A phrase combining two contradictory terms. Oxymorons may be intentional or unintentional.

P

Parable: A story intended to teach a moral lesson or answer an ethical question.

Paradox: A statement that appears illogical or contradictory at first, but may actually point to an underlying truth.

Parallelism: A method of comparison of two ideas in which each is developed in the same grammatical structure.

Parody: In literary criticism, this term refers to an imitation of a serious literary work or the signature style of a particular author in a ridiculous manner. A typical parody adopts the style of the original and applies it to an inappropriate subject for humorous effect. Parody is a form of satire and could be considered the literary equivalent of a caricature or cartoon.

Pastoral: A term derived from the Latin word "pastor," meaning shepherd. A pastoral is a literary composition on a rural theme. The conventions of the pastoral were originated by the third-century Greek poet Theocritus, who wrote about the experiences, love affairs, and pastimes of Sicilian shepherds. In a pastoral, characters and language of a courtly nature are often placed in a simple setting. The term pastoral is also used to classify dramas, elegies, and lyrics that exhibit the use of country settings and shepherd characters.

Pen Name: See *Pseudonym*

Persona: A Latin term meaning "mask." *Personae* are the characters in a fictional work of literature. The *persona* generally functions as a mask through which the author tells a story in a voice other than his or her own. A *persona* is usually either a character in a story who acts as a narrator or an "implied author," a voice created by the author to act as the narrator for himself or herself.

Personification: A figure of speech that gives human qualities to abstract ideas, animals, and inanimate objects.

Picaresque Novel: Episodic fiction depicting the adventures of a roguish central character ("picaro" is Spanish for "rogue"). The picaresque hero is commonly a low-born but clever individual who wanders into and out of various affairs of love, danger, and farcical intrigue. These involvements may take place at all social levels and typically present a humorous and wide-ranging satire of a given society.

Plagiarism: Claiming another person's written material as one's own. Plagiarism can take the form of direct, word-for-word copying or the theft of the substance or idea of the work.

Plot: In literary criticism, this term refers to the pattern of events in a narrative or drama. In its simplest sense, the plot guides the author in composing the work and helps the reader follow the work. Typically, plots exhibit causality and unity and have a beginning, a middle, and an end. Sometimes, however, a plot may consist of a series of disconnected events, in which case it is known as an "episodic plot."

Poetic Justice: An outcome in a literary work, not necessarily a poem, in which the good are rewarded and the evil are punished, especially in ways that particularly fit their virtues or crimes.

Poetic License: Distortions of fact and literary convention made by a writer—not always a poet—for the sake of the effect gained. Poetic license is closely related to the concept of "artistic freedom."

Poetics: This term has two closely related meanings. It denotes (1) an aesthetic theory in literary criticism about the essence of poetry or (2) rules prescribing the proper methods, content, style, or diction of poetry. The term poetics may also refer to theories about literature in general, not just poetry.

Point of View: The narrative perspective from which a literary work is presented to the reader. There are four traditional points of view. The "third person omniscient" gives the reader a "godlike" perspective, unrestricted by time or place, from which to see actions and look into the minds of characters. This allows the author to comment openly on characters and events in the work. The "third person" point of view presents the events of the story from outside of any single character's perception, much like the omniscient point of view, but the reader must understand the action as it takes place and without any special insight into characters' minds or motivations. The "first person" or "personal" point of view relates events as they are perceived by a single character. The main character "tells" the story and may offer opinions about the action and characters which differ from those of the author. Much less common than omniscient, third person, and first person is the "second person" point of view, wherein the author tells the story as if it is happening to the reader.

Polemic: A work in which the author takes a stand on a controversial subject, such as abortion or religion. Such works are often extremely argumentative or provocative.

Pornography: Writing intended to provoke feelings of lust in the reader. Such works are often condemned by critics and teachers, but those which can be shown to have literary value are viewed less harshly.

Post-Aesthetic Movement: An artistic response made by African Americans to the black aesthetic movement of the 1960s and early '70s. Writers since that time have adopted a somewhat different tone in their work, with less emphasis placed on the disparity between black and white in the United States. In the words of post-aesthetic authors such as Toni Morrison, John Edgar Wideman, and Kristin Hunter, African Americans are portrayed as looking inward for answers to their own questions, rather than always looking to the outside world.

Postmodernism: Writing from the 1960s forward characterized by experimentation and continuing to apply some of the fundamentals of modernism, which included existentialism and alienation. Postmodernists have gone a step further in the rejection of tradition begun with the modernists by also rejecting traditional forms, preferring the anti-novel over the novel and the anti-hero over the hero.

Primitivism: The belief that primitive peoples were nobler and less flawed than civilized peoples because they had not been subjected to the tainting influence of society.

Prologue: An introductory section of a literary work. It often contains information establishing the situation of the characters or presents information about the setting, time period, or action. In drama, the prologue is spoken by a chorus or by one of the principal characters.

Prose: A literary medium that attempts to mirror the language of everyday speech. It is distinguished from poetry by its use of unmetered, unrhymed language consisting of logically related sentences. Prose is usually grouped into paragraphs that form a cohesive whole such as an essay or a novel.

Prosopopoeia: See *Personification*

Protagonist: The central character of a story who serves as a focus for its themes and incidents and as the principal rationale for its development. The protagonist is sometimes referred to in discussions of modern literature as the hero or anti-hero.

Protest Fiction: Protest fiction has as its primary purpose the protesting of some social injustice, such as racism or discrimination.

Proverb: A brief, sage saying that expresses a truth about life in a striking manner.

Pseudonym: A name assumed by a writer, most often intended to prevent his or her identification as the author of a work. Two or more authors may work together under one pseudonym, or an author may use a different name for each genre he or she publishes in. Some publishing companies maintain "house pseudonyms," under which any number of authors may write installations in a series. Some authors also choose a pseudonym over their real names the way an actor may use a stage name.

Pun: A play on words that have similar sounds but different meanings.

R

Realism: A nineteenth-century European literary movement that sought to portray familiar characters, situations, and settings in a realistic manner. This was done primarily by using an objective narrative point of view and through the buildup of accurate detail. The standard for success of any realistic work depends on how faithfully it transfers common experience into fictional forms. The realistic method may be altered or extended, as in stream of consciousness writing, to record highly subjective experience.

Repartee: Conversation featuring snappy retorts and witticisms.

Resolution: The portion of a story following the climax, in which the conflict is resolved.

Rhetoric: In literary criticism, this term denotes the art of ethical persuasion. In its strictest sense, rhetoric adheres to various principles developed since classical times for arranging facts and ideas in a clear, persuasive, appealing manner. The term is also used to refer to effective prose in general and theories of or methods for composing effective prose.

Rhetorical Question: A question intended to provoke thought, but not an expressed answer, in the reader. It is most commonly used in oratory and other persuasive genres.

Rising Action: The part of a drama where the plot becomes increasingly complicated. Rising action leads up to the climax, or turning point, of a drama.

Roman à clef: A French phrase meaning "novel with a key." It refers to a narrative in which real persons are portrayed under fictitious names.

Romance: A broad term, usually denoting a narrative with exotic, exaggerated, often idealized characters, scenes, and themes.

Romanticism: This term has two widely accepted meanings. In historical criticism, it refers to a European intellectual and artistic movement of the late eighteenth and early nineteenth centuries that sought greater freedom of personal expression than that allowed by the strict rules of literary form and logic of the eighteenth-century neoclassicists. The Romantics preferred emotional and imaginative expression to rational analysis. They considered the individual to be at the center of all experience and so placed him or her at the center of their art. The Romantics believed that the creative imagination reveals nobler truths—unique feelings and attitudes—than those that could be discovered by logic or by scientific examination. Both the natural world and the state of childhood were important sources for revelations of "eternal truths." "Romanticism" is also used as a general term to refer to a type of sensibility found in all periods of literary history and usually considered to be in opposition to the principles of classicism. In this sense, Romanticism signifies any work or philosophy in which the exotic or dreamlike figure strongly, or that is devoted to individualistic expression, self-analysis, or a pursuit of a higher realm of knowledge than can be discovered by human reason.

Romantics: See *Romanticism*

S

Satire: A work that uses ridicule, humor, and wit to criticize and provoke change in human nature and institutions. There are two major types of satire: "formal" or "direct" satire speaks directly to the reader or to a character in the work; "indirect" satire relies upon the ridiculous behavior of its characters to make its point. Formal satire is further divided into two manners: the "Horatian," which ridicules gently, and the "Juvenalian," which derides its subjects harshly and bitterly.

Science Fiction: A type of narrative about or based upon real or imagined scientific theories and technology. Science fiction is often peopled with alien creatures and set on other planets or in different dimensions.

Second Person: See *Point of View*

Setting: The time, place, and culture in which the action of a narrative takes place. The elements of setting may include geographic location, characters' physical and mental environments, prevailing cultural attitudes, or the historical time in which the action takes place.

Simile: A comparison, usually using "like" or "as," of two essentially dissimilar things, as in "coffee as cold as ice" or "He sounded like a broken record."

Slang: A type of informal verbal communication that is generally unacceptable for formal writing. Slang words and phrases are often colorful exaggerations used to emphasize the speaker's point; they may also be shortened versions of an often-used word or phrase.

Slave Narrative: Autobiographical accounts of American slave life as told by escaped slaves. These works first appeared during the abolition movement of the 1830s through the 1850s.

Socialist Realism: The Socialist Realism school of literary theory was proposed by Maxim Gorky and established as a dogma by the first Soviet Congress of Writers. It demanded adherence to a communist worldview in works of literature. Its doctrines required an objective viewpoint comprehensible to the working classes and themes of social struggle featuring strong proletarian heroes.

Stereotype: A stereotype was originally the name for a duplication made during the printing process; this led to its modern definition as a person or thing that is (or is assumed to be) the same as all others of its type.

Stream of Consciousness: A narrative technique for rendering the inward experience of a character. This technique is designed to give the impression of an ever-changing series of thoughts, emotions, images, and memories in the spontaneous and seemingly illogical order that they occur in life.

Structure: The form taken by a piece of literature. The structure may be made obvious for ease of understanding, as in nonfiction works, or may obscured for artistic purposes, as in some poetry or seemingly "unstructured" prose.

Sturm und Drang: A German term meaning "storm and stress." It refers to a German literary movement of the 1770s and 1780s that reacted against the order and rationalism of the enlightenment, focusing instead on the intense experience of extraordinary individuals.

Style: A writer's distinctive manner of arranging words to suit his or her ideas and purpose in writing. The unique imprint of the author's personality upon his or her writing, style is the product of an author's way of arranging ideas and his or her use of diction, different sentence structures, rhythm, figures of speech, rhetorical principles, and other elements of composition.

Subjectivity: Writing that expresses the author's personal feelings about his subject, and which may or may not include factual information about the subject.

Subplot: A secondary story in a narrative. A subplot may serve as a motivating or complicating force for the main plot of the work, or it may provide emphasis for, or relief from, the main plot.

Surrealism: A term introduced to criticism by Guillaume Apollinaire and later adopted by Andre Breton. It refers to a French literary and artistic movement founded in the 1920s. The Surrealists sought to express unconscious thoughts and feelings in their works. The best-known technique used for achieving this aim was automatic writing—transcriptions of spontaneous outpourings from the unconscious. The Surrealists proposed to unify the contrary levels of conscious and unconscious, dream and reality, objectivity and subjectivity into a new level of "super-realism."

Suspense: A literary device in which the author maintains the audience's attention through the buildup of events, the outcome of which will soon be revealed.

Symbol: Something that suggests or stands for something else without losing its original identity. In literature, symbols combine their literal meaning with the suggestion of an abstract concept. Literary symbols are of two types: those that carry complex associations of meaning no matter what their contexts, and those that derive their suggestive meaning from their functions in specific literary works.

Symbolism: This term has two widely accepted meanings. In historical criticism, it denotes an early modernist literary movement initiated in France during the nineteenth century that reacted against the prevailing standards of realism. Writers in this movement aimed to evoke, indirectly and symbolically, an order of being beyond the material world of the five senses. Poetic expression of personal emotion

figured strongly in the movement, typically by means of a private set of symbols uniquely identifiable with the individual poet. The principal aim of the Symbolists was to express in words the highly complex feelings that grew out of everyday contact with the world. In a broader sense, the term "symbolism" refers to the use of one object to represent another.

T

Tall Tale: A humorous tale told in a straightforward, credible tone but relating absolutely impossible events or feats of the characters. Such tales were commonly told of frontier adventures during the settlement of the west in the United States.

Theme: The main point of a work of literature. The term is used interchangeably with thesis.

Thesis: A thesis is both an essay and the point argued in the essay. Thesis novels and thesis plays share the quality of containing a thesis which is supported through the action of the story.

Third Person: See *Point of View*

Tone: The author's attitude toward his or her audience may be deduced from the tone of the work. A formal tone may create distance or convey politeness, while an informal tone may encourage a friendly, intimate, or intrusive feeling in the reader. The author's attitude toward his or her subject matter may also be deduced from the tone of the words he or she uses in discussing it.

Transcendentalism: An American philosophical and religious movement, based in New England from around 1835 until the Civil War. Transcendentalism was a form of American romanticism that had its roots abroad in the works of Thomas Carlyle, Samuel Coleridge, and Johann Wolfgang von Goethe. The Transcendentalists stressed the importance of intuition and subjective experience in communication with God. They rejected religious dogma and texts in favor of mysticism and scientific naturalism. They pursued truths that lie beyond the "colorless" realms perceived by reason and the senses and were active social reformers in public education, women's rights, and the abolition of slavery.

U

Urban Realism: A branch of realist writing that attempts to accurately reflect the often harsh facts of modern urban existence.

Utopia: A fictional perfect place, such as "paradise" or "heaven."

V

Verisimilitude: Literally, the appearance of truth. In literary criticism, the term refers to aspects of a work of literature that seem true to the reader.

Victorian: Refers broadly to the reign of Queen Victoria of England (1837-1901) and to anything with qualities typical of that era. For example, the qualities of smug narrowmindedness, bourgeois materialism, faith in social progress, and priggish morality are often considered Victorian. This stereotype is contradicted by such dramatic intellectual developments as the theories of Charles Darwin, Karl Marx, and Sigmund Freud (which stirred strong debates in England) and the critical attitudes of serious Victorian writers like Charles Dickens and George Eliot. In literature, the Victorian Period was the great age of the English novel, and the latter part of the era saw the rise of movements such as decadence and symbolism.

W

Weltanschauung: A German term referring to a person's worldview or philosophy.

Weltschmerz: A German term meaning "world pain." It describes a sense of anguish about the nature of existence, usually associated with a melancholy, pessimistic attitude.

Z

Zeitgeist: A German term meaning "spirit of the time." It refers to the moral and intellectual trends of a given era.

Cumulative Author/Title Index

Cumulative Nationality/Ethnicity Index

Baum, L. Frank
The Wonderful Wizard of Oz: V13
Bellamy, Edward
Looking Backward: 2000–1887:
V15
Bellow, Saul
The Adventures of Augie March:
V33
Herzog: V14
Humboldt's Gift: V26
Seize the Day: V4
Benitez, Sandra
*A Place Where the Sea
Remembers:* V32
Bloor, Edward
Tangerine: V33
Blume, Judy
Forever...: V24
Borland, Hal
When the Legends Die: V18
Bradbury, Ray
Dandelion Wine: V22
Fahrenheit 451: V1
*Something Wicked This Way
Comes:* V29
Bridal, Tessa
The Tree of Red Stars: V17
Brown, Rita Mae
Rubyfruit Jungle: V9
Buck, Pearl S.
The Good Earth: V25
Burdick, Eugene J.
The Ugly American: V23
Burns, Olive Ann
Cold Sassy Tree: V31
Butler, Octavia
Kindred: V8
Parable of the Sower: V21
Patternmaster: V34
Card, Orson Scott
Ender's Game: V5
Cather, Willa
Death Comes for the Archbishop:
V19
A Lost Lady: V33
My Ántonia: V2
Chabon, Michael
*The Amazing Adventures of
Kavalier & Clay:* V25
Chandler, Raymond
The Big Sleep: V17
Choi, Sook Nyul
Year of Impossible Goodbyes: V29
Chopin, Kate
The Awakening: V3
Cisneros, Sandra
The House on Mango Street: V2
Clavell, James du Maresq
Shogun: A Novel of Japan: V10
Cleage, Pearl
*What Looks Like Crazy on an
Ordinary Day:* V17

Clemens, Samuel Langhorne
*The Adventures of Huckleberry
Finn:* V1
The Adventures of Tom Sawyer:
V6
*A Connecticut Yankee in King
Arthur's Court:* V20
The Prince and the Pauper: V31
Collier, Christopher
My Brother Sam is Dead: V38
Collier, James Lincoln
My Brother Sam is Dead: V38
Conroy, Frank
Body and Soul: V11
Cooper, James Fenimore
The Deerslayer: V25
The Last of the Mohicans: V9
The Last of the Mohicans (Motion
picture): V32
*The Pathfinder; or, The Inland
Sea:* V38
Cormier, Robert
The Chocolate War: V2
I Am the Cheese: V18
Crane, Stephen
The Red Badge of Courage: V4
Maggie: A Girl of the Streets: V20
Crichton, Michael
The Great Train Robbery: V34
Crutcher, Chris
The Crazy Horse Electric Game:
V11
Staying Fat for Sarah Byrnes: V32
Cunningham, Michael
The Hours: V23
Danticat, Edwidge
Breath, Eyes, Memory: V37
The Dew Breaker: V28
Davis, Rebecca Harding
*Margret Howth: A Story of
To-Day:* V14
DeLillo, Don
White Noise: V28
Desai, Kiran
Hullabaloo in the Guava Orchard:
V28
Diamant, Anita
The Red Tent: V36
Dick, Philip K.
*Do Androids Dream of Electric
Sheep?:* V5
Martian Time-Slip: V26
Dickey, James
Deliverance: V9
Didion, Joan
Democracy: V3
Doctorow, E. L.
Ragtime: V6
Dorris, Michael
A Yellow Raft in Blue Water: V3
Dos Passos, John
U.S.A.: V14

Dreiser, Theodore
An American Tragedy: V17
Sister Carrie: V8
Ellis, Bret Easton
Less Than Zero: V11
Ellison, Ralph
Invisible Man: V2
Juneteenth: V21
Emecheta, Buchi
The Bride Price: V12
Erdrich, Louise
The Beet Queen: V37
Love Medicine: V5
Eugenides, Jeffrey
Middlesex: V24
Fast, Howard
April Morning: V35
Faulkner, William
Absalom, Absalom!: V13
As I Lay Dying: V8
Intruder in the Dust: V33
Light in August: V24
The Sound and the Fury: V4
The Unvanquished: V38
Fitzgerald, F. Scott
The Great Gatsby: V2
Tender Is the Night: V19
This Side of Paradise: V20
Flagg, Fannie
*Fried Green Tomatoes at the
Whistle Stop Café:* V7
Foer, Jonathan Safran
*Extremely Loud & Incredibly
Close:* V36
Ford, Richard
Independence Day: V25
Fox, Paula
The Slave Dancer: V12
Frank, Pat
Alas, Babylon: V29
Frazier, Charles
Cold Mountain: V25
Frederic, Harold
The Damnation of Theron Ware:
V22
Gaines, Ernest J.
*The Autobiography of Miss Jane
Pittman:* V5
A Gathering of Old Men: V16
A Lesson Before Dying: V7
García, Cristina
Dreaming in Cuban: V38
Gardner, John
Grendel: V3
Gibbons, Kaye
Ellen Foster: V3
Gilman, Charlotte Perkins
Herland: V36
Glass, Julia
Three Junes: V34
Golden, Arthur
Memoirs of a Geisha: V19

Forster, E. M.
A Passage to India: V3
Howards End: V10
A Room with a View: V11
Fowles, John
The French Lieutenant's Woman: V21
Golding, William
Lord of the Flies: V2
Lord of the Flies (Motion picture): V36
Graves, Robert
I, Claudius: V21
Greene, Graham
The End of the Affair: V16
The Power and the Glory: V31
The Third Man: V36
Hardy, Thomas
Far from the Madding Crowd: V19
Jude the Obscure: V30
The Mayor of Casterbridge: V15
The Return of the Native: V11
Tess of the d'Urbervilles: V3
Huxley, Aldous
Brave New World: V6
Ishiguro, Kazuo
Never Let Me Go: V35
The Remains of the Day: V13
James, Henry
The Ambassadors: V12
The Bostonians: V37
The Portrait of a Lady: V19
The Turn of the Screw: V16
Kipling, Rudyard
Kim: V21
Koestler, Arthur
Darkness at Noon: V19
Lawrence, D. H.
The Rainbow: V26
Sons and Lovers: V18
Lessing, Doris
The Fifth Child: V38
The Golden Notebook: V27
Lewis, C. S.
The Lion, the Witch and the Wardrobe: V24
Llewellyn, Richard
How Green Was My Valley: V30
Maugham, W. Somerset
Of Human Bondage: V35
The Razor's Edge: V23
McEwan, Ian
Atonement: V32
More, Thomas
Utopia: V29
Orwell, George
Animal Farm: V3
1984: V7
Rhys, Jean
Wide Sargasso Sea: V19
Rushdie, Salman
The Satanic Verses: V22

Sewell, Anna
Black Beauty: V22
Shelley, Mary
Frankenstein: V1
Frankenstein (Motion picture): V37
Shute, Nevil
On the Beach: V9
A Town Like Alice: V38
Spark, Muriel
The Prime of Miss Jean Brodie: V22
Stevenson, Robert Louis
Dr. Jekyll and Mr. Hyde: V11
Kidnapped: V33
Swift, Graham
Waterland: V18
Swift, Jonathan
Gulliver's Travels: V6
Thackeray, William Makepeace
Vanity Fair: V13
Tolkien, J. R. R.
The Hobbit: V8
The Lord of the Rings: V26
Waugh, Evelyn
Brideshead Revisited: V13
A Handful of Dust: V34
Scoop: V17
Wells, H. G.
The Island of Dr. Moreau: V36
The Time Machine: V17
The War of the Worlds: V20
White, T. H.
The Once and Future King: V30
Woolf, Virginia
Mrs. Dalloway: V12
To the Lighthouse: V8
The Waves: V28

European American

Hemingway, Ernest
The Old Man and the Sea: V6
Stowe, Harriet Beecher
Uncle Tom's Cabin: V6

French

Balzac, Honoré de
Le Père Goriot: V33
Boulle, Pierre
The Bridge over the River Kwai: V32
Camus, Albert
The Plague: V16
The Stranger: V6
Dumas, Alexandre
The Count of Monte Cristo: V19
The Three Musketeers: V14
Flaubert, Gustave
Madame Bovary: V14
Gide, André
The Immoralist: V21
Hugo, Victor
The Hunchback of Notre Dame: V20
Les Misérables: V5

Japrisot, Sébastien
A Very Long Engagement: V18
Leroux, Gaston
The Phantom of the Opera: V20
Maugham, W. Somerset
Of Human Bondage: V35
The Razor's Edge: V23
Saint-Exupéry, Antoine de
The Little Prince: V30
Sartre, Jean-Paul
Nausea: V21
Verne, Jules
Around the World in Eighty Days: V30
Journey to the Center of the Earth: V34
Voltaire
Candide: V7

German

Hegi, Ursula
Stones from the River: V25
Hesse, Hermann
Demian: V15
Siddhartha: V6
Steppenwolf: V24
Mann, Thomas
Death in Venice: V17
The Magic Mountain: V29
Remarque, Erich Maria
All Quiet on the Western Front: V4
All Quiet on the Western Front (Motion picture): V36

Guyanese

Braithwaite, E. R.
To Sir, With Love: V30

Haitian

Danticat, Edwidge
Breath, Eyes, Memory: V37
The Dew Breaker: V28

Hispanic American

Allende, Isabel
Daughter of Fortune: V18
Eva Luna: V29
The House of the Spirits: V6
Benitez, Sandra
A Place Where the Sea Remembers: V32
Cisneros, Sandra
The House on Mango Street: V2
García, Cristina
Dreaming in Cuban: V38
Hijuelos, Oscar
The Mambo Kings Play Songs of Love: V17

Subject/Theme Index